Halfway to Revolution

Halfway to Revolution

Investigation and crisis in the work of Henry Adams, William James and Gertrude Stein

Clive Bush

Yale University Press
New Haven and London 1991

Designed by John Nicoll

Set in Linotron Bembo by Excel Typesetters Company, Hong Kong
Printed in Great Britain by Bell and Bain Ltd., Glasgow

ISBN 0-300-04729-0
Library of Congress Catalog Number 90-71195

In memory of Muriel Rukeyser

Organize the full results of that rich past
open the windows:

from 'Poem out of Childhood' (1935)

Contents

Acknowledgements

The writing of this book would not have been possible without a fellowship from the American Council of Learned Societies to study at Yale for the academic year 1980–1, nor without the granting of sabbatical leave from the University of Warwick during 1985. I am also grateful for hospitality extended to me at Branford College, Yale, by Rory Brown and John Merriman during 1983. In the United States I would like to thank Professor Alan Trachtenberg who has encouraged my work for many years now, and the lively American Studies department he has created at Yale. Meeting younger scholars in the field of American Studies in the United States has always been a great privilege. In particular I would like to thank for many different kinds of advice, conversations and general support: Jean-Christophe Agnew, Robert Byer, Ed Burns, Harriet Chessman, Ulli Dydo, Joyce and Richard Lowry, Karen Lucic, Angela Miller, and Bryan Wolf. My thanks are especially due to Joel Pfister for our many arguments over the years and for our friendship. Among the older generation of scholars I should like to thank Leon Katz for encouraging my interest in Stein many years ago – long before the current avalanche of commentary on Stein had really begun. I should also like to thank R. W. B. Lewis for conversations about William James, and the James family. My general evaluation of James in the following pages differs from his because it draws on a European way of thinking in which the radical tradition (including various Marxist traditions) in philosophy is part of normal critical thinking. Nonetheless I hope this book will be in part a tribute to his high seriousness and critical skill. Finally, in social terms my many visits to New Haven would have been the poorer without the home-from-home that Margaret and Matthew Coyle have always provided for me in West Haven.

In England I have had the benefit and privilege of stimulation by a lively group of young scholars at King's College, London University, in the English graduate seminar and on the staff of the intercultural studies journal *Talus*. Here I should especially like to thank Gilbert Adair, Marzia Balzani, Hanne Bramness, Steve Want and Shamoon Zamir. At Warwick University Richard Bradbury and Duncan Webster were a delight to work with, and a constant source of information and intellectual stimulation. I am grateful in different ways also to Edward Countryman, Mair Evans, John Goode, Peter Larkin and John Rignall for support and advice. Above all, however, I should like to thank my colleague, Dr Edward Gallafent, not only for undeviating support and unswerving friendship, but for his administrative skills, and his sense of humour which has cheered the spirit in a very difficult time for British universities.

Finally, if this work succeeds in its ambitious intellectual scope in any way it will undoubtedly be owing to the continuing friendship and encouragement of the poet and critic, Professor Eric Mottram, of King's College, London University. In a period when commercially fashionable critical modes, and books marketed towards instant, bland recognition in hierarchically competitive institutions have imperilled the intellectual project at root, his example of absolute critical integrity has helped keep alive in England for some thirty years and more the adventure of cultural studies and difficult thought.

Acknowledgement is made to the Estate of Gertrude Stein for permission to quote from her writing. I regret it has not been possible to quote directly from the correspondence of Richard Wright.

London, March 1990   C.B.

Introduction

Society, in a subtler sense, cannot 'afford' a single miscarriage of justice, a single inequity in the dispensation of its laws, the violation of the rights of even the tiniest minority, because these undermine the moral basis on which society's existence rests.

HANS JONAS[1]

Professors always judge things to be outside the subject, a proof that they know better than I do where the line is drawn.

MICHEL SERRES[2]

Men believe that a society is disintegrating when it can no longer be pictured in familiar terms. Unhappy is a people that has run out of words to describe what is going on.

THURMAN ARNOLD[3]

Our wisdom in social questions is almost always retrospective only. This is, or ought to be, a humiliating experience for human beings; if justice is beyond us, we would like at least to claim knowledge.

JAMES BURNHAM[4]

'There would be absolutely no need', wrote Raymond Williams, 'to reject the concept of literature...if it still meant what it did in the eighteenth-century: a group of written works of a certain level of seriousness, capable of sustaining an attention that others could not'; and in his work on 'metaphor' the French philosopher Paul Ricoeur states that literature provides a discourse in which 'several things are meant at the same time'.[5] These two statements are of importance in understanding why the three authors under discussion in the following pages, Henry Adams, William James and Gertrude Stein, are seen to fall within the domain of 'literature', whatever traditional genres (history, psychology, philosophy) have been assigned to them. In order to describe discourses where several things are meant at the same time, a criticism must be invented in order to recognize pluralities of strategy and meaning. If properly attempted, the result should be neither eclecticism nor avoidance of 'ideological' content, for one of the lessons of this book is that multiplicity has a shape which can be described.

Choosing among the possibilities in a time of absolute critical diversity is a challenge rather than a burden if scepticism is reserved for procedure rather than for a melancholy a priori truth lost somewhere between nostalgia and prophecy. In her book on Alfred North Whitehead, Dorothy Emmet says, 'there is a mysticism which is the other side of scepticism, and which, like it, is the child of despair; the mysticism, that is to say, which does not examine the truth of its content, while scepticism knows the search is vain,'[6] It is such scepticism that Wilkie Collins (a favourite author of Gertrude Stein) parodies, in *The Moonstone*, in his quizzical account of his over-cosmopolitan heir apparent. The narrator is the faithful retainer, Betteredge: '"This question has two sides," he said. "An objective side, and a subjective side. Which are we to take?" He had a German education as well as a French.'[7] The answer proposed in this book, however, will not be that of the faithful retainer. Betteredge reaches for his English pipe and reads *Robinson Crusoe*, thereby seeking solutions in individualist common sense while simultaneously befuddling sense itself. In this book, however, one type of befuddlement will be avoided wherever possible. The jargonizing language of much contemporary criticism will be eschewed, though not to the extent of refusing necessary complexity.

This book differs in two respects from much contemporary practice. First, it does not attempt to flog a single thesis through recalcitrant material in order to prove that some method has been authenticated. Second, its choice of critics and criticisms is catholic. Too many contemporary monographs take the subjects of last year's conference papers, some scholastic redefinition of 'post-modernism', or the latest nuance in esoteric feminism, or the 'economy' of reception, and forge an instant heuristic which then tends happily to get forgotten once the sacrifice has been laid on the threshold of the in-house gods. The scientific project must proceed by way of contemporary addition, but the humanities should have a different attitude to time and value. They ought, therefore, to recognize as one of their first premises that the revaluation of the great achievements of human culture, from Knossos to Venturi, from Hildegard von Bingen to Stockhausen, from Aristotle to

Sartre, provides a non-dogmatic standard for more contemporary cultures and criticisms. The evaluation of the new, and the encouragement to proceed in new directions, can only come from a deep knowledge of historical achievement. The past is a burden only to those who have no real love of the present, and no creativity with which to address the future with hope.

The critics drawn on in this book range from Aristotle to Serres. On the way it is hoped gently to remind contemporary critics that Aristotle may have had something of interest to say on the subject of emotions and ethics, or that the generation of the Thirties and Forties in England and the United States were not all chasing after false gods, that a Simone de Beauvoir or a Sartre or a Merleau-Ponty are not simply *passé*, that a Dorothy Emmet or an Agnes Arber or a James Burnham or a Lewis Mumford or a Helen Merrill Lynd or a Thurman Arnold are as worth rereading as the latest redefinition of 'post-modernism'. Contemporary theorists will be found in abundance throughout the following work, but they will take their places alongside their historical predecessors.

Criticism shares with literature that enigma of 'metaphorical discourse in that it "invents" in both senses of the word: what it creates, it discovers; and what it finds it invents'.[8] Adams, James and Stein demand an inventive criticism in just this sense. All three resist easy categorization. Historians and critics are divided over the respective merits of Adams's historical and literary work, orthodox philosophers and psychologists have found James's work difficult to co-opt along specialized lines. While Stein was more simply a 'writer', only now are critics in any numbers really taking her work seriously, and then not very much along those historical lines which would show how deeply she was engaged with problems of philosophy and psychology. The work of all three invites considerable intellectual effort in which many levels of meaning have to be responded to at the same time.

Encyclopaedic knowledge is not demanded, rather an intellectual openness and a certain courage not to be intimidated by professionalized subject demarcations. One of the unintentional discoveries of this study was the degree to which earlier generations of critics seemed to be much more wide-ranging in tone and reference, and much more fearless in their judgements, than is generally the case at present. In the corporate-speak of 'post-modernist' academic 'discourse', style and content become all things to all persons. The dissenting judgement is rare, the range of possible criticisms shortened to a priori prejudices or house fashion. Writing to the American poet Charles Olson, Carl Sauer, the American geographer, once said:

In particular, I doubt whether the American mode and mood of life is such that we are sighted to the large and long-range view by so much as a partial question as to the course of history. Indeed, the Europeans are the best minded to contemplate historical forces and processes.[9]

Nonetheless Americans have often shared with Europeans a capacity for larger and longer-range views and have not infrequently gone beyond them. In the literary and cultural tradition the work of such authors as Edmund Wilson, Lewis Mumford, V. L. Parrington, Daniel Boorstin, and currently Richard Slotkin – to name, somewhat invidiously, a very few – come to mind.

If this book falls into an America-versus-Europe debate it will have failed of its purpose. It is almost inevitable that tensions between Europe and America will increase in the next few years. In fact, however, American and European critics, historians, social analysts, cultural historians and literary critics – indeed humanistic commentators in general – face a common cause in defending the humanistic tradition as a whole. Marc Chénetier has accurately seen the European humanistic academic situation as being in a last privileged moment before 'the commodified and market-oriented academic and intellectual situation. . . gradually takes over most of the Western institutions of higher learning'.[10]

Sauer was not, however, altogether wrong. What he saw as a kind of 'national' difference between Europeans and Americans was in fact more of a sign that in the United States the process of professionalization was earlier. In a polemical mood, Brooks Adams, Henry Adams's brother, noted the change as early as 1903:

In the United States capital has long owned the leading universities by right of purchase. . . . What is of moment is that capital has commercialized education. Apparently modern society, if it is to cohere, must have a high order of generalizing mind – a mind which can group a multitude of complex relations, – but this is a mind which can, at best, only be produced in small quantity and at high cost. Capital has preferred the specialized mind and that not of the highest quality, since it has found it profitable to set quantity before quality to the limit which the market will endure. Capitalists have never insisted upon raising an intellectual standard save in science and mechanics, and the relative over-stimulation of the scientific mind has now become an actual menace to order because of the inferiority of the administrative intelligence.[11]

In the late twentieth century the problem of the relation of intellectual freedom to competitive capitalism and of what governments consider necessary in the way of training populations remains as urgent as ever.

Brooks Adams's linking of the question of specialization to the exigencies of power remains exemplary. In their own ways Henry Adams, James, and Stein were to challenge the right of science and technology to speak for all aspects of human life. Of the three, only James remained inside the university for the whole of his life, and then as an increasingly deviant intellectual within it. All three resisted the blandishments of modern scholarship as defined by Alfred North Whitehead, whose usually genial tone sharpens in the following passage:

> But modern scholarship and modern science reproduced the same limitations as dominated the bygone Hellenistic epoch and the bygone Scholastic epoch. They canalize thought and observation within predetermined limits, based upon inadequate metaphysical assumptions dogmatically assumed. The modern assumptions differ from older assumptions, not wholly for the better. They exclude from rationalistic thought more of the final values of existence. The intimate timidity of professionalized scholarship circumscribes reason by reducing its topics to triviality, for example to bare sense and to tautologies. It then frees itself from criticism by dogmatically handing over the remainder of experience to an animal faith or a religious mysticism, incapable of rationalization.[12]

Besides 'canalizing thought', there are many other evasive tactics in modern literary scholarship. Anglo–American critics tend to market 'continental' philosophers in such a way as to neutralize their efforts by turning their thought into sets of techniques. That imaginative and generous anthropologist of an earlier generation, Paul Radin, once said: 'It is generally a significant symptom when scholars become too articulate about their methods,' and he continued:

> The generous view would be to assume that this is a sign of approaching maturity, that we are prepared now to look back on our work with critical objectivity and desire method to guard us more efficiently than ever against error. But I'm afraid there's no warrant for such optimism.[13]

In fact no single method or approach will help to uncover the diverse strands in the work of the three authors who occupy the central place in this book. One of the more sensitive critics of Adams, Vern Wagner, has said: 'Many of the finest books we know cannot be readily classified', and after citing some major American works he adds: 'In one sense all of them are prose but looked at otherwise they are at least poetic if they are not poetry.'[14] It is perhaps in retrospect no accident that the first full-length study of Adams was the poet Louis Zukofsky's MA thesis at Columbia. The critical approach in this book will attempt to respond in multiple ways to the multiply-layered texts under consideration.

The kind of paradigmatic multiplicity which is being argued for here has historical justification. The last years of the nineteenth century and the early years of the twentieth century saw a revolution in human knowledge whose effects are still being measured. In every field of human learning the parameters and the contents of the subjects were changing. Naturalism in literature challenged the autonomy of the individual. Scientific secularism challenged the Christian view of individual worth, and the rise of sociology and anthropology emphasized group behaviour and social structure while deliberately expunging from their respective briefs all traditional political questions. In terms of liberal economics the age of the entrepreneurial individual was, for the mass of the population, over. America itself changed startlingly, from a largely self-employed and family-business economy in 1870 to one where in 1900 12 per cent of the population owned 99 per cent of the wealth. The sciences passed out of range of common-sense knowledge, or, perhaps more accurately, the early, long and expensive training needed to grasp the fundamentals of science placed them out of range of the mass of the people. It is little wonder that the 'Henry Adams' of Adams's *Education of Henry Adams* wondered who, where, and what he was. Adams's 'pessimism' – that officially un-American state of mind – stemmed largely, as will be demonstrated, from his concern that the dynamics of power had escaped democratic controls. Indeed, standing where Orwell stood in 1940 Adams would have shared that English writer's equal 'pessimism', together with his concern that a literature to meet the changed circumstances of the later twentieth century might not even be possible:

> Almost certainly we are moving into an age of totalitarian dicta-
> torships – an age in which freedom of thought will be at first
> a deadly sin and later a meaningless abstraction. The autonomous
> individual is going to be stamped out of existence. But this means
> that literature, in the form in which we know it, must suffer a
> temporary death. The literature of liberalism is coming to an end
> and the literature of totalitarianism has not yet appeared and is
> barely possible.[15]

In intellectual life as a whole the forms of knowledge were changing at the turn of the century. Narrative history had already given way to history of institutions. The eighteenth-century 'science of nature' in the humanistic sciences was replaced by 'psychology'. After Darwin the mechanical model of the world so beloved by the eighteenth-century *philosophes* surrendered to a biological one. In terms which will later have to be challenged for their usefulness, fixity gave way to process, and mechanism to organism. Even a superficial glance at the texts of Lyell, the geologist, and the texts of Darwin shows how analogies of civic events in the former give way to domestic analogies in the latter as a means of directing explanation in what Collingwood called the 'pseudo-historical' sciences.[16] Collingwood's term 'pseudo-historical' is an important reminder that the characterization of the 'historical' in the nineteenth century is a complex matter. Evolution, for example, as a rational time and as a theory of process in nature, has not always been as carefully distinguished as it should have been. Indeed nineteenth-century writers, from Comte to Marx, were prolific with their theories of rational time.

Historical time was singularly less historical at certain levels than it was to those in the late nineteenth and early twentieth century who were vigorously reacting against it – sociologists, anthropologists and linguists. Foucault came to a similar conclusion about the rationality of nineteenth-century concepts of history:

> The nineteenth century is commonly thought to have discovered the historical dimension, but it only did so on the basis of the circle, the spatial form which negates time, the form in which the gods manifest their arrival and flight and men manifest their return to their native ground of finitude.[17]

The twentieth century equally was to be a century of generalizing timeless structures. Inheriting Quételet's revolution, statistics came to the aid of the theorists of institutions, and, joining with natural selection, gave a powerful impetus to the synchronizing social sciences. Arguing that technique superseded liberalism, Ellul, quoting Sartre, pointed out that 'statistics can never be dialectics,'[18] which (however that treacherous term is conceived) nonetheless ruled out questions of change and power from social analysis. It was, therefore, not as difficult for rising economists and social scientists to de-emphasize 'history' as their strident claims to do so sometimes suggested. In any case the rational times of so-called historical 'process' could conveniently reproduce themselves in the models of the social scientists. Sahlins pointed out that Durkheim, for example, while negating 'political econony', was 'forced to reproduce at the level of society, viewed as a kind of supersubject, the same economism he refused as constituting at the level of individual'.[19]

At the turn of the century, there were many ways of characterizing the nature of historical process. The choice was multiple between the two extremes of Bergsonian right-wing cultural irrationalism and evolutionary vitalism, and those Marxists who, as Stuart Hughes points out, were undergoing in the 1890s an 'aberrant and peculiarly insidious form of the reigning cult of positivism'. As a result in the 'transition' from philosophy to psychology – both arrested and abetted by William James – explanation itself seemed 'grounded in epistemology and metaphysics and terminated in psychology or sociology'.[20] The 'ground' was in practice quickly forgotten.

These intellectual changes were inextricably linked with the rise of professional life among the middle classes, a phenomenon which must be seen in relation to the larger historical changes in the late nineteenth century.[21] Among many characterizations of the last quarter of the nineteenth century in America, with its genteel tradition, robber barons, national 'incorporation', its 'urbanization', mass immigrations and its accelerated capital accumulation, it is possible to call it also the era of the rise of the social scientist and economist. Accompanying their origins was a promise of a 'shift from a stress on moralism and reform to a stress on objectivity and science'. Many social scientists were 'mugwumps' of Eastern birth and members of a pre-Civil War social élite: 'they felt their values increasingly menaced by Greenbackers and labor unions.' They first took refuge in theory to protect themselves from politicians and masses alike, later shifting to a more pragmatic and functionalist view of their subject – arguing, for example, 'The applicability of free trade – as a kind of idealism'.[22] With appropriate reluctance, newly equipped with jargon and enhanced status, they forged a new link between 'science' and 'government'. Since that time, there has been, with few exceptions, little cause for optimism that economists are willing to include political values in their calculations or rely on more than a pious hope of 'trickle-down' to the economically dispossessed. In the words of one contemporary economist, 'successfully developing countries' now have one thing in common and that is 'one-party systems, some of them outright dictatorships'.[23] Such perhaps is one political result of the triumph of economic method in the late twentieth century.

The present work will study a historical drift from a political view of the world to a social one, for the original impetus to write this book came from a reading of Hannah Arendt's famous study, *The Human Condition*, originally published in 1958. Arendt theorizes the nature of the social and the political from Greek and Roman thinkers. Her aim is to distinguish terms which have a long history of being confused, and to suggest that our contemporary world not only has its own version of this confusion but practices it in fact. Arendt argues that traditionally the *polis* is the public area of political speech, the *societas* the sphere of the household (οἶκος). The first was the sphere of freedom, the second the sphere of necessity. Her book attempts partially to document and more especially to theorize the incursion of the second into the first, and to assess the consequences of that incursion. The blurring of the two realms in our own time – from the middle of the nineteenth century onwards – has certain effects:

> In our understanding, the dividing line is entirely blurred, because we see the body of peoples and political communities in the image of a family whose everyday affairs have to be taken care of by a gigantic, nation-wide administration of housekeeping. The scientific thought that corresponds to this development is no longer political science but 'national economy' or 'social economy' or *Volkswirtschaft*, all of which indicate a kind of 'collective housekeeping'; the collective of families economically organized into the facsimile of one super-human family is what we call 'society', and its political form of organization is called 'nation'.[24]

The consequences of this victory of society are many. One of them is a new conformity. The true political realm in contrast has always been characterized by debate among those who held different views. The ideology developed to sustain 'society' Arendt sees reflected in the rise of economics as a science:

> It is the same conformism, the assumption that men behave and do not act with respect to each other, that lies at the root of the modern science of economics, whose birth coincided with the rise of society and which, together with its chief technical tool, statistics, became the social science par excellence. Economics – until the modern age a not too important part of ethics and politics and based on the assumption that men act with respect to their economic activities as they act in every other respect – could achieve a scientific character only when men had become social beings and unanimously followed certain patterns of behaviour, so that those who did not keep the rules could be considered to be asocial or abnormal.[25]

Arendt goes on to explain that statistics are perfectly valid when dealing with large numbers and long periods. Historical meaning, however, might well depend on rare events, particular acts which the statistical view actually rules out of court. The dead of the First World War probably would not show up as part of global population statistics for the period 1914–18. The fact, however, should be the despair of statistics in its incapacity to describe the world in human terms, not a despair of history. Equipped with her distinction between *polis* and *societas*, Arendt can criticize with some irony Marx's withering away of the State, defend freedom from its modern characterization as unsolvable subjectivity, as determined or undetermined will, make new distinctions between labour and work, redefine the nature of activity, reassess the political nature of 'story', defend unpredictability, and claim ultimately that the highest human action takes place in the contemplative life. Feminists, of course, have argued that the radicalization of the 'social' will produce its own political effects. But the equalization of roles in the domain of the οἶκος and the coming to power of women in the by now socialized domain of political institutions (and current and recent women national leaders are good examples), as yet promise little reclamation of the political domain for freedom in these terms. Even so the Conclusion of this book will expand the Arendtian thesis in many different directions by drawing on a multiplicity of theorists to describe a world in which democratic political action is endlessly subverted by hegemonic means, as well as by actual relocations of the sources of power.

The aim of this book is to look at three well-known American writers of the late nineteenth and early twentieth century in the context of what Arendt calls 'the rise of the social'. What Whyte says of 1890s figures like James, Dewey, Beard and Veblen applies equally to Adams and Stein: 'They were not rebels against society; what they fought was the denial of society's power, and they provided an intellectual framework that would complement, rather than inhibit, the future growth of big organization.'[26] They are 'modifying figures'[27] not revolutionary ones. In what follows they will be placed alongside other writers to whom they were indebted, and who commented variously on the same changes. The aim is not to create a genealogy but to suggest a community of problems, texts, and historical attitudes which all three share and deal with in various ways. Literary critics and cultural hisorians will have few problems with the comparison of Henry Adams and William James, but may demur at the inclusion of Gertrude Stein, in spite of Stein's connection with James. Unlike the two men, Stein has only recently generated a large critical following. Critics of Stein have been somewhat seduced by current critical fashions, and, given the radical nature of some of her writing, the effort is scarcely surprising. With due note taken of these, I shall be arguing for a much more 'historical' Stein.

In consequence this work will inevitably oppose a number of

current critical assumptions and evaluations, perhaps most of all in connection with James and Stein. James's reputation in the 1980s almost deserves a study in itself. The main books have been by Barzun and Myers, and Frank Lentricchia has announced 'The Return of William James'.[28] Thus James is claimed by right, centre and left. Barzun is always worth reading, though I disagree more or less completely with 90 per cent of what he has to say. On the whole I prefer his writing on Berlioz, and on Darwin, Marx and Wagner to that on James.[29] Myers's enormous book on James is a rather dull, synchronic and careful paraphrase of the main positions of James. It does, however, come alive in the very considerable footnotes which will be of great use to James scholars. Lentricchia's article is a shallow attempt to climb on a bandwagon, emphasizing the worst aspects of James's legacy of anti-intellectualism, here thinly disguised in the author's 'regular-guy' attitudinizing. His reduction of the idealist philosophical tradition to psychology is ludicrous for one supposedly on the left.[30]

Stein criticism during the last few years has generated more heat than light. Obviously I disagree with Marjorie Perloff's statement that Stein's work, unlike Eliot's, 'requires no great knowledge on the part of the reader'.[31] Besides being simply wrong, the statement tends to prohibit access to the more complex work and confuses apparent content with the question of reading at different levels of age, experience, and comprehension. Linda Mizejewski thinks, alongside Stein critics Bridgman, Hoffman and Weinstein, that the interest in Stein's texts 'must centre on its method not its meaning and that its method is directly concerned with the presentation of an alternate means of perception'.[32] If her summary is accurate then I disagree with all four. The location of 'interest' at the level of a method whose reference is epistemology is an old modernist criticism trick. The present book takes the view that form is a part of meaning and vice versa.

Of the feminist critics Catherine Stimpson seems the most intelligent and accurate, and the following statement is exemplary: 'her [Stein's] literary language was neither "female", nor an unmediated return to signifiers freely wheeling in maternal space. It was instead an American English, with some French traits and a deep structure as genderless as an atom of plutonium. It could bend to patriarchal pressures, or lash against them.'[33] Harriet Chessman has summarized the main feminist positions in her work on Stein, *The Public is Invited to Dance*, and the book is valuable also in that it shows a very intelligent capacity for close reading as well as a truly humanist sensibility and general warmth of heart.[34]

Part of the reason for the current desire to haul Stein into feminist criticism or to make her into an exemplar of modernist or post-modernist aesthetics lies in the need to overstate a case to oppose the stultifying conservatism of what most modern English departments conceive to be the parameters of historical 'modernism', and critical enquiry. It seems odd in the 1990s that most English departments do not even gesture in the direction of French, German, Spanish, Italian and Soviet contributions to modernism, and pleas still have to be made to include Stein in a coercively limited view of a period still defined only by Eliot, Pound, Joyce, and Lawrence, with Wallace Stevens occasionally dragged along for the ride.[35]

The position taken in this book is that there have been eighty or more years of reading 'modernist' texts and that there are certain formal structures that the more advanced reader will have no difficulty with. It is not necessary to explain every parataxis, or deviation from formal syntax, or every departure from Aristotelian plot patterns, or even laboriously to point out narrators who seem as happily 'unreliable' as the South Sea Islanders questioned by Henry Adams. It is not necessary to note every heroic simile in Milton as a heroic simile. It is occasionally at least as interesting to attempt to assess what it means.

This book is concerned above all with meaning. Therefore standard academic monograph practice is not followed here. This work seeks multiple theses and contextual readings to try to demonstrate that various and flexible response which any great work of literature demands. The range is from philosophy and aesthetics to ethics and politics.

Adams, James and Stein had two important things in common: an awareness of the new 'social world' and a concern that the discourses they had inherited in their respective fields had in some way to be modified. They had other things in common also; membership in a *haute bourgeois* class, Harvard, and being American at a time of extraordinary social and political change. All three were 'cosmopolitan', though only Stein chose permanently to live in Europe. The aim of the present study is to suggest that the breakdown of conventional discourse – history for Adams, psychology for James, and the language of common sense and narrative structure for Stein – are in some way related to the social and political changes of their time. The argument will cover all the fields with which they were engaged, and some others which provide instructive parallels. Consequently, note will be taken of philosophical, psychological, linguistic, historical, sociological and literary developments in their own period, but not for the sake of being 'interdisciplinary': that modish academic behaviour directed towards new strictures of methodology.

Reading an important work of literature demands whatever it takes, and is only in the end one reading. The guiding principle of the present study can be found in a few sentences from Sartre:

> Our critical investigation, on the other hand, will make use of everything that comes to hand because, in an individual life, each *praxis* uses the *whole* of culture and becomes both synchronic (in the ensemble of the present) and diachronic (in its human depth); and because our investigation is itself a cultural fact.[36]

This book, also, will make use of 'everything that comes to hand'. It is a book that will deliberately employ short 'digressions' in the hope of subverting any sense of the one true 'path'. So-called 'intertextuality' is taken for granted, but it is not regarded as an aesthetics suspended over some ineffable silence or absence. The aim is to give a reasonably, though in no way determinately, informed sense of the intellectual debates in which the text emerged – with always, at the edges, a feel for the historical moment.

Adams will be examined in the context of his contemporaries, the anthropologist Lewis Henry Morgan and the Scottish historian, Buckle, alongside many other famous nineteenty-century names. Some attempt will be made to give a sense of the polymathic reading with which any statement of Adams engages. James will be looked at in terms of the philosopher John Locke, and also in terms of the English constitutional historian Bagehot, whose work, it will be argued, helps to place James's political attitudes. The full international context of James's scholarship will be insisted upon, and moments chosen to illuminate his own syntheses and directions, both for similarity and contrast. In Stein's case the range of contexts is from popular eighteenth-century novels to contemporary detective fiction: from philosophers like Alfred North Whitehead to contemporary American poets. The largest 'digression' in the work is the chapter on language which links some of the more philosophical aspects of the pages which precede it to historical linguistics. The aim is to provide a heuristic for reading the work of Stein more richly, as well as to place her historically. Informing all the readings is the shadow of the Darwinian revolution in every field of the human sciences.

What is asked of the reader is a slightly different way of reading criticism. The digressions (and they are for the most part short) are not in fact digressions at all, but as much a part of the critical exegesis as the direct commentary on the highlighted texts of the three main authors. The criticism has been made as lively and as creative as possible, while always bearing in mind that its aim is to illuminate the more profound creativity of the great writers of the past.

Hierarchies of genres and canonical texts have been challenged. The focus is on the texts themselves. The aim is to give a sense of what it feels like to read them in the 1990s. In that sense the project differs from that of the conventional literary critic, the historian of science, the philosopher, and the linguistic historian. Darwin did not just discover natural selection with Wallace and announce it to the world in 1859, though such a statement would certainly satisfy the working scientist. The text of *The Origin of Species*, understood historically, is a prose poem of considerable intricacy and complexity. Its very use of English is in the grand style of Shakespeare and Milton. Read in full intellectual and scientific context, it provides enormous lessons about the relationships between science, cultural and political values, ways of viewing the world, rhetoric and persuasion, philosophy and even metaphysics.

The Conclusion will attempt to make concrete some of the historical pressures under which this book was written. It is important to demystify the objective authority which any printed page exerts, to make explicit the values on which judgements in the text are based, to demonstrate the relevance of historical study to contemporary concerns, and to make some analysis of what those contemporary concerns actually are. This book was written in the 1980s and hence came into being, for Anglo-American readers at least, in the context of 'Thatcherism' and 'Reaganomics'. Some effects of pressures on the contemporary university and how they affect intellectuals working in the humanities will be examined in the conclusion. This book will attempt to restore an older sense of intellectual breadth to critical enquiry. The inability to imagine or to have confidence in this tradition has been a failure of courage among many academics. In Raymond Williams's words: 'Is there never to be an end to petty-bourgeois theorists making long-term adjustments to short-term solutions?'[37]

Sartre's definition of critical investigation re-states more analytically the words of Raymond Williams and Ricoeur with which this Introduction began. Not only did Adams, James and Stein write works of a certain seriousness in which 'several things are meant at the same time', but they believed that that was the only way they could write.

The paradigmatic uncertainty existing in all branches of knowledge at the turn of the twentieth century made these writers always creatively uncertain in their modes of procedure. The early critical response, too, was various, especially in respect of James's work, and it was more conflicting and hotly argued than Jamesian criticism seems to be at present. The following study will not evaluate the three evenly nor seek to moralize them into some kind of hierarchical position in relation to one another. The main aim will be to find out what is of relevance in their work for our time. Inevitably, given the volume of work the three generated, a selection has had to be made, but longer and more difficult texts have not been neglected for that reason – for example, Adams's *History of the United States* (1884–91), James's *Principles of Psychology* (1891), Stein's *Making of Americans* (1902–11) – and cross-references to other texts not specifically analysed will be plentiful.

Part One
Henry Adams: Towards the Social World

Chapter 1
Opening the Field

It was Henry Adams, the direct descendant of two American Presidents, who, in a long lifetime of writing history, cultural analysis, and fiction, was to give an incomparable account of those contemporary historial, political, and technological changes which would culminate in what will be called the 'social world'. True, his experience was in some respects limited. His upper-class Bostonian background gave him a unique insight into the implications of shifting American power patterns at the political and social levels. But one does not go to him to understand the lives of ordinary people at this time, nor for evidence – at least directly – of many issues which have become of increasing interest to contemporary historians: the closing of the frontier, the huge growth in immigration, the unique life and culture of ethnic minorities, and what are euphemistically called 'industrialization' and 'urbanization'. In one way the world of Henry Adams is the world of Henry James: a world of cosmopolitan travel, of drawing-rooms in time-worn European cities, of an American class background as solid as that of an Old Harrovian or Old Etonian in Victorian England. Not the least of the contradictions Adams fought was the patrician call to duty in an America which was interested neither in patricians nor in public service. If William James was a preacher without a pulpit, Adams was a politician without a constituency. Yet, as contemporary scholars dig up the diaries of immigrants, reinstate the disadvantaged groups, challenge the positivist and nominalist biases of conservative historians and indeed literary critics, it is worth having another look at Henry Adams, whose direct and indirect commentaries on his time are still important both for their content and for the formal procedures governing that content. In strictly political terms Adams pits a peculiarly intelligent conservative response, at every level, against that nineteenth-century liberal ideology which has become the nexus of values of the Far Right in the twentieth century. The result was what one critic has very accurately called, 'a political explication of the meaning of power in society'.[1]

If Adams's was a view from the hotel balcony, it was not that of an average tourist. His family inheritance at the political level made him happiest in Washington. Coming as he did at the end of a line of distinguished New England historians, Adams's intellectual appetite was voracious, his consciousness of the 'American experiment' acute. His experience in England during the Civil War acquainted him with actual international diplomacy, seven years as a Havard professor editing a major journal put him in touch with most of the main intellectual currents of his day. However banal his theories of history, however misjudged his apparent search for reassurance in scientific truth, and however tortured and deflective his comments on social and cultural life, there is something in Henry Adams that holds the attention.

Perhaps his contradictions are peculiarly Victorian: the acute melancholy and the passion for travel and activity; the absolute devotion to the writer's task; the contempt for progress betrayed by a somewhat nationalistic pride in it. He portrayed himself as a recluse, yet his letters sparkle with social grace. To have spent an evening with him over cigars and brandy in Cuba would recall the world of Conrad – a delight in the glitter of 'sound fellows' who could spin a yarn over a world where late nineteenth-century capitalist dog ate dog. There is nostalgia tempered by irony. Adams's many close friends, men and women, bear witness to his charm, and capacity for conversation.

At every level, and indeed in every work – whatever its precise generic nature – there is a sense of that rapidly shifting world of late nineteenth-century America. The sense is there, whether in the early part of his career he is discussing the sequences of diplomacy in the administrations of Jefferson and Madison, or the medieval politics of a Bernard of Clairvaux in the later part of his career. No other American writer except perhaps Mark Twain has put so fully on record what it was like to live in that world so much on the threshold of our own. For in post-Civil War America the liberal tenets which sustained England in its mid-century heyday broke down. The bourgeois individual began to give way to mass man, the small business to corporate power, party to 'pressure group' and the free-market economy to the stirrings of 'planning' on a world-wide basis. The discoveries and speculations of biology 'de-centred' man. Science itself bowed out of the public domain. Its increasing prestige (dependent on the need for long, specialized training) gave rise to an increasing nervousness about its role in actual society. God himself 'died', and worse, with him seemed to fade the faith in language itself – indeed in all of the humanistic arts. Not the least unfortunate aspect of the separation of scientific endeavour from all other forms of human knowledge was the breeding of a contempt for that knowledge among those who were increasingly in receipt of the lion's share of available resources.

In Adams's own field of history, the traditional forms of biography and narrative gave way before the new sciences of anthropology and sociology in all their variant forms. In literature itself naturalism mirrored a world indifferent to the human condition, a world in which the fatalism of the capitalist, drunk on statistics, had replaced the drama of Christian history. Even family life, atomized by the requirements of industrializing society, underwent profound changes, though women, for the first time in any numbers, became conscious that their lives might break free of exclusively domestic necessities. It is in this context that Adams posed his questions about the relations between oppositions which seemed to confirm that capitalist fatalism at every level. The oppositions of science and religion, labour and capital, the roles of men and women, art and science, politics and big business seemed to have an autonomous force like that of nature. What forms of language and style could make sense of it all?

I

It had been easier for Adams's grandfather, John Quincy Adams. For both Henry Adams and his brother Brooks, their grandfather's Enlightenment dream, already turning sour by the 1830s, not only seemed an antique memory, but the dream itself seemed to have been employed to further the excesses of the age which succeeded it. Quincy Adams's New England values of public service built on the premises of the free individual were being corrupted by the survival of the slogans of 'states' rights' and of 'trade and private adventure' into a corporate age. The old liberal values had become a theology which concealed and diverted attention from the reality of the trusts and capital accumulation. Alongside these factors, for Brooks Adams as for his brother, was a new factor undreamed of in the early liberal consensus: technology. For faith in technology had, at the very least, become ambiguous by the 1890s:

> Eli Whitney's cotton gin was certainly one of the most famous and successful of the applications of science to a supremely bountiful gift of God in making American cotton serviceable and cheap to the whole human race. But it propagated slavery, it turned the fair state of Virginia into an enormous slave-breeding farm, where

forty thousand blacks were annually exported to the South, and thus inexorably induced the Civil War.[2]

Even that greatest of mechanics, in the eyes of the eighteenth-century Deist, God himself, by the 1830s seemed to be devoting himself more to utility than benevolence. Of the existence of an 'Omnipotent Spirit' Quincy Adams entertained 'certain involuntary and agonizing doubts'. For Brooks Adams, looking back on his grandfather's life, the man who cultivated his garden and searched the planetary system for truth had become an anachronism. As the younger Adams saw it, Quincy Adams's passion for education and science had 'unwittingly ministered to the demon'.[3]

And yet there is no better place to begin a commentary on Henry Adams's work than to resurrect a forgotten work of John Quincy Adams, the *Report upon Weights and Measures* (1821), which was officially commissioned by Congress, and then administratively buried. In many respects the work anticipates both the grandsons' speculations on the relation of abstract truth to society, the competing claims of institutional and individual life, 'technological creep', and the relation between knowledge and belief. Brooks Adams again gives an accurate summary of the work in question: 'Science could not believe it could be sound and yet literary, artistic and historical. For the *Report upon Weights and Measures* is a vast effort at generalization. It was unprecedented. It deals with history and philosophy quite as much as with physics.'[4]

In composing his report for Congress Quincy Adams had to consider and evaluate two established systems of weights and measures: one English, which had been adopted in the United States through an obvious continuity of tradition, and the other French, which Napoleon, with the help of distinguished mathematicians, including Laplace, had created by fiat in his reforming of the civil code. Adams saw that the problem of measurement involved every aspect of human intercourse in relation to nature. Like money and, as will later be demonstrated, language itself, measurement was at once necessary and alienating. The word Adams uses to describe its originating force is 'society': 'Measures of surface, of distance, and capacity arise immediately from domestic society. They are wants proceeding rather from society than from individual existence.'[5]

Quincy Adams cites Renaissance (and ultimately classical) theories of measurement to affirm that measurement is human not divine. In the words of Protagoras, 'man' is the measure of all things. The traces are still there in words like 'span', 'pace,' 'digit', 'hand', 'foot', and so forth. In a pre-industrial society this not only makes the relations of architecture fit a 'human scale', but is also a source of diversity. Nonetheless, Adams also notes, in the decimal system the fingers of the human hand suggest a group code; thus they are 'supplied by nature' (*Report*, p. 7). There is a problem here crucial to questions to be raised later in relation to Henry Adams. Like his grandson, Quincy Adams refused to interpose a conscious theory of knowledge between nature and artefact. Nature as unmediated model is in fact a nonsense. A contemporary example would be Le Corbusier's complex computations of measurement units based on the human figure for his sometimes inhuman architectural scale. It is after all how you conceptualize from the figure of the hand that is important. For the 'hand' is already an abstraction and the 'rule of thumb' is more a rule than a thumb.

Adams begins with a fable of origins:

> When a child goes forth into the world to make a settlement for himself, and found a new family, civil society commences; government is instituted – the tillage of the ground, the discovery and use of metals, exchanges, traffic by barter, a *common* standard of measures, and mensuration by weight, or apparent specific gravity, all arise from the multiplying relations between man and man, now superadded to those between man and things.
>
> (*Report*, p. 9)

The 'child' is instinct with Lockean and Rousseauean qualities. His 'growth' provides a metaphor of natural process which analogically relates to the 'development' of society. The bias is therefore psychological and anthropological. Unlike Marx and Hegel, who relegate the family to the domain of necessity, Quincy Adams, closer to Vico here, predicates civil order on domestic institutions and makes them a basis of commercial and agricultural activity.

Quincy Adams is clearly seeking a law of history, and like his more famous historical and sociological predecessors, and like his contemporaries in the nineteenth century, is obliged to think in threes. His search is for what he calls a 'theoretic history'. In fact it is less a theoretic history than a paralleling of phases of the history of measurement with social development.

> Thus in tracing the theoretic history of weights and measures to their original elements in the nature and necessities of man, we have found linear measure with individual existence; superficial capacious, itinerary measure, and decimal arithmetic, with domestic society; weights and common standards, with civil society; money, coins, and law; arising in successive and parallel progression together.
>
> (*Report*, p. 11)

Individual, social, civil form a line which intersects with linear, decimal and 'uniform metrology'. It is a kind of correspondential and metaphoric thinking by which Adams hopes somehow to relate history and scientific knowledge in a smooth progressive curve. But even at the theoretical level the parallelisms come unstuck. If, as he argues, the Jews define their history from a single family, and the Greeks form 'associations', the generalizations of theoretic history fall apart.

Already Quincy Adams is speculating on the philosophical problems of unity and multiplicity which were to occupy his grandson, and on all the same subjects: abstract science, domestic and civil society, law and political economy. What is useful in this work is the realization that 'standards' are a kind of working hypothesis rather than a truth. Discussing the 'ton', for example, he says: it 'is in its nature combined with the art of the ship builder, and with the whole science of hydraulics and of navigation' (p. 27). 'Its nature' is different from 'nature' per se. The risk of an oppressive uniformity is everywhere in Quincy Adams's mind. Reformers in these matters, he continues, should look to the 'errors and mutabilities of the law' which they embody rather than complain of the absence of 'an immutable standard from nature' (p. 45).

Nonetheless the attraction of French theoretical elegance is strong. Baym states that 'John Quincy Adams discovered (in Pascal's own phrase) the esprit de geométrie coupled with the esprit de finesse in the very style of the man'.[6] Pascal was to be an important writer for Henry Adams also, and his statement that 'We know the truth not only through our reason but also through our heart',[7] guided Henry Adams's entire writing career. It was one thing to admire French elegance, quite another, in this case, to bring it down to earth. What abstraction from nature could guarantee theoretical constancy: a swinging pendulum, a measurement dependent on a quarter of the Equator or a quarter of the meridian? The French decided on the meridian, measuring an actual meridian from Dunkirk to Barcelona by triangulation.

At this point in his argument Quincy Adams bursts into rhetoric; a late paean to the dream of progressive science in the democratic service of man. Going metric foretells the millennium:

> . . . if the Spirit of Evil is, before the final consummation of things, to be cast down from his dominion over men, and bound in the chains of a thousand years, the foretaste here of man's eternal felicity; then this system of common instruments, to accomplish all the changes of social and friendly commerce, will furnish the links of sympathy between the inhabitants of the most distant

regions; the metre will surround the globe in use as well as in multiplied extension; and one language of weights and measures will be spoken from the Equator to the Poles.

(Report, p. 48)

The right-wing Christian reaction soon put an end in France to hopes of a 'reform' of the calendar. Indeed the system seemed to work better for space than for time. Quincy Adams still needs to bolster his critique of the French system from 'nature'. Nevertheless the standards taken from the measurement of the earth had 'no reference to the advancement and powers of the human body' (p. 70). In addition Adams cites one French navigator who, after trying to steer his ship 'decimally', recommended that the National Assembly of France decree that the earth should perform precisely four hundred revolutions a year. In our own time, as the French metrification system finally triumphs in Europe, contemporary changes have been not without 'frauds upon the scanty pittance of the poor' (p. 14), as Adams feared, and even as this is being written, the binding of British Parliamentary reports in Hansard has gone metric, and complaints of its unwieldy size have come thick and fast from the noble lords of the upper House.[8] 'Nature', comments Quincy Adams, has no 'partialities for the number ten' (p. 85). In fact two views of nature clash in Adams's argument; an Enlightenment belief in mechanical order and a Romantic view of a variousness which is human in that it resists mechanical order. The clash, however, enables Adams simultaneously to criticize the a priori inflexibility of the French system and to praise its theoretical complexity, while suggesting that theory is not truth.

The most important problems the *Report* raises are the interrelations between orders of knowledge. It suggests limits to the order of mathematical truth as uniquely relevant to civil society, while promoting a vigorous investigation of that relation. It suggests, too, that solutions are not to be found (any more than with Marx) in hypostasized orders, nor in custom, but in a human process which connects human beings to nature via metaphorical thinking in their relations with each other. The mode of description (with such pre-transcendentalist conceits as 'gravity and extension will not walk together with the same staff', (p. 114) is an attempt in terms of metaphor to investigate the human values proposed by the new styles of measurement. The 'staff' is not the measure common to gravity and extension but a reminder that drives towards what in science was to be called 'the classical synthesis', while appearing to give support for a human project, also ran the risk of confusing truth with unity.

So to Henry Adams himself. The essays of the late 1860s and '70s give a good indication of the range of Adams's interests and of the ways in which he began to organize the relations between those different intellectual fields which took his attention. The typical preoccupations are all there at the beginning of the career, though the treatment and the tone vary towards the end. With characteristic mid-Victorian energy Adams covers topics as diverse as education, the 10th edition of Lyell's *Principles of Geology* (1867), anthropological speculations on the 'primitive rights' of women; there are several essays on economics and finance, contemporary politics, and one essay on Napoleon at Santo Domingo. Here are early speculations about politics and economics which were to be taken up again in the biographies, the *History*, and *The Education of Henry Adams*. Early thoughts about the role of women point towards their later treatment in the novels, and in *Mont-Saint-Michel and Chartres*. An interest in the history and philosophy of science is already apparent. A search for a theory of history that would fill the gap left by the apparent collapse of traditional philosophy under the weight of new scientific discovery is also clearly in evidence. Adams was to be interested primarily in the relations between these problems; between ethnology and the process of time revealed by the new geology, between conventional history and economics, and between society and politics.

'My article on Lyell humiliated me. It was so damn neatly put together and not an original idea in it,' Adams confessed to his father, Charles Francis Adams.[9] Jordy, the first commentator to take Adams's scientific interests seriously, disagreed. It was a fine well-balanced piece.[10] Although it gives every appearance of being reasonably written, it is not, however, the neat exegesis that Adams himself suggests nor as 'well-balanced' as Jordy claims. It is in fact rife with the most interesting prejudice, not to mention considerable cunning, for as an ambitious young man Adams wanted to make his mark in the literary establishment. Samuels notes that the essay did in fact help ensure Adams a job on the *North American Review* of which he later became editor.[11] A priori, the obvious biases include the fact that Agassiz, the most famous American biologist of the period, and who had never really accepted Darwin's theories, had been a much admired tutor of Adams at Harvard, and that Lyell (who was personally well acquainted with America) was an intimate of the Adams family and a staunch supporter of the Northern cause in the Civil war. Adams, like Lyell, never quite brought himself to accept evolutionary theories.[12]

Adams begins the essay with the famous declaration by the English geologist Hutton: 'In the economy of the world, I can see no traces of a beginning, no prospect of an end.'[13] Then Lyell is presented as a great theorizer after a rather dull period of fact-collecting. Adams cunningly associates fact-collecting with superstition and theory-building with enlightenment. After all, as Lenin said, is not 'intelligent idealism closer to intelligent materialism than unintelligent materialism.'[14] The case is not, however, so simple. There were theorists aplenty before Lyell and, if anything, Lyell was the prosaic one, with his temporal metaphysics disguised within an empirical logic. But at the level of presentation Lyell too was anything but bald and prosaic. He was hotly arguing his case within a charged atmosphere. Adams's ambiguities reflect the then-current paradox that while Hutton was regarded as too speculative, Lyell depended upon him for his 'steady state' theory of the earth. Like his grandfather on the metric system, Adams emphasizes the rather one-dimensional view of the earth which he encounters in Lyell: 'He seems to feel a certain amount of pleasure in lopping away fanciful excrescences which other men foster, and in treating the earth's marvellous history in that wholly scientific spirit which admits only what is enough, and no more than enough, to produce the result observed' (*Historical Essays*, p. 467).

Adams feels the chill of the imperial progress of scientific over other forms of discourse. He goes on to remark that 'Sir Charles is essentially a conservative philosopher, at least so far as concerns a rigorous adherence to a strictly defined method' (p. 468). Adams, like his grandfather, is at least ambiguous on method. How could he respond critically to Lyell's conservatism and not give himself away? Leyll's prestige was enormous at this time and there were personal debts. Against this was Agassiz's catastrophism which, if it could not fit with the best current theories – stemming mainly from Lyell – was more likely to have a psychological appeal to an incipient historian, not to mention a scion of New England watching America being torn apart in the bloodiest war in history. So Adams niggles away with one arm tied behind his back. If 'Sir Charles's books have not the charm of a lively imagination, they have at all events a certain solidity which gives them high authority' (p. 469). Phrases like 'yet we are required to believe', 'most probably is', 'certainly the most reasonable', betray dissent beneath a strategy of prudence.[15]

Adams shows his hand a little more clearly in his discussions of climate and geography, important to him, perhaps, because arguments from climate and geography were part of a historical vision of man which had stretched from Montesquieu to Buckle and Taine.[16] It was, after all, his old teacher, Agassiz, who had linked palaeontology and arguments about climate in his theories of glaciers. Critics have noted that, contrary to Agassiz's intentions, this unwittingly helped 'progressive theories' of the earth's history, first by 'emphasizing the progressiveness of the fossil record and then linking it with embryology'.[17] Adams contents himself by observing that if climate changes can happen once they can happen many times, though he also throws in a cautionary note about the 'cyclical' nature of Lyell's time patterns. These are cautionary notes rather than opposition to Lyell, but they add up to a significantly ambiguous statement.

Adams is already concerned with questions of heat loss and of the apparently sudden nature of changes in climate. He also asks Lyell to square his assertions with the prestige sciences of mathematico-astronomy and physics. Lord Kelvin (who was to occupy Adams in his heat-degradation theories in later years) had maintained a famous opposition to Darwin, for example, by refusing to agree with the geologist and the biologist over the enormous lengths of time with which geological and species changes were accomplished.

Adams on species is even more devious in argument than Adams on geology. His essay reflects Lyell's own ambiguity on species change. Originally anti-Lamarckian – as Cuvier had been – Lyell announced his conversion to Lamarck's evolution, knowing that Darwin wanted to avoid association with Lamarck's theories. Throughout the essay Adams refers again and again to 'Lamarck and Darwin' as if they were representatives of the same theory. Adams refuses to consider the differences between them, and contents himself with placing the psychology of classification in an ironic light: 'Every physiologist has enjoyed a delicate sense of his own omnipotence over forms which have had the misfortune to be discovered for the first time. He is at liberty to class them as varieties, or to invent for them a new species, according to his individual views of their – and of his own – importance.' (*Historical Essays*, p. 485).

Adams does show himself conversant with some of the weaknesses of Darwin's theory. He points out the unconvincing nature of the 'breeding' analogies which even Huxley, Darwin's able English explicator, had played down, and on the gaps in the fossil record. Lyell, says Adams, has been forced, against his praiseworthy conservative nature, to accept the 'doctrine peculiarly disagreeable to his special cast of mind, that the creative energy which shaped the world has not yet ceased to act and that when active it moved by leaps, creating new forms at will' (p. 487). Lamarck never argued for random arbitrary species creation – rather progression from multiple creations – and Darwin never talked about creative energy, and denied multiple creations vigorously, though his notebooks show he had entertained the idea in 1838.[18]

What clearly disturbs Adams at this stage is the randomness of evolutionary process, the arbitrariness of classification and the loss of certainty. He shows himself, however, more willing to theorize than Lyell, but like Lyell somewhat unwilling to accept the consequences of Darwin's revolution of the world picture. In a technique which was to become familiar, Adams argues by positing simplified oppositions. He polarizes the argument over embryology by putting von Baer and Agassiz on one side and Darwin and Lamarck on the other. He tries to hang on to special creations theory and evolution by suggesting that embryos recapitulate evolutionary forms of life before reaching their ideal type. He cites Agassiz and von Baer as evidence. However, Agassiz had suggested at least three types of parallelisms, and von Baer saw the embryo's progress neither as fully recapitulative, nor as continuous or absolutely reflective of the various stages. Adams does not (nor did many others) discuss Darwin's special use of embryological evidence of descent as the bond between living organisms and the past. Lyell is finally praised because he 'sought a permanent and natural, not a rare and fortuitous development' (*Historical Essays*, 498).

In this 'purely scientific' discussion there is therefore rather more than objective exegesis. Adams already shows himself interested in conceptualizing a theory of development which he looks for in science. He can avoid an awkward philosophic impasse by switching the course of the argument to psychology. He shows himself unconvinced that the present is a guide to the past, but is very nervous about the fact that it might not be. He places himself in the conservative camp in order to ironize its position. He is reluctant to accept the notion of chance in historical process and yet he is sceptical about either linear or cyclical views of development. He already shows an interest in prediction. Perhaps a regard for Lyell's personal loyalty, memories of Agassiz, a nostalgia for the coherent world of special creations (coinciding neatly with his eighteenth-century childhood, as he was to call it in the *Education*) distorts the account of Darwin. The tone of the essay places the issues of science in a wider context. One suspects already a scientistic search for analogies of process.

Certain it is that the issues raised here remained with Adams all his life. In the 1890s he is still inveighing against Darwin. In the South Pacific he writes, 'Darwin says that the coral islands have miraculous powers of sinking, while all the coral islands I have seen are perfectly stupid evidences of rising.'[19] The tone is ironic – but still betrays Adams's sympathies. And later still, in 1909, he is recommending Jean Henri Fabre's work because the great French entomologist is anti-Darwin.[20] Here, too is another clue. The French – given Cuvier's influence – took a long time to accept Darwin.[21] Like his grandfather, this American had a more than secret scorn for English metaphysical untidiness, and under a pragmatic common-sense set of strategies, was capable of at least invoking French tidiness against it – while calling down a plague on both their houses.

The underlying problem in Adams's meditation on geology and species was how to recognize the particular event in a new scientific world whose laws suggested that time upset the security of classifications and structures. Although, prima facie, the content was remote from geology and species change, Adams was pursuing the same question in his essay, 'The Primitive Rights of Women', of 1876.[22] The German historian Niebuhr believed that 'early history must be of institutions rather than of events'.[23] Adams, too, turns his attention to the institutions of law and marriage. The movement from events to 'populations of events', to use Toulmin's phrase, brought under scrutiny hitherto invisible structures of human behaviour, while like most structural analysis, it tended to ignore time and history. A movement away from the historicizing of events to structures of events in Adams's time can be seen in virtually every field of enquiry. The methodology of the analysis applied to 'institutions' tended to be legal and psychological. Adams's essay – which relied on Sir Henry Maine's *The Early History of the Property of Married Women* (1873) and McLennan's *Studies in Ancient History* (1876) – must also be placed in the context of the 1870s when demands for a new view of women were becoming increasingly energetic. Were women to be characterized in terms of society, where structures of private life purported to be the secret reason of public life, or in terms of civilization, where the patterns of non-public life and subjectivity were traditionally ignored? And what was the relation between the two as their boundaries became increasingly blurred?

Because the terms of Adams's discussion are legal and psychological, they offer ambiguous comfort to those seeking in his work strong evidences of support for a new view of women. At one level Adams looks like a liberal, challenging the autonomy of custom as divinely given. It is not to be doubted that the wedding ring is a 'symbol of marital power' (*Historical Essays*, p. 2), that contemporary marriage is a decline from a golden age of communitarianism, that property is the substantial ghost in the machine of marriage, that women in societies other than the America of Adams's day had a better deal (thereby undercutting American confidence in the perfection of their own institutions), and that on given historical occasions women are every bit as powerful and competent as men. Against this, however, are ranged the entire terms of the discussion; not to mention some of the assumptions with which Adams was working.

First Adams describes the essential patriarchy of Roman law (*patria potestas*) and contrasts it with the more 'elevated' medieval Christian view of women 'with its high moral ideals, and its passionate adoration of the Virgin Mother' (p. 3). Here Adams sets out the terms of a discussion which will culminate in *Mont-Saint-Michel and Chartres*. The Roman and the Christian are viewed as absolute contrasts. Adams does not consider that the 'Virgin Mother' in fact denigrates women by denying their erotic life, and that the Christian concept subverts their historical role by making a powerful biological drive towards motherhood into a sacred compulsion which is then used to deny women's human right to a multiplicity of life. Given the dubious poles of the argument, however, Adams proceeds to modify them. In fact by subverting these typical oppositions he makes a number of both positive and negative points.

Between the Roman and Christian paradigms of primitive society, for example, he places the ancient 'communal societies' – those stock-in-trade Utopias of nineteenth-century ethnological historians. One senses in Adams an old New England anarchist pleasure when he describes these communities, as if the spirit of the most famous New England Utopian experiment of his own immediate past, the community of intellectuals, teachers, and workers at Brook Farm, lingered as a memory. Unlike Hawthorne, however, who criticized just such a community in his novel, *The Blithedale Romance* (1852), by using the terms of the Gothic to depict women crushed between male leadership drives, Adams praises the early communal societies for their 'system of relationship through women', and the matriarchal patterns of family organization (p. 4). Adams is also still enough of a classicist to look back on this 'golden age' when paradoxically 'mankind was not denounced by the thirst for gold, when all men were of one family, and all the products of the earth or of industry were held by brothers [in a matriarchy?] in common' (p. 5).

Adams now switches from myth to psychology. It is the instinct for property which changes Utopia. For Hegel and Marx the family occupied the domain of necessity and for Engels, too, the relation between marriage and property was variable. For Adams the relationship is an essentialist one. Instinct creates an ahistorical psychology of behaviour and subsequently makes it the basis of institutions: 'the institution of marriage had its origin in love of property' (p. 6). Like Engels Adams also draws on the work of the famous early American anthropologist, Lewis Henry Morgan. While both make use of Morgan to throw doubt on an official Victorian consensus about marriage which operated legally in favour of men (Adams notes that Native American women have the right of divorce, the right to return to their families and the right to dismiss their husbands), Adams tends to deal with 'patriarchy' ironically, so that 'matriarchy' comes out as merely affirming the traditional legal status of the marriage relation – except that this time it is the woman who rules: 'In most cases she was the head of the family; her husband came to live with her, not she with him and her children belonged to her clan, not to their father's (p. 11). Unchanged law and social organization confirmed the status of women in Adams's Utopian fiction as it did for men in his own society.

Evidence for these claims was to be found in mythology, which delivered its special insights to the social truth of the ethnologist of the period. The resultant structural emphasis, however, enables Adams to look at models for the relations in what might be called a kind of cultural study of sex roles. In Egyptian mythology, Isis (fertility), Adams observes, mediates the claims of Osiris (creative light against darkness) and Horus/Ra (the son). Within this triad, which Adams describes in an almost Hegelian manner as 'ever returning upon itself' (p. 14), Isis plays a crucial role. Adams states that when the Christians took the Egyptian triad (probably through Alexandrian civilization) they 'dethroned the woman from her place', and he continues, 'Yet even then, notwithstanding this degradation, the irresistible spread of Matriolity, the worship of the Virgin Mother, proved how strongly human nature revolted from the change' (p. 14).

There are several problems here. The first is the assumption of a binary sexual force within culture which can be simply symbolized. The semiotic of the Virgin Mother does not necessarily imply the semantic of the feminine as an essentialized alternative to the masculine. Nor is there, in history, an automatic compensatory process located within 'human nature'. The relation of the images of a culture to actual history is hardly simple. In some sense Adams is heir to Herder's conviction that mythology reveals the spirit of the race. Adams's paean to the spirit of the Aryans, and his persistent search for images of control in the submerged histories of law and property, must be seen for what they are. Not an admirer of Darwin, Adams's emphasis on 'structure' can lead, nonetheless, to the worst kind of social-Darwinist sentiment: '. . . the race which followed this path [law and property] with the most vigor must have been the strongest race and the best befitted to conquer. Such a race had a natural instinct for law. . .' (p. 15).

In the first instance then Adams sees marriage only in the 'bourgeois' terms of legality and property; terms which he accepts as the basis of society. The 'instinct' for these operates as a kind of natural selection enabling strong races to conquer. There are further difficulties when Adams turns his attention to the ancient epics. In a lively and empathetic style he retells the story of Penelope with long quotations from the *Odyssey*, and comes to the conclusion that Penelope's action 'was contrary to the advice and wishes of her relatives and connections on both sides. She was perfectly independent' (p. 23). There is an unresolved contradiction in Adams's argument throughout this essay which holds to the supremacy of family institutions, while valuing those institutions according to the degree to which women are free of them. There is the same ambivalence over Roman law. The piety of the Roman matron and child counterbalances the law's extravagant logic. This 'compensation' however operates across two entirely different levels of human order and consequently cannot be 'economically' evaluated.

Like Vico, Adams now moves from epic to early medieval poetry, searching for a guide to the origins of human institutions; and more specifically history's treatment of women. '*Njalsaga*, like the poems of Homer, turns on the character of a woman' (p. 26). Hallgerda who murders three husbands and lives comfortably off their combined incomes is spoken of thus: 'No Norse pirate, no Danish jarl, enjoyed more completely than she the legal rights of a free citizen' (p. 31). Women's accumulation of property through divorce was to be a twentieth-century problem of sexuality and economics, feeding the mass society's appetite for melodrama. The particular 'irony' also indicates an all-too-familiar male nervousness about the 'ruthlessness' of an 'independent' woman. A similar ambiguity will occur again and again in Adams's admiration for the strong woman. The image is usefully directed against the genteel tradition but it negates as much as it affirms. There is another famous moment in *Njalsaga* where man and wife die in a burning house together rather than facing the prospect of only one of them being saved.[24] Adams does not mention it.

Adams now complicates his argument a little. A wedding ring represents a civil contract rather than a mere receipt of sale. Also the Church's role not only has the effect of elevating women but degrades them with its emphasis on male asceticism. Women, Adams argues, were thrown towards the Church in the absence of civil rights – the implication being that such compensation is not altogether healthy. Equally the medieval image of Griselda, the endless sufferer, is seen to be a regression from the Hallgerdas, Brunnhildas, and Fregundas. What is more interesting than this commonplace (for the time) image of brawny Germanic types being replaced by women instinct with Christian submissiveness, is Adams's realization that it is an image manufactured by the State: 'These medieval conceptions belonged to a time when the most pressing necessity of society was concentration, and when discipline was the chief lesson to be learned' (*Historical Essays*, p. 38). More than twenty years before Brooks Adams's book *The Law of Civilization and Decay* (1899), Henry Adams is interested in the propaganda of centralized power and its social effects. The piety of the Griselda image directly serves this power. 'Then', says Adams, 'the family, like the State, took on the character of a petty absolutism' (p. 39). One valuable lesson to be learnt from the essay then is the way sexual images are created to serve the interests of the power structure. In his essay on Pocahontas, for example, after debunking Pocahontas as a myth Adams concludes: 'The Virginia Company had no interest in denying the truth of a story so well calculated to draw popular sympathy toward the colony.'[25]

In the end, therefore, Adams sees history as a fight between rival institutions; between the family and the law. The one is a woman's realm, the other a masculine one. Both in turn are dependent on the economics of 'centralization'. But by a series of inversions, ironic subversions and an emphasis on the psychology of image-making Adams subverts the simple opposites he had started out with. Sometimes there is a nostalgia for ideal sexual roles, more often, however, a startling insight into the relation between sex roles, law, religion and power. This seems valuable in spite of a number of clearly sexist prejudices.

Adams's early essays on economics, 'The Bank of England Restriction, 1797–1821' (1867), 'The Legal Tender Act' (1870), and 'The New York Gold Conspiracy' (1870), are perhaps best looked at together.[26] Like the other early essays they show Adams searching for an historical causality which operates at a quasi-structural level. All three essays also indicate something of his response to the irrevocable changes in the American economy which occurred during the Civil War. No American reading Adams's account of the way the Bank of England handled its finances during the Napoleonic wars could fail to draw the comparison. In evident contrast to the United States (and John Quincy Adams's defeat over the National Bank issues in the 1820s should not be forgotten), the Bank of England 'exercised a controlling influence even upon the remote provincial trader' (*Historical Essays*, p. 180). Adams criticizes the lack of a free-floating interest rate – usury laws were still in force – and also the over-reliance on credit control. The sharp cut-back in the money supply which sacrificed so many businesses during England's invasion panic in 1793 Adams sees as unnecessary: 'A bolder course might have been adopted; the discounts might have been liberally increased, the gold paid out to the last guinea' (p. 185). Adams is in effect arguing that the history of political decisions about capital is at least as important as the history of contingent events, diplomacy, battles won and lost, and Carlylean heroes, and a lot more amenable to structural analysis. The question of the relation of government to economics was, therefore, not a result of Adams's interest in British history, rather it reflected the bias of a historican already concerned with abstract causality in an America moving into what Marx called the era of capital accumulation. It also provided a useful parallel with which to criticize the Legal Tender Act of 1862, which Adams saw as a key historical moment on the threshold of that era.

In his essay on the Legal Tender Act, Adams uses a technique he was to apply in his *History of the United States*. One figure will represent a passing power structure and an opposing one will characterize the emergent structure. Adams's sympathy with the loser will be the basis for attacking the winner. Characterology will directly symbolize the transformation from a publicly-controlled order to a secretly-controlled one. Thus in this essay Gallatin represents the old liberal economists who, even in wartime, insist on raising bonds on the open market. Spaulding is the pragmatic representative of the new speculator, happy to print money and damn the consequences. The latter receives the full weight of Adams's Bostonian sarcasm: 'Spaulding naturally applied to the situation the principles of finance he had learned in shaving notes at a country bank' (p. 286). All this is rather patrician satire, but what is more important is that Adams attacks the concomitant propaganda of necessity: 'the unwarrantable plea of necessity', as he calls it. It is on the basis of such a plea that the new bosses of the trusts are able to bolster up 'their scandalous schemes against the pressure of sound economic laws' (p. 301). Patrician or not, Adams is concerned about the shift of power in American life and the breakdown of political control in relation to the new social-economic order. The side effects are potentially destabilizing. Adams quotes William Pitt Fessenden, Senator from Maine, who remarked that the effect of the speculators 'must fall heavily on the poor by reason of the inflation' (p. 311). Adams is blunter when he says the effect will be 'to deliver labor to the mercy of capital' (p. 308).

The basis, however, for making these observations is instinct with nostalgia. In the essay on the Bank of England, Adams had approved of the somewhat fictitious separation of that Bank from the British Parliament. Throughout his discussion, and despite his normal sensitivity to propaganda, there is an un-ironized cynicism in which the political doctrine of the separation of powers becomes a diversionary image for a treasury thus freed to oil the works of an 'efficient' eighteenth-century heaven of mercantile economy with its 'regularly self-balancing principle' (p. 195). On the other hand

Adams is sceptical of the so-called 'currency school' of economics, and in that respect is quite close to Marx. He laments the breeding of 'a race of economists who attributed an undue degree of power to currency, and who delayed for years a longer and more philosophical study of the subject by their futile experiments upon paper money' (p. 235).[27]

Twenty-five years later Brooks Adams was to write a book on the gold standard and would also use Bank of England policy after 1815 to argue his case. Both brothers, a quarter of a century apart, are sceptical of certain aspects of what is currently called 'monetarism'. Neither is a radical economist, but both are critical of certain hypocrisies of the system. Brooks Adams says, for example, that the theory that 'monetary distress tends to produce fall of prices; that fall of prices encourages exports and diminishes imports; is erroneous.' In fact, as he points out when he criticizes the British Lord Overstone, 'monetary distress does not, generally speaking, encourage exports, because when all the world is poor no one can buy'.[28]

Neither Brooks nor Henry Adams had a theory of circulation and they relied heavily on Mill and Maclaren. Certainly money is not viewed as representing a social relation of production, but rather as 'natural objects with peculiar social properties'.[29] The Adams brothers do not distinguish between money as such and capital, nor between different moments in the process of capital within production. Brooks was a bimetallist, which for Engels would have put him firmly in the Utopianist camp.[30] Nonetheless Brooks Adams can be as sarcastic about Lord Overstone (founder of Lloyds bank) as Marx: and Henry Adams himself can describe, in almost as lively a polemical style as Marx, the effects of the changes for which his own theories are only partially adequate. In short, as with Marx, what is valuable in Adams's writing today is the rage against injustice and scepticism about fatalisms offered by the powerful.[31]

If the theory of economics had its weaknesses, the emphasis on economics at least enabled Henry Adams to avoid moralism, and sentimentality. For Adams, history has forsaken the battleground and entered the stock exchange. The heroes are the 'great men of incorporated capital', like Cornelius Vanderbilt 'who by means of his credit and capital again and again swept millions of dollars into his pocket by a process curiously similar to gambling with a loaded dice' (*Historical Essays*, p. 320). Adams's attention is chiefly focused, however, on the 'robber barons'; specifically Jay Gould and James Fisk Jr. whose property was, 'in effect, like all the great railway corporations, an empire within a republic' (p. 325). So a new empire is born within the decayed ideal of republican virtue. As for a number of commentators and cartoonists of the period, the new power appears in the guise of aristocracy. The great men of incorporated capital build themselves opera houses, palaces, and expensive brothels. Adams then proceeds to tell the well-known story of the Tammany ring.

Adams is reacting to the emergence of a new order: what Alan Trachtenberg has called the 'incorporation' of America. Adams is worried by the breakdown of actual justice and the threat to law and 'society': 'Thus Gould and Fisk created a combination more powerful than any that has been controlled by mere private citizens in America or in Europe since society for self-protection established the supreme authority of the judicial name' (p. 332).

While Adams briefly expresses his view that things will eventually settle down after the credit bonanza of the Civil War, the main tenor of his argument is much less sanguine. He is among the first to see the new power of the corporation rising from the fiction of the limited company, and among the first also to see that the American Constitution provided no effective counter-force: 'Under the American form of society no authority exists capable of effective resistance.' He adds, 'Nor is the danger confined to America alone. The corporation is in its nature a threat against popular institutions spreading so rapidly over the whole world.' (pp. 365–6) It is power that Adams is interested in. Recalling the days of the Federalists, he says that power had also been their chief concern; 'not merely power in the hands of a prince, of one assembly or of several, of many citizens or of few, but power in the abstract, wherever it existed and under whatever name it was known' (p. 368).

It is then precisely the question of power 'under whatever name it was known' that will be the key to all of Adams's writing. These early essays suggest something of the range: from philosophy to psychology and from the manipulation of image to economics. All the topics will be taken up again in one form or another: the displacement of political power from representative assembly to corporation, the manipulation of sexual images for business propaganda, the relation of the family to the state, and a metaphysics of order passing from religion to science. Within what Adams saw as the deserts of anti-intellectualism in his own time, he attempted to theorize the changes across multiple fields of information. From the first Adams, like his grandfather, saw that the need was for an education adequate to actual changes of social process. Thus Boutwell, Secretary of the Treasury, is seen as one whose 'common sense' is inadequate to the actual complexities of incorporated America: 'he believed in common schools and not in political science, – in ledgers and cash books, but not in Adam Smith or J. S.

Mill, – as one might believe in the multiplication-table, but not in Laplace or Newton' (p. 367).

II

Having outlined the parameters of Adams's interests and begun to outline and criticize some of his theories, it is now necessary to place him firmly in a historical context and to see precisely what options were open to him in his own time. Each of the areas of knowledge (history–economics; ethnology; science) will now be theorized in turn. Adams began his university career just at that point when American universities began to reorganize on the basis of professional specializations. C. Wright Mills relates the changes to the massive increase of wealth during the Civil War, 'the elective system within the universities' and to 'industrial and business divisions of labour'.[32] From the late 1890s to the 1920s Harvard's endowment, for example, rose from $10,000,000 to $86,000,000. The emphasis, says Mills, is increasingly scientific, professional, and utilitarian. It is against this background that Adams must be placed. Many American students read *The Education of Henry Adams* to test what they mean by 'education', few read it as a satire upon the actual development of capitalist education (more facts and less knowledge) in which specialists, emerging triumphant from the market of competitive education, play into the nervous hands of corporate bosses who do the 'integrating' in their own interests. Looking back on his education at Harvard before the First World War, Buckminster Fuller saw very precisely that it was 'the old strategy of "divide and conquer"'.[33] Adams's own search for links between areas of knowledge was already doomed as an educationally acceptable enterprise in the years following the Civil War.

Nonetheless, for a period after the Civil War there were networks of methods and areas of knowledge that linked philology to ethnology, ethnology to sociology, history to philosophy, and both back to ethnology and philology. History, in many minds the key humanistic discipline of the century, lent its premises to almost every area of study. Not the least of the fascination in reading Adams is to watch how methods of history he inherited gradually break down. Ethnology and sociology, hardly yet defined as subjects, were to challenge history's claim to priority in the study of man. Philology posed the question of comparative method. Similarly ethnology turned to the same method to sketch a slow progressivist theory of cultures, as did sociology itself. Given the rapid secularization of knowledge and the growing prestige of 'hard science', most of the humanistic disciplines tried to authorize their own procedures by claiming the prestige of 'scientific method' as well as seeking analogies of process in sciences such as physics and biology. All sought for predictive laws, especially given the hope around the mid-century that there would be a 'classical synthesis' (the notion that electricity, magnetism, light and heat would yield to a unitary explanation) in science.[34] Comte was generally in favour of physics as a model. Herbert Spencer was to prefer biology. William James was to pronounce a plague on both their houses in his *Principles of Psychology* (1891).[35]

Adams, in his later phase, was particularly anxious to relate the breakdown of the classical synthesis in science with the loss of certainty in classical economics, and to register the consequent shock to liberal premises about the nature of man. By 1894 he was professing an ironic nostalgia for 'my old set of John Stuart Mill'.[36] There was more than a dash of the anarchist in Adams. It was part of the tradition he inherited from New England and his view of the changes within society may well have been reinforced by recollections of Comte, who had said: 'The passage from one social system to another can never be continuous and direct. There is always a transitional state of anarchy which lasts for some generations at least; and the longer it lasts the more complete is the renovation to be wrought.'[37]

The liberal premises with which Adams had been familiar since childhood seemed to have all but disappeared. In spite of political claims the United States had joined an imperialist order in which it slaughtered Cubans and Filipinos, as the British slaughtered Malays, in order to 'give them the comforts of flannel petticoats and electric railways'.[38] In his familiar bantering tone Adams noted that the 'reaction of fashionable society against our old-fashioned liberalism is extreme, and wants only power to make it violent'.[39] In the event he did live to see World War I. But there were larger changes: 'As I view it, the collapse of our nineteenth-century J. S. Mill, Manchester, Chicago formulas, will be displayed – if at all – by the collapse of Parliamentarianism, and the reversion to centralised government'.[40] Adams's vision was accurate. In our own time wars are mainly fought in Third World countries and the parliamentary democracies increasingly enact diversionary dramas on behalf of, to use Adams's term, 'centralised' power; that is, an international banking system and interlocking corporate interests which, even if granted good intentions, are scarcely open to democratic scrutiny.

For revisions of historical theory, therefore, Adams was naturally attracted to economics. His drift to what Samuels calls an 'obsessive interest in currency questions'[41] was based upon a real perception of a later phase of capitalist development. There is a tinge of moralism in Samuels's word 'obsessive'. Socialist and capitalist tended to pre-

dicate human behaviour on 'money', and Adams was no less than a
good Puritan to realize that 'where your treasure is there will your
heart be also'.[42] However, in historical terms, these are the years
of the bimetallism controversies. The gold standard had been established in 1873, and the 'free silver' advocates worked on the assumption, an erroneous one, as Marx pointed out that it was
shortage of cheap money that caused the fall of prices at a time of
expansion and led to stagnation resulting from capitalists' hoarding
gold. By the 1890s the money question had become a plank in the
first extensive populist party's programme; and William Jennings
Bryan went down in history with his speech which concluded, 'You
shall not press down upon the brow of labor this crown of thorns;
you shall not crucify mankind upon a cross of gold.' Nor a cross of
silver – as anyone at the time with a more complex view of
economics might have suggested.

For Adams, currency seemed to be an invisible clue to history. Like
fossils, the coinage seemed to bear within itself a symbolic clue to the
very process of time. In fact with the avidity of a Lyell or Darwin
hunting fossils, Henry Adams collected coins: 'we haunt low
quarters where I bargain for coins with dirty pawn-brokers and
greasy Greek peddlers'.[43] The project was not new. As far back as
1817 the German historian Böckh, in his *Public Economy of Athens*,
had used coins in the Berlin Museum to describe the invisible
movement of currency as a 'scientific cause' of social change.[44] 'The
Greek coinage', said Adams, 'is a delight in itself, and tells the history in unmistakable pictures. Troy or Byzantium on one side, and
Syracuse on the other, were the Russia and America of the world
before Christ, and Athens was the England, or at least one of the
Englands.'[45]

Before criticizing these very typical Adamsian historical analogies, two important points should be made: the first being that
Adams is interested, no less than Marx, in the notion of cipher; the
whole process of symbolization. Adams wants an active investigation of the symbols of exchange. The second point is that 'money'
(following Marx) in a fully developed international market becomes
a universal form of value.[46] But whereas Marx insisted that the basis
of the reality of the abstraction is labour – ultimately labour power –
Adams insisted that society danced to the tune of its own abstractions
which faced it like an independent fateful secret of history.

Nonetheless Adams's global or universalist view of history,
evolved within currency questions, owed much to an America
already developing an internationally corporate power base.
Adams's view to some extent contradicts his own distrust of corporate power by virtue of the fact that currency becomes a

universalist metaphor of process in his own work. Capitalist accumulation (to which currency bears too simple a relation) becomes a metaphysical figure which synchronically decodes the shifts of power in history. Brooks Adams characterized it in terms of organism: 'As consolidation advances, fear yields to greed, and the economic organism tends to supersede the emotional and martial.'[47] Within the vitalistic terms of 'organism' Brooks Adams regrets the fetishizations of a process which leaves subjective and ethical factors out of the new economic society.[48]

In what are arguably two of the greatest novels in English of the period, Henry James's *The Golden Bowl* (1904) and Conrad's *Nostromo* (1904), romantic aristocracy, romantic entrepreneur, and romantic revolutionary go down before gold and silver respectively, and in both cases these metals are in turn symbols for the underlying power of the new American corporate boss. It would be a pity merely to dismiss the Adamses' sub-allegorical route of currency metaphysics as merely inept economics or idealistic historicism which at one level they certainly are. Because the Adamses do not include labour within their speculations, actual human behaviour is placed in a posture of hostility against it own abstracted activity. A fundamentally binary pattern is established in which contradiction is reduced to paradox. In the typical Adams historical description the weak and virtuous go down before the strong and irresponsible with both dancing to the dictates of an unmanifest destiny. Nonetheless, within the terms of irony and contradiction which such a method exposes, much can be learnt about the ideological chaos which faced Adams as an erstwhile liberal historian confronted with an era which denied most liberal premises in practice.

On actual socialism Henry Adams is typical of the upper classes. Not too much should be made of the fact that he read *Capital*. His annotations reach only to chapter 10 of the first volume. And the suspicion is confirmed by an annotation in chapter 3 where Marx writes, 'a change in the value of gold does not interfere with its functions as a measure of value. The change affects all commodities simultaneously.' Adams underlined the last three words and wrote; 'and equally? And are debts commodities? and is not gold itself a commodity?'[49] Adams's drift is towards seeing the commodity itself as an essentialized physical basis of human activity. Earlier he had noted, 'Is not labour itself a commodity, measurable by money? Or is it also to be realized?'[50] Adams's point of view is in fact non-dialectical, and progresses smoothly from money through commodities to labour; that is to say it is the point of view of the owners of the means of production. Like most of his class he felt that government intervention led straight to state socialism.[51] Yet at the same time he disliked the revisionist Bernstein's *Evolutionary Socialism* (1899) both for its jargonizing and because it preached the 'bankruptcy of the only idea that our time has produced'. [52] Adams felt strongly that both socialism and capitalism were bound to economic centralization. He believed that state socialism was inevitable and that corporate power was much the same thing in spite of its much-vaunted image of opposition. He would have been very sceptical of the Utopia of Edward Bellamy's one big trust.[53] Nonetheless the appearance of natural power haunts the results of human activity and Adams's 'economic' theories reflect it. Merely to dismiss this appearance as another fatalism is to ignore the fact that the development of a teleology is not only a recognition that the world is suffered as a structure, but is also a response to a particular historical situation. The terms of Adams's teleology are therefore important.

From the beginning of his career Adams showed himself as anxious as any nineteenth-century historian – Thierry, Buckle, Comte, or Taine, among countless others – to penetrate the veil of events and deliver an unchanging truth about historical process. Historical logic was confused with the question of truth; intelligibility with teleology. The sheer refusal at one level actually to historicize within historicisms was manifest: 'America or Europe, our own century or prehistoric time, are all alike to the historican if he can only find out what men are and have been driving at, consciously or unconsciously'.[54] All that can be saved here is the impulse towards theorizing; and the notion that there is a structure of events that is not available to common sense. The liberal view of 'man's nature' was a double-edged sword. Proposing a universalist psychology, it refused to encounter actual people in actual conditions, and assumed that all 'human' problems were in need of the same solution. By designating the other as absolutely oneself it ran the risk of solipsism and of reducing freedom to necessity. Adams was only one among dozens seeking for a law of history clothed with some kind of materialist aura. In Germany at the end of the century Engels (who himself cannot escape the charge of scientism) noted, 'philosophical, especially natural philosophic systems have been springing up by the dozen overnight,. like mushrooms, not to mention the countless new systems of politics, economics. . .'[55].

At the beginning of his career Adams stood uneasily between the legacies of romantic biographical narrative (models which he might have found in a Carlyle or, nearer to home, a Parkman or a Motley) and a newly emerging 'institutional history', dependent on studies of law, the family and primitive society. Braudel's sophisticated arguments about the nature of historical time will help to focus the discussion a little more clearly. For Braudel the 'social', that is the collective forms of life, run at different times. Intelligibility is not perceptible in the linear time of contingent events, or rather in such a time intelligibility is severely limited. A slow time, which has its grounding in the very history of the earth itself, illumines the different dynamics of economic cycle, the stasis of social science time, the banality of Rankean segmental narrative time, and confronts head-on the 'excessive *longue durée*' of the anthropologist (Braudel has Lévi-Strauss in mind). 'Anthropological' time courts the danger of 'forgetting, perhaps even of denying the inimitable essence of each individual'.[56] For all the Bergsonian echoes, Braudel reminds us that time might not be simply the province of the philosopher and that, paradoxically, a theory of time is essential to conceiving the very process of history itself. The problem remains, however, of how one time relates to another.

It was without such concepts that Adams confronted the possibilities available to him and he sensed that the times of narrative and institutional structure might not be reconcilable. History seemed to be neither a pattern of contingent events from which meaning 'emerged' statistically, nor a 'fiction'. Nor did it seem merely to play variations on a 'universal mind' whose meaning was given by some psychologizing God. Adams read both Guizot, the French liberal historian, and Michelet, the Romantic historian of the French Revolution. These two give some idea of the options available to Adams. Guizot, whose politically liberal principles, Samuels observes, 'harmonized' most closely with the 'creed of the Adams family', stated, 'I am convinced that there is, in reality, a general destiny of humanity, a transgression of the aggregate of civilization; and, consequently, a universal history of civilization to be written'.[57] The problem with the 'aggregate of civilization' was that this fundamentally statistical image tended towards pure synchrony. Change had to be characterized by 'tendency' to keep the subject historical at all. 'Civilization', grounded in the 'common-sense' meaning of the word, simply 'emerged' between the external condition of man and his internal nature. The notion of individual and society (as if the one could check the other without being constituted by the other through actual activity in relation to nature) was a fundamental weakness at the heart of the theory.

By contrast Michelet defended the 'Literary art' of the traditional historian. Nowadays, following Barthes's 'discovery' of binary vertical associative axes in Michelet's subtexts,[58] it is possible to conclude that he differs from Guizot by emphasizing 'vertical' binary patterns rather than 'horizontal' ones (individual and society within narrative), but not only are the two cases not so symmetrically opposed, they are misleading when so characterized. When Michelet heightens his great moments by invoking 'binary' images of a psycho-pathological nature (the levels of the Gothic) he displays the contradictions inherent at the political level in terms of the private – specifically the erotic. That same lively sense of contradiction is not to be found in the 'pallid' liberal equations of Guizot's exegesis. However susceptible Michelet's images are to archetypal reduction by structuralists, the whole direction of his writing is against any structuralist project. Michelet sensed correctly that the 'new history' of his time was itself a reflection of the depersonalization of the factory system and the 'atomization' of persons into functional elements whose unity was beyond their individual control. He said of statistics, 'They are unable – even if they are correct – to make us understand the people. They give partial and artificial findings which have been taken from a particular angle and which are easily misinterpreted'.[59]

Adams would have agreed, and similar problems arise in the interpretation of his own work. In spite of much commentary on him as 'scientific' historian, critics have rarely made distinctions between Adams's actual historical practice, his interest in the philosophy of science, general epistemology, his use of analogy and his relation to the field of options available to historians of his own time. In fact he seriously doubted that there could be a 'scientific history' at all. Like his grandfather, Adams was always to remain deeply ambiguous about system as such. This is reflected in the fact that he seems to have ignored the debates about the rival epistemologies of social science and history in Paris in the late 1890s and early 1900s.[60] He also said very little about historical method beyond a few practical tips he wrote to his friends. Adams had no sophisticated sets of distinctions between hypothesis, theory, and law. He failed on the whole to distinguish logics of method and justification. He constantly confused an empiricism of procedure with an empirical logic. He had the idealist's scepticism about the unintelligibility of the contingent and the empiricist's scepticism about dogma. Every work writes a footnote to the Pascalian paradox that 'Multiplicity which is not reduced to unity is confusion. Unity which does not depend on multiplicity is tyranny.'[61] The drive towards unitary explanation which science seemed to promise only offered Adams numerous analogies for the historical effects of capitalist accumulation and the seemingly fatalistic development of technology.

Then there was the question of time. Linear time had played an important role in the old biographical and narrative history. Forms of history emerging in Adams's own time were increasingly concerned with the synchronic structures of social institutions. In studies of law, the family and the Church, time was already slowing down as social scientists struggled towards patterns of statistical order. A belief in the truth of narrative seemed to dissolve along with a sense of the specificity and unpredictableness of individual human life on which personal moral values had traditionally been based. Adams's own search for a law of history led him in two different directions at once and reflected the bifurcating paths of history's successors. The paths diverged towards scientific abstraction and towards the social psychology of domestic life. In the one he hoped to recover abstract truth and in the other he hoped to salvage the multiplicity of Pascalian feeling.

What must be recognized is that Adams confused the need for theory with a desire for a priori law. He could criticize severely the English historian's empirical mystifications, but at the same time he tended to confuse reflection with objectivity and hermeneutics with teleology:

> Unless you can find some basis of faith in general principles, some theory of the progress of civilization which is outside and above all temporary questions of policy, you must think and act under the control of the man or men whose thought, in the times you deal with, coincides most nearly with your prejudices. This is the fault of almost every English historian.[62]

In an un-English way, the plea for theory is there as a guarantee of freedom within the *practice* of historical discourse. Adams was to search for a theory that was essentially timeless: 'above all temporary questions of policy'. It works perhaps better in the ethical than in the political domain. Eventually this type of reasoning was to lead him towards scientific analogies for historical process. Even so the scientist's view of time could only be defined as a vague sense of progressiveness within a fatalism pragmatically defined as the aggregate work of the total project. Adams was acutely aware of the endless task of the scientific project which Whitehead once compared with Greek tragedy.[63]

In spite of his apparent search for truth in abstract statistical laws of history, Adams was in fact more interested in the specificity of the process than in any absolute truth. There was for him a sense in which the process of time was tragic because in the end it was particular and personal – a fact which the newer disciplines relating to the study of man (no less than positivist Marxism) seemed to ignore. Unable to rely on Pascalian faith, Adams felt that a sense of life must be brought into the dynamics of present process. In a letter of the mid-'90s he makes his point by being more romantic even than Goethe as he suggests that Faust after all did cheat the devil:

> Do you know that I have travelled to every place on earth which
> travellers have described as most fascinating, in the hope of
> finding one where I should want to stay or return, and have found
> that Faust had a sure horse on the devil in his promise about
> passing hour: Bleibe doch, du bist so schon! Three days in any
> place on earth is all it will bear. The pleasure is in the movement,
> as Faust knew when he let the devil in to the preposterous
> contract.[64]

The self-irony here is highly complex. For all the appearance of
allegiance with the Faustian project, Adams realizes it is preposterous. Time will not be cheated by movement in space. Adams
questions a familiar American tendency to see history as, in the
words of Charles Olson, the twentieth-century American poet, 'the
practice of space in time'.[65]

In fact Adams moves in more public moments to a theory of
space–time for his characterization of history. As in Darwin's
theory of species change, space is characterized by interactive areas
exhibiting different times and speeds of development:

> That Salisbury made a dead point of getting George Curzon for
> his chief lieutenant [narrative–diplomatic] points to India as a
> centre of interest; and of course India means silver [economic–
> monetary], which is in fact a race question [ethnological]. On the
> other hand Sir Alfred Lyall assures me that India just now is doing
> well, and is not uneasy about silver. The easier India is, the
> uneasier Lancashire is, and the harder the Lancashire men will
> press for bimetallism. Perhaps the result lies with the Irish
> [political–ethnological], and if our American Irish are instructed
> from here to urge bimetallism, you may see a new deal [ethno-
> graphic–political].[66]

Adams once remarked to Henry Osborn Taylor, 'To me accuracy
is relative. I care very little whether the details are exact, if only my
ensemble is in scale.'[67] And LaFarge, Adams's artist companion in
the South Seas, said of him, 'Adams's historic sense amounts to
poetry, and his deductions and remarks always set my mind sailing
into new channels.'[68] Adams's poetic sense of history, however, was
also the result of careful reflection among the options available to
him. There were many historical models for an 'ensemble' in his
own time, but the one which perhaps most usefully shows a combination of interests parallel to Adams's own, and which he did read,
was Buckle's *History of Civilization in England* (1857), which Adams's
teacher at Harvard, Richard Owen, had denounced as 'gloomy and
scandalous'.[69] Perhaps that was enough to have attracted Adams
to it.

It is worth giving the British historian Buckle more than a passing glance. In Buckle's *History* there are parallels of method and content with Adams's own historical writings, particularly those of the late period. It was the cracking-up of Buckle's proposed principle of liberal civilization that occupied Adams even while he was using the areas of interest and the methods advocated by the earlier historian to advance a fundamental criticism of some of Buckle's assumptions. They shared, for example, a search for a 'law' of history which would decode the narrative structure of events. Like many other nineteenth-century historians they sought for both methods and analogies in the natural sciences. For Adams as for Buckle the gods of natural science overshadowed the positivist historian. Thus for Buckle free will and fate go down before a uniformity, variously derived from analogies with Newtonian physics and Lyellian geology, which gives to teleology a kind of ontological status. History exhibits, then, 'a character of uniformity, that is to say [the actions of men] under the same circumstances, always issue in precisely the same results'.[70] The twin motors of Buckle's system are the contradictory ones of material causality and a metaphysics of generally advancing 'intelligence'. In his own copy of Buckle's work, Adams underlined the sentence; 'I pledge myself to show that the progress Europe has made from barbarism to civilization is entirely due to its intelletual activity'.[71]

It is easy to dismiss Buckle's conviction of the progressiveness of 'intellectual events' as simply another nineteenth-century historicism. Buckle's acknowledged philosophical hero is Descartes, whom he uses in rejecting the evidences of common sense as 'delusions of nature' (Buckle, I. 425). History will be interpreted by a secret knowledge and thus taken out of common perception. The way is open for the professionalizing managers of the twentieth century: 'The real history of the human race is the history of tendencies which are perceived by the mind, and not of events which are discovered by the senses' (I. 600). Some time before Adams, Buckle turned to the philosophy of scientific method and to epistemology for 'keys' to the science of history itself. Like Michelet he, too, invoked Vico and declared an interest in the philosophy of method itself 'which bears the same relation to science that science bears to art' (Buckle, II. 255). In a series of progressive abstractions the philosophy of method becomes prior to the actual practice of both science and history.

Yet as much as he asserts that the physical world provides analogies, theories of process, and even a psychology for the social world, and that there are 'opposites but no contradictions' (II. 225), cracks and contradictions emerge at many levels in Buckle's ambitious enterprise. In his second volume a strangely personal tone comes to the fore as the intellectual historian dramatizes his own voice within this objective account of universal progressive enlightenment. Buckle is forced, like Adams, to admit 'failure'. The original vision of an isomorphic movement of science and history, each endowing the other with its insights and methods, has failed. The universal laws, those geometric truths conceived in the purity of Cartesian scepticism, falter as they did for Adams's grandfather and were also to do for Henry Adams. Above all the main problem occurs, as for the two Adamses, where abstract knowledge engages the human world. Thus, for example, Buckle characterizes the political economist as a man who

> ...blots out one part of his premises, in order that he may manipulate the remaining part with greater ease. But we must always remember, that political economy, though a profound and beautiful science, is only a science of one department of life, and is founded upon a suppression of some of the facts in which all large societies abound. It suppresses, or what comes to the same thing, it ignores, many high and magnanimous feelings which we could ill afford to lose. We are not, therefore, to allow its conclusions to override all other conclusions. We may accept them in science, and yet reject them in practice.
>
> (II. 343)

The key figure who unites theory and practice for Buckle is the doctor; a prestige man of science in the Scottish Enlightenment. Buckle's view that the *doctor* is a key figure of *society* will be of great importance for the discussion of William James and John Locke in Part II of the present book, and for certain key issues within Gertrude Stein's work. Even more than the geologist, the doctor is a 'practitioner' first and foremost. Among a number of considerations Buckle is concerned with the method needed to mediate the claims of science and life:

> What chiefly characterizes the most eminent physicians, and gives them their real superiority, is not so much the extent of their theoretical knowledge, – though that, too, is often considerable – but it is that fine and delicate perception which they owe, partly to experience, and partly to a natural quickness in detecting analogies and differences which escape ordinary observers. The process which they follow, is one of rapid, and, in some degree, unconscious induction.
>
> (II. 433)

What is subtly criticized here is the ultimately idealizing logic of the Scottish theorizers. What is advocated is a complexity of scientific theorizing as a process in which not all the elements are conscious or logical. There is a defence of analogy in perception and in the framing of hypotheses. Buckle characterizes the physician as standing somewhere between art and science. Indeed what is remarkable in this passage is the defense of intelligence and experience operating together through creative analogy, allowing intelligibility to include an almost phenomenological theory of perception.

Although Buckle's work is but one among dozens of historical works in Adams's library, it is particularly useful to have read it in a little detail for the styles of 'ensemble' it practises, and for some of the underlying tones and contradictions which were to be peculiarly close to Adams's own. Adams shared with Buckle a search for a predictive law of history, a recognition that history could not divorce itself from science and technology, an interest in French science and thought, and a belief in a kind of 'mental history' which underlay contingent events. Like Buckle he was torn between the Romantic and Enlightenment aspects of himself, and displayed an increasingly personal melancholy at the 'failure' of 'rational' structures of history. Like Buckle, too, he took a keen interest – a Lockean interest – in education as such. Unlike Buckle, however, Adams became increasingly sceptical of the whole field of liberal ideology, not to mention the whole idea of progress.

While a narrative of contingent events could not supply history with the rationality Adams sought, the displacement of emphasis from 'civilization' (the liberal dream of progress, scientific reason, free trade and personal liberty) to 'society' appeared to offer some solutions. Ethnology, sociology, political economy began to pull the ground from under the historian's feet while temptingly offering the fruits of their own not inconsiderable discoveries. The asking price was a distortion of historical time – even a burial of it. But if the lineality of traditional history seemed itself to be blind to an emerging reason of structure, the new 'institutional' disciplines also developed their secret teleologies and offered new truths to history. Traditional historical truths nonetheless were now to be distrusted. The actual historical collapse of the Roman Empire, Adams argued on one occasion, 'showed very curious energy for a corpse. It adopted a new and very strong, centralized religion just at that time.'[72] The 'long time' of law and the Church showed the strength of 'society' no matter what happened to 'civilization'. In another letter he once wrote, 'history is simply social development'.[73] For Adams it moved along the lines of least resistance like 'water' – a typical analogy for process in Adams's work.[74] There is no doubt that Adams felt that his *History of the United States* had 'failed' because it did not study America in terms of race or of society.[75] Yet as a historian Adams was to remain sceptical of the new social sciences' claim to truth.[76]

The impulse to study society came from many directions. Reviewing Freeman's *History of the Norman Conquest* (1867) Adams commented: 'Historians of the present day, following the lead of the philologists, have begun to study society and institutions at the foundation, by analysing and comparing the varied elements of primeval times, together with the forms which they assume in early history.'[77] Society and race could almost be used as synonyms under certain circumstances.

Primitive society – that key concept of an imperialist age – became both a model and an investigative area for the conscious and unconscious anxieties of Europeans and Americans alike. Placing primitive society at the 'base' of 'social evolution' buried its actual place in history in a temporal metaphysic, and also made it a testing ground for any experiment the ethnologist or sociologist wished to conduct. The range was from scientific curiosity to neurotic projection. Philology also lent its support to the study of legal institutions. Sir Henry Maine's biographer says of him that he 'made his special domain the study of jurisprudence and political philosophy from the standpoint of the comparative philologist, and wrote, as one admiring contemporary suggested, as if he were a political embryologist'.[78] 'Embryology' and 'philology' could supply each other with analogies of method, procedures and hypotheses. The structure of comparative generalization reinforced the hypothesis of 'mind'. Samuels notes that it was Herbert Spencer who 'pointed the way by suggesting that society was essentially mental energy, mind in a state of motion, travelling along right lines'.[79]

By the time of Morgan's work on anthropology the traditional historian's domain had been mined and was ready for sabotage. Morgan objected that the historian placed too much weight on individuals 'in the production of events', and added, 'The work of society in its totality, by means of which all progress occurs, is ascribed far too much to individual men, and far too little to the public intelligence.'[80] But where was the public intelligence to be found? Was it conscious or unconscious? Where was it if not in events? How would you characterize mental 'energy'? Two areas in particular where it was felt these questions could be posed were in 'primitive society' and the 'family'. While attention focused on these twin domains undercut the traditional subject-matter of historians as well as their notions of time, they also invited a new kind of conservatism. As Comte, another major influence on Adams, remarked: 'We must not omit the striking property of domestic organization, – that it establishes the elementary idea of social perpetuity, by directly and irresistibly connecting the future with the past.' It further encouraged 'that universal respect for our predecessors which is an indispensable condition of all social economy'.[81] For Marx and Hegel, on the other hand, the family was simply an area of necessity prior to freedom. An apparently unresolvable contradiction immediately arises. How could the family be at once a kind of ur-historical truth and simultaneously excluded from the public realm of actual power? The very term 'society' seemed to bury this important question.

As for primitive society (linked to the family by structuralist analogy), it was Frederick Jackson Turner, the famous historian of the American frontier, who attacked the idea of primitive society as an 'embryonic' and 'social' model for advanced society. He declared it was one of the 'weirdest delusions that ever afflicted American [and one should add English] intellectual life, . . . that the roots of Anglo-Saxon democracy are to be traced back to tun-moots of barbarians in the forests of northern Germany'.[82] Guizot also, as a Frenchman, dismissed the 'Teutonic origins' theory as the 'puerilities of learned patriotism', but when he himself talked of that 'more profound, more powerful unity: that which results not from the identity of government and destiny, but from the similarity of social elements, from the similarity of institutions', he, too, was opening the way to an ahistorical synchrony which obliterated the distinctions of the public and private realm in the conviction that 'society and government – mutually imply one another'.[83]

Toulmin has argued that it was some twenty years later than the period discussed here (from the 1860s to the 1880s) that the 'historical' terms 'primitive', 'advanced', 'differentiation', and 'evolution' were replaced by terms like 'structure', 'function', and 'interaction', although as late as the 1890s 'it was still an accepted commonplace that sociological and anthropological theory had an essentially historical dimension'.[84] The argument advanced here is that the dates are correct but that the content needs qualifying. For it is not history but liberal evolutionary historicism that qualifies the prior set of terms, and paradoxically this very historicism, while a powerful heuristic device, was more closely allied to a dehistoricized stucturalism than has hitherto been realized. In fact it was one means by which more variously conceived history could be excluded from the social debate. It passed on its gift of the aura of time to the new disciplines of ethnology and sociology. The symbolic time offered served as a powerful aid to creating valuable hypotheses with which to investigate society: that semi-stasis of institutional, 'primitive' and 'domestic' life. But it also firmly banished real questions of the relations of power to actual historical events in their uniqueness and unrepeatability. Since 'ethnology' (and in particular the work of Morgan) seemed to Adams to upset historical procedures, its role in Adams's intellectual picture is of first importance.

The increasing number of works in ethnology (early anthropology, myth, magic, religion) during the nineteenth century can be traced to many sources. From the end of the seventeenth century to the end of the nineteenth century the European and American encounter with the 'primitive' mingled brutal imperialism with a multiplicity of exchanges of knowledge and forms of life. That encounter was fundamentally historical, and Harris points out that during the nineteenth century 'anthropology began as a science of history',[85] a fact which illumines and helps to account for Adams's preoccupation with it. In an excellent review of the subject Paul Radin recounts how the German interest in 'primitive culture goes back to the Romantic movement of the early nineteenth century and the speculations on the history of civilization which date specifically from the time of Herder'.[86] Radin also documents the gradual drift from a cultural and historical method to a 'scientific' one, and outlines the main features of this debate (specifically the growth of religion from animism to monotheism and social organization from the totemistic clan and mother-right to individualized monarchies, republics, and father-right). He points to the great English ethnologist, Edward B. Tylor's, paper, 'On a Method of Investigating the Development of Institutions', as an important turning-point in the subject and comments: 'Therewith the youthful and somewhat blustering discipline was delivered up without further ceremony to the tender mercies of the statisticians.'[87] It is yet another significant moment in a world changing, in the argument of the present book, from civilization to society. Radin's mild wit is directed against the scientism of the Boas school, while acknowledging its undoubted achievements. Ethnological theory with its roots in the writings of Rousseau and Montesquieu passed its a priori legacies to the nineteenth-century ethnologists. For Bachofen, McLennan, Morgan and Tyler, 'primitive peoples were only pawns in the larger game'.[88]

The issue is not whether these early writers on theories of primitive societies were right or wrong in any absolute sense. Their project differs also from that of the kind of historian of anthropology who is anxious to sift history for the purity of scientific origins. They were expressing a suspicion of human beings writing 'scientifically' about other human beings, and proposing an examination of the styles of ensemble which made up their descriptions. In any 'objective' discourse there is always a 'projection' of conscious, and unconscious, values on to the distanced human subject. One suspects that the Calvinist clergyman who tipped Morgan off about the

development of the monogamous family from somewhat more pro-
miscuous arrangements, was arguing primarily from a firm belief in
his own values and from a conviction of original sin. Indeed the latest
and most detailed commentator on Morgan speaks of the whole
process as 'a series of moral reforms'.[89] On the other hand one
cannot but suspect that Engels's fierce championship of Morgan's
discovery of structured but diverse sexual relations among early
forms of marriage was assisted by his own large love of life and
sexual unconventionality. Any notion of social structure as an inert
teleology is therefore rejected in the ethnological argument and it is
proposed, in Sartre's words, that 'Structures are created by activity
which has no structure but suffers its results as structure.'[90]

Since actual history had to be denied, ethnologists had to propose
other ways of making continuous patterns and structures within
history intelligible. It has already been noted that legal and
constitutional history, or rather an historical time defined by legal
and constitutional change, was one of these ways. With the German
armies triumphing over Louis Napoleon, with the collapse of the
Commune in France, the myth of primitive democracy legitimized
conquest as German ideological hegemony entered the domain of
ethnology.[91] Some of Adams's interest in these questions can be
gauged by looking at his letters to Morgan and the work on Anglo-
Saxon law which he put out with the aid of his students at Harvard
in the 1870s. He informs Morgan that he has been teaching 'the
origin of political and legal institutions' especially in relation to
the Germans, and he says, 'I am very curious to know whether
our American Indians had any trace of the political and judicial
organization which characterizes the earliest Germans known to us.'[92]

Adams does not on the whole discuss the relations between
political and judicial organization, nor between private society and
the state. Perhaps this was inevitable given an American concern for
the separation of powers. For Morgan a synchronic alliance of the
trusts with the law seemed to constitute an independent 'force' of
history. The origins of society itself are neatly summed up by Adams
in another line to Morgan: 'Communal institutions, ancestral and
sun worship, family customs, and private redress sanctioned by
public opinion, are the first germs of society that I can as yet see'.[93]
Society thus includes the idea of institutions, religion, family life and
law. It excludes actual history, the power relation between 'society'
and 'state', actual politics and moments of change – that violence of
history in which new orders emerge.

An essay by one of Adams's students on 'Anglo-Saxon Family
Law', on the very eve of the publication of Morgan's book *Ancient
Society* (1877), gives a good picture of the issues as Adams was

currently teaching them at Harvard. Family law belongs to the domain of custom, and custom is seen as offering 'the most stubborn resistance to innovation'.[94] There are two major influences on custom; one is the Church, which softens its harsher features, and the other a growing power of the State. The original kinship-based law and order is challenged by the growth of rich families which develop 'police organizations of a purely political nature'. Under mother-right, members of a family had redress against the head of a house-hold, under father-right as in the Roman family such an arrangement was impossible. The writer also remarks that Morgan's new work on Ancient Society 'will be looked for with interest by all students of comparative history'.[95] The account reads like an historical allegory of the era of the robber barons. The more social (not political) organization of the German tribes seems to be a repository of those liberal values Adams feared were under pressure in an age of capital accumulation.

The distinction between social and political at one level is of course a fiction. At another it is a distinction between necessity and freedom. For Adams ancient society held out a Utopian vision where men lived without priestcraft, possessing an 'instinct' for reconciling liberty and law, and where there was arbitrary power neither in the family nor in the state. Society seems to be defined by being 'pre-State'. As Morgan said in the *League of the Ho-de-no-sau-nee or Iroquois* of 1852, the league itself was merely 'an elaboration of the Family Relationships' which are 'older than the notions of society or government'.[96] However, in the typical 'historical' transition be-loved by nineteenth-century ethnologists, from 'hunter' to 'pas-toral' to 'civilized' states of society, the family relations also represent a kind of sub-constitutional reason which survives actual change. The family is both prior and structural. The family also becomes a correlative of the liberal political principle of 'least government'. A sexual, or indeed sexist, bias then enters the picture. An opposition emerges between female-oriented institutions which are basically apolitical and male-oriented states which are fully political. As a symbolic narrative this opposition reflects a certain conservatism at a time when women in the United States were pressing for the vote. The 'slow time' of institutions has the greater 'truth', but deprives the disenfranchized of any actual opportunity for change.

As an instance, however, of what was possible in civilized char-acterizations of the 'primitive', it is impossible to overlook E. B. Tylor's masterpiece, *Primitive Culture* (1871). Adams shared the English ethnologist's search for general and predictive laws, and like Tylor Adams had a more than ambiguous sympathy for myth, magic, and poetry. Indeed, counterbalancing Tylor's statistical and empirical thunderings against superstition is a clear Romantic sympathy with the animistic past. Lockean assumptions about the universality of human nature, differentiated only by education, connect the 'primitive' irresistibly with the 'civilized'. The past cannot quite be thrown off: 'Many a white man in the West Indies and Africa dreads the incantations of the Obiman. . .'[97] And Adams would have agreed that, 'Fully to understand an old-world myth needs not evidence and argument alone, but deep poetic feeling' (Tylor, I. 305). That deep poetic feeling was one way the nineteenth-century scholar might legitimize a regard for everything left out of the scientific picture. More negatively it also enabled him, particularly in relation to mental life, to make myth a way of articulating the relation between sanity and madness in his own world. The study of myth, Tylor wrote, makes it possible 'to realize a usual state of the imagination among ancient and savage peoples, intermediate between the conditions of a healthy prosaic modern citizen and of a raving fanatic or a patient in a fever ward' (I. 315). In this extra-ordinary statement in which sickness is hierarchically defined as society's historical base, myth reveals a half-way stage or boundary between society's reason and madness. No longer is the 'primitive' the Enlightenment projection of a freedom guaranteed by nature, but a dangerous and dynamic area of 'mind' in which the order of society is confronted with the disorder of its own fears and repressions.

And yet at the same time the mythic is clearly important to Tylor. A nostalgia for the animistic past is, perhaps, more than mere escapism and sentimentality: 'In those moments of the civilized man's life when he casts off hard dull science, and returns to childhood's fancy, the world-old book of animated nature is open to him anew' (Tylor, II. 208). The strains of the absolutist compulsions of positivist and materialist modes are very clear. Tylor thus adopts the vision of the child as if a somehow innocent vision could recapture what is lost in the pragmatic and future-oriented compulsions of the scientific project. Tylor had no scientific discourse available to him to handle his sympathies, such as Monod's view, for example, that animism was a 'projection onto animate nature of man's awareness of the intensely teleonomic functioning of his own central nervous system'.[98] Yet long before Freud Tylor recognized the importance of those areas scientific discourse traditionally ignored. Whether he looks at riddles, children's games, gestures, sneezing, poetry, interjections or dreams, 'such facts are to be worked as mines of historic knowledge' (Tylor, I. 71). Tylor's deep but cautiously admitted respect for the 'primitive' is directed towards a position where 'heirlooms of primitive ages may be claimed in the existing psychology of the civilized world'. (I. 429). The very word 'heirloom' suggests their value, while 'psychology' invites all the ambiguities the imperialist powers felt towards the 'primitive' representatives of the liberal's 'mind of man'.

Of the four types of myth which, in Tylor's words, have a bearing on the 'early history of opinion' – that is, 'philosophical or explanatory myths', misunderstood real descriptions, myths where real events are ascribed to legendary figures, and myths 'made or adapted to convey moral or social or political instruction' (I. 368) – Adams was particularly interested in the fourth type. In fact he is very interested in the relation between 'opinion' and power via 'myth' and the necessary contradiction between this function of myth and myth as the bearer of the psychological and personal, is shown in a passage from one of his letters:

> This then was Anurajpura; the bo-tree: six dagobas with relics; and one or two temples more or less Brahmanic, that is, rather for Siva or Vishnu than for Buddha, though Buddhism ran here a good deal into Brahmanism. As long as Buddhism flourished, Anurajpura flourished. . . . When Buddhism declined, the place went gradually to pieces, and nothing but what was almost indestructible remains. Of course we cared little for the historical or industrial part of the affair, but came here to see the art . . . all the art seems to me pretty poor and cheap. . . . Not a piece of work, big or small, have I seen that has a heart to it. The place was a big bazaar of religion, made for show and profit. Any country shrine has more feeling in it than this whole city seems to have shown.[99]

There is of course irony in cutting out historical and industrial aspects of the phenomenon described. They are to be classically reunited in the famous chapter in the *Education* called 'The Virgin and the Dynamo'. Buddhism is a 'power', and it is the 'aura' of that power which fascinates Adams: for him 'art' is inextricably bound up with power via its chosen 'myths' and thus linked to 'opinion'. Where the art is debased, society itself is valueless – 'cheap'. Unless the images of the myth are addressed to the 'heart' they become subservient to 'show and profit'. Adams's eighteenth-century 'feeling' exhibits nostalgia for the 'country-shrine' – perhaps even that country shrine of Gray's famous 'Elegy in a Country Church-yard'. Adams underlined in his copy of Pascal the following lines: 'La force est la reine du monde, et non pas l'opinion; mais l'opinion est celle que use de la force.'[100] This statement is the key to a great deal in Adams, and to the times in which he lived; the times of Hearst and Pulitzer and the rise of the press syndicates.

Linked with investigations of institutions, myth and religion, were proliferating studies of women's roles, sexuality, and the family. The most famous, of course, was Engels's 'The Origin of the Family, Private Property and the State', of 1884. Adams as far as I know did not read it, and its spirit was utterly opposed to most of his thinking on the subject. Engels's delight in exposing the hypocritical shams of Victorian society is hardly shared by the publicly reticent New Englander. Adams was not inclined to blame men for the institution of monogamy. Nor was he interested in the relation of the 'atomized' family to the economic and industrial system, nor to the plight of women workers. Adams would not have dreamt of analysing male–female relations by using class critiques, nor did he look forward with any optimism to a time when really equal economic relations might produce a new form of marriage, dissolve or confirm it as an institution as such. Adams's suspicion of Darwin prevents him from approaching social organization in anything like Darwinist terms. Even if he thought it, it is difficult to imagine Adams publicly describing 'Protestant monogamy' in the 'average of the best cases' as 'a wedded life of leaden boredom, which is described as domestic bliss'.[101] However, given the tragedy of Adams's own marriage and his keen interest in the 'social' dimensions of historical development, it is not surprising his concerns overlap with those of Engels in many points of theme and detail.

Both thought the Englishman, McLennan's, work very inferior to Morgan's, and their own work is tinged with denigration of English work in the field generally.[102] Bachofen's work *Mother-Right* describes how an original sexual promiscuity gives way to monogamy only very gradually in history, and shows that in the early stages women have a high degree of respect and status owing to the fact that kinship is reckoned in the female line. Engels himself casts doubts on what he calls the 'sheer mysticism' of the concepts of 'father-right' and 'mother-right', but nonetheless praises Bachofen as a pioneer and as one who proposes that forms of marriage change. Engels's irony directs itself towards a supposed loss in status of women. Adams, on the other hand, tends to idealize the role of women as the *sine qua non* of the entire social fabric. Whereas Engels uses Bachofen ironically to deflate the hypocrisies of the middle classes, Adams uses him to reinforce a heroic conception of women based on their biological role. And yet like Engels Adams is keen to bring women back into the general public culture. He would certainly have agreed with Engels's characterization of the 'social status of the lady of civilization, surrounded by sham homage and estranged from all real work'.[103] Adams also would have agreed with Engels and Morgan that the materialist base of a culture is crucial in social organization. He shared Engels's love of Provençal poetry which in Engels's words 'steers full sail towards adultery'.[104] Adams, however, was not quite so enamoured of such matters in contemporary art. He thought Wagner's great *Liebestod* in *Tristan und Isolde* rather too decadently erotic. Both would have agreed with Morgan that the family was an evolving not a static social structure, but whereas Engels took this as a sign of hope and new freedom for women, Adams saw nothing but decline and failure.

The question of Adams and women has been endlessly discussed; for an account of the various commentaries, see the notes.[105] Adams's public pose may be gauged from a letter of his English friend Spring-Rice:

> He found his wife dead on the floor one day and the next was the first day since they had been married that they were separated. Since then he has regarded life with a frivolity which rather shocks people who don't know him well; but I can quite understand that there are griefs so great that after them one is independent of joy or sorrow or the respect of men.[106]

Certainly Adams was deeply shocked by his wife's suicide. But all the evidence shows that he was able to build around the loss, and to enjoy considerable well-being with close women friends and his many nieces.

The worst aspect of Adams's more deliberate views on women may be stated briefly and these views are set out here simply so that the picture may be complicated, if not reversed in meaning, later on. Given his deification of the biological role of women it is not surprising that Adams alleged that American women were 'failures'. No woman would want to live up to such nonsense. Like Michelet he admired the great women rulers of history. Catherine the Great is admired for her machismo as much as anything else.[107] From an issue of the *North American Review* during Adams's editorship which dealt with numerous books on Germanic and 'Aryan' mythology, we learn, with a sense of wearisome repetition, that the 'female principle has altogether a large place in the Teutonic religion', and that the 'Virgin Mary has been shown. . . to be only the substitute of the Germanic goddess of love'.[108] In Adams the notion of motherhood as divine fertility is as heroic a myth as it was for all those competent but dreary late nineteenth-century realist painters with their square-jawed women bearing sheaves of corn on their heads. It may be conceded that Adams somehow admired the 'principle of womanhood' through his reading of John Stuart Mill, but even Samuels permits irony to creep into his own discussion of these issues: 'The *Chartres* made clear that if in the eleventh hour the world was to be saved from apaches and trade unions, the woman must regain her sovereign authority through maternity'.[109]

The *Chartres* is more ambiguous than that remark suggests, but the comment does highlight the worst elements in the case. The making over of the biological role of women into a coercive cultural myth suppresses the diversification of human possibilities for women, not to mention women's actual erotic life. It is not even necessary to argue this from a contemporary point of view. Michelet, for example, was perfectly clear on the subject in the mid-nineteenth century: 'By a monstrous perversion of ideas, the Middle Ages regarded the flesh, in its representation, woman, as radically impure. The Virgin, exalted as Virgin and not as Our Lady, far from raising actual womanhood to a higher level, had degraded it.'[110] There is worse, however, to come. Adams was not averse to reading Eduard Drumont's nasty anti-Semitic outpourings. Drumont was a writer who once described one of de Chevé's characterizations of women thus: 'Poetisée, grandié, adorée, elle apparait dans une auréole comme la femme germaine qu'entourent de respect et d'hommages des guerriers vaillants.'[111]

However, Adams was far too self-reflective and ironic to sympathize fully with such a debasement of the courtly-love tradition. Indeed it is his wit that saves him. Here for instance is Adams writing from that classic site of sexual Utopias, Samoa. Heroic sexuality takes actual form in survivals of the giants of ancient days (Adams was rather short in stature): 'When the giants have dismissed me, and I can sprawl on the mats among the girls, I begin to be happy, and when the handsomest one peels sugar-cane with her teeth, and feeds me with chunks of it, I have nothing more to ask.'[112] One cannot resist quoting at this point his geologist friend Clarence King's encounter with 'female primitives' not in Samoa but in the Far West. Confronted with 'Six foot Susan', a farmer's daughter, in what King calls 'two acres of tranquil pork', King manages to escape heroic matrimony: 'Her full, grand form and heavy strength reminded me of the statues of Ceres, yet there was withal a very unpleasant suggestion of fighting trim, a sort of prize-ring manner of swinging the arms, and of hitching the shoulders.'[113] Perhaps the American tall story meets male sexual nervousness at this point and creates the tradition that leads to Thurber's cartoons.

Adams said of Morgan's *Ancient Society* when it came out in 1877: 'It must be the foundation of all future work in American historical science, and I earnestly hope that no time will be lost in pressing the same class of inquiries among the existing tribes of Indians which have come least in contact with civilization.'[114] Morgan's book attempted to show how in like populations under natural selection society was subject to an invisible process of change. As in Tylor's work, a continuity of mental experience weaves a thread through the evolutionary spiral so that the 'savage', including contemporary 'survivals', becomes the past of Western man's psychic present: 'We have the same brain, perpetuated by reproduction, which worked in the skulls of barbarians and savages in by-gone ages; and it has come down to us laden and saturated with thoughts, aspirations and passions, with which it was busied through the intermediate periods.'[115]

For Morgan that ur-family, the *gens* (an exogamous 'primitive' family unit with matriarchal kinship), was 'social and not political' (Morgan, p. 214). One result of this declaration is the depoliticiza-tion of America's own Native Americans, conceived of as the last stage of family-based society before the State emerged. They are simply 'society' in an 'ethical' period. They do not constitute a political entity. It is a matter beyond irony that Morgan's contem-poraries were busily committing acts of genocide against this 'ethical' society. Certainly it is with a degree of unconsciousness that Morgan can also state: 'Liberty, equality, and fraternity, though never formulated, were the cardinal principles of the gens' (p. 85). The political values of the bourgeois revolution in France are proposed as the aesthetic social values of the defeated in incorporated America.

Morgan's definition of 'political' is basically Lockean. In order to attain political status a man must first own property. The family, with the ghosts of the *gens* and other stages of development within its contemporary structures, is not a unit of the political system 'although individualized by property rights and privileges, and recognized as a legal entity by statutory enactment' (p. 227). Morgan commits himself to few points of relation between the *societas* and the *polis,* though he does say that father-right and monogamy coincide with the growth of property, a common argument which prompted Engels's famous remark that 'The sale of his children by the father – such was the first fruit of father-right and monogamy!'[116]

Morgan refers his reader to the French writer, Fustel de Coulanges's, noted work *The Ancient City* (translated 1874) in order to supply some kind of connecting link between the state and society. Fustel's argument is close to Morgan's own in many basic features, though ostensibly it deals with political and urban man rather than with social and family-based man. The Frenchman's theory is religious and psychological. Politics and material life are conspicuous by their absence. Fustel wrote in the shadow of the fall of Paris and the failure of the Commune. He was presented with the failure, therefore, of both the state and the group formed spontaneously in relation to need. Fustel described society of the ancient world held together by the religion of the family in the face of political and military failure. The unity is maintained by the rites of death. Worshipping ancestors are buried under the 'stone of the hearth' on which the sacred flame is kept burning. In 'religion' then lies the authority for the 'union of two beings in the same domestic worship. . . to reproduce a third who would continue the worship'.[117] In Foucault's words the 'political socialization [is] achieved through the "responsibilization" of couples with regard to the social body as a whole'.[118]

Fustel de Coulanges certainly does not approve of the consequent isolation of the family in Roman civilization, nor of the religion which sustained that 'autonomization' under conditions of need: 'The domestic religion, both in life and death, separated every family from all others, and strictly rejected all appearance of community. Just as the houses could not be contiguous, so the tombs could not touch each other; each one of them, like the house, had a sort of isolating enclosure.' (Fustel, p. 83.) For Fustel the state simply develops from the family as a mystic teleology. In fact warring families produce warring states. A picture emerges of isolated warring cities needing to control the intimate aspects of family life down to the last detail: 'The ancients, therefore, knew neither liberty in private life, liberty in education, nor religious liberty' (p. 297). Fustel rewrites the classical political struggle between patrician and plebeian as a synchronic model for his socialized history. The tense order within the family somehow becomes a war between the haves and the have-nots in the *polis* as such. Fustel depicts them as 'hostile societies (p. 342).

Fustel de Coulanges finds it difficult to sustain the basic contradiction that social history is the secret key to scientific history while asserting that it is simultaneously superseded by political history. As if to bolster the need to assert the authority of social history, he casts about for other connective factors of process. Here he is very close to Adams in his choice of money, law, and technology. These are *social* forces like religion. They are also conservative forces, though occasionally one supersedes the other. Money, for example, 'according to the expression of the lawyers, [was] *res nec manicipi*, and could pass from hand to hand without any religious formality, and without difficulty could reach the plebeians' (p. 364).

Failing a theory of labour and production, Fustel is forced back on simple fatalistic Manichaean struggle: 'If the patrician alleged a sacred custom, the plebeian replied in the name of the law of nature'

(p. 397). No value emerges in struggle and there is a scepticism about the nature of any ideology. Liberty is simply the belief of the rich and tyranny the belief of the poor. 'Public interest' simply replaces 'religion' as the urban organizational base. Life is need is hierarchy. The organization of the army corresponds with 'perfect exactitude to the political organization of the city' (p. 432). It is important, therefore, to remember that that doyen of statistical sociology, Emile Durkheim, was to dedicate his Latin thesis on Montaigne to Fustel de Coulanges.

Thus the problem for which Morgan referred his reader to Fustel de Coulanges was scarcely solved. Marxists who have devoted some time to the problem believe that there could be some sort of law in primitive societies. Hence, as Stanley Moore points out in a useful article, one could regard *Mutterrecht* as a form of 'law'. For Engels 'public power' existed de facto in any society, 'state power' occurred when that power was separated from the people.[119] In a sense Engels concurred with Fustel de Coulanges in his conviction that enforcing agencies as such were not so necessary in a 'primitive society' since public opinion was more effective. Thus Marx could deny executive power in primitive society but still acknowledge effective law. Lenin's view, as is well known, was, by contrast, that there can be no law without a state. The views of Marx and Engels now seem more flexible in that their slightly less rigid definitions open the way to reconciling the separate domains of anthropology and history.

Politically Lewis Henry Morgan was a liberal Whig. The not negligible values implied in this position in Morgan's time inclined him towards an at least theoretical defence of Native Americans against removal policy, a commitment towards furthering women's education, a sometimes articulate distrust of the effects of capital accumulation after the Civil War, a belief that the middle classes held the balance of sanity inside society, a sympathetic support for the secular world view coming in on the heels of Darwinian science, a defence of the 1870 Commune in France, London working men and a loathing of aristocracy. He opposed slavery out of a spirit of benevolence since he believed black people to be a separate species. His lecture, 'Diffusion against Centralization', at Rochester's Atheneum and Mechanics' Institute in 1852, shows him anticipating the broad phenomena Henry and Brooks Adams were to take up in the 1890s.

As a good liberal Morgan was against monopolies. Nonetheless he bought up railroad stock after Civil War and won a quarter of a million acres of railway land for various clients involved in railway and mining cartels – those key agents of the centralization he so opposed. One wonders if he perceived any contradiction between his work on behalf of land-grant agents and his study of Native Americans which he thought would provide proof of the unity of all mankind. In the famous Erie Railroad 'war', as a member of the standing committee on railroads Morgan interviewed Jay Gould on the propriety of issuing convertible bonds and let him off rather lightly with 'questions that made both of them appear as champions of free competition fighting off the dragon of monopoly'. Even so he declared that 'The time is not far distant when the people will be compelled in self-defence to deal with these corporations to the utmost limits of legislative power'.[120]

Morgan did not undertake to resolve these contradictions practically, and there is a certain fatalism in his view of history. Resek gives us more than a clue to this fatalism in the very methodology of Morgan's approach to the subject: 'Preferring to deal with tribal structure, marriage, and inheritance customs, Morgan avoided narrative history. The vacuum, he thought, was filled by the concept of evolution'.[121] But of course the times of evolution and political history are different. Evolutionary time cannot substitute for narrative history. The time of evolution is a hypothetical time, the time of narration is bound more strictly to history; which is not to say that its events need to be presented within strict linear order. What Resek's important comment suggests is that the exclusion of the order of narrative discourse from 'social' history invites an historical metaphysic (undisclosed) to support a logic of process which suppresses actual political history.

In fact a quality of 'evolving' or an evolutionary aesthetic clothes the three organizing social factors (kinship, sex, and property) in Morgan's historical dynamic. Images of natural selection are scattered throughout *Ancient Society*.[122] The secret teleology of institutions becomes a 'moral' or 'mental' economy. Here we move into the realm of (benevolent) Social Darwinism: 'The institutions of mankind have sprung up in a progressive connected series, each of which represents the result of *unconscious* reformatory movements to extricate society from existing evils' (Morgan, p. 59; my italics). It is thus that Morgan surrendered political will, and his continuing emphasis on territory ownership as conferring sovereignty scarcely modifies his postion. Following Fustel de Coulanges again, Morgan argues that when the State takes over from the *gens*, 'the *gentilis*, changed into a citizen', is dealt with through his 'territorial relations and not through his personal relation to a *gens*' (p. 255). However the *gens* remains a permanent 'social' organizing force up to and including the monogamian family.

Like Darwin, Morgan is faced with breaks in the record both temporarily and spatially, and similarly he focuses an 'aggregating eye' on the natural-selection process within the historical 'mind of man':

> It results in disconnected regions of space, and in widely separated ages of time, articulate in a logically connected chain of common experiences. In the grand aggregate may still be recognized the few primary germs of thought, working upon primary human necessities, which, through the natural process of development, have produced such vast results.
>
> (Morgan, p. 255)

In some senses Morgan's evolutionary hypotheses aid and abet the very conditions he attacked so passionately. In a symbolic narrative the 'primitive' is decreed to exist outside real history and politics. The *gens* is ambiguously made the ground of truth of social organization and cut adrift from actual history. Its essentialist slow 'becoming', generalized out of early dispositions to social statistics, makes it more difficult to reconcile with materialist factors and contingent events.

Adams's enthusiasm for Morgan was no doubt owing to the fact that Morgan seemed to make a science out of the new social history. In his own actual contact with 'primitives' as he travelled world-wide in the 1890s, Adams's response varied from the ironies of an eighteenth-century satiric vision to an interest in genealogy, kinship, and custom.[123] In Oceania in 1890 he wrote: 'Our steamer is filled with plaintive-looking native women – the old-gold variety – who vary in expression between the ferocious look of the warriors who worshipped Captain Cook and then killed him, and the melancholy of a generation obliged to be educated by missionaries.'[124] Thus the humour reveals a pattern of response running from old echoes of 'nature's noblemen' – women in this case ('old gold' has extra irony given that Adams was occupied with the bimetallist problem at the time) – to a cultural awareness of the impact of Western influence on once 'untouched' tribes. Like Morgan himself and many an anthropologist later, Adams often finds himself blocked in his questioning of 'primitives'.[125] In more practical terms Adams once helped to finance the excavating of the Dordogne caves, and at the most positivist end of the general response measured the physique of Pacific islanders with a tape measure and took photographs of them with his Kodak.[126]

At this point it is necessary to broaden the scope of the discussion a little. In some ways Adams's interest in science has been better documented than understood.[127] He was always lamenting his lack of expertise in the subject and yet was suspicious of its actual role in society: 'Science is far worse than the Church, and its changes are much more rapid. I dare not stir a step without two cardinals to protect me.'[128] Adams never quite lost his Enlightenment belief that science and general truth were somehow connected. At best this affirmed the entire intellectual project of science, at worst it could degenerate into scientism. Passionately interested in progress, Adams nonetheless had the historian's scepticism: 'Cincinnati and Pittsburgh are the ideal product of a thousand years of nature's effort to attain perfection. As for me, I am left somewhere behind among the Miocene monkeys.'[129]

It is important to place Adams's interest in science in perspective. He said that the *North American Review* under his editorship was 'not a scientific journal... we must restrict ourselves carefully to the general characteristics of scientific thought'.[130] Adams's interest in science was that of an intelligent layman in a period when being an intelligent layman in relation to the range of scientific activity was becoming more and more difficult, if not impossible. His insistence that different areas of knowledge should be related was a conviction under general threat from the development of the corporate university which needed specialist, vocationally oriented programmes to service its backers' interests.

At the intellectual level, and in a period of what Toulmin has called 'paradigmatic multiplicity',[131] Adams found himself forced to give up the notion of unitary truth even though he was only ambiguously to accept 'multiplicity'. As Hamill has pointed out, paradigms can refer to theories, procedures, and to philosophical assumptions.[132] Adams on the whole confined himself to theory and philosophy, and was faced like many others with the key problem of the legitimacy of scientific theories as models (evolution/entropy) for the processes of human affairs in a newly secularized world. To proclaim 'paradigm failure' (which Hamill further points out became the central 'paradigm for his interpretation of history') was a way of questioning the authority of scientific metaphysics assumed by scientist and lay person alike.[133] Late in life Adams declared: 'Forty years ago, our friends always explained things and had the cosmos down to a point, *teste* Darwin and Charles Lyell. Now they say that they don't believe there is any explanation, or that you can choose between half-a-dozen all correct.'[134] At the very least Adams's search for a theory contradicted the average social scientist's postivist mechanisms and the average scientist's naïve empiricism. Further Adams was fundamentally concerned with the contemporary lineaments of the age-old relation between knowledge and power. He foresaw the increased actual power of scientific and technological advance playing into the hands of fewer and fewer people until all pretence of democracy was destroyed: 'Law, in that case, would disappear as theory or a priori principle, and give way to force. Morality would become police.'[135]

Adams's pronouncements are sometimes unclear because of his careless use of the word 'force'. Sometimes it is a simple mechanical cause, sometimes an underlying power which is undisclosed, sometimes the kind of sovereignty that the law essentializes. Adams's use of the word cannot always be said to escape Engels's charge that scientific explanation sometimes resorts to a kind of mystificatory vitalism.[136] Adams's use of the word makes most sense at the level of social belief and propaganda. It also makes sense when he talks about actual energy resources in the productive process. Had he lived now he would have taken a lively interest in the politics of oil and nuclear power. In his own time it was coal: 'carboniferous capitalism' as the historian of the city, Lewis Mumford, in his somewhat autonomizing language, has called it.[137] Adams is in fact interested in the links between belief and technological development. and between science and social power. As a French social scientist contemporary with Adams remarked: '. . . cette conception de la cause *pouvoir causant* s'impose dans la recherche sociologique avec une obsession beaucoup plus tenace que dans les autres sciences.'[138]

It is time, however, to confront a more difficult question. Why did Adams, as interested in philosophy as he was, and eager as he was to ironize contemporary scientific truth with reference to the old philosophical achievements, attempt no formal or informal philosophy of science? Part of the answer lies in the time in which he was writing. It was also a matter of artistic strategy and philosophic and political stance. That he did refuse more philosophically-oriented questions seems clear. Later in life he wrote: 'Bergson does not much amuse me. I like my Schopenhauer and I like my Kelvin – I like metaphysics and I like physics – but I don't much care to reconcile them, though I enjoy making them fight.'[139] In a typically conservative move Adams posits extremes of metaphysics and physics as a rhetorical gesture. The impact of Schopenhauer on late nineteenth- and early twentieth-century thought was extensive and he was doubtless responsible for some of the more melancholy and reactionary qualities of certain of Adams's poses. During Adams's editorship, E. Gryzanovski wrote a long article on Schopenhauer for the *North American Review*. Gryzanovski saw Schopenhauer as mediating the respective philosophies of Descartes, Spinoza, and Leibniz, adding that the philosophic world was divided between 'Dualism, Monism, and Pluralism. A compromise seemed impossible'.[140] The effect was to aestheticize contradiction and take a hedonistic view of melancholy.

The other interesting point that Gryzanovski made in the same article was in relation to Schopenhauer's marginalization of unitary conscious life:

> The 'reflex action' of the motor nerves, and the various phenomena due to what Dr Carpenter has most properly called 'unconscious cerebration', are incontrovertible proofs of the great decentralisation prevailing in our system, and of the existence of many subaltern offices scattered through the body, of whose cooperation or subordination the Intellect can never be conscious, although it may discover both through observation and inductive reasoning.[141]

Was there a multiplicity of unconscious directiveness within the body itself paradoxically opaque to anything except empirical science? This notion would have attracted Adams by virtue of the promise it held out of multiple ways of knowledge, while not giving up a certain unity in method. At one level, in fact, there was not very much of a fight between Schopenhauer and Kelvin, since both conspired to reduce the role of epistemology and consciousness.

The choice of Kelvin was therefore apt. Adams got to know Kelvin's work through his geologist friend King (already encountered above in the 'two acres of tranquil pork'). King was anti-Darwin and so was Kelvin, who had argued from his knowledge of thermo-dynamic heat exchange that the lengths of time assumed by Lyell and hence by Darwin for geological and evolutional change were inaccurate.[142] King had argued in a lecture called 'Catastrophism and Evolutionism' that evolution proceeded by leaps.[143] Through King and Kelvin, therefore, Adams could pass from geology to physics for his analogies of history, and the very term 'degradation' (taken from heat mechanics) was to be used by Adams for his de Maistre-like pessimistic prognostications. Further Adams was inclined to hold to that deep Cartesian rupture between epistemology and the facts of empirical neurophysiology in order to maintain another strong opposition of a slightly different kind; that is, between that unresolvable rupture and the intelligence of feeling. The aim in less abstract language was to fend off the Cartesian predators from the Pascalian hearth.

The impulse to maintain these divisions and to make an irony out of the consequences came less from a concern with science as such than from political and psychological factors. There is a sense that Adams could let his Schopenhauer and Kelvin fight because he cared relatively little, in the end, about either. He was sceptical of certain attempts to join them. For example he did not much like Mach's psychophysics, and his patience came to an end with extreme contemporary inductivists like Karl Pearson.[144] On the other hand, he himself can be accused of exactly the kind of 'scientism' which Sartre has criticized in Engels. The word 'dialectical' in the following passage has been bracketed to let the same criticism apply to the worst aspects of Adams's 'scientific' history:

> The procedure of discovering [dialectical] rationality in praxis, and then projecting it, as an unconditional law, on to the inorganic world, and then returning to the study of societies and claiming this opaquely irrational law of nature conditions them, seems to us to be a complete aberration. . . . Engels's mistake. . . was to think that he could extract his [dialectical] laws from Nature by non-dialectical procedures – comparison, analogy, abstraction and induction.[145]

And yet guilty as he is of the same procedures, there is also a greater scepticism in Adams about that 'irrational law of nature' Sartre speaks of here. To keep the terms, Adams seized precisely on that 'opaqueness' to undercut the entire structure. Indeed when Jordy quotes Adams, 'Nothing in the history of philosophy is more distinctly marked than the effort of physics and metaphysics, since 1890, to approach each other',[146] such a statement can be interpreted in several ways. First, it can be seen as indicative of the collapse of unitary truth, the abandonment of the attempt to find the 'classical synthesis' in physics characteristic of the middle years of the nineteenth century. Second, it can indicate the dependence of the new science on highly 'metaphysical' concepts; concepts which no longer rely on common sense. Third, it offers the hope of correspondence between philosophy and science. Fourth, it rejects both philosophy and science and calls for a more humanistic reason which both metaphysics and physics seemed to deny in Adams's own time. At a time of paradigmatic uncertainty, and because Adams was neither a professional philosopher nor a scientist, it is easy to see why he would have wanted to back off from the epistemological questions.

It is also possible to draw a parallel between the refusal of the epistemological debate and Adams's view of sexual roles. In this respect, and in another article in the *North American Review*, Gryzanovski cites two maxims of Comte. The first is that 'the woman is to be excluded from all public and professional life', and the second is, that 'man should think under the inspiration of woman, his reason being subordinate to woman's feeling'.[147] There is a deflection here, therefore, of purely intellectual questions on to questions of 'social psychology'. The results are both positive and negative. There is undeniably a relation between 'male' public exclusiveness and authoritarianism extending from the economic realm to the psychological. Adams was absorbed by images of power which drew on sexual division. He distrusted Comtean positivism,[148] yet like Comte he was tempted to keep logic public and intuition private. At one level Comte's statements reinforce the nonsense that the truth of 'intuition' belongs to women and 'logic' to men. At another level to exclude women from public life preserves sexist division. Advocating thinking 'under the inspiration of women' in private, grounds logic in feeling without acknowledging the irrational as a creative source, and simultaneously confines women to an irrational social space which can be conveniently ignored. Adams's own work will indeed demonstrate his wish to let the two positions fight and thereby show themselves unstable.

Like Sartre, Adams suspected that for science there 'is not any formal structure, nor any implicit assertion about the rationality of the universe'.[149] In this sense, too, Adams knew he did not have the concept of truth at his disposal. He is in fact close, at his best, to Toulmin's historical sense of the scientific project: 'Within a historically-developing scientific enterprise. . . the significance of our concepts can be adequately shown by referring neither to the relevant empirical subject-matter alone nor to the formal structure of the science alone.'[150] Adams himself, therefore, gropingly examining the entrails of common-sense science, perceived – if dimly – that the artist and writer too must be thrown back on trying to understand a creativity common to both the scientific and artistic worlds. Referring to the 'rule of Phase', the American poet Zukofsky speaks of Adams's wondering and innocent gaze in the midst of a world it was no longer possible to 'know' with certainty; seeking to accept form without determinacy and learning to live with it, Adams '. . . even in disillusion, wrote poetry and perhaps fact'.[151] In this sense too Ezra Pound once said that 'Poetry agrees with science and not with logic'.[152]

In closing this chapter which has discussed some of the implications of the fields of enquiry that the early essays have opened up, a word must be said about technology. One of the more plausible uses of the word 'force' in Adams was to do with the actual forces of production. With the power of technology to release energy in Adams's own time there developed a concept of technique, as Ellul has called it, which constituted a symbolic presence as powerful as any 'material base'. Adams can sometimes be criticized for offering a 'feeling of concreteness' in his view of social forces while ignoring the actual relations of men within the social organization of production.[153] And yet he understood very well the nature of 'aura', in Benjamin's words, 'the transposition of a social reaction on to the relationship of the lifeless or of nature to man', the domain in short of the sacred.[154] For it is precisely the power of the fetish, the material embodiment of human praxis returning to men as a sacred object, with which Adams is most concerned.

It is here, too, that Adams's interest in 'ethnology', 'hard science', and technology meet. For the role of propaganda and 'belief' has become more important, not less, as the process of automation and technological advance qualitatively restructure the relationship between people and the ends of their production. Marx himself did not face the modern question of what would happen when the techniques of 'aura' ensured the lack of consciousness of alienation as such. There is a very important sense in which, in Ellul's words, Adams knew that 'Technique supersedes liberalism'.[155] For liberalism shared with traditional socialism and with bourgeois capitalism a view of 'efficient' man. In the spirit of his grandfather's critique of the metric system, Adams paid ironic tribute to the gods of technique imaged in the machine with its totalitarian equation of freedom and necessity. Paradoxically, in the aura such a world produced, Adams's ultimate loyalty to analogy was to retain an almost direct power subversion. The battle was not only for people's labour power but for their minds. History, in an ironic subversion of liberal truth, actually does become 'mental', not as a revelation of unconscious laws of aggregating and statistical 'social facts', but in efficient techniques of psychological control serving power structures whose ability to moderate the forces they have unleashed seems increasingly fraught with danger.

Chapter 2
From Hero to Social Type

The kinds of changes described in the preceding chapter had a profound effect on the conception of the human subject. This chapter describes the course of a shift, in Adams's perception of the subject, from political hero to social victim. The new synchronizing 'social sciences' of anthropology, sociology, and statistics had this in common, that they replaced the ethical subject with a legal and social one. Adams was to move from historical writing to the novel to chart some of the consequences of these changes.

I

Many critics, usually historians, tend to think of the monumental *History of the United States during the Administrations of Jefferson and Madison* (1884–91) as Adam's finest work. But no more than any other work by Adams can it be described as impartial, objective or even 'scientific'.[1] Adams's *History* is written in a deliberate and self-consciously chosen mode. This was partly dictated by circumstance, for he had at his disposal, thanks to his personal fortune, many hitherto unexamined documents, and was clearly right to exploit them. This, together with his experience at the Court of St. James's during the Civil War, may well have pushed him towards a type of diplomatic history with its biases ingenuously concealed within an apparently innocent narrative of events.

History as a discipline inherited from eighteenth-century thinkers a scepticism about testimony (Bayle, Voltaire), while advancing many theories of continuity and process. It was also in some ways a Romantic phenomenon, a reaction to rationalist ideas of the Enlightenment with its tendency to play down the past in its theory of natural man. But the later nineteenth-century's concern with the slow time of institutions as a subject for study also introduced a conservative bias into history. Niebuhr, in his *History of Rome*, had already begun to study the evolution of institutions. And historians of historiography also point to Savigny's *History of Roman Law in the Middle Ages* (1815 f.) as a crucial intellectual exercise linking the classical concerns of the eighteenth-century writers with that quest for institutional origins which also coincided with the Romantic interest in the Middle Ages. The key area of interest was the convergence of Roman law and Christianity in the early medieval period.

The search for 'origins' and 'survivals' was also a favourite pastime, and tended towards a playing down of the violence of historical change. Long before Darwin, nature had supplied analogies for an evolutionary and continuous characterization of time. Leibniz himself had declared:

> Nothing happens all at once, and nature never makes jumps. I call that continuity. In starting from ourselves and going down to the lowest it is a descent by very small steps, a continuous series of things which differ very little – fishes with wings, animals very like vegetables, and again animals which seem to have as much reason as some men[2].

Savigny showed how Roman institutions survived into the European Middle Ages, and as late as 1883 Seebohm's *English Village Community* attempted to prove that the Roman villa was the ancestor of the manor. Maitland's *History of English Law* of 1895 marked a change in these serene attempts to prove continuities, by showing how it was the Normans who re-introduced Roman law into England after the Conquest. Mommsen's *History of Rome* (1856 f.) achieved a kind of classical balance between Carlylean hero-worship and the force of institutional time. The key structural question was how to reconcile local historical time – the traditional narrative time of biography – with the *longue durée* of institutional change.

It was Ranke who set the stage for nineteenth-century historians. His famous phrase, that the historian '*will bloss zeigen wie es eigentlich gewesen*', needs, however, to be placed against Braudel's description of the effects of such positivist empiricism: 'A gleam but no illumination; facts, but no humanity'; and he provides a reminder that in 'its own covert way, narrative history consists in an interpretation, an authentic philosophy of history'.[3] At the opposite extreme was the Herder tradition of organic history, in which the soul of a people was racially revealed in poetry and literature. Language itself, like geological remains, gave clues to the original essence of the spirit of the people. Indeed, in a convergence which must be noted here for the later discussion of Gertrude Stein, Humboldt's influential essay of 1812 on the Basques equated the investigation of grammar with the investigation of history itself. Throughout the German century a philologically-inspired history revealing the 'psychological' essence of man accompanied a 'realistic' study of institutions.

Law and psychology, narrative and poetry, the varying orders of historical time and the intense and finite responses of the individual life, struggled for priority in the nineteenth-century historian's discourse. Grimm had claimed that poetry and law were of the same kind of human creation, but the precarious alliance had a short life. It was Ranke's pupil Waitz who argued that the German tribes showed a highly developed degree of folk spirit in their instinct for the institutions of family, army, class, and the laws of inheritance. Order was ranged now on the side of the Romans and now on the Teutonic side. Rome could be held responsible for the success *and* failure of civilization. The Teutons were alternately barbarians and original democrats. By the end of the century Mommsen's divisions of historical subjects and categories had become disciplines in their own right. The battles of psychologists, sociologists, economists and narrative historians to lay claim to the past and the right to describe the human condition had begun. Unfortunately there was to be little sign subsequently that they would co-operate.

There were, however, partial attempts at synthesis, not to mention other modes. The exponents of *Kulturgeschichte*, from Vico to Burckhardt, refused to pretend to objectivity; they frankly embraced theoretical structures and expounded hypotheses. From Voltaire onwards, however, this movement was apolitical, concentrating for the most part on the development of aesthetic consciousness. Voltaire's *Essai sur les moeurs* (1756 f.) emphasized customs and manners, a perspective which was to be taken up with enthusiasm by the ethnologists. The range of works in this tradition vary from revelations of folk soul to Riehl's *Natural History of the German People* (1854 f.), where nature in the shape of the movement of produce from the land, the dynamics of the city, and inertia of the countryside describe the total condition of the State. In this analysis the family provides stability against the unpredictability of political change. Gooch has described Burckhardt's *Culture of the Renaissance*, which appeared in 1860, as providing the 'psychology of an epoch'.[4] A more scientific view of psychology some forty years later was Lamprecht's American Lectures on *Modern Historical Science* of 1904. Lamprecht attempted to sum up scientific history, and proposed a unity of political and psychological approaches to historical phenomena. In this respect he praised the work of the German experimental psychologist Wundt, which he regarded as a key to future efforts. Wundt will be encountered again in the discussion of William James.

From the outset Adams was acquainted with international scholarly history. He knew what his options were. The large question he put to himself was whether a discourse centred on law and institutions characterized 'history' better than one centred on events or biographies. One of the few English books Adams admired was Sir Henry Maine's history of *Ancient Law* (1861), which showed law slowly evolving from a basis in status to that of contract – a historical metaphysic once given short shrift by Engels.[5] Adams wanted to discover that secret movement of historical reason which almost every historian was asserting lay in the study of institutions. But he was sceptical about all methods, most of all dogmatic ones. In a letter to Maine, for example, he tells the historian how he had asked his students to overthrow every argument in Maine's book, adding that he did not feel the exercise proved much: it might make his students good lawyers, but it left the mystery of ancient law untouched.[6]

With scepticism, however, went a great range of possibilities. Adams was widely read in German, French and English history. His first European education was German, his intellectual preference was French. From early on he had a number of important friends among English liberals and was well acquainted with a number of English historians. The first major problem that presents itself, therefore, is why he ignored most of the models. In the *History* there is none of the wide-ranging discussion of institutions of a Mommsen, nor the geopolitics of a Humboldt. Social history as such is crammed into a brilliant preface of 100 pages or more. There is no obvious tripartite movement of time, very little on the development of American law, customs or institutions. At first glance the history is primarily Rankean, a narrative of diplomacy emphasizing continuity and causality. The wide-ranging questions Adams asked of Justin Winsor, the Harvard librarian, about technological inventors, banking, medicine, religion, intellectual life and the American conservative spirit, emerge only in flashes in the actual narrative.[7] Nonetheless the various historical questions raised already will have a bearing on a reading of this work and will be recalled as occasion demands.

Adams opens in a very American manner with the 'problem of geography'.[8] Thus he begins with that sense of space which has always haunted the American imagination both actually and meta-physically: from the new earth of the Puritans to the conquest of actual space in the twentieth century.[9] But 'space' is also for Adams an epistemological category, for the 'eighteenth century ruled su-preme' (*History*, I. 15). Process within that space will be character-ized by symbolic interactive co-ordinates dancing to an undefined but broadly-assumed first cause. Like Newton's gravity, 'central-ization' in Adams's *History* will act to coordinate the atomized event as a characterization of activity in space. The 'tendency' of develop-ment in space can therefore be perceived at *any* point in time, that is, at any point in the narrative. Adams's choice of '*moment*' and '*milieu*', to use Taine's terms, always reflects a forward-driving future of the development of the 'force' of capital accumulation: a fatalistic centralization which will subvert liberal choice and whirl heroes in its vortex. At the turn of the century, 'Cornelius Vanderbilt was a boy six years old, playing about the father's ferry at Staten Island' (I. 27).

But if liberalism was to quake before the manifest destiny of embryonic capitalist heroes, that 'mental history' so progressively reassuring to the liberal historian, and lodged secretly in the social domain of institutions, is also under threat. In the new social world of Jacksonian democracy, Adams observes, that true privacy which sustains the public life is threatened: 'By day and night privacy was out of the question' (I. 45). The frontier experience itself (*pace* Turner) actually threatens the stability of domestic institutions. Adams speaks of the disease called milk-sickness, or the still more depressing homesickness, or the misery of nervous prostration, 'which wore out generation after generation of women and children on the frontiers and left a tragedy in every log cabin' (I. 58). He gives the facts a peculiar twist towards mental suffering, as if the liberal historian's 'mental history' had been infected by a virus which attacked the collective brain. The 'home-sickness' is a disease of the institution of family life and undermines that truth of society which the historian sought. ('Nervousness' as an American social 'disease' will be further explored in the discussion of James and Stein.)

Adams is ambiguous about the effects of capital accumulation. On the one hand he berates the populace for the crude materialism it produced together with its accompanying anti-intellectualism: 'Until they were satisfied that Knowledge was money, they would not insist upon high education' (I. 74). There is also, it must be admitted, a naïve, bombastic nationalistic pride in the inevitability of the future of American power. Nonetheless the lament of the failure of 'education' for 'mental development' is already present. The 'intellectual seriousness' of a Jefferson is seen as doomed before more pragmatic events. The problem of the division of the active and contemplative life haunts all of Adams's writing. At the psychological level, a section on 'American Ideals' concludes Adams's Tocquevillean introduction. Adams's new American man is not the property-conscious agrarian of Crèvecœur, but a man gripped by a conception of the future: 'his dream was his whole existence' (I. 173).

In the sequence from Jefferson's inauguration to Monroe's mission to France to negotiate over Louisiana, Jefferson is depicted as acting contrary to 'tendency', and shown as preferring states' rights to Federation, believing in the State only to the extent of negotiating foreign affairs. Adams skilfully draws a personal drama of progressive alienation, and Jefferson, like the defeated Indian chief in Parkman's histories, is accorded sympathy only at the tragic conclusion.

The secret rationale of the narrative is the emergence of centralized power. Actual events become signs pointing to a foregone conclusion. The narrative proceeds dualistically not dialectically. Adams sets up contrasting pairs of figures which oscillate somewhat unconnectedly about a prefigured fate. Belief and conventional morality are judged irrelevant to the march of events, and go down before the fatalism of biological decline – as the language of the following sentence shows: 'Throughout the period of Spain's slow decomposition, Americans took toward her a tone of high morality' (I. 30). The irony here is typical. On the one hand the pathological event censures Americans for their unfeeling righteousness, but the basis of the censure appears to be their ignorance of historical fatality, which in itself of course pre-empts any morality at all.

Like any historian of his century Adams is deeply interested in continuity. The conflict between figures thus becomes paradoxical, not contradictory. The aristocrats of Europe, for example, are shown to be as locked in intrigue as any of Eisenstein's Boyars, but the result is secret and unforeseen. It is not a synthesis which bears the marks of its conflicts but a result which Adams as omniscient narrator has well in hand. Jefferson's mediator with Napoleon is Dupont de Nemours, and the family-conscious Adams comments: 'Dupont's name was then as well and honorably known in France as that of his descendants was to become in the annals of the United States' (I. 410). The past of French diplomacy is pregnant with the future of American capitalism. In this first volume of the *History*, technical narrative is already sophisticated. At the end of chapter 9, for example, the appearance of Aaron Burr at a Virginian banquet shows him at the summit of his influence and dramatically preserves – given the reader's expectation of his fall – a cliff-hanger-like tension between this volume and the next.

In the context of secret fatalistic power the event is invariably an irony. By forcing a large gap between a secret narrative time (the long climb of American power) and the vividness of local event, 'human nature' is pitted against 'cosmic nature', almost as if Rousseau had walked into the plot of a Hardy novel. Tragedy and comedy become forms of behaviour: masks of the hypostasised 'man' of the 'human comedy'. The solemnity of the peace negotiations at Amiens is torn apart to reveal Napoleon in his bath-tub quarrelling with his relatives: 'Between the water and the wit the three Buonapartes recovered their tempers, while the valet who was present, overcome by fear, fainted and fell on the floor'

(II. 36). Like all comedy the moment of contradiction is reconciled through a wit which is often conservatively directed. The fainting valet, in this often noted passage, however, not only preserves the 'people' from the spectacle of symbolic power being reduced to a human reality, but has an even less democratic sub-text which reinforces the charisma of the emperor with or without his clothes.

Conversely the actual event may subvert conscious belief and law. Only the more attentive reader will note Adams's irony when he contends that the Louisiana Purchase was the 'logical outcome' of the Declaration of Independence and the adoption of the Constitution (II. 49), for the Purchase was legally and constitutionally invalid. Law and belief go down before the first revelation of a mass consensus in favour of Empire. Events symbolic of centralization oppose events symbolic of the fading power of the Constitution.

But Adams's fatalism has a positive side. The darkness of the vision may be compared to that power of blackness which characterized the work of a Hawthorne or a Melville. No less than these great novelists of the mid-century, Adams registers the tragedy of an over-confident America being brought within the pale of human history. In the following passage the actual event of the Burr – Hamilton duel offers a landscape of tragic proportions:

> The death of Hamilton and the Vice-President's flight, with their accessories of summer-morning sunlight on rocky and wooded heights, tranquil river, and distant city, and behind all their dark background of moral gloom, double treason, and political despair, still stands as the most dramatic moment in the politics of the Union.
>
> (*History*, II. 190)

The dramatic moment points, then, with all the ambiguous moral symbolism of a Hudson River School landscape, to the illusion of the benignly privileged American landscape as an analogue of natural virtue.

The inexorable nature of power or force undercuts every liberal illusion. Sometimes it refutes the 'common law' as in Chase's impeachment (II. 244). Sometimes, characterized as natural force, it defeats both law and military might. Adams's constantly hawkish tone can sometimes be extremely tedious, and demonstrates that ever-constant tendency of more right-wing commentators to reduce the capacity of human beings to make their own history. Hindsight may convert the intelligibility of any event to teleology. Thus the American navy's action against Tripoli pirates *anticipates* a coming struggle with England to be *proved* in the War of 1812. There is little to no freedom in Adams's characterization of the event. Where goals are inconclusive they become symbolically potential. The War of 1812 was perhaps the least inevitable of all wars in history, yet failing actual confirmation of this Adams makes it serve as a symbolic rehearsal for future American power – particularly in the area of naval technology.

In the same spirit, leaders are representatives of abstract power. This power is hardly ever political – that is, it represents neither the popular will nor alienated sovereignty – but poses as a sign of material life unmediated by labour or praxis. Jefferson represents exhausted power (pacific agrarianism) and wages a titanic losing struggle against rising power (militarily aggressive capitalism). There is little emphasis on Jefferson as a popular leader and on the representative quality of his antipathy to the war. Modes of material life are polarized (Marx for example saw continuous capitalist connections between agriculture and industry) as metaphysical opposites, and then given representative heroes who abstractly denote a linear path from one to the other. Jefferson is represented as 'losing power gradually': an almost biological descent to the tomb which serves as a legitimation of historical inevitability.

Yet Adams is aware of the possibility of different historical modes. He can show himself preoccupied with the different versions of history given by the perspectives of traditional history and law: 'The quarrel between law and history is old, and its source lies deep. . . . The lawyer is required to give facts the mould of theory; the historian need only state facts in their sequence.' (III. 45) Yet it has already been shown how 'facts in sequence' are a consequence of theoretical thinking – so, in absolute terms, the contrast is invalid. At one level Adams is merely disguising his role as omniscient narrator. But he is also asking here whether history should not have a theoretical mould as well, and whether the 'social' law of legal institutions will be of any help to the historian.

In one sense the quarrel is one of rival descriptions of historical intelligibility. Adams knows that the law as such is secondary, not primary, in relation to power. His distinction between lawyer and historian occurs in the context of a discussion of Pitt's decision to impound neutral ships with the connivance of the law in the shape of Sir William Scott. If history makes law and not vice versa, how can the study of institutions help us understand the truth of history? Sir Henry Maine, whose *Ancient Law* Adams taught to his Harvard students, was quite clear on the subject:

It is taken absolutely for granted that there is somewhere a rule of known law which will cover the facts of the dispute now litigated, and that if such a rule be not discovered, it is only that the necessary patience, knowledge or acumen is not forthcoming to detect it. Yet the moment the judgement has been reported, we slide unconsciously or unavowedly into a new language and new train of thought. We now admit that the new decision has modified the law. The rules applicable have, to use the very inaccurate expression sometimes employed, become more elastic. In fact they have been changed.[10]

Maine admits discontinuity within praxis. Thus the principle of continuity cannot be found within legality itself. Adams states: 'History has nothing to do with law except to record the development of legal principles' (History, IV. 265).

The intelligibility of sequences of facts, therefore, has to be found elsewhere. Sometimes it is in the apparently autonomous development of technology. Sometimes it seems to be usefully characterized by scientistic analogies: 'The law of physics could easily be applied to politics; force could be converted only into equivalent force. If the embargo – an extension of force less violent than war – was to do the work of war, it must extend over a longer time the development of an equivalent energy.' (IV. 289). An almost Emersonian law of compensation reveals at this stage the static equivalence-ridden dynamic of Adams's view of history. A Spencerian fatalism is the net consequence of 'scientific' rules of process. In order to become 'mature', America must join in 'the same bloody arena', unable longer to evade the 'law of Nature and the interests of life' (IV. 289).

Chief among the laws of nature are the 'laws' of capital. During the years of the Madison administration, capital gradually centralizes in New England, 'towards the banks of Boston and New Haven' (V. 19). Before it ancient ideals of statesmanship crumble. Southern statesmen particularly are the doomed bearers of this antiquated dream, which 'redeemed every mistake committed in their names' (V. 190). But if 'centralization' stated that necessity was a fatalistic reason of history, it also helped Adams to avoid certain types of sentiment. For example, he would never have contemplated a 'frontier thesis', and, possibly under the influence of Fustel de Coulanges's study of the city, he could write: 'Perhaps the growth of New York City and Philadelphia pointed to a movement among the American people which might prove more revolutionary than any mere agricultural movement westward' (V. 290).

The nearest Adams gets to declaring the fatalistic thread which runs through his narrative is when he discusses the Indian wars, and specifically in his treatment of Harrison and Tecumseh. The inexorable law of history destroys not only ambassadors and nations but the life of the primitive races also. Tecumseh's defeat '. . . offered an illustration of the law accepted by all historians in theory, but adopted by none in practice; which former ages called "fate", and metaphysicians called "necessity", but which modern science has refined into the "survival of the fittest"' (VI. 69). Adams accurately points to 'Darwinism' as a politically legitimating metaphysics. It is interesting that the biological concept, Spencer's not Darwin's, is used to characterize genocide, while analogies drawn from physics (energy, exhaustion, mathematical statistics) tend to show the rise of American power and its centralization; as if the 'harder' sciences provided alibis for the successful and the 'softer' ones compensatory tragic truths for the defeated.

Resistance to the onward sweep of Manifest Destiny is variously characterized. Sometimes it is heroic, sometimes pathetic, sometimes ill-conceived, and sometimes it shows a futile benevolence which lends a human tone to necessity. Daniel Webster is proud, to the end of his life, for example, that he attacked Monroe's conscription. But on the whole the fatalism of history dangles its puppet-like characters as much as ever Thackeray did in *Vanity Fair*. Blakeley's famous privateering sloop *The Wasp* is an exemplum of American technological force. It is perhaps fitting that Blakeley should disappear at sea without trace, like an undifferentiated molecule in an entropic system. But Adams is at least a little ambiguous in his enthusiasm for the development of American power. He regrets that 'the Rights of Man occupied public thoughts less, and the price of cotton more, in the later than in the earlier time' (IX. 104). Failure in such circumstances is moral, he seems to suggest, though morality itself is unrealistic. John Randolph of Roanoke, the supreme Adamsian failure, goes heroically to his doom alone and with eloquence.

Against fatalistic materialism the traditional institutions, whether the family, the law, or the Church, stand impotent. Like Melville and Hawthorne, Adams regrets the passing of the Puritans' sense of evil and criticizes the Utopian fantasies of the Unitarians with their hopes of 'perfection on earth altogether strange to theology' (IX. 183). The New England Church moves to disunity as the State moves to unity. In the process that combination of tough political and moral reason of the Puritan legacy disintegrates into moralistic Utopianism.

Only when he has unburdened himself of the wearisome labour of the nine volumes can Adams really criticize the threatening 'unity' of the corporate American State: 'the corruptions of such a system might prove to be proportionate with its dimensions, and uniformity might lead to evils as serious as were commonly ascribed to diversity' (IX. 219). One victim of unity was the heroic individual of liberalism. The *History* is Adams's swan-song for the Carlylean hero in whose struggles against necessity lay the Romantic life-affirming truth of history itself. The people were being transformed into a society in which political giants like Jefferson, not to mention a Napoleon or a Pitt, were no longer permitted to exist. Of the traditional linchpins of middle-class society, the Church, the Law and the Army, only the last seemed to be relevant to the State in late capitalist development. The future was not political history but social history: 'The scientific interest of American history centred in national character, and in the workings of a society destined to become vast, in which individuals were important chiefly as types' (IX. 222).

Adams registers a profound disquiet at the new society America has become. For a historian committed to time, the atemporality of the new social types destroyed even the old evolutionary continuities of traditional narrative discourse. Like Conrad's 'best of old fellows', Adams poses as his own Marlow to unfold an allegory of the last days of Romantic capitalist enterprise. What was to be the fate of story in the new America? 'Without heroes, the national character of the United States had few charms of imagination even to Americans' (IX. 224). And it is imagination that Adams feels to be lacking in this aggressive materialist society. No doubt he projected the impotence of his own class on to the tone of the discourse, but the questions he asked were nonetheless relevant: 'What interests were to vivify a society so vast and uniform? What ideals were to enoble it? What object, besides physical content, must a democratic continent aspire to attain? For the treatment of such questions, history required another century of experience' (IX. 242).

Some of the questions were to be taken up in his two novels. The novel after all was the primary form of discourse relating to private and domestic life. It dealt precisely with those 'social types' so ambiguously felt by the discourse of history to be relevant to its own project. Was it for this reason that *Esther* (of the two novels the one chosen to discuss here) was to be preferred by Adams to all nine volumes of his *History*?

II

Esther takes up the rhetorical questions about the nature of social types flung out at the end of the *History*, and reads like a parable of the decline from civilization to society, studied through the relations of art and science, nature and law, the social psychology of belief and the ethnographic evolution of the family. The questions are framed through that most popular of themes in Victorian fiction: 'The

Minister's Wooing' (the title of one of Harriet Beecher Stowe's equally witty and melancholy novels). Rid of the confines of formal history, Adams adopts a style closest to that of his best letters, where he can throw around his enthusiasms for ethnology, art and law with grace and skill.

The very formality of the structure of character-types echoes Goethe's *Elective Affinities* (1809) and foreshadows Gertrude Stein's *The Making of Americans: Being a History of a Family's Progress* (1902–11). Indeed Stein's title could serve as a subtitle for *Esther*. Each Adams character represents a formal view of life: for Science we have Roy Strong, a geologist; for the Church, the Revd Hazard; for the Law and Police, Mrs and Mrs Murray; for the Army, Mr Dudley; for Art, Wharton; and for Ethnology, finally, the battle between matriarchy and patriarchy is fought out in the roles of the three main women characters: Esther, whose problems dramatize Arnold's two worlds, 'one dead the other struggling to be born'; a Polish-French whore whom Adams graciously associates with the 'dead' world of 'European' culture; and Catherine Brooke – a prophecy of the new American type. The plot could not be simpler: the fashionable clergyman is refused by Esther because she cannot be a believer. But against this simplicity must be set a symbolic complexity of treatment as Adams plays with all the possibilities of describing society that he has learnt from his reading of the ethnologists.

The problem of social structure in the perspectives of nineteenth-century ethnology is bound up with questions of marriage and matriarchy. Adams's and King's ironic allusions to the older type of heroic women have been noted above, as have Adams's discussion of the 'primitive rights of women', his adulation of the Virgin as an icon in the belief system of matriarchy, his thoughts about the code of courtly love, and finally his rather orthodox, though ironic, belief that women should somehow be fertility symbols denoting the biological continuity of the race. Adams's interest in the family as such, the relation of the family to religion and property (as in Fustel de Coulanges), and the general terms of the arguments about tribal and social organization in people like Bachofen, Tyler and Morgan, all provide the necessary clues in 'social science' with which to trace some of the key arguments in *Esther*.

Adams asks himself, if history is to be social history, what types will emerge within evolutionary selection? The artist of the book, Wharton (the penniless little boy from Cincinnati who has the misfortune to march backwards in time towards Europe and towards perishing types like *femmes fatales*), is himself full of declining 'energy' and poses this question to the clergyman: '"... I never yet met any man who could tell me, whether American types are going to supplant the old ones, or whether they are to come to nothing for want of ideas. Miss Dudley is one of the most marked American types I ever saw.'''[11]

Esther herself is a 'modern type' – her atheist views are moulded by her Army father and the geologist Roy Stong – and she confronts the last gasps of clerical patriarchy in her wooing by the clergyman. The clergyman falls in love with Esther on a classical social site: a hospital – that is, a domain which is neither public nor private. This domain is ruled over by women led by Mrs Dyer, who conducts all the affairs of the hospital with 'masculine gravity' (*Esther*, pp. 32–3). The order of the hospital is directed to helping the 'diseased children' which are its charges. Mrs Dyer is a lawyer's wife and finds fault with everything 'except the Middle Ages and Pericles' (p. 30). Confronted with this matriarchal synthesis of Hebraism and Hellenism, Esther feels impotent and resorts to telling the children stories. In this milieu of what Arnold called the 'strange disease of modern life',[12] the primitive discourse of story faces the efficient social impersonality of the lawyer's wife. The diseased children are an image of the fact that somewhere along the line society has failed to provide the means of heroically continuing the race.

It is here, then, that the minister confronts Esther in a classic moment of post-Hawthornean pictorial symbolism:

> Mr Hazard was not to blame if the scene before him made a sudden and sharp picture on his memory. The autumn sun was coming in at the window; the room was warm and pleasant to look at; on a wide brick hearth, logs of hickory and oak were burning; two tall iron dogs sat up there on their hind legs, and roasted their backs, animals in which the children were expected to take living interest because they had large yellow glass eyes through which the fire sparkled; with this a group of small individuals whose faces and figures were stamped with the marks of organic disease; and in the centre – Esther.
>
> (*Esther*, p. 54)

The scene arouses Mr Hazard's 'primitive' instincts – that is, he falls in love.

Mr Hazard's view of this cultivation of the household gods stirs him deeply. Fustel de Coulanges had said that it was precisely the cult of the household gods that ushered in the male hegemony of law and order, the strictly separate roles of family and state in the Roman *polis*, and was the point of overthrow of the gentile organization which he, like Adams, believed had been liberal in its view of women's roles. At one level therefore Hazard mistakes for a private landscape what is essentially a gentile matriarchal landscape, or one at least balanced precariously between family and State. The scene recalls the dream world of the folk: 'the old narrative fireside mode of story-telling',[13] that primitive past identified in the present with the mentality of disadvantaged groups (women and children) – an interpretation which is reinforced by Esther's story.

This story, counterbalancing the fashionable abstractions of Hazard's sermon earlier, is about 'Kings and queens in tropical islands and cocoa-nut groves, with giants and talking monkeys' (*Esther*, p. 55). The giants in fact indicate the childhood of the race, according to the biblical account, and the monkeys their ancestors according to science. Hazard confronts the history of the race in myth which his own ideology and unconscious psychology is impotent to deal with. Unable to interpret the signs, the minister turns the picture before his eyes into sentiment. Adams's strongest point is that Esther is not to be viewed, here, as a cross between Virgin and social matriarch, administering to sick children surrounded by icons of the 'hearth'.

But Esther herself cannot escape the effects of rejecting that role. After turning down marriage with the minister, the last image she is associated with is not fire but water. Adams makes an important symbol out of Niagara Falls – doubly ironic here because the Falls were a traditional place for American nineteenth-century honey-mooners. Did Adams also think of the Nile, that ancient river of fertility and the cult of death, where he had spent his own honey-moon with a chronically depressed young wife? The image of water is a naturalist symbol, frequently employed by Adams. Certainly the Falls are an image of the ancient gods. They are explicitly contrasted with Athene, the Acropolis and the Aegean. Perhaps also Adams is recalling Arnold's sea of faith, with its 'long withdrawing roar'.[14] Here more particularly, however, the treacherous wisdom of the Hellenic gods is contrasted with an impersonal image of 'force'. The ice, snow, water and mist are like different thermodynamic phases of Nature's own heterogeneous substances, with only the rainbow as an ironic reminder of ancient covenants against impersonal annihilation. After an argument with her cousin Strong, the geologist, about faith and scientific scepticism, Esther characterizes any concept of immortality as a 'great reservoir of truth, and that what is true in us just pours into it like raindrops' (*Esther*, p. 273).

This tough-minded scepticism is the weapon with which Esther confronts the minister whose dogma – in a magnificent moment, one of the best in nineteenth-century fiction – is revealed to be a mask for his own sexist insecurity. When Hazard makes the mistake of appealing to the 'natural instincts of your sex' in the face of her disbelief in immortality, Esther replies:

> Why must the church always appeal to my weakness and never to my strength! I ask for a spiritual life and you send me back to my flesh and blood as though I were a tigress you were sending back to her cubs. What is the use of appealing to my sex? The atheists at least show respect enough not to do that!
>
> (*Esther*, p. 299).

Esther can be seen retrospectively as a forebear of Ursula at the end of Lawrence's *The Rainbow* (1915), or Stephen Dedalus at the end of Joyce's *A Portrait of the Artist* (1914), or Fitzgerald's Amory at the end of *This Side of Paradise* (1920). She at least has the guts to know what she does not want and will take unhappiness rather than live a lie. This moment, though ambiguous, the hint of de-naturing is still there, exhibits a defiance of the compulsions of the sexual, intellectual and religious legacies. The vision of women as needing to be 'protected', instinct with primitive intuitions and historic failure, is shown to be inadequate. She at least challenges the patriarchal inheritance. Both atheist father and clergyman had got on well because the one handed her to the other, thus exhibiting the sexist psychologies they shared irrespective of their conscious ideologies. Strong, too, who asked Esther to marry him when she was at an emotional disadvantage, is rejected. All this is sufficiently positive to place against the conventional ending of the novel, which implies that she will now be unhappy for life.

Esther's companion, Catherine, by contrast pits the Western 'innocence' of the newly born psychological type against the role she is called on to play in sitting as a model for a St. Catherine painted by the artist Wharton. The name 'Brooke' might be a parodying reference to George Eliot's St. Teresa-like heroine in *Middlemarch*. 'Catherine' is undoubtedly a reference to Adams's somewhat macho Catherine the Great. Surely Adams is also recalling the passage in King's book about the acres of 'tranquil pork' when he makes the minister compare Catherine's idea of a picture to that of his Cincinnati parishioner who, 'looking at this harvest as solemnly as Wharton is looking at his picture, said that what he liked most was the hogs he could see out of it' (p. 60). Catherine cuts through the contorted psychological sensibilities of decaying Eastern types almost as fast as she can shoot and drive horses. Like King's six-foot Susan, 'There is something about me', she says, 'that scares them all off the ranch' (p. 195). It is through her that Adams criticizes the whole cluster of feminine character-types: those melancholy neurasthenic Eastern women vaguely interested in art and victims of male demands on them to be the angel of the house. Catherine is glad she does not have to sit for Esther's sketching: 'I should have to sit for melancholy, or an angel, or something I'm not fitted for by education' (p. 194).

Catherine is in fact the reincarnation of the strength of the past directed towards the future. That Adams sees her in terms of a reincarnation of the woman of the *gens* is made ironically explicit when Strong, the geologist, teases her with a question asked by a friend who was a professor of linguistics: '"He asked me what *gens* you belonged to. I told him I guessed it was the grouse *gens*. He said he had not been aware that such a totem existed among the Sioux. I replied that, so far as I could ascertain, you were the only surviving member of your family."' (p. 69)

But Catherine escapes the historicizing categorizations of linguist and geologist as well. To see her as a 'Madonna of the Prairie', linking the cult of the Virgin with *gens* matriarchy, is no more truthful than Hazard's perception of Esther as Madonna of the Hearth. Wharton's picture, says Strong, is to show 'how an American Saint ought to look by the light of science' (p. 81). He then 'drew a portrait of Catherine under the figure of a large Colorado beetle, with wings extended. When it was done, he pinned it against the wall' (p. 81).

Catherine, however, survives the violence of the patriarchal gaze whether directed through religious, artistic or scientific spectacles. Adams's irony is sophisticated and even extends to a critique of sentimental heroines of nineteenth-century fiction. Catherine also survives Strong's experiment of making her read *The Old Curiosity Shop* in the new church under the pictures of the martyrs because he wants to note the effect on a 'Sioux Indian'. She isn't one.

The other woman of note in the novel is the *femme fatale* who is to be responsible for the destruction of the artist.[15] Adams almost runs out of historical equivalents to describe her. She has superb eyes and an eastern trend. She is at once Semiramis, Medea, a Clytemnestra with gypsy charm, a maenad with a French accent and a Jezebel thrown in for luck. She is the archetypal complement of the fertile heroic woman: that is, she is erotic and a trap for artists. Wharton has to be rescued by lawyers as he sits impotent with a broken paint brush in his hand and his forehead red with paint like a mark of Cain. Here the reality is firmly out of joint with Wharton's disrupted vision of Petrarch and Laura: the sexual myth of the 'society' that is on its way out.

Having made his opposites fight, Adams tentatively gives us some clues as to the power which holds society together under the multiple failures of inherited custom and belief. The lawyers, those experts in social history, are the key, and they restore order out of chaos. Mr Murray deals with the scandal of Wharton's whore. Mrs Murray deals with Esther. Social appearances must be preserved and pragmatism rules supreme. It was Mrs Murray who had originally advised Esther to marry Hazard, with the words (and the implicit puns are unavoidable): "Women must take their chance. . . . Marriage makes no real difference in their lot. All the contented women are fools and all the discontented ones want to be men – ." (p. 41) The 'law' swiftly and ruthlessly applied keeps 'society' together, invalidating the claims to such competence on the part of Church, Science and Art. Mr and Mrs Murray perform much the same function as the appalling ex-colonial Assinghams in James's *The Golden Bowl* (1904), and Adams is as ambiguous as James in his characterization of them. Esther's father, for example, hearing of Mr Murray's action in relation to Wharton's whore, an action backed by the police, says, "I suppose he means to terrify this poor creature into a sacrifice of her rights" (p. 146). In the absence of a social, indeed a political theory which has some relevance to actual conditions, Adams fears that society will indeed 'become police'.

Testing his available analyses from the ethnologists, the hard scientists, geologists, atheists, lawyers and priests, Adams finds them all wanting. But at least like his heroine he refuses alibis for action in 'creeds outworn'. As Esther says, and it sums up the interior voice of the novelist across style and content; "Whose first attempt in a new style ever paired with its conception?" (p. 124). The old style no longer provides a resource. The price is too great. As Esther says with grim humour, "One learns theology fast when one is engaged to be married" (p. 180). But the twilight of the gods was to haunt Adams, and the subjects announced here, continuing as they do that complex of issues of the early essays and the *History*, were to be taken up again in perhaps his greatest work, the *Mont-Saint-Michel and Chartres*. There as here, what was to haunt Adams was that in a 'society' become police, without faith or theory, without respect for the past and the richness of myth, and where the only hope was in the carelessness of one-dimensional scientific truth, the historian's sense of time and story might itself be annihilated.

D

Chapter 3
A Poetics of Social Hegemony

Adams moved from the social fiction of *Esther* to a deeper exploration of social power and belief, art, politics and poetry, in the first of
the two major late works. In *Mont-Saint-Michel and Chartres* form and
subject-matter constitute a kind of poetics of the contradictions
of social hegemony. *Mont-Saint-Michel and Chartres* and the pos-
thumous *Education of Henry Adams* stand together as the crowning
achievement of his career. Perhaps they stand together a little lop-
sidedly, rather like the twin spires of Chartres cathedral itself. In
some senses, like *Esther*, the Chartres is a model of *social* reconstruction, in that special nineteenth-century meaning of the word analysed above. That is, Adams gives us the Middle Ages in terms of its
beliefs, as mirrored in customs, artefacts, marriage and sexual habits,
shrines, art, architecture, science (in a broad sense of society's
'knowledge') and ethics. Law (of custom) and medieval studies were
also associated.[1] In one sense the work is again a fictional ethnology,
with the authorial voice deflectively masking and revealing its own
tone: 'tone', that is, in the sense of an attitude towards the materials
engaged.

For the past of the early society that Adams engages with here is
very much the past of his own present, fully and ironically realized
in the 'reconstruction'. As with so many other writers of his time,
Adams turned back to the Middle Ages for a variety of reasons. In
some sense it was a personal '*recherche du temps perdu*', for he had
taught medieval history at Harvard thirty years earlier, during the
first years of his marriage. He had given lectures, he said, 'cribbed
bodily out of Fergusson and Viollet-le-Duc'.[2] To write a work
which examined the cult of the Virgin would also have had that
'attraction of opposites' for someone so strictly reared in the New
England post-Puritan milieu.

Equally, however, it was a way of coming to terms with that
'eighteenth-century' Adams which he was to describe so wryly in the

Education. Alfred North Whitehead, writing about the eighteenth-century philosophers, gives a clue: 'Their hatred of the Gothic architecture symbolizes their lack of sympathy with dim perspectives. It was the age of reason, healthy, manly, upstanding reason; but of one-eyed reason, deficient in its vision of depth.'[3] As much as Hawthorne, who had described his most famous heroine in terms of the Madonna, Adams was to pit his own dim perspectives against 'one-eyed reason'. All reconstructions of the past bear the mark of a contemporary perspective. The increasing nostalgia for the Middle Ages in late nineteenth-century Europe and America was clearly fostered by a sense of revulsion from the disasters of late nineteenth-century capitalism. Every response, however, within the general 'escapism' was particular and can be valued accordingly.

Adams was not insensible to the resurgence in religion of High Anglicanism and Catholicism which, from the Oxford Movement to the Neo-Thomist revival in France, often signified the revolt of the upper classes against conditions they themselves had helped to foster. Like Péguy in 1905, Adams made his own pilgrimage to Chartres. Unlike T. S. Eliot, however, who actually joined the Anglican Church and wrote pamphlets in support of Anthony Eden's Conservative Party, Adams became a scion of neither Church nor State.[4] The dash of 'anarchism' in his 'conservative Christian anarchism' was always too strong, as was his Puritan rationality. Adams's medievalism is therefore to be studied in all its particularity. His portrait of the Middle Ages is marked by lacunae. He shows little interest in the craft movement as such, though he has a highly developed sensibility in relation to stained glass. He plays down the violence of a Europe organizing in terms of rival kingships. He almost completely ignores actual social conditions. He does not directly allegorize medieval 'romance' as did William Morris in his splendidly decadent fables, nor does he involve us in the technicalities of medieval architecture, whether 'cribbed' out of Viollet-le-Duc or anyone else. Diligent American scholars have discovered that his sources in some instances were the obvious ones and not particularly recondite.[5]

Adams was in fact one of us. And the ironic strategy of the book is to insist on it. He threw together some reasonably reliable guidebooks, loaded up his camera, pocketed his binoculars, got into his car and went to 'do' the Normandy cathedrals. Like Gibbon and like Michelet, Adams wanted to communicate what it *felt like* to encounter the monuments of antiquity; for Chartres was as different from early twentieth-century America, for Adams, as the Forum had been for Gibbon in eighteenth-century England. As early as 1895 Adams wrote to his friend, the English MP Charles Milnes Gaskell:

'The Normandy trip turned out well; charming weather; easy journeys; a new world of architecture; and to me also a new variety of scenery and people. I bagged a dozen new churches, and a few castles and châteaux, besides Mont-Saint-Michel.'[6]

This same tourist, however, had numbered among his friends some of the most distinguished historians of his time, and two of America's great artists, one the painter John La Farge, the other the architect H. H. Richardson. The tourist, also, had a dozen or more distinguished works behind him: formal history, novels, biographies, and essays on everything from political economy to ethnology. Every interest of Adams is signalled here. If ever he found a form in which to rehearse his sense of late nineteenth- and early twentieth-century America it was, paradoxically, this meditation on the culture of Mont-Saint-Michel and Chartres.

In fact the continuous stream of historical analogies linking Adams's own present consciousness with the objects of his contemplation seems to work much better here than it does in the *History*. The monuments of Chartres cathedral and Mont-Saint-Michel become images of meditation which Adams seeks to locate within the contemporaneity of his own sensibility. The passages on architecture, for example, reveal something of a Beaux-Arts perspective. Ironic comparisons abound. God the father, symbolizing 'military energy' at Mont-Saint-Michel, is compared with 'Washington who never lied'.[7] Adams's contemporary interest in the social psychology of public icons is thus signalled. In the same spirit Adams can declare that the Virgin 'illusion for illusion' gives a better return on capital than 'the bourgeois get for their investments' (*Chartres*, p. 97). The convention of courtly love (which Adams calls throughout 'Courteous Love') is compared with 'the balance of trade, the rights of man, or the Athanasian Creed' (p. 224). In our own time, when trade figures, moralistic toutings of civil rights by superpowers, and travelling Popes in Pope-mobiles are the 'content' of 'news', Adams's irony does not come amiss. He is questioning the propaganda effect of stage-managed political display. Power manipulates its denizens through images and always has done, but the key question is who makes the images, for what purpose, and what social function is served.

Like a good teacher also, Adams invents analogies to attempt a 'relevance' of past to present. He uses his cross-references to provoke a satire on the mores of his own time. The objects of attack are the sentimental tradition, the split between piety and pragmatism, technological optimism, the illusion of 'progress', the tenets of bourgeois society from sex to politics and from economics to theoretical science. The *Chanson de Roland* is invoked to make

Bayreuth seem feeble and decadent (p. 25). The organizational capacity of Mont-Saint-Michel is praised for its efficiency – did
Adams have the trusts in mind by comparison? Certainly the new
tall buildings going up in New York are compared with the Norman towers (p. 54). Adams invites a test of their relative value. The
culture of Chartres is shown as international, not narrowly provincial. Books published in the Middle Ages, says Adams, seem to be
distributed with greater rapidity than in his own time (pp. 139–40).
Historical comparisons of male and female sexual behaviour are too
numerous to summarize here.

The relation of theoretical science to the power structure is also
a key issue. Is it possible to learn from Bernard of Clairvaux or
Thomas Aquinas how intellectual life may control and fashion
society in ways which might be relevant for a world revolutionized
by the discoveries of Kelvin, Madame Curie and Einstein? Perhaps
the most savage comparison is between the paternalism of the
Church, with its rigorous suppression of civil rights and its tolerance
of diversity in practice, and the rigorous touting of civil rights in
America with repression and conformity of behaviour in practice.
Adams is not suggesting there should be a 'return' to the Middle
Ages. The point is that this 'fiction' of the Middle Ages provides a
commentary on present practice. In choosing Thomas Aquinas's
system to comment on in the concluding stages of the book, Adams
recalls the words of Pope Leo XII: 'on the wings of St. Thomas's
genius, human reason has reached the most sublime height it can
possibly ever attain' (p. 344).

Again the point is not that Adams thought this exaggerated
statement true as such (Adams's view of Thomist theology is
ambiguous and used for strictly non-theological purposes), but that
it serves as an ironic corrective to his own America. The past, too,
has its perfections. The stance illuminates the essential modesty of
the historian who here criticizes those Americans whose ignorance
of the past sometimes leads them to the absurd and dangerous belief
that they alone are 'the last best hope of mankind'. The forms of life
Adams chooses, then, to present in his imaginative social reconstruction of the Middle Ages, and the ways in which those forms are
presented, amount to a study of what Ellul has called 'sociological
propaganda'. Adams, too, is interested in that 'general climate, an
atmosphere that influences people imperceptibly without having
the appearance of propaganda; it gets to man through his customs,
through his unconscious habits'.[8] In the climate produced by unconsciously moulded habits, the figure of the Virgin looms large
as an icon of social belief. Adams's account of the sexual politics of
the Virgin warrants a more detailed examination.

With the study of the cult of the Queen of Heaven and of courtly love, Adams was writing again on a subject that had haunted him since he wrote on Pocahontas in the 1860s. There is much conservatism, contradiction, and some banality in his description of the Virgin, but nonetheless a fascinating series of problems emerges in Adams's treatment of the image. Into his portrait he poured not only his fundamentally Pascalian scepticism about the nature of reason, but also his sense of private failure, his sometimes wildly compensatory sentimentality, his theories of female roles in 'primitive societies', and his search for analogies with which to berate the tendencies of his own time.

Some idea of the range of response can be seen in the following quotation, which opens the eleventh chapter of the work, on the three Queens of France: Eleanor of Guienne, Mary of Champagne and Blanche:

> The twelfth and thirteenth centuries, studied in the pure light of political economy, are insane. The scientific mind is atrophied, and suffers under inherited weakness, when it comes in contact with the eternal woman – Astarte, Isis, Demeter, Aphrodite, and the last and greatest deity of all, the Virgin. Very rarely one lingers with a mild sympathy, such as suits the patient student of human error, willing to be interested in what he cannot understand. Still more rarely, owing to some revival of archaic instincts, he rediscovers the woman. This is perhaps the mark of the artist alone, and his solitary privilege. The rest of us cannot feel; we can only study. The proper study of mankind is woman, and by common agreement since the time of Adam, it is the most complex and arduous. The study of Our Lady, as shown by the art of Chartres, leads directly back to Eve, and lays bare the whole subject of sex.
> (*Chartres*, p. 196)

Each of these representations is a double-edged sword. Placing the Virgin outside political economy debars women from real life while also criticizing political economy for its 'one-eyed reason'. By making her a goddess of the matriarchy Adams affirms the then current assumption by Bachofen and others that women's role has been diminished over the centuries; thus attacking the notion that women are naturally inferior. At the same time the idealization of the role projects a preposterous male fantasy of the essentialist moral superiority and divinity of women on to actual women. Such a fantasy can only be designed to retain women in subjection. Similarly the attribution of the absence of logic at once damns the positivistic mechanisms of some traditionally male thought, while insinuating that the 'feminine' mind is devoid of any form of consious reasoning.

As a repository of archaic traits the Virgin affirms that the legacy of custom and of unconscious behaviour are powerful organizing factors in social organization, but at the same time turns them into a potential fatalism.

Finally the artist as privileged bearer of truth may suggest relations between the domains of sex, politics and culture – outlawed from other forms of knowledge – but the romantic isolation suggests that such forms of knowledge cannot become universal. Here, however, the author's own secret voice comes into play: 'perhaps' he knows what an artist is ; his 'we' states something he is confident about; mankind, however, is in 'common agreement'. The three levels of confidence about the materials in the three suggested voices (artist, author, people) do not necessarily reflect the truths of their content. Adams is suggesting degrees of truth in an argument which engages both consensus and disruption of consensus. It is an argument which also assumes that the relations between myth, society and art are at least as intellectually complex as anything produced by 'the scientific mind'.

To keep the terms of nineteenth-century discussion, the Virgin is a powerful image in 'mental history'; that is the 'force' which governs 'social' history. As such she is part of that *longue durée* of which the thirteenth century is but the final moment in a movement which begins after the birth of Christ – indeed stretches behind it into ancient history. And as such she stands as an icon of the enculturation of natural process presented as a sign of sovereign power. Adams implicitly attacks genteel Christianity by reminding it of the sexual and erotic origins of its own rituals: 'Chartres was exclusively intended for the Virgin as the temple of Abydos was intended for Osiris' (p. 98). By building a distinctly un-Christian version of the Virgin – paralleling the Tristan legand with the 'primitive love' of old Icelandic and Native American societies – Adams proposes a biological key to all mythologies: 'Men were, after all, not wholly inconsequent; their attachment to Mary relied on an instinct of self-preservation' (p. 250).

Nonetheless the problems remain. When Adams remarks, 'the pain of childbirth was a pleasure which she wanted her people to share' (p. 72), we may see it as overturning the Christian emphasis on sharing the death of Christ only; and inviting through its symbolism of birth an identification with the real process of life rather than with a spurious immortality. However, the vicarious symbolization of shared pain is reactionary. Control of the painful process of childbirth is rightly a feminist issue. Similarly the political symbolization of the life-giving mother deflects the erotic into a sexual psychology of dependence used to ensure continuity and order.

Adams's account of how St. Bernard, for example, is given milk from the breast of the Virgin's image is a case in point.

This 'milk for new-born babes' is a familiar symbol of Christian discourse and allegorically represents the receiving of the spirit. Nonetheless in radical psychoanalytic terms it is an image of regression, in which real sexual exchange becomes an equasive, static incorporation of sexual opposites, and in which one of the parties is symbolized as an infant dependent on the other. This 'infant' then receives the authority of the parent in order to continue the condition of patriarchy. Here the very distinction between matriarchy and patriarchy (as a Utopian logic rather than as specific practice) falters, much as Bachofen, Adams and some contemporary feminists would like to value one above the other. The figure of Virgin and child is also a symbol of combination: a search for 'unity' which is a 'vicious cycle, in which subject and object are confused; active and passive, male and female roles are exchanged in the desire and pursuit of the whole'.[9] Here the sacred suggests endlessly unrelieved tensions within the stasis of the image. And while still on the subject of sexual pathology, it must be admitted that Adams also emphasizes those essentially patriarchal moments in which men are pleasurably viewed as wounded or humiliated before women.

Sado-masochism involves a regressive substitute for what is forbidden, a rite of initiation for those about to inherit power: 'In the desire to be beaten by a woman, the woman is both father and mother; a composite figure, a Sphinx.'[10] It is in this sense that Adams's Virgin is bisexual; not the bisexuality which we all have in varying proportions, according to culture and genetic inheritance, but a symbol of unresolvable oppositions posited as the unity of Nature which serves as a religious icon of authoritarian continuity and control. This is the deep psychology of Adams's portrait of the Virgin at one level, and its worst aspect. However, it is important to remember that Adams is actually suspicious of Unity itself. If Unity exists, he says, in which and toward which all energies centre, it must explain and include 'duality' and 'infinity' within the discourse of sexuality; whether as polarized male–female roles or as the 'eternal woman'. Only diversity will remain. But at this deep level diversity can scarcely be directly contemplated, except as an anarchistic irony which confirms almost as much as it challenges the sexual iconography of sovereignty.

There are, however, positive aspects to Adams's anarchistic stance. The illogicality of the Virgin does enforce the values of the heart against that of mechanistic logic and the fatalism of political economy. In some ways the presentation here compares well with the role of a figure like Azdak in Brecht's *The Caucasian Chalk Circle*. The Virgin is a figure which is finally powerless though dressed in the symbols of authority. She is a carnival figure which precisely inverts the normal logic of power, producing satire but only minimally offering countervailing praxis. As a figure, too, which straddles the private and public domains through the 'social' discourse of the law, she is a Utopian glimpse for Adams of an end to contradiction. In his pessimistic allegory the face of the Sphinx still bears the marks of the human visage. In the *Education,* the Dynamo will take the place of the Virgin, as human figures for human power disappear finally from the public domain.

The matriarchal perspective of mother and child as a controlling symbol of the social order is imperfectly paralleled within *Chartres*'s terms of address. Adams initially sets up the tone of the discourse by referring to himself as 'uncle' acting as a tourist guide to his 'niece'. Of course Adams had many actual nieces and visited the cathedrals with them. What is more important, however, is that the imagined dialogue is an old narrative device (a play within a play) in which the ideal reader is invoked to unmask the content, while at the same time the narrative so produced offers the presence of the author as true content behind apparent content. Adams called this work 'a five-act drama, of the twelfth century, to best *Macbeth*'.[11] In this sense alone perhaps the masked presence of the author as chief character in his drama is as strong in Adams as in Shakespeare.

Adams's prologue to the work provides some initial playfulness as to the appropriate surrogate reader. He rejects the notion of father and son, flirts with a parallel in nephew (Macaulay reading with his uncle) and finally lands on niece: 'The relationship, too, is convenient and easy, capable of being anything or nothing, at the will of either party, like a Mohammedan or Polynesian or American marriage' (p. xvi). Adams would have remembered through his reading of Morgan that 'primitive marriage' was distinctly catholic in its non-exogamous inclusion. Adams makes the further point that 'One cannot assume, even in a niece, too emotional a nature, but one may assume a Kodak' (p. xvii). Technology replaces sex. The point of view, therefore, is a truly complex one. It depends on a social relation which is linked to the erotic childhood of the race but which has now become merely a primitive survival; an unconsciousness buried and yet strangely haunting. The niece or old 'wife' of the *gens* is officially no longer emotionally dangerous, and her point of view is that of technological realism: the Kodak. Adams had actually taken pictures of 'primitive' Polynesian tribesmen with his own Kodak. Now the 'primitives' themselves go photographing the remains of 'ancient society'. Adams gives us, from the depths of his irony, the deep psychology of the innocent gaze which from Locke to Freud invoked the image of the child.[12]

Uncle and niece pose as a double innocent paradoxically holding 'nature' up to the mirror of an architecture which displays in its own haunted glass the remains of a vanished world strangely linked with their own. It is a way for Adams to speak of the 'reflex action of the complicated mirror which was called mind', and he adds 'the mark of mind was reflective absorption or choice' (*Chartres*, p. 370). These phrases from the middle of the discussion on St. Thomas's philosophy place the Adamsian perspective somewhere between a Lockean epistemology of mind and the Romantic philosophers. Given this fact, it is not surprising that verbal echoes and even phrases from Wordsworth penetrate the narrative at many points. The innocence of this child, unlike Locke's, however, is an already complicated perception which articulates the 'primitive' capacity to link art with the knowledge of unconscious life – at least as its starting point:

> The man who wanders into the twelfth century is lost unless he can grow prematurely young. One can do it, as one can play with children. Wordsworth, whose practical sense equalled his intuitive genius, carefully limited us to a 'season of calm weather', which is certainly best; but granting a fair frame of mind, one can still 'have sight of that immortal sea' which brought us hither from the twelfth century; one can ever travel thither and see the children sporting on the shore. Our sense is partially atrophied from disuse, but it is still alive, at least in old people, who alone, as a class, have the time to be young.
>
> (*Chartres*, p. 2)

Unlike Wordsworth, however, there is no progression from sense experience to memory and reflection. Rather there is an identification of those social outcasts (the young and the old) as people who deliver their intuitions from the margins of society: intuitions which reveal that 'sense of the past' in an almost literal way as a deep truth of contemporary consciousness. But behind uncle and niece is Adams himself, ready to dissolve the world of his own creating. He steps in to break the illusion of supended time, as Prospero will bury his books or Titania wake from the dream. Or indeed, as in the masterpiece of that other assiduous photographer of young girls, as an Alice will awaken from a dream of logic dissolved on the other side of the mirror.

Two such moments occur, at the end of the nineth and tenth chapters respectively. At the end of the first Adams imagines his senses bewitched by the voice of 'the children of the *maîtrise*':

> . . . you or any other lost soul, could, if you cared to look and listen, feel a sense beyond the human ready to reveal a sense divine

that would make that world once more intelligible, and would bring the Virgin to life again, in all the depths of feeling which she shows here – in lines, vaults, chapels, colours, legends, chants – more eloquent than the prayer book, and more beautiful than the autumn sunlight, and any one willing to try could feel it like a child, reading new thought without end into the art he has studied a hundred times; but what is still more convincing, he could at will, in an instant, shatter the whole art by calling into it a single motive of his own.

(*Chartres*, p. 177)

The 'sense divine' is that addition to the Lockean psychology which Wordsworth himself had to make and which, in an American tradition stemming from the same source, Jonathan Edwards was also obliged to add to his synthesis of Calvinism and British empiricism. Here, to keep Edwards's terms, the 'religious affection' is what art itself adds to system and form (the prayer book) and to the pure evidence of the senses (the autumn sunlight).

But there is a sense in which Adams is tougher-minded than Wordsworth. The sense of loss is more absolute. There is a truth, closer to Blake perhaps, that the condition of childhood is both magical and irrecoverable. And yet that childhood is also one of lost Eros, in Adams's terms of the primitive, and of the lost role of women. One senses at these moments that the power of Adams's feeling is neither for childhood nor religion but for his own lost wife, and beyond that again the Hawthornean truth that recognition of failure (that most uncharacteristic American truth), is the basis of all human truth:

It was very childlike, very foolish, very beautiful, and very true – as art, at least; so true that everything else shades off into vulgarity, as you see the Persephone of a Syracusan coin shade off into the vulgarity of a Roman emperor; as though the heaven that lies about us in our infancy too quickly takes colours that are not so much sober as sordid, and would be welcome if no worse than that. . . . For seven hundred years Chartres has seen pilgrims, coming and going more or less like us, and will perhaps see them for another seven hundred years; but we shall see it no more, and can safely leave the Virgin in her majesty, with her three great prophets on either hand, as calm and confident in their own strength and in God's providence as they were when Saint Louis was born, but looking down from a deserted heaven, into an empty church, on a dead faith.

(*Chartres*, p. 195)

Here the counter-movement of the abstract world of the coinage re-
enters, pointing to the degeneration of any image within a changing historical culture. And by implication the parallels move from
Persephone to Caesar and from the Virgin to the American President. Even while denying art any contemporary significance Adams
asks us to judge the 'devaluation' in a world which has made its
insignificance possible.

Adams's historical pictures of time are, then, first presented as manifest paradox. As in the *History*, every event in this book seems to be
located within a profoundly dualistic pattern. Art, philosophy and
the dramatization of human relations are proposed as paradox. But
the strategy of presenting ambivalence in these domains is undercut
by an irony which always challenges the very terms of paradox. The
oppositions in the *Chartres* are readily apparent. There are dualities of
North and South Europe, Gothic and Norman, the architecture of
arch and spire, towers and portals, line and colour, love and law,
heroes and heroines (Pierre–Blanche), types of theologians and
theology (Bernard–Abelard), intellect and the forces of nature. As
a narrative strategy, to proceed by oppositions is as old as 'creation
myths', but what Adams does is to break the process down so that
a series of small-scale dualities appears within the larger ones – a
procedure not unlike a Liszt étude, where the traditional sense of
harmonic base is challenged through small-scale contrasts. The sense
of process (since dialectics is not directly proposed) emerges almost
vitalistically. As in a chromatic sequence, the moment of harmonic
meaning is also a moment of transition.

For the most part Adams is content to describe the instability
and transience – indeed the restlessness – of his paradoxes: 'One
must live deep into the eleventh century in order to understand the
twelfth; we shall find the thirteenth in many ways a world of its
own, with a beauty not always inherited, and sometimes not bequeathed' (p. 11). There is a typically French sense of history here
perhaps. It is best described by Collingwood: 'The French historian
seeks, following Bergson's well-known rule, *s'installer dans le mouve-
ment*, to work himself into the movement of the history he is studying, and to feel that movement as something that goes on within
himself.'[13]

Adams's whole sense of these centuries represents a kind of hover-
ing between what Sartre calls accumulation and transition. Sartre's
example interestingly enough is Adams's own: '. . . the whole feudal
period of the eleventh, twelfth and thirteenth centuries is a perpetual
turmoil: there were events everywhere, yet there was no emergence
from the Middle Ages because the elements for doing so did not

exist.'[14] Adams tends to let the accumulations of events and tran-
sitions oppose each other. Certainly he sees more 'transition' in
these three centuries than Sartre and perhaps rightly so.

The moment at the centre of the paradox becomes for Adams
neither a precise consequence of the past, nor a direct cause of the
future. He rejects the lineality of dates, and tends to spatialize them
to describe the more statistical time of institutions: 'Ordinarily a
date is no great matter, but when one has to run forward and back,
with the agility of an electric tram, between two or three fixed
points, it is convenient to fix them once for all' (*Chartres*, p. 35).
Dates become coordinates in a grid rather than moments of historical truth. Dates sustain an almost ideogrammic tension within a
given space. Part of the reason for this was neither philosophical
nor a question of historical method, but *technological*.

Two technologies are important. The first is the automobile (an
18 hp Mercedes) which enabled Adams to 'bag' his cathedrals. The
second is his Kodak. In 1896 Adams wrote of the first: 'These inven-
tions infest France, almost as much as Bloomer cycling costumes,
but they make a horrid racket, and are particularly objectionable.'[15]
He soon, however, adjusted to them:

> The auto is made for the aged. The sense of going–going–going
> in the open air, dulls thought, and induces a sort of hypnotism or
> mental lethargy, with swift visions of landscape and escape. . . . It
> becomes a hazy consciousness, a sort of dream without charac-
> ters. . . . The auto is a great tyrant. I have to invent space for it.[16]

Negotiating his fixed points, therefore, Adams is forced to invent
a new and dreamlike space. The rapid shifting of point of view
within the landscape paradoxically also enabled him to reassemble
the sequence of time. The evidences of survivals could be gathered,
brought home and fixed in evolutionary sequence.

The photographs must have contributed to the same effect. Scat-
tering them about the floor of his Paris apartment, Adams could
pick out the frozen details and reassemble them into the grand design. Here Adams builds (not without humour) his ideal church of
the transition out of the imperfection of the architectural record: 'So
too the central tower or lantern – the most striking feature of Norman churches – has fallen here at Mont-Saint-Michel, and we shall
have to replace it from Cérisy-la-Forêt, and Lessay and Falaise'
(*Chartres*, p. 9). The irony, however, suggests that such a project is
doomed. He says later, 'no law compels you to insist on absolute
repose in any form of art' (p. 66).

Restlessness, an American restlessness, such as Adams's much-
admired Tocqueville saw in American life, haunts the book. It is the

deep structure of paradox itself: the latent tension of unresolvable contradiction. This perspective sees opposition everywhere. For example, Adams reviews the rival French and Norman designs for towers: the Norman is the 'practical scheme which states the facts, and stops; while the French will be the graceful one, which states the beauties, and more or less fits the facts to suit them.' Adams adds, 'both can sometimes be tiresome' (p. 55).

The Form versus Ornament debate was raging fiercely in Adams's own period. It may not be too bold to speculate that the 'marriage' of the Norman and the Gothic which Adams so emphasizes in his description of the nave and choir of Mont-Saint-Michel came out of a contemporary debate. For did not his friend H. H. Richardson, the architect who built Adams's own house in Washington, synthesize the heavy downward thrust of Furness's buildings – so reminiscent of the Corliss engine which Adams had admired at the Chicago Exposition of 1893 – and that upward-thrusting movement of Sullivan's buildings? Between Furness's 'Norman' and Sullivan's 'Gothic', Richardson designed his own 'Transition'.[17] It can be seen in the surviving photographs of the house Richardson built for Adams: in the stretched-out massive double-arched front, with the windows diminishing in size upwards to give a sense of relief from the vaulted base. The effect is restlessness; a tie between security and escape. Perhaps it points to the fundamental psychology of the family dwelling.

Hugo Münsterberg (who was to teach Gertrude Stein behavioural psychology), in a remarkably perceptive passage had made his own parallels between America and the Norman or 'Romanesque':

The positive features which especially strike the European are the prevalence of the Romanesque and of the sky-scrapers. The round arch of the Romans comes more immediately from southern France; but since its introduction to America, notably by the architectural genius Richardson, the round arch has become far more popular than in Europe, and has given rise to a characteristic American style, which is represented today in hundreds of substantial buildings all over the country. There is something heavy, rigid, and at the same time energetic, in these great arches resting on short massive columns, in the great, pointed, round towers, in the heavy balconies and the low arcades. The primitives force of America has found its artistic impression here, and the ease with which the new style has adapted itself to castle-like residences, banks, museums, and business houses, and the quickness with which it has been adapted, in the old streets of Boston as in the new ones of Chicago and Minneapolis, all show clearly that it is a really living style, and not merely an architectural whim.[18]

For Adams, however, one pole of the debate could be 'tiresome'. His interest was in paradox, to see if the movement within the transition would hold any clue to the final paradox of unity and multiplicity. It is the illusionary stability of paradox that interests Adams and also its psychology. It is in fact the historian's sense of time that subverts the sequences of Adams's paradoxes. A paradox is a structure without real time. The psychology of the structure of unresolvable paradoxes runs to melancholy, therefore, and Adams brings it out in many places. But perhaps it is exposed as clearly as anywhere in his discussion of the *Roman de la Rose*, the medieval allegorical masterpiece of social manners. In a Swinburnean mood Adams says, 'The undertone of sadness runs through, felt already in the picture of Time which foreshadows the end of Love.' A quotation from the translation thought to be by Chaucer follows:

That there nys man that thynke may
What time that now present is;
Asketh at these clerkes this;
For or men thynke it readily
Thre tymes ben ypassed by
The tyme that may not sojourne
But goth, and may never returne,
As water that down renneth aye,
But never drope retourne may.

(*Chartres*, p. 274)

The final image recalls Esther's meditation on Niagara. In a sense Time is interested in neither unity nor diversity, it has 'settled few of the disputes. Science hesitates, more visibly than the Church ever did, to decide whether unity or diversity is ultimate law.' (p. 289.) Once again Art will supply the key.

The parallelism of past and present in the methods of art now finds its object not in architecture but in literature. Just how subtly Adams can bring his meditation on paradox to bear on his theme of time and process may be seen when he recalls Flaubert in this moment in the farewell to Normandy:

But here we must take leave of Normandy; a small place, but one which, like Attica or Tuscany, has said a great deal to the world, and even goes on saying things – not often in the famous *genre ennuyeux* – to this day; for Gustave Flaubert's style is singularly like that of the Tour Saint-Romain and the Abbaye-aux-Hommes. Going up the Seine one might read a few pages of his letters, or of 'Madame de Bovary', to see how an old art transmutes itself into a new one, without changing its methods.

(*Chartres*, p. 55)

The same paradoxical tension persists. Beneath Flaubert's 'masculinity' lurks the restlessness of the wanderer and of the bored and doomed woman. 'Going up the Seine' is an image which links past and present: an image perhaps of time itself or a return to the source of the primitive which is the basis of the psychological truth of art in Adams's terms. Of course Flaubert's famous description of a journey up the Seine is in the book Adams does not mention: *L'Education sentimentale*, the very title of which could serve also as a subtitle for the *Chartres* and indeed link it and Adams's own *Education*. The paradox of the eternal question of dualism seems immovable, says Adams; you can read Flaubert's *Letters* or *Madame Bovary*. At every level, then, Adams knows here the value of his omitted reference: the hope of an end to paradox in the education of the heart.

The question of paradox then is something more than an aesthetic and something less than a philosophy. Adams conducted a search beneath the dualisms of common sense for a form of art which would dissolve their oppositions. However, by shifting the ground from under the traditional discourses of architecture, poetry, philosophy, and science, by playing with and inverting their respective languages towards an analysis of social power, Adams stumbles on the only resource left to him: the power of analogy. For in analogy lie all the resources of the creative act. Its operations differ from logic in that meaning constantly escapes the formal contrasts of what it seeks to bring together. It creates a form of multiplicity which is proportion but not order.

Having begun with St. Michael, continued with the Virgin, Adams now figuratively moves to God. Towards the end of the book he goes deeper into the heart of his meditation. Adams asks: What is the nature of the historical process? As with every other question of the book, the answers of the Middle Ages are turned over in the light of late nineteenth-century questions. How does syllogism confront a potential dialectic? What is the relation of analogy and metaphor? How does St. Thomas square up to Poincaré? These questions by Adams will move towards defining a relation between speculative and poetic discourse, and perhaps come closer to turning the very notion of paradox into that of contradiction and tensional truth. Of the many contemporary theorists of metaphor and analogy, two only are chosen here; one the biologist Agnes Arber, and the other Paul Ricoeur. The first has the advantage of being an actual scientist, a biologist, and as such sympathetic to the more vitalistic aspects of Adams's thought; the other, as a contemporary French philosopher whose work takes in the whole range of the contemporary debate, has the added advantage of continuing in our own time that

French tradition of speculation to which Adams himself was so much attracted.

Just how relevant Arber's discussion is to an understanding of Adams can be readily shown. Like Adams, Arber was attracted to Indian thought, and had an unusually sympathetic view of the idealist tradition to which Adams himself in later years was more and more, if sometimes reluctantly, attracted:

> Indian thought seems to have recognized the need to pass beyond the naïve conception of Oneness, more fully than Western philosophy, though Heraclitus, writing before the birth of Socrates, realized that the Unity of all things is not simple oneness, but is the tension of opposites; unity in the manifold; the harmony of strife; order within change.[19]

It was almost certainly this aspect of Indian thought which attracted Adams and within the terms of a very similar discussion. Eric Mottram points to the most positive aspects of Adams's engagement with Buddhism: 'He had that essential modesty which knows that the Buddhists are right; everything is coherent in any case.'[20] Unlike many contemporary theorists Arber speaks of the 'delight' of recognition within the manifold and equates it with Spinoza's 'definition of pleasure' as 'the passion by which the mind passes to a higher state of perfection'. (*Arber*, p. 21).

Adams was also attracted to Spinoza, and the Neo-Thomists tended, as Adams does, to use him against Descartes. Like Adams and the Neo-Thomists, Arber pursues the contrast between Descartes and Spinoza: 'Unlike Descartes, Spinoza treated the concepts of body and mind as both referring to the same reality; this reality was, however, held to assume an entirely different character according to the "attribute" – extension of thought – under which it was considered' (pp. 98–9). Like Adams and *unlike* the Neo-Thomists, Arber is not attacking the Cartesian tradition of scientific scepticism in order to reaffirm a reactionary religious doctrine, but rather to overcome the limitations of certain mechanistic defects in the Cartesian philosophy of nature in order to enrich the possibilities for scientific thought. As it was for Adams, it is a way of attempting to reconcile the opposed camps of mechanist and vitalist:

> The mechanist, starting from the physico-chemical standpoint, interprets the living thing by analogy with the machine. The vitalist, on the other hand, supposes a guiding entelechy, which summons order out of chaos; he thus adopts a dualistic attitude. The elements of truth in both these views are recognized, and their opposition is resolved in the *organismal* approach to the living

creature. This approach is conditioned by the belief that the vital co-ordination of structures and processes is not due to an alien entelechy, but is an integral part of the living system itself.

(Arber, p. 101)

A theory of analogy within this system becomes crucial. Its key terms are proportion and relation. Duality becomes heuristic, a means of testing the relations between the subject and the subject's sense of the other: the microcosm – macrocosm view of the world during the Renaissance, for example. Most interesting for this argument is that Arber criticizes Darwin for his failure to recognize the completeness of his breeding analogies in relation to the development of the organic world. In other words he did not do enough of what the 'hard' scientists said he should not do. But Arber also points to the Middle Ages, where the argument from analogy 'found its focal points in the theory that man himself could be understood by analogy with the scheme of things as a whole and vice versa' (p. 36).

Arber returns the discussion to the Middle Ages and to Adams. Here Ricoeur can be profitably taken up. Discussing the Thomist system from a viewpoint which will need a name as composite as Adams's 'Conservative Christian anarchist' – that is, from a 'left-wing, post-existentialist, post-semiotic Christian philosospher', Ricoeur meditates on Thomas Aquinas's 'onto-theology' as an attempt to heal (and yet at the same time reaffirm) the split between speculative and poetic discourse; a distinction held to be true since Aristotle.[21] The Thomist doctrine of analogy is seen to establish theological discourse at the level of a science and to free it from poetical forms of religious discourse. Collingwood actually saw it as a first step in the secularization of Christian thought: 'It was in the thirteenth century that St. Thomas Aquinas threw overboard the conception of divine substance and defined God in terms of activity, as *actus purus*. In the eighteenth Berkeley jettisoned the conception of material substance, and Hume the conception of spiritual substance.'[22]

The doctrine of the analogy of being was born of the desire to encompass in a single doctrine the horizontal relation of the categories of substance and the vertical relation of the created things to the Creator. The question is then how the conceptual order relates to questions of ontology. Analogy for example functions at levels of names and predicates, but the 'condition of possibility' lies in the order of being. Thus the discovery of being as act becomes a kind of ontological keystone of the theory of analogy and the deeper meaning lies in 'causality': 'It is creative causality, therefore, that establishes between beings and God the bond of participation that makes the relation by analogy ontologically possible' (Ricoeur, p. 276).

But then it might be asked – what kind of analogy? The sequence of categories and the hierarchy of the divine still appear to be ir-reconcilable. In fact Aquinas never quite solves the problem. *Pro-portionalis* balanced between a perfection of effect and cause and an imperfection of the finite and the infinite tended to throw its weight behind a more secular 'ordering principle inherent in being itself' (Ricoeur, p. 277). The conception of unity and the conception of the real are placed in a mirror-relationship with each other. And in a statement which must be noted for the later discussion of Gertrude Stein, Ricoeur extends this principle to the ontology of language: 'In that interplay of Saying and Being, when Saying is at the point of being forced to silence by the force of the heterogeneity of being and beings, Being itself revives Saying by means of underlying con-tinuities that provide an analogical extension of its meanings to Saying' (p. 277).

The problem that now arises is that if unity and diversity (multi-plicity) are required to be assigned to efficient causality, then even causality has to be thought of as analogical. This defeats the whole purpose of the exercise, because the aim of speculative discourse is to keep analogy (proportion) and metaphor (participation) distinct. There is therefore a profound paradox at the heart of Aquinas's system: 'at the point of greatest proximity the line between analogy and metaphor is most firmly drawn' (Ricoeur, p. 278). Analogy is closest to metaphor, paradoxically, when it is defined as propor-tionality. Two predicative modalities intersect in a 'composite mo-dality of discourse' in which 'the speculative verticalizes metaphor, while the poetic dresses speculative analogy in iconic garb' (p. 279). Thus the weight is thrown on to the act of predication – of clear interest to someone who comes from a Marxist tradition – in which meaning emerges. Here analogy and metaphor intersect: the one rests on the 'predication of transcendental terms, the other on the predication of meanings that carry their material content with them' (p. 280).

So Ricoeur meditates on the system from the point of view of language and epistemology. His aim is to create a dynamic scheme in which speculative and metaphorical thought interact. At the nega-tive level dead metaphor produces metaphysics, or an endlessly self-authenticating circle of reference, as in Ricoeur's paraphrase of Derrida that 'there is no discourse on metaphor that is not stated within a metaphorically engendered conceptual network' (p. 287). For Ricoeur, however, the process of pure structure is not metaphor idealistically engendering metaphor as truth, but metaphor itself is a perpetual transcendence of structure in which new meaning emerges. Structure is here characterized as an inert moment in a process, not a transcendent truth in which metaphor endlessly engenders and explicates metaphor.

There are other places, in addition to the last part of the *Chartres*, where Adams's own treatment of St. Thomas can be observed. Pursuing Adams's deliberations through his pencilled annotations in editions of Descartes, Pascal, books on the new science and Aquinas himself, is a fascinating business. On Descartes, for example, Adams's viewpoint varies. He can argue like Mill that the idea of a circle must come from circular substance, on the other hand he can insist on the revolutionary power of analogy as predication within concept-building: 'all hypothesis is unscientific. Every generaliz-ation is hypothesis. God is unscientific.'[23] Certainly Adams comes at Descartes from the Thomist point of view, and he scribbles against Descartes's 'Response to the 9th Objection': 'Is substance more real than form or energy?'[24] In his annotations in books on Thomas Aquinas Adams's pencilled notes play ironically against the vertical and the horizontal axes of the Thomist system. Against an assertion that 'tous les êtres sont refermés en lui', Adams writes, 'conversely is he shut up in all beings, as causes in effect and sees only himself? How does this differ from Pantheism?'[25] Adams ironically reverses the intellectual love of God of Spinoza: God's intellectual love of us is pure Pantheism and robs us of free will. Here Adams plays off Descartes against St. Thomas. And it is this same scepticism that he brings to any a priori reason or hint of it in Aquinas. When Jourdain quotes Aquinas: 'Quaedam rationis ordinatio ad bonum commune, ab eo qui curam communitatis habet promulgata', Adams writes, 'Much law has been and is daily recognized as not for the common good and has to be repealed or ignored – does such law fall within the definition?'[26] Indeed the question of liberty is crucial. In l'Abbé P. Carbonel's *Historie de la philosophie* (1882), Adams underlines: 'Quant à l'action de Dieu sur la créature, comme Spinoza, elle détruite la liberté. Leibniz craint même que la théorie cartésienne de la création continuée ne mène à la négation de la liberté.'[27]

The notes are most extensive in Maumus's two-volume work, *Saint Thomas d'Aquin et la philosophie cartésienne* and betray Adams's anxiety for the freedom of human action and intelligence within a theory of natural correspondence. As the reference to Leibniz shows, if the continuity of nature, however conceived, becomes the reason of history, liberty is negated. It is not simply that Adams sets Descartes against Thomas and Spinoza against Thomas – both ends against the middle; the clash is conceived within the milieu of

Darwinism. For Arber, analogy in its creative play banishes the
fatalism of the mirror from a theory of natural correspondence.
Adams could not be so sure. Nonetheless Adams's annotations
in Maumus become more and more sarcastic, and nowhere more
so than when Maumus derides the stance of scepticism:

> Le scepticism ne se contente donc pas de dégrader l'homme: il est
> une insulte à Dieu.

> [Adams] voyons! doucement! and St. Thomas who refuses to let
> us assume the existence of God![28]

Yet the interest in process remains; particularly that aspect of the
Thomist system which, as in Ricoeur, can be used to discuss the twin
operation of analogical and metaphorical practice within concept-
formation and stylistics. Against Maumus's discussion of three
phases in the generation of the 'idea' ('L'image fournie par la sensation, un travail d'abstraction opéré par l'intellect agent et enfin entrée
de l'idée') Adams wrote 'image = species?/ travail = energy?/ idea =
concept?'[29] The weak point in Adams's meditations, which so
closely paralled Ricoeur's here, is that of energy. Adams still hankers
after an idealistic metaphysic of process. Ricoeur replaces 'un travail
d'abstraction', which Adams had even more simplistically rendered
'travail = energy', with that act of predication which underlies both
analogy and metaphor.

What Adams appears not to discuss at all, however, is of course
the post-Kantian solutions to some of these problems. And yet in
some ways that omitted reference is still somewhere in the background. That Adams was perfectly aware of the problems of Romantic philosophy can be seen in his comments opposite Maumus's
discussion of Kant and Fichte. Then as now, however – or until
relatively recently – to take Romantic philosophers seriously was
to tar the perpetrator of such a deed with an extreme left- or right-
wing brush. When Maumus writes of Kant's transcendentalism,
Adams commented: 'The question is how to conceive Unity? Experience gives only Multiplicity. Is Unity only an idea or concept
in our Mind?'[30] Modern philosophers no longer see clear divisions
between idealist and empiricist philosophy, but in the nineteenth-
century such a division was in general taken for granted.

In the final stages of the Chartres Adams wrote a last tribute to St.
Thomas: 'The field embraced all that existed or could ever exist.
The immense structure rested on Aristotle and Saint Augustine at
the last, but as a work of art it stood alone, like Rheims or Amiens
Cathedral, as though it had no antecedents' (p. 354).

Within the structure of the work of art Adams could admit discontinuity; that fall of speculative discourse into metaphor. The work of art insisted on the discontinuity of creativeness itself; an inventiveness within the given. Adams's technique is to dissolve a philosophical discourse of concepts by revitalizing metaphor. For example, he takes the geometric reason of Cartesian thought, over-lays it with the image of the Trinity, and produces something which is neither philosophy nor theology: 'God as a double consciousness, loves Himself, and realizes himself in the Holy Ghost. The third side of the triangle is love or grace.' (p. 350) Adams presents philosophy and theology 'as art' – perhaps the most persistent two words in the book. In the notion of the Trinity he can admit what he cannot admit in Descartes, or Spinoza, or even St. Thomas. The Trinity becomes an image of the interaction of Form and Content. The concept of the self-splitting God is the means by which Adams can admit reflection and consciousness and make an intelligibility of act within the forms of nature. Here Adams truly does make his own structure out of Descartes (consciousness), Spinoza (a parallelism of mind and nature), and St. Thomas (creative act). There is also an ethics. It is an ethics connected with praxis, and because it is con-nected with praxis it incorporates the unexpected. 'Grace' within Christian theology uses the notion of the unexpected. It escapes purpose and is fundamentally undesigned in the sense that it has no antecedent. For Adams it summons creativity from logic and repetition. It is a form of loving the world and trusting the new.

Behind the debate on St. Thomas is yet another argument. It is one which haunted the early years of the nineteenth-century: the debate between separate and single-source creations: the first spatial, and fixed in the certainty of the categories of God's monism; the second evolving through generation and time. For Aquinas, Adams says, time is diminished: 'Time had nothing to do with it. Every individual that has existed or shall exist was created by the same instantaneous act, for all time' (p. 354). This unity is architectural and spatial. Adams in fact hurls the world of Linnaeus and Newton synchronically back at Darwin and Kelvin, Curie and Poincaré. The effect, however, is neither scientific nor theological, nor philo-sophical. Adams is not advocating the truth of eighteenth-century science, but he is paradoxically reminding the nineteenth- and early twentieth-century scientists that their own truth is relative and time-bound. Truth shifts even in the grandest architectural design. Indeed Aquinas's fundamental mistake was to ignore the fact that 'time comes into it'. A geometricizing epistemology is inadequate. Adams takes care to quote Pascal's scoff at Augustine, 'a meridian decides truth' (p. 365). So he returns to his grandfather and to the problem of measure.

Thus Adams examines creativity and structure, and in a century of arrogant specializing sciences insists on the pre-eminence of art. There is also, however, a politics: a politics of contradiction. On the vertical axis of his own created world Adams places Saint Bernard of Clairvaux and William (Guillaume de Champeaux) who represent Plato, the Roman arch, mystery, orthodoxy, the establishment, realism and bureaucracy. On the horizontal axis is Abelard, who represents Aristotle, the pointed arch, mathematics, dialectics, conceptualism, nominalism, revolution and democratic creativity. Abelard of course loses. Adams's class identification of the psychology of nominalism with dialectics is a paradox which betrays a general Anglo-American prejudice. In the end, however, Adams will claim the radicalism of the negation of the negation for art itself. On Bernard's side the authoritarianism of the mystificatory bureaucrat points to a 'society become police': though here, too, is a countervailing recognition of the need for the pragmatics of power and order. So imperfect oppositions fight. It is difficult to suppress the thought that Adams is writing an allegory of the politics of labour (diversity) and capital (unity) of his own time at the level of behaviour and ideology. His description of tolerant patricians includes some harsh judgements but perhaps does not satisfy at the political level. But at least it serves as a reminder that behind rival modes of discourse there is an actual politics.

Adams leaves his equations open-ended. In an appeal to freedom of judgement his work opens up response and admits new forms and contents. For Adams resolves, or at least rehearses, his contradictions poetically. That is, he directs our attention to *poiesis*; the 'making' of new meaning. His prose has the deep and dense quality of poetry itself. Discussing the concluding sections of the *Chanson de Roland*, Adams says: 'The action of dying is felt, like the dropping of a keystone into the vault, and if the Romanesque arches of the church, which are within hearing, could speak, they would describe what they are doing in the precise words of the poem' (p. 30). This meditation on architecture is itself poetry. The upward thrust of art maintains itself by a movement which imitates the downward pull of gravity, but paradoxically sustains itself against it: an imperfect imitation which destroys the notion of imitation. In Ricoeur's words the 'bond of participation' (the dropping of the keystone into the vault) makes the relation by analogy ontologically possible. So Adams undertakes to re-make his cathedral by recreating the already created. The cathedral is a given which makes the book possible. He speaks therefore what has already been spoken; a renewal within the created.

Adams's book ends with the Gothic cathedral – one final paradox – for the movement of the work comes to rest in transition:

> Perhaps the best proof of it is their apparent instability. Of all the elaborate symbolism which has been suggested, for the Gothic cathedral, the most vital and most perfect may be that the slender nervure, the springing motion of the broken arch, the leap downwards of the flying buttress – the visible effort to throw off a visible strain – never let us forget that Faith alone supports, and that, if Faith fails, Heaven is lost. The equilibrium is visibly delicate beyond the line of safety; danger lurks in every stone. The peril of the heavy tower, of the restless vault, of the vagrant buttress; the uncertainty of logic, the inequalities of the syllogism, the irregularities of the mental mirror – all those haunting nightmares of the Church are expressed as strongly by the Gothic cathedral as though it had been the cry of human suffering, and as no emotion had ever been expressed before or is likely to find expression again. The delight of its aspirations is flung up to the sky. The pathos of its self-distrust and anguish of doubt is buried in the earth as its last secret. You can read out of it whatever else pleases your youth and confidence; to me, this is all.
>
> (*Chartres*, p. 377)

Here Adams moves beyond paradox towards that turning point in apparent stasis; a transition which might be characterized in terms close to Hegel's negation of the negation.[31] Or more appropriately, perhaps, logic, historiography and narrative are dissolved into poetic image.[32]

Almost every moment of Adamsian process is here. 'Substance' is potentially dissolved (danger lurks in every stone). The 'arc' of the meridian becomes an analogy of 'tensional truth' showing strength in its very imperfection. Unlike the Norman arch, the Gothic breaks into successive fragments to leap higher. Restless, vagrant, uncertain, irregular, unequal, suffering, haunting and nightmarish – these are the emotional qualities with which the courage of art flings its aspirations against the sky. The downward and upward movement suggested by the images recalls not only the 'marriage' of Richardson's architecture, but also of Heaven and Hell. Is the 'leap downward' the leap paradoxically of the Romantic version of Milton's Satan? Is the strain that is thrown off that of the very vertical analogy of St. Thomas's 'being'? Does the revolutionary act of metaphor dissolve the dead structure of static oppositions? Here Adams questions – as does Pascal – the uncertainties of logic and recalls the lost heaven of the childhood of the race. The faith is in an equilibrium 'beyond the line of safety'. It is the risk taken by the

poet towards 'complexity, multiplicity, variety, and even contradiction' (*Chartres*, p. 375). In a positivist age Adams claims an intelligibility for emotional life. The error and uncertainty at the heart
of metaphor – those irregularities of the mental mirror – are claimed
as a process of truth. In the words of William Carlos Williams, 'It is
NOT to hold the mirror up to nature that the artist performs his
work.'[33] In the final deliberate disengagement of authorial voice,
Adams resists the appeal to the child and moves beyond 'confidence'
to an appeal to the *work* of the artist, making the final analogy of
the transition correspond to the very span of human life itself. It
is Arber's delight of recognition within the manifold that he celebrates here. For a brief moment Adams's dualities, still restless
and unceasing, fail to fight.

Chapter 4
The Arts of Transition: *The Education of Henry Adams*

Seeking some impersonal point for measure, he turned to
see what had happened to his oldest friend and cousin the
ganoid fish, the Pteraspis of Ludlow and Wenlock, with
whom he had sported when geological life was young; as
though they had all remained together in time to act the
Masque of Comus at Ludlow Castle, and repeat 'How
charming is divine philosophy!'.

HENRY ADAMS[1]

measure. **1**. The action or process of measuring. **2**. Size or
quantity. **3**. The width of a printed page. **4**. Duration of
time. **5**. An instrument for measuring. **6**. A standard
criterion, test. **7**. (Math.) A submultiple. **8**. Satisfaction (of
appetite, need, desire). [. . .] **11**. Moderation. [. . .] **16**. A
plan or course of action.

from the *OED*

Adams's autobiography was his last attempt at 'measure' in the face
of a natural philosophy which had become less than 'charming'. In
The Education of Henry Adams, he appears to let the mask slip. Here
is no surrogate Esther, nor Blanche, no Gallatin nor Abelard to
disguise the tone he adopts on the burning issues of law and sex,
history and science, and the other topics which have appeared
steadily but in varying constellations through the entire career. And
yet the 'Adams' who appears, as critical jargon has it, is 'unreliable',
in spite of the bold tactic of the advancement of the narrator in the
third person singular. Adams might have begun 'Call me Adams',
much as Melville's narrator in *Moby Dick* had invoked the name of
Ishmael. It is thought that Adams did not read Vico's *Autobiography*,[2]
but Vico, too, had referred to himself in the third person singular,
precisely to subvert the Cartesian ego with its solitary consciousness
reflecting on a world radically detached from it. It is at any rate a
reason Adams would have relished. He refers quickly to his old

master Carlyle by stating that 'The object of study is the garment, not the figure' (*Education*, p. xxiv). Adams confronts us with his 'presence' as draped as Saint-Gaudens's sculpture of his dead wife. In Carlylean terms the outer appearance is but a symbol manifesting different orders of concealment, revelation and silence.

The *Chartres* and the *Education* stand in symbiotic relation the one to the other. There are many direct and indirect references in the latter to the former. The pose of tourist, of life rather than of ancient culture, is readopted. The current processes of culture and anarchy are again hurled against the relics of the liberal dream. Again and again Adams's search is not only for the line of history which most guarantees intelligibility but for that moment of contemplation with which to restrain Faust's passing hour. The two once again are incorporated into landscape descriptions which affirm the analogies of art against the fragmentation of specialized discourse. In a radically American perception, the forests of Normandy become an escape from the city and contemporary time; a place where like a contemporary Hester Prynne, Adams might reinvent the province of art torn from a forbidden pleasure: 'In the long summer days one found a sort of saturated green pleasure in the forests, and the gray infinity of rest in the little twelfth century churches that lined them, as unassuming as their own mosses. . .' (p. 369). Here again the horizontal line of nature and the verticality of the analogy of being intersect. The mosses as the object of the simile not only help Adams create the sense of place but also recall Hawthorne's *Mosses from an Old Manse* and further link the sense of place with the line of the story itself.

Correlation and transition are the terms of reference. And once again there is the doubly ambiguous hope – 'ignorance required that. . . social and political and scientific values of the twelfth and twentieth centuries should be correlated in some relation of movement that could be expressed in mathematics. . .' (p. 376). Again, too, the problem of sex and society re-emerges. Shuttling between the St. Louis Exhibition of 1904 and Normandy, Adams leaves his options open: 'He could suggest nothing. The Marguerite of the future could alone decide whether she were better off than the Marguerite of the past; whether she would rather be victim to a man, a church, or a machine.' (p. 477)

The two works share these and many other characteristics: a concern with the active and passive life, the intersecting movements of landscape and time, sexual tragedy, intellectual life and feeling. Unlike as in Matthew Arnold's work, culture and anarchy seem to be different perspectives of the same object: simultaneous presences whose interaction may give birth to a new order. In order to come to terms with the *Education*, and by implication with the work that has gone before, five aspects only of this dense and multiple book will be taken up. First there is the notion of character type, which from Jefferson to Senator Hay, from Pocahontas to Héloïse, has been a concern of Adams in relation to the very meaning of history in both its political and social dimensions. Then there is the question of time – apparently absent as a metaphysic from the new concepts of social order. These issues in turn throw up the problems inherent in the whole architecture of liberal thought, and, further, the relation of knowledge (science in its broad and narrow sense) to consciousness. Finally a summary of the role of the notion of 'society' will be attempted by looking at one of Adams's last efforts to define it.

The suspicion that the living cannot rely on constant identity feels as if it should be a modern thought. However, a passage from the fourth-century *Corpus Hermeticum*, which so delighted Renaissance scholars, states: 'Know then, child, that all that is in the world, without exception, is in movement, either diminishing or increasing. And that which is in movement is also in life, but there is no necessity that every living being should conserve its identity.'[3] Adams's *Education* will attempt to give intelligibility not unity to the fragmentation of the subject.

There is a double, paradoxical definition of type in the *Education*, for the author himself, glimpsed in the opaqueness of himself as text, is a type which shifts from that 'eighteenth-century child' (*Education*, p. 11) to the multiple twentieth-century man. Adams gets the vertical analogy of being in motion by ironizing the fixed order of creation as a symbol of the individual's development: a wry and symbolic recapturing of phylogenesis by ontogenesis. This vertical thrust, the Buddhist ascent out of contraries to the acceptance of multiplicity, cuts across the play of categories in which duality is both posited heuristically and unceasingly destroyed in the inner movement of metaphor. It is within these terms that Adams's view of himself as a constant failure must be seen. 'Failure' is the turning-point of metaphor and Aristotle's 'mistake'. Failure in intellectual terms is the prime agent of what modern commentators have called the 'category mistake'. Adams's whole epistemological emphasis is on how category mistakes might be used for historical description and planned in the process of creating art. A familiar Adams strategy will assert the duality of types while subverting any confidence in their opposition.

The initial terms which posit the type are Burkean, with the addition of Montesquieu's notion of character modified by climate and geography, and articulated through by now familiar Wordsworthian echoes and verbal play. A sense psychology in which 'education' proceeds through aesthetic contraries determined by climate is then the first 'style' of education considered by Adams. Ironically, however, Adams posits the cultural availability of knowledge in contradictory relation to the Romantic model of the natural growth of knowledge. He describes himself as being 'thirty years old before his education reached Wordsworth' (p. 36). If you cannot know what you need to know at any given moment, Adams suggests, then the revelation of the type you are might come too late. Throughout the book there is an almost desperate plea for an education in which intelligibility and present process might intersect. Experience on the Wordsworthian model, of sense impression moving through reflection on memory to stoic stasis, for Adams has been revealed at a moment midway in his own life rather than at its end. Unlike Wordsworth, Adams was to be haunted by the contrary states of beauty and fear to the end of his life, and he had little confidence in nature for a correspondent metaphor of the essentialist egotistical soul. In a challenge to traditional American moral – geographical terms for personality and type, Adams says: 'Always he felt himself somewhere else' (p. 52).

What Adams does in fact is to push the old premises of originally-created categories towards a position of extreme paradox. Thus in the search for 'types' of survival, he is forced to multiply the categories until the whole monistic mental architecture falls to pieces. In literary terms the result is a stunning series of portraits. The search for constant types is presented as a strategy within the work only to point up the vagary of the event and the fragility of the passing moment. Time and history are the ghosts in the machine of portraiture. Palmerston's laugh was 'a laugh of 1810 and the Congress of Vienna' (p. 135). In the marvellous 'portrait' of Louisa Quincy Adams the surface may resemble the frozen elegance of Sèvres china, but what is remembered is her determination to rejoin her husband in Russia through the retreating Napoleonic army. The genteel category of the 'feminine' is dissolved in the social movement of the individual against the political 'march of events'. The result is neither social nor political nor representative of manners.

The literary mode for the subversion of category is satire. And no less than in Gertrude Stein's Making of Americans, which will be examined in the same spirit later, Adams's dualities are directed towards articulating a loss of faith in the old order and scanning the relics for the new. The American 'Southern type', as tested on the senses, is 'sensuous' enough but also 'haunted by suspicion, ill-balanced, and provincial to a degree rarely known' (p. 100). In this 'paradox' the Burkean psychology of beauty and fear fails to come into equilibrium. There is little 'calm' of the Wordsworthian kind in the correspondence here of thought and sensation. Nor can the moral dualisms of geography be relied on to create social types, for the Northern trust bosses are morally equated with erstwhile Southern slave-owners. Nor can race be relied on. Like Engels, Adams can accuse the English of having 'untidy minds', but he insists that the absence of that unity which constitutes type might itself be a virtue: 'it was scrappy, and everyone knew it, but perhaps thought itself, history and nature, were scrappy, and ought to be studied so' (p. 221).

But it is of course the 'American' type in which Adams is most interested. Here the portrait of his geologist friend Clarence King is important. For Adams he is a kind of Steerforth to his own David Copperfield: the Byronic hero caught out of his time. He is doomed in events and disappears in a satiric violence which invites all the pathos of the mode, and yet: 'King loved paradox; he started them like rabbits, and cared for them no longer, when caught or lost; but they delighted Adams, for they helped, among other things, to persuade him that history was more amusing than science' (p. 313). It is when paradoxes are started 'like rabbits' that the possibility of knowledge fleetingly reveals itself; caught (static) or lost (dead) they are no longer of interest.

Of the new American type Adams doubts even the truth of a paradox set in motion:

> That the American, by temperament, worked to excess, was true, work and whiskey were his stimulants; work was a form of vice; but he never cared much for money or power after he earned them.... At Washington one met mostly such true Americans, but if one wanted to know them better, one went to study them in Europe. Bored, patient, helpless; pathetically dependent on his wife and daughters; indulgent to excess; mostly a modest, decent, excellent, valuable citizen; the American was to be met at every railway station in Europe, carefully explaining to every listener that the happiest day of his life would be the day he should land on the pier at New York.
>
> (*Education*, p. 297)

Installed in the pure process of capital the actual sensuous world is relegated to second place. Emasculated before the world of women and art (in the terms of Adams's satire), the American can only repeat that transition (Europe to America) as a myth of existential impotence. Real history and time are lost as the new American becomes a victim of habit without aim, work without ends, and power without goal.

Then there is the question of time. In classic nineteenth-century fashion Adams addresses the problem from a triple perspective. The retrospective gaze over his own life, divided in three, is made into an analogy for three modes of society. The eighteenth-century, the period of Adams's 'childhood' represents the lost world of Revolutionary America; the second, his early adulthood, registers the shocks to the liberal consensus in society and science; the third is his own movement towards old age and a period of 'anarchy' in both economics and science. Having, Comte-like, distinguished his three periods of time, Adams also casts about for ways in which to characterize process within time. It is again possible to distinguish at least three, and they relate to each other. The first engages the problem of sequentiality, the second the notion of acceleration and stasis, and the third is a search for a mode of description which will present multiple times simultaneously.

First then the problem of sequence. In the following definition of 'society' in America Adams both emphasizes and subverts the idea of 'historical' sequence:

> Society in America was always trying, almost as blindly as an earthworm, to realize and understand itself; to catch up with its own head, and to twist about in search of its tail. Society offered the profile of a long, straggling caravan, stretching loosely towards the prairies, its few score of leaders far in advance and its millions of immigrants, negroes, and Indians far in the rear, somewhere in archaic time.
>
> (*Education*, p. 237)

That 'straggling caravan' with its twin connotation of merchant and pilgrim, practicality and piety, shifting towards the desert of the future symbolizes horizontally the actual moment of the great period of immigration. All the sequences are present. Lineality presented spatially engages a paradox of immobility. Second, the image of the earthworm struggling to catch its tail offers a further simultaneity of a not quite perfect interaction between beginning and end. The 'immigrant', the 'negro' and the 'Indian' – all three inaccurate and degrading definitions of types – are part of the same body, offering the contradiction of a blind social unconscious out of key with the mental reason of the advance guard of society. It is the tail against the head in Adams's image, and the head against the tail. The image cuts across the confidence of Americans that theirs is lineally progressive society. The psychological presence of the rejected cuts across the time-bound pattern of social evolution.

Then there is the ubiquitous characterization of time as acceleration. That ever-flowing stream of Newton, to use Adams's favourite image of water, is seen to be subject to reversals of direction and stoppages, not to mention headlong accelerations. The notion of acceleration leads Adams to computations of breakdown in analogies of entropic stasis in works like *The Degradation of the Democratic Dogma* (1919). In the *Education*, too, Adams can, not without justice, state: 'the American boy of 1854 stood nearer the year 1 than to the year 1900' (p. 53). Everyone since Adams's time has experienced the constant acceleration of change, political, economic, technological and social, which gives, in Melville's words, not so much a sensation of progress towards some defined aim as that of 'rushing from all havens astern'.[4]

In the deep contrary motion of Adams's thinking, there is, however, an opposing image. It is in fact the image of the Eternal City, of Rome itself. It is the city which inspired Fustel de Coulanges's examination of public and private life, and for Adams contained within itself the contrary motion of the 'failure' of 'two great experiments of Western Civilization: Christianity and Roman Law'. And in a truly Hegelian moment Adams suggests, 'nothing proved that the city might not still survive to express the failure of a third'. Adams drives home his point: 'Rome could not be fitted into an orderly, middle-class, Bostonian system of evolution. No law of progress applied to it. Not even time sequences'. (*Education*, p. 91) Through Adams's ironic exaggerations the 'city on a hill' of American Puritan optimism turns into a 'Catholic' psychological symbol of the survival of the past within the present as a simultaneous presence of splendid failures.

It might be pertinent here to recall Freud's great analogy of Rome in *Civilization and its Discontents* (1930):

> ...suppose that Rome is not a human habitation but a psychical entity with a similarly long and copious past – an entity, that is to say, in which nothing that has once come into existence will have passed away and all the earlier phases of development continue to exist alongside the latest one... indeed the same piece of ground would be supporting the church of Santa Maria sopra Minerva and the ancient temple over which it was built. And the observer would perhaps only have to change the direction of his glance or his position in order to call up the one view or the other.

Freud goes on to comment that to represent historical sequence in spatial terms can only be done by juxtapositon. The same space cannot have two different contents. It shows us how 'far we are from mastering characteristics of mental life by representing them in pictorial terms'.[5] But for the poet, however, the terms of analogy can create multiple times (multiple historical contents) within the same space. Perhaps, too, Freud's disclaimed analogy is more plausible than the logic of his overly mechanical – indeed Euclidean – view of 'points' and 'space'.

After the great historical crisis of public events in the book – the Civil War – Adams turns, in a justly celebrated passage, from the violence of irreversible historical time to the 'moral geography' of the lovely Welsh border country of Wenlock Edge. It is one of the greatest prose descriptions of landscape in Amercian literature. Here, as in Freud's image of Rome, multiple layers of time are present in the same space. To keep the nineteenth-century terms, 'mental history' is revealed in a Gibbonian moment of the contemplation of the landscape; not as American 'potential' but as the 'relics' of time itself. Historical memory is 'given' in the Buddhist sense. Time sequences shift from a hierarchy of becoming towards a spatial simultaneity of being. Adams experiences, in meditating on the relics of the medieval past, the times of Roman history and the Dark Ages: 'the shepherds of Caractacus or Offa... would have taken him only for another and tamer variety of Welsh thief' (*Education*, p. 22). Again the effect is neither historical nor scientific. In a poetic violation of logic, history accuses Adams of being a thief of time. The ghosts of the past, like the shades Odysseus summoned from Hell, appear to tell Adams that he has left the work of time and story undone. Visually all times are present: the moment of the summer afternoon, Roman, medieval, Renaissance time, the nineteenth-century – Thoreau-like, in the 'steam of a distant railway'[6] – and the still-slower moving time of evolution itself. Again progression is subverted. The quotation at the head of this chaper, which juxtaposes the fossil of the Pteraspis at Ludlow[7] with the acting of Milton's *Masque of Comus* at Ludlow Castle, challenges the sheer confidence of the Scientific Revolution in its 'youth' ('how charming is divine philosophy') with the ambiguous certainties of Adams's own youth and the Darwinian revolution. 'Sported' in the quotation is an echo of Wordsworth's 'Immortality' Ode.[8]

The final time is personal. There is a great emptiness in the *Education*. For against all the metaphysics, the scientific characterization and the differing modes of time, the sense of the individual life and its infinitesimally brief time is reaffirmed with tragic intensity. The death of Adams's sister confronts one with the absurdity of death and a Conradian, almost existential, view of the 'horror, the horror'. Yet this too seems a mask for that great temporal lacuna in the book, the twenty years of marriage and his wife's death. This is the presence which paradoxically begins the taking up of 'absence' after that 'gap' in the 'record' with the phrase 'Once more!' It parallels the 'once again' of 'Tintern Abbey', that other contemplation of Welsh border landscape where space in a great romantic gesture also becomes time, and in which an almost erotic contemplation of the 'sister' affirms that only in art can time itself be held at the edge of the stream:

> If I should be where I no more can hear
> Thy voice, nor catch from thy wild eyes these gleams
> Of past existence, wilt thou then forget
> That on the banks of this delightful stream
> We stood together.[9]

Tougher-minded than Wordsworth, and less inclined to stoic contemplation, Adams's 'once more' becomes a kind of courage to take up the threads of time again in the absence of love, a task made easier by the discovery that time itself is neither logical nor sequential nor causal. It is to be found neither in the Newtonian stream, nor in the Rankean sequence, nor in Bergsonian psychology (no psychologizing of temporal feeling can obliterate the fact of death, or betrayal in love), nor in the Darwinian statistical and evolutionary model. In an answer that was certain to be irrelevant to physicist, historian, psychologist, and biologist alike, Adams gathered their insights into a multi-layered image of space – time: a truly poetic synthesis, which used the recognition of tragic irreversibility to find the courage to say 'once more'.

For Adams, looking back on his own lifetime, the first casualty of multiple time was liberalism. Here he portrays it at the moment of its 'classical synthesis':

> The Paris of Louis Philippe, Guizot, and de Tocqueville, as well as the London of Robert Peel, Macaulay, and John Stuart Mill, were but varieties of the same upper-class bourgeoisie that felt instinctive cousinship with the Boston of Ticknor, Prescott, and Motley. Even the typical grumbler Carlyle, who cast doubts on the real capacity of the middle class, and who at times thought himself eccentric, found friendship and alliances in Boston – still more in Concord. The system has proved so successful that even Germany wanted to try it, and Italy yearned for it. England's middle-class government was the ideal of human progress.
>
> (*Education*, p. 33)

One must give Adams credit for perceiving that this ideal was creaking in every joint. As a conservative member of the ruling class he knew as well as the socialist that what was undermining liberal values was the effects of 'acceleration': 'the world was producing sixty or seventy million tons of coal, and might be using nearly a million steam horse-power, just beginning to make itself felt' (p. 33).

He further adds: '...he had no idea that Karl Marx was standing there waiting for him, and that sooner or later the process of education would have to deal with Karl Marx much more than with Professor Bowen of Harvard College, or his Satanic free-trade majesty, John Stuart Mill' (p. 72). The conservative Adams was radical in this sense, that he insisted society had better think fearlessly and openly about its options.

Adams's view of process is unsatisfactory in that it attempts to combine Comte's historicizing metaphysics with the vitalism of pseudo-Marxian 'productive forces', as 'base'. He lacks Marx's best insight; the hope of intelligibility opening up a new vision of human society if all the relations of freedom and necessity are examined together from the point of view of *collective* need. Nonetheless Adams has two further interesting points to make. The first is that it is the writers who stand at the points of transition between cultural orders, and can give us a sense of what it feels like at that historical point with the aim of at least alerting their readers to what is actually happening:

> Thackeray and Dickens followed Balzac in scratching and biting the unfortunate middle class with savage ill-temper, much as the middle class had scratched and bitten the Church and Court for a hundred years before. The literary world had revolted against the yoke of coming capitalism – its money lenders, its bank directors, and its railway magnates.
>
> (*Education*, p. 61)

And Adams further reminds us that just registering the 'unhappy consciousness' is not enough: 'The process that Matthew Arnold described as wandering between two worlds, one dead, the other powerless to be born, helps nothing' (p. 108).[10]

In the margin of his own copy of *Culture and Anarchy* Adams wrote, against Arnold's comment that 'without order there can be no society': 'surely a dangerous concession for him to make: Order is neither Hellenism nor Hebraism, but pure Philistinism, as he has painted it.'[11] Conservative as he was, Adams feared the effects of the frightened bourgeoisie calling indiscriminately for more 'order'. And with equal truth he could see that 'in the social disequilibrium between capital and labour, the logical outcome was not collectivism but anarchism' (*Education*, p. 339). Adams's satire reveals and faces contradiction. He would always admit that 'the Army and the Navy have saved me and mine so many times that I'm not going back on it, whatever it does.'[12] Such accurate admissions are not common within liberalism. Just as Adams saw new kinds of power subverting a once-revolutionary liberal ideal, so his commentary at least makes an implicit plea for a new thinking to challenge the excesses of new forms of power. Hence the importance of his reflections on science, and indeed upon the notion of consciousness itself.

Since Descartes's time 'consciousness' has become a much battered concept. The notion of reflection as such has suffered from multiple intellectual fatalisms. Social Darwinism, mechanistic psychology, Freudian psychoanalysis, linguistics, semiology, structuralist anthropology have one thing at least in common: the notion that purposeful consciousness plays little part in human behaviour. In the next section there will be a closer look at how a late nineteenth-century American philosopher, William James, approached the problem, and in the subsequent discussion of Gertrude Stein's work the problem of consciousness will be taken up again in relation to early twentieth-century linguistics. To admit that it is possible to be aware of being aware seemed to Adams, as to so many others brought up within the tradition of British empiricism, to invite an immediate descent into solipsism. Adams could attack Descartes's confidence in reflection by implicitly challenging the notion of a God who safely held the key to the world of that 'other' posited by the Cartesian *cogito*. In his own copy of Descartes's works Adams wrote, therefore, against Jules Simon's introduction 'is not self-consciousness a defect, since it implies a non-ego'?[13]

Conversely, within an idealistic approach to the problem Adams was paradoxically attracted to Hegel.[14] In Albert Schwegler's *Handbook of the History of Philosophy*, in the section on Hegel, Adams underlined: 'Self-consciousness then, as universal self-consciousness or reason, describes another series of successive stages, until it appears as spirit, reason that, filled and identified with the rationality of existence and the outer world, dominates the natural and spiritual universe as its kingdom. in which it knows itself at home.'[15] Hegel's metaphysics of processs, with its quasi-vitalistic parallelism of mind and history, undoubtedly appealed to the late Adams for all the reasons Marx rejected it as a theory of history.

Again, against Descartes's 'Second Meditation' he wrote, 'What is a "thing"? Logically one infers "I am a thought in action". The thought alone is assumed in cogito', and a little later he adds, 'penser then is sentire or consciousness, not reason'.[16] Adams would have agreed with contemporary Marxist existentialists that consciousness is not the originating source of the act, and with the nineteenth-century psychologist that consciousness lies in the domain of sensation not reason.

Two points must be made. The first is that Adams was again happy to make his opposites fight and to explore the paradox of nature-as-mind facing mind-as-nature. Second, Adams was not interested in philosophy as such. He preferred to subvert its oppositions by shifting the level at which the subject was discussed. Adams can achieve a kind of shot-gun marriage of Descartes and Hegel by saying in effect, I accept Cartesian reason because Hegel makes reason unite the spiritual and natural worlds, and I can accept Hegel because that reason is in fact feeling or sensation according to British philosophers! Behind these annotations, Aquinas and Spinoza can again be sensed: Aquinas for that 'thought in action' and Spinoza for the pantheistic universality of reason.

Adams treats the philosophers much as he treated the theologians in the *Chartres*. He changes their logical connections into analogical ones. The important point here is that this is also precisely how he treats scientists. No less than with the theologians, Adams is searching in their work for analogies of process with which to write a prolegomena to a reason of history. This can readily be demonstrated by reference to a few of the annotations in books in his library on scientific subjects. Thus he notes in Lucien Poincaré that while mechanistic models are reversible, in physics *'la reversibilité n'existe pas'*. Adams remembers his grandfather again when Poincaré asserts in his discussion of *'la valeur d'un arc méridien'*, that natural unity no longer exists and that its authority rests on consent not truth.[17]

In fact, Adams scores more than one palpable hit against the scientists' own wild analogies, particularly when he moves out of the strictly scientific world. As Jordy suggests, the aggressive annotations in Pearson's *Grammar of Science* display Adams's acute perception of Pearson's scientific arrogance.[18] When Pearson states that more will be achieved by pure science than technology, for example, Adams writes ironically, 'More what? money? virtue? science? method? what is it we want?' Even with his 'amateur philosophizing' Adams is able to ask pertinent questions about Pearson's naïve evolutionism and progressivism. When Pearson claims that 'the scientist postulates nothing of the world beyond sense', Adams writes, exposing the secret idealism of such a statement: 'He projects the mind into it and defines it as modes.'[19]

Adams is no fool. He is genuinely open to learn from science. For example, with commentators of his time rushing about with the notion that 'relativity' is some kind of metaphysical truth, Adams can write against Stallo's discussion of the problem, 'The relations are real but relativity is not.' And in a brilliant note against another discussion he writes, 'The object of a concept is already a synthesis of objective and subjective elements when the intellect takes cognizance of it.'[20] At this moment he readmits consciousness and, more important, the idea of the object as a phenomenon in Merleau-

Ponty's sense. In this way Stallo's comments are readopted. Adams, not unlike Pound and the Imagist poets, was to look for a way in which to use images as a means of defining sets of relations while retaining a sense of concreteness. He also shared those poets' fundamental sense of the creativity of metaphoric thought.[21]

As for analogies of process, Adams can take multiplicity from Henri Poincaré's *La Science et l'hypothèse* (1903), or an image of transformatory vitalism from Oliver Wendell Holmes's account of the blood and nutrition. Adams revives the ancient controversies of religion, philosophy and science as a heuristic strategy to plead for multiplicity, to question goals and values and to advocate a dialogue between disciplines. Among his achievements is a sophisticated approach to the philosophy of sensation. He also advocated the notion of the phenomenon in pleading for creativity in the way any world is experienced, and he made a place for the multiplicity of art in an age of specialized discourses. He abandoned the notion of unitary truth as a quest for knowledge on an analogy with the multiplicity of contemporary science, and then turned that notion against the claim of science itself to be the sole truth of human experience. Multiplicity also entered the historical domain, as a concept disturbing all those neat triadic nineteenth-century pseudo-histories. Before leaving Adams one of his last attempts to describe process will be examined. It contains all his strengths and weaknesses: it is the chapter on 'The Virgin and the Dynamo', towards the end of the *Education*.

In the Beaux-Arts setting of the Chicago Exposition (1900), Adams questioned his scientist friend Langley and discovered that he 'said nothing new, and taught nothing that one might not have learned from Lord Bacon, three hundred years before' (*Education*, p. 379). Commentators do not seem to have remembered what Collingwood once called 'Bacon's celebrated gibe that teleology, like a virgin consecrated to God, produces no offspring',[22] which is clearly a key to the passage. Bacon was meditating on Aristotle's four-part division of causes and was advocating that the notions of form and final cause should be distinguished. In modern terms Adams was asking whether his 'phenomena' of the Virgin and the Dynamo were hypotheses or truths. It is a by now familiar tactic. His solution will lie outside the terms of the initial question. Nonetheless teleology will be ironically abandoned, for Adams has made it plain that he 'inherited dogma and a priori thought from the beginning of time' (*Education*, p. 26).

The key question is: How innocent is design? Is it an innocent idealism constantly subverted in practice? That is, is it inherently sterile? What is the relation between it and its consequence? To keep the terms of Adams's analogy, what 'child' does this holy mother produce – are the causes natural? What is the relation between cause and effect: between the dirty coal-house which feeds the dynamo and is so reminiscent of 'carboniferous capitalism', and the great, silent electricity-producing dynamo? In every punning sense of the phrase there are 'arguments from design'. Do the Virgin and the Dynamo have designs on us or for us? What does design include and what does it leave out? Surely again Adams must have remembered Carlyle: 'it is false altogether what the last sceptical century taught us, that this world is a steam engine. There is a God in this world.'[23] At one level Adams is telling us of the discontinuity between technological phases. At another level he is insisting that the products of thought return as strange and alienating to human beings via the productive process. The entire human environment is changed with a new invention and relearning even the most simple responses becomes urgent.

The dirty coal-house also seems to indicate that the source of energy is in nature, and an old source of power in a new guise. The very products of time (coal) transformed to a new energy seem to become 'a symbol of infinity'. But is the transformation to be seen as sacred by men hallucinating in front of their own technological brilliance? Adams's irony suggests that old problems exist with the compulsions of the new. Much like McLuhan, Adams celebrates the entirely new world of electricity: particularly the fact that electricity upsets sequence in its concept of instantaneous feedback and field application. It makes 'the Rhine more modern than the Hudson' (*Education*, p. 415). There was no point in going like Carlyle's Teufelsdrockh to seek the infinite power of the primitive in Northern Norway when electric lights blazed at Hammerfest (p. 413). What was this new power?

Adams's annotations to works on electricity show him searching for clues. A letter of the great English physicist Clerk Maxwell to R.B. Litchfield, cited in Campbell and Garnett's *Life of James Clerk Maxwell* (1882), caught Adams's eye. He underlined a passage which asserted that the great scientists of electricity had one thing in common, 'a freedom from the tyranny of words in dealing with questions of order, law, etc., which pure literary men never attain'. Adams was stung enough to write in the margin, 'within ten years (1906) all the scientists were asserting the contrary about science'.[24] That is, he is saying, there is no central privileged discourse in spite of the dazzling discoveries associated with electricity.

Like Hegel, Adams believed the human world could not be described solely in the language of mathematics. He wanted to save words, indeed language itself, as a great measure, perhaps the most important measure of human life. He knew that there was a great tyranny in silence – the chief distinguishing characteristic of the dynamo's 'aura':

> As he grew accustomed to the great gallery of machines, he began to feel the forty foot dynamo as a moral force, much as the early Christians felt the cross. The planet itself seemed less impressive in its old-fashioned, deliberate, annual or daily revolution, than this huge wheel, revolving within an arm's length at some vertiginous speed, and barely murmuring – scarcely humming an audible warning to stand a hair's breadth further for respect of power – while it would not wake the baby lying close to its frame. Before the end, one began to pray to it. . . .
>
> (*Education*, p. 380)

This passage might be compared with one by John Borwick, the chief technical adviser to *The Gramophone* on a recent visit to Japan:

> Computer-assisted design and the assembly of complex integrated circuits involved perhaps the highest technology we saw anywhere, in clean-air working areas. I was amused to find that entering these areas obliged us to remove our shoes and don special slippers – just as we did on entering various shrines. . . .[25]

Adams had Melville's great insight that to link the domain of power with that of the *sacred* ('the transposition of a social reaction on to the relationship of the lifeless or of nature to man')[26] was a hazardous business, and that the writer's reinvention of language was a powerful countervailing force. If society no longer needed language then Adams could see nothing but the order of despotism. What education, he asks, will give the sleeping child a consciousness of the power within which it was born? When he quotes Hamlet's 'The rest is silence' at the end of this chapter of the *Education*, it concludes his attempt at measure. He knows that the absolute discontinuity between himself and the child is in fact the hope of the future. Adams's act of writing – imaged as St. Thomas's analogy of being as act – places story against the synchrony of nature. Without the paradox of discontinuity and measure which great art itself practised there was little hope for a future. Conversely, without the lessons of the past in story the child would be doomed to the fatalism of repetition.

Once again Adams insists that the defeated world of art is also the defeated world of the erotic in his own society. Only Whitman, says Adams, had insisted on the power of sex. Within Adams's notion of the erotic lay the 'empathy' of women,[27] the diversity of the emotional and hence the illogical, an alternative 'reason' as unconscious life, and a power which could be evil as well as good. Ignoring it, Adams suggests, deprives art of its true power as well as diverting society's energy into blindly regressive paths. Americans lack, he said, a sense of tragedy or a sense of evil: 'in Amercia neither Venus nor the Virgin ever had value as force – at most as sentiment. No American had ever been truly afraid of either' (*Education*, p. 383). Although he could only use the powerful terms of analogy, Adams was surely correct in his instinct about the relations between sexual psychology and power. He knew that the displacement of the erotic, however dimly understood, was in some ways connected with the behaviour of a society rushing full speed ahead, blinded by the gods of technology and science. To pay for Saint-Gaudens's magnificent statue for his wife's grave Adams sold two-thirds of his stocks in American railroads.[28] Adams's image of a man in an accelerating car with his hand on the gear lever, dragging his neglected wife into the same neurosis of anxious speeding directionlessness, was in some way related to what he rather clumsily called 'the amount of force controlled by society' (*Education*, pp. 445, 389). He was writing before the discoveries of Freud related compulsion to repression, before Reich investigated the mass psychology of fascism, or Riesman informed us of the lonely crowd, before Weber had investigated the Protestant ethic and McLuhan had spoken of the fundamental reorganization of the mental field by a new technological invention.[29]

A last point must be that in an indifferent world Adams defended the special knowledge and pleasure that literature gave. Henry James, Adams said, 'had not yet taught the world to read a volume for the pleasure of seeing his burning glass turned on alternate sides of the same figure' (*Education*, p. 163). Nor had it learned that art itself might give, in a lonely and impossibly multiple world, a sustaining comfort: the 'only sensation of home' (p. 258). That statement must be taken seriously and literally set against American psychologizing critics. It is a plea for the deep peace of the active life of the mind. In the great image of the pen working for itself within a process, un-unified but 'never arbitrary', truth may yet be recognized as sequence; that is a story which includes time and tragedy. The 'pen becomes a sort of blind man's dog to prevent him falling into gutters' (p. 389). It is the oldest image of the artist; the blind poet seeking a reintegration with the world out of manifest impotence, and transforming it in the process.

Part Two
A Metaphysic in Reserve: William James and Some Dilemmas of the Liberal Centre

Chapter 5
Adams and James

In 1917, in one of his last letters to his close friend Elizabeth Cameron, Adams referred to 'our beloved William James'.[1] It was the last moment of a friendship in a life of letters characterized by that 'no holds barred' witty seriousness which often marks exchange between committed intellectual peers. In busy lives apart, the paths of William (and Henry) James and Adams only occasionally intersected, but always with something struck out of the crossing. They had their class and cosmopolitanism in common. Henry James wrote in 1879 of sitting up with the Adamses in London, 'till one o'clock this morning abusing the Britons. The dear Britons are invaluable for that.'[2] Adams wrote of Henry that on principle he did not read his friends' books. However, he thought *Daisy Miller* 'really clever', though he 'broke down' over *The Portrait of a Lady*.[3] Socially Adams seems closer to Henry, and intellectually closer to William. Artistically and generically, his work situates itself somewhere in between.

With William James, Adams crossed intellectual swords from the early 1870s until the end of his life. Beneath their mock-fierce exchanges, however, neither would budge on their respective positions. They recognized each other's seriousness though comedy often characterized the tone of their exchanges. When James asked for a copy of the *Education* in 1907, he said he did so because he 'found himself accused (along with others) of having made of Cambridge a conversational desert... properly only blood could wipe out such an insult...'. To which Adams replied that he had thought himself safe, 'unless indeed, you got hold of them!' – in that case, he added with all the theatricality of feigned surrender, 'I was rather inclined to weep and wail in advance, for I knew your views better than my own.' In 1909, Adams wrote to Margaret Chanler, advising her to 'borrow William James's copy [of the *Education*], in hopes that he may have marginally noted his contempt for me'.[4]

Emerging briefly from that darkness which characterized his last years, Adams gives a glimpse of his pride in the Jameses: 'You, at least, and your brother Harry, have been our credit and pride. We can rest in that.'[5]

In a sense both Henrys had an advantage over the philosopher. They were artists. So, as noted by Matthiessen, Henry James could remind Adams that they both – in words recalling Melville's exchange with Hawthorne two generations earlier – could face that 'unmitigated blackness', because they had the advantage of that 'queer monster, the artist'. Henry James confessed he still found 'my consciousness interesting – under cultivation of the interest'. Creativity was that 'act of life', and the artist 'an obstinate finality, an inexhaustible sensibility'.[6]

It is clear – even without adapting the excessively psychologizing theses of some commentators – that William James was frustrated in his early attempts to become a painter. In a sense it undoubtedly made more difficult his task of finding a form in which to attempt a multiple response to the world. Both Adams and James were intensely sceptical of academic formulas and suspicious of the movement, beginning in their own times, towards that state or corporate institution which universities have increasingly become. Both reacted against institutional inertia – though in somewhat patrician tones. Complaining of lack of time to write, Adams declared: 'Here I sit, at the regular meeting of the College Faculty, while some thirty twaddlers are discussing questions of discipline around me.'[8] James himself was deeply aware of and suffered from that professionalization of the universities (particularly in his own field) throughout the late nineteenth century. He wrote of the 'Ph.D. octopus' while near-contemporaries mechanized their numerous graduate offspring as much as their subjects, and he uncompromisingly declared: 'But the institutionalizing on a large scale of any natural combination of need and motive always tends to run to technicality and to develop a tyrannical Machine with unforeseen powers of exclusion and corruption.'[9] Official academic psychology responded by ignoring him.

James stayed within the academy but in spirit he moved out of it towards a larger public: one craving reassurance in an America and England doubting their ideologies and goals. James was world-famous from the turn of the century onwards, and to more than psychologists. As one commentator put it: James's books 'are selling by the thousands, . . . businessmen are caught disputing over their lunches', while 'matrons and maids display equal eagerness.'[10] He became a pundit to the nation, supplying an Emersonian 'uplift' tonic to individuals caught in the toils of fading mid-nineteenth-century liberal values. There was also a bravery in the man which, while it did not always make for clarity, compels admiration. From his recovery from his psychological crisis of the 1870s to his fearlessness (as Freud noted) in facing his own death, he had the virtues also of the Puritan inheritance.[11]

Royce noted the influence of Carlyle. The 'everlasting yea' was undoubtedly one source of *The Will to Believe*.[12] While Adams retreated inwards, doubting the entire ideology and psychology of Carlyle, Mill and Arnold, James strenuously, even stridently, reaffirmed the tone if not the detail of that vision of confident individualism. Paradoxically Adams's inward vision gave him a perspective on public change which was sharper than James's. James, by contrast, in affirming confident individualism struck a more sympathetic note in the public response while blurring key issues of public power.

These public and private perspectives lock into a kind of stasis when the two men are looked at together. Adams, always speculative and with a tendency to abstraction, loved the movement of travel and society. James, in theory more practically oriented, hated his year of field-work with Agassiz in South America. James argued himself into a belief in the future, Adams shrugged his shoulders over it with a historian's scepticism. Both 'Victorian' men were typically reticent about their personal lives. Henry James spoke of Adams's 'austere seraglio',[13] though Adams was certainly more worldly than William James. Adams complained of a whole range of American attitudes to issues of sex, and he had more flexible genres with which to take them on. James was partially caught by the terms of academic discourse, though there are more than enough hints of a sensibility more 'puritanical' than Adams's – even if the argument is not taken as far as by one commentator who declared (without irony) that James was 'insensible to the carryings-on of the id in human nature'.[14]

In Adams's work there is always a sense of the public, and indeed of time – however metaphysically characterized. By contrast, in James the psychological sense of self is depicted classically, for an American, in spatially posited terms. James posed a synchronically 'innocent' space within which the psyche was structured. This can be given a more precise cultural and historical meaning by citing Hoffman's description of an American valuation of self as 'dependent upon a visual recognition of space available infinitely'. Hoffman goes on, however, to characterize this space as an abstraction which Americans suspect and to which the 'Jamesian' solution of intuition

and voluntarism acts as a half-truth at best.[15] James's synchrony of
the self was an important theoretical part of his future-oriented
vision. The past as such had to be negated – in true American style.
James's *Principles of Psychology* had as its longest chapter 'The Perception of Space', and the publication of the work itself coincided
with the closing of the frontier. The psychologist had a number of
things in common with Turner's romantic frontiersman, replete
with 'American' values. Neither would have welcomed Hegel's
observation that America would only begin to define itself and be
comparable with other countries when 'that immeasurable space
which that country presents to its inhabitants shall have been occupied, and the members of the political body shall have begun to
be pressed back on each other'.[16] Even that most transcendental
of philosophers, however, could not have foreseen how the marketing of visions of endless space could render Americans distinct from
the inhabitants of other countries long after the 'spirit' had lost its
'geographical basis'.

In psychological terms the shadow of the free individual in free space
haunts James's theory of self, and dogs his more moralistic moments. He tried, as one commentator puts it, 'vigorously to save the
individual-moralistic perspective within the confines of scientific
psychology'.[17] From the perspective of scientific psychology, religion was simply 'not science', and by that gesture science itself
gripped the obliterated individual as much as ever religion had with
its vision of always-to-be-realized revelation. Brave recent attempts
to rescue James's theory of self within existentialist and phenomenologist definitions encounter many problems also. Sartre's claim
that existence precedes essence cannot be matched exactly with
James's notion of 'human action' preceding psychological axioms.
For Sartre ontology, under Heidegger's directive, was a means of
setting the world at a distance while simultaneously allowing the
new to enter the Open. Sartre's metaphysic is engaged, James's
held in reserve. Sartre's ontological, Marxist and psychoanalytic
premisses would have been anathema to James. Moreover Sartre,
both as a dramatist and an existentialist and Marxist philosopher,
had a notion of the public and private self as much more interactive.
One cannot imagine James theorizing the group, any more than
Sartre falling into the trap of individual-and-society obscurantisms.[18]

   James and Adams also differed on their attitude to the will. James
was always suspicious of the unconscious, which he tended to
characterize as 'spiritual' and removed from the real world, thus
preserving faith in the radical incompleteness of human knowledge.

Adams by contrast was disposed to accept a more human sense of the mystery of creativity. As John Diggins has shrewdly argued, 'Unlike James's "belief", Adams's notion of "faith" could not be produced by the experience of the will alone since it is faith that makes the activity of will possible.'[19]

Both Adams and James were 'tough-minded' in their refusal to ignore intellectual arguments for the death of God. As with his Virgin, the humanized face of God ministering to the needs of personal defeat, Adams was interested in the religious icon as the measure of political power. As such it was central. For James religion was both marginalized and central. It represented at once a fringe – a way for James to acknowledge a repressed side of himself, and to encounter the 'people' in their 'folkiness' – and the continuing presence of a way of thought no longer intellectually valid. The undoubted positiveness of James's courage in insisting on the widespread presence in society of a set of religious phenomena must be measured against the terms he imposed on that insistence. One senses that Adams trusted his feelings more than did James, but though more drawn to actual religions, he never fully surrendered himself to Buddhism.[20] James had, to follow an argument of Maritain, little sense of that *actus secundus* as a 'super-abundance of existence'.[21] Perhaps Adams was simply more attracted to the Buddhist's and Catholic's sense of the givenness of the world, James to the Puritan seizure of the world as practical action. The danger of the one is pure metaphysics and the danger of the other is 'rightness'.

In their attitudes to science, James and Adams again offer a significant contrast. First, Adams was more concerned with the physical sciences, though he was a life time admirer of Agassiz and did acquaint himself with 'such leading British exponents of physiology and psychology as Maudsley and Bain'.[22] James was temperamentally unsuited to experimentation, although his founding of the first American psychological laboratory and his engagement of Hugo Münsterberg to manage it is well known. James's reputation as a scientific psychologist was highest at the very moment he began to pull away from scientific psychology.[23] Yet the impact on him of biological science, specifically the work of Darwin, was lasting, though it was directed more towards a revision of philosophy than towards a revision of science. Adams always mistrusted Darwin. Adams and James both doubted the claim of science to be the model of all human thought and the sole instrument of human progress. Neither man would have shared John Dewey's quasi-imperialist belief (for all its practicalism) in the general truthfulness as such of the scientific project, that 'practical faith at work engaged in subjugating the foreign territory of ignorance and falsehood step by step'.[24]

In terms of pure philosophy – or as pure as it ever gets with these decidedly impure philosophers – the contrasts become even more urgent. Levenson, perhaps straining a little to find a philosophical point of comparison between them (equating Adams's search for historical reason with James's solution to the problem of the will), has to admit the differences between them are much more interesting: 'For Adams the solution to the ultimate problem lay in the assertion of mind, while for James it lay in the assertion of will.'[25] Adams was not, however, as pure a Cartesian as a number of commentators have claimed,[26] nor as uninterested in will as his often Hobbesian perspectives on the nature of power suggest. As a self-confessed admirer of Locke, James was bound to engage those obliquely Cartesian moments within Locke himself. Locke disputed thinking as a guarantee of essence ('' 'tis doubted whether I thought all last night, or no') but not as one of the operations of the soul.[27] James objected to the static quality of Locke's associationism, not his epistemology. Yet it was James's anti-Cartesianism that led him, along with so many others in the Anglo-American tradition suspicious of epistemology and dialectics, into a fundamental difficulty about the location of the subject. James, as one commentator suggests, viewed as his 'major problem, . . . having to account for the relationship between the world of objects and the world of consciousness without recourse to positing a dualism of subject and mind'.[28]

James's declarations about the nature of 'consciousness' are many and confusing. At the opening of The Principles of Psychology, mechanism rules. Writing to Bergson, however, James heaps on to the psychological function of attention most of the traditional aspects of idealistic consciousness. While bravely maintaining that it 'is neither the duplicate nor the instrument of conscious life [sic]', attention is the part which 'inserts itself in events – something like the prow in which the ship is narrowed to cleave the ocean'.[29] The passive verbs typically posit the presence of the masked subject.

James's 'temperamental distrust of the dialectics and inner inconsistencies of things'[30] is well known – and comes out most clearly in his Kierkegaardian response to Hegel:

But the real offers us these terms in the shape of mutually exclusive alternatives of which only one can be true at once, so that we must choose, and in choosing number one possibility. The wrench is absolute – 'Either–or!' Just as when I bet a hundred dollars on an event, there comes a moment when I am a hundred dollars richer or poorer.[31]

Here is James, like the Puritan or Marxist, insisting on the absoluteness of evil and contradiction. Yet at what level must this contradiction be taken? At the micro-level James is surely right. No less than Marx on Hegel, James is reminding us that there is a 'real world out there'. At the macro-level, however, the 'bet' is a great deal more complicated, linked to exchange of money, the ideology and anthropology of gambling, that relation between winner and loser (indeed the dependency of the one on the other) and so on. This is not so much philosophy as a contradiction within liberalism itself: that the truthful admission of reality at a personal level will not necessarily work for society as a whole.

Sartre's critique of Kierkegaard is relevant here. Like Kierkegaard, James 'asserts unrelentingly the irreducibility and the specificity of what is lived'. Unlike Kierkegaard, James could not openly assert the transcendence of the divine, as a means of handling that 'specificity' at the metaphysical level. However, the psychology of their situations is comparable. Sartre is right to see the German philosopher and the Dane as linked. So it is possible to say, with Sartre, that Hegel is right because 'the philosopher of Jena aims through his concepts at the veritable concrete; for him, mediation is always presented as an enrichment...'. At the same time Kierkegaard is right because 'grief, need, passion, the pain of men are brute realities which can neither be suppressed nor changed by knowledge'.[32]

James was hardly alone in misinterpreting Hegel as having equated consciousness with 'consciousness of consciousness', with inner life, with metaphysics, with incomprehensible jargon, with morbid introspection spiralling into solipsistic nihilism. In those years before the First World War, James's own philosophy of brute realities seemed to Europeans and Americans to clear the air, while omitting the finer realities of truth and meditation. In the popular imagination, and indeed among certain intellectuals, the American philosopher beckoned the time-stained, sometimes morbid, sometimes metaphysically obfuscated, 'continental' philosopher towards the clarity and simplicity of the American future. It is not without irony that Stuart Hughes sums up the mood:

I doubt whether ever before or since an American thinker has enjoyed such prestige on the European continent. For with the advent of James – with the publication of his *Varieties of Religious Experience* in 1902, and more particularly with the *Pragmatism* of

1907 – the intellectual horizon seemed to·clear: everything became simple, direct, unequivocal. No longer was it necessary to break one's head over Kantian metaphysics and Teutonic hair–splitting. The sage from the New World had once for all displayed how the most vexing problems of traditional philosophy were simply not worth the trouble of worrying over them.[33]

Yet there were dissenters. Adams may have read *The Principles of Psychology* when it came out, but his extraordinarily interesting marginalia are to be found in an edition of 1902.[34] This is significant, in that from the early 1900s onwards Adams was more fully immersed than he had ever been in philosophy and speculative thought, in preparation for his two late great works. His marginalia in James's *Principles of Psychology* show, as does hardly anything else in their relationship, the fundamental differences between the historian and the philosopher-psychologist. In the first 200 pages and more of the first volume Adams goes straight to the Achilles heel of James's thought. With a mischievous sense of paradox, he submits James's struggling empiricism to a set of typically idealist probings.

Adams mocks all those Jamesian evasions created by the deliberate suppression of the subject. When, in the chapter on the 'Automation Theory', James attempts to define consciousness both within a Darwinian framework and against the determinisms of post-Darwinians, by suggesting it is capable of 'loading the dice' (*Principles* [1902], I. 138–9), Adams ironically notes that *en route* James has made consciousness into a cause, an organ, a state of mind and an active agent. James's adoption of the dualism of high and low brains as poles of an essentially physiological continuity brings out the Adams who loves the scepticism of paradox: 'Is it double? in the lowest sphere and in the highest. It chooses. It is not the ego? but helps!' (I. 141). Passive and active constructions are noted by Adams in all their contradictions: 'Consciousness is distributed: it steers. . .' (I. 144). And in a Cartesian mood Adams asserts, 'Can anything be conscious except the ego?' (I. 163). A few pages later he is grumbling: 'We have not yet had a definition of consciousness. What is it?' (I. 164). Against James's declaration that 'A state of mind must be a fully conscious condition' (I. 173), Adams writes, 'Conscious of itself or what?'

When in the 'Mind Stuff' theory chapter James argues that the identity of successive ideas is to be found only in the 'cognitive or representative' (*sic*) function in dealing with the same objects, Adams raises the ghosts of Aristotle, Locke and Hegel in three questions: 'Consciousness of a real object? Consciousness of a sense impression?

Consciousness of a consciousness?' (I. 175). Just a few pages later, he quotes the 'old, old formula', *cogito ergo sum*, and adds: 'All this to return to the old dispute without answering the old question' (I. 182). When James argues, 'We must avoid substituting what we know the consciousness is, for what it is conscious of' (I. 197), Adams acidly replies, 'Thus far two hundred pages have been wholly given up to it.' James's boldly asserted correspondence theory and almost mechanistic continuities of body and mind also attract Adams's attention. When James writes: 'The dualism of Object and Subject and their pre-established harmony are what the psychologist as such must assume...' (I. 220), Adams replies: 'Stupendous assumption: Leibnitz alone ever dared assume it.'

Another set of closely linked comments centre on the famous image of the 'stream of thought' (or 'stream of consciousness', as it is more popularly known): an image which will be commented on in some detail later. Adams's expostulations at least put a question mark over what is one of the most famous passages in American literature and which still evokes reverence, as Barzun's commentary shows.[35] Barzun accepts personal 'ownership of the stream', as a priori truth. In contrast here is Adams:

Is thought a stream?
Has it a starting-point or an end?
Why not call it an ocean with streams in it?
Or the inter-reflections of mirrors?
Or a pot, boiling what falls in it?
Or a magnet with lines of force?
Or a condition, like time and space?
Does thought think, or do I think, or does the earthworm think?

This chapter answers that the thought thinks, and that the thing outside the thought has a pre-established harmony with it.

(*Principles* [1902], I. 290)

In fact Adams continuously harries James over the very issue which most commentators take as given: that is, the importance of the role of the subject. At least Adams, in common with those who have seen incipient phenomenology in James's work, admits that there are inconsistencies and contradictions.

Again and again Adams brings the historian's sense of time to the future-oriented and spatial bias of James's thought. When James in fact admits that the mind dissolves in biological ageing, Adams underlines his statement that the 'old paths fade' (I. 661), and his comment is acute, pointing to his refusal to let the past fade into

mental blankness and stoic insipidity. One may imagine personal and
professional reasons for this. Against the Wordsworthian 'fading'
Adams insists: 'Paths do not fade. They are obscured. This proves
the path-analogy error. The memory is in the sensitiveness.' (I. 661.)
Adams sought to defend historical memory against the psychologist.
The remarkable and brilliant phrase, 'the memory is in the sensitiveness', draws the definition of memory away from mechanistic
imprintings fading through time, and towards a human and creative
sense of the past. In a similar mood, against James's ultimately
Lockean analogy of facts hooking themselves together in the mind,
and fishing things up from below the surface, Adams comments,
'This is properly not memory but the reasoning faculty of creating
relations' (I. 662). For Adams memory was creative, for James it was
an adjunct of habit.

In the second volume, at the end of the chapter on 'The Perception
of Things', Adams writes that 'Surely all this chapter is as chaotic as
a dream?' (II. 133). Significantly, it is the chapter where James has
discussed various states of hallucination, which Adams brushes aside
(perhaps feeling slightly shaken in his lingering Cartesian convictions) as a 'form of disorder or chaos' (II. 137), adding, 'all we need
to know is whether they are morbid or normal.' Typically, he goes
on to doubt whether they can be characterized separately and concludes, 'Is the chaotic mind the healthy state, and is the ordered
intelligence normal?' R.D. Laing would have approved. Many of the
remaining annotations are Adams's defence of intelligible instinct
in the face of Jamesian assertions of will. Against James's famous
declaration, 'Freedom's first deed should be to affirm itself' (II. 573)
– that ethical imperative of classic liberalism – Adams writes 'Freedom seems rather to consist in keeping one's mind free to choose'
(II. 573). The gesture seems perhaps more relevant now, in the
propaganda-ridden twentieth century, than in the nineteenth century.

James's Carlylean calls to work-for-the-night-cometh Adams
meets with scepticism. As James utters his battle cry, Adams is
doubting we have adequate means of understanding the modes of
resistance. When James waxes fulsome on the hero holding 'himself
erect' in the 'game of human life' (II. 579), Adams writes, 'Twaddle!',
and against 'lords of life', writes, 'or slaves?' Adams's comments on
The Principles of Psychology range therefore from a quasi-Cartesian
critique of James's refusal to look at the question of consciousness in
any orderly way, which opens up doubts about the quality of the
psychologist's critical perception, to the ethical problem of Carlylean
will.

James, in a way, wanted to make the subjectivity of feeling
objectively natural, and Adams was certain that would rule out the

possibility of critical thought as such. These two issues (consciousness and ethics) will be raised again later. The next chapter, however, will deal directly with what most commentators ignore: James's actual stance on social and political issues.

Chapter 6
William James: The Self and Politics

A great part of the current image of William James is that of Jacques Barzun's magnanimous man. The tributes and the moments are well known and not to be doubted: the teacher rushing up undergraduate stairs to look after sick students, the staff-room eccentric, the anti-imperialist protester, the spontaneous William who embarrasses brother Henry by setting a ladder to a wall to take a peek at G. K. Chesterton, the lively boy who invents curses that people shall have lumps in their mashed potatoes, the lecturer who takes serious issues out of the university and brings them before a wider public, the serious philosopher with the engaging style, the popularizer of pragmatism; the inventor of a distinctive American philosophy, and so forth. As with all images, there is a mixture of truth and untruth in the caricature. There are, of course, as many Jameses as Lovejoy's romanticisms and pragmatisms – but the one that is beginning to emerge in our own time is perhaps best caught by Barzun. It is the James of the liberal centre: the 'magnanimous man', whose resurrection measures the values of our own culture and finds them wanting.

Here are the timeless values of tolerance, erudition, Nietzschean strength and Shavian common sense seen within the context of the 'tragedy' of the West.[1] James is our memory of the life of culture before 1914, whose spirit strolls with light grace through the collective memory of high civilization, a mixture of dedicated scholar and Yankee wit. Along the path of Barzun's 'stroll' we find a familiar characterization of the 'existential misery' of the 'Europeans', a refusal to admit any difficulty in James's various views of consciousness, a total lack of precise historical contexts, monolithic and overgeneralized characterizations of the 'modern state' which 'interferes' with 'individual liberty'. Intellectually, Barzun's anthologizing of great thoughts from great thinkers in which to place James performs just that act of saccharine parataxis that James complained of in Palgrave's *Golden Treasury*.[2]

So what did William James stand for? His critique of the Utopian society of the middle-class liberal arts college of Chautauqua has also often been noted.[3] He hurled the 'real life' of 'zymotic diseases, poverty, drunkenness and crime' against the Utopian liberal arts college. But did not his remarks have something of that *nostalgie de la boue* which characterizes an upper middle-class project and which often attempts to ally the upper and lower classes against the middle? Mark Twain was much more sophisticated when instinctively he linked gentility with violence in *Huckleberry Finn*. In addition, did Alice James (William's wife) accept so easily the Barzunian role of angel in the house? She had studied the piano with Clara Schumann. James doubtless found his wife's playing very therapeutic, but what did she feel when he sneered at Boston Symphony audiences? Was James capable of making a distinction between a real love of music and a well-polished, untuned piano in a bourgeois parlour which no one except the children played?

At this point it is instructive to look at James's actual politics and at some aspects of his institutional behaviour. What did politics have to do with philosophy and/or psychology? Did it have to do with one, both, or neither? In England with his father, and conducting the crucial diplomatic negotiations with England during the Civil War, Henry Adams contemplated the fact that Gladstone seemed not quite sane, that Russell was verging on senility, and that Palmerston seemed to have lost his nerve. He concluded: 'Politics cannot stop to study psychology.'[4] Adams's injunction to the historian was, of course, fruitfully flouted in his own practice. The problem in general, however, has haunted much political writing in the twentieth century, particularly after 1945. With a few exceptions up to that date, commentators would have agreed with Adams's statement and its obverse. In our own time, however, a 'politics' will include not only an economics, but theories of group behavior, theories of personality, ideas about sexual roles, institutional structure and techniques of mass persuasion.

From the mid-1870s, in spite of the beginnings of professionalization and specialization within higher learning, James's writings attempted to encompass a totality which was already splitting at the seams. For this reason the connections, say between a politics, psychology and institutional practice, are laid bare in ways which later would have been unthinkable. The discourses were still connected. John Dewey could insist, unlike most commentators of his time and subsequently, that 'psychology is a political science', because 'experience' differed under different regimes.[5] Specialization, however, pulled academic discourse away from the political

arena. Indeed specialization within the human sciences was as much a
function of 'professionalization' as the need to divide and analyse the
subject-matter. Nonetheless James never felt its full force and his
writings show it. C. Wright Mills could note without difficulty:
'That there is a close correspondence and interaction between his
[James's] social-political views and his epistemological, metaphysical, and psychological opinions is clear.'[6] One correspondent of
James's, however, thought that the relation of philosophy and
politics in the United States was less of a concern than in Europe:

> We, therefore, as it seems to me, take this matter of philosophy
> much more seriously than you have occasion to do, on whom the
> necessity is not impressed by social and political and ecclesiastical
> and economical problems, clamouring for a solution, and by the
> hostility of man to man, and nation to nation, the seething
> commotion called Europe.[7]

Hodgson's realization that philosophy is linked with political and
social pressures is not equalled by his endearing *naïveté* about
America. James had no illusions about the myth of republican
innocence, but he was much exercised as to what philosophy fitted
the 'seething commotion' of America. (Indeed where do 'ideas' go in
America? They seem to disappear into the thin air of the Rocky
Mountains or peter out, transubstantiated into technique, in a
thousand Ph.D. theses: libations to patron–advisers in a statistical
game of numbers which is as highly organized as averages in an
American football game.)

Theoretical thinking itself in James's time was likely to be
characterized as 'a priori', that is 'European': it is a racist time-scale
that always posits 'Europe' as permanently 'behind', and therefore,
of course, as 'un-American'. James's own onslaught on 'idealism',
however, is partially not an intellectual argument at all, but a response
to the fact that no single discourse seemed to be able to cope with the
extraordinarily rapid transformation of society in the United States
from 1880 onwards. In a sense James's clear attempt to pick up what
he thought were the discredited discourses of classical philosophy,
Christian exegesis, and liberal sentiment, within the framework of a
critique of current psychological practice, was likely to lead to heroic
failure. Inevitably, therefore, any discussion of James's politics will
have to pick its way across the fragments of those discourses. The
particular 'mix', however, will be characterizable.

The approach here will differ from that of the generation of Benda
in the 1920s, which spoke of the *'trahison des clercs'*, and yet again
from those, like Eric Bentley and Barzun, of the '40s, who believed
that the philosophy of James was the one of which the world stood

most in need.[8] What characterizes these opposing views as having something in common is a belief that 'ideas' have *direct* political consequences. Paradoxically the political events to which both sets of critics were reacting – the foreground to World War II – inaugurated a new era of anti-intellectualism accompanied by physical terror, not to mention new media marketing the 'white noise' of Orwellian Newspeak, which guaranteed the neutralization of any idea. Mussolini had declared: 'James taught me that action should be judged rather by its result than by its doctrinary basis. I learnt of James that faith in action, that ardent will to live and fight, to which Fascism owes a great part of its success.'[9] When H.W. Schneider took up the task of defending James from such an outrageous charge he said: 'The *fascisti* are not mere hard-headed "men of action" who spurn all speculation and attend to business. On the contrary nothing is more characteristic of a fascist than a passionate devotion to theorizing.'[10] Against this should be placed both the experience and writing of someone like Gramsci, who called for a concrete study 'for each country [of] the cultural organization which keeps the ideological world in movement and to examine its practical fuctioning'.[11]

Schneider's was a common simplistic defence and it would be one not unattractive to Barzun. The attempt to align a political ideology with whether one thinks or acts (assuming the two genuinely separable) is however a nonsense. The illogicality in Mussolini's statement is not whether James advocated a practicalism judged by results – for which there is some evidence – nor whether he advocated faith in action and a will to live and 'fight', for which there is considerable evidence, but what fascism owed to these statements. The answer is nothing – except perhaps what Mussolini believed it did. Speculative and practical types characterize all ideologies and creeds. Jesus was speculative (the Sermon on the Mount), St. Paul was speculative and activist, and Constantine was activist. Marx was speculative, Lenin activist and partly speculative. Washington was activist, Jefferson partly speculative and partly activist. To pursue this line of reasoning gets nobody anywhere.

The lacuna in Mussolini's argument was one also to be found in Schneider's defence: the assumption that a description of behaviour can be articulated essentially in terms of a characterology dependent on an ideology. It ignores the educational level of a people, their common political experience, the means of distribution of message, irrational, emotional appeal, and above all terror. Mussolini's 'success' was a result of thuggery and of manipulating propaganda within a legacy of historical circumstances arising out of the aftermath of the First World War. It was not a result of a dualistic characterology, philosophy, and psychology being somehow weighted down on one side rather than the other.

Yet James's more popular writings, built round a belief in (not the truth of) the will, and the kind of moral uplift which the accruing 'advantages' were assumed to bring, can be read as a crude advocacy of pure stance unchallenged by intellectual scrutiny. There is nothing in such a belief to make it more difficult for a Mussolini to attempt to co-opt the position. The very individualism of such a belief as well as its easy solutions to 'pessimism', are parodied once and for all in Sartre's *Nausea*:

> 'No reason for existing . . . I suppose, Monsieur, you mean that life has no object. Isn't that what people call pessimism?'
>
> He goes on thinking for a moment, then he says gently: 'A few years ago I read a book by an American author, called *Is Life Worth Living*? Isn't that the question you are asking yourself?'
>
> No that obviously isn't the question I'm asking myself. But I don't want to explain anything.
>
> 'He concluded', the Autodidact tells me in a consoling voice, 'in favour of deliberate optimism. Life has a meaning if you choose to give it one. First of all you must act, you must throw yourself into some enterprise. If you think about it later on, the die is already cast, you are already involved. I don't know what you think about that, Monsieur?'
>
> 'Nothing,' I say.
>
> Or rather I think that that is precisely the sort of lie that the commercial traveller, the two young people, and the white-haired gentleman keep on telling themselves.[12]

The problems of James's 'practicalism', the difficulties of defining pragmatism, have long been the stock-in-trade of Jamesian commentary. Barzun's suggestion of functionalism helps little to clear up the 'verbal mess'.[13] Few would doubt that relativism, plurality and imperfections of truths are the only assumptions a fair society can make in proceeding with its affairs. Yet the issue remains as to how and on what grounds it can be known whether those truths are plural, relative and imperfect. Pragmatism distrusts principles, yet pragmatically people are supposed to stick to them and so on. The specific content of human affairs can only, in the last resort, be judged by a combination of theoretical and practical means in open, public debate.

Neither Adams nor James had much inclination for actual political or public life. Yet Adams was practically involved in foreign affairs for the Union in the 1860s and James is largely known politically for his public statements on American imperialism in the Philippines at the turn of the century. Individualist as he was, so the argument goes, James always supported the weak against the strong: the Boers and the Irish against the British, the Filipinos against the United States. He wrote to Godkin in 1889 that in his earlier years his whole political education was 'due to *The Nation*'.[14] Yet this liberal middle-of-the-road journal was not the only factor in James's political outlook. C. Wright Mills has argued shrewdly that James's model for society was that of a profession. After completing his medical course James wrote: 'I feel it both in its scientific "yield" and its general educational value as enabling me to see a little the inside workings of an important profession and to learn from it, as an average example, how all the work of human society is performed.'[15] The professional model of society is crucial, and it will be seen in the last part of this book what effect such a model had on Gertrude Stein. Mills argues further that this model often came into conflict with James's 'personalism'.

One of the problems with a medical professional model is the notion of social health. Health, to reduce a potentially complex argument, is itself based on the notion of the self-regulation of an organism tending towards replication and stability. It invites normative and centrist versions of social truth. Whatever opposes it is therefore 'pathological', or, to use a familiar Americanism, 'sick'. (James's notions of the 'sick'- and 'healthy'-minded character, which were derived from his medical and professional training, will be considered later.) Unlike many intellectuals, James was to characterize the Haymarket riots of 1886 as the 'work of a lot of pathological Germans and Poles', in contradistinction to that 'healthy phase of evolution, a little costly but normal', carried on by the Knights of Labor.[16] Did James also think it was 'normal' for those who had crushed the pathological also to crush the healthy when business propaganda made the Haymarket riots into an occasion to break the Knights of Labor in their turn? 'Healthy individualism' had its limits when confronted with a fundamentally political situation. In this respect one commentator remarks that 'It is not insignificant that the philosopher who begged his reader not to miss the joy of being alien and different continually pictured the "Asian spirit" as threatening the West'.[17]

In addition there is a significant presence within the American cultural tradition of an alliance between religion and medicine, from the 'New Thought Alliance', founded by patient-disciples of Phineas Parkhurst Quimby and insisting on 'therapeutic' approaches to social problems (healthy beliefs cure disease, etc.) to Christian Science's answers to Beard's American 'nervousness'. If Americans could relax they would not be so imperialistic![18] Images of health and sickness in the social field exhibit the worst aspects of analogies used as principles. In James they sometimes rode roughshod over actual political detail. The man who would write 'The Moral Equivalent of War', ostensibly against Roosevelt's remark that an occasional war was good for a nation, could also write, in his enthusiasm for German re-unification, 'I hope the French will get a good thrashing from somebody soon.'[19]

Thus the particular bundle of contradictions here is shaped by an undeclared model of therapeutics and social organism. The mind–body problem was also another undeclared factor in shaping James's attitudes, for example, towards women. He had no objection to women being educated, but he did not think they should be independent.[20] Both Adams and James of course had watched extraordinarily gifted women (wife and sister) die as a result of what seemed weak physiological constitutions. Henry James summed it up acutely with his usual brilliant gift of phrasing when he spoke of his sister Alice's 'tragic health' as the only solution to the practical problem of life.[21] Henry's perception seems a little in advance of William, but then he did not have medical expertise to contend with. The worst aspects of that medical expertise can be seen in Charlotte Perkins Gilman's famous short story, 'The Yellow Wall Paper'.

William James never quite lost his 'body' bias. One solution for women was heralded by the sisters of Norway: 'They tell us that in Norway the life of the women has lately been revolutionized by the new order of muscular feelings with which the use of the ski, or long snow shoes, as a sport for both sexes, has made the women acquainted.'[22] There is no doubt that it is possible to have quite revolutionary 'muscular feelings', skiing in Norway (as the author knows), but it is to be doubted whether it solves the set of problems involved in 'neurasthenia' beyond a certain behavioural positiveness. Quite clearly Nora and Hedda Gabler should have done a little more skiing. Women were not the only oppressed group to be recommended 'sport'. James's statement should be placed in context with the popular belief of his time that 'more sport' was a solution to an America weakened by 'over-tension'. As one history of sport in America puts it: 'early in the twentieth century, industry began to promote athletics among its workers as a means of keeping them content.'[23] As in the 1980s and 1990s sport was more than a means of 'health'.

The terms of health were increasingly political. James could write to Renouvier of the 'singularly artificial yet deeply vital and soundly healthy character of the English social and political system as it now exists. . . I know nothing that so much confirms your philosophy as this spectacle of an accumulation of individual initiatives all preserved. . . '.[24] The language here is semi-Darwinian, semi-therapeutic, and semi-sociological. The fragments of ideology it puts together are: an eighteenth-century view (largely from France) that the England of the Glorious Revolution was the acme of political success, a metaphysics of accumulative process, and liberal individualism. This is not the England of Gustave Doré. It is the upper half of Disraeli's two nations. Within the very term 'health', then, are a large number of concealments and assumptions.

It is revealing to contrast William James with his sister Alice who, for all her apparent withdrawal from the world as a result of her 'tragic health', sometimes seemed very much more in it than her activist brother:

> I shall always be a bloated capitalist, I suppose, an ignominy which, considering all things, I may as well submit to, gracefully, for I shouldn't bring much body to the proletariat, but I can't help having an illogical feminine satisfaction that all my seven per cents and six per cents with which I left home have melted into fours. I don't feel four per cent quite so base!. . . What one of us, with the sentimental, emotional sympathy, ever stood by his fellow, starving, and watching his dwindling wife and children for weeks? And yet at every strike thousands of the unfed, unclothed, and the unread, stand or fall together and make no boast.[25]

Alice subverts her opening line with an irony rivalling Adams and with an ability to limit substantive propositions reminiscent of her brother Henry. There is irony, too, in her equation of body with proletariat and an implicit challenge to the result of that equation. Her active *mind* does indeed subvert here the truth of 'health's' guide to the world.

James's public pronouncements on politics, notably his response to the American occupation of the Philippines, were made at the high point of the imperialist era. The *New York Evening Post*, in which he published letters and which was to print his address to the Anti-Imperialist League, took a broadly liberal line. A leader of 4 March 1899 stated that 'the colonial Empire of Great Britain undoubtedly represents, on the whole, a great triumph of civilization and philanthropy', but it regretted that 'the operations of the English army in the Sudan have, in a way, brought as much shame and compunction to philanthropic people in England as the exploits of our soldiers in the Philippines have caused Americans'.[26] Thus imperialism as such was not questioned – or possibly was put down to 'tragic necessity' – within the somewhat contentless notion of moderation.

James's first letter to this paper hopes that time will 'apportion

justly the blame for the Philippine situation', and lays the phenomenon squarely on the American sense of manifest destiny. He
speaks of 'the hollowness of this whole business which is so pleasing
our national imagination, the mission, namely which we suppose
Providence to have invested us with, of raising the Filipinos in the
scale of being'. James points to the psychology of the situation: 'dim,
foggy, abstract good will, backed by energetic officiousness, and
unillumined by accurate perception of the concrete wants and
possibilities of the case'. The 'consciousness of goodness' (James
means 'sentiment') is the enemy of a 'rational settlement'.[27] James
does not advocate complete military withdrawal, but a replacement
of blundering with efficient staff at Manila, a payment of a heavy
indemnity, and low-profile help. It is a professional solution – that is,
it concentrates on technique while disregarding the facts of power.
James also feared that American benevolent sentiment would quickly
turn to bloodthirsty demands for revenge if many American soldiers
were killed. Two points are worth highlighting. The first is that
James takes public sentiment as cause, and the second is that he
believes efficiency will be some kind of palliative and remedy. How
'efficiency' will be determined he does not consider.

James's largest statement on the war occurs four years later, after
the subjugation of the Philippines' people had been accomplished
with an appalling combination of violence and terror.[28] He now
advocates independence for the Philippines (although he does not
envisage it for fifty years), and unhesitatingly damns the activities
of the intervening four years with an ironic body model: 'In
the physiologies which I studied when I was young the function
of incorporating foreign bodies was divided into four stages –
prehension, deglutination, digestion and assimilation.' McKinley, he
states, offered America's late allies an alternative, 'insalivated with
pious phrases', of 'instant obedience or death'. The anti-imperialist
prophecies have all come true:

> . . .the material ruin of the islands; the transformation of native
> friendliness to execration; the demoralization of our army, from
> the war office down – forgery decorated, torture whitewashed,
> massacre condoned; the creation of a chronic anarchy in the
> islands, with ladronism still smouldering, and the lives of Amer-
> ican travellers and American sympathizers unsafe anywhere out of
> sight of army posts, . . .

> ('Speech', p. 8)

Meanwhile the public has become bored with and indifferent to the
whole affair.

James then offers his solutions. First, he advocates leaving the past
to the historians: 'Let us drop yesterday and its sins, then, and forget
them.' Otherwise, he suggests, the anti-imperialist will be in danger
of becoming a caricature:

> To the ordinary citizen the word anti-imperialist suggests a thin
> haired being just waked up from the day before yesterday,
> brandishing the Declaration of Independence excitedly, and
> shrieking after a railroad train is thundering to its destruction to
> turn upon its tracks and come back.

In practical political terms the 'better half of the Republicans' are the
people to amend the situation in the Philippines, for 'Political virtue
does not follow geographical divisions. It follows the eternal division
of each country between the more animal and the more intellectual
kind of men, between the tory and the liberal tendencies. . .'.
Another practical suggestion is to repeat incessantly phrases such as
'Independence for the Philippine Islands', and 'Treat the Filipinos
like the Cubans', because 'phrases repeated have a way of turning
into fact' [!].

Finally James says that 'Angelic impulses and predatory lusts
divide our hearts exactly as they divide the hearts of other countries'.
America is now to be seen as part of an international company of
nations, for it has, once for all, 'regurgitated' the Declaration of
Independence and the Farewell Address:

> We are objects of fear to other lands. This makes of the old
> liberalism and the new liberalism two discontinuous things. The
> older liberalism was in office, but the new is in opposition.
> Inwardly it is the same spirit, but outwardly the tactics, the
> questions, the reasons, have to change. American memories no
> longer serve as catchwords.
>
> ('Speech', p. 8)

James predicts that the future will continue to see a kind of Manichaean struggle and he ends: 'The Lord of Life is with us, and we
cannot permanently fail.'

This address gives a good idea of the strengths and weaknesses of
James's political position. On the positive side, he calls American
terrorism by name, he outlines the hypocrisy of the way 'public
opinion' abandons the mess it has created, he calls for a certain
practical realism in facing up to altered circumstances; he advocates
independence, he recognizes the immediate irrelevance of historic
American principles, and realizes that any new liberalism has to be
international in character. On the negative side, however, is his
attitude to the past. To abandon the past may be good politics (a

F

British Prime Minister once said a week is a long time in politics),
but is positively harmful to analysis and to the capacity to learn from
mistakes. If a wise policy is to emerge the brief cannot be given only
to the historians; neither can a judgement of events simply be handed
over to the 'verdict of posterity'.

Futher, while in any pressure group there are caricaturable 'protest
types', James ignores the very possibility of malicious caricatures
being made by the controllers of public opinion to discredit genuine
criticisms of national policy. The burden of truth is not simply on
someone else's observation of the behaviour of the critic. Moreover,
while the principles of the Declaration of Independence may be
'realistically' irrelevant to American foreign policy, this does not in
and of itself make them untrue. American domestic policy has found
it necessary to base a code of civil rights on 'idealist' grounds, and
rightly so. James throws out the baby with the bath water. To
caricature, as he does, the advocate of such truths as a shrieking
hysteric is irresponsible and is a gesture more characteristic of right-
wing politics than the liberal centre James seeks to hold together.
Indeed the whole question of 'types' is at issue here. James's 'eternal
division' of the animal and the intellectual is also suspect – not to say
theological and medieval.

An item in the same newspaper a day later gives some idea of the
temper of the times. The leader reports a mass meeting at Cooper
Hall in protest at the arrest of an anarchist who had been speaking at
a mass meeting. The leader comments that 'Mr Turner was arrested
in true Russian style', and adds that 'the British authorities had never
deemed it worthwhile to pay any attention'. It goes on ironically,
'Under our law Tolstoi himself would probably have been barred
out.'[29] Up until the Thatcher era a spy in England was regarded
merely as a military threat, while in the United States this crime was
blasphemy against the divinity. James probably under-estimated the
danger of type-casting in an America controlled as never before by
mass media whose assortment of behavioural types would be
produced under a metaphysic of 'general threat'.

Since James's politics were bound up with a view of society which
was, in part at least, contoured by a stint in medical school, it is
important to survey his actual institutional behaviour. Again the
image is of the reluctant professional universally beloved by all who
came into contact with him. The awkward case of Santayana is
simply the exception which proves the rule. It must be said,
however, that the image is substantially close to the truth. The many
testimonials to James's work and teaching cannot be impugned. But
once again there are certain flaws in the image which are worth

mentioning in the current spate of Jamesian hero-worship. In personal terms the tolerant James of the liberal image is a half-truth at best. The James of the 'either-or' stance has already been discussed. Lovejoy spoke of a 'touch of Puritan austerity', and his 'somewhat choleric nature', and says further that he was no 'lover of amiable compromises or of higher syntheses'. One consequence of this was his 'inveterate tendency to oppose theology and religion to each other in the strongest possible way'.[30]

This separation of theology and religion in James has its roots deep in the American philosophico-religious past and is crucial. As far back as the mid-eighteenth century Jonathan Edwards had attempted to hold together Calvinism and Lockean empiricism. His invention of the 'religious affection' was an attempt to appeal to the heart and mind simultaneously. However, the Lockean shift to 'sense' opened the way for religious experience to be determined almost in the sense of a biologically-given experience. Speculative and practical life became increasingly separated. Transcendentalism and business-backed revivalism equally pushed the very concept of the experience of religion towards sentiment. In *The Varieties of Religious Experience* James attempted to create a psychological model for de-intellectualized religion.

James, of course, could not rely on the great intellectual and emotional synthesis of the Puritan tradition to be found in a Milton. Nor, one suspects, would he have taken kindly to the religious sects whose general 'enthusiasm' also included a political 'enthusiasm'. While not as biased in general against 'enthusiasm' as his admired Locke (James had no axe to grind on behalf of an Established national church – in any case America did not have one), James would have preferred his case-studies of enthusiastics to remain decently apolitical. As for a more intellectual religion, he would have shared Harriet Beecher Stowe's view, in an authorial comment in her novel *The Minister's Wooing* (1859): 'It is not in our line to imply the truth or the falsehoods of philosophic theology which seem for many years to have been the principal outlet for the proclivities of the New England mind, but as psychological developments they have an intense interest.'[31] In intellectual terms the wide distance between conceptual thought and religious practice joined with a general distrust of the idealist tradition in philosophy to create a serious problem about how moral life could be described and thought about.

These issues are mentioned here because they help to throw light on James's involvement in the Abbott affair. The story is told in C. Wright Mills's *Sociology and Pragmatism*. Mills is broadly sympathetic to James, though he is certainly not the quasi-reincarnation of James which the editorial introduction to that volume claims. Mills's

discussion is useful in that it takes into consideration the background
to the professionalization of American universities in the late
nineteenth century. One consequence was the alliance of 'big money'
with 'hard science'. Appropriately, Mills cites a passage from the
inaugural address of Charles W. Eliot (possibly Harvard's most
famous president), in which he said: 'Philosophical subjects should
never be taught with authority. They are not established sciences. . .
[they are] full of. . . bottomless speculation.'[32]

Speculative thought was unauthoritative, hard science was authoritative. The idea is still adhered to among second-rate scientists, but
today scholars are much more sceptical of such positivist declarations, and much more sophisticated about the role of concepts in
science. The problem with Eliot's declaration is that it assumes that
the danger of dogmatism is higher in philosophy than in established
sciences, which is not necessarily true. It also assumes, and this is
worse, that speculative thought and its practice in some way lack
'authority' within the human world. Eliot's own dogmatism was to
equate authority with certainty, and to assume that science could
deliver it.

James's role in the Abbott case can be seen much more clearly
against this background. James's increasing preoccupation after the
Principles was to prise as much of the human world as possible away
from a coercive scientific 'centre'. In attempting to 'save' what he
thought was valuable in human experience he had to abandon the
prestigious modes of the only intellectual discipline which seemed to
have 'authority'. Francis Ellington Abbott's work struck right across
James's own fears and taboos. Confronted with the ailing nineteenth-
century God, Abbott revised his ideology (he moved from Uni-
tarianism to humanism) and his practice (he not only abandoned
but attacked the church). He further attempted to put his revised
principles into practice by joining quasi-political pressure groups,
and daring to pose challenges to philosophical practice inside the
academic world. He applied Eliot's 'bottomless speculation' to social
practice, challenged the rising scientistic snobbery, and insisted
not only that philosophy and science should be connected but that
'philosophy' should not 'sit modestly at the feet of science', so that it
became 'modernized'.[33]

Adams, of course, would have agreed absolutely. Abbott's fault
was that he chose the wrong mode, the wrong genre, and the wrong
set of institutional circumstances at the wrong time in which to
publish his views. All this would have been enough to rattle James,
but he would not have bothered to attack Abbott in the way he did if
the discussion had remained at this level. The following passage
from Abbott's work *Scientific Theism* (cited by Mills), which James

told Hodgson 'makes me groan [so] that I cannot digest a word of it', would have touched directly on James's socio-political sensitivities:

> What wonder that, in the hands of those who insist on their rights to reduce theory to practice, philosophy is so often found pandering to the moral lawlessness of an Individualism that sets mere personal opinion above the supreme ethical sanctions of the universe? In human society, individual autonomy is universal antinomy.[34]

It hardly seems indigestible. However, this defense of theory as the bulwark of maintaining a holistic perspective on social needs, the description of individualism as 'moral lawlessness', not to mention the frank 'idealism' of the 'supreme ethical sanction of the universe', would have caught James on the raw.

Strangely, Abbott had a glowing testimonial from that most supreme of American individualists, Ralph Waldo Emerson. In his own time Peirce both admired and defended him, and at least one modern commentator sums up (generally approvingly) the issues at stake:

> Peirce (and Abbott) are correct in holding that science is not nominalistic but realistic. For scientists do believe that the past is a guide to the future and do believe they have a basis for making predictions. Such being the case scientists are realists. This argument, of course, does not prove that there are real laws, but it does indicate that the philosophical basis of science is realistic, not nominalistic. Even this is no new discovery, since philosophers generally recognize a difference between what is philosophically demonstrable about the nature of scientific laws and what the scientist actually thinks about them when he is engaged in scientific activities.[35]

The fundamental linkage of past and present, the distinction between the logic of justification and the process of discovery, and the relation between empirical practice and hypothesis-building, are missing in James's sometimes intemperate oppositions. Because James was a reluctant scientist, because his own background was in medicine and psychology, and because his experience of scientific practice was in the distinctly unengaging intellectual domain of mechanistic psychology seeking to free itself from the older humanist discourses, he over-reacted to the very possibility of scientific speculation at one end of the scale and to any possibility that humanistic discourse might revitalize itself theoretically in relation to older models at the other. In the Abbott affair it appears that the balance of justice was not on James's side. While all the details are not known (it is possible,

for example, that Abbott like Peirce might have made a difficult
colleague), it is hard not to sympathize with Abbott. In 1890 Abbott
was attacked by Royce in the *International Journal of Ethics*, defended
by Peirce in *The Nation*, and answered again by James in *The Nation*.
In spite of his later efforts to popularize his *own* views, James took
the institutional line, regretted that the issue had been brought
'before the large public', and imputed a 'pathalogical' (*sic*) motive
to Abbott's conduct. Abbott's career was ruined and after increasing
poverty the wretched man poisoned himself and in 1903 was found
dead on his wife's grave.

Here the contradictions must be left to speak for themselves. In some
sense James's view of politics and society is peculiarly modern in
its emphasis on liberal sentiment and therapeutics. He is much less
the moderate man than the prevailing image suggests. There are
weaknesses in his view of society and culture. There is an in-built
division in his thought between psychological and moral life and the
distribution of power in a political sense. His individualism and calls
to action tend to divert attention from the content of behaviour
towards its outward form. His somewhat naïve anti-idealistic stance
threatened to some extent the cause of thinking as such. Worst of all,
the 'medicalization' of social discourse opened up a series of evasions
which have been analysed in the late twentieth century by numerous
feminist theorists, and perhaps most famously of all by Foucault.
Nonetheless against this must be set the fact that, unusually for his
time and ours, James was prepared (in accordance with the best
aspects of his practicalism) to step outside academia and speak out
against an increasingly imperialist America taking steps whose
consequences continue down to the present day.

Chapter 7
America and Europe: Locations of Sensations and Healthy States

When William James was born the elder Henry James led Ralph Waldo Emerson up to the chamber to catch one of the first glimpses of the new-born child. What the transcendentalists bequeathed to James was neither dogma nor a set of philosophical positions. Rather it was a habit of mind, an intellectual consensus about books read and traditions absorbed. James himself inherited the transcendentalists' intellectual curiosity, their self-reliance, their bohemianism, their advocacy of liberal causes, their practical idealism, their Utopianism and their tendency to mysticism.

William James's father, Henry James Sr., had, for example, corresponded with Faraday on abstruse questions concerning the Sandamanian sect. He had mistrusted Emerson's radical views on nature. He was intimate also with the details of the American philosopher's quarrels with Carlyle.[1] Henry James Sr. was at the end of the long line of what Perry Miller called the 'New England Mind'. Practicality was the nebulous socialism of Fourier, piety the consolations of the melancholy Swedenborg. Perhaps Henry James Sr. spoke more truly than he knew when at a literary party he commented on Hawthorne, the most famous dissenter from New England Utopianism, that he 'had the look all the time, to one who did not know him, of a rogue who suddenly finds himself in the company of detectives'.[2]

William James, however, overturned a number of the premises of his father's thinking.[3] The father's notion of individual damnation and collective salvation became the son's individual salvation and collective damnation in a secular psychology formed within the atmosphere of an emerging social Darwinism. The terms of the argument are, however, recognizable from father to son. Essentially religious problems were to remain a frame of reference. From his father, too, James inherited a mistrust of conceptual thought as such. The father's more secular view of 'right affections' – ultimately traceable to Jonathan Edwards and Locke – was curiously to be

paralleled by the son's psychological investigations into pre-
conceptual feeling, which in some quarters would lead to the charge
of anti-intellectualism.

American philosophy first took formal shape in the hands of the
great New England divine, Jonathan Edwards. It is perhaps not
surprising that the very philosopher who was to hold together the
mind and heart of religious experience in such a way that they fell
apart almost immediately afterwards should also have taken some
early American steps towards a practical psychology. It was within
the same New England project that James took up the task 140 years
later. Edwards retained a philosophical Platonism to support an
idealist's notion of God's justice, and a Lockean empiricist psychology to create a religious 'sense' to underpin those rational ideas in
experience. Holy love becomes empiricist sense.[4] If Edwards was
faced by the collapse of Puritanism, James was faced with the
collapse of liberalism as a ruling ideology. Edwards might also be
seen as the father of behaviourism in America, in that he too devised
a system of tests (in the spirit of empiricism) for human behaviour.
Edwards was faced with the problem of how to tell a truly converted
man from a false one; James believed that the social value of the
'college bred' (the very phrase an attempt to marry culture and
biology) was that you should be able to 'know a good man when you
see him'.[5] Minister and psychologist both offered criteria to determine who was saved and who was socially valuable.

The camp meetings of the fiery Jonathan Edwards and the
Harvard of William James might appear worlds apart. Santayana,
however touched on connections which might be searched for in
vain in books on the history of psychology. The Harvard professors
were, he tells us, 'consciously teaching and guiding the community,
as if they had been clergymen; and it made no less acute their moral
loneliness, isolation and forced self-reliance, because they were like
clergymen without a church.'[6] After publishing *The Principles of
Psychology* James became increasingly the secular clergyman. Conviction of sin in the congregation had become a well-bred melancholy
in the post-Lyceum audience. James's 'sermons' were directed towards the inwardness of bourgeois anxiety. The middle class needed
reassurance about that disappearing world of romance and daring
which had characterized its own origins.

The famous Dr Beard's 'nervous' age certainly stalked the James
family.[7] William, Henry and Alice all had serious nervous break-
downs in the 1860s. Alice, whose courageous and spirited diary has
already been cited, died of 'neurasthenia', though she was 'relieved'
in fact to discover she had cancer. One look at the photograph of
Alice James which Leon Edel reproduced in his edition of the diary

gives us a powerful view of this atmosphere. Here is the woman who damned the practices of the British Empire in her correspondence, yet felt sceptically grateful for her capital invested at 7.5 per cent. A great silk bow and full sleeves gather richly to her neck as if to prop up the chin and keep the spine rigid. The hard-set down-turned lines of the mouth, inward-turning eyes, the hair swept back from a broad Irish brow suggest a marble will in the face of dissolution. Indeed neurosis stalked upper-middle-class America as much as it ever did Wittgenstein's Vienna or Durkheim's France. The James family, it must also be added, had the means to give their neuroses leisurely treatment.[8]

These details are mentioned to emphasize some of the more intangible co-ordinates of James's attitudes to 'psychology'. It was Edwards who made salvation a matter of psychological health and James who confronted clinically a modern version of medieval accidie within himself and his own family. Henry and William fussed over each other's health continuously and with minute descriptions of symptoms. Henry's letter to William on their father's death lingers like a forensic scalpel over a detailed preparation.[9] The James family toughed it out. Perhaps William James's remark about Darwin sums it up: 'I have just been reading Darwin's life... and, whilst his nervous system makes bad nerves respectable, the tale of it shuts the mouth of all lesser men against complaining.'[10]

It is important to remember that the literary and the psychological worlds were still capable of speaking to each other at this period. Eugene I. Taylor's recent work has discussed James in the context of the 'literary psychologies' of the early nineteenth century, claiming for example that Hawthorne's *Scarlet Letter* is, in a sense, an exegesis of psychosomatic medicine.[11] That is not all it is, of course, but it is a timely reminder of how closely the two disciplines converged. In a sense Taylor's point was already made by James himself in a much-quoted letter to his novelist brother:

> I am just now in the middle of his [William Dean Howells's] *Hazard of New Fortunes*, which is an extraordinarily vigorous production, quite up to Dickens I should say, in humour, detail of observation and geniality, with flexible human beings on the stage instead of puppets. With that work, your *Tragic Muse*, and last *but by no means least*, my *Psychology*, all appearing in it, the year 1890 will be known as the great epochal year in American literature.[12]

Indeed, as Hocks has shown, William's philosophy and Henry's structures of character in his novels have many areas in common.[13] Even Whitman's poetic drama of 'separateness' and 'adhesiveness' in 'Song of Myself' is clearly kin to the following definition by James of man as a bundle of desires: 'The expansive embracing tendency, the centripetal, defensive, forming two different modes of self-assertion sympathy and self-sufficingness.'[14] Curiously enough, Whitman's terms were drawn from phrenology – that proto-science of brain localization and hopeful mind–body syntheses. James, too, was interested in phrenology and he used to ask for photographs of prominent European psychologists when he corresponded with them, in order to study their heads.

There is little doubt that James's American experiences gave a direction and shape to his reception of European philosophy and psychology. It is now time to look at what he culled from three major European countries, in spite of the fact that, as he once said: 'A man coquetting with too many countries is as bad as a bigamist, and loses his soul altogether.'[15] For James, England was fundamentally a 'healthy' state, though like many English people he preferred the 'Continent' for a vacation. In no other country has he been so honoured, and James returned the compliment in spite of his fierce nationalism. Like most travellers he could blow hot and cold according to mood. The year 1901, for example, seems to have been a bad trip, for he spoke of the absence of charm and intellectual deadness. Seven years later, giving eight lectures at Oxford in 1908, he had a 'blessed 9 days' at the beautiful little Cotswold village of Bibury and in truly 'mellow' mood spoke of the Genius of the Anglican Church and vowed that if he were an Englishman he would vote against all change at Oxford. Leaving out the slum life, as he said, the good nature of England was much to be admired. And on the whole he did leave out the slum life. Visits to Sussex and to the Lamb House at Rye would have confirmed his conviction: 'Everything about them is of better quality than the corresponding thing in the U.S. – with but few exceptions.'[16]

It was, however, the intellectual life of England which presented a rich field both of exploration and challenge. James's primary intellectual allegiance was to the philosophical and psychological tradition of British empiricism, whose great names included Locke, Berkeley, Hume, Hartley and John Stuart Mill. Charles Darwin, however, had perhaps a greater effect on James's work than any of these, and he will be held over (with the American natural historian Agassiz) for later consideration. Mill was to be the dedicatee of *Pragmatism*, but it was 'dear old John Locke', as James would refer to him, who was to be fundamental.

Indeed there are a striking number of points of similarity between James and Locke, in spite of wide difference of history and culture.[17] They were both somewhat conservative politically though ideologically liberal and their tolerances were somewhat selective. Locke could damn Penn's constitution for Pennsylvania, approve of people knocking off Quaker's hats, insist on Catholics being barred from political power, and all in the name of the moderate Anglican centre. The philosopher who enshrined life, liberty and property at the heart of the bourgeois's quest for freedom from aristocratic privilege could also frame a constitution for the Carolinas in order to 'avoid a numerous democracy'. Both men had difficulty in deciding on a career. Both hated war. Together they span the great bourgeois moment of history: Locke at its period of young fresh confidence, James at the onset of its decline. They shared a nucleus of attitudes: an 'English' separation of emotion and philosophy, a somewhat theoretical belief in the right of rebellion, a strong individualism (both kept notes on great men), a scepticism of excess, a hatred of disputing in public, a dislike of actual experimental science. There was a touch of the Gothic about them, a pleasure in 'mystery for the sake of mystery'. Locke's Oxford latitudinarianism was close in spirit to James's pragmatic view of religion, and it separated him from the more idealistic line at Cambrige which, from the Cambridge Platonists to the neo-Hegelians, had had importance for the Harvard School of Theology. Neither of them had any feeling for, nor much sense of, history. Both wrote with a strong sense of the difficulty of the structure of their work, and with a penchant for what Cranston calls 'commercial idioms'.[18]

At the beginning of their careers, which both decided on with difficulty, they trained in medicine. The importance of this for Locke cannot be overestimated.[19] One commentator has argued that 'what differentiated Locke from the other great figures of his period who concerned themselves with the perennial problem of spirit and knowledge is probably the fact that he was a physician, not a mathematician'.[20] Locke knew Thomas Sydenham, the outstanding physician of his time, and Cranston cites a passage from Sydenham's work designed to show the proximity of their ideas:

> The function of a physician [is the] industrious investigation of the history of diseases, and of the effect of remedies, as shown by the only true teacher, experience. . . . True practice consists in the observations of nature: these are finer than any speculations. Hence the medicine of nature is more refined than the medicine of philosophy.[21]

James would have concurred absolutely, though whereas for Locke it was a matter of establishing empirical medicine as such, for James, nature, experience and philosophy became facets of a single diffuse set of problems which he encountered in a career that moved from medicine to psychology and from psychology to philosophy. There were differences, of course. The era of Romanticism stood between James and Locke. But however much he was to 'impeach' English empiricism, James's debt to it was fundamental though ambiguous.

John Stuart Mill was also important for James, not least in that Mill was the means by which the 'mental philosophy' of Locke and Hartley was preserved and modified in the nineteenth century. In 1872 James wrote to Renouvier, the man who was to deliver him from German mechanism and English materialism, that while the philosophy of Mill, Bain and Spencer carried all before it, its practical effect was both determinist and materialist.[22] More than philosophy, however, what attracted James to Mill may have been the life as revealed in the *Autobiography*. The emergence from nervous collapse, 'the state, I should think, in which converts to Methodism usually are, when smitten by their first "conviction of sin",' would have especially interested James, as well as Mill's 'conversion' when, as he recounts, the reading of Marmontel's *Mémoires* changed his life and enabled him to take on responsibilities for the family on his father's death.[23]

As for the late nineteenth-century English idealist philosophers, James was to use models of analysis derived from Darwin to attack the neo-Hegelians Edward Caird, T. H. Green and F. H. Bradley. These were the English philosophers who helped James map out his field of opposition and so, too, shaped his intellectual course.

Locke thought of literature as intellectual time off, but in James's life English literature played a large role. It was under the influence of H. G. Wells's *Harper's* article, 'Two Studies in Disappointment', that he seems, almost uniquely in his career, to praise the notion of abstract principle. Strangely he appears astonished that Wells has been able to put his finger precisely on what is wrong: 'Exactly that callousness to abstract justice is the sinister feature, and, to me as well as you, the incomprehensible feature of our U.S. Civilization'. Adams would have known better than either why it was 'incomprehensible'. Yet James will not let go of his medical model. The 'national disease', he continues to Wells, is the 'squalid cash interpretation put on the word success'. He praised Wells's *The Future in America* of 1906 as '*the* medical book about America'.[24] The American social future was to be therapeutic.

References to English writers abound in James's work, and they are often linked with his own views of life and above all of personality. Comparing Henry James Sr. with Carlyle he spoke of the 'smiting *Ursprünglichkeit* of intention' of both, their reliance on intuition not reason, and their 'deep humour'.[25] G.K. Chesterton, in spite of his 'mannerism of paradox' is praised for his remarks on 'success' in *Heretics*.[26] Kipling's *The Light that Failed* he saw was 'indecently true to nature', but he recognized, 'after all that my ethics and his novel were the same sort of thing.' He later met Kipling and in spite of the fact that the English novelist did not like 'Yankees', James called him a 'regular little brick of a man'.[27] Ruskin was the 'noblest of the sons of man', though one feels James preferred the art work to the writings.[28] But if Locke was the most influential English philosopher, Wordsworth, who wrote under his shadow, was the most significant English writer for James – and more so than Milton, whose *Paradise Lost* he used to learn by heart. Milton would, however, have prepared the way for Wordsworth.

Wordsworth's poetry took on the paradoxes of Lockean psychology: that vision of a world half created and half perceived. In Wordsworth's poetry the child develops behaviourally under Burkean stimuli of beauty and fear, and in adulthood identity becomes predicated on memory's view of the past, with Locke's logical identity becoming a mysticism of being. Inherent in this individualistic educational process is the empiricist paradox of the senses: at once Epicurean pleasure and the means by which character is formed. The bridges built over the sensationalist chasm of fact and understanding are memory, habit and reflection, underpinned by the doom-laden awareness of biological ageing. Wordsworth's *The Prelude* is the key poem of nineteenth-century middle-class sensibility. Progress towards death underwrote bourgeois melancholy and bourgeois will. The latter was inspired by visions of remembered innocence and pre-Tolstoyan moments of ecstatic insight. Its radical individualism had the effect of isolating 'character' from 'society', with stoic melancholy in the balance. These observations are not intended to 'explain' the poetry as such, but they may help align its *themes* with James's own sensibility. The trancendentalist tradition in America saw Wordsworth primarily as a religious poet, but it was another work of his which led James to claim the English poet's importance for his own life.

It was as a result of reading Wordsworth's 'The Excursion', in Italy in 1873, James wrote, that he finally felt himself

> ...in a permanent path, and it shows me how for our type of character, the growth of the whole dominates the particular moments. All my moments here are inferior to those in Italy, but they are parts of a long plan which is good, so they content me more than the Italian ones which only existed for themselves.

Perry, quoting this in his anthology, mentions the moment as being very important.[29] The idea that the whole dominates the parts is conceptually simple, but the results for James's philosophy were to be profound. Still casting about for a career, James seems to shun those Italian moments which, for the nineteenth-century American, might have represented a place at once of ancient sin and ancient pleasure. America was the place to recollect in tranquillity evidence of the senses encountered in Italy. The 'long plan' endows James with Wordsworth's 'more sober eye'.

James never perhaps reconciled the artist and the philosopher in himself. The one was taboo to the man of earnest life, the other was earnest but dull. Psychology, on the other hand, ran the risk of falling between the two stools. Whatever else may be said about James's encounter with literature, it almost certainly saved him from the oblivion other psychologists of his generation have fallen into. 'The Excursion' was a poem of the romantic figure of the wanderer, a figure perhaps more at home in German than in English literature. At any rate James had a deep knowledge of Germany and its culture, and it is that country which now claims our attention.

Germany, ever since the first Harvard professor of modern languages, George Ticknor, had gone to Göttingen to learn the language in 1815, had become the spiritual home of the American academy. In the nineteenth century a spell at a German university was *de rigueur* for an American scholar, and it was what chiefly distinguished the American university man from his English counterpart. What primarily appealed to James in Germany was a serious-mindedness, a sort of Düsseldorfian moral picturesqueness, and Prussian discipline (in moderation). James was deeply involved with the pyschological work of the great eighteenth-century German philosophers and later psychologists. References to Leibniz, Kant, Herbart, Hering, Lotze, Fechner, Helmholtz, Stumpf, Wundt, Ebbinghaus, G. E. Müller and Mach all found their way into James's *Principles of Psychology*, along with a number of lesser names. James read all of them, and met most of the living ones in person. In terms of the history of ideas James's theory of continuity between mind and body probably owes something to Leibniz, from whom came the seeds of 'parallelism' in psychological theory: the notion that the mind and body work by parallel laws. James was less sympathetic to Kant, who compromised between Lockean sensation and Leibnizian intellectual materiality and denied that the real could be known. As is well known, Kant substituted 'categories of understanding' which came from within: 'a priori *Ausschauungen*' (modes of appearance). In the twentieth century these modes of appearance became the psychological field of the Gestaltists.[30]

Kant's successor at Königsberg was Johann Friedrich Herbart, who rather like Jonathan Edwards held things together in such a way that, on his demise, they tended to fall apart. Herbart's 'psychology' was a synthesis of experience, philosophy, metaphysics and mathematics. From a contemporary psychologist's point of view the mixture seems somewhat contradictory, since Herbart insisted that mathematics dealt only with mental laws and not experimental data. Nonetheless, in separating physiology from psychology and mathematics from psychology, Herbart's work had several important results. In the first place 'psychology' was established as an academically acceptable discipline. Secondly it inherited also a set of internal contradictions. At Herbart's door can be placed both an intellectual ancestry for Pavlov's 'conditioned reflex', derivable from his notion that active ideas struggle for survival between the poles of inhibition and freedom, and Freudian repression. For Herbert no idea (*Vorstellung* – the nearest German equivalent to Locke's idea) is ever lost. It is only submerged and continually struggles, on the threshold of consciousness, for freedom. A machinery of the soul was to emerge from the contradictory directions in which Herbart's thought led.

For Herbart's successor at Göttingen, Rudolph Hermann Lotze, these mechanics of the soul became a physiological psychology. Lotze retained a philosophical view of physiological fact, however, and James cites him in *The Principles of Psychology* as holding a position opposed to his own: closer to Helmholtz's (Kantian) tendency to speak of unconscious inferences, and the synthetic impact of sensations. Lotze's position on the mind–body problem was tempered by his clearly medical biases. The overall tendency of his work placed ancient mind–body problems in an increasingly observational and above all clinical light.

Lotze had been trained in medicine, and so had the next and perhaps most important figure in German psychology generally. Gustav Theodor Fechner (1801–87) was one of James's heroes. It is easy to see why. Like James he was trained in medicine, he distrusted materialism, and wrote on aesthetics and Buddhism. Unlike James, he was interested in exploring the relations of mathematical physics and psychology. Overwork and poverty caused him to have a nervous breakdown while he was still in his thirties, a factor which, as in the case of Mill, may have drawn James to him. He is best remembered for his 'psycho–physics' and thus joins the ranks of those who sought for unified mind-body theories, much as the physical scientists of the mid-century sought a 'classical synthesis' for a grand theory of electricity, magnetism, light and gravity. Fechner secures his place in the history of psychology by his formulation of what came to be known as the 'Weber–Fechner law'. His starting-point was the old problem of the identity, correspondence, or parallelism of physical and mental life. James was to admire the metaphysics and damn the science. Positivist historians of experimental psychology, of course, reverse the evaluation, praising Fechner for pioneering psychology along statistical lines from a position of 'neutral' observation.

When James went to Germany in 1868, his aim was to study with the great Helmholtz and Wundt. Helmholtz, one of the greatest German scientists of the nineteenth century, also began life in medicine and surgery and first became distinguished in physiology. The impact of physiology – in which James also began his career as an instructor – on nineteenth-century psychology was overwhelming. The French scientist Magendie had already established the distinction between the motor and sensory nerves by cutting nerve roots in the spinal cord. Paralysis, he observed, accompanied cutting off the anterior but not the posterior root. The result was to provide a physiological basis for the distinction between nerves for sensation and movement. Parallel to this work was research on the brain. Researchers were increasingly able to localize different physiological functions in different areas of the cerebrum. More and more the philosophical notion of sensations as intermediaries seemed to receive experimental proof, whether investigated by Kantians like Johannes Müller, who was instrumental in establishing physiology as an independent science, or by an empiricist (with some Kantian traces) like Helmholtz.

For James the results of German work in the field were on the whole chilling. As he wrote on his honeymoon to the American professor. Francis J. Child:

> The only Psyche now recognized by science is a decapitated frog whose writhings express deeper truths than your weakminded poets ever dreamed. She (not Psyche but the bride) loves all these doctrines which are quite novel to her mind, hitherto accustomed to all sorts of mysticism and superstitions. She swears entirely by reflex action now, and believes in universal *Notwendigkeit*.[31]

The problems of Psyche and motor and behavioural paths were to haunt James through at least the first chapter of *The Principles* not without unintentional Gothic effects.

Helmholtz was interested in physiology from the standpoint of physics, and psychology from the standpoint of both. The result was two classics of physiological psychology: *A Handbook of Physiological Optics* (1856–67) and *On the Sensations of Tone* (1862). Wordsworth's 'mighty world of ear and eye' was investigated on the principle that 'no other forms than the common physical and chemical ones are active within the organism'.[32] Using the opthalmoscope (which he invented), Helmholtz turned the observing eye on its own functions and structure. Most of him was severely empirical. He argued for example that geometrical axioms were the product of experience. James's encounter with Helmholtz in the *Principles* is one of the most interesting in the whole work. James accuses him of a certain lack of 'empiricist' rigour in the *Optics*, but it is precisely Helmholtz's adoption of the notion of unconscious inferences that makes him so valuable in contemporary theories of perception.

Helmholtz was not in fact a psychologist as such, though he made important contributions to the psychology of space, colour and tone perception. Wilhelm Wundt (1832–1920), however, is reckoned by the empirico-behavioural school to be the father of modern psychology. Wundt's reaction to James's *Principles* (James hit him fairly hard in several places), that it was more a work of literature than psychology, illustrates one of the first uses of the word 'literature' to designate intellectual sloppiness, a tendency by no means absent in behaviourists of the recent past.[33] Wundt, for James, was the model of the German professor, a Napoleon without genius, 'a being whose duty is to know everything, and have his own opinion about everything, connected with his *Fach*. . . a finished example of how much *mere* education can do for a man'.[34] James's lively protrait of 1887 in a letter to Stumpf is worth reading *in toto*, for it applies to many a character in our contemporary professionalized universities. Even that severely positivist historian of psychology, E. G. Boring, called Wundt a man 'unrelieved by fun and jollity'.[35] Nonetheless there is a degree of unfairness in these characterizations, and now that Boring's hugely detailed work on the history of psychology is being challenged for its overly empiricist bias, Wundt's other interests and qualities are being brought forward to give a rather different view of the man.

Perhaps James was reacting to the fact that Wundt took the fact of consciousness for granted; and that his *Völkerpsychologie*, which was a study of the 'social' (customs, ritual, institutions, family, tribal relations), insisted on the 'social determinants' of thought. Daniel N. Robinson, whose argument is followed here, has even suggested that throughout his career Wundt stood 'as the champion of an experimental psychology of individual consciousness, and as something of a reluctant Hegelian in his treatments of the human will, human society and human history'.[36] This would have been enough to make James suspicious of him. It is something less than disingenuous, therefore, to present Wundt as a dogmatic empiricist. Like Helmholtz he began in medicine and physiology, and his major work was on 'physiological-psychology', which he revised many times between 1873 and 1911. In Wundt a version of English empirical philosophy becomes adapted to the experimental psychological laboratory. Wundt obliterated the distinction between 'inner' and 'outer' experience. Physics and psychology, material and immaterial, differed only in the viewpoints taken of them.

However accurate his assumptions were, James took much the same attitude to these forerunners of experimental psychology as Melville had to the German higher critics of the Bible. There was a sense of loss and of admiration combined. However, there were other German psychologists, men like Hering, Brentano, Stumpf and Mach, whose work may be seen as foreshadowing the Gestalt psychologists and even the phenomenological psychologists of the modern era. James was to maintain a correspondence with Stumpf, whose ideas on 'space perception' had taken his attention. Stumpf owed his philosophical bias to Hering, who argued that space perception is intuited rather than learned. Like Husserl, the phenomenologist who saw in James's work foreshadowings of his own, Stumpf was a pupil of Brentano, who represented a kind of reaction to the severely experimental Leipzig school.

As with Charles Sanders Peirce, there was something of the medieval schoolman in Stumpf. Music, as in the Middle Ages, was the greatest of the arts. In his work physics, mathematics, sensations, physiology, psychology, the emotions, and ethnology are all incorporated into a search for a philosophical logic of sound. But his musical expertise demanded that he think both theoretically and emotionally. His famous quarrel with Wundt was an illustration of the fact that expert musicianship led to better results in studying the phenomenon of sound than unenlightened 'experimental method'. His personal memoir tells us that he met his wife through music: 'Beethoven's great, wonderful trio in B minor had brought us together.'[37]

Finally Brentano, whose life as a radical Catholic has its own intrinsic interest, took psychology back to philosophy by distinguishing between experience as 'structure', and experience as 'act'. The act of seeing, he argued, is different from the object of seeing and is the province of psychology. Significantly, 'feeling' is no longer a 'content', but the very basis from which the mind takes hold of the world. As Watson puts it, 'loving-hating is the motivating source of psychic life.'[38] Brentano's 'act-psychology' also quickly established itself in opposition to Wundt's experimental psychology.

As far as the psychologist in James was concerned the German experience was early and profound. It is also relatively easy to document, given the length at which James summarized current German work in the *Principles*. Less easy to document is the effect of German literature. He did not think much of German criticism, but in an early letter to his parents from Germany he spoke, somewhat dutifully perhaps, of 'the enthusiastic, oratorical and eloquent Schiller, the wise and exquisite Goethe, and the virile and human Lessing [who] have in turn held me entranced by their Drama'.[39] In the same year, 1867, he wrote a notice which was published in *The Nation* of Professor Herman Grimm's *Unüberwindliche Machte*.[40] His dislike of Hegel, including the *Aesthetics*, was early, and continued throughout his life. One senses he did not like Nietzsche, whose political sensibilities he accurately perceived were autocratic.[41] Goethe, however, after an initial uncertainty, was his great love. It was the eighteenth-century Goethe that seemed to have appealed to him, someone whom he could place with Wordsworth on the primacy of 'sensation':

> The man lived at every pore of his skin, and the tranquil clearness and vividness with which everything painted itself on the sensor- ium, and found a cool nook in his mind without interfering with any of the other denizens thereof, must have been one of the most exquisite spectacles ever on exhibition on this planet.[42]

James's stay in Germany, for all the effect it had later in his career, was not a happy one. The loneliness of the foreign student can be readily imagined, as can the temperamental antipathy to the mechanisms of Wundtian philosophy. As for so many American intellectuals, from Jefferson to the present day, it was French philosophers who seemed to offer a way out.

'To Descartes belongs the credit of having first been bold enough to conceive of a completely self-sufficing nervous mechanism which should be able to perform complicated and apparently intelligent acts' – so James wrote in The *Principles of Psychology*, adding that Descartes had not thought to extend his observation beyond the animal kingdom. James enlisted Locke against Cartesian conscious- ness, stating that the pages in which Locke attacks the Cartesian belief are 'as spirited as any in his *Essay*'.[43] Later James was to reject Descartes's 'substantialist' view of the soul, which he held in common with many other philosophers: not as being untrue, but unnecessary. It was indeed Descartes, as much as Locke, who stood behind nineteenth-century psychology and for precisely the reason which James gives. The basic philosophical problems dogged nineteenth-century psychology as much as they still dog our own psychologies. It was Descartes who placed thinking at the centre of problems of existence and knowledge; as has already been shown, Adams thought that James himself had scarcely solved the issues. The paradox was that mind itself was unknowable; but since both organic and inorganc matter possessed the geometric properties of

length, breadth and depth, theoretically there was no distinction
between the two. Descartes could rely ultimately on a metaphysic.
James felt himself obliged, in the name of science, to give no
appearance of having one.

It is, then, in questions of mind-body dualism that Descartes is
important for the history of psychology. It is worth remembering
that Descartes's mechanistic view of human physiology and behaviour was in part encouraged by his experience of automata,
operated by water fountains in the French royal gardens. Neptune
shook his trident when the unsuspecting visitor stepped on a hidden
pedal: a moment which was no doubt accompanied by derisive
aristocratic laughter. Descartes thought that human behaviour could
be explained similarly, by hidden, mechanistic springs of action.
Mind and body were thought to be connected by 'vital spirits' which
passed from the heart through the brain to the muscles. Habit and
custom made artificial connections between mind and body, the
point of interaction being the pineal gland: 'Descartes, as is well
known, thought that the inextended soul was immediately present to
the pineal gland.'[44]

Descartes insisted on dualism. Mind and body had different
functions, 'the heat and movement of the members proceed from the
body, the thoughts from the soul'.[45] Thus the one could contemplate
the other. The effect was to give the observing eye a kind of
neutrality, and the body itself the appearance of a machine
responding to stimuli.

Descartes illustrated the principle with an image which was to
haunt the psychological textbooks: a man, or in James's *Principles* a
child, burnt by fire. Here for psychologists is the first moment of
knowledge which leads to survival. 'Educating the hemispheres',
James called it in his first chapter in the *Principles*, where he is already
straining to narrow the gap between 'lower centres' and 'hemispheres'.

By quoting Bachelard it is possible to throw a question mark over
the whole set of assumptions in this grotesque image of a child
'learning' by being burnt by fire:

> . . . fire is initially the object of a general prohibition; hence this
> conclusion: the social interdiction is our first knowledge of fire.
> What we first learn about fire is that we must not touch it. As the
> child grows up, the prohibitions become intellectual rather than
> physical: the blow of the ruler is replaced by the angry voice; the
> angry voice by the recital of the dangers of fire, by the legends
> concerning fire from heaven. Thus the natural phenomenon is
> rapidly mixed in with complex and confused items of social

experience which leave little room for the acquiring of an unpre-
judiced knowledge.[46]

All that is necessary to add here is that deep within the vision of the
body as a machine is an impulse towards authority and control.

From its first beginnings psychology is a Janus-faced science. It is
possible to regard reflex action as a vitalist or mechanist action: secret
and open simultaneously. Aarslef's comments on Condillac's mechanical statue are relevant here. He argues that it does not offer a
purely materialist and mechanistic conception of man: 'the statue is a
structural device designed to show that the sensations suffice to
produce a habitual and instinctive assurance of the existence of the
outside world', and he further quotes from Condillac's *Essai*:

> Thus when I treat the ideas that the statue acquires, I do not mean
> to say that it has knowledge of which it can render an exact
> account to itself: it has only practical knowledge. All the light it
> has is properly speaking instinctive, that is to say, a habit of
> conducting itself according to ideas of which it does not know
> how to render account to itself.... To acquire knowledge of
> theory, it is necessary to have language....[47]

This passage anticipates a set of problems which will be taken up
from many diverse perspectives. What is instinct? Practical knowledge, or unreflected action? James was forced to confront these very
issues. The problem of language also is crucial and it will be
re-examined later in the discussion of James's famous 'stream of
thought' image. Indeed what sort of a person is the mechanized man?
The right-wing philosopher–physician La Mettrie was to prove in
the eighteenth century that the mind–body mechanism existed by
observing that the facial muscles of a beheaded prisoner continued to
twitch.[48] For mechanism involves many interconnected questions
about the relation of mind and body, of reflex action, of the relation
of motor to sensory response, not to mention old questions of will
and freedom. Certain it is that absolute dualism cannot be maintained. As R. D. Laing once said: 'The cut-off cannot be seen by the
cut-off mind.'[49]

Cartesian mechanism drew the attention of subsequent psychologists to the nervous system itself, for which, in turn, models were
sought in physiological structure. The result, from the mechanist–
vitalist debates of the eighteenth century to the behaviourist/
psychoanalytic debates of the twentieth century, has been that
psychology occupies a divided kingdom. The role of the subject, reflective intelligence, automatism, unconscious drives, conditioning,

cognitive development, knowledge and its validation are still key issues in psychology.

As a place to be, James did not take to France as he took to England, Germany and indeed Switzerland. He once wrote, 'Otis Place is better than Languedoc and Irving Street than Provence.'[50] Early in his life he found George Sand morbidly introspective and Balzac's *Modeste Mignon* 'so diseased morally [*sic*] I could not finish it'. However, later in his life he could speak of Sand's *Histoire* and her letters, with the revelations of the Musset episode, as 'beautiful and uplifting'. Sand was 'an "absolute liver" harmoniously leading her own life and neither obedient nor defiant to what others expected or thought'.[51] Of Zola's *Germinal* he said that it was 'a truly magnificent work, if successfully to reproduce the horror and pity of certain human facts and make you see them as if real can make a book magnificent'.[52]

Catholic France, it is clear, had its darker side for the Protestant Harvard man. Nonetheless the handful of French intellectuals whom James came to know were very important. The principal ones were Renouvier, François Pillon to whom he dedicated the *Principles*, Henri Bergson, Emile Boutroux and Pierre Janet. The last two he met relatively late in life, and Bergson was not an influence but someone whose work James discovered with a sense of recognition, as having parallels with his own. It is Renouvier who is the most important. It is well known that James claimed that Renouvier's work pulled him out of depression towards that Carlylean 'everlasting yea', though Schwen plausibly argues that his marriage to Alice Gibbens was probably more important, and made him a 'healthy man'.[53]

From Renouvier James drew the notion that philosophy is a question of temperament defined within psychological process. For all its scientific apparatus, this was to be the overall message of the *Principles*. From Renouvier also James got his structural pattern of arguing dualistically: philosophy is pushed into 'either–or' positions and helped out by psychology – generally in terms of a suspended judgement. Renouvier's philosophy of faith and risk was to become the foundation of pragmatism. It will be shown later, too, that Renouvier's philosophy had a profound effect on Durkheim and thus helped underwrite that notion of 'society' which is the sustaining metaphysic of Jamesian individualism. In addition Renouvier's doctrine of phenomena apprehended in shifting relations led to pluralism. James wrote in his diary for 30 April 1870:

> I think that yesterday was a crisis in my life. I finished the first part
> of Renouvier's second *Essais* and see no reason why his definition

of free will – 'the sustaining of a thought because I choose to when I have other thoughts' – need be the definition of an illusion. At any rate, I will assume for the present – until next year – that it is no illusion. My first act of free will shall be to believe in free will.[54]

James also discussed Henri Bergson at length in *A Pluralistic Universe*. He had 'killed intellectualism definitely and without hope of recovery'. He liked Bergson for setting limits to logic, for his notion of flux, the *'devenir réel* by which the thing evolves and grows', and for his intuitive sympathy with things.[55] Both men had an ability to move between philosophy, science and psychology (for example, Bergson wrote to James that his 'unconscious' was analogous to the as yet unperceived nature of matter), and both men were committed to what Sartre has called the 'illusion of immanence' by assigning a cognitive role to concepts and to immediate experience.[56] Both men exploited evolutionary theory, though Bergson's treatment of it stressed vitalistic possibilities. James was more interested in adaptiveness and chance. Both attempted to get rid of subject–object dualisms, both emphasized continuity. There was, said Bergson, in James 'Un ardent foyer. . . dont on recevrait chaleur et lumière'.[57]

Both Bergson and James, in Adorno's words, 'postulated an immediate–intuitive awareness, of the living against conceptual–classificatory thought', an awareness which bears ready comparison with Husserl's 'essential insight'. Here in Adorno's critique of Bergson are some of the questions which can also be addressed to James. In his emphasis on intuitive, immediate experience did James also see it like 'thunder from heaven'? Adorno insists that 'intuition' is not a simple antithesis to logic:

> Whatever is at work in rational cognition also enters into inspirations – sedimented and newly remembered – in order to turn for an instant against all the devices over whose shadow thought by itself cannot leap. Discontinuity in intuition does honour to continuity falsified by organization.[58]

The question of continuity will be important. James, antipathetic to anything approaching dialectics, will give some strange answers. In view of recent attempts to haul him into the phenomenologists' camp, his account of experience and method will have to be looked at carefully.

The three major European countries, England, Germany, and France, by no means constitute the sum of James's contact with cultures other than American. He had friends and contacts in Italy and Switzerland. Tolstoy was a favourite author. It may be imagined that the liberal Christian structure of Tolstoy's conflicted heroes would have appealed to James, no less than that Tolstoyan moment in which ecstasy lights up a world rich and dense in its complexities but closed and claustrophobic in its individual possibilities. Dostoevsky's depiction of abnormal states must have appealed to the psychologist. Throughout James's encounter with American and European intellectual traditions there runs a thread which must now be exposed more clearly. What claims did the somewhat heterogeneous emergent discourses of psychology have to describing the minds and bodies of human beings? James's conclusions were to lie in the direction of the therapeutic, and the issues of medicine, mechanization and society will now be theorized more closely.

It was Mark Twain who, in *Huckleberry Finn*, summed up a contemporary division of interests among professionals that is of some relevance to James: 'Revd Hobson and Dr Robinson was down to the end of the town, a–hunting together; that is, I mean the doctor was shipping a sick man to t'other world, and the preacher was pinting him right.'[59]

After returning from Brazil in 1866, James entered the Harvard Medical School. On the law faculty at Harvard was Oliver Wendell Holmes. The Holmes family was on intimate terms with the James family. O. W. Holmes Jr., the Supreme Court Justice, was a life-long friend of William James, and Holmes Sr., who was not only a distinguished physician and a novelist of some standing but a lively essayist, noted for shrewdness and wit, anticipated in many ways the complex of problems to which James addressed himself. These were fundamentally psychological problems and stemmed from that breakdown in the discourse of social and moral understanding made acute in New England by the death of God.

One moment from a long correspondence between Harriet Beecher Stowe and the elder Holmes illustrates the point. Mrs Stowe wrote to Holmes about his novel *Elsie Venner* (1861), which is about an erstwhile New England medical student confronted with a genetically determined *femme fatale*, expressing

> . . . an intense curiosity concerning that underworld of thought from which, like bubbles, your incidents and remarks often seem to burst up. The foundations of moral responsibility, the interlacing laws of nature and spirit, and their relations to us here and hereafter, are topics which I ponder more and more, and on which only one medically educated can write well. I think a course of medical study ought to be required of all ministers.[60]

The shift of moral authority is from minister to doctor, who now has a more expert psychological brief on the 'interlacing laws of nature

and spirit'. For the doctor that dualism translated itself into a very
ancient problem of definition: Was medicine a science or an art?
Holmes, who had saved the lives of hundreds of women in childbirth
by insisting that puerperal fever was a result of unhygienic conditions, was sceptical of science as such. With the exception of opium,
wine and the 'vapours which produce the miracle of anaesthesia',
wrote the 'amiable autocrat', 'I firmly believe that if the whole
materia medica, as now used, could be sunk to the bottom of the sea, it
would be all the better for mankind – and all the worse for the
fishes.'[61] Holmes had already addressed the problem of doctors in
Elsie Venner, especially in chapter 22 of that novel entitled 'Why
Doctors Differ'.

The doctor stood at the intersection of art and science, society and
the patient. Was the authority scientific, moral, social or technical?
Henry James's thoughts on the matter can be gauged from the
account of Dr Sloper in *Washington Square*. James opens his novel by
outlining the great prestige of medicine in the United States, and in a
typical reversal the rest of the novel ironically denies that this
phenomenon is a 'healthy' state of affairs. Medicine, James explains,
is honoured because it is liberal, and this liberalness draws on two
sources of credit: practicality and science. 'It was an element in Dr
Sloper's reputation that his learning and his skill were evenly
balanced; he was what you might call a scholarly doctor, and yet
there was nothing abstract in his remedies – he always asked you to
take something.' Just as William James insisted that theology and
religion should be kept apart, Henry appeared to feel that the art of
doctoring and science should be kept apart. In the novel the scientific
doctor has lost his wife and destroys his daughter's happiness
thought his authoritarian paternalism. Henry James's ironies cut two
ways, however, and perhaps there is more than a hint of a criticism
of his brother's advocacy of 'experience' when he continues, 'he [Dr
Sloper] was an observer. . . even a philosopher. . . . He admired
experience and in twenty years he got a good deal.'[62]

Medicine in short inherited all the previous problems of theology.
In the words of a contemporary doctor–priest: 'medicine is a moral
enterprise and therefore inevitably gives content to good and evil. In
every society, medicine, like law and religion, defines what is
normal, proper, or desirable.'[63] In our own time there have been
many commentators on the precise configurations of social and
political meanings, epistemologies, attitudes to science and technology, various psychologies, economic patterns, class and sexual attitudes inherent in society's perception of the art and science of
medicine. Medicine tells us how society sees itself. Illich speaks of
the 'intensity of an engineering endeavour that has translated human

survival from the performance of organisms into the result of technical manipulation', of how 'diagnosis' characterizes the 'other' in peremptory and inhuman ways, how professional power is the result of power politically delegated to the class of university élites, how permission to act beyond traditional authority is guaranteed by the 'ritualization of crisis', how even any form of suffering or attempts to cope with it outside permitted patient–doctor roles are labelled 'deviant', how our very deaths are taken away from us in a process which Illich sums up as a 'medicalization of life'.[64]

James himself incurred the wrath of the Harvard Medical School in 1898 when he defended the plurality of medical truths in a public hearing at the Boston Court House. He spoke out for the right of Christian Scientists and others not to take the proposed legally required professional medical examination. He opposed the religion of certified science in the service of professionalism because it limited the field and practice of medicine as such, whether or not the Christian Scientists themselves were also guilty of authoritarian practices.

The implications of being robbed of our deaths, as Rilke would have put it, are also partially outlined in a statement by Foucault: '. . . from the experience of Unreason was born psychology, the very possibility of psychology; from the integration of death into medical thought is born a medicine that is given as a science of the individual.' The capacity to see ourselves as subject and object is a historical phenomenon and implicit in the philosophies of both Descartes and Locke. However, Foucault describes how Descartes's faith in a world lit by a geometry of light is replaced by a more opaque world which is surveyed by a slow gaze conveying its own light. It establishes essence. Since the object may now equally be a subject, clinical experience is possible: 'one could at last hold a scientifically structured discourse about an individual.'[65] The more mechanistic aspects of Descartes's thought led to the science of mind of the late nineteenth century, and James was to face a contemporary choice between theories of will and the science of mind, 'Whereas all the phenomena of nature could be likened to a machine, the soul, and especially its noblest attitude, the will, resisted the simile.'[66]

A belief in perpetual discovery and perpetual innocence also characterizes the experimenter. It was most completely expressed by the eighteenth-century physician Jenner: 'Why think? Why not experiment?'[67] Most important of all, however, is the development of the method of technique. Foucault's description of what Illich calls engineering 'the dreams of reason' is relevant to his discussion of clinical uncertainty. Uncertainty could now be treated analytically as 'the sum of a certain number of isolatable degrees of certainty that were capable of rigorous calculation'. As a result the object of perception itself became a 'modal event'. The uncertain evolution of the disease could be expressed in an aleatory series. Here Lockean probability moves into clinical practice. Philosophically the 'combinative variety of the single forms constitutes empirical diversity'.[68]

Foucault describes crucial changes in the social description of disease, with family medicine, individual perception, a medicine of spaces and classes changing to clinical experience, a new notion of collective perception, and a concern with time and a free field of enquiry. After the Revolutionary period in France the new role of medicine is that of establishing health, virtue and happiness in the State. Illich's description of the culmination of the process, the modern origins of which are uncovered by Foucault, is more direct and less structurally discursive and opaque. These sophisticated contemporary critics give philosophic and social accounts of what novelists from Mary Shelley to William Burroughs have described as that face of evil when secret knowledge becomes its own authority and manipulates the needs of others in cold blood. Illich speaks of the 'depersonalization of diagnosis and therapy' which has 'changed malpractice from an ethical into a technical problem', and a shift in the sensibility of the servants of state so that 'until proved healthy, the citizen is now presumed to be sick'.[69] The parody of legal language here reminds us of the potentially colossal misuse of power which the phenomenon involves.

Teasing out the details of this historical shift of sensibility is, however, difficult. Dewhurst's book on Locke as a physician helps to trace moments of convergence between philosophy, science and medical practice which will be of help in looking at James's many layered texts. Dewhurst argues convincingly that it was not so much Boylean atomic theory that influenced Locke's philosophy as the practice of the Boylean laboratory and Sydenham's clinical emphases which were most significant. Thomas Sydenham, as ex-cavalry officer and 'essentially a man of action', was suspicious of speculative theories and declared:

> True knowledge grew first in the world by experience and rational observation, but proud man, not content with the knowledge he was capable of, and which was useful to him, would needs penetrate into the hidden causes of things, lay down principles, and establish maxims to himself about the operations of nature, and thus vainly expect that nature, or in truth God should proceed according to those laws which his maxims had prescribed to him.[70]

The traditional rift between clinical medicine and experimental science is clearly observable here. Both Locke and Sydenham apparently were selective about what 'hidden' causes they looked into.

Anatomical dissection did not attract them, studying the body's secretions did. Was it simply a preference for bodies whose movements could be observed in life, rather than for dead bodies which were as inert as the principles they warned against?

When Matthew Baillie published the great *Morbid Anatomy* in 1793 it was accompanied by a series of engravings. The figure illustrating emphysema depicts the lung of Samuel Johnson.[71] The moment can be used symbolically to introduce, or rather anticipate, problems of language which will become more and more important to the argument. The anatomist and the compiler of dictionaries proceed on atomistic principles. In a dictionary words are isolated without breath, as in anatomy the parts of the body are isolated without life. The respective relations of the morbid anatomy and the dictionary to life and speech involve an intervention not only of philosophy but of language itself. The clinic and the schoolroom connect statement with perception. In medicine the doctor and the philosopher, Foucault argues, meet on common ground: 'The doctor's discursive, reflective perception and the philosopher's discursive reflection on a perception come together in a figure of exact superposition since the world is for them the analogue of language.'[72]

As both a doctor and a philosopher Locke's reflections on language are of relevance here. Writing under the shadow of the scientific revolution, Locke's task was to a degree more difficult and more Herculean than it had been even for Francis Bacon. Locke's insistence on the 'social' basis of language's intelligibility is fundamental. As with the late nineteenth-century linguists, Locke's view of language was instrumental. Like them he saw social habit as the means of forging the bond between the sound and the idea. A tendency towards a synchronic view of language is implicit in Locke's view of linguistic epistemology: 'Words become general, by being made the signs of general Ideas: and Ideas become general, by separating from the circumstances of Time, and Place, and any other Ideas, that may determine them to this or that particular Existence.'[73] On other occasions Locke's comments verge on the idealistic. It is in the 'power of Words, standing for the several Ideas, that make that Composition, to imprint complex Ideas in the Mind, which were never there before, and so make their Names be understood' (*Essay*, p. 425). This understanding comes without reference to a particular society or an accustomed bond. Locke was, of course, faced with a new world of science which was making reality unavailable to common sense and to ordinary language.

Paradoxically however, it is in the moral and ethical domain that Locke is most concerned with the inadequacy of language. It is the names of 'Mixed Modes' (where Ideas are presented to the mind and the mind works on them) that give him most trouble. He could envisage a kind of correspondence, truth guaranteeing the accuracy of language *vis-à-vis* substances, but such a correspondence – although he could pay lip-service to it – was not so easy to perceive in descriptions of the human world. In this world the Mind 'takes a liberty not to follow the Existence of Things exactly' (p. 429). Again, how you follow exactly or not something that cannot be known is something of a mystery. There is a world of controversy in the word 'exactly'. Locke, one of the founding fathers of empiricism, is forced to create an 'Archetype' to name what we cannot experience. What we cannot experience is for most of us, interestingly, deviance and crime. Empiricist by temperament, as James would have said, Locke makes his archetypal namings of unexperienceable actions seem like a Gothic revenge on the clear language of science, for his 'mixed modes' include Murder, Parricide and Incest.

Behind Locke's scepticism about the efficacy of language in the moral sphere stands the religious and political turmoil of his own era. Locke's views on language cannot be separated from his attempts to hold a latitudinarian centre between the freely democratic scrutiny of the word by the sects and the tradition-bound commentaries of Catholicism. Locke's own diatribe against 'huffing Opinions' (p. 438) must be seen in this light. His advocacy of moderate manner and behaviour in relation to language practice, while of obvious pragmatic value, may also be seen as something of a diversionary tactic against the actual content of social meanings in genuine contention.

Locke's more pressing concern, however, was to try and adjust thoughts on language to the needs of science, and then to reflect on the implications of that for social discourse. His real achievement is to separate naming from essence and thus to confer on naming a heuristic possibility:

> . . . all we can do, is to collect such a number of simple Ideas, as by Examination, we find to be united together in Things existing, and thereof to make one complex Idea. Which though it be not the real Essence of any Substance that exists, is yet the specifick Essence, to which our Name belongs, and is convertible with it; by which we may at least Try the Truth of these nominal Essences. . . . (449–50)

(*Essay*, pp. 449–50)

Idea (a word that has multiple meanings in Locke) is thus here the prospective essence that may be named (unlike Things) in the trying of truth.

In spite of the empiricist pressure towards absolute clarity, Locke
is aware of the richness and diversity of language operations, and
sometimes in surprisingly modern ways. For he has the advantage of
empiricist introspection as well as the disadvantage of empiricist
metaphysic. Nowhere is this more striking than in his discussion of
grammar. He rejects the dictionary approach and in his discussion of
particles, for example, he demonstrates that the variety of semantic
implications of individual words is a result of the way they work
within the entire sentence. Just as the perspective of the entire
sentence can alter the individual parts of speech, so individual parts
of speech can take on the meaning of the proposition sentence
(p. 479).

Locke is, however, more democratic in terms of science than he
is in terms of civil discourse. There is no sense of words Trying
(testing) truth in Civil Discourse as there is in Philosophical Discourse. Instead he becomes more and more insistent about clarity.
Again one has to go outside the text for reasons. In the discourses
of law, religion and morality Locke concedes the problems are immense. His response to this is almost to abandon the notion that
language can be a means to truth. Maintaining that we have
'sufficient reason' to interpret the 'legible characters' (that is, non-
written ones) of God's Works and Providence, Locke argues on the
basis of his 'Natural Religion' that we do not in fact need books and
languages to understand religious and moral truth (p. 490). As a
polemical gesture in the weariness of religious dispute his statement is understandable. Apart from that it is extremely dangerous,
since it bars this kind of truth from all discussion. A certain anti-
intellectualism creeps in, a phenomenon which will be characteristic
as well of James's discussions of religion. The language of natural
religion bypasses that social use of language on which Locke has
previously insisted.

Mid-way between the inexpressibleness of religion and the clarity
of science lies the complicated human world and the concerned
figure of the doctor, defeated by language, and poised between
science and art. 'Society' is clearly more open to biological than to
physical analysis, but even in biological discourse there are insuper-
able problems. One problematic word is the word 'life' itself.
Locke's choice of the difficult word was not arbitrary, it would have
been fundamental to his clinical practice:

Life is a Term, none more familiar. Any one almost would take
for an Affront, to be asked what he meant by it. And yet if it
comes in Question, whether a Plant, that lies ready formed in the
Seed, have Life, whether the Embrio in an Egg before Incubation,

or a Man in a Swound before Sense or Motion, be alive, or no, it is easy to perceive, that a clear distinct settled Idea does not always accompany the Use of so known a Word, as that of Life is.

(*Essay*, p. 503)

The *Essay* is the liberal classic of the English seventeenth century, directed to the feelings and sentiments of the rising bourgeoisie and mercantile trader. Could Locke's lively colloquial writing (as James's after him) with its business metaphors, 'propriety of speech' and 'clear notions' as a 'common measure of Commerce and Communication' (p. 514), encompass the complexity of 'Life' itself?

Locke ironically presents himself as likely to fail in this aim since 'Eloquence, like the fair Sex, has too prevailing Beauties in it, to suffer itself ever to be spoken against' (p. 508). Passion produces only lies, and pleasure only deceit. There is a Puritanism in Locke and a fear of letting go of a 'centre' which is in fact just as amenable to criticism as the sects and the Catholics. Maurice Cranston has argued that Locke is a representative of the new mercantile England. Indeed his great patron Lord Ashley was the 'complete progressive capitalist in politics; he might almost have been invented by Karl Marx'.[74]

Locke knew that while nature is given, 'tis Men...who range them into Sorts, in order to their naming' (*Essay*, p. 462), and he knew also that the world, whether it was gold in its differing states, or species in their multiplicity, was hard of definition. Living in a period of rapid social change, Locke's brilliant notion of nominal essences open to the act of naming secured him the advantages of the ontological act of setting the world at a distance, without himself being accused of arrogance or essentialism. At the same time, in the human world this same notion registered his doubts relative to individual passion and to social cohesion. Clarity seemed challenged everywhere, and posed particular and peculiar difficulties to biologist and medical man alike. One wonders whether Darwin, who of course abandoned the notion of fixed design but was also an inveterate speculator on philosophical subjects, ever read the following in the *Essay*:

There are Fishes that have Wings, and are no Strangers to the airy Region: and there are some Birds that are Inhabitants of the Water; whose Blood is cold as Fishes.... There are Animals so near of kin both to Birds and Beasts, that they are in the middle between both: Amphibious Animals link the Terrestrial and Aquatique together; Seals live at Land and at Sea, and Porpoises have the warm Blood and Entrails of a Hog, not to mention what is confidently reported of Mermaids, or Sea-men.

(*Essay*, p. 447)

James, the Darwinist and reader of Locke, was, like both his English predecessors, concerned about the crucial issues of physical and mental classifications in relation to human beings. In the next chapter the relevance of these multiple problems of definition, of bodily and psychological authority, legitimations of social and psychological practice through scientific discourse, problems of the normative assumptions of professionals, and the relation of epistemological questions of psychological judgements, will be taken up in relation to the Darwinian revolution. The problems relating specifically to language will be held over, and dealt with in Part Three.

Chapter 8
Philosophizing a Social Pathology:
Agassiz, Darwin; Adams, James

The importance of the Darwinian revolution lay in multiple transformations of every sphere of intellectual life. Through James and
others it had a powerful influence on American psychology, and
through the pragmatists as a whole, on American philosophy. It had
historical importance for biology, not only for its revolutionary
theory of natural selection but also for biology's attempt to free itself
from the prestigious science of physical mechanics in order to
establish a right to describe the world. Its challenge to religious
views of the world is well known or, more accurately, well ad-
vertised. In social thought the impact was various and had more
effects than can be lumped under 'social Darwinism'. It is proposed
here only to examine a few of the moments of this revolution, which
continues to provoke controversy in all fields even in our own time,
and to direct that examination in the first instance to a last comparison of Adams and James, and then towards James's work as a
whole.

I

Locke and Darwin have already been compared on the score of
classification and naming. There are many other points of comparison between the English empiricists and Darwin. Greta Jones has
argued that the role of sensation and experience in creating ideas is at
the heart of Darwinian biology and social theory, and further that
Darwin used associationist psychology as the 'mechanism by which
these initial attributes in the animal became the sophisticated
apparatus of human faculty'.[1] Locke's clinical experience had already
helped to shape the interaction of biology, philosophy and social
practice. His theory of language presupposed a steady state of what
might be called linguistic organism, a notion which would find its
way through Darwin to Saussure in the late nineteenth century.
Perhaps Lockean probability helped form a strand in Darwin's

populationist theories. Like Locke Darwin relied on analogy, and he thought that linguistic parallels were of significance to his general argument. Darwin was also once a medical student and he appears to have enjoyed actual scientific experimentation about as much as Locke and James. It is not without significance for Darwin's and James's psychology that in 1827, at an Edinburgh University club called the Plinian Society which Darwin attended, 'a certain Mr Gray had submitted his theory that "the lower animals possess every faculty and propensity of the human mind', and that one W. A. Browne proposed that the mind and thus consciousness had an entirely material basis.[2] While Darwin's work was a conscious effort to break with the physical sciences, it continued consciously or unconsciously its common links with English social and psychological thought.[3]

In the United States the American school of evolutionism tended to stress the internal factors of development (authogenesis) and a 'regular, goal-directed process of individual growth'.[4] This clearly had ideological implications. The socialist Wallace, by contrast, had observed badly adapted species in the forests of the Amazon which had, for him, ruled out regularity and equilibrium in nature. Indeed Darwin's followers could use various combinations of internal and external factors (genetic/environmental) to justify almost any ideological requirement. They could use explanations according to nature as they had always been used, to challenge fixed hierarchy as well as to justify social order.[5] Recent work has questioned previous all too easy assumptions about the relation of biology to social theory. The English philosopher taken up by Americans to justify social hierarchy, Herbert Spencer, was a Lamarckian not a Darwinist, and Lamarck's theory did not require struggle.[6] Spencer once astonished a group of Pittsburgh businessmen by criticizing the effects of 'struggle' in their own home town.

The American pragmatists also used the legacy of Darwin in very different ways. James used it to create a new psychology, Peirce conceived it as the 'cosmic growth of concrete reasonableness', to be understood by means of his own newly furbished logical concepts.[7] Indeed Peirce distinguished three modes of evolution: 'fortuitous variation' (tychasm), inner mechanical necessity (anacasm), and evolution by creative love (agapasm).[8] James himself was to vary in his use of Darwin from the positivistic materialism of the early parts of the *Principles* to a more metaphysical 'extension of spontaneous chance to the whole of nature and its laws' in the later philosophical work – a movement in fact inspired by Peirce.[9]

James, of course, took Darwin's side against Agassiz. Agassiz, as has been mentioned, was a friend of Adams. A brief four-way comparison will help clarify some of the interlocking issues at stake. Both Adams and James began their intellectual careers when the prestige of Darwin was at its height. By the 1890s, however, Darwin's work was under attack from many quarters. The discontinuity of the fossil record remained a weak link in his argument, and the physical time required for his evolutionary periods was questioned by the physicist Lord Kelvin and others. Radioactivity had not yet altered the picture with its suggestion of infinitely slow decay. Some biological structures seemed obviously non-adaptive, others seemed in a state of permanent stasis. Natural selection itself seemed a peculiarly non-creative force and pre-Mendelian blending inheritance seemed to suggest a perpetual averaging-out of variation rather than a movement of change.[10] James, who became increasingly sceptical of any scientific model for human behaviour was also less and less concerned with what happened in science. In contrast Adams, who had never accepted Darwin's theories as wholeheartedly as had James, remained to the end of his life more actively engaged with the developments of science.

Agassiz's annotations in his own copy of *The Origin of Species* may serve as a useful point of reference for his opposition to Darwin.[11] Agassiz underlines Darwin's statement of doubt that variability is an inherent and necessary contingency, and questions whether the domestic breeding analogy is adequate: 'his results concerning species are founded not in an investigation of species themselves but in an investigation of breeds,' he writes in the margin (*Origin*, p. 122). Darwin's attempt to prise the classification of species from the question of original, separate creations is met with scepticism.[12] Agassiz defends design in a Lamarckian sense as existing somewhere between environment and organism.[13] Everywhere he challenges Darwin's scepticism of religious accounts, and defends structure against instinct. When Darwin marvels at bees making cells 'which have practically anticipated the discoveries of profound mathematicians', Agassiz writes: 'That their mathematics are identical with their organization – a result of structure and not of instinct. It is not by instinct that the leaves grow arithmetically on the trees' (p. 172). Agassiz doubts that any organs have actually developed, since there is no evidence that one has ever developed into another. When Darwin admits that it is difficult to conceive of transition and that there are no leaps in natural process, *natura non facit saltum*, Agassiz comments: 'What does this prove except an ideal unity holding all the parts of one plan together' (p. 194). Indeed Darwin's continuity *is* something of a metaphysic. His further uncertainty over internal versus external agents of change is seized upon by Agassiz. When, for example, Darwin asserts, 'Mountain breeds always differ from lowland breeds,' Agassiz writes: 'And when animals descend the slopes?' (p. 198).

Adams's own response to Agassiz acts as a foil to James's. Adams's connections with Agassiz went back a long way. His wife, Marian Hooper, had attended a high school run by Mrs Agassiz at which Agassiz himself gave lessons.[14] As late as 1903 Adams is writing to Agassiz's son about 'Darwin's eccentricities': 'never was there a scientific theory which rested on a slenderer basis of evidence – unless it may be the parallel roads theory, or the evolution theory itself.'[15] Adams is referring here to Darwin's theory of the formation of coral reefs and his scepticism, as he toured the Pacific – given our hindsight as a result of contemporary plate techtonics theory – is not without some justification. He was keenly aware of current paradigmatic shifts in science, as he wrote to his English friend Milnes Gaskell in 1903:

> Forty years ago, our friends always explained things and had the cosmos down to a point, *teste* Darwin and Charles Lyell. Now they say that they don't believe there is any explanation, or that you can choose between half-a-dozen all correct. . . . The one most completely thrown over is our gentle Darwin's Survival which has no longer a leg to stand on. I interpret even Kelvin as throwing it over.[16]

Adams's sympathies with French intellectuals also would have made him less sympathetic to Darwin. The tradition of Descartes, Cuvier and Claude Bernard who viewed the organism as a rationally ordered system, made French scientists slow to adopt evolutionism until early in the twentieth century.[17] As one amusingly extreme critic of *The Origin of Species* put it: 'What metaphysical jargon clumsily lured into natural history! What pretentious and empty language! What childish and out-of-date personifications! Oh lucidity! Oh French stability of mind, where art thou!'[18]

Adams was attracted to Agassiz for some of the same reasons he was attracted to Lyell. Lyell's world exhibited a classical cyclical stability over long periods of time, with violent change and unrest operating only at the micro-level. Agassiz had a metaphysically stable and rational view of the unity of nature.[19] Evolution was confined within the micro-level of embryonic development and was in turn guaranteed by a teleology.[20] To a degree biology and physics fought out their cosmic analogies within Adams's own sensibility. Lyell had written:

> As the present condition of nations is the result of many antecedent changes, some extremely remote and others recent, some

gradual, and others sudden and violent; so the state of the natural world is the result of a long succession of events; and if we would enlarge our experience of the present economy of nature, we must investigate the effects of her operations in former epochs.[21]

If Adams learnt something here about the 'economy' of nature and history, and something about a metaphysics of time, he also had to cope with thermodynamic's view of degeneration. Both would tend to work against an evolutionary perspective.[22]

Adams's chapter on 'Darwinism' in the *Education* in fact challenged just that Darwinian sense of continuity: 'Natural Selection led back to Natural Evolution, and at last to Natural Uniformity. This was a vast stride.' Adams's ironic meditations on Darwinian continuity and Lyellian uniformitarianism are masterly, and the famous passage on Wenlock Edge is a poetic attempt to mediate their contributions as well as subtly to characterize a whole English cast of mind. Adams's conclusion was predictably sceptical: 'he was conscious that, in geology as in theology, he could prove only Evolution that did not evolve; Uniformity that was not uniform; and Selection that did not select.'[23]

In contrast, James flatly preferred Darwin. As a young man he wrote: 'The more I think of Darwin's ideas the more weighty they appear to me, though of course my opinion is worth very little – still I believe that the scoundrel Agassiz is unworthy intellectually or morally for him to wipe his shoes on.'[24] Later he became a little more generous. James had been lonely and unhappy collecting fishes with Agassiz in Brazil in 1865. Agassiz himself was fond of quoting Goethe's lines:

Grau, teurer Freund, ist alle Theorie,
Und grun des Lebens goldener Baum.[25]

James, however, was to find defining that '*Leben*' as problematic as had Locke. He knew that the 'raw experience' of collecting fishes was not satisfying enough for him, and he mistrusted Agassiz's penchant for unifying metaphysics. James was also no scientist and consequently had no basis for relating hypothesis and practice. Darwin, in Sedgwick's words, however, had 'never been able to look steadily in the face of nature except through the lens of a hypothesis'.[26]

James discovered on the Brazilian journey that he was 'cut out for a speculative life', but not for applying speculation to nature. Indeed he tended to keep the two realms separate: 'Man's activities are occupied in two ways: in grappling with external circumstances, and in striving to set things at one in their topsy-turvy mind.'[27] James

saw Agassiz as wholly preoccupied with the former and rather
indifferent to the latter. This does Agassiz less than justice. The
philosopher of experience longed 'to be back to books, studies, etc.
after this elementary existence'.[28] Yet Agassiz did create in James
that tolerance towards those irreducible empirical details that no
scientist can afford to ignore. James could say he learnt of Agassiz
that 'No one sees further into a generalization than his own knowledge of details extends'. For Darwin, on the other hand, abstraction
and the world's concrete fulness, to adopt James's phrase, were not
opposed.[29] James was to prefer pure speculation to practice and what
was abstract and what was concrete remained a problem.

Adams's and James's last exchange of letters was ostensibly about
metaphysics. Whereas in *A Letter to American Teachers* Adams
advocated for the historian a knowledge of the more philosophical
aspects of scientific history, James replied that the 'second law' (of
thermodynamics) was 'wholly irrelevant to history', and reminded
Adams of the empirical practice of scientists and their gentlemen's
agreement to believe each other until a newer revolutionary concept
had been hit upon.[30] He continued by asserting the difference
between the quantity and quality of 'energy' and by pointing out the
irrelevance of the macro- to the micro-levels of energy deployment.
James added two postscripts (the second following by postcard),
both containing analogies. The first was of a clock. However far the
weights are up or down the mechanical operation of the hands is
constant. The second was of the 'hydraulic ram', which runs no
matter what the force of the stream. From his reading of Bagehot,
James would have remembered that 'Mr Babbage taught us years
ago that one great use of machinery was not to augment the force of
man, but to register and regulate the power of man. . . .'[31] James's
response to Adams's apparently fatalist metaphysics somewhat overlooked the fact that Adams had said that the 'Vital Enemy was
independent of mechanical law'.[32]

James was reacting, not absolutely without justice, to Adams's
scientism, but it was not a profound reaction. James's own model of
the universe running with constancy within declining 'force' and
finally expiring with a surfeit of contentment was an ironic reaction
to Adams's pessimism and melancholy. In some ways he is telling
Adams what he had already said. James would have concurred with
Adams's statement that 'the energy with which history had to deal
could not be reduced to a mechanical or physio-chemical process' (*A
Letter*, p. 11). But Adams had insisted that grand theories of nature
do have an effect on us; they have their aura. Adams's notion of
acceleration was immensely important to a century in quest of
hi-tech transformations. No less than Abbott, Adams wanted a new

set of theoretical possibilities for society, because he knew that 'the law that history was not a science, and that society was not an organism calmed all serious effort' (pp. 13–14). Adams was pleading for plausible theory; an intellectual effort placed at the service of society free of the scientisms invoked by physicist and biologist alike. Adams was more sophisticated than James allowed him to be, and one can but imagine Adams's reaction when the famous philosopher read him a lesson on how gentlemen scientists behaved.

In James there was, strangely, a quietist streak – in spite of declarations of Carlylean will to effort. James's version of happy entropy was not for Adams, who had declared, 'A society in stable equilibrium is – by definition – one that has no history and wants no historians' (*A Letter*, p. 186). Adams defended reason against instinct and mechanism alike. He was highly critical of American-style progress. In that respect James was more stoic. Adams could in fact cite his old friend Agassiz to the effect that man 'is the last term of a series beyond which, following the plan on which the whole animal kingdom is built, no further progress is materially possible' (p. 64). In a strange way it was James who had accepted Darwin relatively unquestioningly, as a set of analogies to feed philosophy and psychology. Adams remained much more sceptical because he was more aware of the current actual turmoil in science itself.

Why was Darwin so important for James? It is necessary to explore a few of the implications of Darwin's theories for social and psychological developments in the late nineteenth century in order to provide some contexts for a reading of James. Increasingly the nexus of issues in biology seemed to provide the terms of discourse for both psychology and sociology. E. O. Wilson's notorious, and notoriously marketed, post-Vietnam *Sociobiology* (1975) has numerous ancestors.[33] It has been frequently pointed out that 'social Darwinism', for example, is but one of many historical examples of the interdependence of biological and social theory in Western culture. 'Organism' or biologically based theories of social order were much older than Darwinism. In the Romantic period this mode of analogous thought had a conservative political bias. In the later nineteenth century it was adopted by liberals to form the basis of a sociological view of society. Society was now held together by a widely diffused sentiment, not by authority and political sovereignty.[34]

Darwin himself applied concepts of social science to biology in the first instance, only to have them re-borrowed by sociologists.[35] Had he not existed, the general intellectual mood in the nineteenth century would have experienced 'a conscious search for a biological underpinning to the social sciences'[36]. Darwin argued on the one hand that 'the war of nature is not incessant, that no fear is felt, that death is generally prompt, and that the vigorous, the healthy and happy survive and multiply' (*Origin*, p. 129), yet on the other hand he could often use imperialist analogies to characterize struggle. His overriding principle of continuity places him in the conservative camp, yet his advocacy of abundance, his principle that 'the greatest amount of life can be supported by great diversification of structure' (p. 157), would tend to suggest a more liberal approach to the life of nature. We have not altogether learnt in our own time that no single mechanism governs change or stability: 'Perhaps the various mechanisms are not even analogous.'[37]

Given the contradictions within Darwin's work itself, it is not surprising that *The Origin of Species* could be adapted to almost any ideological position. A new statistical fatalism which Darwin's work did encourage, and which guaranteed a more sophisticated control of the status quo, was best summed up by the American biologist Asa Gray when he said of Darwin: 'Instead of Morphology versus Teleology, we shall have Morphology wedded to Teleology.'[38] Change could now be programmed into predictive process in spite of another emphasis in the theory, on chance as guaranteeing the new. Socialist responses are well known. Engels saw the analogy of the normal state of the animal kingdom, applied in a thoroughgoing way to English society in a famous phrase, as a 'bitter satire on mankind'.[39] The Italian socialist Enrico Ferri once said: 'In a society of fools the most foolish is fittest.'[40]

Patrick Geddes of the University of Edinburgh – perhaps best known as a mentor of Lewis Mumford – turned biological theory in a direction which, though less well known, is important for our argument. Geddes was originally in the medical faculty and, with a number of others, attempted to marry late nineteenth-century English liberalism to a notion of social organism and social health. He used the biological model to advocate state intervention, city and ecological planning, but his notion of organism did not include supporting trades unions or allowing workers to bargain on pay. Geddes saw a sort of up-dated medieval guild system as the basis for 'social organic health'.[41]

Social theory had indeed excluded questions of power and sovereignty from its argument. Natural selection after all needed no human agency to reject what was bad and to preserve what was good: 'We see nothing of these slow changes in progress, until the hand of time has marked the long lapse of ages, and then so imperfect is our view into long past geological ages, that we only see that forms of life are now different from what they formerly were' (*Origin*, p. 133). Darwin's backward glance rhetorically allows him to preserve Humean scepticism. The principle of continuity, as the historians of science say, in a rather neutralist term, did not include 'transitivity'. The same sort of 'ecologism' can be seen in the work of a widely read commentator like Bateson, whose pronouncements seek a metaphysical basis in Zen and the Bible and are innocent of the 'unhealthy' taint of economics and propaganda, while admirable in their attempt to recover mind for human purposes.[42] That Darwin can, therefore, be used for many social perspectives, does not mean it is not important to think through the relation of social to biological theory. The two have always been fundamentally linked at the levels of hypothesis, analogy, and social judgement, and it was with a certain innocence that Ghiselin argued that Darwin used Malthusianism merely as a heuristic device.[43]

In the same spirit Wittgenstein wrote that 'Darwin's theory has no more to do with philosophy than any other hypothesis in natural science',[44] yet it is hard to see how Darwin could, without Locke's 'addability' and 'instrumentalism' (his admiration for Aristotle, who stands behind Locke, is well known), have written: 'The key is man's power of accumulative selection: man adds them up in certain directions useful to him' (Origin, p. 90). The domestic analogy implied purposiveness, in co-operation with genetic variation, and was irreducibly an important social metaphysic as well as a scientific hypothesis. The populationist aspects of Darwin's theory seemed to imply non-human-oriented universalist drift, and this in turn has often provided commentators on twentieth-century mass society with an alibi for their sense of impotence. Darwin's theory depended upon 'large numbers of individuals being kept' (p. 98). While living beings tended to develop in many directions, thus guaranteeing the importance of an empirical approach, they also developed along lines determined by inherited characteristics – that is, there was certain a priori patterning. Together this double tendency pruned nature of ill-adapted organisms (hence a priori the process was healthy), which left a residual pattern assuming a kind of 'universal purposefulness'.[45]

There are moments in The Origin of Species, doubtless rejected by serious historians, which show cracks in this confident populationist theory, but they are not without significance when a more holistic approach to the text is taken. Certain organisms are unfortunately unable to keep up their 'distinct breeding', and in an endearing English aside Darwin explains: 'on the other hand cats, from their nocturnal rambling habits, cannot be matched, and although so much valued by women and children, we hardly see a distinct breed kept up' (Origin, p. 99). This amusing cameo of unconscious assumptions and connections, in which the underbred are judged valuable by the socially discounted, poses the serious question of the

role of populationist theory in social ideology. Is the natural to be
equated with the normal, and what implications for social truth does
a scientific theory propose which assumes large numbers of those
designated countable as statistically programmed in closed spaces?
Perhaps the contemporary rejection of metaphysics has paradoxically created a metaphysical innocence.

It is in fact difficult to think about individuals, lineages, entities,
groups, definitions of organisms, modes of interaction and so on
without posing some of the classical metaphysical questions. A
recent book whose various contributors explore some of the parameters of these overlapping discourses shows that the debates are as
lively as ever. The Marxist contributors are, as usual, useful in
reminding us of the irreducibility of human life to biological
formulas and organismic abstraction, but their a priori of social
labour tends to ignore (unlike Marx himself) technological change
and to characterize the nature–tool dichotomy too simply. Human
beings produce, after all, in the produced.

When one commentator in this work takes evolutionary models
into the social sphere, some of the old problems emerge in a new
guise. Here, the model of expressive practical 'dualism' becomes an
unwarrantable a priori, reflecting a piety–practicality division that
would not have been unfamiliar to James. In an attempt to overcome
the opposition of the two, the writer asserts that expressive action
can be a means of adaptation, and his example is revealing: 'For
example, the oppressive practices of football hooligans are very
nicely adapted to resisting and remedying the humiliations they
perceive themselves [sic] to have received in the world of work and
school.'[46] Perhaps only a social philosopher could perceive revenge
as remedy. The Darwinian 'nicely adapted' is little short of scandalous
here. But the terms of feedback and behind that again of homeostasis
(disruption–compensation) have, from the nineteenth century to our
own time, provided those who equate the terms of life with those of
society, with authoritarian models of description. From Claude
Bernard to Durkheim and from Durkheim to Talcott Parsons, as
Toulmin has shown, concepts of homeostasis have dominated social
thought. They are conservative theories 'which explain only how
existing institutions of a society adapt their operations in the face of
external changes so as to defend themselves in their present forms,
not how they can modify these forms to take better advantage of
external conditions'.[47]

Turning from these contemporary discussions about evolutionary
discourses, John Dewey's *Influence of Darwin on Philosophy* (1910) can
profitably be taken up to *re-historicize* the argument for issues in
James's own psychology and philosophy. Dewey himself pointed to

the Aristotelian *eidos* (translated by the scholastics as 'species') as a concept of constancy in change, and as a principle of knowledge as well as of nature. For Dewey, Darwin had claimed biology for a principle of transition without purposive design. By undercutting fixity, Dewey argued, Darwin was bound to 'transform the logic of knowledge: he emancipated, once for all, genetic and experimental ideas as an *organon* of asking questions and looking for explanations'.[48] Dewey's 'logic' is a strange mixture of metaphysics, ethical exhortation and psychology, and its intended purity tends to fall apart into a metaphysics and a method. As with so many others of his period, his main argument is directed against 'epistemology' as an ungrounded mentalism: 'The things that pass for epistemology all assume that knowledge is not a natural function or event, but a mystery' (*Influence*, p. 97). Dewey abstracts from Darwin an autonomous transition, a naturalization of consciousness and the familiar Lockean mental operations of additiveness and instrumentality. He cites James's *Does Consciousness Exist?* (1904): all there is is 'an additive relation – a new property possessed by a non-mental object, when that object, occurring in a new context, assumes a further office and use' (p. 104).

The deep contradiction within Dewey is that while he admits psychology is a 'political science', because different political systems produce different 'experience', he also declares that 'consciousness is but a symbol, an anatomy [*sic*] whose life [*sic*] is natural and social operations' (p. 244). Thus the gap between political experience and our consciousness of it is taken up and reconnected into a smooth self-confirming circle by the undeclared truth of natural and social operations. The circle is not, however, quite closed, for Dewey sees that there is a 'need of a language for reading the things signified' (p. 244). But again the influence is Lockean. A technique of language will make for correct adjustments to conditions. For Dewey evolution is the discovery of 'a general law of life' and a 'generalization of all scientific method' (p. 262). The historical controversies over Darwin's method as a science have been forgotten as Dewey re-abstracts the latent philosophical empiricism of Darwin's text into a clinical tool with which to recreate homeostatic health in the social world.

Dewey's own metaphysic is 'individual experience' and it sustains this vision of 'philosophy-as-method' by claiming priority for psychology as such: 'Given the freed individual, who feels called upon to create a new heaven and a new earth, and who feels himself gifted with the power to perform the task to which he is called: – and the demand for science, for a method of discovering and verifying truth, becomes imperious' (p. 287). Here an old American Utopian drive and sense of religious calling enter secretly into the apparently neutral ground of methodology. Not by their fruits but by their method ye shall know them. Method becomes manifest destiny and is supremely practiced in psychology, which is 'the attempt to state in detail the machinery of the individual considered as the instrument and organ through which social action operates' (p. 302).

The Origin of Species was, then – in all its homeliness of style, its passionate rhetorical persuasiveness, its cunning delay of abstraction until the conclusion, its deployment of rival philosophies – a text not only for biologists but for philosophers, psychologists and sociologists. Empiricists could take comfort in the givenness of the domestic analogy by going on to construct a synchronic model for life itself, conservatives, scientific and social, could take pleasure in genealogical patterns, socialists could read irony into struggle, philosophers could ponder rival metaphysics of change (did Natural Selection add things up or wave a magician's wand?),[49] statisticians could equalize the 'functions' of life and death, biologists could find an extremely plausible model of species change and development, and if the religious despaired of confirmation of Holy Writ, they could at least take comfort in the vision of an English God as a super-comprehensive stock-breeder. Darwin had biologized Carlyle's Nordic tree of History and turned historical consequence into descent. Indeed, in Stanley Edgar Hyman's words, we have a 'poetic vision of struggle, adaptation, and triumph'. While Hyman's thesis – in his still undervalued book – is overly Freudian, he accurately locates the strain of the exotic, the dramatic and the surreal in Darwin's vision. It is no exaggeration to claim that Darwin's use of the image of the 'tangled bank', with which he concludes his work, has a lineage going back to Shakespeare.[50]

When Darwin's work passed into psychological discourse its richness was almost inevitably reprocessed into analytical formulae. For philosophers, scientists and psychologists who wanted to know whether natural selection was a method of analysis (variation–selection), and for sociologists who pondered social process, Darwin's dreams about the results of undreaming pigeon-fanciers and his mixing of the unconscious and the methodical seemed ripe for 'tidying up'. Yet the strengths were in the untidiness, in the deftness in mediating that 'fuzzy boundary' between the logical and psychological which Ghiselin locates in the very concept of explanation itself.[51] In James's passage from biology to psychology it was Darwin who was to incline him to link the emotions with instincts, and it was English empiricism which would lead him to stress receptive and cognitive aspects of mental conduct.[52] It is ironic that the one chapter of The Origin of Species which proliferates in socio-economic images of struggle is the chapter on instincts.

As for Darwin's own relation to psychology, one commentator stresses that he had 'historicized associationism'.[53] Actually it is probably more accurate to say he had given it historical metaphysic. Association became the mechanism by which animal attributes developed into human faculties. It emphasized the origin of ideas as mediators between the senses and the environment. Greta Jones argues that in Darwin's work, *The Expression of the Emotions in Man and Animals* (1872), he ran the full gamut of associationism from contiguity of ideas to the physiology of the nerve reflex.[54] For James this, too, would come to mean that in one sense 'all our theories are *instrumental*, are mental modes of *adaptation* to reality'.[55] How far James stuck to this Darwinian view of things must now be determined precisely.

II

In 1880, in an article in the *Atlantic Monthly*, James spoke of 'A remarkable parallel, which to my knowledge has never been noticed . . . between the facts of social evolution on the one hand [and the mental growth of race], and of zoological evolution as expounded by Mr Darwin. . . .'.[56] Earlier in the year James had made his first reference to 'a text book in psychology'.[57] His 'remarkable parallel' attempted boldly to adapt Darwin's theory of selection to a science of mind. In the article James mounted an attack on Spencerian fatalism by describing the mind as purposefully 'picking out what to attend to, and ignoring everything else, – by narrowing its point of view'.[58] James here registers, somewhat passively, not merely a problem from his reading of Darwin but something of a capitulation to a particular view of scientific methodology. He had to fight two opposing tendencies in himself: a holistic and ultimately religious feel for taking in the totality of the world, and a rather more specialized Puritan sense of having a duty to invoke the 'rigour' of empiricism and to take on board the scientists' increasingly clamorous invasion of the 'life-world'.

James continued by arguing that Darwin's genius was to keep two things distinct: the causes of variation, under the title of 'tendencies to variation', and the maintenance of peculiarities by natural selection. He then applies this model to an individualist sociology. The Carlylean great man is a 'variety' selected by the 'visible environment' – a euphemism for society as a whole. Societies in turn become species:

> The mutations of societies, then, from generation to generation, are in the main due directly or indirectly to the acts or the examples of individuals whose genius was so adapted to the

receptivities of the moment, or whose accidental position of authority was so critical that they become ferments, initiators of movement, settlers of precedent or fashion, centres of corruption, or destroyers of other persons, whose gifts, had they had free play, would have led society in another direction.[59]

Darwin is thus invoked to save the liberal individual. The difficulty socially, however, is of the same order as the biological difficulty. How is that purposive residue guaranteed? What is there to stop an ultimate averaging out, or indeed a degeneration? James's answer is more great men: 'Leaders give the form.'[60] James notes that England has lost effective form while Germany in the figure of Bismarck has gained it. The liberal world of 'self-and-society' is biologized into 'genetic variation and social environment'. James recommends as evidence for his own thoughts that 'golden little work', Walter Bagehot's *Physics and Politics* of 1872, which a recent critic has called 'a defence of liberal democracy by use of a Darwinian analogy'.[61]

It is worth pausing over Bagehot and his volume. James's admiration for *Physics and Politics* has not been sufficiently noticed. It gives many clues to the relations between science, psychology and politics which will be of first importance for understanding James himself. Much about Bagehot would have appealed to James. A conservative liberal, he had taken over *The Economist* from James Wilson, who had founded it to represent Free Trade principles during the struggle against the Corn Laws. However, Bagehot had dismayed liberal friends by his reaction to the 1848 revolution and Louis Napoléon's *coup d'état*. In a series of letters to *The Inquirer*, he said he believed that the only secure basis for people doing their duty was 'that they should not know anything else to do', and that the only guarantee of political stability was that they should be incapable of comprehending any other condition of political life than that to which they had been accustomed. (This principle, endemic in English conservatism, also characterizes English ruling-class thought of the 1980s and '90s.) The entry in Leslie Stephen's 1885 *Dictionary of National Biography* states that this position pervaded Bagehot's *Physics and Politics*, published more than twenty years after the Napoleonic coup.[62] James had probably not read, nor would even have been very interested in the details of Bagehot's work on the British Constitution, but aspects of the British writer's political position in terms of behaviour and psychology certainly struck a sympathetic chord in James; and, taken together, these aspects do help to clear up some puzzles about James's ambiguities – for example on the notions of 'success' and 'experience'.

The sources of power for Bagehot lay in sentiment (ultimately therefore in psychology) – not in Hobbes's historically constituted power, nor in Locke's contract. In *Physics and Politics* he dismisses, for example, Locke's debate with Filmer as relatively unimportant.[63] With Bagehot a political theory of government becomes a social one. The key was psychological control of a country of ignorant and respectful poor. As Geoffrey Best says, 'The mid-Victorians of course have no historical monopoly of deference: but deference does seem to have been remarkably strong in their time, and Bagehot was its Darwin.'[64]

Darwin will turn out to be a key figure in this new psychology. However, deference is a complicated notion, and should not simply call up visions of forelock-tugging estate servants. It was a *modus vivendi*; a bargain struck 'between the traditional middle classes and their potential rivals'. Class and economic position were not necessarily determinants. With the proper manner, which would include cleanliness, independence, respectability, you could be one of Samuel Smiles's 'nature's gentlemen': 'you are expected to pay your own way, to look after yourself, to keep out of trouble if you could and to bear [*it*] manfully, i.e. uncomplainingly, if you couldn't.'[65] Excellent advice to the upwardly mobile, but a crippling social ideology for thousands of the poor and for those who had been victims of injustice. A contemporary historian has said of Bagehot: 'there was at the bottom of him, a moral vacuum'.[66] It has also been noted that Bagehot's famous phrase, 'the cake of custom', had 'considerable influence on William James'.[67]

Bagehot was not much troubled by questions of free will and evolution: 'Every Freewillist holds that, upon the whole, if you strengthen the motive in a given direction, mankind tends to set more in that direction.'[68] This was to be James's psychological and ethical conclusion. 'Habit' – a key to James's psychology – was also a mixture of evolutionary and psychological theory. Bagehot said that the 'clock-work of material civilization' was unpossessed by 'savages' (*Physics*, p. 19). Youthful nations (and hence children and young people of contemporary times) had 'soft minds' needing to be 'fixed by hard transmitted instincts', which echoes James's thoughts in the *Principles* that 'It is well for the world that in most of us, by the age of thirty, the character has set like plaster, and will never soften again.'[69] So also Bagehot's words: 'it is the continued effect of the beginning that creates the hoarded energy of the end' (*Physics*, p. 11), are echoed in James's 'we must take care to launch ourselves with as strong and decided an initiative as possible' (*Principles*, I. 127) – something James, incidentally, quite failed to do in his own life.

James, in fact, got that idea of the social application of Darwin's theory to the selection of great men by society from Bagehot. He is right to claim, however, that the application of natural selection to the realm of mind is his. More accurately, it is possibly Bagehot's Darwin-derived social model that helps construct James's mental model, and principally because he always has at the back of his mind its ethical (and ultimately political) import. James, like Bagehot, is interested in belief. Belief is a vital ingredient in Bagehot's theory of imitation – in turn a key to deferential emulation – and it is primarily psychological: 'having its seat mainly in very obscure parts of the mind' (*Physics*, pp. 92–3). It can be, for Bagehot, almost a transmitted instinct tending towards preservation. This is absolutely true, he says, in savage people and has some truth in civilized ones also, though a too strongly held belief is hard to distinguish from superstition and rigidity. Neither James nor Bagehot is ever quite clear on the subject of belief, for both fail to discuss the relation of individual to social belief.

They are much clearer on the 'custom-making power', which, if the pun may be forgiven, constructs their individual psychological constitutions. Much of James's work is a gloss on the following by Bagehot:

> The first thing is the erection of what we may call a custom-making power, that is, of an authority which can enforce a fixed rule of life, which, by means of that fixed rule, can in some degree create a calculable future, which can make it rational to postpone present violent but momentary pleasure for future continual pleasure, because it ensures, what else is not sure, that if the sacrifice of what is in hand be made, enjoyment of the contingent expected recompense will be received. (*Physics*, p. 137)

The 'fixing' power of natural selection is made a personal and national ethical imperative. Its twin characteristics of variation and selection give the political theorist some problems. Who will vary and who will select? Even within variation, inheritance seems to exhibit continuities and discontinuities. Darwin can in fact be used conservatively and liberally. The conservative Bagehot states, 'Natural Selection means the preservation of those individuals which struggle best with the forces that oppose their race' (p. 84). The liberal Bagehot who has read Darwin closely can say 'we find like men in contrasted places, and unlike men in resembling places' (p. 85).

Bagehot psychologizes the liberal 'mind of man'. The unknown power of variation of favoured nations throws up 'mental prerequisites' which are seized upon and made firm (p. 135). He cites Huxley on mental reflex action: 'the brain gives rise to actions which are as completely reflex as those of the spinal chord', anticipating James's mechanism of the opening chapter of the *Principles*. However, Huxley introduces a distinction between natural and artificial – so that by analogy, 'By the help of the brain we may acquire an infinity of artificial reflex actions' (pp. 4, 5). But the most important aspect of Bagehot's argument is that he provides an explanation for how conscious action becomes unconscious. Just as Hobbes assumed that, theoretically, historical change once occurred, so the psychologists assume that historically, in society and in the individual, a conscious act did once take place. Bagehot speaks of a 'power which the nervous system possesses, of organizing conscious actions into more or less unconscious, or reflex operations' (p. 7). There is an ethics and a politics behind these psycho-physiologies of society.

Bagehot knew a priori who should be admired – gentlemen of the House of Lords – which at least gives a gouty weight to his behavioural abstractions: 'this unconscious imitation and encouragement of appreciated character, and this equally unconscious shrinking from and persecution of disliked character, is the main force which moulds and fashions men in society as we now see it' (p. 97). Bagehot's psychological consensus in the service of obedience is far from even the conservative liberal image he is credited with. Few would disagree that some order in a society is better than none. But as a rule of ordinary political life this reduction bears the taint of crisis-mongering as a means of control. The Terror of 1848 haunts Bagehot's liberal politics. Like a latter-day Burke, he transforms Sir Henry Maine's 'status' into a politics of charisma and image. We will naturally select those who will save us. James's praise of Bagehot's work reveals a highly conservative bent in his own thinking.

In James's essay, 'Great Men and their Environment', Bagehot's psycho-social Darwinism is evident. Great men are variations thrust up by unknown causes, to be selected by something called 'the visible environment'. This visible environment turns out to be a mental environment of psychological sentiment. On these grounds James can judge that Bismarck shows the mental state of Germany to be better than that of England, or that Boston is dying for want of an abundant variety of great men. James hurls his 'Darwinian' mental evolutionism, however, against Spencer's fatalism:

And I can easily show that throughout the whole extent of those mental departments which are highest, which are most characteristically human, Spencer's law is violated at every step: and that, as a matter of fact, the new conceptions, emotions and active tendencies which evolve are originally produced in the shape of random images, fancies, accidental outbursts of spontaneous variation in the functional activity of the excessively unstable human brain, which the outer environment simply confirms or refutes...selects in short....[70]

So Darwin's 'chance' is thrust against Spencer's fatalism. But at what level? Unpredictability is, says James, the highest order of mind. But if social sentiment will naturally select what is unpredictable it has to take on the counter-evidence of socially conservative history. In fact James protects himself from this conclusion by switching to an ethical level. Good societies do this, bad ones do not. James does not consider that society may be just in rejecting the unpredictable, nor that it may not have the power to carry out its choices. That unpredictability may be extremely dangerous for a society is also not considered.

The advantages and disadvantages of James's model are not difficult to sum up. First, he admits the irrational into human social organization, with all its power to challenge the sanity of possibly oppressive organization. But he does not consider that it also may disrupt good organization. Second, the model provides a more flexible way of discussing social change than either positivistic or idealistic social science. Mind is also defended in its creative pre-conceptual activity and the irrational selectiveness of society can, James suggests, have some unknown purposive element on the same model. But James atomizes the creative moment (the Great Man) and then robs it of its power by insisting on the slow continuity of society. Bagehot's buried politics emerge as technique. Also limiting the field may not be the best thing for a society. Finding possible models of multiple development might be better. Within the model of natural selection, there is only a *passive* creative element. For James creativity is reserved for the individual, but not for collective decision.

Henry Adams, as might be imagined, had objections to James's article. Adams would have known that one argument against natural selection was that variation and selection might cancel each other out so that no purposive residue was left. He also disliked James's old-fashioned view of historical change:

> With hero worship like Carlyle's I have little patience. In history heroes have neutralized each other, and the result is no more than would have been reached without them. Indeed in military heroes I suspect that the ulimate result has been retardation. Nevertheless you could doubtless at any time stop the entire process of human thought by killing a few score of men. So far I am with you. A few hundred men represent the entire intellectual activity of the whole thirteen hundred millions. What then?[71]

Adams's élitism exposes James's liberalism. Adams could not be dragged into believing in purposive automatic social sentiment, and he was politically and culturally too astute to be taken in by Bagehot's 'custom-making power'.

In 'The Sentiment of Rationality', first published in 1879, James converted Bagehot's social sentiment into a theory of motives for intellection. Hence the sentiment of rationality. Jones reminds us that Bagehot was one among a number of post-Mill liberals of the generation of 1860 and 1870 to rediscover 'feeling' as a politically reactive force.[72] 'Feeling' makes choices when politics fails: as James says, 'The transition from a state of puzzle and perplexity to rational comprehension is full of lively relief and pleasure.'[73]

James characterizes the sentiment of rationality in various ways. First it is a feeling of the absolute presentness of things in a poetic sense. James quotes Whitman but he could equally have quoted Keats's negative capability, or that 'blessed mood' of Wordsworth's in 'Tintern Abbey'. James calls it 'a sort of anaesthetic state', though that is hard to reconcile with the more aware mood of 'I am sufficient as I am', which he quotes from Whitman. To get to this state there are several routes. One is the philosopher's method of reducing 'manifoldness to simplicity' (*Will to Believe*, p. 58). James again follows Bagehot's directive; 'In the interest of sound knowledge it is essential to narrow to the utmost the debatable territory. . .' (*Physics*, p. 11a). The 'economy of means in thought', says James, 'is the philosophic passion par excellence'. This reduction within explanation he then illustrates:

> Who does not feel the charm of thinking that the moon and the apple are, as far as their relation to the earth goes, identical; of knowing respiration and combustion to be one; of understanding that the balloon rises by the same law whereby the stone sinks; of feeling that the warmth in one's palm when one rubs one's sleeve is identical with the motion which the friction checks. . . .
>
> (*Will to Believe*, p. 58)

James's heart ingenuously runs counter to his head. He has the intention of celebrating philosophic 'economy' but the result is quite the opposite. These examples of 'scientific law' give the effect of the many-in-the-one, not the one-in-the-many. Aristotle's perception of the similar in the dissimilar,[74] the heart of metaphor, seems to appeal to James, for it is his concrete examples, not the abstract law, which here arouses a sense of wonder. James recaptures the actual multiple world and a feeling of creativity while innocently explaining the psychology of a philosopher looking for an economy of means. Of course there is a philosophical pleasure – or perhaps one should say scientific – in that search for the elegant One to explain the Many. But James's actual language suggests that he is on the other side; that his pleasure is in multiplicity. The sentiment of rationality is an attempt to synthesize the two in a psychology, but the moment James begins to list his examples the heart, rather than the head-plus-the-nervous-system, comes to the fore. Then he states that the sister passion to simplification is clarity: the passion for a part rather than the whole. This is clearly the psychology of empiricism and is apparently in constant opposition to the other. Oddly, for a philosopher who is always supposed to be closer to this tradition than the other one, James gives us no racy examples of 'clarity'.

In a characteristic movement James links the history of philosophy to his dualistic psychology, which in turn of course has been constructed in the first instance from philosophy. He pits Spinoza against Hume, to claim 'that the only possible philosophy must be a compromise between an abstract monotony and a concrete heterogeneity' (*Will to Believe*, p. 61). Whereas Adams let his opposites fight, James attempts to find a 'common essence'. Essence is the basis of classification, and since classification has to ignore the untidy, real world in order to function, the main characteristic of essence is that it can never be complete. The reasoning is tricky. James wants to separate 'abstract essence' and 'living fact' yet give them a kind of ontological association. Abstract essence turns out to be 'the attribute invoked as universal principle' – not a heuristic device as in Darwin. The data which escapes it is 'associated empirically with the said attribute but devoid of rational kinship with it' (p. 61). A second-level empirical association guarantees the relation of data outside the class with that inside it, but it cannot be known. Here James hovers about the mystic centre of empiricism. He already has his Lockean metaphysic in reserve. Only 'attributes' can be known; substance, that metaphysic of living fact, escapes us.

There is a psychological pressure behind James's logic. It has been noted how much he loathed collecting with Agassiz, and his mood here is like that of 1865. James cuts his world in two. If you are going to be a philosopher then the best theoretical philosophy is the simple classification of things. If not, not, as Gertrude Stein would have said. With a certain lack of irony James then quotes Agassiz's favourite passage from Goethe, those lines in which 'the golden tree of life' is said to be better than 'grey theory'. He goes on to damn the entire scientific enterprise. Supposing, he says, you attain your goal of a unified system, you would reach the deep peace of the sentiment of rationality. Unfortunately, says James, now switching to a psychological explanation, the mind just does not work like that.

Whitman, in his Preface (1855) to *Leaves of Grass*, captures James's mood:

> Has any one fancied he could sit at last under some due authority and rest satisfied with explanations and realize and be content and full? To no such terminus does the greatest poet bring...he brings neither cessation or sheltered fatness and ease. The touch of him tells in action.[75]

Whitman, of course, could rely on Hegel and other idealist philosophers. James specifically rejects Hegel, but is curiously close to Whitman nonetheless. His final position is one of Romantic psychological paradox. 'The peace of rationality may be sought through ecstasy when logic fails', and he goes on to cite Whitman and Wordsworth yet again.[76]

This is a typical pattern of Jamesian argument, to be repeated in part or whole many times. The strategy is to invoke philosophic dualism by an a priori reduction to psychology, attempt logically to justify the move with a theory of scientific procedure, damn science by claiming that the richness of the world escapes its methods, and claim only partially satisfying alternatives in 'religious experience' – the emotion of ontologic wonder eternally unsatisfied before brute fact. It is perhaps best to leave James's strategy as a bundle of contradictions.

The reduction of philosophy to psychology has the merit of exposing concealed emotions and unadmitted motives in many a philosopher, but it also has the demerit of downgrading actual theoretical procedure through unwarranted simplifications. Invocation of method as a kind of ground of truth, though common to many scientists, is too simplistic a way of describing what actually happens in scientific procedure. In hypothesis-building and in the consensus about practice there are both imaginative and logical factors at work. Ecstasy, which is set against logic and which James invokes in his search for religious peace, is only one aspect of religious experience and it is doubtful whether the kind of ecstatic feeling saint and poet share is precisely the same.

The second part of the essay on rationality, which first appeared as 'Rationality, Activity and Faith', in the *Princeton Review* for July 1882, attempts to give a 'practical aspect' to the more theory-oriented earlier essay. Actually, as the three terms of the original title indicate, it proceeds on at least three levels: philosophic (rationality), pragmatic–ethical (activity), and religious (faith). Like others of his time James blends 'appeals to metaphysical, explanatory, and methodological percepts...'[77] within a single argument. His feelings about that perpetual incompleteness of 'ontological wonder' point more to

a psychologically observed behaviour than to a philosophical consideration of ontology. The problem of 'being' is in fact repressed.

By eschewing metaphysics in the traditional sense James invites
ambiguity at another level of his argument. If there are attributes
inside and outside the classification of substance, to what do the
attributes outside it belong? And do these two types of attribute
point to the same being; one knowable, the other always escaping
knowledge? How can they be related empirically except in their
common being as appearing to sense? Or is there a further reality to
which both these attributes (in fact they are two-level Lockean Ideas)
point? Their mere appearance to sense hardly relates them except in
so far as James assumes a further coherence in nature itself. James's
intuition of reality is primarily religious. He seems neither to delight
in the scientist's local coherences nor in the philosopher's theorizing
– given his characterization of this divide. He also justifies conceptualizing on two quite different and indeed opposed grounds.

The first is instrumental: concepts are teleological instruments.
The second is aesthetic – a psychological drive towards simplicity
and elegance. For James takes no pleasure in the actual solution of
actual problems. Between practice and 'art for art's sake' there is no
connecting logic, only a psychology which buries its metaphysics.
Rationality therefore depends on psychological realities. In the
second part of the essay James gives some clues as to what these are.

They may be briefly summed up as pre-cognitive attention, a
reflex action and a retrospective confirmation of that action by belief.
Truth for the mind is tested, in a phrase from the first version of the
essay, by 'the aesthetic constitution of our practical nature' (*Will to
Believe.* [Historical Collation] p. 375), a phrase which yokes mind
and body with all the vagueness of Jamesian vigour. It is the
psychology of the way truth is arrived at that interests James. Like
Jonathan Edwards, James has a series of tests for his sense-beyond-
sense lying in the aesthetics of our 'practical essence'. The first test
is that of custom, the second that of banishing uncertainty from
the future. The first test is psychologically verified. Empiricists
notice that if things appear regularly in a certain order that order is
accepted as true. This 'daily contemplation' of a 'certain order' begets
'acceptance'. Thus something can be explained by passing 'easily
back to its antecedents', and it is known (that is, it can be used
practically) when it can be used to predict things accurately.

It should be noted that James here rules out conscious reasoning in
his psychology of truth. Expectation – building on Darwin – has a
purposive utilitarian quality. We attend an object, it upsets us, we get
used to it (a somewhat passive form of selection) and incorporate it
if it is useful to us. Again, there is not much that is creative in this

multiple-choice view of the world. Like the tests examiners devise for unfortunate pupils, truth is only a choice between already selected data. The only practical result for the pupils is to pass the examination and win approval by flattering the examiners, who will enable them to join the sacred company of believers in multiple-choice tests. There is no possibility of explaining something which might in fact involve a rejection of antecedents. It is not possible to explain Einstein by reference to Newtonian geometry. Thus James psychologizes the 'truth' aspects of natural selection. That 'use' also might be problematic does not occur to him. Building nuclear power stations is useful to those without jobs but not very useful to those who have to live downwind of them.

As for the reference to the future – so notable a part of Jamesian thought – it operates on a confusing number of levels. Ethically it means you have to have faith, logically it is a nonsense, for you cannot determine a thing by a future – James merely plays on the common-sense ambiguity in 'determine': will and limit. Psychologically 'determination' associates two emotions; a sense of the future, which we all need in order to keep going, and certainty. Mere certainty of a future (unspecified) does not necessarily keep us sane, as anyone who has just been informed of a terminal illness knows. James's 'desire to have expectancy fulfilled' rules out any possibly sane desire not to have expectancy fulfilled. Indeed, is it expectation that is selective or is there a further selection of expectancy embedded in variation? The outside world seizes our attention. But what limits what? James remains deliberately unclear because he refuses the question of consciousness.

Having got the world into our attention, he continues, somehow a further selection takes place through our active and emotional powers. These are preserved if our faculty of faith or 'unconstrained' belief is confirmed. This makes a nonsense of any ground of truth whatsoever. If faith is the Christian's 'evidence of things unseen' (before? or now?), then there is some room for the new. If 'unconstrained' means our belief is free to change, the same applies. But if 'unconstrained' means intensive, then we will only accept what we already know, which may or may not preserve us. Depending on how you read James's deliberate ambiguities it is possible to interpret him in almost any direction. In fact there is a conservatism in his invocation of continuity and psychological intuitionism. James psychologizes consciousness and then turns it into religious faith – trying to reassure us that even if we do not think, everything will turn out all right.

James was accused of anti-intellectualism by an earlier generation of critics, and at moments like this – in spite of the barrage from his intellectual stockpile – it is hard not to agree with them. For James demotes reason by saying that its 'essential factor' is the 'determination of expectancy'. He slants his case by saying it is 'philosophical craving' (as if thinkers were all somehow recognizable addictive behavioural types) that is the truth of their activity. He argues that it is necessary to recognize ethical purposes in natural selection and religious faith, or distress results, just as an unknown object troubles its observer and then turns out to be useful when it is recognized. Because it is not rational to believe, James argues that it is better in the last resort not to be rational, since practically everything works out anyhow: 'It is far too little recognized how entirely the intellect is built up of practical interests. The theory of evolution is beginning to do very good service by its reduction of all mentality to the type of reflex action' (p. 72). James leaves entirely undetermined what the truth of the 'practical' is. He appears unable to accept his own suggestion that the multiple world might have other truths than natural selection, or faith which guarantees certainty.

James also has the empiricist's difficulty in determining on what grounds some things are noticed and others not:

> We comprehend a thing when we synthesize it by identity with another thing. But the other great department of our understanding, acquaintance (the two departments being recognized in all languages by the antithesis of such words as *wissen* and *kennen*; *scire* and *noscere*, etc.), what is that also but a synthesis – a synthesis of a passive perception with a certain tendency to reaction?
>
> (*Will to Believe*, pp. 72–3)

Our passive perception gives us no active grounds (like natural selection) for acting. As a description of the role of the unconscious James's description here is exemplary. It gives an almost psychoanalytic account of the attention. We attend what we know not and do things that surprise us. But James did not actually approve of the unconscious as an explanation. He wanted natural selection concretely to synthesize the world of the practical and the world of the thought-about. For James idealism and materialism are not problems in the history of philosophy, nor moments in scientific thought, nor pleasurable acts of thinking, nor aspects of culture and of the life of the mind. They are not even part of the history of religions, or social thinking. They are pointers to an emotional dualism in human psychology.

James now forgets what he has said about certainty and invokes faith directly from religion, to compensate for the fact that there is no certainty in the cold materialistic scientific world of natual selection. So he moves straight into the rhetoric of uplift and reassures us that

'The inmost nature of reality is congenial to powers which you possess' (p. 73). Emerson had said, of course, that 'Everyman's condition is a solution in hieroglyphic to those inquiries he would put'.[78] Emerson at least emphasized questioning, and 'puzzling out' a world divulged to us as symbols. The emphasis is on creative play and richness and the interplay between world and thought. Idealism at least has the advantage of not being practical, and of joy in being. James insensibly reflects the American 1890s – winning or losing is all. He does make success an ethic: an almost Calvinistic one: 'If my inborn faculties are good, I am a prophet; if poor I am a failure: nature spews me out of her mouth, and there is an end of me' (*Will to Believe*, p. 78). And for someone who theoretically dislikes idealism, James also says, 'whenever we espouse a cause we contribute to the determination of the evolutionary standard of right' (p. 82). He gives no grounds for determining whether the 'evolutionary standard' is right or wrong. James is too timid to insist that 'nature' is obviously immoral, because he craves that Arnoldian 'power not ourselves' to keep his own faith going.

Like many 'religious' people James perhaps found it difficult to accept the fact that you could both be moral and not believe. He has been called a Romantic, but he did not have the Romantic guts to defy God. He is more of a psychological latitudinarian, for he refused tragic disappointment as much as he refused the Epicurean's scepticism. 'Scepticism in moral matters is an active ally of immorality. Who is not for is against. The universe will have no neutrals in these questions' (p. 89). That 'either-or' is coercive because James offers only 'neutrality' in between. If as a European I dislike both American and Soviet foreign policy, it does not mean that I am neutral. It means I can positively call a plague on both houses and suggest a third alternative. I may be crushed because I am not on either winning side, but I reserve the right not to be called immoral, or foolish. I do this out of certain principles and a priori judgements, without regard for whether 'the entire human race' will justify me in a posterity in which I can have little personal interest, since I accept the finality of my death. James's 'social verdict' is a bloodless secularization of the Christian judgement seat with pietistic overtones.

Thus 'natural selection' in one guise or another affected virtually every area of human understanding – with the exception of 'hard science'. It was, as Frederick Pollock's *Mind* article of 1876 put it, 'the master key of the universe'.[79] James used it as a key to ways of discussing mind and will, 'social evolution' and 'mental growth'. It was the means by which physiology attempted to swallow up British associationism and which James would attempt to oppose while using similar arguments. Philosophically it was seen as a way of reconciling an empirico–utilitarian tradition with 'the poetic ideals of the transcendentalist'.[80] For Dewey, looking back in 1910, it had transformed also the 'logic of knowledge, and hence the treatment of morals, politics and religion'.[81] Its effects on political thought are of direct relevance to James. Bagehot shifted the ground beneath traditional debates about power and representation, filling the vacuum with psychology and theories of social sentiment. Bagehot was responding to new relations between political and economic power, and to the actual political events of 1848; phenomena not without relevance to post-Civil War America. Ultimately the drive towards a 'science of mind' had political as well as psychological implications. It downgraded traditional philosophical and political questions with implications for problems of explanation, method, the role of consciousness, epistemology and metaphysics.

James's *The Principles of Psychology* will now be read in the light of these issues. The aim will be to test Ralph Barton Perry's old claim of 1935 that James 'constructed an image of human nature which after forty years is not yet obsolete', and the claim of his more recent biographer, Gay Wilson Allen, that 'William James was pre-eminently the philosopher of freedom and human dignity, and in his philosophy he criticized and prepared for the crises of humanity in this revolutionary century'.[82] Did William James, as Bentley – citing Whitehead – claimed, open up 'a new epoch, as yet unnamed in human thinking'?[83] James's psychologizing and his view of philosophy go together. This makes more difficult the notion that he moved from one to the other in any simple way. Specialized professional claims on James are highly dubious. All the areas he touched on must be seen together and these must include the history of psychology, philosophy, issues within the history and philosophy of science, and literature. The approach to the text will therefore be holistic and it will be closely examined for its particular moments.

Chapter 9
The Principles of Psychology

James wrote his psychology at a time when the fate of philosophy as well as psychology seemed precarious, though for different reasons. The extraordinary rise in the prestige of science seemed to sound the death-knell of pure philosophy. This was hardly a new phenomenon. Indeed as 'long as there has been cosmological speculation, science has constantly robbed metaphysics of what it thought to be its own'.[1]

Psychology in James's time was in a deeply unsettled state. Only four years after James's *Principles* was published, for example, Freud was still working and publishing in neurophysiology.[2] James's *Principles* was published at a time when psychology was not simply poaching on philosophy but claimed to replace it altogether. It was taking it into its own chaos. It is little wonder that James wrote humorously to Stumpf that his *Principles* was 'so unclassic in form, that I confess it seems not altogether right to inflict the whole of it on a foreign nation with whom my country is at peace'.[3] Not the least of the problems of the relation between philosophy and psychology in the *Principles* is that 'principles' are offered in 'non-classical' form. After all, how could you investigate the principles of a subject when the very means of determining principle had been replaced by the subject itself?

One result was an anti-intellectualist strand in James in which a kind of common-sense therapeutics would replace abstract thought. Like Dewey, James said it was 'experience' that was a 'reconstitutive function' (that is, a kind of mental tonic), which led those hostile to him to wonder 'whether he had not confused those activities which, since the time of Aristotle, philosophers had sought to keep distinct, namely, knowing, making and doing'.[4] In explicating 'experience' within pragmatism, one of James's most acute critics, John E. Smith, reveals (somewhat unconsciously) both 'therapeutic' and 'professional' values when he says that for James the 'living through' of personal endurance, the 'acquisition of skills', 'is the actual career of the subject itself'.[5] Individualism, specialized skills and the notion of a career receive particular emphasis at the end of the nineteenth century. James's writing will engage not so much a general theory of personality as a set of historical values which were then currently being associated with a new professional class.

I

It is hard from a philosopher's perspective to look at James's treatment of philosophy with a great deal of sympathy. What Lovejoy said of James's use of pragmatism to test the truth of belief applies equally well to James's attitude to philosophy: 'Professor James's usual method of peacemaking is to try and annihilate both combatants in the quarrels of which he disapproves, using his pragmatic formula as a bludgeon to that end.'[6] For James made a psychological drama out of philosophy. His two actors were Idealism and Materialism. These days, when philosophy is no longer looked at as two systems facing each other down and when critics have rediscovered relations between British and continental eighteenth and nineteenth-century philosophies, there are problems in understanding James's procedure.[7] James rarely quotes at any length from actual philosophers in the *Principles*, yet he speaks all the time about their camps being traditionally opposed, as if that were a received and undisputed fact.

At the same time, however, psychology did grow out of a number of philosophical propositions. James was to follow Hume in ways which were seized upon by behaviourists. James's emphasis on 'habit' is a case in point. Watson explains the relevance: 'Hume held that the principle of connection between our ideas is habit. Habit is the universal law of mind. Not only our external perception, but all our experiences are explained by habit. As it has been put, 'Empiricism becomes associationism".[8] James could not, therefore, given his subject-matter, avoid philosophical issues. Critics have often pointed out discrepancies between James's alleged allegiances and his practice. While not adapting a Kantian creative consciousness, he appeals to an analogy of one. He refuses an intuition of space and time in Kant's sense, but appeals to affective grounds in human nature, to some extent like Kant also, and indeed Nietzsche. In spite of James's refusal of a priori categories, many have seen him as lapsing towards idealism, especially in his theory of truth.[9]

In fact James's appeal to truth breaks the philosophic urge to system. He could disconcertingly switch levels of that appeal – from reason to experience or feeling. A number of commentators have noted James's reaffirmation of Cartesian dualism, for example, in the

Principles.[10] In *The Will to Believe*, James had criticized Hegel's concepts of time and the ego from the point of view of space's ability to determine the 'relation of the items that enter it in a far more intricate way than does time'.[11] At moments he seems melodramatically opposed to Hegel, who was every empiricist's archetypal idealist. Like others in Anglo-America, he attacked the obscurity and otherworldliness of Hegel's project. It was 'experience' which was to save mankind from the hell of Hegelian solipsism and a priori dogmatism.[12] Yet in the *Pluralistic Universe* the shadow of Hegel emerges more positively. Hegel's contradictions in unity, however, James saw as 'paradox': 'Somehow life does, out of its total resources, find ways of satisfying opposites at once.' While this appears to bring Hegelian process to a grinding halt, in another mood James can say, 'He plants himself in the empirical flux of things and gets the impression of what happens', as if Hegel, too, were building on some kind of Lockean sensationism.[13] In one important sense James knew that he could not avoid what he saw were the eternal questions of philosophy. For if psychology was to replace philosophy it not only faced those eternal questions, but it would need some other kind of discourse for making a critique of itself.

There are, of course, historical reasons for James's philosophical preferences. Jean Wahl's almost forgotten book of 1925 gives valuable clues to what James, in purely philosophical terms, was immediately confronted with. Wahl traces the rise of the British Hegelian Movement whose ideas 'crammed' journals like the *Journal of Mental Science* at the end of the nineteenth century. Curiously their goals were not unlike those of James: 'it was hoped, that it would be possible to overcome agnosticism in metaphysics, associationism in psychology, and utilitarianism in morals.'[14] James's respect for Bradley – though disagreeing with him philosophically – is well known. Bradley in fact fitted in somewhere between Hegel and James. His emphasis on the transitory relations of appearance, on immediate experience, on the concrete, his suspicion of categories, a disposition to pluralist assumptions, could meet James half-way coming from another philosophical direction. Hence James's ambiguity about Hegel in the *Pluralistic Universe*.

James has many strategies of using philosophy. He uses it as a principle of criticism, as a means of historically defining its redundance, as a way of berating the repetitions and naïvetés of contemporary psychology, as a dualistic strategy of argumentative procedure, as a ground of his own synthesis, and as a foil for unreconstructed appearance. But of all the philosophers, it was Locke who was most important for James. His influence was pervasive in spite of James's rejection of his empiricism in *Radical Empiricism*.

James and Locke have already been compared in personal terms, and in relation to that common background in medicine which offered models for mediating the claims of knowledge and life. Commentators have also, of course, seen the general significance of Locke's work for psychology, in addition to the particular relation between Locke's *Essay* and James's *Principles*. Klein's *History of Scientific Psychology* (1970), a work in which James is clearly the most important touchstone, summarizes Locke's importance for contemporary psychology-or rather, 'scientific psychology', as Klein prefers to call it. Stating that Locke's *Essay* is primarily an epistemological rather than a psychological exercise, he concludes that significant fragments of it point towards the recognition of neural processes as immediate antecedents of experienced sensations, anticipate knowledge about the effect of sensory deprivation on perception, have important things to say about the psychology of visual depth perception, habitual behaviour, and theories of the self and individuality.[15] Yet epistemology cannot be so simply separated from psychology. Locke's double representation of reality in sense and intellect has a tendency to speak of contents of consciousness and mental events at a philosophical price, that of raising an ontological problem of 'whether there is any real material world at all'. Linschoten, whose argument is followed here, goes on to quote Berkeley's quip: '*Esse est percipi*'.[16]

It is well known that Locke used Gassendi's critique of Descartes, summed up in yet another Latin tag which goes back in fact to St. Thomas's endorsement of Aristotle's *De Anima*: '*Nihil est in intellectu, quod non prius fuerit in sensu*'.[17] Locke was 'thoroughly familiar with Descartes's work, with Gassendi's sensationist attack on this work, with Pascal's suspicion of rationalism'.[18] Locke's relation to Gassendi and Epicurean philosophy has come under increasing scrutiny in the last few years. Epicureanism provided the means for the seventeenth-century English scientist Boyle to satisfy a 'two-fold demand for physical explanation and for a method of enquiry'. It helped, on lines rather different from that of the actual Epicureans, to provide for 'a method of enquiry, a cosmology and an ethical doctrine'.[19] In the *Principles* James accepted Locke's distinction between truths which needed sensory evidence and those which could be held by examining concepts, which Locke, of course, had in turn adopted from Descartes. James went on to Americanize his philosophy, however, by claiming that metaphysical truths were grounded in 'sentiment' – as Jonathan Edwards had done.[20]

What James hoped to do was to place Locke's 'sense' against pure physiology. Bodily events had first to be felt before they became data for psychology.[21] Empiricism demotes in importance the relation of

Being to the representations of sense, and whereas this was a problem for Berkeley, James was later to invoke simple 'Faith' to make the connection.[22] By these means James could challenge the primacy given to bodily events by the materialists, and also any relation between those events and sense. Paradoxically, therefore, the investigation of sense led to the construction of psychological laboratories whose operators quickly forgot the representative nature of sense itself and invoked it as the baseline of truth. Such was not the original intention. After the first psychological laboratory had been installed under James's initiative at Harvard, James Elliot Cabot said: 'The ignoring of the physical side of mental phenomena has had the natural effect of exaggerating the importance of materialistic views'.[23] Ironically it was originally thought that the laboratory would cure this.

In comparing Locke's *Essay* with James's *Principles*, Eisendrath comments: 'How similar their discursive moods, their lack of dogmatism, and their receptivity to new evidence; how close their range of topics.'[24] Cranston calls Locke's *Essay* a 'very English book', in the sense that its tone was at once moral and pragmatic.[25] Locke and James accept the basic premiss of empiricism, that knowledge is sense-derived. As far as the *Essay* and the *Principles* are concerned, they accept the difference between intuitive and demonstrative knowledge, the necessity for 'faith' outside these knowledges, and one could also link Locke's notion of 'sensitive knowledge' with the qualities James gives to the psychological category of attention.

There are differences of emphasis, however, among the common problems. James was more troubled about the decentring of the sovereign subject which Locke's confident empirical procedure adapted: 'The Understanding, like the Eye, whilst it makes us see, and perceive all other Things, takes no notice of itself: And it requires Art and Pains to set it at a distance and make it its own Object'.[26] James, in the context of late nineteenth-century psychology, could not afford Locke's declared intention not to 'meddle with the Physical Consideration of the Mind' (*Essay*, p. 43). But he shared Locke's distrust of the 'unconscious': 'For to imprint anything on the Mind without the Mind's perceiving it, seems to me hardly intelligible' (pp. 49–50). James shared also Locke's emphasis on memory and habit in building knowledge, so an ethical approach to learning and cognitive development is common to them both. The senses take on physiological 'Appetites to good', so ethics is brought down from innate truths to practical natural good. There are behavioural desires for happiness and aversions to misery. Locke in fact has two ethical bases. One is a behavioural instrumentalism: 'Practical Principles derived from Nature, are there for Operation, and must produce Conformity of Action, not barely speculative assent to their truth, or else they are in vain distinguish'd from speculative Maxims.' The other is purely rational, for God has 'joined Virtue and publick Happiness together' (pp. 67, 69).

Historically the latitudinarian Locke needed to defend himself from Dissenters. His ethical practicalism, which James shared, left judgement to the mercy of permitted practice. You cannot let your belief terminate in practice if you are not permitted to do so. Writing under the shadow of Hobbes, Locke had to admit this. He knew action was governed by Leviathan (p. 8). James ignores Leviathan in his greater reliance on Bagehot's sentiment. In general the shadow of the Publick still haunts Locke's definition of Society, whereas in James it has virtually disappeared. James merely exhorts the individual to renew the fight. Locke had a much more practical sense of what to do with profligate atheist wretches in the shape of the 'fear of the Magistrates Sword' (p. 88).

With Locke, James would have agreed that Knowledge is derived from Experience, but only at the largest level of generalization. For Locke 'Observation' operates internally and externally: on objects and the operations of mind. James, unlike Locke, tended to emphasize memory and habit rather more than 'considering' and 'reasoning'. Indeed certain definitions Locke uses for his Ideas have an almost rationalist ring. He continuously emphasized the epistemological dimension of his argument, while James, in common with the other pragmatists, avoided it. However, Locke did emphasize the psychological effects of the operations of Mind, 'the satisfaction of uneasiness arising from any thought', thus including feeling in intellection for selective purposes (p. 106). James did not emphasize reflective reasoning to anything like the extent that Locke did.

Indeed Locke's epistemology is disconcertingly diverse in its parameters. The process from simple to complex ideas – later rejected, by James – is only one side of him. Ideas coming from reflection, for example, and those dependent on sensation and reflection would seem to defeat a linear account of their origin. But Locke's view of sensation does have a psychological and ethical base. Ideas (sensations) of pleasure and pain rouse us from our 'lazy lethargick Dream' (p. 129). To that extent James trusted the senses less than Locke to galvanize us into activity. Locke was caught between a doctrine of natural organism and the need to be a Christian. As a doctor he saw a balance-producing function in bodily response. Too much light causes our eyes to hurt: 'Which is wisely and favourably so ordered by Nature, that when any object does, by the vehemency of its operation, disorder the instruments of Sensation, whose structures cannot but be very nice and delicate, we might by the pain, be warned to withdraw, before the Organ be quite put out of order, and so be unfitted for its proper Functions for the future' (p. 130). Like the Anglican poet George Herbert, however, in his famous poem 'The Pulley', Locke kept aside a little restlessness for ethical and spiritual reasons.[27]

Locke's excursions into Natural Philosophy, as he called them, also had certain implications for psychology. In maintaining the difference between 'the Qualities in Bodies, and the Ideas produced by them in the mind', Locke used the old Aristotelian distinction between primary and secondary qualities (*Essay*, p. 140). Ideas relate to secondary qualities. Locke's problem, also experienced in the late nineteenth century, was how far psychology could be investigated on the philosophical precepts held by the natural sciences.[28] In nineteenth-century psychology idealists could identify mental events with primary qualities and neural events with secondary ones, and materialists could do the opposite. Could Locke's affective elements of consciousness (pleasure, pain, etc.) be reduced to more fundamental ones? While strategically maintaining Cartesian dualism, Locke was nonetheless affected by certain metaphysical implications of the theory of primary qualities, and of the methodology of the physical sciences. Boylean atomism (simple to complex elements), Newtonian action at a distance (Locke's 'powers'), and notions of continuity all figure in his epistemological descriptions. The nineteenth-century associationists, too, 'invoked the principle of the continuity of nature and the precepts of the scientific method'.[29]

When he turns to more obvious psychological issues, Perception, Discerning, Space, Duration and so on – staple areas of investigation for nineteenth-century psychologists – Locke's medical emphasis, if it may be so called, is on the body. In simple perception the body cannot help attending its object: senses select some impressions, screen out others. Disease, blindness, habit, all escape our will yet produce effects. Pain and pleasure as well determine physical and moral health. Memory is a physical capacity open to the ravages of Fever. Against this 'crisis' (originally a medical term – politicized in the late nineteenth century), clear and distinct ideas are necessary. Metaphor, common conversation, custom, inadvertency, wit, irregularity in the succession of ideas, enthusiasm, indeed any lapse in the 'one constant, equal, uniform Course' of Newtonian time itself, is likely to mislead our understanding. Rational will is the only defence.

It has recently been argued that the nineteenth-century psychologists came to blows over the problem of volition which challenged nineteenth-century views of what scientific scope, methods, explanations and assumptions in fact were. James took 'will' out of the scientific debate eventually – having attempted in the *Principles* to incorporate it along biological – selectionist lines to placate the scientists. Here is Locke on the subject: Given the constant state of uneasiness which psychologically undermines us, Locke conceives the will to be automatically called up for natural and ethical reasons: 'we look beyond the present, and desire goes with our foresight, and that still carries the will with it.' And Locke continues:

> For the *will* being the power of directing our operative faculties to some action, for some end, cannot at any time be moved towards what is judg'd at that time unattainable: That would be to suppose an intelligent being designedly to act for an end, only to lose its labour; for so it is to act, for what is judg'd not attainable; and therefore very great *uneasinesses* move not the *will*, when they are not capable of a Cure: They, in that case, put us not upon endeavours.
>
> (*Essay*, pp. 257–8)

Prudence co-operates with the self-regulating mechanism of desire passively to produce Cure; on the metaphysical assumption that the world is authoritatively orderly. When we choose wrongly Locke has a medical anecdote to confirm this pragmatic view of the world: 'And therefore 'twas a right Answer of the Physician to his Patient, that had sore Eyes. If you have more Pleasure in the Taste of Wine, than in the use of your Sight, Wine is good for you: but if the Pleasure of Seeing be greater to you, than that of Drinking, Wine is naught' (p. 261 n.). As Buñuel knew in his film, *The Discreet Charm of the Bourgeoisie*, a certain anxiety over eating characterizes the class. Locke's 'use' has a definite utilitarian ring to it. There is no point, says Locke, doubtless recalling Hooke, in having 'microscopical' eyes capable of penetrating into the 'radical Texture of Bodies', if 'he would not make any advantage by the change, if such an acute Sight would not serve to conduct him to the Market and Exchange' (p. 303). Such a statement not only marks Locke's revenge on Boylean pure science, but suggests that 'good use' is automatically verified by market principles. In today's multiversity, perhaps Locke would be on the cost-effective administrator's side, rather than that of the pure scientist or arts professor.

James's direct use of Locke in the *Principles* is various. Neglecting Locke's more Cartesian aspects, James emphasizes his attacks on the *cogito* (*Principles*, I. 198). He accepts Locke's dualism which he calls 'mind knowing and thing known' (I. 214), and the 'theory of ideas' which builds simple into complex mental events – though he challenges the assumption that sensations are simple ideas, since we never get the same sensation twice (I. 225), and in other chapters (VI and IX) he speaks of compound states. James quotes Locke in his 'The Consciousness of Self', emphasizing in the telling phrase, 'club-worth', the social aspects of the individual sense of worth as a gloss on Locke's statement in the *Essay*: 'Nor is there one in ten thousand who is stiff and insensible enough to bear up under the constant dislike and condemnation of his own club' (I. 283). Like Locke, James advocates a prudent self, sacrificing immediate desire for future ends, though without Locke's notion of desires fighting each other, and with a greater moralistic emphasis (I. 300). James approved Locke's *legal* defence of consciousness as sanity. Descartes's Being, dependent on thought, implied a man responsible before God, whether sane or insane, crippled or healthy. James approves, as Locke did, of pleas of diminution of responsibility. Person, said Locke, is 'a Forensic Term appropriating Actions and their Merit; and so belong[s] only to intelligent Agents capable of a Law and Happiness and Misery' (*Essay*, p. 346). This definition of 'person' as a forensic term, that is as a definition dependent on law and health, is of central importance to the entire argument of the present book. It will simply be noted here and taken up in detail in the discussion of Gertrude Stein, and in the Conclusion.

James goes on to approve Locke's distinction between consciousness and personal substance in order to moderate feelings of retribution by those who would refure extenuating circumstances of bodily condition (*Principles*, I. 331). Casually admitting consciousness here, James puts, however, a greater emphasis on bodily condition (I. 352 f.) and, again like Locke, on the capacity of illness to disturb memory. James rejects metaphysical conceptions of the self (unlike Locke), but continues many of the latter's psycho-pathological arguments. Discussing the associationist theory of self, James asserts: 'Locke paved the way for it by the hypothesis he suggested of the same substance having two successive consciousnesses, or of the same consciousness being supported by more than one substance. He made his readers feel that the important unity of the Self was its verifiable and felt unity. . .' (I. 332).

James also quotes Locke on the notion of conception, where he states in the *Essay* that we can have an Idea of bitter even if sugar tastes bitter to us in a fever. James advises us to read the whole passage. He gives Locke's example an empiricist explanation by saying that conception depends on repetition and memory, and then on recall of memory simply. On discrimination and comparison James quotes Locke *en bloc*. The passage in question is the one in the *Essay* where Locke warns against analogy, metaphor and allusion, and speaks of the need for clear and distinct Ideas (I. 458). James argues against the exclusively analytic quality of Locke's argument and states that psychology needs both synthetic (associationist) and analytic approaches. On another tack, James feels that even Locke's and Hume's simple ideas are too much of an initial abstraction.

In his chapter on 'Association', James replaces Locke's Ideas by 'Things Thought of' as the elements of association, and hopes thus to save causality in brain processes:

> The psychological law of association of objects thought of through their previous contiguity in thought or experience would thus be an effect, within the mind, of the physical fact that nerve currents propagate themselves easiest through those tracts of conduction which have been already most in use.
>
> (*Principles*, I. 531)

Whether the 'effect. . . of the physical fact' is really different from a Lockean Idea, except in so far as it can retain multiplicity of impact (not simply a simple-becoming-complex impact), is open to doubt. However, James gives Locke the credit and quotes him:

> 'Custom', says Locke, 'settles habit of thinking in the understanding, as well as of determining in the will, and of motions in the body; all which seem to be but *trains of motion in the animal spirits* (by this Locke meant identically what we understand by *neural processes*) which once set a-going, continue in the same steps they have been used to, which by often treading, are worn into a smooth path, and the motion in it becomes easy and, as it were, natural.'
>
> (*Principles*, I. 531)

Custom, then, unlike the later simplifications of a Bagehot, operates on three levels: understanding, will and body. With 'continuity' it constitutes in Locke and James a virtual metaphysic.

Associationism was the most important legacy bequeathed by the English philosophers to psychology, and it was quintessentially an English invention. The English philosophers are ransacked by James in this chapter for matters relevant to late nineteenth-century psychology. Associative machinery throws up variations of connections among things and the mind then selects what is already associated.

Locke is also recalled in James's chapter on 'The Perception of Reality'. James opposes Cartesian doubt with 'Belief' as a way of cognizing reality, and so turns an intellectualist argument into a psychological one. He quotes Bagehot in speaking of the 'emotion' of conviction (II. 913). To prevail, a conception we believe in must 'terminate in the world of orderly sensible experience' (II. 929). James advances his argument by referring to Locke: 'Among all sensations, the most belief-compelling are those productive of pleasure or of pain. Locke expressly makes the pleasure- or pain-giving quality to be the ultimate human criterion of anything's reality' (II. 934). It has already been shown that for Locke this was associated with a rather utilitarian ethic and an Epicurean stance: a paradoxical combination. If pleasure (for the Physician's Patient), consisted in getting drunk rather than seeing clearly, the implicit irony suggests that value is independent of the disturbance of the receptive senses. Locke hovers, too, over James's last chapter. Indeed at one point James confesses: 'in truth I have done nothing more in the previous pages than make a little more explicit the teachings of Locke's fourth book' (II. 1255–6). Cranston calls the fourth book of the *Essay* the 'most incomplete and tantalizing yet in many ways the most important'.[30]

In many ways Locke opens more subtleties than he can cope with – which is the great merit of the untidiness of his argument. He disputes the nature of truth as a physician facing claims of natural philosophers, as a Christian determined to keep final truth for God, as a philosopher who puts the real world in doubt, and as one nonetheless prejudiced enough by the new science to doubt any steady truth conveyed by ordinary language. If real truth occurs when 'signs agree as our Ideas agree' (*Essay*, p. 573), then the required correspondences and means of testing face an almost impossible task. One of the most significant of Locke's arguments occurs when he places his physician's sense of the interconnectedness of living substance against the physicist's (Boylean) atomism. The implications are philosophical and methodological. Instead of limiting the area of enquiry atomistically in order to search out the things opaque to the senses, the scope of the enquiry is widened to include the observable with the opaque as part of a continuous scale. Arguing that even physical bodies need other physical bodies in order for their properties be known (the empirical enquiry of similarity and dissimilarity), Locke asserts: 'it is more so in Vegetables, which are nourished, grow and produce Leaves, Flowers and Vegetables in constant succession' (p. 586). And a little later he states categorically: 'This is certain, Things, however absolute and entire they seem in themselves, are but Retainers to other parts of Nature, for that which they are most taken notice of by us' (p. 587).

Locke then argues against Descartes's notion of self-evident truths because he wants to claim that there are other sorts of truths besides those of geometry and because as a Christian, he wishes to retain the notion of revelation. Those other sorts of truths are the structures and interplay of his Ideas which he wishes to free from their dependency on a priori maxims.

Anticipating James, Locke wants a plurality of truths and indeed types of knowledge. Maxims have mainly pedagogic value. Mr Newton, 'in his never enough to be admired Book', merely proceeded by showing the 'Agreement or Disagreement of the Ideas, as expressed in the Propositions he demonstrated' (p. 599). In a phrase once used by Huckleberry Finn, Locke is telling the truth here but with 'some stretchers'. And what is stretched is the notion of Idea, which if applied to Newton becomes very metaphysical indeed. Further, Locke's refusal of creativity to axioms is just, but his proposed use of them to 'stop the Mouths of Wranglers' (p. 601) is less than just, for it denies the possibility of a democratic synthesis between disputants occurring in a creative way. When Locke turns to positive pedagogy, his theory of how we acquire new knowledge is again ambiguous: 'he that would enlarge his own, or another's Mind, to Truths he does not yet know, must find out intermediate Ideas, and then lay them in such order one by another, that the Understanding may see the agreement, or disagreement of those in question' (p. 611). While this is excellent pedagogic practice, it fails to account for discontinuity and untidiness in creative thought as such. The plea for continuity will be repeated in James, as will the problem of whether or not truth can be found in method.

Continuing his meditations on truth and knowledge, Locke then considers our knowledge of the existence of God and Things. He argues against Lucretius' *Ex nihilo nil fit*, so amenable an argument to atomistically-minded natural philosophers: 'Because it is not reasonable to deny the power of an infinite Being, because we cannot comprehend its Operations. We do not deny other effects upon this ground, because we cannot possibly conceive the manner of their Production' (p. 629). Practicality needs us to take things on faith, just as Darwin's unknown principle of variation had to be taken on trust. The lesson is both pious and practical. It can also then be used as an argument for trusting knowledge from the senses: 'For it takes not from the certainty of our Senses, and the Ideas we receive by them, that we know not the manner wherein they are produced' (pp. 630–1). Reviewing how our senses help to frame our knowledge, Locke concludes that their testimony is adequate to our Condition, which perhaps we should gloss as our general health. We do not in fact need absolute certainty for our general health. Indeed lack of certainty encourages faith, which paradoxically helps us to be prudent and practical: 'He that in the ordinary Affairs of Life, would admit of nothing but direct plain Demonstration, would be sure of nothing, in this World, but of perishing quickly' (p. 636).

It is a merchant venturer's theory of practical knowledge of risk and prudence in skilful balance. Truth may be single but we need to adapt our methods of enquiry 'to the nature of the Ideas we examine' (p. 643). In natural science, when we enquire after the nature of 'substance' Locke suggests that we can trust neither Reason nor Experience, though Experience is the better guide. He has the practice of the laboratory in mind. Locke assumes a priori the imperfection of the human faculty on religious grounds, and so concludes that experience cannot deliver certainty either. He is quick to say he does not wish to disparage scientific and technological advance, but that we should not make a religion out of it: nor take 'doubtful Systems, for complete Sciences' (p. 647).

Locke's world, to use his own term, is a 'twilight' world. In this world he assesses degrees of probable truth which are psychologically connected to the nature of inducement as to what to believe. There is something in belief not manifestly concerned with reasoning and with a linear connection of ideas. Locke has no theory of power, in his subsequent discussion of individual and social beliefs, and consequently adduces a somewhat mechanical argument as to where error lies. Is it in our memory, or in our first judgement, or in our memory of that judgement? Probability can lie in common assent, in repetition delivering constancy, in the lessons of history – although in the latter case Locke gives us a psychological example: that people perfer private to public advantage. He argues legally rather than politically, or socially, or religiously. But the legal argument disguises a political, social and religious argument. Testimony from witnessed written documents is doubtful, so is testimony from traditional report. Locke balances the Church of England between Puritan reliance on the Word and Catholic veneration of tradition. Revelation can give us structures which help us to a 'wary reasoning from Analogy'. It may also lead us to new truth, however, and here Locke admits, to put it in modern terms, the role of metaphysics in building hypotheses (p. 666). In this sense faith is not opposed to reason. In a long discussion of the syllogism, a fairly limited mode of reasoning, Locke shows his preference for 'native rustick Reason' (p. 679).

Faith and reason can also be related in a psychological and ethical stance towards the world. They still need distinguishing, however, on occasions, for the threat of dissenters persists. After all, if those who have the power to call what they do reasonable, when they are unjust, anyone who opposes them is *ipso facto* unreasonable. Since Protestant Dissenters made much of being justified by faith alone and claimed a personal interpretation of the Word, Locke's argument addresses itself primarily to that. In the latter case he argues that since words are simply agreed conventions by which people express their ideas to each other, it is obvious we cannot receive new revelations in words. Locke is no poet and is not prepared to admit that words might have a funtion other than to communicate our ideas clearly. That they might be metaphoric aids to conceptualizing the new never occurs to him. Locke wants to make faith reasonable and reason faithful.

As the work comes to its close it is clear that extra-philosophical concerns dominate more and more. Locke holds steadfastly to the twilight of Anglicanism against the inner light of the sects: 'For strong conceit like a new Principle carries all easily with it' (p. 699). Indeed he sometimes appears to have a domino theory of any new principle – as if society accepted them so easily. There are contradictions in Locke's argument and they are between authorities. If inner light must be brought to the test, is that not to doubt what he has said elsewhere about Ethics and revealed truth? What happens when the modes of the practical and the revealed intersect, and when a situation makes it difficult to judge between what methods are appropriate for different subjects because the subject boundaries are difficult to distinguish? Or when, given a new problem, the methods might have to be invented?

How far, then, in the last chapter of the *Principles*, did James make Locke's fourth book more explicit? James says his use of Locke is 'politic'. In fact he uses Locke, who stood for common-sense experience in the nineteenth-century image, for his more rationalist concepts: for example, the inner agreement of ideas in general propositions. Locke, as has been shown, only uses the term 'experience' for the doubtful truths of science. In fact James confirms, denies and distorts Locke. First James:

> Impressions, as we well know, affect certain orders of sequence and coexistence, and the mind's habits copy the habits of the impressions, so our images of things assume a time- and space-arrangement which resembles the time-and space-arrangements outside.
>
> (*Principles*, II. 1217)

And then Locke:

> Words become general, by being made the signs of general Ideas: and Ideas become general, by separating from them the circumstances of time, and place, and other ideas, that may determine them to this or that particular sequence.
>
> (*Essay*, pp. 410–11)

James's impressions reflect exterior order. Locke's Ideas serve cognition by excluding exteriority. The role of Ideas, for Locke, is at once passive and active: passive in the sense that we can only know the world by their permission, active in the sense of their separation from time and space.

Locke denies certainty in the relation of the order of sense with the world – allowing in different spheres only degrees of probable order. Thus Ideas for Locke relocate experience in an ahistorical psychological time, while being heuristic in the sense that we may through them discover a world beyond the known. They are radically imperfect in a fallen world, for they only allow us degrees of probable truth. Clearly James's summary of the psychologist's assumptions falls far short of the philosopher's subtlety.

In some instances James will assume as a general truth what Locke consigns only to the order of natural philosophy. For example, James wishes to .retain the notion of the progression of experience in Locke's sense (the child gaining its senses on the way to adulthood), and in an ethical sense as, for example, in the typical Wordsworth poem. In this latter sense, James says, experience is educator, sovereign helper, friend; there is something real about it and it ought 'to be kept sacred' (*Principles*, II. 217). Unlike Locke, however, James's emphasis is psychological and ethical as opposed to epistemological and ethical. Locke could not have called experience 'sacred', for as a Christian he could depend on other orders of the real. James has no such recourse at least officially. James's overt intention in the *Principles* has been to show the correspondence of the mental world with what was known physiologically about the brain, and to suggest continuity between physiological response and mind itself. Their respective characterizations of 'experience' are therefore crucial.

Locke has already made 'experience' radically unreal and while, James states, we ought to agree with the 'scientific animus of anti-super-naturalism' (II. 1223), there exist 'other more recondite natural agencies' than those in the scientific description of experience. James uses Locke's doubt of appearance to argue for a probability that there are other natural agencies which are not known. This entirely reverses Locke's emphasis. At this point James brings in his Darwinian model of mind. Exterior, adaptive, conscious, environmental pressures meet in the brain with interior, unconscious, variable and accidental modifications. James calls the former the front-door approach and the latter the back-door approach. He says he will confine 'experience' to the 'front door'. What he means by the 'back door' he says will emerge later. Susceptibility to music and drunkenness are, however, the first examples of the latter. James's Romantic view of the ecstatic and his conviction that music is a survival of the primitive (so much for Bach and Beethoven) – it has no adaptive utility – are questionable, but for the moment they will merely be noted.

When he moves on to describing mental categories James loosely follows Locke, except in the first instance when he speaks of the 'genesis' of elementary mental categories and thus adds a broadly Darwinian tone. To elementary sensation he also adds 'feelings of personal activity'. He puts emotions, desires, instincts, ideas of worth, aesthetic ideas into the same bag of atomistic elements, as a second category. Locke had a physician's view of emotions and desires. They were part of the grand scheme of nature to preserve us. Where they failed they had a further purpose: 'that we finding imperfection, dissatisfaction, and want of complete happiness', might be led to seek greater happiness in God' (*Essay*, p. 130). Locke's view of ideas of worth was merely a secondary pragmatic principle of social cohesion, for the rules of clubbableness failed the highest principle: that of following God's laws directly. By lumping these 'elements' into the same psychological category James buries Locke's religious and socio-ethical distinctions.

James then takes up Locke's forms of thought (ideas of time, space, number, difference, resemblance, causality, subject, attribute, logic) and empirically asserts their natural origin. But James has a problem of how to prove this without entering on an old-fashioned epistemological debate. The answer is psychogenesis. Locke used a linguistic analogy to mediate consensus in change. James uses a Darwinian analogy. Abstract discoveries come about as 'lucky fancies' (chance variations) and *après coup* they correspond to some reality (*Principles*, II. 1228). James extends this individualist cognitive model to social knowledge. Elements of consciousness as such are socially preserved lucky variations. In this way he incorporates Kantian intuitions and Lockean organism into a single model, and preserves the notion of Ideas for pre-cognitive brain reactions. James gives subjective spontaneity to elements of consciousness but not to the relations of time and space, for these are conceived within a metaphysic of evolution.

Opposed to Kantian intuition of time and space, James nonetheless makes evolution a metaphysic (and therefore intuitive at one remove) on the basis of Newtonian time and space characterizations. Newtonian time and space is an environment which sensibly effects us from without and thus can be truly called 'experience'. Here Locke's sense-derived categories of time and space are coupled with associationist continuity, reinforced by Newtonian absoluteness, further coupled with environmental determinism, and hence create a philosophico-mental underpinning to the authority of habit. However, James then adapts Locke's internal relations, the mind's activity about itself (the operations it observes in itself about them), to images outside mere time – space relations (environment). James shifts the emphasis from epistemology to psychology. It is not Ideas operating with Ideas, part sense-derived and part relationally derived, but feelings or sentiment as a sixth sense operating about Lockean Ideas. It is how Ideas 'befall' in a mind 'gifted with memory, expectation, and the possibility of feeling doubt, curiosity, belief, and denial' (II. 1230). Experience is thus separated from thinking and attached to sensibility and even to intuitive judgement.

James then associates thinking with the way of proceeding in the natural sciences, and like Locke denies certainty to the scientific project. Locke does this partly by denying representation of the real to Ideas and the senses and partly by criticizing the scientific method which limits the nature of problems. James emphasizes the second critique, and reverses his earlier ideas about economy. The scientist's proposed simplified unity is, he adds, more like a religious faith than a demonstration. Here James comes into line with Adams's critique of the scientific project. However, to a degree James simplifies the notion of laboratory practice. Devising tests may be quite as imaginative an operation as the 'lucky variation' of the hypothesis, or the ability to assess an unlooked-for result.

In his discussion of the methods of science, paradoxically, James wants to preserve 'truth' for cognition pure and simple: 'Instead of experience engendering the "inner relations", the "inner relations" are what engender the experiences here' (II. 1234). Like Locke, James had an antipathy to actual experimenting, and both men used the necessary recognition of the partial truth of scientific knowledge quite unwarrantably to damn the practices of science as partial in relation to itself. James's 'artificial experiences of the laboratory' rightly condemns the unreflective mediocrity of much that passes for science in our own times, and scientific arrogance in arrogating all experience to its own descriptive discourses, but his model of scientific practice is not adequate or relevant to the condemnation.

As usual James wants to keep the inner and outer worlds separate. He is caught in a complete ambivalence as a result. He is committed to the naturalism of the scientific project and admits that the correspondence theory of truth fits science the best. However this gradually growing certainty is only valid within a small area of human understanding. In ethics it does not hold at all, and in aesthetics only partially. Locke ultimately fell back on revelation and God to protect him from restlessness, and the wearisomeness of endlessly incomplete knowledge. James invokes timeless 'Orientalism' as revealed to travelling English aristocrats in search of 'statistics', to expose the way 'science' has become an 'idol of the tribe'. The Turkish Cadi replies to his Illustrious friend and Joy of his Liver:

> But thou wilt say unto men, Stand aside, Oh man, for I am more learned than thou art, and have seen more things. If thou thinkest that thou art in this respect better than I am, thou art welcome. I praise God that I seek not that which I require not. Thou art learned in the things I care not for; and as for that which thou hast seen, I defile it. Will much knowledge create thee a double belly, or wilt thou seek Paradise with thine eyes.
>
> (*Principles*, II. 123 n.)

What James cannot achieve by God he seeks by Modammed and aristocratic hippies. Not for nothing is he the heir of transcendentalism.

Turning to the 'a priori' sciences of classification, logic and mathematics, James considers these as essentially aesthetic modes. Instead of classification being an intuition of God's monistic order, as in the eighteenth century, James invokes serial logic, difference, similarity, and comparison as an intuition of genetic mental change (the back-door way). Instead of *cogito ergo sum* James offers *sentio ergo cogito*. Rational propositions depend on intuitive comparisons – Ideal truths for comparison: 'It is, for some unknown reason, a great aesthetic delight for the mind to break the order of experience, and class its materials in serial orders...' (II. 1242). How you know experience thus becomes a problem, for you have to know it somehow before you break it. James confines aesthetic reason to logic, and indeed to syntax. Creative construction is limited to continuity, and successions of attributes, and to complementary equations operating about the 'is' of comparison like a series of conditional ontologies. The hightest act of reason is to skip along the line of propositions which in any case is metaphysically continuous underneath. James confines reason to genetic explanation and excludes the speculative which must, as the French say, following Husserl, supply its 'horizon'.

No amount of keeping the system moving through evolutionary paradigms alters this separation for James. His instinct is to turn speculative truth into a kind of secular revelation which acts as an insurance policy. In this way he takes up Locke's distinction between 'mental truth' and 'real truth' (II. 1257), noting the strange descent in status of the a priori. Here James conflates Locke's different modes of knowledge to make a rather sweeping statement, affirming that 'we still have to go back to our senses' to find what the reality is. At this point he drops Locke's epistemological complexity, and his distinctions.

Whereas for Locke Religion and Science filled two separate realms, for James science rushes into the vacuum left by the death of God. James gives us the psychology of hypothesis, not its epistemology: 'The craving to believe that the things of the world belong to kinds which are related by inward rationality together, is the parent of Science as well as of sentimental philosophy (Psychology)' (II. 1260). Locke kept his feelings about science separate from religion by stressing the uncertainty of the probabilities revealed by the former. The success of science in James's time (after all he has said on the subject of the idols of the tribe) allows him to assert by analogy a faith in 'other ideal relations not yet so verified' (II. 1262), in other areas of human experience. Thus a model of understanding, radically discontinuous from other understandings, becomes a psychological model to ensure faith in other areas of human experience. It is a trickle-down theory of success and as such is a nonsense. James can only fill up the gap by exhortations to confidence: 'The widest postulate of rationality is that the world is rationally intelligible throughout, after the pattern of some ideal system. The whole war of the philosophies is over that point of faith' (II. 1269).

James concludes by examining Lamarck and Darwin on their views of transmitted habits or instincts. James perfers Darwin's internal factor to Lamarck's external ones, perhaps because so little is convincing on either side and because the unknown principle of variation at least keeps the debate open. Indeed, James closes his great work with an affirmation of scepticism worthy of Locke, but much more pessimistic. Having surveyed with generous completeness the range of available literature, James concludes, not with Locke's hopeful twilight in which the Christian perspective at least saw Things darkly, but with a conviction that when the insights of psychology have been gathered and its biological history hypothesized, 'The more clearly one perceives the slowly gathering twilight close in utter night' (II. 1280).

II

In fact the great conclusion of James's *Principles* was that psychology could depend neither on biological nor on physical explanation. A vacuum was thus created as to what model of explanation *was* possible for psychology. Pluralistic explanation was prudent, but the line between it and confusing of levels and procedures was thinly drawn. Scepticism about all available models was a fine negative stance, and perhaps inevitable in the closing years of the nineteenth century, before the great scientific breakthroughs of the early modern era. However, absolute plurality was hardly an encouraging model for those actually engaged in the business of psychology. In fact the psychologists ignored James and got on with their work.

More important, however, is the fact that when James accused science of metaphysical dogmatism and consequently attempted to split its practice from its metaphysics, he also robbed it of creative possibilities.

In fact James refused psychology's various models of explanation on a priori grounds, covered himself against the charge of dogmatism by in turn querying philosophy's 'traditional' dualism (empiricist-idealist), and then attempted to find a synthesis in a Darwinian science of mind. The net result was a displacement of the focus of truth from both theory and practice on to method, in spite of a scepticism about method. Unlike Adams, who was sceptical of all scientific explanation, from Lyell to Poincaré, especially when transposed to discourses other than its own, James never challenged Darwin's actual model. As a result the metaphysic of natural selection becomes a mental method from which epistemological concerns are excluded. This has enormous implications for James's philosophy. Santayana said that 'his radical empiricism and pragmatism were in his own mind only methods'.[31] What Santayana saw critically, most Jamesian commentators have taken positively. James's account of intelligence was defended by John Dewey, who called it a 'teleological instrument'.[32]

James himself, however, was finally ambiguous about method. In *The Will to Believe* he said: 'Science has organized this nervousness [about error] into a regular technique, her so-called method of verification; and she has fallen so deeply in love with the method that one may even say she has ceased to care for truth by itself at all'.[33] James is on the verge of attacking method as an idol of the tribe, but in *Pragmatism* he reaffirmed his claim that pragmatism did not stand for special results: 'It is a method only'.[34] On the other hand he would have agreed with Adorno in the late 1930s, that 'the primacy of method has today already gone so far that only those research tasks can be undertaken which can be discharged by means of available devices'.[35]

Sidney Kaplan, in a little-noted article, speaks of 'a school of method in the Harvard Yard' during James's time there. He compares views on social reform held by James, Frank Taussig the economist, and Francis G. Peabody the theologian. Kaplan makes the point that in spite of an apparently liberal methodology, or perhaps because of it, the efforts of all three seemed to confirm rather than challenge the status quo in an America where, in 1900, 12 per cent of the population owned 90 per cent of the nation's wealth. The work of all three men was interdisciplinary; all three admitted the presence of 'real life', wanted to be concrete and factual, emphasized 'scientific method' on the hypothesis–verification level, and admitted social change on a historico-evolutionary model. Translated into politics, this model admitted only the 'solution' of personal regeneration, ultragradualism, and a mistrust of alternative ideologies, normally characterized – or rather, dismissed – as wholesale panaceas:

> Biblical texts and a vague evolutionism on the one hand and a pragmatic pluralism on the other, have eventuated in the view summed up more simpy a few years later by Harvard's Eliot: 'the effect of the trades unions is to destroy individuality and limit freedom; moreover they make it impossible, or rather very difficult, for a man to do his best in his daily work; and they deprive all their members of the satisfaction which comes from doing one's best'.[36]

'Method' thus became the guarantee of the 'free' individual.

Out in Chicago Dewey gave a less sophisticated but socially more transparent account of method: 'This conviction of the value of the individualized finds its further expression in psychology, which undertakes to show how this individualization proceeds, and in what aspect it presents itself.... [This] means that philosophy be a method; not an assurance company, nor a knight errant.'[37] Then as now, there was often confusion between empirical logic which more or less determined (or over-determined) procedures, and empirical procedures themselves with their honest and untidy relations between hypothesis and experience.[38]

The alliance between the plurality, and at its worst confusions, of explanations and the deification of method left traditional epistemological concerns in philosophy without apparent relevance. The attack on epistemology and consciousness as merely offering evidence for the degenerate, aristocratic, abstract, unscientific, 'continental', self-absorbed, unpractical, stubbornly unadaptive, un-future oriented, mystical, potentially revolutionary, unstable, Utopian ways of thought came from all quarters. Consciousness was more un-American than George III. Like Lincoln Steffens in the Soviet Union, the pragmatists had seen the future and they knew it worked. But it was not only the pragmatists. To anyone working in the behavioural or social sciences, problems of consciousness and epistemology were simply not relevant. Actual science appeared to get along fine without them. Lovejoy meditated with casual innocence: 'Theoretically, epistemology, since it professes to determine the criteria of truth, and the scope of real knowledge, should affect natural science as vitally as theology. But in practice it has not usually done so.'[39] Modern commentators have hardly been more sophisticated when they speak of 'epistemology as social process'.[40]

By 1919 the psychologists had jettisoned the entire philosophical vocabulary of just a generation earlier. In the introduction to *Psychology from the Standpoint of a Behaviorist*. Watson abandoned the 'crude dualism', as he called it, of 'structural psychology', and he added that Behaviorism – 'a purely American product' – was so pure that 'the reader will find no discussion of consciousness, and no reference to such terms as sensation, perception, attention, will, image and the like'. Like the wicked 'European' influences they were deporting more physically in the same year, American psychology could get along without them. Watson's book has to be read in the context of the managerial revolution and the invention of 'human engineering'. Among many other things to be noted in the book is his suggestion that silent observers, technically trained, judge the 'assets' and 'liabilities' of 'personalities'. Within the free market of behaviour, 'consciousness' is a superstitious irrelevance. Further, 'From the behaviorist's point of view the problem of "meaning" is pure abstraction. It never arises in the scientific observation of behavior'.[41] Not the least of the ironies of the pragmatists' downgrading of epistemology was that it led to the abandonment, in 'scientific' psychology, of their entire structure of discourse.

Consciousness had different meanings for them all, but none really included will, reflection, or imagination. Mead, no less than Watson, saw it as a means of control and behaviour adaptation: 'successful social conduct brings one into a field within which a consciousness of one's own attitudes helps towards the control of the conduct of others'.[42] At most consciousness was regarded as a kind of anticipatory attention. As for James himself, his attitude to consciousness 'varied greatly at different times and in relation to different subjects'.[43] Commentators brandish phrases like 'teleology of consciousness', 'functional' not 'ontological' consciousness, 'modes of attention' and so on, each of which can be aligned with some preferred philosophy.[44] Indeed the commentary can become extremely ingenious. Attempting to steer a path for James between phenomenologists and logical positivists, Eisendrath states: 'Experience, or conceptually, "I think", is the basis of all our construction of the world, and so does accompany all our objects, as Kant says. This positing of experience as precondition of the world is the basis for James's phenomenology.'[45] One's assent to such a statement must depend on accepting the equivalence of that first 'or' and the ambiguity of the word 'posit'.

Psychoanalysts, who also like to claim James for their history, make use of this automatic positing by saying that James really meant unconscious when he said conscious: 'What is striking in James's explanation [*Principles*, I. 563] is the seeming autonomy of the intended thought in picking up associative material, in the same automony which Freud's repressed material seems to enjoy in creating dreams.'[46] But James distrusted just the kind of unconscious creative symbolism which such statements imply. In *A Pluralistic Universe*, following out the directives of radical empiricism (relations being themselves part of experience), James talked about 'states of consciousness' being able to separate and combine freely, keeping their own identity unchanged while forming parts 'of simultaneous fields of experience of wider scope'.[47] Consciousness is again in the same order as experience while holding aloof in terms of mere identity. In fact, says one commentator, 'James strenuously rejects all formal statements of epistemological idealism and therefore cannot, at least within the framework of his philosophical orientation as it is generally understood, appeal to the genuine creativity of consciousness'.[48]

What James substitutes is interest, which one commentator argues correctly is as fundamental to him 'as consciousness to Hegel because James construes interest to be the integrating factor in human experience'.[49] 'Interest', however, is a word with legal, economic, social and even spiritual connotations. It points to a relation of feeling to objects, mediated by a code whose terms have become automatic through habit. It relies on credit, it cannot alter its parameters. It has all the atmosphere of that 'kindly leading' of experience (the credit system) verifying our ideas.[50] It is not Newman's 'lead, kindly light' but lead, kindly experience, objects, relations between objects, and hopeful selections of chance. Interest can weight the dice, praise the Lord and pass the ammunition. Interest is unearned, but it is hardly grace. Santayana's words are still timely:

> To deny consciousness is to deny a prerequisite to the obvious, and to leave the obvious standing alone. That is a relief to an overtaxed and self-impeded generation: it seems a blessed simplification. It gets rid of the undemocratic notion that by being very reflective, circumspect, and subtle you might discover something that most people do not see.[51]

For the much more democratic Sartre, consciousness is an act of self-transcendence, both towards the object and towards others: 'Joy, sorrow, melancholy are consciousness. And we must apply to them the great law of consciousness: that all consciousness is consciousness of something. In a word, feelings have special intentionalities, they represent one way – among others – of self-transcendence'.[52]

There are many hints in James of something similar, but they remain hints. For Linschoten, James used 'consciousness' as 'awareness', 'self-awareness', 'voluntary reasoning to ends', and – with inevitable Cartesianism – an 'entity different from the body'. James's 'stream of thought' (consciousness) breaks the synchrony of Lockean ideas and ascribes cognitive functions to sensation, perception, and language. James's field of experience is likened to the phenomenologist's situation, and James's consciousness can even include the body's intentionality: the body being the source of a Husserlian horizon of experience. However, Jamesian 'experience', while corresponding to the phenomenologist's 'given' fails the phenomenologist's sense of 'being-given-to someone'.[53]

No one has better demonstrated than Wilshire the project that failed in James's *Principles*: the physical – mental correspondences given up after the first chapter, the 'intrinsic referentialness of mind' which 'snowballs'; the totality of experience becoming prior to objects, in turn prior to mental states in turn prior to brain states. The *Lebenswelt* is the founding level of meaning. Meaning is prior to truth though unacknowledged. Wilshire reminds us of all the difficulties of James's refusal of consciousness, though he does not put it quite that way, for the phenomenologists have their own problems about that seamless web connecting mind and world. Wilshire does point out, however, that the notion of 'experience' is essentially a metaphysical one and that James's functionalism in practice had to refer to mental states and their objects simultaneously.[54]

Giving the history of the phenomenologists' relation to and use of James, one large summarizing article about this essentially late-'60s phenomenon goes further and attempts to relate James radically to Sartre and Merleau-Ponty, relying on Sartre's *Transcendence of the Ego*. But if James adopted 'a non-egological theory of consciousness on phenomenological grounds',[55] Sartre surely never did. The fact that the World has not created the Me and the Me has not created the World becomes two objects for Sartre's 'absolute impersonal consciousness', which in turn is the *condition* for the ego to appear endangered before the world. Sartre and James did, however, in their different ways attempt to 'plunge man back into the world'.[56]

That world was only revealed in experience, and Whitehead was probably putting it rather mildly when he said that the 'word experience is the most deceitful in philosophy'.[57] Locke could invoke the word against the Dissenters: 'no Suppositions of any Sect, are of force enough to destroy constant Experience.' On the other hand since Ideas are how we come by experience and since their generalizing capacity makes known the unknown particularity of nature by 'separating from them the circumstances of time, and place', it is clear that two meanings of experience are here invoked.[58] As the Dissenters probably found out, the appeal to experience robbed them of their own right to it. In fact both Dissenter and Latitudinarian could appeal to experience. The seventeenth-century Richard Coppin, urging the radical doctrine that God had revealed himself to the poor and ignorant, said: 'This is a marvellous thing indeed to all that know it not; but experience goes beyond all things.' Locke and James would have agreed precisely with that last phrase in a different context. John Robinson, like James, appealed to the future for his doctrine of experience in the farewell sermon to the Pilgrim Fathers in 1620. The very experienceabilty of America was guaranteed by God's future revelations.[59] Experience could be appealed to as a manifestation of both inner light *and* teleology. It could also deny both of them.

It is important to remember that Locke, like James, lived historically. Locke tempered into social generalization and organism the fierce confrontation of political reality and power in Hobbes. As Christopher Hill puts it:

> Locke's ideas – by Hobbes out of the Protestant ethic – were less ruthlessly logical, less brilliantly clear-cut, less shocking to traditionalists. They fitted the world in which kings ruled by the grace of God but could be turned out if they did not rule as the men of property wished; in which the Church showed men the way to heaven but bishops were appointed by politicians.[60]

For the relevance of Hill's comments to James's time one might substitute the Senate, ruling by the American Constitution, for kings; the robber barons for the men of property; liberal individualism for the Church; and the Supreme Court judges for bishops.

It was Benjamin Franklin who declared that 'Experience is the worst teacher', and Sartre powerfully characterized its conservative psychology thus : 'Experience was much more than a defence against death; it was a right – the right of old men.'[61] In *A Pluralistic Universe* James could write, 'Direct acquaintance and conceptual knowledge are thus complementary of each other; each remedies the other's defects.'[62] James had no philosophical way of characterizing mind and experience, so the result was a bland parallellism underpinned by appeals to faith in moments of crisis. Neither did James have any intellectual apparatus for characterizing contradiction, so he turned to moral exhortation to fill the vacuum.

It is precisely James's refusal of a more engaged and reciprocal view of the world that is the problem. Heidegger said that 'Experience is the name for the referral of the objective back to the subject'.[63] However, James's attempt to identify the mental with the physical through the notion of pure experience, which Russell called 'profoundly original',[64] had no means of characterizing that referral. When in *The Meaning of Truth* James says the truth of cognition 'terminates in experience',[65] the feedback from experience to cognition is obliterated. In a sense experience is impoverished by depriving it of that power of referral. One commentator, setting out with the intention of putting James straight on 'experience', ends by stating that 'pure experience theory is a bog'.[66] It is indeed hard to know how to characterize language, or to describe chaos as self-ordering. Philosophers are not on the whole too happy to be told that philosophy is not a technical matter and that our 'dumb sense of what life honestly and deeply means' is the most important part of our attempt to know the world.[67]

In his book *The Culture of Experience* (a significant title, for it gives up the notion of philosophy), John C. McDermott attempts to enlist the great twentieth-century poet William Carlos Williams as an ally of James. But Williams had a sophisticated theory of language, which James did not, he was a poet which James also was not, and this meant he could take for granted the metaphoric creativity of his discourse. Williams's strategy (no ideas but in things) has been mistaken for his practice.[68] Indeed McDermott's use of 'radical empiricism' and 'experience philosophy' to characterize 'modern art' in essentially analytic terms like 'process', 'reconstruction', 'event', 'relation', and his claim that this is a metaphysic which is somehow parallel with the 'originality' of modern art, exposes the essential poverty of a philosophy which refuses consciousness as part of a creative act. Predication is obliterated in a synchrony of permanent valueless assemblage. The labour and craft of the artist is ignored as well as the actual historical struggle for recognition.

McDermott's terms parody the worst aspects of the foregoing judgements. In spite of due caution he speaks of 'society' in the pathological terms of diagnosis, is incautious enough to state that James's individualism is closer to Marx than British empiricism (both are in fact far from it), and in his genuine and moving unease about American society can only cite the quietistic aspects of Norman O. Brown's work, castigate Ellul's 'European' pessimism, turn a blind eye to politics by reiterating that 'Space, however, is time undergone', take Dewey's conception of the 'social' as a *deus ex machina*, and then reach for the familiar American recourse of punditry: 'Everything we experience exacts a price and often we must say no if we are to say yes, although both responses are two potentially enriching occasions'.[69] Exit Polonius – Right.

Once the argument is removed from philosophy and its formal procedure, however, reasons can be discovered why James and the philosophers of his time, not to mention commentators, still bother with the notion of experience. Dewey helps give the game away:

> In principle. . . the history of the construction of suitable opera-tions in the scientific field is not different from that of their evolution in industry. It is therefore understandable that for the popular imagination in America, 'science' is not represented by the Willard Gibbses, the Einsteins, the Darwins, but by the Edisons, the Bells and the Westinghouses.[70]

Knowledge thus equals practical experience whose truth is guaran-teed by spectacular (and highly pubicized) technological achieve-ments. C. Wright Mills extends the context further: 'The academic community in America as a whole is morally open to the new practicality in which it has become involved. Both in and out of university, men at centres of learning become experts inside admi-nistrative machines'.[71] Mills goes on to talk of the lack of political education and the lack of foresight, in the consciousness of special-ists, beyond the walls of the academy. James was thoroughly aware of this problem, but offered few positive means of combating it. Some actual examples he gives of 'experience' in the *Principles* will be examined now, as yet another way into this strange and dense text.

First the chapter on 'Habit'. James quotes the Duke of Wellington to the effect that habit is 'ten times nature' (*Principles*, I. 124). Various social examples follow. James tells us of riderless cavalry horses going through motions at the sound of a bugle, indulges in a little slapstick with a quotation from Huxley of a veteran dropping his 'mutton and potatoes' (no officer this one) when leaping to the call 'Attention', speaks of the unquestioning obedience of domestic animals, and tells us of men grown old in prison asking to be taken back once having been set free. A tiger set free in a railroad accident in 1884 is said to have crawled back into its cage in its fear of freedom.

> Habit is thus the enormous flywheel of society, its most precious conservative agent. It alone is what keeps us all within the bounds of ordinance, and saves the children of fortune from the envious uprisings of the poor. It alone prevents the hardest and most repulsive walks of life from being deserted by those brought to tread therein. It keeps the fisherman and the deckhand at sea through the winter; it holds the miner in his darkness, and nails the countryman to his log cabin and his lonely farm through all the months of snow; it protects us from invasion by the natives of the desert and the frozen zone. It dooms us all to fight out the battle of life upon the lines of our nurture or our early choice, and

to make the best of a pursuit that disagrees, because there is no
other for which we are fitted, and it is too late to begin again. It
keeps different strata from mixing.

(*Principles*, I. 125)

Here James brilliantly sets out for us the melancholy bitterness, the
fears and sense of impotence of the American bourgeoisie of the
1880s and its absolute psychological conservatism. Habit is instinct,
not a result of terror. How great a distance has been travelled from
Emerson's 'Whoso would be a man, must be a non-conformist', or
Whitman's 'I, now thirty seven years old in perfect health begin'.[72]
What James in fact does is turn Bagehot's 'deference' and 'sentiment'
into a ten-times-natural fatalistic psychological behaviour out of a
distrust of freedom. For it is not habit but terror and necessity that
keeps the poor bent to their tasks and away from the throats of the
rich. James will always be attractive to conservatives who fear life,
emotions, and have secret desires to control others.

Hill spoke of Locke's fear of literature and music. James's case is
more complicated. He was a psychological Puritan with a passionate
nature which he sought always to keep under warps. The kind of
'moderation' which is produced at the intersection was neither
imaginative nor creative. It is that moderation Melville spoke of in
The Confidence Man: 'The moderate man, the invaluable under-
strapper of the wicked man.'[73] One also might contrast Adams's
insight in the *Education*: 'Chaos often breeds life, when order breeds
habit.'[74] Adams saw the disposition to totalitarianism in Matthew
Arnold's law-and-order reaction to the Hyde Park Riots.

James's chapter degenerates, like many of his commentators, into
punditry. Make useful habits automatic, do not abandon old habits
before you find new ones, and be sure to be successful from the start
otherwise you will become discouraged. Do not read novels or go to
the theatre too much, cultivate asceticism since it will pay off, for it
is like 'an insurance which a man pays on his house and goods'
(*Principles*, I. 130). The reward is to become Superman: 'He will
stand like a tower when everything rocks around him, and when his
softer fellow mortals are winnowed like chaff in the blast' (I. 130).
Here is no Nietzschean noble ecstasy out of tragedy, merely a fantasy
of rigid gratifications turning feeble lusts into dreams of domination
in crisis.

In terms of personal 'experience' James's view is Wordsworthian,
though his solution to biological decline as 'felt experience' is not
Wordsworth's contemplative peace, the quiet sense of rich experience held in the memory – the past for James has no relevance to
American life:

From one year to another we see things in new lights. What was unreal has grown real, and what was exciting is insipid. The friends we used to care the world for are shrunken to shadows; the women, once so divine, the stars, the woods, and the waters, how now so dull and common; the young girls that brought an aura of infinity, at present hardly distinguishable existences; the pictures so empty; and as for the books, what was there to find so mysteriously significant in Goethe, or in John Mill so full of weight? Instead of this, more zestful than ever is the work, the work. . . .

(Principles, I. 227–8)

If the mood is Swinburnean, the form lacks Swinburne's magnificent classicism and Epicurean detachment. The solution is a parody of Puritanism.

As for the consciousness of the experienced self, since James has no theory of consciousness, attention has merely to terminate in objects. And so it does:

In its widest possible sense, however, a man's Self is the sum total of that he can call his, not only his body and his psychic powers, but his clothes and his house, his wife and children, his ancestors and friends, his reputation and works, his lands and horses, and yacht and bank account. All these things give him the same emotions.

An equally instinctive impulse drives us to collect property: and the collections thus made become, with different degrees of intimacy, parts of our empirical selves. The parts of wealth most intimately ours are those which are saturated with our labour.

(Principles, I. 279–80, 281)

Quite how what is collected (including a wife and child) is saturated with one's own labour is unclear. Marx's insight into the fetishism of the commodity (that power not ourselves but from ourselves which animates things as if they were human) is crucial here.

Feeling for James becomes a medium of exchange, not differentiating its object. Experience based on mediating sense can only be altered by alterations in sense. James's search for such experience is a search for a sixth sense – which was Jonathan Edwards's solution to his synthesis of Calvinism and empiricism. For James heightened sense and its experiences are a kind of compensatory fringe, or a vestige: sex, intoxication, music, hypnosis; hysterical women, hashish; all these haunt the fringes of James's mechanistic models, breaking them down from margin to centre.

Sometimes sense experience may degenerate into sentiment: 'The

passionate devotion of a mother – ill herself perhaps – to a sick or
dying child is perhaps the most simply beautiful moral spectacle that
human life affords' (I. 440). Everyone to his own taste in moral
spectacle, but James's combination of sentiment and instinct within
an essentially carnival-like framework of outlet merely re-confirms
crisis. In fact when we see others suffer we experience our own
loneliness. Sentimentalizing that distance as 'moral spectacle' is sheer
cowardice as well as aesthetic obscenity. Is this what James was really
experiencing when he looked at the sick mother and child – as well as
acquiring, perhaps, a permitted framework (distanced by disease) for
actually looking at a woman? The Norwegian painter Edvard
Munch took his revenge on Victorian melodramas of this kind.

James's description of experience and its ethical import is directed
not towards happiness but towards a reduction of pain either by
anaesthetization or intoxication of the senses. As a result the real
world he so much desires, and which all the commentators tell us he
recalls us to, slips constantly away from him. James is not so much
the philosopher of pluralistic experience as the 'pusher' of that
experience to those whose senses no longer record the diversity of
life. Like disillusioned hippies in the American 1960s, James turned
to the fringe and to drug-inspired and religious alterations of the
senses as a result of a society which had lost most vestiges of
'common sense'. 'Pleasure' here is not an issue.

Finally there is the question of James and language. By way of
transition here is his 'experience' under hashish: 'In hashish intoxication there is curious increase in the apparent time-perspective. We
utter a sentence, and ere the end is reached the beginning seems
already to date from indefinitely long ago. We enter a short street,
and it is as if we should never get to the end of it' (I. 601–2). The
relation of the sentence to the very structure of our experience and to
time will be taken up in detail in Part Three and the Conclusion of
this book. It was Gertrude Stein, James's most famous literary pupil,
who was to stretch out that sentence mesmerically, pointing to a
'stored' eternity, in her great work, The Making of Americans (1911).

In The Descent of Man, Darwin gave at least three different
accounts of language, in fewer pages. There is a species theory of
language, needing long periods of time for development (here
Darwin quotes Lyell's Geological Evidences of the Antiquity of Man
[1863]). Second, Darwin has an onomatopoeic theory of language
whereby he argues that language can be traced back farther than species
owing to certain rudiments of speech which imitate pure sounds.
Thirdly he argues, quoting Max-Müller, that descent is an excellent
model for language creation: 'A struggle for life is constantly going

on among the words and grammatical forms in each language. The better, the shorter, the easier forms are gaining the upper hand, and they owe their success to their own inherent virtue.' He concludes:

> Philologists now admit that conjunctions, declensions, etc. originally existed as distinct words, since joined together; and as such words express the most obvious relations between objects and persons, it is not surprising that they should have been used by men of most races during the earliest ages.[75]

James's problem was how to modify this rather conservative and old-fashioned English tradition, while not delivering himself into the hands of the German idealists, with their tradition of creative consciousness and symbolic language. Darwin had read the eighteenth-century Monboddo, who had advocated the verb rather than Horne Tooke's noun as the primordial form. Empiricists tended to favour the noun, idealists the verb. The American tradition had its own versions of these debates. Noah Webster had insisted that language was a natural phenomenon.[76]

These moments from the history of language help to explain James's sometimes contradictory statements about language. In *Pragmatism* he could speak of common sense as the 'natural mother tongue of thought', and in *A Pluralistic Universe* he could state, 'The great transcendentalist metaphor has always been, as I lately reminded you, a grammatical sentence, the absolute flash'.[77] Did James, as Linschoten claims, ascribe a constitutive function of experience to language?[78] The answers have to be very mixed.

Perhaps James wanted his sentence metaphors to be true, as well as providing an index to the real. And in the famous metaphor of the stream of thought the one thing pulls against the other. In emphasizing the movement of the stream and the structure of the sentence James could both have his cake and eat it: he could retain Locke's scepticism about words, affirm their essential relation with ideas, suggest creativity in movement and metaphysically rely on the sentence's essential grammatical stability:

> As we take, in fact, a general view of the wonderful stream of our consciousness, what strikes us first is this different pace of its parts. Like a bird's life it seems to be made of an alternation of flights and perchings. The rhythm of language expresses this, where every thought is expressed in a sentence, and every sentence closed by a period. The resting-places are usually occupied by sensorial imaginations of some sort, whose peculiarity is that they can be held before the mind for an indefinite time, and contemplated without changing; the places of flight are filled with

thoughts of relations, static or dynamic, that for the most part
obtain between the matters contemplated in the periods of comparative rest. . . . *Let us call the resting-place the 'substantive parts',*
and the places of flight the 'transitive parts', of the stream of thought.

(*Principles*, I. 236)

The passage has rightly dazzled commentators. It is as if James for
once lets the creative side of himself go. It contains all his themes, the
metaphysical aesthetic (rhythm), radical empiricism (thoughts of
relations), and the simile of the bird, ignored by most commentators, with its trace of allegory points to the human soul, and suggests
its fundamental participation in the same flux as the natural stream,
secularizing Webster's theological given and naturalizing Emerson's
'Spirit' in and through the world. James's metaphor is, however,
primarily religious and aesthetic, for it suggests that structure is
truth. The stream – so often before James applied to time – is
spatialized in recurrence. The last trace of a historic metaphysic is
expunged, making an enormous isomorphic equation between language and utterance.

The sentence becomes, therefore, for James a rhythmic structure
of the world and further acts as a model for the operation of the mind
itself. Two things are excluded from this model; the position of the
subject and the question of language as such. Consciousness varies
pace with the given – but passively, at a level paradoxically of pre-
conscious certainty. Further the 'stream' is a universalizing image
employing variation and stability towards the goal of 'unity'. Psychologically the impetus is towards quietude. Ultimately language has a
merely analogical relation to the process of mind, and consciousness
is a mystical truth unrelated to either mind or language. Whatever
graceful gestures commentators (those whose own disposition is to
the religious and the aesthetic) invariably find in James's description
of the 'stream of consciousness', problems remain in both religious
and aesthetic spheres.

It is the range of *The Principles of Psychology* that is so dazzling: its
untidiness, its inconsistencies, its anguished attempts to come to
terms with the human psyche, its rhetoric of uplift, its total
scepticism about the scientific and psychological projects to describe
the life world, its elegy for traditional philosophy which is only half
understood because it is so radically simplified, its ambivalence about
a commercialization of spirit which goes back to Locke, its refusal to
admit any argument about the nature of power in human experience,
its Puritan inwardness, its academic learning, its proliferation of
insights and hints which anticipate much in twentieth-century

thought, its rhetorical lurchings between common sense and mysticism, add up to one of the most magnificent failures in American letters. It is the key document of the American mind in a period of social change. It bears witness to ideological confusion, to paradigmatic uncertainty in science, to the weaknesses of liberalism at the level of intimacy and theories about the nature of the person, to the absence (no less than in Adams) of the authority of any single discourse to describe the world. It has the great Puritan virtue of refusal. In the end it fails because it offers nothing positive. Its spirit is satiric and its mood stoic and melancholy. It reflects the genuine anguish of a thoughtful American bewildered in the aftermath of the most costly war in history. It was written in a period of political and industrial upheaval in which bourgeois confidence broke down. Individualism, common sense before passion, tolerance for differing beliefs, friendly competition, liberal Christianity, progressivism linked to the scientific project and technological advance, philosophic learning as a value in relation to the materially active life – all these came more and more under threat. When James did turn like an old Puritan divine from the study to the field, the weaknesses of his negative honesty became only too apparent. To conclude this part, therefore, it will be instructive to turn from the academic to the public and popular James.

Chapter 10
War and Peace in the Global Psyche

James's two best-known works, in reverse chronological order, are perhaps 'The Moral Equivalent of War' (1910) and *The Varieties of Religious Experience* (1902) – the one a short essay and the other a full-length book. In the essay he attempted to modify the notion of war as the ultimate nineteenth-century arena of praxis and individualist moral ennoblement. In the book he confronted religion's use of the irrational and the ecstatic as exemplifying variations on an ultimately unitary truth of the metaphysical other. In both the emphasis is on 'experience'. Paradoxically, both works have relatively little to do with 'experience' in either common-sense or traditionally metaphysical terms. This should not, however, be surprising, given some of the conclusions drawn in the preceding pages. The Darwin-based theories of essentialist behaviour, social organism and sentiment place restrictions on an examination even of psychological responses to aggression. They rule out questions of power and the coercions of Leviathan by restricting the parameters of what 'experience' is construed to be. James, further modifying Locke in this exclusion, neglects the political dimension of the issues almost completely. Furthermore, Bagehot's 'emotion of conviction', while offering itself as a concept to aid the discussion of the irrational in religion and war, scarcely gives analytic terms for explanation. The reduction of the person in Locke to a 'forensic' term discovers a social truth, but only in a somewhat inert body open to a medical and legal gaze claiming to limit scientific excess and political debate equally. The exclusion of all questions of consciousness, with the consequent mystification of experience, poses further problems.

The encounter with Darwin, the ambiguous treatment of method, the search for a science of mind, and James's attempted solution of the problem of social organism in a modification of Bagehot's social sentiment, all tended to downgrade the actual content of human exchange and to offer paradigms of concealed behaviour lying 'behind' the specific and the particular. That 'economy of means' in thought, and the notion of a corresponding truth in the structure of syntax, tended to place meaning itself in some inexpressible realm sealed off from language and therefore from the fundamental means by which men and women interact in whatever forms of life they have in common. In what individualized hell of non-communication could Bagehot's 'emotion of conviction' replace the Hobbesian public or even the Lockean society?

I

James's 'The Moral Equivalent of War' is a classic example of the way to that hell being paved with good intentions. It was first published in 1910 by the Association for International Conciliation. It was a psychological offering to mediate the 'aggression' (that favourite essentialist quality of popularizers of 'human behaviour') evident everywhere in the United States in one of the worst periods of industrial unrest in its history. Thirty thousand copies of the essay were printed as a pamphlet, and it was twice reprinted in popular magazines. On whatever terms, therefore, it was felt to be 'relevant'. But the essay, while clearly directed towards a pressing contemporary need, also depended on a number of nineteenth-century convictions.

An assumption that was widespread in the nineteenth century, and by no means eradicated in our own, was of the moral necessity of war. Barzun quotes the German military theorist von Moltke as evidence for this common obscenity: 'perpetual peace is a dream and not even a beautiful dream. War is an element of the order of the world established by God'.[1] War was the arena of the rites of manhood. It 'hardened' 'character'. The real bravery and self-sacrifice of people at war were turned into propaganda for peacetime behaviour. This was accomplished by a psychological model in which morality was assumed to be contingent on personal survival in a 'crisis' during which the soul was 'tested'. It was but a thin secularization of certain types of religious psychology. The Christian or Mohammedan first dons his armour and then fights the good fight. During the nineteenth century, the proto-socio-biologist was able to reinforce these assumptions of religious psychology with 'scientific' evidence. The importance of the late nineteeth-century debate on 'instinct' is a case in point, and has been well documented by Greta Jones. The instinct debate offered a determinist thesis which supported the truth of pairing marriage, property-holding and territorial struggle. The theory of 'instincts' acquired a 'highly conservative bent'.[2]

Numbers of theorists, German, French and English, hastened to apply the theory to war. Aggression became a psychological, not a moral or political, problem. If James's own tendency to link belief with emotional life is added to these considerations the terms on which he joined in the debate are complete. Aggression was assumed to be innate and irrational. The only hope of controlling it was to divert its inevitable presence to a safe realm. James's 'economic' language of compensation, equivalence, and balance reinforced rather than challenged the ultimate truth of universal violence.

It has already been noted that one form of compensatory behaviour was 'sport', to which Julien Benda, a generation later, gives the full weight of his sarcasm in his discussion of the cult of 'war-psychology': 'This teaching leads the modern "clerk" [intellectual] . . . to confer a moral value on physical exercise and to proclaim the morality of sport – a most remarkable thing indeed among those who for twenty centuries have exhorted man to situate good in states of the mind.'[3] The present author recalls, while earning his own 'liberal' credentials in Cameroon in 1961, the weight the British Government gave to an 'Outward Bound' course as a means of morally uniting different cultures (Ibo, Yoruba, Hausa – to cite the main ones). Climbing, swimming, assault courses were the order of the day to ensure manly co-operation among the élite of the newly independent Nigeria. Four years later the country was torn apart in one of the bloodiest civil wars in twentieth-century history. Physical exercise as a pragmatic means of sustaining health and above all enjoyment is not criticized here. What is criticized is its incorporation into a system of values which at its most extreme depends on rites of physical humiliation as a testing ground for eligibility to join a ruling class. Puritanical psychology, sado-masochistic testing accompanied by an 'uplift' ideology, are manifestations of deep disturbances in any society and culture.

In *The Will to Believe* James gave plenty of evidence for his own conviction of the instinctiveness of warlike behaviour and of its pragmatic truth: 'A war is a true point of bifurcation of future possibilities.' James extended the argument further to assess at a psychological level the truth of feeling. To live with real feeling meant to fight. 'It feels like a real fight', he was fond of saying. For the unbelieving James the God of War was a necessary psychological hypothesis: 'When God is there. . . It saith among the trumpets, ha! ha! it smelleth the battle afar off. . . and cruelty to the lesser claims, so far from being a deterrent element, does but add to the stern joy with which it leaps to answer the greater. . . .'[4]

James joined in Roosevelt's contemporary cult of the 'strenuous life', which reflected an America now using political means to moderate personal and social behaviour. In some ways Roosevelt turned the ideology of the Christian Soldier–Adventurer – that key actor in the bourgeois period of history – into an image of mass propaganda. In 1914, the British Conservative newspaper *The Daily Telegraph* put out a series of War Books, one of which was a reprint of Stephen Crane's *Great Battles of the World*, in which Crane cited the words of the seventeenth-century King Gustavus Adolphus of Sweden to his officers: 'A good Christian will never make a bad soldier. A man that has finished his prayers has at least completed one half of his daily work.'[5] It was Perry, perhaps James's most faithful commentator, who in 1918, after the Great War, made explicit the connection between wartime and peaceful behaviour as a matter of equivalence: 'Entering a war is doing on a colossal scale what a man does when he leaves his duties and pastimes of ordinary life and trains for a Marathon run.'[6]

Perry did so on the basis of James's essay, 'The Moral Equivalent of War'. In that essay James stressed the irrationality of 'military feelings' and pleaded for rationality. Yet at the same time he declared:

> The duty is incumbent on mankind, of keeping military characters in stock – of keeping them, if not in use, then as ends in themselves and as pure pieces of perfection, – so that Roosevelt's weaklings and mollycoddles may not end by making everything else disappear from the face of nature.[7]

The 'economic' language here sustains the psychological. The military characters are to be 'stocked' where moth and rust cannot corrupt. For James 'battle' was the normal condition of mankind as much as 'repression' was for Freud. Unlike Freud, however, James made no pragmatic plea for a rational balance between that condition and the superego. James speaks in fact of 'the fear of emancipation from the fear regime',[8] as if without terror life would not be quite real. Here Sartre's bad faith – the desire to escape Kierkegaardian anguish by pretending we are not free – is psychologized into a natural condition.

R. W. B. Lewis once told the author that James regretted not having experienced the Civil War like his two brothers, Bob and Garth. In his premisses, if not in the intent of his essay, James romanticizes military life, and regrets the decline of war itself, 'in which the destinies of peoples shall nevermore be decided quickly, thrillingly, and tragically, by force, but only gradually and insipidly by "evolution"'. Even Darwin's analogies of the life of nature as the war of all against all are not tough enough for James. He continues with a challenge to anti-militarists: 'So long as anti-militarists prepare to substitute for war's disciplinary function [*sic*] no moral equivalent of war, analogous, as one might say, to the mechanical equivalent of heat, so long they fail to recognize the full inwardness of the situation.'[9] The key words here are 'disciplinary function', 'substitute', and 'inwardness'. Substitution – to use the language of the rhetoricians for a moment – contains within itself both resemblance and deviance. James identifies a 'trope' of 'disciplinary function' whose own axiomatic function makes 'equivalent' war behaviour and peace behaviour as 'substitutions', dependent on the trope's need to perform an algebraic sum in which substitution and restitution constitute zero.

Here we reach the deep nihilistic centre of James's logic. In simpler terms there *is* no 'moral equivalent' of war. Myers's recent claim, that James's strongest point is that 'there may be a moral equivalent for the pugnacious impulse', is casuistical nonsense.[10] To essentialize the aggressive instinct and then make equivalents for it is a familiar twentieth-century game for those who refuse to confront the specificity of violence in its full context: situational, ideological, political, sexual, psychological and above all historical and particular. There is an intelligibility of violence which behavioural equivalence-mongering obscures in order to obliterate questions of how power is distributed in any society. Here liberal apologists are as bad as those who actually believe in the face value of all James says. Dewey's accurate objection is tucked away in Myers's notes: '. . . the idea that most people need any substitute for fighting for life, or that they have to have life made artificially hard for them in order to keep up their battling nerve, could come only from a man who was brought up an aristocrat and who had lived a sheltered existence'. Myers adds that this is the only negative comment Dewey ever made about James.[11] Jamesian apologetics in the Reagan–Bush era reach a new peak. James calls for good fears (God and the enemy) as opposed to bad fears such as socialists have: 'poverty if one be lazy'.

In the industrial-conciliation debate it is clear which side James is on. In the fear regime it is important to have the correct fears. Further the equivalences unrealistically assumed here are between fear and poverty, work and wealth. Ultimately James says he believes in some sort of 'socialist equilibrium' – presumably when socialists have 'inwardly' recovered from their fear of povery, and their sense of history as an ongoing and changing process. The effect of James's equivalents, substitutions and equilibriums is not to mediate at all. Rather they polarize real complexities into either-or dogmatisms in order to create conditions for heroic behaviour. The resulting rhetorical dramas obscure an actual massive evasion of collective and social issues, as well as mystifying the entire subject.

At this point James floats his 'Peace Corps' idea for the 'whole youthful population'. Unfortunately the 'whole population' is not quite that implied by James's terms of universalist psychological behaviour. After all there is no point in sending an eighteen-year-old coal-miner down a mine shaft for his moral improvement. In practice James's 'moral equivalent' is only for the sons of the upper classes: the 'gilded youth'. These are to be 'drafted' off to get the 'childish-ness' knocked out of them and to encourage manly virtues in what is clearly for James a dangerously 'pacific civilization'. The 'moral battleground' is in fact the space of industrial urban America. James ends by quoting H. G. Wells's *First and Last Things* of 1908:

> When the contemporary man steps from the street, of clamorous insincere advertisement, push, adulteration, underselling and intermittent employment into the barrack yard, he steps on to a higher social plane, into an atmosphere of service and co-operation and of infinitely more honourable emulation.[12]

That higher social plane (itself based on the terror of unemployment) of course legitimizes murder in the interests of the State.

The popularity of James's essay was no doubt owing to its appeal to the sense of chaos people felt under the rapid changes occurring within American society at this time. Its behavioural bias appeared to bypass the conflict of ideologies and to relocate actual social conflict in the safe area of 'education' for the young – as if eighteen-year-olds were more of a threat to society than the decisions of those who actually held power. The best that can be said for the essay is that it articulates a whole series of fears: the threat actual industrial life posed to that upper half – if half it was; dismay about workable ideology in face of the clear shortcomings of positivist Marxism and traditional Christianity; and a threat to the bourgeois theory of personality which needed conflict in order to dominate its own versions of the status quo. There is an air of 'punishment' in James's prescriptions for the young, just as countries which offer 'civil service' instead of 'military service' construe that 'civil service' as the most menial tasks the society can find.

By far the worst aspect of the essay is, however, its refusal to dis-cuss the actual content of these equivalences of behaviour. There is a craving for order at almost any price. The great conservative virtues, obedience, lawfulness, honour, loyalty and bravery, are put at the service of a militarized version of peaceful behaviour. All content is expunged. Obedience to whom? On what terms? Service on behalf of what? Honour under what principle? Loyalty and bravery to what end? James cannot make up his mind whether the gilded youth ought to be in 'industry', for their moral uplift, or in the army so that they can be sanitized away from the world of industry. In fact James sets both the world of the army and the world of the industrial masses against the middle, as a vicarious correction to his own deeply alienated sense of life.

Further there is a Hobbesian sense of aggression and conflict as 'essential' to human life but without the Hobbesian political vision. As such the essay played straight into the hands of a rising class of managerial employers who would carry out 'industrial conciliation' on their own terms and who could now draw on that essay's moralistic assumptions, reinforced by psychological truth, to effect their own deferred hopes for 'equilibrium'.

II

The other most famous and popular work of James was *The Varieties of Religious Experience*. Here he confronts head-on issues which he was to take up again in later works. Throughout *Pragmatism* (1907) and *A Pluralistic Universe* (1909) his close involvement with religion and religious psychology becomes plainly evident. Pragmatism – in reality a theory of truth – also had a use as a 'happy harmonizer of empiricist ways of thinking with the more religious demands of human beings'.[13] These religious demands, however, seemed to have little to do with the historic theory and practice of religion as such. In *A Pluralistic Universe* James was officially to declare his lack of interest in the content of traditional religion – of whatever kind:

> The theological preaching that spoke so livingly to our ancestors, with its finite age of the world, its creation out of nothing, its juridical morality and eschatology, its relish for rewards and punishments, its treatment of God as an external contriver... sounds as odd to most of us as if it were some outlandish savage religion.[14]

The progressivist assumptions and the historical intolerance would have riled Adams. St. Thomas Aquinas joins the Polynesians in this justification by contemporaneity. James's view of religion confines itself to the Christian, and his definition betrays his own historical context. The world's age only becomes important after Darwin, the creation out of nothing (*pace* Lucretius) is relatively a non-question then as now, the juridical morality applies more to the Hebraic tradition and Puritanism than to the teachings of Jesus. James himself was not immune to a morality of rewards and punishments. God as an external contriver was not much different from James's own 'metaphysic in reserve', suitably psychologically camouflaged. In fact James attacks religion on these grounds because he believes that it is on these same grounds that he can defend it.

James's religious experience was a carefully marked-out area of the 'mystical', initially untouched by historical religion, thought, psychology or common sense. In the shock waves produced by the death of God, James also characterized that experience as a need: 'This need of an eternal moral order is one of the deepest needs of our breast.' Further, by psychologizing an essentially Protestant tradition, he could add, 'I myself believe that the evidence for God lies primarily in inner personal experience.'[15]

Thus for James 'religious experience' is neither historical, theological, eschatalogical, moral (in the first instance) nor mythical, social or political. It excludes the anthropologist's custom and ritual, and even the psychologist's notions of health, sexuality and pathology. In a specifically American tradition, James narrows religion to Edwards's 'religious affection': that sense beyond sense paradoxically delivering its effects to the scrutiny of the empirical gaze. But perhaps it is less a metaphysic in reserve than a therapeutics in reserve, directed to the special pressures of American life: 'When the outward battle is lost, and the outer world disowns him, it redeems and vivifies an interior world which otherwise would be an empty waste'.[16] No less than for the 'Mind Cure' movement and the gospel of relaxation, James's evidences of 'experienced happiness', these essentially ecstatic intuitions, are assumed to be powerfully psychological underpinnings of the moral life which promise deliverance from madness.

That madness – a kind of existential terror – is for James fundamentally a personal psychological problem: 'Not the conception or intellectual perception of evil, but the grisly blood-freezing heart-paralysing sensation of it close upon one, and no other conception or sensation able to live for a moment in its presence.'[17] It is the ecstatic freedom from this terror in moments of religious experience that interests James, and his 'varieties' are variations on this one theme.[18] Just one moment will be taken up, the famous one where, suitably disguised, James gives an account of his own 'religious experience': a terrifying one, revolving fundamentally around a hypnagogic vision of a 'black haired youth with greenish skin'. Here is the whole central part of the account:

> Whilst in this state of philosophic pessimism and general depression of spirits about my prospects, I went one evening into a dressing-room in the twilight to procure some article that was there; when suddenly there fell upon me without any warning, just as if it came out of the darkness, a horrible fear of my own existence. Simultaneously there arose in my mind the image of an epileptic patient whom I had seen in the asylum, a black-haired youth with greenish skin, entirely idiotic, who used to sit all day on one of the benches, or rather shelves against the wall, with his

knees drawn up against his chin, and the coarse gray undershirt, which was his only garment, drawn over them enclosing his entire figure. He sat there like a sort of sculptured Egyptian cat or Peruvian mummy, moving nothing but his black eyes and looking absolutely non-human. This image and my fear entered into a species of combination with each other. That shape am I, I felt, potentially. Nothing that I possess can defend me against that fate, if the hour for it should strike for me as it struck for him. There was such a horror of him, and such a perception of my own merely momentary discrepancy from him, that it was as if something hitherto solid within my breast gave way entirely, and I became a mass of quivering fear. After this the universe was changed for me altogether. I awoke morning after morning with a horrible dread at the pit of my stomach, and with a sense of the insecurity of life that I never knew before, and that I have never experienced since.[19]

This passage invites questions at many levels: moral because it is a sensation of *evil*, psychological because it is a *sensation* of evil. It also invites problems of consciousness and will. First, therefore, it will be considered in general terms, and then specifically as a literary text, for not the least interest of the passage is its contribution towards modes of representing an American Gothic.

Possibly James was right to call it a religious experience, though there is in fact nothing particularly religious about it. There is for example no sense of guilt, or worthlessness, merely 'insecurity of life'. If terror of insecurity be a fundamental aspect of religious life, then it is a strong claim. If not, not. Most religious practice however includes rituals covering all of the rites of passage – birth as well as death. James's sick soul also simplifies in terms of therapeutics the potential complexity of the experience of suffering in any given situation or society. Further, the terror is intensely personal, involving feelings of being cut off from others, as he goes on to explain. In some ways the emphasis is modern, in that a Kafkaesque isolation is a strong element of the experience.

Nowhere does James consider that his paradigm of the religious experience (terror – ecstatic relief – confession – morally inspired behaviour) might be, not a naturally spontaneous experience but one controlled by social and indeed political conditions. The 'relief' from the personal is also a strong element in James's description of religious experience. But that relief is proposed only in a metaphysical 'higher'. The attempt to escape the self and the conditions which produce that self are genuine enough. The psychological conditions of late nineteenth-century American life were readily

apparent: the inconceivability of a collective as opposed to an individualist theory of American life, the genuine alienation of the middle
and upper middle classes from the industrial wastes of late nineteenth-
century capitalism, a longing to escape the crudenesses of American
materialism and the naturalist ethic of 'survival', and finally a desire
for reassurance and love where the official ethic was every man for
himself.

Given the paradigmatic uncertainty of traditional ethical and moral
discourse, and the hopelessness James had felt about psychology's
boasted replacements, it is little wonder that he was forced back on
to the scriptural texts of his childhood. I would argue that perhaps
the shame of this confession – for that is its structure – led him to
conceal himself as author. Another reason might well be that James,
like many another humanistic commentator, was intimidated by the
claims of scientific discourse to truth in the human world even
though he had publicly challenged those claims. Further, there were
no modes of discourse available – other than traditional literature –
for connecting discourses about the irrational with discourses about
moral and ethical behaviour. No more than other scientists of his day
was James able to provide a connection between the George Fox
who wandered through Lichfield proclaiming its streets filled with
blood, and the shrewd and brave man who confronted Cromwell
and created the magnificent edifice of Quaker ethics. James as instinctive latitudinarian had Locke's scepticism about 'enthusiasm',
yet the psychologist felt drawn irresistibly towards it. As a good
bourgeois and Harvard professor also, 'the world turned upside
down' had no especial charms.

Practically James acknowledged that religious experience gives
powerful impulses towards change. In more secular terms, however,
he did recognize the role of the irrational in effecting that change. His
mistake was to assume that in irrationality as such there was some
locus of truth. His either–or attitude ensured that there could not be
a creative compromise between the rational and irrational. The
Victorian taboos also, one assumes, were too strong. James cites
R. L. Stevenson on the absence of sexual passion in acknowledged
life. As a result he went overboard in making irrational conviction a
locus of truth. James buries the great Puritan tradition of the social
intelligibility of unreason, and therefore also its invitation to be
publically scrutinized and tested: 'Our impulsive belief is hence
always what sets up the original body of truth, and our philosophy is
but its showy verbalized translation into formulas. The immediate
assurance is the deep thing in us, the argument is but a surface
exhibition.'[20]

This linking of original truth to intuition is fundamentally a reactionary formula. It is not simply 'anti-intellectual', though that is one aspect of it. Under the guise of a necessary incorporation of irrational experiences into judgements about forms of life, James invokes that conservatism which uses as an alibi a retrospective teleology of origin locked in the inexpressible stasis of intuition. But is it possible to say, then, that James simply waxes evangelical about an assurance opaque to others, and refuses the democratic level of language? First everything has to be taken into account. For James does offer his narrative of narratives and invites response. The stories of others confront us in a familiar language even when they represent experiences different from the ones we recognize. The whole business of criticism lies in the confrontation. James's irrational, which he links with the religious, has to be represented. In the following critique of James's moment of terror, recourse will be had mainly to Sartre's *Psychology of Imagination*, with some help, also, from Freud and Merleau-Ponty.

To begin with the 'illusion of immanence' – the notion that the real is given us directly – takes on a particular meaning when both the examples James supplies in his text and the way (to reverse his emphasis) he hangs them together are considered simultaneously. By ruling out a theory of consciousness, or of consciousnesses as such, James is prone to assert certain aspects of the illusion of immanence. Here it is possible to assert, with the phenomenologists, a first distinction between the way consciousness apprehends an object and an image. When the object appears to consciousness in perception it is the result of a series of overlapping profiles: 'we must learn objects, that is to say, multiply upon them the possible points of view. The object itself is the synthesis of all these appearances.'[21] In contrast, the image is determined: 'it suffers from a sort of essential poverty' (*Imagination*, p. 8). The image is determined by the consciousness that accompanies it. The consciousness which plays about an object (reflection) slowly constitutes it and brings it into the open. In contrast the image does not approach the real at all: 'However lively, appealing or strong the image is, it presents its object as not being'. But Sartre adds significantly, 'This does not prevent us from reacting to the image as if its object were before us' (p. 13). Imaginative consciousness – which is the subject of Sartre's work – in fact deals with the object as if it were an image.

Sartre continues his argument by claiming that it is image-consciousness, not the image itself, which is significant. It is temporal in character, not some 'cross-section of the stream of consciousness' (p. 14). James's own metaphor (in the *Principles*) was essentially spatial, in spite of its emphasis on rhythm and on pace. The model of the sentence binds the 'resting places' and the 'places of flight' together in a predetermined spatial syntax – every thought is expressed in a sentence, and every sentence closed by a period. It is almost as if time is captured within spatial determinants. Sartre, however, insists that the spatial metaphors must be dropped. Nonetheless, James's timeless hypnagogic image will be full of unreleased narrative, and therefore temporal, possibilities. Sartre goes on,

> The first condition of the hallucination appears to us to be a sort of vacillation of personal consciousness. The patient is alone, his thoughts suddenly become entangled, scattered: a diffuse and degraded connection by participation takes the place of the synthetic connection by concentration.
>
> *(Imagination, p. 182)*

The hallucination, Sartre argues, is anti-thematic. It does not invite critical consciousness. It involves seeing but not looking. Unlike the object, the content of the hallucination does not invite continuous efforts to understand its multiplicity, its 'over-flowingness'. It is fixed by memory as unchanging, external and outside the will. Yet at the same time there are terms for recognizing what the content of the hallucination is, just as there are in dreams. Freud quotes Hildebrandt with approval: 'We may even go so far as to say that whatever dreams may offer, they derive their material from reality and from the intellectual life that revolves around that reality.'[22] In addition, when represented to others, the hallucinatory image is placed in time even though it is experienced as timeless. It therefore becomes subject to what Freud called 'secondary revision'.[23]

In dreams we can be aware of dreaming. James will not, in representing his experience, give any hint that he submits the experience to secondary revision, he does that at another level. He is 'influenced' by the vision (i.e. magically overwhelmed) and believes it absolutely. Sartre makes the connection: 'If we study the dream and perception somewhat more deeply we shall see that the difference that separates them is, from one point of view, the difference between belief and knowledge.' Whereas knowledge in perception is immediate – I have no need to believe this typewriter is real – and whereas knowledge in reflective consciousness when presented with evidence has no need to believe, in a sense belief is a dream: 'Everything that happens in a dream is something I believe' (*Imagination*, pp. 190–1). James wants to sustain his experience at the level of belief only.

Dreams are, of course, somewhat nearer to waking consciousness than the kind of vision James had. The relation of hypnagogic vision to dream is analogous to that of perception to reflective conscious-ness. The transition from one to the other can be marked. When we say, 'This is only a dream,' Freud comments, 'Here we have a genuine piece of criticism of the dream, such as might be made in waking life'.[24] In pure hypnagogic vision there is no reflective consciousness. However, the moment it is realized as 'interesting' the reflective consciousness has begun to work. The transition to dream is marked by a movement towards locating it in a time and space absent from pure hypnagogic vision.

There is, Sartre argues, no dream world as such, for there is no corresponding object. When the hypnagogic image passes into dream a story has begun: 'Because of the fact that a dream carries us suddenly into a temporal world, every dream appears to us as a story' (*Imagination*, p. 195). As in a story we are caught in its magical world. At its most extreme this world locks reflective consciousness out. An unreal self is imaginatively captured by an imaginary world: 'I am compelled to live the fascination of the unreal to the dregs' (p. 201). Unlike a reader, who is never quite captured by a story, and unlike the merely dreaming who can be critically aware even inside the dream, the sufferer from hypnagogic visions is radically unfree. He is absolutely influenced and absolutely, in turn, believes. The continuance of this state is, however, rare even in the mentally dis-turbed, for already in dreaming the hypnagogic image moves into story.

This account offers one rich possibility for reading James's hallu-cination. His strategy is to persuade us that he is living 'the fascination of the unreal to the dregs'. It is a strategy, for in the text of *The Varieties of Religious Experience*, James is in fact not only telling stories but making a story of his stories. Thus he tells us he is forced to live the fascination – the binding of the spell: 'I became a mass of quivering fear.' Furthermore he experiences an emotion intimately bound up with that binding and with the consequent deprivation of freedom, for he is overwhelmed by 'a sense of the insecurity of life'. From his 'sensation' he is only freed by a fading of the vision in waking life. He does not make that effort of will or consciousness which is normal in such cases. It is as if he wants to be fascinated, in the same way as we want to be overwhelmed in a horror movie: for the pleasure of the fear. In his narrative James makes no effort to rationalize the content of the hallucination. Most commentators make the point that sufferers from hallucinogenic experiences are aware that their experience is true and not true at the same time. This may make space for rationalization. There is a relation between what is known a priori and appearance in hallucination or dream. This is most fundamental at the level of language. Most English-speakers are not alarmed, for example, by the story of Dracula read in Romanian.

Further, it can only be known that the hallucination is startling because its startlingness is inferred from the basis of ordinary experience. This also, of course, provides strategies for coping. There is a sense in which James in his own descriptive narrative deliberately omits for the sake of effect this link between ordinary experience and the hypnagogic image. He does not say, 'That epileptic patient I saw last week must have affected me more than I thought', or, 'must have had a drop too much last night'. Nor does James attempt to extend the content of the vision into dream: 'I think I'm rather different from a cat, Alice always calls me her little poodle.'

The significant question is, therefore, why James does not do what most of us would have done, that is to have recourse to these familiar strategies. There are many reasons, and only a few are suggested here. First, at an intellectual level, James has no theory of reflective consciousness – even though it has broken in once or twice in *The Principles of Psychology*. He still wants to cling to 'empirical truths' of sensation, hence the mere *fading* of the vision. The gulf James places between the hallucinatory image and the world of objects is therefore a priori. Unlike the phenomenologists, James cannot image the role of thought within that constant overflowing of objects which, in other places, he is so good at insisting upon. It is almost impossible, therefore, for him to bring the image back into the world. There is also no possibility for James of Sartre's 'image consciousness'. However, it can be argued that he does bring the image back into the world in spite of himself, by a literary narrative, rather than by a philosophical argument.

James's experience does coincide, however, with Sartre's description at certain points. The narrative gives accurately the classic preconditions for the experience. James is already melancholic and consciously so before the vision. The intention aids the conditions of the image's appearance. In his memory of the event – for the event exists only in memory – James links this intentional feeling with what follows, not necessarily causally as such, but within the magic causality of narrative: 'Whilst in this state...I went...when suddenly'. Similarly, after the fact of the event James consciously withholds the experience from his mother – letting us as readers partake of family secrets withheld from the family. All this is familiar narrative strategy to arouse our (prurient) curiosity. *Psst*, guess what happened to me. It was awful. I didn't even tell my mother. James's narrative strategy, to use Merleau-Ponty's terms, presents a horizon of his own present in which the past appears.[25]

Anticipation and memory within the description itself thus form a narrative. The context surrounding the image forms a narrative which is active rather than passive. That narrative is made, of course, by James who is at once omniscient narrator and narrator within the text. James as narrator confronts the unreal James captured by the vision which is apparently without narrative features – that is, it is suspended in time and place. Nonetheless the experience comes into the world – is in fact simultaneous with it – because it is then given to narrative. Merleau-Ponty writes: 'There is no experience without speech, as the purely lived-through has no part in the discursive life of man'. In the act of narration James subverts his own desire for a metaphysic in reserve; that act of setting 'the unreflective, as an unknowable, against the reflection. . . [he] brings to bear on it'.[26] Considered as a narrative, James's speaker is unusually consciously in control, yet simultaneously, unusually evasive.

James begins with yet another familiar fictional device. He finds a text, adding, 'for permission to print. . . I have to thank the sufferer'.[27] Two strategies of concealment are already apparent; first he disguises himself as narrator, second, he disguises a kind of dialogue with himself as narrator. He is already split in two: the unreal James of the hypnagogic vision and the conscious narrator. There follow strategies to persuade us to enter the text. Of course James says the original text is in French – that classic language of the split Cartesian world, and of detective fiction. The particular experience is authorized also because as an extreme example it has the virtue of that simplicity which appeals to the 'scientist' James. The relation between extreme and simple tends to find its authority within a statistical vision. James also tells us he is translating freely, ensuring that the original with its authority is further concealed from us. His authority, in contrast, is heightened because he is the only knower.

The scene of the narrative is also significant. The dressing room is a space where symbolically one dons the Carlylean disguise, and it is just here at the vulnerable place of identity that James is caught. The narrator James continues to face off the unreal James. For it is conscious memory which recalls the epileptic patient of the asylum. This figure with its key characteristics of 'idiotic', epileptic, being out of control and regressive (knees drawn up foetus-like), also makes a symbolic configuration. Among many meanings James associates health with sanity: that first assumption of the therapeutic vision. Indeed here is a nightmare which accurately reflects the flaws in that identification. Sanity becomes merely the whim of chance when it is identified with pure physiology. The asylum, too, that space of the professionally and socially excluded, returns in almost classic Freudian fashion. For the narrator continues his absolutely conscious account – even supplying psychological reasons for the unreal James's panic – as part of the descriptive unveiling of the hallucination. The cat and mummy – icons of the Egyptian cult of death popular with Victorians – give Poe-like images of Gothic authority to the scene.

At the climax of the account the unreal James of the remembered confrontation with the image identifies with the remembered perception of the live object: 'That shape am I, I felt potentially.' At the same time, he marks his distance from that object. He knows that it is real and unreal at the same time. At the very climactic moment of horror he is thus not absolutely taken over. 'Potentially' wards off the absolute entry into hallucination. It also signals a pragmatist nightmare of a contentless future incapable of justifying a present action.

James's narrator also makes a footnote comparison with Bunyan's fear and trembling in the face of the unpardonable sin, and thus links the 'fear of existence' with the moral world. It would be difficult to find the 'fear of existence' as such playing any part in Old Testament or New Testament teaching. The 'fear of existence' in this context is a nineteenth-century phenomenon governed by the fact that the entire belief system of Christianity is under threat. James sticks doggedly to his psychological reduction. Unlike Bunyan he will not extend his image into narrative. There is no journey as a result of the dream. Cat and mummy do not enter the narrative and the little man with greenish skin and black hair remains unthematized.

However, at the level of feeling James does thematize. As narrator he drags the emotion into time. The 'insecurity of life' is such as he never knew before and never experiences again. That comment comes from a perspective of distant time – the narrator, in a familiar gesture, bowing out of the story. Possible consequent narrative within the magic time of the story is reduced to a few months: 'for months I was unable to go out in the dark alone.' Then, as noted, he conceals the event from his mother. Instead he appeals to other texts of Christian comfort. Within the values of the culture James inherited there was probably little else he could do. Interestingly, however, he breaks, on his own behalf, the paradigm which the book as a whole supports. There is no consequent moral decision or renewed life. The nihilism is repeated: 'man's original optimism and self-satisfaction', concludes James, as a result of such experiences, 'get levelled with the dust'.[28] It is perhaps a rather American conclusion – the corruption of an original optimistic dream which, when corrupted, leads to abject pessimism.

It is possible to interpret James's story in many ways. At a social level the asylum haunts the normal world with its own fears writ large. At a psychological level the entire history of New England Puritanism, with its failure to reconcile empiricism and religious theory in the 'religious affection', leads to a degeneration of 'religious experience' into an aestheticism of terror. At a fictional level the story is a dense pattern of concealment and evasion of some interest. At a philosophical level it displays a failure to come up with an admitted workable definition of consciousness. At a religious level it demonstrates the shock waves of the implausibility of religious description after the death of God, and the inadequacy of psychological explanation to fill the gap. At a socio-historical level it exemplifies a late nineteenth-century fascination of the upper bourgeoisie with the 'world of spirits'. ·

There is also a political dimension. James was a sufferer in a real sense from that obsessive concern with the self inherent in the Puritan and Protestant tradition. Hence all his heroic and ambiguous calls to escape the self and to be in the world. James's difficulties are most succinctly articulated by Merleau-Ponty:

> The normal person does not find satisfaction in subjectivity, he runs away from it, he is genuinely concerned with being in the world, and his hold on time is direct and unreflecting, whereas the sufferer from hallucinations simply exploits his being in the world in order to carve a private section for himself out of the common property world, and constantly runs up against the transcendence of time.[29]

Finally it might be asked, is it a good story? In one sense the answer has to be no. The compressed narrative of the image is, for all the over-consciousness about it, not trusted to produce a story. Another theme plays about it. It is the theme of James as narrator playing with the structures of revelation and silence. One suspects he rather gruesomely enjoyed his little *jeu d'esprit*: a moral equivalent, perhaps of the poverty of philosophy. James never went as far as the Dodgson who became Lewis Carrol. He was a little too solemn to imagine the sharp chin of a dream-Queen digging into the 'innocent' with the question 'And the moral of that, my dear?' But *The Varieties of Religious Experience* – indeed all of James's 'professional' and unprofessional work – does pose the question of tale and teller. James himself wanted to be seen as a writer of literature. The sad thing was that he was ultimately defeated: by the state of the art in psychology, the professionalizing specializations of the university context, by the reduced capacity of religious discourse to describe moral and emotional life, by the peculiar constraints of a post-Darwinian social discourse, and doubtless by all the personal problems of an extra-ordinary family (including the problem of having one of the nineteenth-century's greatest novelists as brother) which American psychoanalytic critics are so enthusiastically uncovering.

Not the least of James's liberal dilemmas was how to reconcile the scientist, the artist and the philosopher in himself among disintegrating scientific paradigms and humanistic discourses. For another turn of that famous brother's burning glass, it is now time to look at Gertrude Stein's rehearsal of not dissimilar problems. However, her account will be from the point of view of one who was disposed to accept the role of story-teller rather more readily.

Part Three
Beyond the 'Fourth Natural Kingdom'[1]

Chapter 11
Gertrude Stein and the Legitimation of Society

> I do still think Darwin the great man of the period that formed my youth.
>
> GERTRUDE STEIN[1]

Gertrude Stein has so often been hailed as a precursor of the post-modernist era that any attempt to situate her in her own time runs the risk of appearing to cavil at the achievement itself. Nonetheless, to ignore the immediate cultural and historical past from which she emerged and in which she found the terms with which to transform the very language of literature is to limit a full evaluation of her work. Gertrude Stein was in fact a young contemporary of both Adams and James. She not only shared their ambitions for literature but proposed a renewal of that literature within a framework of the kind of problems – in philosophy, psychology and historical metaphysics – which Adams and James had also addressed. Often regarded as a pure aesthetician, she was in fact as interested as they in the emergence of America as a society.

It is well known, of course, that Stein was a pupil of William James. As far as is known she never met Henry Adams, though there may have been some near-misses. For example, on 17 September 1909, the art historian Bernard Berenson wrote to Adams, 'Last night I dined with Leo Stein, a Californian painter-metaphysician, etc. He spoke without an idea that I knew you and spoke of your history as one of the few most intellectual and thorough he had ever read. You really flatter yourself about being so unread.'[2] The remark, as well as linking the Steins through Berenson with Adams, raises two important subjects which were to occupy Gertrude Stein as much as they ever did Adams. The first is the meaning of history, and the second the nature of the artist's role in society – a society which seemed increasingly to ignore serious and difficult work.

Like Adams, Stein was to attempt to look at society 'scientifically' and to judge the results in relation to traditional modes of understanding in literature and related arts. She shared Adams's sense of being an outcast and was as keen as he to assess the relation between the personal and public domains. Like Adams, she had a typically nineteenth-century view of history as 'mental history', and she searched with equal dedication for the 'laws' of social behaviour, though the range of her materials was different. Like Adams, too, she was occupied with the relation of the family to public and to creative life. She would have agreed with Adams that women rather than men were to be of significance in twentieth-century society and art. In economics she was a conservative, as Adams was. Like Adams also, she liked to play games with traditional issues in philosophy from the vantage point of the artist. No less than Adams she searched for 'types' which would give clues to the inner workings of 'social evolution'. There was similarly a shared interest in metaphysical philosophies of process and change.

In personal terms, too, they had much in common. They enjoyed to the full the love of the good life of the late nineteenth-century bourgeois. Both were fascinated by Roman culture. Both loved Provence. They shared a love of Shakespeare. Both were fiercely nationalistic in their advocacy of American culture. Both loved cars and motoring about the French countryside. Nonetheless, it is of course strange to think of them sharing the Paris of the pre-First World War era. Adams, at least according to his self-image, was an increasingly lonely eighteenth-century 'survival', burying himself in the culture of Provence and declaring the current art and music to be inadequate and decadent. Stein, on the other hand, was coming into contact with the exciting new work of Picasso, Matisse and Cézanne, and having her first experimental prose pieces published in Stieglitz's *Camera Work*.

With William James the connections with Stein are perhaps more obvious. While it is clear that James had little understanding of her experimental writing – that is, the little he saw – for Stein he was one of those 'geniuses' who, along with Picasso and Whitehead and sundry lesser lights, she claimed as crucial for her work. There is no doubt that ways of thinking learned with James provided important parameters for her work throughout her life. Nevertheless there is much evidence that in taking on the Jamesian legacy Stein also transformed it: both inevitably, because her literary modes enforced such transformation, and also consciously and creatively.

From James, Stein acquired a habit of mind in which literature, philosophy and psychology could be placed in the service of one another. Both attempted to straddle humanistic and scientific areas of thought and broke disciplinary boundaries in the attempt. They were fascinated by traditional philosophical questions and attempted to carry these questions into the resistant modes of psychology and literature. Both turned to an investigation of language and method as a means of carrying the attack further, and temperamentally both were empiricists with a lively sense of the limitations of the tradition. Darwin was an important figure for them both, and they shared with differing degrees of emphasis the Darwinian contribution to psychological questions, particularly those which concerned problems of habit, environment, language, emotional expression and time. They were further fascinated by the nature of behaviour in pre-conscious states, problems of perception and, true to common philosophical tradition, they tended to downgrade epistemological questions which involved 'consciousness' and reflection. Both were interested in the nature of belief and they shared a certain fatalism about the human condition.

Again like Adams and Stein, James and Stein combined an easy cosmopolitanism with fierce nationalism; both loved painting but James, unlike Adams, disliked music. James, however, cannot simply be viewed in relation to Stein. The differences are very important, for the simple reason that their forms of discourse are different. Literature does not *illustrate* philosophy, any more than philosophy *explains* literature. They may meet, however, in particular syntheses on the common ground of criticism. At the conceptual level, too, there were differences.[3] Stein was to be nervous about a Darwinian model of mind, though in 'Composition as Explanation' she flirted with a Darwinian model of reception theory. Stein was much less disposed towards concensus than James, as Harriet Chessman has shown.[4]

The public recognition of Stein, which really began on a large scale during her visit to the United States in 1935, has hindered as much as helped the serious study of her work. There was a touch of vanity, vengeance and exuberant energy in the way, as Adams might have said, she 'entered the twentieth century' in 1935, stage-managed by the novelist and impresario of the Harlem Renaissance, Carl Van Vechten. She criss-crossed America by air and road, making newspaper headlines, a Rip Van Winkle roused from European entombment, delivered wise-cracking *bons mots* in a style which surely echoed back through Mark Twain to Benjamin Franklin, offering endless advice and adoping the pose of a pundit whose cultivated *naïveté* delighted an America still in the depths of the Depression. So successful was she that on arrival in Hollywood the first question the temporarily upstaged film stars put to her was: Who is your publicity agent? Ironically, while Stein was responding to airplanes, soda fountains, Ford motor cars and radio, the public found in her a reassurance of the 'survival' of a 'lost' America, an

America untouched by technology, or depression, or capitalist disaster.

Her actual work was still not much read. Political radicals in criticism, with two very distinguished exceptions (Richard Wright and Hugh MacDiarmid), damned it as mystificatory, decadent and bourgeois,[5] and equally the commissars of the new anti-Marxist Establishment, the Southern school of New Critics, had few means of understanding its ambitious intellectuality. Stein's lonely integrity made her resistant to categories. In some ways she was an aristocrat with an aristocrat's taste for popular culture, with all the contradictions that involved, and which are so well exemplified in *Three Lives* (1909). 'Picasso', she once wrote to Van Vechten, 'is mad about those negro photographs of yours.'[6] While her sexual preferences made her always ironic about 'normal life', she was scarcely a sexual liberationist. Her relation with Alice B. Toklas was monogamous, and as one recent commentator has pointed out: 'Stein never was a member of [Natalie Clifford] Barney's circle of international lesbians. . . and thought. . . Barney somewhat corrupt.' The relation with Alice B. Toklas has been endlessly discussed, with the dominant role being ascribed now to the one, now to the other.[7] Certainly Toklas shared intellectual interests with Stein and was much more than a secretary and typist. In so far as Hemingway's famous letter is to be trusted, Stein disliked homosexuality in men.[8]

Between the public image and the private concerns, and beyond the bohemian fringe, was the serious artist.[9] One thing always emerged and that was Stein's absolute commitment to the writer's task. It was for this that the early career as a doctor was abandoned, but its memory was to play an important part in her work.[10] To live with another woman lifted the burden of childen and family life. One theme that goes through her work (and it suggests that her choices were not made easily) is the relation between art and necessity, and between creativity and existence. She wrote her first book for children just a few years before her death. The liveliness of the wit directed against the stultifyingly boring deification of the natural process belongs also to her own age: the wit for example of the theatre of Oscar Wilde: 'We have married perfect husbands, and we are well punished for it.'[11]

In political terms Stein was a conservative. A mixture of liberal sentiment and populist attitudes put her firmly on the side of reaction. Stein left America at the end of the nineteenth century, at a time when the values of liberal individualism were becoming a point of nostalgic reference and when radicalism though lively was diffuse. A radical as such could mean anything from membership in a

Temperance League to being a feminist. In a time of disillusion she had an admiration for leaders, whether General Grant, Susan B. Anthony or Mussolini.

Her most revealing comments on politics are in her letters to 'Kiddy' in the 1930s. Kiddy, W. G. Rogers, was one of the 'dough-boys' Gertrude Stein met during her ambulance-driving days in World War I, and he became a lifelong friend. Rogers scented reaction in many of Stein's attitudes and pressed her closely on a number of issues. It is evidence of her affection for Rogers that she unburdened herself so fully. Stein was scarcely alone among writers in not disapproving of Mussolini as such, and of fascist Spain. In spite of the fact that Franco had moved in with the army against the democratically elected majority of the country, she wrote (Stein's spelling and punctuation are kept):

> You see in Spain and in a certain xtent in France you cannot change the government when the people no longer want it, we ourselves had some such difficulty in the civil war, after all it does happen, and the Reds in Spain did not really any longer do what the people wanted beside after all here in France and I know a lot more about it than I did once anybody gets in power its hard to dislodge. Like Tammany.[12]

Fatalism about actual power distorts the facts in this argument. Stein's attitudes at root, however, reflected the oldest of American political beliefs. Deep inside her was a small-town Jeffersonian individualist, pragmatic, even rural. Like Montesquieu whose writings influenced the ideology of the American Revolution, she believed in the geographical basis of history. Thus she thought that England had a constitutional government because it was an island, that America was too large a land mass to be a democracy, and that the 'Latins' did not have the temperament for it.[13]

Stein's attitudes to the New Deal were, therefore, predictable. But she also allowed them to be publicized. In the mid-1903s she wrote a series of articles for the *Saturday Evening Post*, a magazine which, as was most of the American press at the time, was conducting a savage campaign against the New Deal. The issue in which her first article, on 'Money', appeared had a cartoon showing the New Deal Octopus strangling the 'American pocketbook', the 'American home', the 'American citizen', as well as American business, industry and government. In the same magazine one would find Stein's comments: 'So until everyone who votes public money remembers how he feels as a father of a family, when he says no, when anybody in the family wants money, until that time comes there is going to be a lot of trouble and some years later everybody is going to be very unhappy.'[14]

Thus, in an all-too-familiar propagandist proposition, the assault on collective caring is mounted by an appeal to paternalist family psychology and idealist self-sufficiency, and further turned aggressively against the mass of the unemployed. Stein called for a 'spiritual [sic] pioneer [sic] fight' against collectivism, and Rogers recalled that 'to my great distress she criticized severely the current trends of democratic government'.[15] There was, of course, much to criticize, but the terms of the criticism seemed to create a basis for something a great deal worse.

Stein's lively interest in history and current politics contradicts her declaration that 'no writer is really interested in politics'.[16] Recalling her days at Radcliffe she declared: 'I had been very interested in constitutional history...that was about the time of Cleveland's second administration and we talked politics a lot but the reading of the written English word was really the thing that held me.'[17] While the preference is clear, the interest in 'constitution' (in the United States of course a written one) and in the professional, legal and structural aspects of political life remained crucially important throughout her career.

Her attention was to be focused on the *societas* not on the *polis*, and the problem of writing and 'society' would be investigated in terms of behaviour and psychology. What emerged was a set of assumptions perhaps most positively summed up by Kenneth Rexroth, speaking here of movements in European culture between 1870 and 1929 (his 'They' refers to Blaise Cendrars, Pierre Reverdy and the young Louis Aragon):

> They believed and hoped that the arts would be the instrument of a fundamental revolution of the human sensibility as such. They believed that the word or pictorial image would be used to subvert the dead syntax by which human self-alienation had been grafted into the very structure of the brain and nervous system. They believed that the Revolution of the Word would liberate a new life meaning for man and sweep away dead shells from which meaning had become exhausted or had turned malignant.[18]

The relation of the word as essence and sign to the essence in turn of psychology and behaviour was of course much more complex and problematic than such a swift bypassing of questions of politics and intelligibility would suggest. Yet Rexroth's instinct was right. There is a connection between dead syntax and alienation, though the assumption that it is unmediated is incorrect – that is, 'self-alienation' is not an autonomous act but a response to others. In considering Stein's relation to these issues it is important to describe the historical foreground which gave her the terms with which to approach the problem of society.

Stein was to turn a half-psychological, half-literary gaze on to society as such and to register at the local and particular level the disturbances of the quasi-private and quasi-public domain of the social. She was always amazed at the freedom, the casual freedom, of people talking to her on the streets of New York – people who had heard her on the radio or read of her in the papers. She also observed a strange fracturing of the emotions as a result of what she took to be an absence of American 'daily life'. Much as Thoreau before her had registered the 'lives of quiet desperation', she noted: '...in America there is no daily life.... the American not living every minute of the day in a daily way does not make what he has to say exciting, and to move as everything moves, or to move as emotion but to move as anything that really moves is moving.'[19]

Stein had an acute sense of new ways of life being created in America. The following passage registers Adams's sense of 'society become police', but without overtly making the judgement. It is there, nonetheless, in the writer's fidelity to detail:

> And also then there is the stewardess and the pilot and that is what makes it so real and unreal, she is just nice and talks United States and is helpful and friendly in the best United States way and he, in the best United States way, is well-informed and kindly and protective and in the best United States way there is a pistol hanging low to shoot man and sky in the best United States way and the pistol I know is a dark steel-blue pistol.[20]

For Stein the key question was to be: what is the relation between language and social psychology? The partial answer she gave was a result of investigating both together. The two cannot ultimately be separated. In order, however, to investigate what their historical relation was as she herself would have thought about it, it is necessary to look first at the kinds of psychology and philosophy with which she was engaged.

Some important clues are provided in a letter to Robert Haas:

> I was at Radcliffe of course and I began specializing in science. I was awfully interested in biology but gradually it turned into philosophy and psychology. I do still think that Darwin is the great man of the period that formed my youth, and I often meditate about his expression of emotions in man and animals, aside from William James, Münsterberg and Santayana I did not work with anybody in particular, English courses when I was at Rad-

cliffe were not particularly interesting, and as I had read day and
night for many years in the Mechanics and Mercantile libraries of
San Francisco, I really did have a pretty close and intimate feeling
about it.[21]

It is precisely the passage from biology to psychology through a
set of quasi-philosophical problems which formed the framework
within which Stein approached literature.

The book Gertrude Stein refers to in the above letter is Darwin's
The Expression of the Emotions in Man and Animals of 1872, which,
with 'A Biographical Sketch of an Infant' of 1877, is his major contribution to psychology. Darwin had claimed for behaviour the
same kind of evolutionary pattern as he had claimed for physical
characteristics. Expressive actions, originally produced to relieve
or gratify emotional impulses or sensations, can be inherited as a
result of becoming habitual through repetition, even when the
original emotional cause is absent. Free from this original motivating cause they come to be imprinted on the nervous system itself.
Paradoxically, for a work which emphasized repetition and habit,
the effect of these arguments was to widen the role of irrational
behaviour in human life. With the 'will' relegated to exercising
choice far back in evolutionary time, gesture and expression become
unconscious and ahistorical existents. There are two unconscious
mediations in Darwin's argument, and they relate to the kind of
evidence he used to back up his theory. The first concerns his use
of literature as evidence for his theory, and the second the kinds of
beings who best deliver themselves for the pursuit of the intelligibility of emotional expression.

Darwin's work on the psychology of emotions is strangely the
most 'literary' of all his works. Quotations from Shakespeare,
Homer and Milton, and from many other writers both ancient and
modern, are drawn on to provide 'evidence' for the analysis of facial
and bodily expression. In holding the literary mirror up to nature
Darwin invoked an extreme mimetic view of literature. Literature
delivered the facts of experience. When these facts of experience
are to do with emotional life, however, Darwin cannot rely on
traditional common sense to give the experience its aura of reality.
In the popular consciousness, then as now, poetry was simply 'the
spontaneous overflow of powerful feelings', and Wordsworth's
corollary, 'by a man who has also thought long and deeply',[22] was
conveniently forgotten. Darwin himself admitted in his biography
to an early interest in literature, and the power of the English literary
tradition in *The Origin of Species* is very strong. He also confessed to
losing that interest in literature, and it is possible, given that in

nineteenth-century biological thought ontogeny was thought to recapitulate phylogeny, he felt literature belonged to the more primitive – that is, the more youthful – period of his own life. Certainly the view was commonplace: at worst it is a rather arrogant rationalization of a fear of literature, and at best a rationalization of the fact that Darwin preferred to do something else. With so many progessivist schemes of human history, and an increasing assumption that all truth was scientific truth, literature got stuck somewhere down the evolutionary ladder.

Darwin used Shakespeare's and Milton's descriptions of human emotion rather as symbolic fossils. The ultimate referent of Darwin's expression of emotions was, to borrow a phrase from Whitehead, 'naïve experience'. Whitehead used the phrase to justify his own peculiarly Platonizing empiricism: 'the ultimate appeal is to naïve experience and that is why I lay stress on the evidence of poetry.'[23] It must be one of the sillier statements about poetry made by an intelligent man in the modern period, but it reveals the arrogance of someone convinced of the historically determined superiority of the scientific project. 'Naïve experience' for Darwin is curiously both present and absent. Its past was clear enough in earlier, 'primitive' societies – even one's own at an earlier stage of development. Its present was determined by what could be characterized as 'naïve'. Darwin associated it with those people (as well as with animals) who lacked the power to declare themselves other than naïve.

Thus the facts of gesture and emotional expression, Darwin said, are best observed in children, animals, primitives, the insane and those undergoing electric shock treatment. It is people on the 'fringe' of society – either within one's own society or outside it in another society – who deliver a half-conscious truth for those who most vigorously defend the centrality of their own claims to truth. The spatial image 'fringe'/'centre' is value-laden, as already observed in James. 'Fringe' is designated by those who assume their own values to be 'central'.

Indeed much of the unintentionally appalling humour of Darwin's book lies in the centrist biases of his informants, who are missionaries, colonial officers, police, travelling academics, and even romantic kings like Rajah Brooke who observed, for example, that 'the Dyaks of Borneo. . . open their eyes widely when astonished, often swinging their heads to and fro and beating their breasts'. The abstraction of the 'facts of behaviour' from their dramatic context reveals with cruel clarity the cultural biases of the observer. Darwin cites, for example, a young man 'not very liable to blush' who 'will blush intensely at any slight ridicule from a girl whose judgement on any important subject he would disregard'.[24]

The following more extended example reveals even more clearly the buried assumptions of the objective gaze confronting the facts of human emotional expression:

> Mr Scott informs me that the workmen in the Botanic Gardens at Calcutta are strictly ordered not to smoke; but they often disobey this order, and when suddenly surprised in the act, they first open their eyes and mouths widely, then they often slightly shrug their shoulders, when they perceive that discovery is inevitable, or frown and stamp on the ground from vexation. Soon they recover from their surprise, and abject fear is exhibited by the relaxation of all their muscles; their heads seem to sink beneath their shoulders; their fallen eyes wander to and fro; and they supplicate forgiveness.[25]

The act of divorcing the physiology of expression from the qualitative context of a dramatic situation was not the objective undertaking that Darwin thought it was. The abjectness of the controlled is not a fact of human nature but a gesture to ward off punishment through an appeal to the insecure arrogance of the controllers.

Before we explore the significance of these matters in relation to Gertrude Stein, one question begs for attention: the question of language. Darwin himself uses the analogy of language for the inheritance of half-conscious choices fixed through habit. In Darwin's century the 'pseudo-historical' sciences had often provided analogies for one another. Geology and language were frequently compared. Words, said Emerson, for example, are 'fossil poetry'.[26] The problem immediately arises of how 'natural' is selection in relation to language, and at what level. Darwin was writing about language within a relatively impoverished English tradition of language theory,[27] and he scarcely had the equipment to discuss issues which still foment debate in our own time. But here and there in his work he does take up the question of language, and inevitably it had to come up whenever he thought about human development. In his notebooks of 1837 Darwin is already struggling with the question:

> Probably, language commenced in some necessary connection between things and voice, as roaring for lion, etc. (in same way alphabet arose from letters, symbol or word beginnng with sound of letter) – crying yawning laughing being necessary sounds . . .not produced by will but by corporeal structure.[28]

Darwin glosses over the difficult part – 'symbol of word beginning with sound of letter' – suggesting that he wanted a theory which in its insistence on the continuity between biology and mental life pushed to one side the problem of symbolization.

Darwin had what Merleau-Ponty once called a 'prejudice in favour of the world' which led psychologists who followed his work to resort to a philosophical mechanism. In our own time 'sensation and judgement' have lost their apparent clearness.[29] Husserl's view might also be recalled, that intentionality with its intuitive presence banishes both idealism and realism; or one might say further, with Derrida, that the thing in itself is already a '*representamen* shielded from the simplicity of intuitive evidence'.[30] The unfortunate workmen in the Calcutta Botanic Gardens had in fact created a body language out of terror. Within the terms of an address to others, the game of language is one of power and politics. The results of that *are suffered as structure*. Similarly, language as pure structure is also suffered in history as the inert legacy of others. The signs are not existents generalized in neutral language. The wandering to and fro of the 'fallen eyes' of the Calcutta workmen are selected as evidence from the point of view of the powerful, whose neutrality of stance is granted without consent.

A further note must be added here on Darwin's legacy to James on the subject of the emotions. In Darwin's work there is still a sense of the human world, of 'civilization', a feeling that individuals interact with one another. It is there in the abundant quotations from literature, and even in the short example of imperialist psychology discussed above – the colonial officer (unlike the officers of the World Bank) is after all obliged to communicate with his victims. When James banishes the emotions to the psychological hinterland of the natural his discussion falls back on the more mechanistic aspects of the emergent behavioural sciences in Germany and France. For Darwin the intelligibility of an emotion could find its reference in an identifiable past which survived in the 'primitive'; women, children, and colonized races. The effect of James's discussion is to push the emotion into an absolute unconsciousness. James reacts emotionally to his own proposition by stating that merely descriptive accounts of the emotions are 'one of the most tedious parts of psychology'.[31]

Nonetheless it is precisely at this most tedious point of the argument that James enunciates the psychological theory for which he is most famous; the celebrated James–Lange theory of the emotions, in which emotion is predicated on physiological reaction not the other way round. Thus we are sad because we cry, happy because we laugh, and so on. One example James gives is a personal one. He recalls how he fainted as a child when he saw a horse bled: 'with no feeling save that of childish curiosity'.[32] The emotion for the tough little fellow bypasses consciousness and triggers an automatic physiological reaction. Significantly, James's example is of himself as a child, where the case for study is purest. Primitiveness equals scientific limitation of field. For James emotions are either to be made safe in unconsciousness (shut your eyes and think of England, as Victorian ladies were told), or they are to be governed by the strong hand of cultivated habit.

The aim seems to be to keep both positions in maximum tension, like reason and unreason in a detective novel, where the further aim is to preserve the authority of the author in relation to a public playing a game necessarily lost. For there is in fact both cultural bias and judgement in James's description of physiological manifestation on an ethically loaded scale of 'crudity' and 'refinement' – as if gentlemen sweated while ladies merely perspired. He describes a continuous, unconscious route of judgement from physiological reaction to those subtle emotions which are 'moral, intellectual and aesthetic feelings'.[33] James in fact anticipates the seamless world of Whitehead's sentient aesthetics.

At this point it is instructive to generalize the critique of Darwin and James on emotional life. Following Sartre, it is clear that to take an emotion as a fact or as an existent is to isolate it from other phenomena. An emotion is an attempt to seize the world and as such has 'its own essence, its peculiar structures, its laws of appearance, its meaning'.[34] There is much more, therefore, than unconscious psycho-physiological disorder. A bodily condition manifests itself *as* terror or *as* love. Sartre comments on James:

> The reflective consciousness can always direct its attention upon emotion. In that case emotion is seen as a structure of consciousness. It is not a pure, ineffable quality like brick-red or the pure feeling of pain – as it would have to be according to James's theory. It has meaning, it signifies something in my psychic life.[35]

Theories of psychology and society do not emerge in a vacuum. There is a political context for theories of the emotions, as Darwin's example of the Calcutta workmen suggested. In the first years of the twentieth century employers were not indifferent to the economic and industrial chaos of the 1890s. Slowly the fatalism of social-Darwinist struggle was countered by the progressivist's dream of scientific management and human engineering. Neither Americans nor Europeans were strangers to the idea of model work-places. Early in the nineteenth century Richard Owen had created New Lanark and New Harmony successively, one on either continent. Utopian experiment was rife in the restless 1830s and '40s. Lewis Mumford summarized the historical impulse in his first book, *The Story of Utopias* (1921). What was new in the first and subsequent decades of the twentieth century was a wholly 'scientific' approach addressed to the industrial situation. It was characterized by an appeal to abstract principles of method, technique and efficiency. American psychology was to be the actual and theoretical discipline through which far-reaching changes in American industrial practice were proposed.

Hugo Münsterberg (whose descriptions of American late nineteenth-century architecture have already been cited) was Gertrude Stein's teacher at Harvard; as well as being a psychologist, he was a widely published writer on cultural and social affairs, whose work establishes a clear link between experimental psychology and social and industrial life. William James had brought Münsterberg over from Germany, where he had studied with Wundt, to run the psychological laboratory at Harvard. James was never really enthusiastic about his German colleague's work, and Münsterberg repaid the compliment by seldom referring to James's psychology and by alluding to his philosophy with an 'ironic smile'.[36]

Münsterberg called his book, *The Americans*, of 1905 (which was translated and expanded from an earlier version written in German), both a 'social psychological experiment' and 'a philosophy of Americanism'. Although the relation between these two concepts is never really examined in the work, Münsterberg clearly expected the method of 'social psychological experiment' to reveal the 'philosophy of Americanism'. He explains further that 'the chapters on economic and political problems are the least important of the book, as they are meant merely by way of illustration'.[37] James at least had attempted to mediate rival philosophies of psychology. For Münsterberg the truth of the scientific gaze is self-sufficient and self-evident.

Exteme common sense is here identified with absolute idealism. Münsterberg notes, for example, that the subjugation of inferior races is 'simply a quiet aristocratic complement to the inner workings of the Constitution' (*Americans*, p. 10). The gaze of the social scientist replaces that of the helpful colonial administrator. In fact Münsterberg's book is at one level an apologetic in 'social science' terms for the American business culture in which the 'Spirit of self-initiative' and not 'greed nor the thought of money' (p. 239) will bring about the desired millennium; provided correct habits can be induced. It is in this spirit that Münsterberg defends the increasing specialization of the worker's task. Far from dividing and alienating workers from each other and the product, specialization guarantees 'the highest mastery. . . and lets the workman see even more the complexity of what is going on' (p. 174). The relation between intelligibility and behaviour is announced from the point of view of the owner of the means of production, and then assumed also to fall within the experience of the employee as self-evident truth.

It is with the same bland benevolence that Münsterberg also justifies American policy in external affairs. Here the therapeutic concept of hygiene replaces utilitarian habit. In relation to the seizure of Cuba, for example, 'that which was done under [Governor] Wood's administration for the hygiene of a country which had always been stricken with yellow fever, for the school and judicial system of that people, is remarkable' (p. 209). Here the equation of nature and nurture, assumed in the naïve behaviourist's discourse, becomes propaganda for the justification of conquest. Münsterberg's arguments 'reasonably' remove the possibility of qualitative reasoning: 'socialism may not spring directly from envy, but a people given to envy are very ready to listen to socialism; and in America socialism remains a foreign cult, which is preached to deaf ears' (p. 538). Poor socialists envy, while poor capitalists emulate.

Münsterberg's metaphysics of moral characterization structure his political prejudices, from foreign affairs to domestic circumstance. He laments the fact that American women see domestic work as a chore: work which German women undertake with joy, and concludes: 'the social self-assertion of women, in which every American believes with all his heart, is just as little likely ever to lead to universal suffrage for women as American industrial self-assertion will ever lead to socialism' (p. 572). What is important in this argument is not merely its obvious anti-feminist polemic, but the terms in which that polemic is put. The argument needs to confine women to the domain of the social. 'Social self-assertion' must be preserved as depoliticized behaviour. The moment the philosophic spirit of American self-assertion leaves the arena of social truth it becomes distinctly un-American.

These objective psychological truths were not proposed in a vacuum. In the rather modest relief from industrial repression known as the 'Progressive Era', reform was everywhere being debated. Trusts were being severely criticized, the woman-suffrage campaign was reaching its peak, culminating in 1911 in the winning of the vote for women, and even socialists were to receive more than a million votes in 1919. However, within the structure of Münsterberg's thought, ideology becomes sentiment and the liberal essentialism of 'moral character' moves from the pages of literature to the psychological laboratory as an a priori metaphysic. It was Münsterberg's boast that by the turn of the century America had over forty psychological laboratories, and that they were bigger and better than their European counterparts.

Münsterberg's arguments become even clearer in a work he published some ten years later, called *Business Psychology* (1915). Here any pretence to an older American liberal ethic is dropped, and there is a straightforward advocacy of 'social psychology'. In this book Münsterberg refers to Frederick W. Taylor's classic *Principles of Scientific Management* of 1911, and gives qualified approval to the scientific-management movement, which had, he asserts, achieved much with 'mere common sense and experience'.[38] Undoubtedly the movement contained within itself good as well as bad results. Mumford wrote that it directed attention to the industrial process as a whole and 'treated the worker as an integral element in it', but that its weakness was that it regarded 'the aims of capitalist production as fixed'.[39] From whose point of view the worker becomes that 'integral element' Mumford does not however consider. Ellul contends that Taylor's separation of goal from mechanism, the emphasis on means and method and contentless efficiency, reduced the entire political and historical process to a kind of fatalistic autonomy.[40] In technological terms, as Wiener points out, Taylorism was a kind of half-way stage towards the actual automated factory of our own day.[41] Technics, however, is only a part of the story.

Braverman cites Drucker's important point that scientific management took 'tools and techniques largely as given'.[42] The implication is, therefore, that management was hardly tackling the problem from the workers' point of view, since radical thinking about the role of labour in relation to the whole technological process was refused. There were no thoughts about reorganizing technology. It was more 'economic' to reorganize people.

There were, however, problems with the psychological mechanization of the worker. When Taylor's principles were actually put into effect in the famous experiment at the Hawthorne, Illinois, plant of Western Electric in 1927, it was found that production did not actually increase. Better results were gained when individualist psychology was replaced by *group* psychology, and when the social group producing the goods was made more cohesive. Therefore the next stage was the need for an administrative élite which would actually organize society as such. In Whyte's classic words:

> They will adjust him. Through the scientific application of human relations, these neutralist technicians will guide him into satisfying solidarity with the group so skilfully and unobtrusively that he will scarcely realize how the benefaction has been accomplished.[43]

The techniques of the benefaction put to utilitarian use the psychological categories of Jamesian psychology: repetition, memory training, attention analysis, and the freedom of the will.

Münsterberg in his 1915 book goes on to distinguish between social psychology and group psychology. The distinction occurs in the context of a remark about language:

> For instance the mental processes involved in the use of language, or the acts of initiation or suggestion, of subordination and self-assertion, belong to social psychology. In group psychology on the other hand, the question is not how a group of men work together and how they influence one another, but what mental characteristics are common to them as a class wherever they may be found. (*Business Psychology*, pp. 236–7)

Here even social interaction is banished, language itself is silenced together with its fundamentally political mode of a dramatic exchange between persons, and what emerges is a despot's dream of atomized human units, constituting a group whose unity is a class of mental characteristics directed to the despot's ends.

Nor does Münsterberg shirk what is necessary to achieve such ends. For example, one class of mental characteristics defines the female group. The Harvard psychologist, armed with results from forty laboratories, delivers the following verdict:

> The average female mind is patient, loyal, reliable, economic, skilful, full of sympathy, and full of imagination; on the other hand it is capricious, over-suggestible, often inclined to exaggeration, disinclined to abstract thought, unfit for mathematical reasoning, impulsive, over-emotional.
>
> (*Business Psychology*, p. 241)

Ever of a practical turn of mind, Münsterberg then demonstrates the utility of this psychological truth. He turns to the problem of factory fires. Many fires had recently caused appalling loss of life, particularly in factories employing women and children.[44] According to Münsterberg these disasters had not been brought about by inadequate inspection, poor safety regulations, greedy employers, badly designed buildings and lack of proper warning systems and fire-fighting equipment. There was one main cause; the hysteria of women, who panicked at the least provocation. Münsterberg concludes that a 'few strong men' should be strategically placed 'to force the women in the right direction toward the exit and to direct their hysterical excitement toward a place of safety (*Business Psychology*, p. 242). The issue is, however, more than a feminist one, for the example demonstrates the implicit authoritarianism of the psychologist's view. The 'few strong men' are the complement of his vision of order.

Always reasonable and sane, Münsterberg depicts a world of helpful experts directing carefully analysed humanoids towards the place in society selected by 'trained psychologists' (p. 257). There will be tests for memory, association, attention, feelings, reaction times, all of them impartially administered in the full confidence that 'there is no mental type for which society has not a place where he can do useful work. . .'. A vision of peace, happiness and success, concludes Münsterberg, is within reach and it can be achieved by 'psychologists only' (p. 288).

Münsterberg did, however, have problems with some of the younger professors, who displayed 'a sort of reactionary mood against the modern high estimation of specialized work'; some even had the audacity to emphasize 'the cultivating value of *belles-lettres* as opposed to the dry details of scholarship' (p. 412). Münsterberg must surely have had Gertrude Stein in mind when he wrote this passage. He seems unaware of the contradiction between the professionalization of the university and the lonely romantic intellectual he admires. Gertrude Stein would in fact have concurred with him on the following point: 'The genius, who in his day is always incomprehensible to the masses goes to waste; and the man who sees beyond the vulgar horizon fights an uphill battle. . . . It is no accident that America has still produced no great world genius' (p. 26).

At any rate Gertrude Stein was to quit the psychological laboratory and herself strike out on a rather lonely artistic existence, perhaps to join the ranks of those American artists and geniuses, such as Whitman, Emily Dickinson, Winslow Homer, Willard Gibbs and Charles Ives, whom Münsterberg thought did not yet exist. But before she left the laboratory Gertrude Stein, with Leon Solomons, wrote two papers on her experiments there. They posed a set of problems which were to occupy her in differing ways well into her literary career.

The first essay, 'Normal Motor Automism' (with Solomons), addresses itself to the problem of the 'second personality' – what James had referred to as 'the divided self'.[45] The aim of the two investigators was to show that automatic behaviour and 'hysterical' behaviour were analogous. The hoped to reduce attention artificially, to prove that there were two types of attention; one physiological, the other associative. The experimenters found that the best kind of literature for distracting the subject's attention was of an 'emotional' kind.[46] It is clear that Stein was not interested in 'automatic writing' as such (*Motor Automism*, p. 9) – as Skinner's well-known and unhelpful article of 1934 suggested[47] – but rather in certain problems her essay somewhat naïvely set out to investigate: If you suspend the idealist notion of consciousness, what are the links between 'automatic' and 'associative' behaviour? Where does language come into it? What is the relation of repetition to habit-formation in language and in social terms? What is the relation between 'emotional' language and automatic behaviour? What is the relation between the emotions and creativity? Eventually Stein's meditation on these problems was to steer her away from mimesis and conventional grammar. The article concluded by stating: 'without a full knowledge of the past history of the patient, it is not possible to tell just where the limits of habit lie' (*Motor Automism*, p. 24). In short, the conclusion leads the way to invoking 'past history': a narrative – the 'story' of which would lie in conscious rather than unconscious memory. Story was to be much more apparent in the second of the two articles, 'Cultivated Motor Automism'.

The whole tone of the second essay (by Stein alone) seems more literary than psychological. Stein observes that induced behaviour is most effective when it is rhythmical in nature, that is apart from the best students, who tend to break the pattern. No less than Adams or James, Stein was early fascinated by the cognitive process of learning. What does 'education' mean in these terms – to what extent does it take account of the 'type' or 'character' under inducement? Stein describes a pattern of learning which involves constant reversion to the old way, 'then the new, and then a slight return to the old, like the struggle between two themes in a muscial composition, until at last the new movement conquered and was then freely continued' (p. 28). The language is Darwinian, of course; two themes in music do not 'compete' for 'survival'. Classification remains a problem. It is not clear whether Stein's subjects are best classified as 'Harvard or Radcliffe types', or in terms of their motor reactions, or in terms of their ability to learn unconsciously. But shifting the categories of character always has satiric possibilities, and there is a wry proposal of categories here. In the first group of subjects are 'girls in literature' and 'men in law'. That Stein decides these are passive types is her oblique comment on what she thinks of such socio-sexually determined roles. Throughout the essay freedom is proposed in resistance to both habit and types. Münsterberg must have thought the contaminating influence of '*belles-lettres*' overwhelming in such a paper.

With the advantage of hindsight, it is clear that even though Stein gave up psychology in favour of writing, some of the basic questions remained. A fascination with dualistic characterology is observable in her early work. Philosophical questions of ontology and epistemology enter her discussions of the creative act and the learning process in the context of literature. The relation between attention and behaviour, and between conscious and unconscious attention will remain an important problem. The relation between conscious and unconscious rhythm will engage both the form and content of her experimental writing.

There were deeper questions too. If psychology, which laid claim to being *the* description of human behaviour, expunged philosophical questions from its discourse, what role was there for critical intelligence? Where did the critical viewer fit in? These questions were to come to the fore again in Stein's meditation on painting and in her 'portraits'. Was the language of description neutral? – If it was not, was it possible to incorporate an awareness of viewpoint into the very language of description? What life was there still in the old philosophic chestnuts of perception and conception?

The questions multiply. Did the divided self exist and on what terms? What is genius? What are the conscious and unconscious factors in creativity? Over all these hung two questions which were hardly new to the American artist: What is the relation of the artist to the world of scientific discourse? What right does the artist have to speak for others? Those questions, which for James were posed between materialism and spiritualism, fatalism and freedom, monism and pluralism, became for Stein pivotal questions for the artist. Finally one writer who claimed to know the world of science, as well as of philosophy and literature, was the philosopher Alfred North Whitehead. By way of answering some of these questions in terms Stein herself would have pondered, those aspects of Whitehead's philosophy which show some degree of convergence with the questions raised will now be considered.

It was in 1915 that Gertrude Stein and Alice B. Toklas spent a weekend with the Whiteheads in their country cottage at Lockeridge in Wiltshire.[48] It would be useful to have a record of what they talked about. As it is, it is possible to speculate on their mutual interests in philosophy, memories of William James, the relations between the arts and sciences, and perhaps the relations between English and American culture. The attractiveness of Whitehead to Americans was to be confirmed later in his career. In the words of one commentator: 'There was a certain congeniality between the outlook of Whitehead's American books and a great deal of what was best in American philosophy.'[49]

It is with caution that one approaches Whitehead's work. As Collingwood once said of him, 'he is always a difficult writer to read, and even after long study one is often not sure how far he has solved by implication problems which he appears to have ignored.'[50] Commentators therefore, not surprisingly, quarrel over his philosophical allegiances; Russell maintaining he is in the English camp of honest, rugged, clear empiricism, others detecting a secret allegiance to idealism. Was he really a Platonist? Some have seriously doubted it.[51] One critic plausibly finds in Whitehead remarkable similarities to Kant – specifically in the notion of 'interpenetration', and in the 'analogues of experience' where 'all appearances are, as regards their existence, subject, a priori to rules determining their relation to one another in time'. Further, Kant's 'extraordinarily modern terms' such as 'field' and 'contexts of possible experience', the relation of our knowledge to which forms a kind of transcendental truth which precedes empirical truth and makes it possible, are also close to a number of Whitehead's formulations.[52]

It was James, of course, who had argued that 'concreteness' was gained by substituting fields for 'stable things and changing thoughts'.[53] Much has been written on the relation of Whitehead to James and other philosophers of his immediate generation. The actual relations are more difficult to assess.[54] None the less Whitehead acknowledges the influence of James's dependence on 'feeling' and quotes approvingly from *The Principles of Psychology* that 'sensation is the feeling of first things'.[55] Indeed James and Whitehead share, not only their admiration for Locke, but the whole instinct for the empiricist tradition. However matter is defined, there is a strong feeling for its otherness. From sense perception, says Whitehead, we are aware of something 'self-contained for thought'. 'Events' which replace old-fashioned atomic matter are comparable because they 'body forth permanences'. Whitehead can speak, too, of the 'ultimate fact' of 'multiple relations'.[56] Science, he affirms, is 'rooted in what I have called the whole apparatus of common-sense thought'.[57] None of this would have been contested by James. Both were happy to 'replace' traditional philosophical questions with related questions about scientific method. Both argued that our experience comes in drops or pulses, 'each of which has a unique character and an indivisible unity'.[58] But Whitehead would have disagreed with James's scepticism about the unity of the individual soul. He ascribed, not completely accurately, to James and Hume a profound rejection of 'a self-identical Soul-Substance'.[59] Nonetheless their thought coincides with differing emphases over wide areas: in the notion of 'field', 'fringe', 'continuity', 'inheritance', 'feelings of relation', and 'tendency'.[60]

As a pupil of James and Münsterberg, Gertrude Stein would have been more than prepared for certain key Whiteheadian issues. Three problems are raised here by way of rehearsing analogous questions in Stein: first, the 'idea of nature', in Collingwood's phrase; second, the implication of this idea for the creative arts; and third, the problem of language, which constitutes an important lacuna in Whitehead's thought and which raises at the same time key political and social questions about his work.

More orthodox philosophers have responded in rather negative ways to Whitehead's philosophy. Those with a positivist bent have distrusted his metaphysics; pluralists suspect his teleologies, materialists his conception of 'matter', determinists his emphasis on the role of chance and the dependence on statistics, and realists the difficult location of primary data in the neural process when they are also phases of that process.[61] There is in Whitehead's world a drive towards an autonomous unfolding of nature, the intelligibility of which is covered by frankly embracing a metaphysic. Certainly Whiteheadian process is different in many respects from that of Hegel. Hegel rejected the notion of mathematics as the ultimate court of appeal for the philosopher. There is no element of contradiction in Whitehead's theory, instead there is 'a hierarchy of categories of feeling rather than a hierarchy of categories of thought'.[62]

The extent to which feeling is intelligible is a problem which goes back to James and Münsterberg, and indeed to Bagehot and Darwin. Like them Whitehead was keen to emphasize the 'unconscious' nature of process, as well as its continuity of operation. American critics of Whitehead have been quick to reinforce the point: 'Hegel and Marx were wrong; the conflict of uncoordinated opposites is a disaster. The conditions of synthesis, in every form of existence, are aesthetic contrast rather than strife.' Subjective experience simply 'emerges' in 'pulses' guided by an 'internal teleology' whose point of reference is the objective world.[63] 'Process' is at once the connectiveness and the general shape within which the two elements find they are identical. The traditional ontological distinction between being and becoming is thus supposedly overcome: 'The present moment is constituted by the influx of the other into that self-identity which is the continued life of the immediate past within the immediacy of the present.'[64] Time is autonomous. The past is agreed. An absolute continuity is made into sufficient intelligibility: 'thus perishing is the initiation of becoming. How the past perishes is how the future becomes.'[65]

Lacking the radicalism of Hegel's 'negation of the negation', the order of process in nature becomes a naïve analogy for human activity and experience. Continuity and repetition become key aspects of process. At one end of Whitehead's scale of nature the process of recurrence and non-recurrence could be expressed in statistical laws; at the other end, the domain of human history, there is a binary fatalism far more dogmatic than anything in Hegel. 'It is God's adventure', says one critic; 'to that extent the Whiteheadian universe is less humanistic than Christianity'.[66] Whitehead went even further, at one level re-echoing Lyell's Stoic adoption of Greek cyclical time, whereby Fate in Greek tragedy 'becomes the order of nature in modern thought'. According to Whitehead this should not produce unhappiness but rather a 'solemnity of the remorseless working of things'.[67]

The tone of that last statement is close to the final pages of *The Origin of Species*. In fact the general theory of evolution was at least as important for Whitehead's philosophy as mathematics. Both could of course find common ground in statistics. The theory of evolution was, according to one critic, 'for Whitehead – who was born in 1861 and once visited Darwin's house – a real and living force, not an item in intellectual history.'[68] Biology occupied the other end of the world of things from that of physics: 'Biology is the study of larger organisms, whereas Physics is the study of smaller organisms.'[69] Whitehead's picture here of the absolute compatibility between the two scientific disciplines is very different from what Darwin himself actually experienced. Whitehead's effort to generalize throughout nature in non-mathematical terms can lead to banality, but the terms of his punditry were not so very different from those of Stein herself: 'The process of living often contains both repetition and anarchy. It also contains creativity which instigates repetition and reason, which controls anarchy.'[70] The problems of the relationship of repetition to creativity, and of both to anarchy and control, were also ones which Gertrude Stein set herself, and as usual they were compounded by the attempt to bypass the question of consciousness.

Like James, Whitehead needed to play down the notion of the consciously experiencing subject. The fate of 'consciousness' in the nineteenth century was in fact very much linked to the growing interest in unconscious states: a project which was to culminate in the work of Freud. L. L. Whyte's book, *The Unconscious Before Freud*, gives the entire foreground to the nineteenth century's onslaught on Cartesian reflection. Already by the end of the eighteenth century and the beginning of the nineteenth, the French philosopher Maine de Biran was speaking of 'sensation without awareness'. Marx opened a Pandora's box with his avowal that 'Life is not determined by consciousness, but consciousness by life'. Just prior to James, Carpenter coined the term 'unconscious cerebration', and in the United States Oliver Wendell Holmes declared: 'The more we examine the mechanism of thought, the more we shall see the automatic, unconscious action of the mind enters largely into all its processes.' Nietzsche, perhaps most famously, spoke of the 'absurd overvaluation of consciousness', and coined the term 'id' for the unconscious. He even went so far as to identify 'consciousness' with illness – a kind of nightmare, one supposes, in which men struggle to sleep more deeply. In a sense Nietzsche summarized the century's speculation: 'The real continuous process takes place below our consciousness: the series and sequence of feelings, thoughts, and so on, are symptoms of this underlying process.'[71] When James asked, therefore, in 1904, 'Does Consciousness exist?', and proposed, as Whitehead was to do later, that it was only a fraction of total experience, he was entering, with an approved bias, an already long-established debate. There is both genuine puzzlement about the terms and equally genuine evasion. It takes relatively little historical insight to see why the term unconscious should have been reviled before 1914 and adopted afterwards as a bearer of truth.

Like James, Whitehead banished consciousness to the psychological category of the attention, and expanded feeling to cover the consequences. In the words of one commentator, '"Feeling" is nothing more than the grasping of an organism of some aspect or another, and the appropriation of this to its own nature. Such may be the action of smoked salmon on the palate, or Mozart on the ear.'[72] Without the privilege of 'cognitive understanding' there is of course no way of telling the difference between smoked salmon and Mozart as aesthetic experience, except that one comes via the palate and the other the ear. Nonetheless Whitehead can reassure us that art does perform a service for civilization, and in cascades of lyrical paradoxes:

> It unlooses depths of feeling from behind the frontier where precision of consciousness fails. The starting-point for the highly developed human art is then to be sought amid the cravings generated by the physiological functionings of the body. The origin of art lies in the craving for re-enaction. In some mode of repetition we need by our personal actions, or perceptions, to dramatize the past and future, so as to relive the emotional life of ourselves and our ancestors. There is a biological law – which, however, must not be pressed too far – that in some vague sense the embryo of the womb reproduces in its life-history features of ancestors in remote geologic epochs. . . . Thus art has its origin in ceremonial evolutions from which issue play, religion, ritual, tribal ceremonies, dance, pictures on caves, poetic literature, prose, music. . . . Art can be described as a psychopathic reaction of the race to the stresses of its existence.[73]

This passage neatly summarizes many of the issues of the preceding pages. They can be viewed as a series of contradictions. First a relation between 'physiological craving' and the 'unconscious' can be noted, together with the proposal that this is a starting-point for art. Undoubtedly there is a connection between the creative possibility of art and emotional life (indeed one suspects Whitehead is thinking specifically of erotic life), but he restricts the possibility of thinking about it to a kind of psychological mimesis whose mode is repetitive re-enaction, and the goal of which is 'to relive' our own emotional life and those of our ancestors. He then invokes (cautiously) the notion that ontogeny recapitulates phylogeny and buries cognitive understanding in the paradox of the 'ceremonial evolutions'. Thus what is creative in relation to the evolutionary process is made conservative by the notion of ceremonial – the enforcement (socially) of continuity. Then art becomes 'a psychopathic reaction of the race' to the stress of existence. Art is thus restricted to therapeutically repetitive norms justified by consensus, for the purposes of easing 'stress'.

This is the wholly neagative side of Whitehead's deliberations. Reading it more positively, no one would deny the role of ritual and ceremony in art – nor for that matter in science. In secular terms there is clearly a need to accept a role for art within evolutionary survival. But it consigns art to the domain of necessity, and views its operations as passive. At the same time there is arrogance in Whitehead's association of 'art' with the 'primitive' and with pre-conscious states. It serves that very unhistorical historical metaphysic which has already been investigated. Cultural evolution becomes an autonomy justified by the notion of socially aggregated ends. Society becomes natural and its intelligibility metaphysical. Consequently it is justifiable to turn the whole discussion around and argue not from nature to society, but from society to nature. What then was Whitehead's view of society? What did he mean by, to use one of his own phrases, social organism?

Dorothy Emmet argues that it was Locke who forecast the main outlines of the doctrine of organism: 'This is certain, things, however absolute and entire they seem in themselves, are but retainers to other parts of nature for that which they are most taken notice of by us.'[74] Like James, Whitehead would have been happy to see Locke as a forerunner of his ideas, and he coined the term 'society' to describe the temporary unities that fall within knowledge.

Like Locke, Whitehead was conservative in his thoughts about social organism. An American commentator represents the position fairly, though innocently:

Whitehead's central doctrine of causal inheritance seems to me to have sprung from his reflections on the characteristics of human society. The reflections are the sort made, on a smaller scale, by Burke in his conception of 'prejudice'. Whitehead uses the actual specific character of human individuals, and the specific part of human society (say New England), and the specific character of a house, or of a tree, as the outcome of an inescapable inheritance transmitted from the past, and of sporadic or purposed deviations [*sic*] from the inheritance. Such a conclusion is obvious to an Englishman who dispassionately considers the institutions, the edifices, the customs about him.[75]

These seem to be accurate comments. But their *evaluation* depends on how far Burke represents the politics of all Englishmen, and how far the essence of an Englishman is in historical fact a dispassionate consideration of institutions and edifices. Mandarin 'objectivity' is not a synonym for either tolerance or 'balance'. The particular Whitehead as opposed to Whitehead-as-Englishman is not so easily generalizable.

The continuity between individual and group is in fact a little rough, for Whitehead, it must be said, manifests distressing prejudices. The contradictions emerge most starkly in the early pages of *Adventures of Ideas*. As much as Buckle, Whitehead lets the smooth evolution of 'mental history' side-step actual history, and seems unaware of the far from continuous and contested process of the generation of ideas. Every historical transition is finally a psychological one. The net result is that adventures of ideas never in fact encounter adventure. Whitehead does not deny that his history will be devoid of prejudice. The question is how to characterize accurately what that prejudice is. It is not a matter of detail: what Whitehead thinks of Gibbon, for example, but of his prejudice in favour of psychological automism in history: 'In every age of well-marked transition there is the pattern of habitual dumb practice and emotion which is passing, and there is the oncoming of a new complex of habit.'[76] In between may be a phase of anarchy involving 'misery and decay of young life' (*Adventures*, p. 15). It must be one of the few references to the Great War in the work. Whitehead never addresses himself to the relation of his paradigm to actual history. Is it really plausible to argue that because the Great War happened it was bound to have happened, and in order to demonstrate the 'phase of anarchy' required in the clash of habits for a social-psychological paradigm? What is in question here is the domain of social history: that retrospective view over generality of custom whose process is without prior decision or consequent reflection; a 'sociology of the Western world', in which 'Men knew not what they did' (pp. 17, 16).

Material life is also relatively unimportant for Whitehead: 'The physical conditions are merely the background which partially controls the flux of modes and moods' (p. 11). The 'flux of modes and moods' suggests a Bergsonian vitalistic structure in which psychological paradigms emerge from feeling. The 'mental history' of Whitehead does not even have the energy of Buckle's intellectual process. Whitehead admits that thinkers do not necessarily change history or constitute a 'political force': and he adds, 'sometimes thousands of years have to elapse before thought can capture action' (p. 71). For Lyell and Darwin the mere lapse of time becomes prime mover of change, but whereas their characterization of time was based on changes they could observe and define, when Whitehead transfers this function of time to the social world he provides no such actual secondary evidence, or details of praxis. Whitehead's 'space–time', however much it works for the new physics, turns history into an aesthetics of 'spatialization': a theme which is scarcely new to students of American culture.[77]

The relation of society to spatialization remains problematic. Whitehead's ultimate characterisation of society as such lurches towards the last limit of individualism:

> The wide scope of the notion of 'society' requires attention. Transcendence begins with the leap from the actuality of the immediate occasion to the notion of personal existence, which is a society of occasions. In terms of human life, the soul is a society. Care for the future of personal existence, respect and pride in its past, are alike feelings which leap beyond the bounds of the sheer actuality of the present.
>
> (*Adventures*, p. 333)

The isomorphism between entity and collective form cannot be carried over so easily into the life world. Here Whitehead verges on Jamesian punditry.

And yet, like Adams, Whitehead realized that the world into which he was born had changed. He knew for example that 'the mere doctrines of freedom, individualism and competition, had produced a resurgence of something very like industrial slavery at the base of society' (p. 46). He knew also, like Adams, that the 'limited liability corporation' had 'considerably modified the effective meaning of the characteristic liberal doctrine of contractual freedom' (p. 80). He attacked Maine's old notion of society as progressing from custom to contract, calling it a 'shallow sociology', and added, 'There is no escape from customary status' (p. 81). Whitehead adds therefore to his notion of socio-psychological continuity the doctrine of absolute conservatism of status: 'individualists and socialists are merely debating over the details of neo-feudalism which modern industry requires' (p. 38). Commerce is praised as taking a benevolent attitude towards the psychological acquisitiveness of man, and as 'an example of intercourse in the way of persuasion' (p. 104).

The great lacuna in Whitehead's thought is a theory of language. Whitehead's impatience with verbal language as such for the purposes of thinking is understandable in a scientist. A. H. Johnson, the author of an important article on the subject, makes a virtue of necessity by saying: 'in a philosophy stressing organic interrelatedness, Whitehead's discussion of the uses of language is not to be found in any one chapter or any book or article.'[78] The logic of this statement is dubious. Language does not simply disappear into inter-relatedness. Nor does the fragmenting of the discussion of language suggest its unity in terms of content. Nonetheless Whitehead's position is carefully summarized in this article, and it is worth reviewing it briefly.

Although Darwin is not mentioned, the Whiteheadian position is close to that advocated by Darwin. Johnson shows that for Whitehead language is an instrument of adaption. It begins as squeaks, goes on to express emotions, and then it communicates. Like Darwin, Whitehead believed that traces of these developments were present in current speech. Whitehead's theory of symbolism attempted to explain language in terms of a process from 'things' (that is, both traditional objects and mental states) to a 'listener', thus avoiding saying 'back to physical objects and mental states' and raising the question of consciousness. For Whitehead words, and especially written words, make memory, and consequently civilization, possible. Further, 'thanks to the instrumentality of words, we can not only converse with others but also hold that internal conversation of self-examination which is essential to self-development.' That is, it is possible to turn this instrument upon ourselves objectively.

Words themselves have a tripartite function: they express emotions, refer (that is, record and facilitate communication) and – the pragmatist view – facilitate action. They bring urges into attention and, for patriotic Englishmen thinking about England, express their emotions, especially when they think of lines like 'this little world/ This precious stone set in a silver sea'. Again, how the emotion is known as patriotism is not discussed. This quotation from Shakespeare might be retained as an example of what is left out of this view of language as instrumentality. There is no discussion of dramatic context, the formality of metaphor, the imagistic conventions, the Renaissance philosophy of the relation of the microcosm to the macrocosm, and so on. There are, however, positive aspects to Whitehead's deliberations.

For example, he stresses the fact that meaning lies in the relations between things, and depends on the system within which the symbol operates. Whitehead distrusted the Oxford philosophers of language (whose 'clarities' will be dealt with presently), and insisted that 'No language can be anything but elliptical, requiring a leap of the imagination to understand its meaning in its relevance to the immediate experience'. He also (in a passage cited by Johnson) equated language with social order:

> Free men obey the rules which they themselves have made. Such rules will be found in general to impose on society behaviour in reference to a symbolism which is taken to refer to the ultimate purpose for which the society exists. . . . The art of free society consists first in the maintenance of the symbolic code; and secondly in fearlessness of revison, to secure that the code serves the purposes which satisfy an enlightened reason.[79]

Who or what power decides what enlightened reason is, however, is left absolutely vague. Whitehead is ever the master of the art of ambiguity.

There is an immediate contradiction between his belief that language somehow expresses the emotional value of common-sense life and at the same time is renewed in masterpieces:

> Language is incomplete and fragmentary, and merely registers a stage in the average advance beyond ape-mentality. But all men enjoy flashes of insight beyond meanings already stabilized in etymology and grammar. Hence the role of literature, the role of the special sciences, and the role of philosophy – in their various ways engaged in finding linguistic expression for meanings as yet uncovered.
>
> (*Adventures*, p. 263)

Here Whitehead seems to be arguing for a general semiotic which embraces both language and scientific language, and in which literature becomes much more than the evidence of naïve experience: just the reverse, in fact. The suggestion that meaning does not only lie in the immediate content of a proposition is valuable:

> No verbal sentence merely enunciates a proposition. There may be an incitement to believe, or to doubt, or to enjoy, or to obey. This incitement is conveyed partly by the grammatical mood and tense of the verb, partly by the whole content of the book, partly by the material circumstances of the book, including its cover, partly by the names of the author and the publisher.
>
> (*Adventures*, p. 280)

Unlike the Oxford philosophers Whitehead seems wary of the exclusive right of the sentence to manufacture propositions. The whole idea of 'subject qualified by predicate', he says is a trap 'set for philosophers by the syntax of language'.[80]

Gertrude Stein shared many of Whitehead's cultural and linguistic ideas.[81] Like him she was concerned with the nature of process defined in terms which would ask traditional philosophical questions and turn them towards an aesthetics and a socio-cultural psychology. With aesthetics she hoped, like Whitehead, to connect the moral and the natural worlds by framing questions whose patterned half-answers would mirror a slowly revealed pattern of the world itself. She too was interested in the problems of language, the nature of time, the psychology of scientific search, theories of creativity, and in the large questions of continuity, repetition and habit. She too would explore epistemological questions in relation to unconscious belief. She would write her own contribution to the relation of nature and mind. She was interested in 'masterpieces', and the nature of their production in relation to general consciousness.

Unlike Whitehead she would, however, insist on the separation of nature and mind. Involved in the difficult and arduous *work* of the artist, that seamless set of correspondences between art and nature would appear absurd. Above all she would take up the challenge of the status of language in relation to scientific discourse, and defend it from the behaviourists and the pitying gaze of the scientist. She too would have to confront the social implications of language which would invoke a political perspective in a world of failing liberalism, and to ponder the problem both of its instrumentality and of its relation to emotional life.

Unlike Whitehead, moreover, Gertrude Stein was fundamentally occupied with the problems of language, and it was this difference which enabled her to approach the many preoccupations she shared with Whitehead from a rather different angle. But before testing these matters in her work it will be necessary to look historically at the language debate, both European and American, which was gathering impetus in her time. Not the least of the results of the following brief sketch will be to diminish the astonishment of those literary specialists who, armed with the latest jargon, discover in Stein's work 'anticipations' of their own characterizations of 'postmodernism'. It should already be apparent that Gertrude Stein did more than cast glances over her shoulder at other areas of intellectual investigation.

Chapter 12
Indices for an Approach to Stein: Language in the Late Nineteenth and Early Twentieth Centuries

Language never gives mere signs.

WALTER BENJAMIN[1]

In the late nineteenth and early twentieth century the theoretical grounds of debates about language were challenged in many disciplines: anthropology, psychology, philosophy, and political and social theory. Then, as now, linguistics, the moment it approached the semantic level, fragmented into many subcategories of its own long-vanished centre. The comparatively few histories of linguistics show that many of the old questions about language persist in new forms and that the magic of language, its definiteness and its elusiveness, its generality and its particularity in any culture, its disclosures and its petrifications of forms of life, its offer of new thought and its persistent constraint, its openness to and opaqueness for logic, its gift of the past and its promise of the future: – all these questions continue as strongly as ever. Stein was interested in the relation of language to all forms and genres of human thinking, from high philosophy to the language of the detective novel, the drugstore and the ethnic minority.

In the face of Nietzsche's onslaught on 'ontology' the relation of language to being has been relegated to mystics and to the religious. It became one of history's famous lost causes. Signs surely were arbitrary, reliant on a socio-cultural consensus whose internal structure was to be revealed by the dispassionate gaze of the linguist. But a paradox emerged (which was apparent to the less than pragmatic), that if signs were arbitrary, what was it they were arbitrary in relation to? Saussure summed up the dilemma more honestly than most: 'language thus has the strange, striking characteristic of not having entities that are perceptible at the outset and yet of not permitting us to doubt that they exist and that their functioning constitutes it'.[2]

In a strict sense the world is not embodied in language. Words do not embody the nature of things.[3] In Heidegger's words, 'words and language are not wrappings in which things are packed for the commerce of those who write and speak.'[4] The emphasis is on 'commerce'. As a pre-packaged commodity language falls away from its relation to the real, because it denies that the real is other than itself. It is in this sense that Heidegger says that 'the essential nature of language refuses to express itself in words'.[5] Something is withheld. That withholding paradoxically initiates the possibility of bringing it into the open. That 'being' is sensed as different makes it possible to speak of it. Thus language is not 'exhausted', to use Heidegger's word, when it has signified the world, nor is it ever merely a sign. Without the relation of language to Being, then, the sense of language as actively pulling the real towards us, or the world as standing within language, that 'house of being', in Heidegger's famous phrase, would be diminished. Language gives us that sense of standing before rather than in the world. It is a feeling analogous to that which Rilke described in his VIII Dunino Elegy: 'the animal is in the world; we stand before it by virtue of that particular turn and intensification which our consciousness has taken.'[6]

However, too often this rich sense of the relation of Being and language has slipped into a stultifying metaphysics. Here the Open is in fact closed, in the voice from heaven which proclaims an order which language merely reflects. Cassirer, in Stein's time the most overtly transcendental of philosophers of the sign, spoke of the 'demand for the Unity of the Deity', which took 'its stand on the linguistic expression of Being, and [found] its surest support in the word'.[7] But this unity, this great absence, or ultimate silence, is a characteristic reference for the Being of language even today. The unity asked for is in fact death. Foucault has said that writing is prepared for by 'one of the most decisive ontological events of language; its mirrored reflection [sic] upon death and the creation. . . of an internal space where speech discovers the endless resource-fulness of its own image and where it can represent itself as already existing beyond itself to infinity'.[8] However, while language is busy spatializing itself in this paradoxical presence of the absence of God,[9] Being itself is impoverished. The Open is closed in the future imagined as Infinity.

Actual theology was undoubtedly historically richer. Aarslef states that 'To Luther the Gift of Tongues had given renewed assurance of the Truth contained in this relationship [between language and cre-ation], and thus in his [Leibniz's] exegesis he replaced the allegorical mode of the fathers with the Protestant study of the truth that lay concealed in the word, in languages.'[10] At least here is the promise of truth in the renewal of that contract between language and creation: a practice of openness in the Open rather than a piquant savouring in sadistic memory of a limit transgressed, or a transgression limited in a static and equasive logic. At the level of syntax, too, Heidegger's intuition of being can paradoxically recall a sense of history in the very structure of the language:

> It no longer even enters our heads that all these things we have known so long might be different, that these grammatical forms have not from all eternity stood there like absolutes, dissecting and regulating language as such; that quite on the contrary they grew out of a very definite interpretation of the Greek and Latin languages.[11]

Ricoeur formally extends Heidegger's insight that the 'essential being of language cannot be anything linguistic'. As a result language, in metaphor, permits a Being hitherto unanticipated to enter: 'Being as we said means being and not being. In this way, the dynamism of meaning allowed access to the dynamic vision of reality which is the implicit ontology of the metaphorical utterance.'[12] Thus while objects cannot be put into words, words enable us to speak about them. Merleau-Ponty, too, has argued that language is a kind of being – perhaps a second-level being. It is, he says, 'much more like a sort of being than a means'; and he continues: 'At the very moment language fills our mind up to the top without leaving the smallest place for thought not taken into its vibration, and exactly to the extent that we abandon ourselves to it, it passes beyond the "sign" towards their meaning.'[13]

Heidegger makes a useful characterization of this motion towards meaning: 'The essential being of language is Saying as Showing. Its Showing character is not based on signs of any   Reciprocally, too, the act of showing depends on a recognition of what may not already be agreed. Herein lies the relation of language to freedom. Showing involves a *dramatic* setting within a 'social' plane. The being of a word, argues Volosinov, is not a matter of 'sign purity' but of 'social ubiquity'.[15] To the degree that we are bound by its ubiquity, and allow ourselves to be 'taken in' in order to situate ourselves for a reciprocal 'showing' in relation to others, the world will turn back to us.

The refusal to discuss 'metaphysics' as 'unscientific' – the neglect of the 'ontology of representation' – led to a remystification of the relation between nature and representation. The sense of being in language rested on the anthropologist's preconstituted ritual or the psychologist's substitution of the secret positivism of repression or automatic behaviour for the absence of God.[16]

The equation of language with secret forms of being in late nineteenth-century America begins with Whitney, the first great

American linguist. The being of language was its method or its instrumentality. Instead of 'linguistic instinct' or 'language sense', Whitney substituted the 'faculty of adapting means to ends, of apprehending a purpose and attaining it'. So language became instrumental – indeed, to anticipate Gertrude Stein, even a kind of 'instrument nature'. Whitney continued that language was 'not less in its essential nature from that other process, not less characteristic of human reason, the making and using of instruments'.[17]

It was against this view of language that Walter Benjamin levelled his own, not unproblematic, view. Language, he said, is not a means of communication: 'The other conception of language in contrast knows no means, no object, and no addressee of communication. It means in naming, the mental being of man communicates itself to God. . . . Only through the linguistic being of things can he gain knowledge of them from within himself.'[18] The discussion here relies on Merleau-Ponty's important insight that 'Every science secretes an ontology; every ontology anticipates a body of knowledge'.[19] In one sense the ontological constantly disappears and re-emerges in the epistemological and vice versa. In Ricoeur's words: 'Language designates itself and its other. . . it is knowledge that accompanies the referential function, the knowledge of its being-related to being.'[20]

Like Benjamin, Heidegger, Merleau-Ponty and Ricoeur, the American linguist and anthropologist Benjamin Lee Whorf was sure that 'language implies a metaphysic', and he went on, in a study of the Hopi Indians, to make problematic that serene assumption of Saussure that the 'stream of language flows without interruption':

> It must be emphasized that these underlying abstractions and postulates of the Hopian metaphysics are, from a detached viewpoint, equally (or to the Hopi more) justified pragmatically and experientially, as compared to the flowing time and static space of our own metaphysics, which are *au fond* equally metaphysical.[21]

The claim is more justifiable as a plea to reverse hierarchical assumptions about the kinds of being disclosed in languages, than as a claim to reinstate metaphysics. Ricoeur in this respect perhaps rather more correctly emphasizes the ontological in relation to the epistemological: 'Kant wrote "something must be for something to appear." We are saying: "Something must be for something to be said".'[22]

In fact the rejection of metaphysics can lead to all kinds of rigidities and innate conservatisms, as for example the re-mystification of science in the grammatical myth-making of Ogden and Richards's influential *The Meaning of Meaning* (1923). In an appendix to this work the anthropologist Malinowski noted the superiority of the 'highly developed European languages', which distinguish so beautifully (that is if one is brought up on a nineteenth-century Latin grammar) the lexical and grammatical aspects of language. Ogden and Richards can 'objectively' note the 'remarkable' way in which 'primitives' confuse the two aspects – like a couple of sun-helmeted colonialists poring over a cabinet of primitive curiosities in darkest Cheltenham.[23] In the 'primitive', in poetry and in the emotions are to be found those hindrances to progress which anyone who writes 'scientific' prose must reject. The rejection of 'being' as 'metaphysics' induces a naïvely mimetic concept of representation: 'so far from the structure of a symbol system being a reflection of the world, any supposed structure of the world is more probably a reflection of the grammar used'.[24] The grammar they require is clear and orderly in the best 'English' way, and reflects a world with the same qualities. Noting, however, with dismay and consternation, 'change and decay' all round them, they propose 'Canons' to patrol the Cathedral closes of clear English. These saintly gentlemen are simplicity (secret atomism), expansion (Jamesian additive truth), actuality (the hypostasization of the real), compatibility (common-sense judgements by specialists), individuality (Baconian one-sign, one-meaning definitions), and definition (denial of the truth of multiplicity).

It is unfair to pursue the analogy of the Church. It should perhaps be exchanged for medicine. For what is attempted is a purge of genetic deviations in a 'eugenics of language'.[25] Like real eugenicists of the body, the world Ogden and Richards project is full of undeclared 'canons': secret idealisms, health specialists and human engineering. The passionate denunciation of metaphysics had the not too subtle consequence of filling their entire argument with a new and perhaps more insidious set of metaphysics. Ontological questions are transferred to the domain of anthropology, where they re-emerge as a natural history of language. So much does the world reveal itself mimetically in the structure of grammar that more advanced cultures develop a genitive case when a sense of property emerges. Long after the challenge of Whitney and Saussure to Darwinian onomatopoeic theories, Darwin is praised for his analysis of sounds as part of an essentialist expression of emotions directed towards survival.

It would perhaps be simpler to say that language re-accompanies the world continously but not repetitively, like feeling itself, for 'feeling is no less ontological than representation'.[26] This position has the merit of radicalizing James and Whitehead in the direction Stein herself was to go. For Stein was to be occupied with how language creates knowledge, and how that language can be spoken about when the only recourse is language itself. In Merleau-Ponty's words: 'since language is neither a thing nor a mind, we can postulate that it is characteristically obscure and ambiguous.'[27]

Certainly Stein hoped to find a language which would represent feeling and celebrate it as a kind of second level of being. In Whitney's time, however, the claimants for language being either one or the other were shrill in their advocacies. In Whitney's words – and it must be remembered that he was situated midway between the German evolutionary linguist Schleicher, who applied theories of selection to language, and Saussurean structure – 'Physical science on the one side and psychology on the other are striving to take possession of linguistic science which in truth belongs to neither'.[28] Ogden and Richards wrote in a period of pervasive scientism which affected other, more humanistically based subjects as well as their own. Their work was part of a long movement of the triumph of 'scientific discourse'. In fact science and scientific philosophy are far from the orderly, temperate, logically evolving phenomena Ogden and Richards thought they were. Paul Feyerabend notes that scientific thought is 'inherently superior only for those who have already decided in favour of a certain ideology'.[29] Science is also a great deal more interesting, adventurous and complex than frequently represented in scientistic narratives of its development. Stein was to parody scientism and to investigate ironically the truth-bearing possibilities of 'primitive' emotions.

There are deep historical roots to all these questions. In the seventeenth-century debate between the followers of the magicians and mystics (Fludd and Boehme) and the scientists, the Royal Society clearly 'won'. It was an important victory, for, in Aarslef's words, 'The nature of language is the crucial problem in the epistemology of the new science.'[30] Equally, however, the epistemology of the new sciences created problems about the nature of language. For while 'science' was perhaps protecting itself necessarily from what Mumford called the 'rabbity thought-warren' of Church and State, there was a price to pay. Mumford recalls

. . . a condition laid down in Robert Hooke's original memorandum on 'the business and design of the Royal Society', namely, its engagement not to meddle with 'Divinity, Metaphysics, Morals, Politicks, Grammar, Rhetoric, or Logick'. This reservation not merely discouraged the scientist from critically examining his own metaphysical assumptions: it even fomented the delusion that he had none, and kept him from realizing his own subjectivity – a theme only recently, and reluctantly opened up.[31]

One important aspect of Mumford's statement is that it shows how language and its relation to knowledge have always been politically related to non-linguistically-oriented discourses.

More particularly, as has been shown with James and Locke, there have always been links between the medical/biological sciences and theories of language. Sir William Jones was influenced by the famous Scottish surgeon and anatomist John Hunter, Schleicher was influenced by Cuvier, and Saussure by Darwin.[32] The very comparative method of early nineteenth-century philology drew its impetus from anatomy, botany and geology.[33] As already noted, John Locke, who viewed language as playing a central role in the life of the mind, serving both to support intellectual facts, experience, and even acting as what Merleau-Ponty calls 'a state of consciousness', was not only influenced by the French philosophers but also by Boyle, the father of chemistry, who expressed the view that words cannot stand for the reality of things.[34] In turn Condillac was indebted to Locke's theory of knowledge.[35]

It is quite clear, therefore, that it is not possible to talk in historical terms about the relation of language to knowledge without seeing how much it has been dependent upon many contexts and discourses whose parameters are shaped by the sciences and philosophy. During the nineteenth century, and lying midway between the sciences and philosophy, was the murkier domain of psychology. From the mid-nineteenth century onwards, the liberal, essentially epistemological view of language as it related to that 'universal mind of man', was under attack from many quarters. The earlier eighteenth-century view was that the mind itself was best studied in language. In Monboddo's words: 'It appears that, from the study of language, if it be properly conducted, the history of the human mind is best learned'.[36] Stein was to concur absolutely, and thereby showed herself as much an 'eighteenth-century person' as Adams. During the same period speculation about the origins of language and about universal grammars were set firmly within an epistemological framework. Epistemological speculation tended, however, to get buried with the emerging prediction of language on psychology. Psychology emerged as a conservative discipline in which the categories of Lockean understanding tended to become, as in James, laws of the mind.

By the end of the nineteenth century the mind had become a place where a certain automatism prevailed. Peirce spoke of the 'law of the mind' being a tendency to acquire habits. At the same time he asserted that 'A symbol is connected with its object by virtue of the idea of the symbol-using mind, without which no such connection would exist'.[37] Is the mind, therefore, merely there to intuit reference? Is it lost somewhere between an intuition of the real and a tendency to acquire habits? It certainly may seem to, for a sense of creative symbolism interacting with the given is not the emphasis Peirce gives. Indeed he recalls Emerson's world of the *Essay on Nature* of 1836, with its sets of correspondences making the relation between the mind and world almost isomorphic. Peirce in fact quotes Emerson in the following passage:

> *Omne symbolum de symbolo.* A symbol, once in being, spreads among the peoples. In use and in experience its meaning grows. Such words as force, law, wealth, marriage bear for us very different meanings from those they bore to our barbarous ancestors. The symbol may with Emerson's sphinx, say to man of thine eye I am the eyebeam.[38]

An 'organic' sense of process implies a naturally ameliorative evolution. So uncertain is Peirce of the relation between the symbol and the mind, that he falls back here on an elaborate conceit of seventeenth-century physiology to connect mind and matter. Experience becomes a kind of god in the machine of the symbol. There is no thought here that the symbol may wither from metaphor to cliché, or that it may be renewed in the face of changed experience. Part of Peirce's problem, as with James, was to avoid the notion of consciousness and to preserve language itself as a relatively stable collective unconscious.

However, with the new priority given to the unconscious as such there was a tendency to revise (in terms of language) the traditional hierarchies of the primitive through to the civilized. Slowly a new modesty began to emerge in the writings of philosophers, anthropologists and linguists. Wittgenstein asserted, 'Everyday language is part of the human organism and is no less complicated than it'. Piaget affirmed that 'There are strong reasons for presuming that primitive child language fulfils far more complicated functions than would first appear to be the case'.[39] Doubts began to be entertained whether any language was quite natural, and its 'second nature' made its relation to first nature problematic.

Whorf turned round Peirce's assumptions about a universal experience being the deciding factor of intelligibility, and suggested that language itself was variable in relation to the form of experience: 'Concepts of time and matter are not given in substantially the same form of experience to all men but depend on the nature of the language or languages through the use of which they have been developed.' In a comparison calculated to provoke, Whorf made an unholy alliance between the aristocrats of the scientific world and the 'primitive' Hopi, and ranged them both against the middle ground of pragmatist and psychologist: 'Hopi "verb forms" [are] nearer expressing that field of vibrations and particle contrast of modern physics than such contrasts as space, time, past, present and future – which are the sort of contrasts our own language imposes upon us.'[40] But the problem of language and its relation to knowledge, tossed out as it was between the pseudo-historicism of evolutionary and post-evolutionary models and the psychologism of behaviourist and Freudian accounts, was not to be resolved so easily.

In this respect it is instructive to go back to the 1870s and see how the American linguist William Dwight Whitney attempted to resolve some of these questions. It will also help to summarize the history of the language discussion just before Stein's own period. Whitney asked himself what kind of discipline linguistics was, and came to the conclusion that it was a branch of 'the history of the human race and of human institutions', further aided by mental and metaphysical philosophy, associational logic, the physiology of speech, physical geography and climatology. He concluded: 'what but an analogical resemblance can there be between the study of things so essentially dissimilar?' Whitney never hesitated to use analogies and parallels, even if the result is a disconcerting multiplicity of theories. A theory, indeed virtually a metaphysic, of 'continuity' informs all his arguments. It is a familiar one, drawn from an analogical comparison with geology – a comparison which he argued was 'most instructive': 'The present must be regarded as the consequence of a gradual accumulation of results in one unbroken line of action.'[41]

Characterizing this process further and elaborating a further analogy, this time from botany, Whitney changes from time to space:

> . . . the arrangement of linguistic families corresponds with the division of plants into natural orders, founded upon a consideration of the whole complicated structure of things classified, contemplating the sum of their characteristic qualities, fixing their position in the vast kingdom of nature of which they are members, and determining the names by which they shall be called. The genetical classification is the ultimate historical fact which the historical method of linguistic study directly aims at establishing.[42]

It sounds like Linnaeus but it isn't. For Whitney is interested in what he calls 'genealogical history'. The process through time of a category is structured by common descent, but it is not monistic, as if Whitney were adapting a pre-Darwinian 'special creations' theory for his family models and then putting them in motion. The problem of space – time interaction is, therefore, solved by the 'historical fact' of 'genetical classification'. It is a brave attempt at a synthesis.

But something more is needed than this aggregate of family patterns. What animates them and moves them is what Whitney calls 'The law of "economy"', which is 'the grand current setting through universal language, and moving all its materials in a given direction – although like other currents, it has its eddies, where a counter-movement on a small scale may prevail. . . .'.[43] Whitney speaks of true economy and lazy wastefulness within a process which works on with 'blind absence of forethought'.[44] In his attempt to give 'economy' a positive connotation in a general economic process which appears totally fatalistic, Whitney draws an analogy with that crisis of liberal economics which believed in individual free enterprise yet found itself overwhelmed by the growth of institutional finance. Thus language is institutional, according to Whitney. But are individuals free to shape their own institutions? Whitney was writing in the 1880s and 1890s during the growth of the trusts.

Economy is essential, too, to the view of language as instrument. What but economy will mediate the survival of the fittest in an age of industrialism? Whitney actually uses the 'analogies' of locomotive and power loom to describe the 'instrumentality of language'. This force, not unlike James's image of habit as a 'flywheel' does not simply determine thought but acts as a regulator – a flywheel, or perhaps to keep the locomotive image, something like Watt's 'governor': 'The powerful reflex influence of language on mental action is a universally admitted fact in linguistics; to allow it is only to allow that rooted habits, barred by each operation from its predecessor, have a controlling influence on action – which is axiomatic.'[45] So perhaps language may be seen as regulating (economically) mind directed towards survival. But quite where the automatism of this 'reflex influence' comes from is not clear. It is not from the emotions, nor does it have its basis in emotion. For the history of language begins only where expression turns to 'intellectual uses'.[46] Whitney does not go into the contradiction of how 'intellectual uses' are axiomatically controlled by 'reflex influence'.

What is transparent in Whitney often becomes obscured in his successors. There is a tendency to equate the emotional with the unconscious, for example, and to predicate all intelligibility on a behaviour directed merely towards survival. The behaviour theory of knowledge reaches absurdity in Ogden and Richards: 'We misinterpret typically when we are asleep or tired.'[47] Typically? As if knowledge came to the merely awake. With descent theories mingling with 'geneticist' theories of language, it was only a matter of time before the development of language was seized by the purposeful and turned into the breeding (perhaps the good breeding) of language. Ogden and Richards spoke of the 'eugenics' of language, inserting the power of the controlling physician into a 'correct' language usage which would ensure scientific knowledge. Korzybski spoke of 'semantic hygiene', and declared that 'the neuro-physiological attitude towards 'meaning' is the only structurally correct one'.[48] But psychology and neuro-physiology, much as they too turned new light on language (for example, in inviting significance beyond the literal, or in treatments of aphasia), still could not fill the gap left by the decline of epistemological and symbolic approaches to language in this period. Condillac's statement that 'the measure of reflection we have beyond our habits is what constitutes our reason',[49] was forgotten in the generation immediately following Whitney. Exactly contemporary with Stein, the effects of Darwinian theory on language theory became more and more pronounced, and this occurred in spite of the fact that Saussure, for example, had valued Whitney because he was opposed to those linguists (like Schleicher) who called themselves Darwinian.

Saussure's work illustrates the entry of Darwinian thought-patterns into the very structure of the argument of the linguist. *Langue* is the virtual stasis of a long-existing generalized population (species), subject only to slow change. *Parole* is the short time of event or variation possibility. The relation of variation to selection is to a degree more conservative than in Darwin himself: '. . . never is the system modified directly. In itself it is unchangeable; only certain elements are altered with regard to the solidarity that binds them to the whole.' While Saussure attempts to hold together the mutual necessity of synchrony and diachrony in terms of the community of speakers, the relation of the two remains problematic. Like Whitney, Saussure had an institutional view of language, but the direct reference to actual social institutions, unlike Whitney, gets buried as a secret structural principle. For Saussure speech 'always implies both an established system and an evolution'.[105] Yet the established system is clearly the more powerful, with its metaphysic of regularity shrugging off most accidental variation.

The contradictions are more difficult to balance in Saussure's discussion of analogy. It is at once a disruptive 'creative force' and a regularizing principle, counterbalancing the 'effect of phonetic transformation'. In yet a third role it is the procedure 'through which languages pass from one state of organization to another'. Puzzling through the dynamics of this function of analogy Saussure falls back on a social image couched in dramatic terms: 'Every ana-logical fact is a play with a cast of three: (1) the traditional legitimate heir. . . (2) the rival. . . (3) a collective character made up of forms that created the rival. . . .'[51] The difficulty is (3). Does the 'collective character' endorse the rival and does the rival represent the forms which created him? Is the rival a variation within the group? It would seem so, for the collective character acts as a conservative force. But in the end the drama would seem to be merely diversionary, for the action is once again dependent on a natural selection in turn dependent on 'economy'. Analogy's capacity for transformation as such is ruled out, only elimination is creative. Its relation with the first term of its comparison is merely deviant and substitutive within a general economy.

The economic and legalistic terms of the discussion once more constitute this 'social' or institutional view of language, but to a much more abstract and much less actually historical degree than with Whitney. As Ricoeur once remarked, in discussing Saussure's 'marriage between associationist psychology and structural linguistics', association 'never confronts a truly predicative operation'.[52] The synchrony of grammar was a kind of liberal view of the free market in which all things worked together in spite of those things which did not. It held in check any individual speaker while absorbing efficiently the quarrels of heirs and rivals. Stein also was to pose the question of the relation of the individual to the strange cluster of meanings given a unique shape in vision of what might be called the grammatical synchrony of society as such.

By the 1920s there was not only some unease about instrumentalism, but also about its inner ally, 'associationism'. Whitney's attempt at a controlled instrumentalism is paralleled by Whorf's attempt at a 'controlled association', which he outlined in 1927, in a letter addressed to the compiler of a dictionary of psychological terms. He preferred the phrase 'controlled connection' or 'controlled association' and again, like Whitney, stressed the need of 'making it known to other men':

> 'Connection' is important from a linguistic standpoint because it is bound up with the communication of ideas. One of the necessary criteria of a connection is that it be intelligible to others, and therefore the individuality of the subject cannot enter to the extent that it does in free association, while a correspondingly greater part is played by the stock of conceptions common to people.[53]

By implication intelligibility is seen once more to depend on an assumed conservatism of (and the language is not without significance) that 'common stock' of conceptions. At least Whorf, however, pleaded for intelligibility within society, and separated the domain of 'association' from publicly communicated speech.

Aarslef cites the classic passage in Locke where the philosopher reveals the need for 'semeiotike' which would reconcile philosophy and public communication. The need is for a discipline of signs:

> the business whereof is to consider the nature of signs the mind makes use of for the understanding of things, or conveying its knowledge to others. For, since the things the mind contemplates are none of them, besides itself, present to the understanding, it is necessary that something else, as a sign or representation of the thing it considers, should be present to it; and these are ideas.[54]

Thus Locke takes into a universalizing mind both the representation of the world (the 'understanding of things') and the public nature of utterance ('conveying its knowledge to others'). The mind is also both total and modest, aware that ideas 'cheat', just as language misinforms. This double deception – a double nonconformity – induces despair as to the role of the subject in actual experience, actually communicating with others. Signs become the method by which things are represented, and the danger lies in the fact that the consistency of the universal mind, operating with arbitrary signs to encode the real, transfers its own methodological consistency to the experience of the real. As initial doubt epistemology is useful, as institutionalization of doubt it is treacherous.

For signs are never quite arbitrary, and essence is not a kind of truth. That eighteenth-century universal mind of man was a double-edged sword. It held out the promise of a fundamental relation with the other – hence the liberal necessity of tolerance – but at the price of assuming what the other *should* know, provided the correct theory of knowledge was engaged. Thus there are limits to this reciprocity-limiting epistemology, both in its relation to sign, world and community, and also within thinking itself. In Merleau-Ponty's words: 'There is no choice to be made between the world and art or between our senses and absolute painting, for they pass into one another.'[55] And at the level of thinking itself, there is a distinction to be made between thinking and representation as such which epistemology may confuse: 'In thinking, the situation is different from that of representation. In thinking there is neither method nor theme, but rather the region, so called because it gives its realm and free reign to what thinking is given to think.'[56]

Among contemporary thinkers, Volosinov is useful at this point. He asserts the precedence of ideology over psychology. In so doing the sign is limited in its arbitrariness ('the complement of compulsion'),[57] while remaining open to a consciousness which takes account of its history with discrimination and without rigidity of method. Against the psychologists Volosinov had the courage to raise the possibility of consciousness once more: 'Consciousness becomes consciousness only once it has been filled with ideological (semiotic) content, consequently, only in the process of social interaction.'[58]

The problem of knowledge via language, therefore, cannot escape a theory of society as such, with its concomitant questions of freedom and necessity. Locke's own definition of freedom in relation to language cited (as was *de rigeur* for the time) original freedom as having been possessed by Adam:

> That same liberty also that Adam had of affixing any new Name to any Idea; the same has any one still (especially the beginning of languages, if we can imagine any such), but only with this difference, that in Places, where Men in Society have already established a language amongst them, the signification of words are very sparingly to be altered.[59]

Society therefore controls and preserves that 'original' freedom whose actual historical moment is not imaginable. Social man (Men in Society) has in fact very little freedom. The myth of Adam can be seen as a heuristic rather than as a historical concept.

Even so it is not difficult to re-contextualize that use of pseudo-history as a structure reflecting Locke's actual historical moment. Men of science were forming a 'society' and a 'royal' one at that. No less than Adam they were busy renaming the natural world, perhaps in a manner rather more like God than Adam. For what was being created was nothing less than a second nature beyond common sense. Meanwhile the multiple descendants of Adam cheerfully went on being deceived. On general names Locke states: 'these have for the most part, in all languages, received their Birth and Signification, from ignorant and illiterate People, who sorted and denominated Things by those sensible Qualities they found in them.'

Men in 'Royal Society' knew the 'cheat of words', commoners didn't. In contrast Leibniz seems to have had a rather less 'them-and-us' attitude: 'The bond of language, of social customs, and even of the common name unites individuals in a powerful though invisible manner and produces as it were a sort of affinity.'[60] 'A sort of affinity' buries the actual connection, but at least it stresses interaction.

How language is unconsciously or consciously used and transformed, the relation of 'special languages' (logic, mathematics, musical notation, cookery terms, Latin nomenclature for botanists, etc.) to so-called natural languages, how we learn them, use them, authorize others to use them, are no less current political questions than in the seventeenth century. Locke's denial of anything but materialistic positivism to 'ignorant and illiterate people', by an epistemologist who knows, is echoed in the twentieth century by Ogden and Richards who connected 'savages' with unconscious psychological behaviour and naïve pragmatism: 'When a savage learns to understand the meaning of a word, this process is not accomplished by explanations, by a series of acts of apperception, but by learning to handle it.'[61] The distinction between mind and hand-work goes back to the Athenian state and its slave-ocracy, and it is curious to observe these twentieth-century commentators re-adapting it to downgrade any activity involving learning which is not 'science'. Already by the late nineteenth century Whitney's words seemed outmoded: 'No study, into which the acts and circumstances and habits of men enter, not only as an important, but even as the pre-eminent and determining element can possibly be otherwise than a historical and moral science.'

Around the turn of the twentieth century the 'neo-grammarians' held sway. Sophistication of techniques of structure produced a view of grammar as orderly, centrally consistent, phonetically uniform, and analogically conservative. Thus in his chapter on 'Analogic Change', Bloomfield could say, 'It is safe to say that the factors which lead to the origination of a form are the same as those which favour the frequency of an existing form'. In full reaction against the 'great Indo-Euopeanists', he continues: 'In turn to describe a language one needs no historical knowledge whatever.' On 'society' his views were absolutely organicist:

> The term society or social organism is not a metaphor. A human social group is really a unit of a higher order than a single animal, just as a many-celled animal is a unit of a higher order than a single cell. The single cells in the many-celled animal cooperate by means of such arrangements as the nervous system; the individuals in a human society cooperate by means of sound waves.[63]

For Bloomfield, mathematics constituted the 'ideal use of language', for his view of language was largely 'instrumental'. Darwinian and indeed even imperialist bias permeated his descriptive language, which was firmly based on a pragmatic recognition of 'speech groups'. Thus a speaker of non-standard English precariously attempting to negotiate his position ('who acquires prestige') in his new class can be described as 'a native of the less favoured group'.[64]

Robbins points out that the neo-grammarians in fact gave important new emphases to work and to principles which had already been accepted as important in the previous decades. The in-variablility of sound-change laws within the same dialect and the universality of analogical changes of words as lexical or grammatical entities were shifted to pre-eminence. The challenge to the neo-grammarians came, as a challenge from margin to centre, from the study of dialects. The detailed study of actual dialect situations showed that the spatio-temporal limits of any speech group 'tolerate certain words changing before certain others when the same sounds are involved, and that dialect interpretation across major isogloss lines may upset the universal application of a sound shift in a particular region'.[65]

Thus against the phonetic uniformity of that universalist space of the neo-grammarian, the 'linguistic geographers' set about making space that was relative and multiple by stressing the individual instance of the particular history of a word in a region. Similarly in anthropology, the centralist importance of Indo-European was being challenged by detailed study of the 'fringes' (to use the Jamesian word), those whom Anglo-American power had marginalized. Ironically it is in the study of the 'Indian' languages of North America that the human issues of language once more received attention.[66] Not that the problems of language and society were to be solved overnight. Saussure warned against the 'linguistic geographers': 'by itself space cannot influence language. . . . Geographical diversity should be called temporal diversity.'[67] Time, of course, would also not solve the problems by itself.

It was the famous American linguist Edward Sapir who insisted on the 'interplay between language and experience', and who rejected the 'cold status' of aligning linguistics with 'mathematical symbolism' and 'flag signalling'.[68] Sapir was adamantly interdisciplinary in his approach to linguistics and culture, and insisted that linguistics had to be tied up with 'anthropology, and culture history, with sociology, with psychology, with philosophy, and more remotely, with physics and physiology'. He rejected the post-Darwinian tendency to 'derive speech from emotional expression', and even went so far as to emphasize language's capacity for symbolism. He declared that sound changes and their regular patterns were 'only superficially analogous to a biological automism' and as for the psychologists, he declared, 'they have been too narrowly concerned with the simple psycho-physical bases of speech and have not penetrated very deeply into the study of its symbolic nature.'[69]

When, however, Sapir writes of the pattern of change in language, attempting to combine the insights of the linguistic geographers with Saussure's emphasis on time, the results seem to call up that Darwinian world which he appeared so anxious to leave. In an effort to see language changing in both space and time, Sapir spoke of the 'drift' of a language; a word which holds within itself both knowing and natural process:

> The drift of a language is constituted by the unconscious selection on the part of its speakers of those individual variations that are cumulative in some special direction. This direction may be inferred, in the main, from the past history of the language. In the long run any new feature of the drift becomes part and parcel of the common accepted speech, but for a long time it may exist as a mere tendency in the speech of a few, perhaps a despised few.[70]

Why 'despised few'? Is it a last-minute attempt to anthropomorphize a process replete with Darwinian language? Sharper than most linguists, Sapir asks himself a question which he cannot really answer: if the general shape of the phenomenon of language change cannot be perceived at the micro-level nor indeed its immediate relation to the macro-level, is the relation of observable variation to the totality of drift unknowable: 'are we not imputing to this history a certain mystical quality?' Like the fossil record language was not only 'spead out in space', but moved 'down time in a current of its own making'.[71] It had drift. For all his liveliness there is a conservative and almost fatalistic aspect to Sapir's thought. The direction of drift was guided only by past history. Where was even Whitney's human agency in Sapir's drift? In the same period Mae West was at least ironic about certain forms of unconscious selection: 'I used to be Snow White but I drifted.'[72]

Nonetheless, at his best Sapir is very conscious of the limits of the specialized commentator on human affairs, and his distrust of the professional psychologist and economist, together with the reductiveness of their arguments, is as relevant now as it was then:

> The sum total of the tacit assumptions of a biological and psychological nature which economics makes get petrified into a standardized conception of 'economic man', who is endowed with just those motivaitons which make the known facts of economic behaviour in our society seem natural and inevitable. In this way the economist gradually develops a peculiarly powerful insensitiveness to actual motivations, substituting life-like fictions for the troublesome contours of life itself.[73]

Like most of the other writers so far dealt with, Sapir placed the basis of intelligibility in 'social psychology'. He was well aware of its inadequacy, and in this respect the new Gestalt psychology was attractive to him, with its emphasis on configuration and patterning. Intrinsically spatial models of Gestalt psychology which preserved nonetheless a degree of epistemological freedom were doubtless particularly attractive to an anthropologist. But the problem of history was still not confronted. In a re-configuration of concepts Sapir speaks of a 'psychological geography' as the definition of the problem which linguists will help to identify and solve. But this same 'psychological geography' which is unconsciously built up on the 'language habits of the goup', conflicts with a definition of 'language' as a 'symbolic guide to culture', unless symbols are merely references to habits.[74]

The clue to Sapir's contradictions is to be found in his attempt to make a separation, as Saussure once did between historical and political economy, between the psychology of the social and the political individual: 'The extraordinary importance of minute linguistic differences for the symbolization of psychologically real [sic] as contrasted with politically or sociologically official groups is intuitively felt by most people.'[75] This will also be Stein's position. One can sympathize with Sapir in the sense that he is writing at a time when socialism seemed to ignore any form of subjectivity. Yet at the same time there is a loss of faith here in the individual's relation to institutions formed by individuals. The strength of his argument is that it speaks of differentiation at a time of oppressively enforced unities.

Sapir's linguistics performed the valuable function of reminding linguists of his time of the wider fields in which the study must operate. It manifested a healthy scepticism towards abstraction and the academic hypostasization of discourse. Its emphasis on drift and group change created a more nearly three-dimensional model for the study of language, and there was some note taken of symbolization. But Sapir had no theory for the dynamics of 'linguistic entities' and their interaction with 'psychological geographies', and his definitions of culture, society, history had all the fuzziness of the avoidance of key political issues. The conservatism of the linguist fought the more tolerant relativism of the anthropologist, illustrating both the strengths and weaknesses of his linguistic liberalism. Finally Stein herself was to be interested in all aspects of the relation of language to culture. She was well aware that her own word- and syntax-based grammar derived from the Greek and Roman worlds.[76]

Since Aristotle – indeed since the pre-Socratics – commentary on the formal structure of language had embodied a world view, an epistemology, an ontology and not infrequently a logic. For Western European grammar studies developed with the conjunction of Aristotelian and scholastic thought. Aristotle's own view of language as grammar mirrored his view of the world as self-realizing substance and accident. Robbins points out that Aristotelian influence was already apparent in the sources of Priscian's grammar (*c.* AD 500) – the grammar most used before the Modistae – via Thrax's *Techne* (*c.* 100 BC). With the Modistae, 'Defining categories were designated *modi significandi essentales*, and Priscian's *accidentia* became *modi significandi accidentales*, covering such categories as case and tense'. Robbins further shows that epistemologically these terms rest on the moderate realism of St. Thomas's interpretation of Aristotle. The mind abstracts the *modi essendi* from things, 'considers them as *modi intelligendi*, and language permits such abstractions to be communicated by means of the *modi significandi*'.[77] This view, containing the origins of Locke's epistemologies, firmly linked grammar with philosophy and suggested a universality of grammar which anticipated not only Port-Royal but more contemporary theories of universal grammar.

In the sixteenth century it was Scaliger who, according to Padley, 'was to restore to grammatical studies the Aristotelian concepts of substance and accident, etc., and to apply them to language in a way that had not been done since the time of the medieval *Grammatica Speculativa*'.[78] In one positive sense that natural conformity of understanding and things – the axis of Thomist divine perception with human perception – lent to language study the dignity of investigating languages as modes of knowledge directed towards the world. As the philosophy on which it was based hardened into constricted generality, so both the structure and the paradigm of reality it represented came to seem less automatic and less satisfactory. These problems are often most clearly manifested in historical theories about the sentence. Owing to Stein's interest in the sentence this discussion of historical linguistics will be particularized in that direction.

Speculation about the functioning of the sentence has occupied linguists since the time of the Greeks, and not only Western linguists. Sophisticated theories were held by Indian linguists from the sixth to the ninth centuries, and even today 'the semantic relation between a sentence and its component words' is 'very far from being solved'.[79] It has already been noted how William James attempted to make the sentence isomorphic with a sense of the structure of the world.

From Aristotle the sentence had, 'unlike the isolated word, affirmed or denied a predicate, or made an existential statement'. Protagoras, a hundred years before Aristotle, had set out 'different types of sentences in which a general semantic function was associated with a certain grammatical structure'.[80] By the time the Renaissance humanists were confronting the same problem, the realization that sentences implied general semantics had had a long history. The '*oratio* or sentence, repeatedly expressed in terms of

Priscian's criterion of the expression of "perfect sense" which ultimately goes back to Dionysius Thrax, is basically semantic'.[81] Syntax and sense were inferred to be congruent through the structure of the sentence itself.

Following the implications of sentence structure, however, the relation of subject and predicate in the Aristotelian-based models had its limitations. The followers of Scaliger were not always careful to perceive noun and verb, for example, as epistemological modes (*per modum permanentis* and *per modum fluxus*); rather, by incorporating a naïve mimeticism, the noun came to represent the essence of the real and the verb an essentialized activity. Indeed the positivism which privileges the lexical over the semantic aspects of words also derives from Aristotelian concepts of substance and accident deprived of their epistemological content. The reductionism involved can be seen in Ogden and Richards, who even went so far as to speak of the 'thing-word' and the 'action-word', and then align the distinction within pseudo-history.[82] The two are distinct in primitive cultures while they converge in advanced ones.

Quite how the sentence form related to reality was another question. The young Darwin cited Monboddo's assertion that languages began in complete sentences.[83] Whitney answered such theories shortly: 'To demand that "sentences" in the present sense of that term, with subject and predicate, with adjuncts and modifiers, should have been the first speech, is precisely analogous with demanding that the first human abodes should have contained at least two storeys and a cellar.'[84] Whitney further presents what was a very common view for his time, that it is writing rather than speech which more progressively engenders the apparently rational goal of the sentence:

And the interjectional employment of common words, or of complete phrases, is a very common thing in the general use of speech; emotion or eagerness causing the usual set formula of the sentence, the combination of subject and predicate, to be thrown aside; and the conspicuous or emphatic elements to be presented alone – a real abnegation of the historical development which, under the growing dominion of consciousness over instinct and of reason over passion, has wrought the sentence out of the root.[85]

Here the 'primitive' is characterized in grammatical terms, in turn dependent (like Darwin's Calcutta workmen) on irrationality and a need to appeal to others. The civilized equally is characterized by clear subject – predicate propositions uttered in calm isolation, uncontaminated by emotional appeal. The relation of the two is historical and yet also psychologically synchronic: the general use of speech being arrayed against the 'dominion of consciousness over instinct'.

Saussure, anxious to maintain a word-based analysis – and ultimately the further atomism of the sound unit – makes the sentence dependent on the word. There are contradictory epistemological assumptions in Saussure's discussion of the sentence. Meaning develops, according to Saussure, in two ways: the first (syntagm) shows meaning developing lineally – the word relating to others lineally in a series; the second depends on associationism. The sentence becomes the 'perfect syntagm', but it belongs to speaking and speaking is 'free'. The problem then rises of in what sense the linear series is formal. Moving, perhaps, beyond the usefulness of the model, Saussure then splits up syntagms. Some belong to *langue* (the formal ones) and some belong to *parole* (the free ones), and he concludes: 'But we must realize that in the syntagm there is no clear-cut boundary between the language fact, which is a sign of collective usage, and the fact that belongs to speaking and depends on individual freedom.'[86] What is more interesting than Saussure's slide into dualism is the location in the sentence structure itself of such terms as 'collective usage' and 'individual Freedom', via syntagmatic patterning.

The implication that sentences have series logic, and that words are dependent on psychological associationism, forming a kind of sub-world of meaning which never quite comes into actual meaning, will be of importance for the discussion of Stein's *Making of Americans*, which attempts to investigate that unclear boundary between structure (collectivity) and association (individual freedom) within the terms of the sentence itself. Contemporary thinkers have also given the problem of the word's relation to the sentence much attention. 'For Frege', states Ricoeur, the 'reference is communicated from the proper name to the entire proposition, which with respect to reference, becomes the proper name of a state of affairs. For Beneviste, the reference is communicated from the entire sentence to the word'.[87]

Problems of philosophy and language were furiously discussed in Stein's time. Eventually of course Oxford philosophy was to dominate Anglo-America with its commissars of clarity. In the '20s, however, there were multiple views of the relation between language and philosophy. Some, like Korzybski (whom Stein knew personally; she was a recipient of his book on business psychology),[88] threw out the whole problem of predication by dismantling the entire subject – predicate structure: 'From the use of a subject – predicate form alone, many of our fallacious anti-social and "individualistic" metaphysics and semantic reactions follow.'[89] 'Semantic reaction' implies a behaviour which bypasses reflection, and so

Korzybski's own advocacy of new predications and new signs is already half-way to automism. Equally, in his discussion of the verb 'to be', Korzybski makes no distinction between the 'is' of equivalence and the 'is of determination', and one would need to oppose to his whole discussion Ricoeur's insight that the verb 'to be' always metaphorically implies non-being and that the tension between the two is not 'markedly grammatical'.[90] Cassirer's vitalism was equally simplistic: 'It turns out that language could not begin with any phase of "noun concepts" or "verb concepts", but in the very agency that produces the distinction between these forms, that introduces the great spiritual "crisis" in which the permanent is opposed to the transient, and Being is made the contrary to Becoming'.[91]

This spiritual path between dualisms hardly permits the relation of language to an experience of the world. Heidegger warned of the dangers of characterizing Being and Becoming so simply. Being, for example, was a 'verbal substantive' and he warned, 'let us not be lured into the emptiest of all forms, the verbal substantive'.[92] For Heidegger the verbal substantive diminished the activity of the world because it reduced the otherness of the personal and therefore the possibility of interaction.

The uneasiness about relations between the parts of the sentence, the hesitancy about the moment of knowledge, the conflict between associationism and linear logic, the ontological confusions, are all part of that paradigmatic (here perhaps literally) uncertainty throughout all forms of knowledge in the first years of this century. The overpowering sense of a world whose silence was unapproachable through language, or glimpsable only through a scientific discourse which revealed that world both as irrelevant to human time and lent its prestige to make fatalistic other models of human behaviour, is very much reflected in the debates about language. The very problem of the sentence demanded an answer to how the subject related to the world and the terms of the activity of that engagement.

By contrast Stein's contemporary, Benjamin Lee Whorf, the American linguist, stressed that the urge towards meaning was primary. Instead of tying the sentence to logic and associationism, Whorf spoke of 'fashions of speaking' which cut across 'typical grammatical classifications'.[93] He had some particularly acute comments on the implications of the logic of continuous time, which he saw as implicit in current characterizations of grammar. These characterizations he thought were dependent on Newtonian assumptions about discrete objects in space and the objectification of continuous homogeneous time: 'Newtonian space, time and matter are no intuitions. They are recepts from culture and language. That is where Newton got them.' The referential continuities implied within the language structure, according to Whorf, lead to a pro rata allocation of value to time, building up a commercial structure which is 'based on time – pro rata values: time wages (time work constantly supersedes piece work), rent, credit, interest, depreciation charges, and insurance premiums'.[94]

Whorf's experience with the Hopi led to the realization that language had a heuristic relation with nature itself, a kind of patterning within the pattern, like Whitehead's world of prehensions – a comparison Whorf actually makes.[95] And for Whorf also there were differing degrees of consciousness within speakers of the same language. Thus, depending on the level of language involved, the degree of consciousness or unconsciousness involved, Hopi and nuclear physicist do not gravitate to some pre-ordained hierarchical position in the human scale. Whorf, as linguist and chemist, also had the authority to assert that referents for so-called precise scientific words can be fairly vague because they are under the 'sway of the patterns in which they occur'. Whorf's sense of reference is ultimately creative: scientists (real ones), poets and lovers 'are alike in being "flights" above and away from the slave-world of literal reference'.[96] Whorf's view of the sentence as culturally relative in its sense of reference, his preference for utterance as reconstitutive of structure, and his insistence on the deep cultural and social significance of the result make this controversial and often misrepresented figure still of great value.

It is possible to sum up by saying that while syntactic forms come closer to the real conditions of discourse than phonetic or morphological ones, they are not entities which encompass the whole of the utterance: 'The category of sentence is merely a definition of the sentence as a unit element within an utterance, and not by any means as a whole entity.'[97] Thus, slightly to modify Ricoeur who cites Wittgenstein and Husserl, the sentence will not wholly refer to a 'state of affairs', nor a word to an 'object'.[98] It is the utterance not the sentence which is the place of meaning. The objectivism of Saussure, as Volosinov points out, was not

> the only high point of abstract objectivism in our time. Looming alongside the Saussurean school is another. . . the sociological school of Durkheim, represented in linguistics by a figure such as Meillet. The compulsory nature of language and the fact that language is exterior to the individual consciousness are for Meillet its fundamental social characteristic.[99]

At its most extreme the marriage of structural linguistics and sociology linked language to necessity, compulsion and alienation.

Against this early twentieth-century view the present argument will emphasize the primacy of gesture and utterance, not as a social but as a political characteristic: 'to the extent that what I say has meaning, I am a different "other" for myself when I am speaking; and to the extent that I understand, I no longer know who is speaking; and who is listening.'[100] Without this recognition language becomes a museum (a fate in our time worse than a prison house) in which gesture is turned into a message from an unknown God or 'society': 'The museum kills the relevance of painting as the library, Sartre said, changes writings which were originally a man's gestures into messages.'[101] The key problem then becomes how to translate the messages of grammar back into the gestures of sign.

From the 1880s onwards, 'society' took over 'history's' role as the metaphysic which sanctioned an increasingly analytic, statistics-based, and 'technical' approach to language. Among the many defined. Society excluded actual politics. It was in some mysterious way continuous with the 'organism' of nature and therefore could be studied as a 'fact'. It was as impervious to ideology as to particular political or social organization. Neither will nor consciousness could account for it, but the promise was that it would be slowly revealed by the 'scientific method'.

The melancholy of the linguists' discourse from 1870 to the 1930s (and beyond) was a result of many overlapping factors: the actual failure of politics and political discourse, the predication of the reference of language on 'society', the habit of motivating speech by unconscious drives whether behaviourist or psychoanalytic, the too-slow rise of semiotics, which arrived only to be built on the basis of new anthropologizing discourses or revised essentialist psychologies.

The key question not asked at the time was, in Merleau-Ponty's words, how the social can be 'both a "thing" to be acquainted with without prejudices, and a "signification" which the societies we acquaint ourselves with only provide an occasion for – how, that is, the social can exist both in itself and in us'.[102]

Such complexities had not troubled Saussure, who was quite direct on the subject: 'Of all social institutions, language is least amenable to initiative. It blends with the life of society, and the latter, inert by nature, is a prime conservative force.'[103] That view of 'society' as Jameson suggests, was close to one conceived in Durkheim's sociology: 'the very thrust of Durkheim's thought, in its attempt to sort out the personal and the individual from the objective and social, is quite consistent with the Saussurean distinction between *langue* and *parole*. . . .'[104]

Jameson states the matter in too compressed a manner, and without properly detailed reference to the issues involved. To get a clearer idea of the relevance of Durkheim's sociology to these issues it is instructive to glance briefly at a small collection of Durkheim's writings, published some years ago, which specifically addressed itself to his thoughts on institutions as such.[105] Durkheim specifically rejected the theses of political philosophers – Plato, Hobbes, Rousseau – with the exception of Aristotle, 'who was the first to see society as a natural fact' (*Durkheim*, p. 45). The question of human freedom 'belongs to metaphysics' and must be ignored by the positive sciences (p. 48).

What must be encouraged is the 'sentiment' of society (shades of Bagehot again), in spite of the fact that Durkheim can criticize others (like Schaeffle's *Gemeinsinn*) for being too serene about that sentiment's efficacy (p. 114). Durkheim's rejection of Marx and socialist thought is well known, thought honest disagreement is not made more attractive by his persistent misrepresentation of socialist thought as having been stated once for all by Saint-Simon. The result was to play down theory ('The work of the scholar is not that of the philosopher', p. 137), ignore the entire relation of human organization to technology, labour, economics and ideology. It is 'religion' which is put in the space left by these deliberate omissions.

But as with James, it is a strange sort of 'religion' – one possessing essentially structuralist forms, as the title of Durkheim's most famous book, *The Elementary Forms of Religious Life*, indicates. It is a religion without eschatology, without emotion, without theology, without a history or a metaphysic of history, without a sense of evil or of isolation or of rebellion, or of any challenge to authority in an elaboration and praxis of truth. Durkheim's world is serene, continuous, with very little sense of conflict. Durkheim understood that structures are formed by results that escape specific and general intentions, but he refused to believe that the political process could monitor those events with practical intelligence.

Equally, intuition of truth is not a reliable guide to judgement, though it plays a role. Durkheim in fact uses 'religion' to criminalize dissent from the 'collective sentiment'. This sits uneasily with his judgement that 'The great moral reformers of all times have condemned contemporary morality and have been condemned by it' (p. 186). This common-sense admission in fact undermines the entire superstructure of his moral collectivity.

In the bright sociology laboratory of Durkheim, where 'literary descriptions of remorse and satisfaction' have been erased, the social scientist is invited, in full imperial confidence of the result, to 'compare the modern conscience of the typical European of today with that of the savage, the unwell, or the criminal' (p. 222). In a line of argument close to Münsterberg's, Durkheim's view of society is one where the 'occupational group' – a 'perpetual entity' – or the specialized task will replace the family as the backbone of society (p. 238). Durkheim's view of the 'professionalized man' is the concomitant of his view of 'society'. The privileging of 'society' as the guarantor of the normal demands the credo that 'man can be happy and can satisfy his desires in a normal way only if he is regulated, contained, moderated, and disciplined' (p. 252). Here is the deep psychology of human engineering, regulation, balance, repetition – in short a totalitarian view of the normal. Instead of a variable rhythm of human life – in which indeed balance and rest play a part – Durkheim prepares the way for an order in which 'society' sanctioned by the State regulates private affairs to an unprecedented extent.

This detour into Durkheim's view of institutions which are de-historicized and unengaged with politics, helps fill out the assumptions which lay behind characterizations of the period, of language first as a social institution and then as pure structure. Simply because structure is inherited – not of our making – it is, however, not therefore objective: there are more complexities than either Saussure or Durkheim dreamed of in 'social questions': 'If I name what I am, I allow myself to be defined within a certain social order, and I become its accomplice. But I cannot remain silent. What then must I become?'[106] In sum the work of Durkheim and Saussure reflected a deep despair of individual action and a lack of faith in human collectivity.

Fortunately not all twentieth-century linguists have been so locked in such a vision. Volosinov stated that it was precisely not the 'inexpressibility' of the collective of language which was important, but the 'whole route between inner experience (the 'expressible') and its outward objectification (the 'utterance'), which lay across social territory.[107] Not the least of the problems lies in an inadequate conception as to what social territory is and a lack of imagination as to what it might become. As sociologist and linguist sought for an absolute purity of context for their work, they thought they had freed themselves from the impurities of history.

Though statistically negligible, it is the writer, the novelist, the dramatist and the poet who hold out possibilities thought to be impossible in terms of the view of language held by the 'scientists'. Merleau-Ponty outlines the recall of language to human direction in the serious writer: 'To become a writer is to learn a personal language. The writer creates his own language and his own public.

He, therefore, recommences the creation of language on a higher level.'[108] Stein as a 'she' would have concurred absolutely. It did not occur to most of the commentators adduced above that the social might be transformed by reinventing the public.

Finally Whorf, looking at the 'appalling sterility of the vast mass of minutiae that this science [psychology and sociology and linguistics could be added] accumulates', advised his students that they would get more from 'the best works of the novelists, playwrights, and poets'.[109] It was at any rate a choice that Grertrude Stein herself made.

In the next chapter one of Stein's most abstract and theoretical texts will be taken up because it combines, in some quite extraordinary ways, the issues of language, philosophy and society which have been looked at here.

Chapter 13
How to Write

J'ai reçu ce soir votre grand sourire grammatical.

Jean Cocteau[1]

Real thinking is conceptions aiming and aiming again always getting fuller, that is the difference between creative thinking and theorizing.

Gertrude Stein[2]

In these days when literary theory seems to be redoubling its efforts, having lost sight of its aim, it is well to meditate on the distinction Stein offers here. *How to Write* at its best engages intellectuality in play and is suspicious of formal reductionism while keeping a kind of creative suspension between the two. Much as some critics would like to hive off Stein's thoughts on language into some never-never land of formal aesthetics, her more abstract thoughts on writing, grammar and language in these pages continue to make fuller the thematic content and creative thinking evident in work already examined:

> Language as a real thing is not imitation either of sounds of colors or emotions it is an intellectual recreation and there is no possible doubt about it and it is going to go on being that as long as humanity is anything. So every one must stay with the language their language that has come to be spoken and written and which has in it all the history of its intellectual recreation.[3]

As in much of Stein's work the range of tones in *How to Write* will go from Mark Twain-like jokes about punctuation to an urgency about revising what Noah Webster (along with Daniel a favourite American) called 'the natural connection between ideas and words'. Grammar itself was a means of order and recognition, a 'digested compilation of customary forms of speech in a nation'.[4] The 'digestion' of custom had its place in Stein's affections. France, for example, is 'a good country for grammar because cooking is so admirably and so simply organized, a continuous illustration of the essentials of grammar'.[5] So grammar is a kind of well-organized nature which, however, will always fall short of that 'intellectual recreation' she demanded as a quality for writing.

Stein's meditations on language also nearly always have a dramatic quality – 'plays', in their many senses of drama, creative play, and chance casts, are often attached to a 'portrait': real or fictional, from Dr Faustus to Henry James. *In Eighteen in America: A Play* (1937), for example, she pits Noah Webster against Daniel to take on questions about how language develops and redefines itself. The peculiarly pragmatic and nationalist activities of the famous American dictionary-compiler are contrasted with the public declamations in support of national unity of the orator. Her very play with their names, as in many other works, suspends conventional reference for multiple purposes: from heuristic parataxis to simple irony. Her main criticism is reserved for a point at which rules for order, dictated by necessity, go wrong – as in her portrait of Woodrow Wilson: 'In a moment he was heartily immersed in the very necessary process of illusion and reason and teaching and surveying. Do not neglect persecution. All language is evil.'[6]

Stein did not like Wilson, so she uses him to illustrate the negative aspects of illusion, reason, teaching and surveying. Language was more than illusion, reason could be part of it, teaching was an auxiliary art like cooking, surveying was too close to naïve representation to interest her. Language was evil, it might be surmised, because it opposed the artist's desire to renew it, and when renewed seemed like a romantic challenge to the sacredness of being itself. Her audiences were perhaps unnecessarily surprised when Stein seemed to punctuate 'like a teacher of grammar' in her lectures.[7] Her commitment to creativity enabled her to make very clear distinctions between composition and explanation when the pragmatics of the situation demanded it.

Critics like to quote Jakobson's work in readying their attention for Stein's use of language. Yet in some ways no work seems less relevant, given Stein's distinction between theorizing and creative thinking. Jakobson makes a clear-cut distinction betwen lexical and grammatical forms, quotes Sapir to suggest a natural referential basis for parts of speech, and sees grammar as playing a 'mandatory role' between 'referential, cognitive value and linguistic fictions'. His dynamic cutting or montage image, as Steiner points out, does not fit Stein's work.[8] Furthermore his either/or attitude to the creative writer – the symmetry or chaos option – is inappropriate for the multiplicity of Stein's games with language. His search for a relational geometry mirrors the kind of objection Stein had to Wilson's 'surveying'.

Here in contrast is Stein's 'definition' of a sentence – one of the many:

> A sentence is money made beautiful. Beautiful words of love. . . .
> Suppose a sentence.
> How are hours in a glass.
> Glass makes ground glass.
> A sentence of their noun.
> How are you in invented complimented.
> How are you in a favorite.
> Thinking of sentences in complimented.[9]

Ironically moral, Stein mocks the familiar analogy of money and language. If for James the sentence embodies reality, for Stein it is, like money, an intervention in reality. A sentence is also, of course, a judgement, and opinion – even an axiom. Webster said it was 'a short saying containing moral instruction'.[10] The force of the 'is' in the sentence not only makes an absolute complement of two uncomplementary halves, but plays with the very thought of bringing new meaning into the Open of metaphor, while mocking that action in a tone of ironic punditry. The effect is one of a kind of democratized 'high sentence'. If judgement is money made beautiful what hope for justice? 'Beautiful words of love' bring in the Ivesian flavour of the camp meeting, suggesting that moral fervour and sentimental religion also have something to do with money made beautiful. This was indeed the case in 1920s America, where Billy Sunday became a millionaire. Abandoning yourself to that kind of meaning – to redeploy Merleau-Ponty – shows a false movement from reference to sign, not the other way round.

Stein also goes through sentence types. After statement there is command: 'Suppose a sentence.' It is the kind of command that brackets its object and makes it conditional. The irony is implicit. How can you bracket off the very means of articulating reality without calling those means into question? There follows a question which is not a question. Stein thought question marks good for branding cattle but not much else.[11] Like William Carlos Williams she did not see much point in pause marks either. If you did not know where to breathe in your writing you had problems which could not be cured by punctuation.

Of course Stein also plays against traditional usage, casting a slightly vengeful eye on what she once called her 'good old public school'.[12] Indeed 'hours in a glass' suggests that shut-upness where the energetic young are held up to inspection, the narcissism of those who are occupied with reflecting themselves, and also the neutral continuity of the passing moments of time. 'Glass makes ground glass' not only has the suggestion of making the opaque transparent, but also the possibility of a revised vision in the transformation of a material to make new means of perception. It is the authoritarian who holds the mirror up to nature and proclaims that what is mirrored there is natural. For the image of (in Allen Fisher's words) 'unpolished mirrors' in Stein, Harriet Chessman cites Emerson's 'The poet turns the world to glass', for the 'blind glass' of *Tender Buttons*, and uses Irigaray to suggest a dissolution between naming and the world by recapturing the possibility of reflection in every sense.[13] So far, then, the sentence suggests an ambiguous public linguistic currency, a possibility that it might not be a ground of reality, that it might be heuristic rather than truthful, and that it might either itself be a cast at reality or be a vehicle for a kind of moral bankruptcy. The contradiction within the image (reflection is at once passive and active) is not really brought out by using Irigaray's synthetic moment of creation.

It is a version of Stein's perpetual question, of how the particularity of the moment engages with a general structure: 'A sentence of their noun'. This suggests that nouns are judgements of reference and that they are complexes not essences – in the spirit, perhaps, of Ezra Pound's 'A true noun, an isolated thing, does not exist in nature. . . . The eye sees noun and verb as one: things in motion, motion in things. . . .'[14] Nouns, too, can afford meanings without sentence structures: certainly part of Stein's strategy since half-way through *A Long Gay Book* (1909–12). As noted above in Ricoeur's comment on Frege and Beneviste, the communication of reference between atomized unit and sentence is still an issue with linguists.

Two non-questions now follow with puns on 'complimented' and 'complemented': a possible spelling trauma in any public high school. Stein compliments reality ('privileges' it in the current American academic slang) by turning predication into complement, thereby suggesting a very close relation between subject and object. It may be said that the problem of predication is avoided rather than confronted, as it could also be said that she diminishes a public response when she turns a question into statement. On the whole, however, Stein upsets grammatical patterns to revise reference. The implication is how do we feel when we flatter the world by making it into an image of ourselves: 'How are you in invented complimented.' There is a thin line between invention and pride: between 'i' and 'e'. The same question with 'a favorite' implies a long-established situation and perhaps takes us back to those 'beautiful words of love'. The puns on 'invented' and 'complimented' invite questions as to what kind of favours are involved in the perception of the outside world. The metaphysical backing here is dependent on correspondence. Thought takes place inside the already complemented in which subject and object are radically joined in terms of declaration. Compliments, the beautiful words of love, can be treacherous in their disposition to cliché. So in the spirit of Stein it is possible to say that a complement is not a complement when it's a compliment. Thus even in this short example Stein challenges the meaning of a 'sentence' across economic, religious, philosophic, social as well as linguistic possibilities of explanation.

How to Write (1928–39) is a work in which Stein meditates on the relation of language to reference via a radical play with those linguistic, philosophical, psychological and epistmeological issues which had occupied her writings from the beginning. 'A noun', Stein says, 'is the naming of anything. There is no hope of their pleasure. It is very nice to change your name about anything'.[15] So Stein begins to demonstrate both the arbitrariness and the magic of naming. The effect is twofold, first, to preserve the freedom of the actual world, and second, to suggest that creative representation changes pleasurably. The sentence that follows the initial statement, as so often in this work, both extends the meaning of the first sentence and offers an example of its content. Naming refers to no substantial reality: 'hope of their pleasure' does not yet actually 'exist'. Name as an abstraction intuits an 'emotion' which as has been shown cannot be considered as existent. The third sentence here gives back to the subject the power of describing the world.

Between naming and the world, however, is the structure of grammar. Stein says, for example, 'No one knows a noun by name' (*How to Write*, p. 188). Grammatical designation of itself fails to bring being into naming. Between the magic of naming and the science of grammar there seems to be no common ground. The first seems to Stein as opaque to the second as that silent continuity Sartre satirized in Parain's silent God: 'A noun is the name of a calling which they have made in their time as known' (pp. 120–21). Given the ambiguity of the term 'calling' in American Protestant culture, there is a sense of evangelical dogmatism in the function of the name as noun. The rhythms of the sentence support the feeling. There is simultaneously, however, a sense both of that calling into the open which Heidegger described in his meditations on ontology, and an ironic sense that the noun's capacity to stand for essence is subject, however passively, to the pressures of historical and social fashion, 'made in their time as known'.

Stein was also keen, like James, to align 'being' with feeling, and to separate both from knowledge, though the philosopher did so seriously and Stein tends to take in a range of tones.[16] 'A sentence is not emotional', she says; 'a paragraph is' (*How to Write*, p. 3). Sentence belongs to the domain of mind. A paragraph does not, presumably, because of its 'natural breaks' and its overall association with Aristotelian beginning, middle and ending: that is to say with its dramatic and narrative possiblities. 'Grammar' – and here Stein took issue with the entire nineteenth century – 'is not grown' (p. 58). Like Ricoeur she believed in the implicit ontology of the metaphorical utterance, and challenges syntax to draw more attention to it. To renew language's capacity to approach being, she turns what is a normally unconscious grammatical paradigm into reference itself: 'A lake is an article followed by a noun a lake which is there' (p. 197). Stein's aim was givenness without prejudice. In this respect she instinctively distrusted the instrumentalist view of language and its commodification as criticized by Heidegger: 'A sentence should never be employed' (p. 15).

Words neither had fixed value for Stein, nor did they project an image of their own silent fluidity. A language speaking only to itself however brilliantly was never her aim. The self-reference of language hoped for from Novalis to post-modernists to some pure language poets, depends upon a secret psychological essentialism, 'mind', or metaphysics. Stein says, 'there is no use in finding out what is in anybody's mind' (p. 16). For Stein *writing* your 'mind' was absolutely preferable to the ineffable beauties of the inexpressible so popular with critics of all generations. That meaning always seems to escape the writer in the act of writing does not mean its truth is located in some essence of language, nor in psychology.

Nor was meaning for Stein to be located in an analytic approach to grammar. Stein parodies the traditional way in which grammar atomizes parts of the sentence. The word 'mingle' in the following sentence suggests a freer interaction of parts of speech while both doubting and anticipating meaning: 'Nouns and verbs mingle in a difficult sentence because they will hope they think so' (p. 203). As for the relation of being and time, in the next sentence the apparent authority of grammar to present being is contrasted with the necessarily historical moment of representation: 'Appointed is grammar at and when is description' (p. 79). Grammar, Stein never fails to insist, is secondary to the world: 'Grammar follows what is the matter' (p. 98). Parts of speech are therefore intermittent in their capacity to describe reality, secondary to the act of meaning: 'A name is a place and a time a noun is once in a while' (p. 207).

Webster had defined the sentence as a number of words containing complete sense or 'sentiment'. Completion of sense as such always

seemed to Stein false to the rhythms of experience: 'How is sentiment maintained. A pause' (p. 15). Good timing is not necessarily
linear, just as good thinking breaks away from its models. As always
Stein's criticism is directed against the psychology of idealism. What
comes into the open is not predictable.

For Stein language was neither thing nor mind. She liked words
which could refer to both structure and act, thereby leaving out the
troubling question of consciousness. The word 'sentence' is a case in
point. It means a judgement, an opinion, and a maxim as well as a
semantically meaningful pattern of words. Webster even points to
Psalm 17 where, in the words, 'Let my sentence come forth from my
presence', sentence means the vindication of innocence. Words have
their meaning in the possibility of sentence in all these ways, and Stein
exploits them to the full: 'A sentence is an imagined masterpiece. A
sentence is an imagined frontispiece. In looking up from her
embroidery she looks at me. She lifts up the tapestry it is partly'
(p. 123).

Stein here makes the sentence into an urge towards creativity and
an index to a text which follows. It is both future and past in relation
to what comes into knowledge via its structure. It holds several
things in suspension. There is the contrast of masterpiece and
frontispiece with embroidery and tapestry, suggesting completion
and beginning, decorative work and art, and possibly some sexual
differentiation of task. There is a move from embroidery, conferred
by the gaze of Stein, to tapestry, the fully public art which then
enters the realm of public display. It is known that Alice B. Toklas
was embroidering the chairs now on view in the Beinecke Rare Book
Library at Yale, and the seat patterns of which were designed by
Picasso at the time *How to Write* was written.[17] As the gaze of
Toklas shifts from work to companion an appeal goes out. A
sentence is asked for in the act of lifting up the work. Sentence is
then the combination of love, craft and knowledge. Here, then, is a
three-way cooperation: (Picasso–Toklas–Stein) design–execution–
response, as a process of the way a sign confronts the world, is
enacted in it and recreated. Thus the 'mind' is 'furnished', and the
'texture' revealed.

Within the sentence there is an act of transformation or, perhaps,
an endless translation of forms. The relation of language to mind
and the quality of knowledge expected had, for Stein, to be worked
out on Locke's premiss, inherited from Boyle, that words cannot
stand for the reality of things. Yet language introduced both doubt
and certainty into appearance. In this way 'sentence' can capture
both. A phrase Stein often repeats to illustrate her response to
knowledge and identity occurs here: 'What is a sentence for if I am I

then my little dog knows me' (*How to Write*, p. 19). 'I am I' is axiomatic in a God-like (dog-matic) way. Fixed identity is natural gaze – dependent and necessary but the opposite of the appeal of Toklas as she lifts the embroidery. In creativity the natural self is put in abeyance. As Stein says elsewhere: 'I am not not longer when I see. This sentence is at the bottom of all creative activity. It is just the exact opposite of I am I because my little dog knows me.'[18]

After God, the Grammarian. The advocacy of grammar as a truth beyond necessary convenience has always been a message from authority. Its metaphysics of authorization are often economy and instrumentality, and it is just these aspects that Stein satirizes:

Grammar does mean arithmetic.
They act quickly.
Grammar matters if they add quickly. If they add quickly they make a connecting of what they are adding and they have added them quickly.

(*How to Write*, p. 93)

If the children of the poor can do their fractions they might make it to clerks, as D. H. Lawrence's school teachers knew. The banality of result confirms the banality of technique as truth. The result is merely additive coherence. Stein's work always directs itself against the inertia of the expected in language:

A sentence says you know what I mean.
Dear do I well I guess I do.
Keep away from that door and go back there, that has not a meaning that has an association...

(*How to Write* p. 34)

Authority does not depend on the 'association'. Real knowing is 'guessing' meaning to subvert the sentence. Against dogmatism Stein offers approximate judgement.

As for grammar itself, Stein meditates on the problem of whether it refers to particular structure or general principle. For herself grammar was an urgent matter – for along with a number of other writers of her generation she broke its common-sense grasp on reality: 'Grammar is undated. Grammar is undated because furlows and furrows are avaricious with hunting hares in partial referring to enable utter with renown come distaste unable' (p. 79). Perhaps grammar here refers to a syntax of habit rather than the guiding principles generally acknowledged. It is dateless then, rather than timeless. Furlows (furloughs), the soldier's leave, and furrows, the farmer's lines in the earth, suggest absence in war and cultivation in peacetime. These 'natural breaks' define a kind of space-time tied to necessity, reinforced by the proverbial sense of 'hunting hares', which plays on the fact that they should be running with them not hunting them, Proverbs like grammar claim dateless truth and Stein challenges us to think again about accepted truth. She liked to take things slowly and the greed of nature hunting down its objects, transferred to other domains, seemed indeed a 'partial referring'. Time is more than leave from war, and space more than cultivating furrows. In symbolic terms furrows are traditionally associated with the brow wrinkled in thought: a pure expression rather than a dramatic understanding of the emotions. Since consensus accepts proverbs and grammar, it 'enables utter with renown' but cannot cope when the fashion changes. Images of greed and distaste inform the tone of the text. Stein was reluctant to keep her 'date' with grammar. Like William Carlos Williams she knew that divorce was 'a sign of knowledge in our time'.[19]

Throughout these 'casts' at grammar, Stein attempts quasi-epistemological definitions based on images of space and time. She was to do the same in *The Geographical History of America* (1935). Grammar she also calls a 'conditioned expanse', echoing the theories of the geographical linguists. In the particular phrase 'conditioned expanse', however, there seems more of a tension between authority and space with a hint of temporal tension, too, as if the one word referred to the past (conditioned) and the other to a rather American future (expanse). Still retaining the spatial image, Stein argues that this conditioned expanse is only a condition: 'There is a difference between grammar and a sentence this is grammar in a sentence. I will agree to no map with which you may be dissatisfied and therefore beg you to point out what you regard as incorrect in the position of my troops in my two sketches.' (p. 72) The 'map' is the 'conditioned expanse' whose accuracy depends on a formal (here emphasized by the tone) agreement. The map and the sketch may stand for grammar and the sentence: a relation between general structure and active structure. Stein was meditating at the time on the career of U. S. Grant, and her own tone is general-like as she revises the ground for marshalling her own compositions.

The sentence was intelligence working within the nature of grammar: that second nature dear to the hearts of the linguists. In her own revision of grammar Stein, nonetheless, wanted to claim also a new and authoritative description of its ground or nature. Like Whitehead she would have liked a correspondence theory of truth between nature and creative thought. In the following 'cast' she sees this second nature of grammar as more fluid than the traditionalists saw it, perhaps as an enabling stance directed to meaning: 'Grammar is the breaking of forests in the coming of the extra sun and the

existence of which it was. Grammar readily begins.' (p. 74) In the
dense forests of words grammar opens a space of light. At the same
time its very essence is defined by the broken trees in a network of
single instance and temporary system. In a sense Stein moves beyond
the organicism of Whitehead in that phrase 'extra sun' but retains its
notion of nexus and relation. For her essential definition is always
retrospective as it provides the condition of renewal.

Two sections of *How to Write* are concerned with the nature of
sentences. Stein offers many definitions in relation to sense, spoken
language, grammar, ontology, epistemology and reference. First she
takes on the most common definition and immediately makes it
ironic: the sentence 'pleases by its sense. This is a fashion in
sentences' (p. 27). If the sense depends on fashionable consensus
then the automatic ability of the sentence to give any new sense is
questioned, yet fashion has its place. Then there is the question of
the sentence's relation to spoken language. Here Stein is ambiguous.
On the one hand she is a child of the nineteenth century, in the sense
that she more readily associated writing with a superior 'mental'
culture; on the other hand the language of the 'folk' had a kind of
romantic truth which constantly subverted that superior mental
culture. Speech was closer to the multiplicity of daily life which
she valued: 'What is the difference between talkative and grammar
grammar makes a parlor a nun's affair. . . .' (p. 56.)
    Grammar's relation to speech here seems constricting – placing
speech under rule and confining it socially – reminding us of
Jakobson's notion of the 'mandatory role' speech plays in utterance.
Yet the possible meanings of this sentence do not end there. A
parlour was originally a room in a monastery for speaking within
silence. Does grammar then confirm the obvious, or does it open
speech within social silence and the silence of thought? Parlour, in
American, suggests both sentiment and a place of business and show.
Hence it refers to but excludes the erotic. Does speech therefore
degenerate there or return to the people? Thus Stein proceeds by
paradox. What is extraordinary in this work is the richness of the
meanings brought into play.
    A new way of reading is required; dreaming over the words and a
kind of quasi-philosophical meditation: 'A reflection is not a sentence
of delight is not a sentence whether they are there is not a sentence'
(p. 157). 'Reflection' here is possibly mimesis and consciousness
and therefore neither judgement nor rule. Emotion is not speech as
such and a sentence never quite captures an ontological moment.
Sentences, too, are to be distinguished from speech. Stein's statement that 'A sentence is never spoken' (p. 208) reminds one of
Andrei Codrescu's line that 'There was a man who spoke in com-

plete sentences and one day he was run over by a train'.[20] Stein
carefully makes her distinctions among the thickets of lingusitic
definition, like Emerson before her, though here the style is
empirical not idealistic: 'A sound is the name of a sense which they
have. A noun is the name of a sense which they have. A sentence is
not made by sound.' (*How to Write*, p. 201)

There is a vigorous defence of the semantic everywhere in Stein
and she commits that defence not to 'society' but to the writer who,
perhaps necessarily autocratically, renews the language patiently and
in solitariness: 'the minute you disperse a crowd you have a sentence'
(p. 29). Against the Saussurean balance of sentence and lineality,
word and association, she opens different forms of connectivness:
'we have known one who is kind. Now that is a very good sentence.'
(p. 30) The ironic self-congratulation stems from an interplay
between one and kind, retrospective knowledge and being. The 'is' is
both in and out of time by virtue of its ungrammatical place in the
subordinate clause. The sentence's disposal of time fascinated Stein:
'A sentence has wishes as an event' (p. 18). If 'event' is taken in the
Whiteheadian sense intentionality becomes concrete as a temporary
moment within discourse. Anything which was too familiar in the
creative act was unreflected, and therefore unstable: 'If there is a
name in a sentence a name which is familiar makes a data and
therefore has no equilibrium.' (p. 166)

Stein revised the sentence as a mediator between the atomization
of available vocabulary and the unconscious world patterning which
Whorf saw in traditional Western grammar. At times, however, she
swings right away from any attempt at syntax: 'The question is if
you have a vocabulary have you any need of grammar except for
explanation that is the question, communication and direction
repetition and intuition that is the question. Returned for grammar'.
(p. 60) Could the sheer piling up of words give a sense of the pure
magic of naming without recourse to syntax? Could in fact words
predicate themselves? It was obvious no word existed without some
shade of reference. Could there exist a vocabulary of thinking prior
to association and synchrony? Put another way, how could she
describe in words that Saussurean structure of *langue* in course of
revision? The attempt was in some ways bound to be a failure. 'A
vocabulary of thinking' cannot be recognized until it crosses the
threshold of utterance, at which point it must make an appeal to
others and thus define itself positively or negatively in relation to a
syntax. Stein slips into her own bogey of idealism here. Vocabulary
becomes mystical essence when the problem of consciousness is by-
passed. Words are not evidences of the senses however (phenomeno-
logically) already meaningful.

Stein also suggests, however, that vocabularies are multiple and have meaning in their capacity to represent demarcated spatial areas – which Whitney, it will be recalled, carefully separated from national boundaries. The notion of linguistic geography becomes important again: 'What is the difference between a vocabulary. A dictionary. A vocabulary outlines the capable district of rendering it account of however it is careless sentenced shattered record near this in sees (p. 381). Dictionaries by implication do not give the whole range of language but primarily point to other dictionaries, suggesting that all classifications and ordering of vocabularies are relative. Then the fiscal images (traditionally providing common analogies for language) creep in once more. Vocabulary both pays, like the silent coin of Mallarmé, and judges, in the double senses of 'rendering it account of'.[21] In one sense districts are there to collect. But does vocabulary need scrutiny because it is carelessly sentenced (judged and structured) or is it the shattered record of thought itself?

Thoughout the nineteenth century writing (record) was supremely the authentic trace of law and judgement, the permanent form of authoritative knowledge, and proof of fact. In addition 'putting on record', the *Oxford English Dictionary* states, was an American phrase – which is not perhaps surprising given that American historical commitment to the word itself. From political and religious directions the written record directed the course of thought itself from the Puritans' scrutiny of the Word to the written Constitution of State. It is said that when the English go to a dictionary they go to compare the definition with their own thoughts about the word in question; the Americans go to find a definition which they consider truthful enough to be used. The record, too, is the persistence not only of the past in the present, but the thought of the present become past – a mechanical state of mind perhaps belonging mainly to one who has given up on the present, as Macbeth's phrase, 'the last syllable of recorded time', indicates.

Stein invites the reader to an active struggle with her meanings and to a sense of play and delight also. The clear suggestion, at any rate, is that vocabulary as such constitutes fragments for rebuilding knowledge. To view Stein's efforts most positively would be to regard the atomization of words as a heuristic precondition for renewing semantics. In any case she makes it difficult to return to ordinary discourse with the same innocence about the structure of grammar and its unconscious ordering of the forms of knowledge itself.

How to Write is not a book to be read straight through. In spite of thematic continuities it is an uneven work and was in fact composed at various times. It varies also in difficulty, from the dense word sequences of 'A Vocabulary of Thinking', which fail almost to enter language at all, to the looser and less elusive patterns of 'Arthur a Grammar'. The bias in the following commentary will be towards reference and content in one of the most abstract, if not the most abstract, text by a major writer in English. There will equally be no drive for certainty or 'correct' reading, but the text *will be read*. As Ulla Dydo points out, Stein's work 'especially at its most imaginative, required great but loose and playful concentration'.[22] That process is begun but not completed in the following response to the work.

Key issues in *How to Write* include the nature of linguistic representation, problems of knowledge, the play between sign and reference, and between sign and sign. The deeper meaning of these issues is once more a meditation on the professionalization of society. It becomes most obvious in 'Forensics', the only section to be dealt with here, for in the very word 'Forensics' Stein was able to combine references to her most pertinent themes. Here is the most 'scientific' practice of the 'art' of medicine, for it addresses itself to messages sent from the dead rather than to signs which will promote life and healing. S. C. Neuman, in one of the few really searching books on Stein, has argued that Claude Bernard's *Introduction à l'étude de la médicine expérimentale* (1865) 'would have certainly formed part of the frame of reference of much of her instruction in medical experimentation'.[23] Bernard himself, of course, was fascinated with the larger problems of life and death, and while his experimental use of curare showed that muscle and nerve could be excited independently of each other, his fascination with the drug exceeded its use as a 'physiological dissection' tool. There is Gothic fascination here, a use of death to explicate life – a process which underwrites Bernard's metaphysic of 'dynamic equilibrium' in the organism: an idea of 'homeostasis', which will be shown in the conclusion to this work to be a key twentieth-century social metaphor.

Stein wrestled with not dissimilar problems, and for her, too, the 'primitive' was part of a promise of renewal in a civilization pulled towards death. In Bernard's words, 'The civilization of a nation is a movement towards death. The upper classes do not go down again. There must always be primitive or barbarous men who become civilized and rise. If this renewal does not take place, society dies like an organism deprived of cellular renewal.'[24] This is a biologist's version of renewable resource, in some respects analogous to what Marx called the capitalist's reserve army of labour. The detached experimenter also needed a metaphysic of renewal to overcome his own dissociation from the life world in the very act of experimenting on living organisms. Stein, too, posed the question, did life need the experience of death to explicate its living processes? Unlike Bernard, Stein was sceptical of a 'science of life', was more disposed to investigate the processes of reason, and distrusted models of 'dynamic equilibrium' as a truth, though not as a literary strategy.

'Forensics' is also a legal term and deals with the relation of medicine and law. In a more general sense it refers to an argument, speech or written thesis. It falls, therefore, crucially, between experiment and telling, and has the task of explaining one structural praxis in terms of another. Philosophically it invites a comparison of law with epistemological problems. It has been noted, for example, that Husserlian concepts 'all unwittingly construe epistemology analogously to a legal content. . . epistemology works in the figure of a contract that is never fulfilled'.[25] Intellectually forensics engages the problems which occur between a specialized and a common-sense discourse: the expert confronts a jury. Psychologically – as in a detective novel – forensics works out the relation between the living and the dead. Its authority is its claim to absolute objectivity. As the late Professor Keith Simpson, one of England's most famous forensic scientists, said, forensics is a work 'not coloured by emotion'.[26] Yet the moment the results leave the laboratory the course of events becomes highly emotional, as Gothic fiction and the popular press attest. The medical witnesses themselves can be caught politically between their obligations as citizens and as members of the smaller group of the profession.[27]

Indeed the relation of anatomy and the clinic, as Foucault describes it at the beginning of the nineteenth century, might serve as a model for that between medicine and law: or the expert and the court-room: the two not necessarily being of 'one mind'. Death, however, was 'entitled to the clear light of reason'.[28] A perceptive French critic notes that 'doctoring' was a key term for Stein even as early as *The Making of Americans*; 'c'est prendre en charge, attentivement, nos besoins'.[29] In this attentive taking in charge, however, Foucault argues that two types of knowledge confronted each other along 'new geographical lines' and in a 'new way of reading time'. Foucault develops his argument in relation to a movement from a localization of origins of disease in organs (volume) to Bichat's 'reading' of disease across tissular space: 'It is the same form of perception as that borrowed by the clinic from Condillac's philosophy: the uncovering of an elementary that is also a universal, and a methodological reading that, scanning the forms of disintegration, describe the laws of composition.'[30]

Condillac's name usefully connects language and anatomy for a prolegomena to the argument advanced here. The 'laws of composition' return us to Stein and the linguists. Throughout the nineteenth century linguists scanned the remnants of the past for a clue to the structure of language. For the anatomists, the problem was how to adjust anatomical perception to the reading of symptoms. The question in slightly altered terms was just as relevant to language. Stein, too, scanned the forms of disintegration in order to describe the laws of composition. She was best on the epistemological and rhetorical aspects, however, of what is in the last analysis not merely a compositional but a political question. As a trained doctor herself, Stein was very much aware of the disjuncture between experiment and discourse:

> experimenting is trying to do something in a way that may produce a result which is a desired result by the person doing it but telling something is not an experiment it is a thing that has to be done since any one inevitably has to tell something in the way it feels that something is what that thing is.[31]

This statement indicates that continuing ancient conflict between the knowledge of things and the practice of a social art in medicine. With 'things', 'desired results' are projected a priori which repetition will or will not confirm. In social practice truth lies in the 'telling'. Stein was fundamentally interested in the relation between knowledge, telling and the public domain. There is a problem with the politics of any specialized discourse, but with the rise of professionalism, indeed with not so much the culture but the cult of the professional, it becomes more urgent. Perhaps all professionalization at its worst follows the model of medicine – permanent crisis, love – hate relations with specialists, a psychology of scientific progressivism, status conflicts, and above all, perhaps, an illusion that the discovery of the constitution of things elicited by neutral procedure will guarantee order in the social realm.

Stein was, in fact, fascinated by the professions as such. Her somewhat ambiguous praise of the French *notaire*, for example, suggests that his ways were mysterious but effective. One wonders, too, whether she knew of that delightful parody of the law, *Forensic Fables by O.*, first published in London in 1926.[32] O.'s legal sketches measure the gap between theoretical and practical intelligence, between logical action and success. They parody legal jargon and constantly demonstrate how the dramatic event outruns speech. The law, the Church, the army, medicine, teaching provided Stein with many of her subjects. In a way the professions were *the* new American *class*, and their activities set parameters for Stein's continuous efforts to distinguish skill and intelligence, analytic and creative skills, technique and imagination, institutional practice and the revision of epistemes. Socially, too, there was the shadow of the politics of professionalism – that energetic participation in the 'rule of nobody'.

Forensics then mediates law and nature, logic and the corpse, the crime and the public. It is asked to re-establish order *post factum*. The details recovered from a flight recorder will surely and scientifically reassure the nervous about flight. A key role of forensics is to assuage nervousness and to lock up disintegration in an empirical heaven.[33] Stein's casts at forensics will exhibit many of the contradictions already manifest in her sections on 'grammar' and 'sentences'. These same contradictions however, are here marshalled and deployed with wit, energy and a rich intellectual playfulness not often to be found in the preceding sections. Could 'forensics' move towards that stillness of reassurance which grammar and sentences also sought?

Stein's chapter opens with: 'They will have nothing to do with still' (*How to Write*, p. 385), perhaps suggesting both a reluctance to leave the dead as dead in thought, indicating a psychological restlessness – and paradoxically a distancing from the dead as a stance. Instead they have 'skill', which is learned as a habit until it becomes almost unconscious. This is parodied in the line: 'A dog who has been washed has been washed clean with our aid in our absence' (p. 385). Stein uses reference to dogs to challenge natural operations. Washing the dog needs time and practice, as Paul Bowles found out, not creative intelligence.[34]

The distinction between natural skilful action directed to necessity and the conditions for educative growth is suggested in the line: 'No distress in elegance'. Growth needs disruption and dissonance. In a characteristic example Stein says:

Quarrels may wear out wives but they help babies.
We hope they will not wear out wives.

(How to Write, p. 385)

The word "appointment' then comes into play with its suggestions of contract, agreement, and a directive towards the future. Stein queries the nature of these modes:

They say it would have been better.
To invite.
Would it have been better.
To say.
Would it have been better
To show
Them this.

Inviting, saying and showing seem to have more openness than appointment. They are less formal, less pre-contracted gestures which open the world more creatively to others. These thoughts show Stein still very much involved with the terms of address.

Within representation, Stein suggests, forensics tends to be rather dogmatic:

Forensics use a plan by which they will never pardon.
They will call butter yellow. Which it is.

(p. 385)

Stein suggests a certain rigidity in the forensic method. Pardon has legal, economic and theological overtones. Parodying an act of affirming the known, Stein suggests yellow keeps its appointment with butter. The same creation of virtue out of necessity is seen in a subsequent example: 'They will also oblige girls to be women' (p. 385).

More positively Stein suggests that forensics has the capacity both to dogmatize and to free the sign it employs. Between the two possibilities lies the entire argument about language, reference and authority: 'What is forensics forensics is an argument to be fought' (p. 386). Stein as always gives us the process. She immediately counteracts this by saying: 'There is no argument in forensics' (p. 386), and in an almost Hegelian effort at synthesis she says, 'Forensics are elaborated argument' (p. 387). Stein then supplies an extended example:

There is a difference between a date and dreary.
Snow at an angle can fall.
But will she.
They may go.
At a certain gate.
For them to call.
Will she need a title.
Must they copy a matter.
Or would they call a cloth annul.
Categoric or a thought.
Heavenly just as bought.
Forensics are double.
They dispute a title and they dispute their trouble.
A title is made for defense. It did not defend him nor did I.
I always do.

(p. 387)

The 'argument' first distinguishes between time and feeling, illustrated by the fact that even in nature snow does not fall in straight lines – the whole difference between 'will' and 'may'. The next lines continue a meditation on appointment: 'At a certain gate./For them to call'. This seems to indicate not only an ambiguity between the place for reference and the place as reference, as an object of a naming, tryst or appeal, but a precise place which is simultaneously open. Copying and entitling ring changes on the same theme, pointing to an activity perhaps suspended between already established legal right (the law copyist in every sense) and something like Peirce's index, a pointing to, or title. 'Must they copy a matter' continues the legal connotations but also calls into question the activity of mimesis in its claim to representation. The alternative is to question authority: the voiding of the claims of the cloth – which refers not only to priestly but also to legal authority.

Stein then shifts more openly and abstractly to the problem she has been approaching all along. 'Categoric or a thought' sums up the debate between logic and metaphor. Both are needed, for forensics are 'double'. 'Title' (law) and 'trouble' (event) are what forensics mediates, since what is already named – the sacredness of title – is no defense in the discontinuities of actual events. Sometimes, indeed, forensics seems only to have to do with the lesser art of the skilful management of daily life: '. . . forensics has nothing to do with advice and why'. That is, its task is only to provide evidence, not to suggest how the case should be argued. Nor does it probe beyond the empirical 'how', to 'why'. Its action seems pragmatic. It has 'only to do with the difference between inconvenience and disgrace' (p. 388).

Is it then that cool, professionalized behind-the-scenes pragmatism and nothing more? In Part III it seems so:

> Forensic are plainly a determination
> Does and do all include obstinacy.
> Particularly for pleasure in clarity.

> (p. 389)

By the end of the section, however, the clear limits offered here seem to have become more confused. Behind Cartesian clarity lurks Cartesian doubt and the more unmanageable world of dream:

> Think forensically. How I doubt.
> It is more than a pleasure to dream more than a
> pleasure. To dream.
> Were he to manage to whom would there be an
> obligation to oblige.

> (p. 389)

Doubt and dream takes up the Cartesian dilemma, and the Lockean response. And from inside the problem Stein poses the question of authority. What exactly is the object of successful management?

What are its obligations? Since obligation is again ultimately a legal term, what are its limits? In a world of open-ended contracts can the place of 'forensics' be 'a remedy in time' – with obvious double meanings here? (p. 390).

Stein falls back on a kind of Whiteheadian process. Judgement is bound up with matter, and constitution is at once separate from and integral to the thing it judges:

> Forensics is in the state. They do feel that they are included in a state. In a State. A state is a piece of a part. Which they make added. Forensics is so true.
> A state apart.
>
> (p. 390)

There is a sense here that 'forensics' never completes its own project. Since it aims at authoritative totality, there is humour in the phrase 'in a state'. Like Toulmin, Stein would like to see a model of common law perhaps for the development of human understanding.[35] But could one trust the 'automism' of its general result? Do the professionals of life and death constitute a power within a power, a state within a state?

Also crucial is that pull of the 'outside', that 'outward criteria' of Wittgenstein – in Stein's own words, 'What everybody is looking at'. This leads to her only half-ironic claim that 'At last I am writing a popular novel' (p. 391). The subject-matter is indeed a staple of popular fiction, but the form and radical experimentation with language would be beyond the audience of that fiction. Like Melville before her, Stein likes to mix generic forms in her writing. So as well as being a 'popular novel', 'Forensics' is also that highest of classical dramatic forms; 'A trilogy'. 'Forensics is an adaptation of a trilogy. She is useful therefore she is not martyred. And they are correct or why do they do so.' (p. 391.) By comparing the popular novel and the classical trilogy Stein is probing the psychology of the needs they serve. Forensics adapts trilogy (the dramatic anthropology of Christ and Dionysius) to social use, not martyrdom and political display. The death displayed by science is oriented towards explanation, not mystery. There follows probably the most brilliant line in the work: 'Forensics consists in disposing of violence by placating irony' (p. 391). Does that then align it with the catharsis offered by Christ and Dionysius? Stein disposes of the often-advanced view that irony resolves real contradiction in untroubled stasis. The comparison of forensics with Greek and Christian sacred drama works both ways. Forensics, Stein suggests, has its drama – the display in the courtroom of the dismembered body – and Greek and Christian cultures have their own ways of holding corpses up to view and their own rigid methodology and perceptions. Science, too, Stein suggests, has its own darkness, rituals and mystery. Whitehead's comparison of the scientific project with Greek tragedy, and scientific method with the psychology of medieval Christianity, made the point precisely.

Stein elaborates all these possibilities as she moves to a conclusion, drawing into richer configurations the themes of authority, structure, change and the rhetoric of epistemological statement. Can we really believe forensics when it asserts that 'calm in time is their remedy'? (p. 393).

> How can they use policy of persuasion. Listen to hints. Forensics begins with the union and organization. After that. Advance in volume.
> They shall stretch. Their conclusions. From here. To there. They will. Prepare. Efficaciously. Just as much. As they have been. In the habit. Of anticipating. Melodiously. In reference. To their analysis. In a garden. Admire forensics.
> If in the meaning of their connection. They disturb. Without it. As much. As they generously instil. Into them. In their allowance. Of whether. They will partly fail.
> Forensics is a distribution unequally.
> Expalin why it matters. That they must bewilder. With whatever. They could crowd. As treasure. And so they fastened. Window curtains. Forensics makes regaining wholly a feather in meditation.
>
> (pp. 393–4)

The 'union and organization' refers just as much to the return of sentence pattern comically broken by random full stops as to social content. But there are other disruptions here in the generally smooth-flowing lines. Meanings of policy, for example, which offer themselves for relevance here, would include 'state', prudence, expedience, projected action, and insurance. Stein's advice to listen to hints while reserving judgement should be taken. 'Volume' can of course refer to the physical state of a substance as well as to the bound pages of the book itself. 'Advance' had both economic and military overtones and the tone at least borders on the comic. It is almost as if at this point Stein is saying: Go on, play your games, for that 'advance' both positively and negatively will 'stretch. . . . conclusions'. For, to use the cant term, 'closure' will be disrupted for all their unity of organization and however elaborately they prepare, as 'efficaciously' suggests. The breaks in obvious sentences (judgements) still shows that a consensus about the world will not come easily, and that an effort less than creative will leave them 'As they have been'.

Then, depending on the interpretation of 'melodiously', Stein builds another view of the analytic process as a harmonious Utopian state signalled by 'in a garden': where of course art, science and nature meet, and states of nature meet states of grace. Less positively, if the symbolic implications are admitted, it is also a place where a 'fall' is inevitable. Indeed the rest of the text seems to chart a continual failure of the habit and practice of mind which 'forensics' has been defining. The unequal distribution refers perhaps at once to honest recognition of inequality, and also to the dissonance of logic itself. The 'bewilderment' will be inevitable whatever hopes of a 'garden' they have. Here Stein uses the oldest images in American writing. 'Crowd' as a verb has the general meaning of 'push'. 'Forensics' pushing 'treasure' (cognate of course with 'thesaurus' – the treasure house of language) into the crowd takes its own risks. The last words are hard to understand, but they seem to suggest an act of withdrawal as well as crowding in order to 'regain' that spent treasury which for meditation, in contrast, is a lightweight affair. Forensics' meditation on death regains in fact nothing except perhaps that 'feather on the breath of God', in the words of Hildegard von Bingen. As for Whitman, the soul is no more than the body.

Stein also seems to question whether the fatalism of forensics is enough. In the following lines, 'cause' shifts its means from philosophy (Aristotle) to law (motive, lawsuit). Following out the legal term, Stein suggests that rigid principles are a consequence of a certain kind of dogmatic emotionalism:

> And wealth, they will use energy in very much with which they will have caused their ought, ought they to comply made it as predetermined, vouchsafed, or with the cause of their relief, that they once knew. It is a gradual cause.

> (p. 394)

'It is the cause' – that classic high moment of Shakespearean drama – is echoed in that last phrase. The gradual corruptions of the logic of competition and need for psychological certainty work inexorably on the psychology of romatic hero of the adventurous mercantile era. Will wealth corrupt romance? Is it in fact the cause of romance? Stein had read enough eighteenth-century fiction to be pretty sure it was. The passage suggests false reassurances in the abstract processes of law, money, and scientific investigation, and the theory of general 'drift' in the 'gradual cause'. The last lines are scattered with phrases better suited to the popular novel. Stein, like Ford and Conrad who also wrote their swan-song for romance in a novel of that title (and in everything else they did), offers the broken phrases: 'treasure', 'a thirst for gold', 'battle and die', to complete her text. Had the world grown grey at the touch of forensics? What cause was Stein referring to? What continuity was possible in logic (Aristotle's four causes), in science – the physics of unequal distribution – in law, in explanation, in politics? Like Adams, Stein could see none.

Even from the evidence of this necessarily tentative preliminary reading, 'Forensics' appears as one of the finest short pieces Stein ever wrote. It exhibits finally the deep bewilderment and difficulty in finding common cause as a writer, an intellectual and as a member of society in the early 1930s. The multiplicity of definition, however, fails to disturb a sense of decay in the decline of Western institutions – the army, religion, law and science itself – and in their ability to manage the world. Ironically 'billed' as a prophet of the future, Stein is in fact a profound analyst of the liberal age which had passed. The world of romance has become a dollar-frenzied machine, but the figure of the contract remains unfulfilled because the emotional underpinning is never confronted. Only sympathy remains as the merely structurally dissected body of the language registers the effects of Sapir's 'flag-waving' in completing yet another sentence:

> Forensics may be athirst for gold. It may with them battle and die. It can as much bequeath and condole. For them. To merit. That they. Should console. Them.

> (p. 395)

Stein's *How to Write* was a mature work of the 1930s. It has been read here as a way into the relationship between Stein's themes and techniques, and between her epistemological interpretations of language and language's relation to the world. In the following chapter her first major work will be considered in terms of a broader semantic approach, taking more account of the thematic and generic implications of the text in relation to interactions among philosophic, scientific, social and literary materials.

Chapter 14
Decline in the West: Gertrude Stein's *Making of Americans: being the history of a family's progress*

> What convinces masses are not facts, and not even inverted facts, but only the consistency of the system of which they are presumably a part. Repetition, somewhat overrated in importance because of the common belief in the masses' inferior capacity to grasp and remember, is important only because it convinces them of consistency in time.
>
> HANNAH ARENDT[1]

> We drove around, we had just missed one homicide it was the only one that happened that evening and it had not been interesting it had been a family affair and everybody could understand everything.
>
> GERTRUDE STEIN[2]

> We will never have a true Socialist Realism until we are able, unafraid, to describe the boredom of Minsk.
>
> KENNETH REXROTH[3]

'Hueffer or Ford you know Ford Maddox Hueffer the editor is moved,' Stein wrote excitedly to Carl Van Vechten in 1924; 'he says it is magnificent and is terribly impressed with it having been done some odd 18 years ago.'[4] The slight exaggeration was pardonable. *The Making of Americans* was finished in 1911, although it was tentatively begun in 1903. Stein had given up hope of publication, for the 900-page novel with its long sentences and paragraphs, employing modes of abstraction and repetition, was never destined to be widely read.[5] Yet for the few who do read it there are many rewards. At its best it has the deep melancholy of Joyce's sense of a society of estrangement and defeat, Lawrence's seriousness about the sexual basis of conflicts registered between independence and family life, Proust's feeling for the psychology of memory, Ford's sense of a world whose habits are bankrupt, and Conrad's shrewdness about the ironies of bourgeois economy and romance. While Stein's world in this novel is not without its own contradictions, it somehow manages to avoid the hopelessness of Joyce's hermetic world, Lawrence's tendency to create mythic paradigms of behaviour, Proust's withdrawn aestheticism, Ford's nostalgia, and the coldness that sometimes blows through the limits of Conrad's irony.

Stein's shrewd gaze focuses on the apparent success of the bourgeois revolution in America: on the American Dream, no less, with its Utopian goal of freedom based on property ownership, its sharp demarcation of male – female roles, its triumph of the average, its psychology of the middle way, its individualism, and its claim to have solved the dynamic of nature and labour through honest business practice, cultured leisure and moderated passion within family life. *The Making of Americans*, written at the height of the new immigrations by one who had gone back to live in Europe on a small private income, is a psychological investigation of the New Americans – not the recent immigrants, though there are immigrant memories, but those who had migrated psychologically from the liberal certainties of *laissez-faire* economics to a world of employees, professionals and trusts.

The sweep of the novel provides neither the possibility of private values such as are still defended in Lawrence, nor the clash between private and public or military life as in Ford, nor yet the rather autocratic intimacy of Joyce. In Stein the world of the private and the public is suspended in the social. The suspension however is a highly active moving state, which includes a nostalgia, in Charlotte Kretzoi's words, 'for a peaceful, domestic, almost Jeffersonian agrarian existence'. Kretzoi adds however a significant analogy for the mode of recall:

> The effort to remember in bits and pieces, the knowledge of something which existed in her mind as a solid whole, as a moment filling a space not entirely filled, calls to mind Niels Bohr's model of an atomic structure in which the fast flitting circling electrons in a practically empty space give the impression of solid material.[6]

The analogy points us to the scientific foreground from which Stein develops her abstractions, though they were in biology and psychology rather than in physics. Yet physics and biology, as was observed in Whitehead,[7] shared a statistical impulse which moved beyond traditional geometries of space and time. The analogy is also useful in that it suggests, as does all scientific activity, that common-sense life most readily gives up its secrets when investigated with highly abstract and imaginative hypotheses. Whitehead's attempted synthesis of the abstractions of the mathematician's description of process with evolutionary paradigms via the vocabulary of traditional philosophy is pertinent to the whole of Stein's project.

The reversal of terms and their references is a case in point. If in Whitehead objects become universal and abstract, and events particular and continuous, so in Stein character becomes static (abstracting its place in society as much as any character of Expressionist drama) and plot continuous and particular. In Kantian terms, relevant for Whitehead as previously noted, the 'analogues of appearance' are already structured and structuring. In the terms of radical empiricism, the Jamesian 'drops of experience', unique and indivisible yet held by relations which are also part of experience, will give Stein a model for attempting to overcome traditional philosophical dualisms such as being and becoming. Yet Stein would not be able to maintain that mandarin metaphysics of process on which Whitehead relied. She was also to doubt radically the isomorphism of repetition and continuity.

However, the terms in which Stein thought are close to those of Whitehead. For both of them repetition and anarchy characterize the 'process of living'. But whereas Whitehead was sure that creativity instigated repetition and that reason controlled anarchy, Stein was to propose that repetition and creativity were the reverse of each other, and that 'anarchy' might well be one important aspect of the whole business of thinking. Thus, where for Whitehead repetition is re-enactment in an anthropological sense, for Stein it is more a spiral of evolving forms. For Whitehead play is ceremonial, for Stein ceremonial is subverted in play. For Whitehead art reacts against madness. For Stein art situates itself in madness, so that it is essentially different from that 'psychopathic reaction of the race to the stresses of its existence'.[8] For Whitehead cultural evolution exhibited 'progress' and could be paralleled with natural organisms. For Stein 'evolution' might progress at the level of nature, and regress at the cultural level. For Whitehead socially aggregated ends overcome historical anarchy. Disturbances at the human level, for Stein, challenged her confidence in whatever aggregate 'unity' any autonomous process seemed in course of proposing.

Similar divergences of emphasis within shared terms can be observed in relation to Darwinian and post-Darwinian psychology. Whereas Darwin's work on psychology drew on the 'evidence' of literature to propose the secret truth of habit-formation through inheritance and repetition, Stein took the abstract modes of habit and repetitive gesture back into literature, both to ironize the procedure and to revise the nature of characterology. Unlike Darwin, Stein knew that 'facts of behaviour' were part of a drama of interaction, the truth of which could not be found on a calibrated scale of

M

inheritance or generalized habit. Stein, often accused of 'primitivism' – whatever that may mean precisely – was to reserve unreflected action as an object of satire, while simultaneously suggesting that its promptings, whether a result of repressed sexuality or fear of death, were the basis for a kind of moral and creative blindness. Similarly with her description of emotional behaviour. Free of James's somewhat puritanical attitude to the emotions, Stein directed a creatively attentive if not absolutely reflective consciousness significantly upon emotional life. Within Stein's own making of *The Making of Americans* there is a significant development also, from the dualisms of Jamesian and Weiningerian characterology such as her notebooks of the period exemplify, to the actual result in the work, where the authorial voice laments its continuous failure to classify the novel's characters.

It is clear that in the period of *The Making of Americans* Stein was working through the James – Münsterberg legacies. Even before then, in her college essays she had been pitting her literary compositions against classes in behavioural psychology. Here is a short extract from one student essay for the composition class; it describes a popular experiment of the time which examined the relation between bodily behaviour and 'automatic writing' which, in turn, would deliver the truth of that second-level personality:

> Next she finds herself with a complicated apparatus strapped across her breast to register her breathing, her finger imprisoned in a steel machine and her arm thrust inexorably into a big glass tube. . . . Strange fancies begin to crowd upon her, she feels that the silent pen is writing on and on forever. Her record is there where she cannot escape it, and the group about her begin to assume the shape of mocking fiends, gloating over her imprisoned misery. Suddenly she starts, they have suddenly loosened a metronome directly behind her, to observe the effect. . . . One is indeed all things to all men in a laboratory.[9]

Among the many levels of significance here is the Poe-like sense of entrapment in the machine, the nightmare of being investigated and exposed, and the experience of impotence. The subject is literally robbed of her words. Experiment has taken the pen from her and spells out incriminating evidence which it will then claim is the truth about her. The metronome is a Poe-like reminder of mechanical time. Stein had a great fear of death. To be observed in that fear went beyond nightmare. Many of the subjects of her first great work are already here: sexual behaviour, the distorted passions of the experimental gaze, the relation of time to behaviour, of author to audience, the problem of consciousness and speech, and the limitations of the scientific method. Stein exposes the nightmare behind – to quote Whyte's words again – those 'neutralist technicians' who guide human beings 'into satisfying solidarity with the group so skilfully and unobtrusively that he will scarcely realize how the benefaction has been accomplished'.[10]

Stein's dryly humorous tone, however – 'One is indeed all things to all men in a laboratory' – shows that there was more than one level of response to the circumstances in which she found herself. She was not to reject science or philosophy as such, nor indeed was she to take some kind of reactive refuge in literariness. Like Henry Admas, she liked to make her opposites fight. She inherited a world in which maleness was associated with intellectual life and the world of the emotions with femaleness. At the simplest level she was to attempt to subvert these received oppositions. She confessed to herself in a notebook: 'my intellect and consciousness is masculine. . . my actual sexual nature pure servant female.'[11] *The Making of Americans* would investigate society within many contradictions of class, sexual identity, conscious mental life and automatic behaviour. The subjects of her discourse were the new American middle classes. Stein's highly ambiguous celebration of those classes will be examined under two headings: first, the conflict between bourgeois life and creative necessity; and second, a preliminary consideration of the terms of her technique.

I

Leon Katz has noted that the chief preoccupation of *The Making of Americans* is 'the conflicts, tensions and solid justification of bourgeois marriage'.[12] Some years after writing the book Stein was (with the rawness of memories fading a little perhaps) more positive about it than the work itself suggests. There is much conflict within the book, little solid justification. Nonetheless she said:

> Even the small bourgeoisie has its charm, at different moments of the world's history they made a fetish of one class's charm against another, but to me they all have charm and aside from class distinction which is inevitable they are all just themselves which is to me interesting. It is a story I tried to tell in *The Making of Americans. . . .*[13]

Some contemporary critiques have attempted, using radical post-structuralist terminology, to see Stein's efforts in *The Making of Americans* as 'a politics of exchange' between men and women within family life.[14] Yet it is hard to see the work as a politics, and there are few moments of exchange as such inside or outside its metaphysics of process. Stein gives us a social psychology not a politics. That in itself is, of course, a political position by default, but not one that can too easily be claimed for a radical critique.

Yet at the level of the social there is little doubt that Stein herself in the early 1900s sought to escape from and to evaluate her own bourgeois early upbringing. There seemed to be more hate than love in her memories of her family, especially as she approached adolescence. If the Herslands of Gossols of the book are anything like the Steins at Oakland, the memory must have been a relatively bitter one.[15] Later in life, in a populist mood, Stein could hold up the small bourgeoisie as a value against an America of trusts and corporations. Yet in the end her attitudes varied little throughout her life. They can be glimpsed in this short piece of 1928, called 'Business in Baltimore':

> Imagining up and down. How many generations make five. If another marries her brother, if another marries her brother, if their brother marries another, if their brother and a brother marry another the sister how many pairs are there of it.... Business in Baltimore makes a wedding....
> She did see fortunes fade.
> Who did see fortunes fade.
> Nobody saw fortunes fade.[16]

Marriage is there for business. The riddling structure invites a calculation of necessity. The multiplication of marriages, like doing business, falls within necessity. Like the fatalism, the secret fatalism of capitalism, it seems to exist outside human will and direction.

Stein's real criticism of American society lay in attacking unconscious assumptions and behaviour. Her baselines were the creativity for which the artist was a model, and the contemplative life. Like Hannah Arendt she recognized that the contemplative life was more difficult, and more energy-consuming, than a life of pragmatic action and she judged her world out of this conviction. She said, 'Activity is a cheap commodity. Mankind never profit from experience. Dr Franklin used to say that experience is the school for fools.'[17] Experience was for her those compulsive repetitions which hindered the Thoreauvian aim of authenticity in life and work. 'One might', she wrote, 'say anything is the same but dance and war are particularly the same because one can see them.'[18] Common-sense life with its undisclosed compulsions was to be the object scrutinized from her own creative viewpoint. An American, indeed even a romantic, impulse to study the forms of ordinary life from non-common-sense perspectives reversed the assumptions of her favourite eighteenth-century forebears, who attacked the disruptions of common-sense life from a pragmatic consensus of what common sense involved. The contemplative life of the artist was the basis of Stein's values, and her especial wrath was reserved for those who made a business out of it. Her anti-Semitic comments in the note-books can be partially explained by Arendt's discussion of the late nineteenth-century Jewish bourgeois's attraction to what Stefan Zweig called the 'Radiant power of Fame'. For the Jewish bohemian entrepreneur 'to live in the aura of fame was more important than to become famous: thus they become outstanding reviewers, critics, collectors, and organizers of what was famous'.[19] Stein's comments on Bernard Berenson and her brother Leo Stein should be seen in this light. A collector herself, surrounded by family collectors and critics, she would have been particularly sensitive to the necessary dis-tinction between the artist, the collectors, the administrators, and bohemia generally.

Against them, she did value the actual bourgeoisie more. Their daily struggles and their feelings about their activities were more interesting. Had they made survival into an art? In the words of one French critic, were they 'comme les êtres humaines qui sont, sans fin, à la fois semblables et dissemblables; distinct et pourtant se répetant les uns les autres, dans les activités fondamentales, manger, dormir, aimer, se reposer, commencer, finir'?[20] Stein was to make distinc-tions of value in the way people performed activities common to all. What was evasive and what fulfilling in these moments? Stein has an almost Burroughsian sense that anything might become addictive. She could speak of creative work, family, routine work, ethics, beauty, love, money and philanthropy as ways, in her words, of 'allying oneself to eternity'.[21] Her critique was directed at patterns of repression and dominance in the most common and intimate forms of living. Changes in small acts of quasi-conscious behaviour were to be made reference points to describe a psychopathology of American living. It was a sombre vision reinforced by her own acute sense of death. 'Normal' death was even 'more depressing than pathological death'.[22] In the novel she would link success-ethic drives with a psychology of the denial of death.

Indeed within the potential banality of her characterology – codified in her notebooks under moralistic types, those who had sentimentality, loyalty, pride, self-knowledge and so on – there is a deeper level, as indicated in her observation: 'most of them have not real fear'.[23] The old-fashioned moralistic terms applied to her characters will be seen to be evasive, involving repetitive habits drugging a true sense of sexuality and death. At its darkest the novel gives us an intimate world of activity without aim, and purpose without intelligibility. There is also wit, however, and humour, as well as a pervasive sense of *Dunciad*-like dullness as a universal moral

condition which stops just this side of tragedy. Against the blandness
of the unreflective habits of group life, Stein set the old liberal ideals
of individualism. Thus she could say, 'Government is the least
interesting thing in human life, creation and the expression of that
creation is a damn sight more interesting.' She disliked the very
notion of 'humanity in groups',[24] but such a notion conflicted with
her training in classifying behaviour patterns. She lived out the
contradiction in *The Making of Americans* of analysing groups while
dissolving the classificatory premises on which that analysis was
conducted. She could do this by directing her attention to behaviour
that went deeper than the then-valuable terms of behavioural
psychology, and also by reserving for herself the right to reject the
artist's task as a form of mimesis. The bewildering world of the
emotions might have been the object of her analysis but it had
nothing to do with her methods and procedure. For Stein, as W. C.
Williams said of her, writing 'must attend to its own comprehensive
organization of materials. And by so doing...rather than by
copying, it takes its place as most human.'[25]

In her notebooks Stein speaks of an experience in Spain soon ofter
first arriving in Europe:

> when I got the awful depression of repetition in history, then
> realization much later that I did not believe in progress, that I was
> in that sense not an optimist, then realizing that I was not a prag-
> matist just recently do not believe all classification is teleological,
> that aesthetic has become the whole of me. . . .[26]

The rejection of progress as such made her stance as an American
writer radical. Her rejection of pragmatism is part of that same
rejection of progress. Classification for the pragmatist is based on the
paradox of design justified by an *ad hoc* future. An aesthetic at least
had the advantage by contrast of emphasizing a present, willed
activity in which conscious choices could be made. Stein rejected all
alliances with eternity, pragmatic and otherwise. In that sense she
rejected William James. Aesthetic meant for her that she could adopt
an abstract design for her work, letting it change and modify in
relation to the materials it encountered. William Carlos Williams
correctly saw a political value emerging when the artist fearlessly
claimed abstract modes of thought: 'To be democratic, local (in the
sense of being attached with integrity to actual experience) Stein, or
any other artist, must for subtlety ascend to a plane of almost abstract
design to keep alive.'[27]

'Difficulty' can scarcely be placed in the service of the demagogue
either, and at this level Stein was democratic. The most positive
aspects of her reaction to bourgeois life within a revised individual-

ism and a practical, not metaphorical, aesthetic resulted in her placing the contemplative against the active life, a radical pessimism against cheap optimism, the freedom of difficult creativity against common-sense habits, a concern for individuals and their difference in the presence of the formation of a mass society, a belief in the radicalism of the artist's task in opposition to the bohemianism of her class, a distrust of moralism, and an acceptance of the multiplicity of actual experience against any formulas of progress or pragmatism.

On the negative side her loss of faith in the actual political process – very understandable for one who had spent her college years in the America of the 1890s – had two results. It turned her to the social rather than the political world, and made her analysis psychological rather than historical. It also sent her scurrying towards epistemology as the basis of her analysis. This had a negative effect on her politics but a very positive effect on her whole approach to language, and the techniques of narrative.

In most of her more difficult works Stein emphasises the structure of composition as it simultaneously delivers its contents. Her work has hence a kind of built-in self-reflective device. In *The Making of Americans* she abstracts as far as possible a Richardsonian world of interior consciousness, drawing attention to her own gaze which is at once involved and alienated. There is a sense in which Stein seeks to expose the classic structure of the novel in its relations with a bourgeois psychology of behaviour, and at a time when confidence in the behaviour had reached its limits. In her preparations for the novel she turned her attention principally to the eighteenth century, the high point of bourgeois mercantile confidence. She had well-established favourites like *Robinson Crusoe* and *Clarissa*, and indeed *The Making of Americans* will explore the psychology of the self-driven man, isolated, dominating, happier in the world of things than of people.

She will describe, too, the women whom that very ideology marginalized, their fantasies coded in a Gothic plot structure which needed the vile seducer as much as the helpful cannibal. Like Adams, and like the present-day producers of American soap operas, Stein was interested in power. She was attracted to these early novels because she knew that they were key texts for understanding her own culture. She grew up at the height of the genteel tradition in America and also at the height of the activities of the Robber Barons. She was attracted to the popular novel, many of them written by women who took the themes of *Don Quixote* into popular genres where the knight's adventures were domesticated and adapted to the needs of the new rising classes, with their uncertainties about every-

thing from their table manners to their clothes. It was this popular
novel, with its contents of sentiment, romance, touches of the
Gothic, and its pervading moralism that Stein seized on. Partial lists
of what she read are recorded in her notebooks: works like *The
Female Quixote*, Mrs Aphra Behn's *Oroonoko* and *Fair Jilt*, Mrs
Haywood's *History of Betsy Thoughtless*, Sarah Fielding's *Adventures
of David Simple*, and Peter Wilkins's *The Fool of Quality*. She pursued
the tradition into the early nineteenth-century, into the works of
Fanny Burney and Jane Austen.[28] From the evidence in her notebooks she seemed to classify her reading in quasi-sexual terms, men
on one side, women on the other. With the male writers and subject-
matter she seemed to be drawn, in the title of one of them, to
'English Men of Action'; men like T. E. Lawrence and Clive of
India. Parkman's elegantly written and sadistic histories of western
adventure also appear on her list. So does Captain Maryatt's *Mister
Midshipman Easy*. Titles appear at heads of blank pages, presumably
for analyses which classify them in terms of a character psychology
derived from Weininger.[29]

It is also clear that she was attracted to autobiography and biography. From a later comment she made, it can be shown that works
of this kind gave her particular insights into the crucial subject of
authorial address. On the great classic work of eighteenth-century
biography she wrote: 'The case of Boswell's Johnson is an interesting
one, Boswell conceived himself as an audience, achieving recognition at one and the same time that Johnson achieved recognition of
the thing Johnson was saying.'[30] The problem of self-inscription into
the text joined with the problem of constantly exposing its technique. Stein was also preoccupied with the question of audience. At
its simplest level it was a matter of personal concern. She was to
remain unknown for a long time, living out a paradoxical position as
one who perhaps had constructed *the* theoretical text about popular
literature. In a mood halfway between bitterness and irony she wrote
to Van Vechten in 1916: 'Alas about every three months I get sad. I
make so much absorbing literature with such attractive titles and
even if I could be as popular as Jenny Lind where oh where is the man
to publish me in series.'[31]

At the earlier end of the classic period of the novel (from Cervantes
to Henry James) were literatures also which prompted Stein to think
about form and structure. From the Elizabethans she took, no less
than did Pound and Eliot, a sense of a language which bore the
liveliness of an oral tradition, resources of wit in relation to
metaphor, and the virtuosity of a prose still open to many possibilities before Bacon and the Scientific Revolution narrowed its range.
From Lyly's *Euphues* she copied out, albeit inaccurately, a quotation

which signals a serious and ironic perspective on *The Making of Americans*: 'In faith Euphues thou hast told me a long tale, the beginning I have forgotten the middle I understand not and the end hangeth not together'.[32] Euphues's satire on Aristotelian narrative was also a satire on the structure of thought implicit in that narrative. Stein, too, would direct 'forgetting', absence of 'knowing', and 'discontinuity' against the Aristotelian certainties of memory, empirical knowledge and continuity. For narrative involves both an epistemology and a psychology in its deployment of time.

The other novel which helped to shake conventional patterns of form in her own deliberations was Sterne's *Tristram Shandy*. Sterne's hero's end was certainly in his beginning, and his complex repetitive projection of his reader 'in series' must have been a resource on which Stein could draw. Sterne's preoccupation with Lockean philosophy and perhaps even obstetrics would have attracted her. Stein was eventually to reject Aristotelian narrative for largely psychological reasons. Her own comments on the period of writing *The Making of Americans* are revealing: 'When I first began writing really just began writing, I was tremendously impressed by anything and everything having a beginning, middle and ending. . . . One would not have been one escaping from adolescence if there had not been a beginning and a middle and an ending to anything.'[33] Aristotelian plot here signals a personal need to end the difficulties of her own adolescence as well as her own youthful fear of death. Aristotelian plot had the advantage of completion, but at the same time its remorseless lineality seemed to falsify the actual multiple world of lived experience. In *The Making of Americans* forms of Aristotelian narrative dissolve as the book moves from childhood to adolescence and beyond.

While a challenge to Aristotelian modes of narrative and indeed the theory of knowledge implicit in it would be presented in *The Making of Americans*, and in many subsequent works, Stein's preparations for her first long novel emerge very much from a classificatory mood. Katz was the first to point out that Otto Weininger's *Sex and Character* of 1906 was a crucial document. It had better be said at once that this notorious anti-feminist classic is fraudulent in its attempts to attribute essentialist characteristics of male and female behaviour to human behaviour in general, via a discourse which swings uncertainly between mysticism and empirical procedure. For Stein its method of dualistic sexual characterology, its notion of sexual affinities which Weininger took from Goethe's *Elective Affinities,* gave her an impulse to classify behaviour abstractly in terms of sexual and emotional paradigms.

It is difficult to know the extent to which Stein accepted Weininger's essentialisms which today read like classic statements of sexist prejudice. As we have seen, she thought of herself as intellectually male, and Weininger equated creativity and 'appreciation of genius' with maleness, while arguing that women with large doses of 'maleness' should be free to develop their own powers creatively. It is hard to deny that Stein's feeling of intellectual privilege added a touch of arrogance to her attitudes to 'female' weakness. Did she agree with Weininger that 'emancipation' was only for women geniuses with 'male' elements? It would have helped to legitimate her own sexual preferences and her role as a writer, while screening out the wider struggle for the emancipation and liberation of women. Weininger also suggested that genius was most likely to be found, not merely in the Carlylean great men of history, but in those who write biography. For Weininger psychology itself becomes theoretical biography. In that sense *The Making of Americans* takes a crucial clue from Weininger. Stein's novel is theoretical biography.

At points in *The Making of Americans* Stein also takes on a distinction, which Weininger derives from Avenarius, between character and essence. Avenarius argued that character was 'adjectival' not substantive. He challenged Cartesian logic to propose that elements are 'ideas'. Thus the character of green, blue, cold, warm, soft, hard, sweet, bitter is 'the particular kind of quality with which they appear'.[34] This appearance Weininger makes dependent on time rather than space, as in the more spatially paradigmed propositions of Descartes. For the appearance of more conscious ideas in the conceptual as opposed to the sensational sense, Weininger adopts an evolutionary metaphysic of time. Like most nineteenth-century historians he sees mental history as a depoliticized autonomy, as if history were only history of ideas. Oddly anticipating Whitehead later, he says: 'Definite scientific conceptions are preceded by anticipations. The process of clarification is spread over many generations.'[35] Character, then, as a 'quality' of appearance in time, and scientific conceptions as gradually evolving organic forms, structure Weininger's view of history. This coincides of course with some aspects of James's evolutionary vitalism.

Weininger may well have reinforced Stein's interest in medieval humours (Ben Jonson was a favourite author) and the concept of organic qualities of appearance as clues to character may well have linked in her mind with conversations with her friend Dr Claribel Cone, who wrote papers on the pathology of tissues:

There must now then be more description of the way each one is made of a substance common to their kind of them, thicker,

thinner, harder, softer, all of one consistency, all of one lump, or
little lumps stuck together to make a whole one cemented together
sometimes by the same kind of being sometimes by other kind of
being in them, some with a lump hard at the centre liquid at the
surface, some with a lump vegetablish or wooden or metallic in
them. . . . It and the state it is in each kind of them, the mixing of
it with the other way of being that makes many kinds of these two
kinds of them, sometime all this will have meaning.[36]

Stein is both parodying and using (because mind and body were seen
by James to form a continuum) the centuries-old desire to predicate
behaviour on bodily substance, and the language of the Elizabethan
humours still, of course, dominates common-sense language description of behaviour. It is impossible after reading Stein, who
continuously draws attention to our common-sense language habits,
to react to contemporary usage innocently. Weininger also had at
least the merit of rejecting the Wordsworthian version of Lockean
psychology which stated that youth was the time of strongest
impressions. He rejects this on the grounds that such thinking leads
to a view in which modern psychology treats people as bits of
receiving apparatus. Yet memory is still a key concept, and Weininger's words sum up Stein's project also: 'Our consciousness and
vision of the past is the strongest ground for our desire to be conscious in the future.'[37]

Weininger's book is therefore a curious one: simultaneously a
chapter in late German idealistic philosophy and a treatise on an
empirical science of character. He retains the Kantian notion of the
'intelligent ego, distinct from all empirical consciousness', which
was perhaps a source for Stein's subsequent insistence on the distinction between human nature and human mind. Yet such a stance
had clear dangers of de-historicization. Nietzsche and Ibsen are
praised, for example, for the 'truth' that 'the timeless, human personality is the necessary condition of every real ethical relation to our
fellow men'.[38] In the last years of her life, when Stein met Richard
Wright, she said she thought of him as a human being rather than as a
black man. Wright was, in spite of his respect for Stein, understandably angry. She was not free from the absolute idealism implied in
the transcendentalism of the 'timeless personality' applied to human
beings in their particular contexts. As Katz says, Stein was in pursuit
of the ultimate human being, a project which, since Emerson at least,
had been an American tradition. Yet in spite of these unpromising
premises, Stein's impulse in *The Making of Americans* was to measure
the forms of ordinary life by the highest standards: the energy-
releasing creativity of the artist.

On the other hand, for Stein the forms of ordinary life were most fully located in the family. She needed at once to defend it as a place of human value and to escape from its repetitive compulsions. Weininger's own attack on the family is most interesting as a cry of rage against the invasion of 'society' into every area of truly public life. The attack is on women as managers of the domain of necessity. However, Weininger's attribution of a 'slave-like' character to women buries logic in the guilt of the slave owner. The symptoms of repression are mistaken for human nature. Indeed dualistic characterology, offered as theory but in fact adopted as underlying truth, discovers without much difficulty the evidence for its pseudo-empiricist gaze: repressive reality made over into natural process.

Unlike Weininger, who thought the mode typical only of the sentimental erotics of Jews and women, Stein availed herself of the possibility of satire. She directed it against the family with a range of tones from the bitter to the indulgent. For Stein the American ideology of the family, enacted with unforgiving alternations of marriage and divorce, seemed to be derived from its permanently unresolved synthesis of excessive sentimentality and obsessive moralism. It was a domain where pragmatism covered the need for competitive possession. Santayana's definition of fanaticism is a clue to much of Stein's writing. Stein depicts a world where all the inhabitants are redoubling their efforts having lost sight of their aim. If memory, too, for Weininger was the hallmark of genius, for Stein it seemed to be a burden carried against creativity. Marianne Moore was wrong when she declared that *The Making of Americans* was a 'living genealogy'. Time and the family in Stein's vision had all the life of a phosphorescent corpse.[39]

The Making of Americans is in many respects, for all its humour and wit, a painful record of Stein's attempt to come to terms with her own singularity. In an enigmatic note she wrote: 'I believe in reality as Cézanne and Caliban believe in it. I believe in repetition. Yes. Always and always. Must write the hymn of repetition. Sterne gave me the right feeling for it.'[40] She wanted to revise a description of the knowable to include a new topography of mental perception, placing reality at the disposal of the subject, as in Cézanne, and one also which would include that 'bottom nature' – that servant nature, the troublesome id. Was it then an alliance of aristocracy of mind and proletariat of body against the middle? Ariel and Caliban in common misdirection of the centrist paternal power? Yet that same middle – the forms of daily life in their ritualized stays against both necessity and disruption, and the *longue durée* of institutional change in 'society' as such – was attractive to Stein. Did not the American dream privilege such stabilities against the inequalities of European life?

In the Thoreauvian tradition Stein asked herself whether that feeling for the wholeness of daily life, what Hauser has called its totality, was not in fact profoundly allied to the 'self-sufficing immanence of art', in that it made partial, in its 'sensually immediate nature', all other forms of organization: social, moral and scientific?[41] She said: 'Americans do not need a narrative of every day of any day, they have nothing to say of living each day that makes it a really soothing thing to say'. The key question then arose. What would happen to narrative: and particularly to the narrative of bourgeois consciousness, if this were true? Aristotelian narrative particularly would be inappropriate. She said: 'American writing has been an escaping not an escaping but an exciting without the necessary feeling of one thing following another thing of anything having a beginning a middle and an ending.'[42]

For Aristotle, beginning-middle-and-ending was a structure not of necessity but of a tragic view of life. It involved a sense of decorum, of finite magnitude (which Aristotle compared with the beauty of living creatures) held in memory, to be re-enacted in full view of a public whose sense of itself and the order it ritually celebrated was sure. It was a view of a world intelligible to the senses possessed by all and in which cause and effect stood within the realm of the probable.[43] Stein's need to abandon the pattern can be explained in a number of ways. First, there was a radical disengagement of the public from her own compositions: no spectators, and no public stage. There was therefore no guarantee of shared decorum. There was also a radical doubt about the truth offered by sense perception and with it of the reasonable connection between cause and effect. Intelligence and unconsciousness seemed to claim separate kingdoms which Stein's studies at Radcliffe and Johns Hopkins offered no means of uniting. There was also a refusal in American life – pointed out by Hawthorne, Melville, Henry James and Adams before her – to accept the nature of tragedy. This meant that the Aristotelian paradigm would only be used ironically. Thus Aristotelian lineality could be contrasted with a pattern of repetition which for Stein best articulated American life: a life in which activity and desire seemed so much at odds.

Stein's title in full, *The Making of Americans: being a history of a family's progress*, also signals multiple instances of the failure of public meaning in the socialized state. 'Making' referes at once to the Americanization of the immigrant, the manufacture in the crude sense of homogeneous mass man, and yet still holds as a hope the Aristotelian sense of *poesis*. Making, however, in the sense of 'making it', refers to the dream of success on the material and sexual levels. Questions of history of course involve the problems of narrative. Stein was aware of the problem of how you describe the passage of time at different levels: 'Literature we may say is what goes on all the time history is what goes on from time to time, and this is what is terribly important to think about in connection with narrative.'[44] Literary narrative then occupies the time Braudel assigns to events. The difficulty was how to relate that to other kinds of time which had their own significance: 'Narrative concerns itself with what is happening all the time. History concerns itself with what happens from time to time. And that is perhaps what is the matter with history and that is what is perhaps the matter with narrative.'[45]

The Making of Americans was to experiment with many narrative times. Aristotelian plot is turned into fable and relocated within a more slowly shifting and longer time. The very notion of the history of the family means that the changes are slow. It is a social and institutional time. Nor in Stein's ironic vision is its change necessarily seen as progress. The *Swiss Family Robinson* was one of Stein's favourite books and not surprisingly, for it was the classic attempt to adapt the individualist ethic of Defoe to the paternalist family. For Stein these models reinforced her attempt to write something between a social history and a psychological anthropology of the family in *The Making of Americans*. It is important to stress the in-between nature of Stein's position. One year after *The Making of Americans* was finished, American business organizations instituted Mother's Day as an attempt to cheer the country up after a year of the greatest labour unrest in American history. Stein rejected a political position, but she also rejected any sentimentalization of the family as such.

The more difficult problem was choosing the time of narrative. Autobiography was generally self-selecting, history could choose any stretch of time, but the problem Stein was unable to solve was the relation between the institutional time of the family and history proper:

> That is what narrative is that twenty-five years roll around so quickly but that one hundred years do not roll around at all but that they end, the century ends in being an entirely different thing and so any century comes to begin and end. That makes one of the great difficulties of narrative to begin and to end and I think it has to do with the fact that the century begins and ends but that no part of it begins and ends. . . .[46]

No less than Adams, Stein faced the question of what was historically significant time, and what was the relation of common-sense

or Bergsonian personal time. There were even more profound questions. Is a stretch of time an organizing heuristic or does it offer a
possibility of truth? What is the relation of private to social time and
to the further public time of history?

The questions can be rephrased, given Stein's involvement with
Darwinian paradigms. Is twenty-five years merely a set of random
variations within the slow time of species change? If only the long
time gives meaning, what effect does this have on the individual's
sense of time? How did you grasp the present if in Hutton's words,
so prophetic of Darwin's own sense of time, the world showed no
evidence of a beginning, no prospect of an end? To what extent did
scientific time at all have relevance to human experience? Lacking a
political sensibility, Stein could not speculate like Adams on the
institutions of law as a model, nor like Marx on periods of capital
growth and intensification. She fell back on a narrative which
incorporated dualisms of Nature and History and which authorized
itself by advertising its epistemological bases as a gesture of openness.

In this respect it is instructive to compare Stein's position with that
of a contemporary whom she probably did not read until after the
War. Spengler's *Decline of the West* was written between 1911 and
1914, and like Stein he was interested in theorizing the relation of
nature and history:

> Nature is the shape in which the man of higher Cultures synthe-
> sizes and interprets the immediate impression of his sense. History
> is that from which his imagination seeks comprehension of the
> living existence of the world in relation to his own life, which he
> thereby invests with a deeper reality.

Lacking a theory of either political or technological change, Spengler
then had the problem of how to reconcile what he called two possible
world forms:

> In the two possible world forms then, History and Nature, the
> physiognomy of all becoming and the system of things all become
> – destiny or causality prevails. Between them there is all the
> difference between a feeling of life and a method of knowledge.
> Each of them is the starting-point of a complete and self-contained
> but not a unique world. Yet after all, just as the become is founded
> upon a becoming, so the knowledge of cause and effect is founded
> upon some feeling of destiny. . . . Conversely, if 'Nature' is that
> constitution of things in which the becoming should logically
> be incorporated in the thing-become, and living direction in
> rigid extension, history may best be treated as a chapter of
> epistemology.[47]

Stein was to experience all the difficulty of reconciling that 'feeling of life' and the 'method of knowledge', and in her revision of the possibilities of syntax she would attempt to break down the very distinction between being and becoming. One effect of this was to suggest that any personal incorporation of the sense of destiny was malign. Like Spengler she attempted to dissect the Faustian spirit with its 'passionate urgency towards infinite future', and that 'will-to victory of science'. In an instructive parallel for this agrument, Spengler at one point turned Goethe and Shakespeare against Darwin:

> In Goethe evolution is upright, in Darwin it is flat; in Goethe organic, in Darwin mechanical: in Goethe an experience and emblem, in Darwin a matter of cognition and law. To Goethe evolution meant inward fulfilment, to Darwin it meant 'Progress'. Darwin's struggle for existence, while he read into Nature and not out of it, is only the plebeian form of that primary feeling which in Shakespeare's tragedies move the great realities against one another; but what Shakespeare inwardly saw, felt and actualized in his figures as destiny, Darwinism comprehends as causal connexion and formulates as a superficial system of utilities.[48]

There are details to quarrel with here. Darwin did not see his system as progressive. Yet the instinct is right. There is much in Spengler's work which would provide a useful heuristic for Stein (chapters on race, language, space, portrait, drama and so on), but the central issue is one of the right of artist and scientist to interpret the world. Did their psychologies overlap or were they opposed? What was the meaning of inward fulfilment in an America where Social Darwinism sanctified drives for success and reduced meaning to survival? What was the relation between experience and the perspective of art, and cognition and law? The by now somewhat voluminous literature on Stein's use of the 'continuous present' in *The Making of Americans* has yet to take on board these issues.

At one level the continuous present was an attempt to escape that onward drive of linear time deprived of Aristotelian tragic catharsis in repetition and ritual, at another level it was an attempt to co-opt the indifference of endlessly continuous nature as a contemplative perspective from which to stay the passing hour of Faust. At another level it was simply an evasion of the recognition that any individual is historically bound and politically engaged. And yet by focusing on the time of three generations and on the particularity of her subjects Stein reversed the Darwinian emphasis on the general structures of quasi-evolutionary change even while employing its strategies.

Within her own terms she could measure futile repetition against real change, pleasurable repetition against repetition compulsion. By challenging the sentence model with its split world of subject and object, its disengaged action in the verb, and its logic of beginning, middle and ending which had seemed to William James to constitute reality itself, she challenged any intelligibility based on lineality and simple mimesis. The strategy of strangeness within the very terms of language would draw attention to that 'tension between reference and compositional game', which Marjorie Perloff has noted.[49] There was more magic in language than could be captured by formal grammar. Stein began a tradition in American writing which broke up the very syntax of the language. In Brion Gysin's words: 'all spells. are sentences spelling out the word lock that is You. Stop. Change. Start again – lighten your own life sentence. Go back to childhood.'[50]

Stein did go back to childhood, and from a developing perspective attempted a complete reassessment in terms of unconscious behaviour of the values of American society. In one sense she had to clear the ground of her own history. Spengler had said, 'The process of historical self-adjustment begins for everyone with the earliest impressions of childhood.' By submitting her own subjectivity to the test of her various knowledges, Stein, in a time of social Darwinists and positivist Marxists, turned again in the words of Spengler to 'the history that is actually lived with and participated in', which 'never reaches more than a grandfather's span'.[51]

Unlike Spengler, however, she was a writer not a cultural historian, philosopher, or critic. Working against and with philosophic dualism, psychological characterologies, Darwinian concepts of nature, time and history, the divided perspectives of literature and science, Stein attempted one of the most ambitious projects in American literature. The abstract modes of thought would be placed at the service of a fiction which would be, not mean, on the premises perhaps which Hegel outlined in his own logic: 'Neither in heaven nor in earth, neither in the world of mind nor of nature, is there anywhere such an abstract either – or, as the understanding maintains. Whatever exists is concrete, with difference and opposition in itself.'[52]

II

With these issues in mind it is time to turn to the novel itself. The subject-matter of Stein's first major work is how Americans come to be Americans, yet anyone might be forgiven for being puzzled as to how the work fits that description. There are few details of family histories which would satisfy a sociologist or historian. There is no sense of actual locality, no mention of developing economics, no

obvious ethnic concerns, no sepia photographs of the imperishable
faces of the ghetto, the brutalities of Ellis Island, no sea crossings
lasting a hundred days, no romance in memory of an abandoned
country, no sweat of pioneers, no treasured family letters, no
struggle of families taking their chances in urban streets or lonely
homestead, no freedom imaged in an untilled hundred acres, no
brindle cow, log cabin, no frontier, and, nearer Stein's own time, no
common man crucified on a cross of gold. Nonetheless Stein's
novel is at least as relevant to an understanding of American culture
as most histories dealing with these subjects. Purged of local names
and details of her own family, Stein's *The Making of Americans*,
written more than a decade after the closing of the frontier, is in fact
an enormous satire – elsewhere I have called it a 'romantic satire'[53] –
on the psychopathology of an emerging mass society.

Katz argues accurately that there is a shift in the writing from the
nineteenth-century world of 'mental tragedy and sorrowful ironies'
to the world of 'passionate indifferentism' of Kafka and Beckett.[54]
Perhaps, however, it is not so much a shift as a disturbed movement
from one to the other, showing a world of liberal values collapsing
into psychological habits under that enormous increase in power
which Henry Adams noted. American society in this vision registers
a gap between socialized discourse and real feeling. It is a society at a
loss as to how to behave even at the intimate level of courtship and
decorating a house. Stein pits a synchronic sense of the 'natural'
family cycle against the inevitability of actual change and the actual
requirements of individual freedom. For her it was not a theoretical
question. As an American herself, she was five times alienated from
centrist American values. She was a woman, a lesbian, a Jew, an
expatriate, and most important of all, an artist. From such a vantage
point she could offer a profound critique of the psychology produced
by the 'normal' world of affairs, the stress of the heterosexual family
and its psychology, and of what constituted knowledge and wisdom
in a professionalizing and consuming society.

The skeleton of the 900-page work can be set out quickly, which
itself indicates that conventional plot is its least important aspect.
The novel concerns two families: the Dehnings and the Herslands.
The first third of the book develops a history of the Dehning family:
the characters of grandfather, husband and wife introduced in middle
age, and their three children: George, Julia and Hortense. The two
families begin to interact almost immediately as Alfred Hersland
comes east to represent an incursion of professional life (he is a
lawyer) into the strictly business life of the Dehnings. The Herslands
also have three children: Martha, Alfred and David jr. The grand-
parents are described and also the relationship between Mrs Fanny

Hersland and her husband and her father (Mr Hissen). She is shown to live a vicarious existence through her husband, children, governesses, servants and other dependents. Various psychological portraits are developed, but the elder David Hersland is among the first to receive any extended attention (*Making of Americans*, pp. 120–49). His portrait intersects with a multiplicity of portraits of the various hangers-on of his wife. From about the beginning of the second third of the novel Martha Hersland is the centre of attention.

Martha emerges slowly out of the multiplicity of portraits which draw attention to their own modes of explanation. She seems to exist as a function of other people's relations with her. A repeated motif of a childish incident in which she sulkily throws an umbrella in the mud brings her to the threshold of sexual life and her college career. The style of the description then becomes more concrete and the book turns into what must be one of the earlier twentieth-century college novels. Stein gives an account of her relations with teachers and her lover Philip Redfern whom she later marries and divorces. Alfred Hersland's portrait dominates the end of this section.

The last third of the book is taken up with the Dehnings. Julia's portrait is given first. Stein portrays her unsuccessful marriage to Alfred Hersland, its effect on the Dehning family particularly and Dehning's own portrait is again resumed. A kind of muted sexual struggle between Julia and her father-in-law and husband is registered and anticipates the last section, which deals with the last years of David Hersland. On page 715 the deaths of Mr and Mrs Dehning are announced casually and the sense of failure between Julia and Alfred becomes intense. The last pages turn into an almost lyrical account of David Hersland's conscious and unconscious sense of himself as he moves towards death. It is the half-tragedy of someone who has half-lived. His grasp on reality seems less sure than his father's before him. It is almost as if Stein is writing out the psychology of a suppressed death-wish as the psychological basis for the very ontology of the family. Hersland slips out of life as little remarked as an unsuccessful mutation within the great familial average whose contours are defined by the impersonality of natural selection itself.

Only a few moments from this enormous book can be looked at here: the content and theory of an overt social criticism within the work, the terms of explanation, and the important questions of address and authorial voice.

In his great work, *The People of the Pusta* (1936), the Hungarian writer Gyula Illyes describes a ritual of family violence all too common in the lives of the impoverished farm servants of the Hungarian plains:

> Up to a certain age parents beat their children, then there is a brief pause. When this is over, the situation is reversed and the children beat their parents. This also is an ancient tradition. There was a famous anecdote about Uncle Palinkas, an old acquaintance of our family. His son used to drag him by the hair through the common room and kitchen and when they reached the doorway of the servants' quarters, Uncle Palinkas would shout, 'Let me go here, son, this is as far as I dragged my father!'[55]

Like most stories of the folk this one has a long history. It first appears in Aristotle's *Nicomachean Ethics*,[56] a work over which it is worth pausing, for it examines at the ethical level – that is, a level which assumes a synchronic essence of man – the interaction between desire, knowledge and conduct. Aristotle understood that there was no simple relation between these areas. Thus, he says, it is hard to tell whether an unrestrained person is so because of the object to which that unrestrainedness is directed, or because of a certain innate disposition, or because of some mixture of the two. One truth may be predicated of the 'universal' in the man, another of the thing. Similarly there are two types of knowledge. There is one when a man is sober, another when he is angry, drunk, or in a state of sexual passion. The emotions for Aristotle actually alter the state of the body so that 'we must pronounce the unrestrained to "have knowledge" only in the same way as men who are asleep or mad or drunk. Their using the language of knowledge is no proof that they possess it.'[57]

Thus there is a difference between the appearance of reason in language and truth.

In a way Aristotle's *Ethics* is a kind of treatise on the emotions. Pleasure and pain structure acts of desire and avoidance, and ethical modes of profligacy and temperance. A fundamentally dualistic pattern emerges: unrestraint and restraint in relation to pleasure, and 'softness' and endurance in relation to pain. Like most of the commentators who have followed him and who attempt an ethics of the natural, Aristotle is constrained to make some emotions more natural than others; or rather more naturally good. Anger, for example, is preferable to desire because it is out in the open. Desire is secret and crafty and therefore more unethical. It is in this context that Aristotle's story indicates the less morally culpable action of anger:

> witness the man who was had up for beating his father and who said in his defenses, 'Well, my father used to beat his father,

and he used to beat his, and (pointing to his little boy) so will my son here beat me when he grows up; it runs in our house'; and the man who, when his son was throwing him out of the house, used to beg him to stop when he got to the door, 'because he only used to drag his father as far as that'.[58]

Commenting on Aristotle's ethical theory, W. F. R. Hardie distinguishes two types of ends (*telos*) of ethics. The one is an aim, or 'direction towards', an activity for some good, the other is directed towards a result of some action. The aim is not the means, it is a kind of impulse. There is thus an ethics of tendency and an ethics of activity. The implicit autonomies of activity within tendency are given a Darwinian twist by Hardie when he argues that Aristotle takes a fundamentally 'biological approach to the study of man'. Indeed Aristotle was Darwin's favourite philosospher. There is also a certain pragmatism in this ethics. As Hardie argues, the 'practical intellect aims at truth in agreement with right desire'.[59]

The fable emphasises that the open relief of feeling within the tendency of the biologically necessary is preferable to the crafty realm of desire. Here now is Stein's version, for it is precisely this fable which opens the novel and sets up a pattern to be confirmed or denied in its working out:

Once an angry man dragged his father along the ground through his own orchard. 'Stop!' cried the groaning old man at last, 'Stop! I did not drag my father beyond this tree.' It is hard living down the tempers we are born with. We all begin well, for in our youth there is nothing we are more intolerant of than our own sins writ large in others and we fight them fiercely in ourselves; but we grow old and we see that these our sins are of all sins the really harmless ones to own, nay that they give a charm to any character, and so our struggle with them dies away.

(*Making of Americans*, pp. 3–4)

Like Aristotle, Stein will examine the relations between desire, knowledge and conduct within an assumed universalist human behaviour. The relation of activity to tendency is crucial. For the artist in Stein lays claim to that *energeia* with which Humboldt endowed language itself. It may equally be compared with Keatsian negative capability, described by Norman O. Brown as 'activity without motion or change or passivity, and therefore, since time is correlative with motion, an activity not in time'.[60] Stein, too, was to be perplexed as to the placing of *energeia*. It seemed to apply to historical and to psychological experience. It is the impediment of this activity or 'frustration' which inhibits its pleasurable nature and creates an awareness of time as death-bound.

Brown points out that 'Aristotle succeeds in formulating philosophically the notion which also underlies the Christian theology of time – that time is relative to Becoming rather than Being, and Becoming is relative to imperfection or evil'.[61] In Stein's telling of the story she has added a Judaic-Christian dimension. Ironically she reverses the Aristotelian – Christian synthesis of Brown's discussion. 'Becoming' biologically dies in the individual and with it 'sin'. 'Being' is reserved in the assumed wisdom of the authorial voice and tone. The implication of Stein's version is that undue importance should not be given to natural process. Further the Christian identification of 'sin' with 'nature' in the myth of the Fall is de-emphasized by invoking the cyclical nature of classical time. 'Tendency' in Stein will be identified with inevitable biological process, and its denial will be seen in her characters as leading to repression-producing anxiety. Stein's 'continuous present' is an attempt to render the voice of the author as truthful, in the sense that it captures 'Being' as a result of that perfect activity which Brown describes.

By contrast Stein's characters are time-bound, trapped in the 'sin' of an endlessly frustrated 'becoming'. The fatalism of neurotic repetition is also represented in the fable, and there is little doubt that Stein saw that the 'making' of Americans produced a society addicted to repetition compulsion rather than to pleasurable repetition, to the Freudian continuities of 'killing the father', and to that 'neurotic time obsession of repressed humanity', which in the earlier chapter on language we have seen Whorf link with the very terms of the language itself. Stein, too, will describe the deep psychology of 'economic' man. Brown quotes Keynes: 'The "purposive" man is always trying to secure a spurious and delusive immortality for his acts by pushing his interest in them forward into time.'[62] So much for Jamesian pragmatism.

Like Brown, Stein will develop her critique of American bourgeois society at the level of behaviour and psychology. The critique in both lacks a historical and political dimension, but it does offer antidotes to linear, progressive or degenerative ideologies of history, castigating Right and Left in the process. So far Aristotle has been used structurally. But by Stein's time that compulsive repetitiveness is no longer a public event. The terms of mass society insist on repression from within. Anger and desire occupy the same interior space. Neither Aristotle nor Christianity had a theory of repression. Stein's achievement is to adopt their terms to describe a universal repression articulated in repetitiveness. Her own method of imperfect repetition in her sentences will, however, implicitly challenge that repetition which represents a deep and futile American psychology of 'beginning again'.

Before linking this discussion more historically with changes in late nineteenth-century American society, it is instructive to turn to one more use of Nicomachus's story in American literature. In his own ignored masterpiece, '*A*' *1–12*, Louis Zukofsky, perhaps under pressure to inform his own son of the value of creative life, meditates on the reach of art philosophy in relation to time:

A poetics is informed and informs –
Just *informs* maybe – the rest a risk.
Or: that a bit of culture
Dies a sudden death
Of a man over ninety
That much culture is little breath –
Infinite things in
Infinite modes
Follow divine nature
Being such.
Or: remember, G. S. begins
'Making of Americans'
With a quote
From Nicomachus' father –
'With patient father and angry son' –
That she said,
'How can you know
More than you do know
And we are still in the shadow
                    of explanation,'
Add to her insight ('in all periods before
Things had been said
But never explained.
So then they began to explain')
Long before 'before'
Too, they had explained a long time.[63]

It is in recreating the created that 'poetics' gives knowledge. The very breath of utterance sets culture against the immensity of time. Knowledge for Zukofsky emerges in the way he sets Spinoza's multiplicity against Aristotle's dualistic categories. Stein too will wrestle with the problem of explanation and metaphor. The 'shadow of explanation' is that ambiguous drive to systematize the knowledge revealed by the senses: a Platonizing impulse which is ever the enemy of poetry. Indeed Zukofsky takes up Aristotle's rebuke of Plato:

How can we know the objects of sense
Without having the sense,

His forms destroy the things
For which we are more ardent
Than for Being of the Ideas
Whatever that is;. . .

Yet Aristotle haunts Zukofsky and toward the end of the poem he picks up the story again:

Or
The man who dragged on the floor by his son
Asked him to stop at the door for he himself
Had dragged his father that far and no more.
When love laughs that carefully it has eyes
And Authority has a nose of wax.[64]

Unlike Zukofsky, however, Stein could not rely on a personal or cultural continuity which might support inventiveness and carefree laughter. *The Making of Americans* is fraught with the melancholy of a very lonely artistic struggle. Yet like Zukofsky Stein judged value in society to the extent that it permitted the free life of contemplation for all – a demand which as Arendt has pointed out was the Christians' reply to the Greeks. Stein had an acute sense of (again in Arendt's words) 'society's victory in the modern age, its early substitution of behaviour for action and its eventual substitution of bureaucracy, the rule of nobody, for personal rulership. . .'.[65] As much as any political theorist Stein saw that contemplation was being subverted by habit and action by behaviour. In late nineteenth-century terms this movement is registered in the rise of the new professional classes (inaugurating the rule of nobody) and in the decline of the self-employed businessman. Bledstein in his book, *The Culture of Professionalism*, provides terms for entering Stein's story more directly.

A political and economic dimension needs to be added to Bledstein's analysis. The professional class was required by the new multi-millionaires to administer its interests. The new technologies also demanded servants with long and expensive training. Both brought lawyers, financial advisors and specialized academics in their train. Bledstein is best on the psychology of these new professionals and on the images they had of themselves and their work. These images worked towards defining the ideal American class. But it was an ideal of a middle which, however, was fundamentally unstable. To cope with this instability a new psychology was needed:

The eighteenth-century citizen had acted on the grounds of reasonable want and socially sensible material interest. The nineteenth-century individual required an additional mental step.

In a calculated manner, he actively willed his action in order to satisfy a drive for self-distinction and self-assertion. Individual wilfulness and desire now upset the balance of the older eighteenth-century equation.

The eighteenth-century equation in actual historical terms was not the 'balance' Bledstein thinks it was, but his point holds. Personal interiorization of conflict, the result of the kind of capitalist society America was fast becoming, needed new mental attitudes. The new class needed reassurances about its worth and identity: 'a basis in universal and predictable rules to provide a formal context for the competitive spirit of individual egos'.[66]

The place where they could find them was in the college and the professionalizing universities backed by big business. Here the specialized task could be certificated. In essence the professions became secret societies for which years of training were required to join the ranks and then 'lifetime affiliation membership'. The public realm was eschewed. George Ade, a Chicago journalist, affirmed that 'the middle class means all those persons who are respectably in the background'.[67]

The ideology offered was that of a self-governing person in a free society. The reality was anxiety, depression, the neurosis of the endlessly incomplete task and a separation, in the nineteenth-century at least, between those who produced wealth and those who controlled it: 'Sustained by an unfinished career and a vertical vision, the consummate mid-Victorian individual – the professional never lost faith in the promise of his "becoming", despite adversity: He never gave up on "making it".'[68] This was the private psychology deriving from and eventually sustaining the culture of professionalism. 'Becoming' in this sense, and 'making it', are precisely the objects of Stein's satire.

By the 1890s so much had the universities abandoned the ideal of the contemplative over the active life, that Eliot, president of Harvard, argued that administrators ought to be paid more than teachers in compensation for their lack of contact with 'bright young minds' and because teachers had 'long uninterrupted vacations' which offered the satisfaction of literary or scientific attainment.[69] For the utilitarian capitalist, thinking is leisure and teaching rejuvenating contact with the young. The difficulty of thinking and the physical and mental demands of teaching are denied simply because any authentic work can only be defined in terms of profit and managerial visibility. This utter nonsense is still marketed in our time by newspapers as anti-intellectual, right-wing propaganda. Given his position, Eliot was hardly likely to draw attention to the changing paymasters of intellectual life. Buckminster Fuller's critique of Whitehead's views on education is relevant here: 'What Whitehead didn't ask was how Harvard could afford those Graduate Schools.'[70] The feedback from those who pay the piper has marked effects on the tune.

Stein records the failure of the liberal professional in more psychological terms in her sections in the book on the midwestern liberal arts college. In its hermetic world questions are posed in a sanitized vacuum. The college complements the bourgeois home in its passional incompletion, sentimentality, power drives, obsessions with sport, health and cleanliness, and in its pervading tone of melancholy. Stein fixes an ironic gaze on that 'typical co-educational college of the west, a completely democratic institution', where the 'democracy was too simple and genuine to be discussed by any one of them' (*Making of Americans*, pp. 431–2).

Redfern, the soap-opera young professor, is a public preacher for women's rights, a mathematician, a psychologist, and a philosopher. He is, in short, a veritable bundle of professionalisms tied together with moralism. In the socialized, professionalized world of the college, public is private and private public, which means there is neither real privacy nor public policy without private intrigue. In Stein's account of sexual conflict we have neither the cynical plottings of a *Liaisons Dangereuses*, nor the cry of an Anna Karenina living out the contradictions of Tolstoy's liberal Christian vision, nor even the ritualized and public psychological performance of melodrama. Stein takes the conventions of romance to measure the gap between the terms of its discourse and new and terrible American loneliness: 'To our new world feeling the sadness of pain has more dignity than the beauty of joy' (p. 438).

The breakdown of family living is registered in both the business context and the professionalized group. Stein is ambiguous about every aspect of the American Dream. There are a few hints, however, for the children when young, of a Blakean child world of unalienated activity. A Blakean sense of threat, however, also surrounds it. No less than in James Fenimore Cooper the 'people' threaten the family:

> And all around the whole fence that shut these joys in was a hedge of roses, not wild, they had been planted, but now they were very sweet and small and abundant and all the people from that part of Gossols came to pick the leaves to make sweet scented jars and pillows, and always all the Herslands were indignant and they would let loose the dogs to bark and scare them but still the roses grew and always all the people came and took them.
>
> (*Making of Americans*, p. 36)

There are hints of symbolism here, and a class nervousness – an almost naturalistic sense of an erotic abundance of the people who threaten to overwhelm the strictly controlled desire of the family. However cultivated the rose, someone (from the lower classes) will want to steal it.

Tocqueville's restless America of the 1830s has become the 'nervous' America of the 1880s – as the title of George M. Beard's now well-known book, *American Nervousness: Its Causes and Consequences*, indicated. The value which lies at the heart of Stein's satire is the capacity for difference and the acceptance of difference: sexual, social, ideological, and religious. The society raised on an ideology of risk and freedom she sees as addicted to homogeneity and insurance. Stein was strung between love of the self-employed who had made money, and distrust of the next generation of employed professionals; she was suspicious of the bohemian incorporation of art, contemptuous of middle-class college women, full of praise for the daily living of American childhood, and unable to deal with the monotony of middle-class adult American life. She did have a sense of the nightmare of women's lives, but perhaps felt her own escape too precarious to feel much sympathy for women who lost out, or for moralistic reformers.

The portrait of Fanny Hersland is a case in point. She lives out the contradictions of being provided with the ten acres at Gossols fenced in with cultivated roses. Dominating the servants gives her 'the dignity of decent family living with good eating being the mother of nice children the wife of a well to do man, and all in simple and expensive clothing' (p. 56). There is rage in Stein's etching of this set of expectations for women. The portrait continues into a Strindbergian bleakness. The manipulation of small irrationalities and emotional scenes has turned sexuality into dominance drives, albeit at a muted and minimal level within the family. Like Adams, Stein sees the American woman as a kind of failure: that is, she fails to be the Bachofen matriarchal power centre. Women in the novel leave families to become nervous professionals and the marriage of 'equals' in the new world appears to leave Stein's women more abused and embittered. It is a bleak and conservative vision. The series of bought educators for the children fail the test of intellectual commitment. Business cycles fail to sustain men emotionally. Even the design of furniture seems unallied to either comfort or need. American 'openness' breeds new forms of emotional power-seeking between the sexes and over all broods a Darwinian spirit of winning and losing which underwrites terror at the most intimate forms of life.

Against this radically nervous society the family itself offers little protection. Like language, the family appears to have a structure which is resistant to individual knowledge and yet reliant on it: 'Family living is a peculiar thing because not anyone, mostly, is deciding family living and always each one is himself or herself inside her or him and family living is in a way a combination that in a way is not coming from any one' (p. 638).

If nineteenth-century writers were aware of anything it was the historicity of the family. At any historical moment the family group reflected the general culture. Stein's sentences seem to present the family abstractly, as abstractly as the limited company. It is neither thing nor process. No one seems in control. Knowledge of what it is varies from member to member. Its group dynamics are hard to pin down and it seems to escape conscious direction. The irrational total effect seems unpremeditated by any one member: 'a combination that in a way is not coming from anyone'. Stein works in and around this passage a series of key verbs which articulate the very consciousness of the family: realizing, knowing, telling, explaining, deciding, expressing and thinking. Stein's not-so-homely soap opera is conceived within a highly abstract epistemological framework which constantly draws attention to itself: realizing – the ontological coming into being; knowing – the epistemological act; telling – the strategy of narrative and language; explaining – the critical act; deciding – involving questions of judgement and perhaps authority. These overlap to form a series of superimposed gestures about knowledge and understanding in a fundamental human situation in which because of passional drives and repressions only half-knowledge is permitted. In a way Stein took this situation as a model for human experience in general, as if human beings acted in a twilight world of half-responses and half-understanding.

To what extent then did the novel's radical technique, with its implied revision of epistemological perceptions – Stein's 'shadow of explanation' – turn the novel into something more than a family chronicle? Stein's phrase 'the shadow of explanation' serves as a starting-point to take some of that long foreground in psychology, the sciences and the language theory towards the work itself. Immediately it signals a paradox. Explanation will not be found in the light, in clarities, or in logic. By reversing the Platonic assumption, explanation becomes shadow; a reality here and now, a kind of darkness which closes round immediate experience in the urge towards description. Explanation creates a rift between itself and experience, yet it clings to and moves with it. Stein signals her concern with explanation in many ways but not least in her ironic characterizations of the 'natural'.

Durkheim said that Aristotle was the first to see society as a natural fact. With a degree of irony Stein proposes 'the making of

Americans' as a natural fact. Yet this natural society Stein ironizes as
a 'secret' beneath common-sense life, for its signs are unreflected
habits, the slow half-conscious gestures of the Herslands or the
Dehnings. Stein looks at them as Darwin looked at the fallen eyes of
the Calcutta workmen, with the difference that here irony is
involved, and the observer is more concerned with what she sees as
their mental habits. The consciousnesses of people in Stein's multiply
peopled world in *The Making of Americans* are at once natural and
secret, leaving the field open for 'explanation'.

A series of questions can be posed. Implicit in Stein's presentation
of her subject-matter is the question: How conscious is emotional
life? Is it a set of habitual reactions inherited from the past? Are the
strongest emotions in Darwinian terms 'ardent love, rivalry and
triumph'? Do these impulses lie behind Münsterberg's spirit of self-
direction, realization, assertion? How do the emotions mediate social
structure? Do they link parent with child, the administrator with the
administered, the rich with the poor, the master with the servant
'naturally'? What role is there for consciousness? Is it, as with Whitehead, a 'variable factor' in an organism's discrimination of its environment? How useful is it to consider the whole world as an
aesthetics predicted on a structure of feeling? What is the relation of
Aristotelian tendency to movement without consciousness, or of the
Lockean idea to motor activity? What is the place of memory in
behaviour? Is it possible, in Whitehead's words, to escape from
customary status? If human consciousness is like one bundle of habits
complexly evolving into another set of habits, what place is there for
the attention? Is attention itself a relation between the physiological
and the 'associative'? Does it operate individually or socially?

A start can be made on some of these questions by taking a passage
which deals with the representation of emotional life. Here Stein
begins to 'explain' the apparently essentialized emotion of (Aristotelian) 'angry feeling':

> Angry feeling again and again is in each one being in any family
> living, being in any living, this is pretty nearly certain. Angry
> feeling again and again is in one being one being in a family, being
> in any living. Angry feeling again and again is in one in different
> ways in one in one being in any living, being in any family living.
> Mostly each one being in any family living, mostly each one being
> in any living is having to have in that one again and again angry
> feeling from each one that one is knowing in the family living.
> Perhaps it is certain that not everyone is having angry feeling in
> that one from each one they are knowing in any living. Perhaps it
> is certain that each one in any family living is having again and

again the same kind of angry feeling from each one being with that one in that family living. Perhaps this is really certain. Perhaps it is really certain that almost every one is knowing and perhaps it is quite certain that mostly every one has that way of feeling angry feeling from some one being in living, from some one doing something, again and again. It is perhaps almost completely certain that each one being in some family living is having some angry feeling about each one in that family living and about each one in a certain kind of way of having angry feeling and in each way of having some angry feeling having it again and again. Perhaps not every one is having a different way of having angry feeling with different ones in their living, perhaps some are not having angry feeling in some way again and again.

(Making of Americans, pp. 762–23)

The paragraph moves from certainty to conditional propositions as if Stein had abstracted still further the technique of Henry James. The self-completingness of statement is subverted in repetition. Jamesian sentiment is made infinitely complex. The confident statement about 'angry feeling' – the ontological presence of feeling, in Ricoeur's words – is made more fluid. So too is the presence of the 'natural fact' of angry feeling. It is fluid but not continuous. Stein undermines the continuity of her own gestures of representation which might guarantee that silent continuity of feeling: 'Perhaps it is certain. . ., Perhaps it is really certain. . . Perhaps not everyone. . .' and so on. If there are different ways of having the same emotion and different ways of understanding them, then the fundamental confidence of Darwin's analysis is undermined. Furthermore if there are different degrees of it then the differing degrees may take on different significances. Stein also makes problematic the relation of 'angry feeling' to both living and family living. At first she equates the two, but then, when she goes on to say that there are different modes of the same emotion in both, the original equation loses its importance.

This, too, however, is only a moment in the process. Having asserted identity she then contradicts it, for 'living' as opposed to 'family living' holds out potential freedoms from family stress. Both the perception of 'angry feeling' and 'angry feeling' itself move from consciousness to unconsciousness and back again. The certainty that the feeling exists because of 'family living' is only reached at one moment in the description and then only in 'Perhaps it is certain. . .'. Finally repetition drops angry feeling altogther from its repertoire of variants. It dies away, suggesting that the tendency of emotional life is merely cyclical and therefore not very interesting. However, the way these feelings are thematized varies in a much more multiple way. One of the ways that Stein confronts the tabooed question of consciousness is to suggest that there is both feeling which cannot be avoided, and feeling which can be directed.

Stein also turned Weiningerian classificatory dualisms into modes: alternating moments in a general movement. Like Whitehead she made the abstract concrete and the concrete abstract. For Stein, Darwinian selection of variants, Aristotelian tendency, and Whiteheadian fate gave her not a metaphysic, nor a method, nor even a secret history, but a confidence that intelligibility could be found by applying methods of abstraction: 'Sometimes it takes many years of knowing someone before the repeating in that one comes to be a clear history of such a one' (p. 291). Knowledge depends on time and it seems half automatic and half willed.

> I have not with ways of living that slow openness of steady realization, that joy in always being certain that it is repeating, I know ways of living are repeating, I am not realizing them as repeating, I know it of them, I do not really truly feel it in them. I do not know whether I am clearly expressing a feeling. I will sometime begin again telling how I am not really realizing ways of living.
>
> (*Making of Americans*, p. 621)

The most crucial distinction in the book is between 'ways of living' and 'realizing ways of living'. In 'realizing' lies the truth of a revised emotional perception confronting its unconscious repetitions. At the level of 'realizing' nothing really repeats. Stein employs the methods of abstraction against the psychology of abstraction.

Darwin had used the analogy of language to characterize the inheritance of half-conscious changes and choices fixed through habit. Stein's technique, as the last example shows, is to make us aware of habits, clichés, and automatic behaviours. She hoped that by subverting the expectations of language, from syntax to expected plots, the unreflected habits of society, too, would be challenged. Stein would have agreed with Heidegger that grammar is not absolute and that words do not embody the nature of things.

The effect of her redeployment of sentences as unstable repetitions also exemplifies Whitehead's point that 'No sentence merely enunciates a proposition. . .' – rather there is an 'incitement to believe, or to doubt, or to enjoy, or to obey'.[71] The imperfect repetitions of the sentences invite contrast and transfer attention to the paragraph. Association, built-up memory, and contrast paradoxically relieve the structure of the sentence of meaning. Similarly the act of repetition sets off the appearance of the new. At another level Stein shifted the interest of the sentence back to rhetoric, as if she were classifying the means of persuasion only then to set the categories in motion again. She knew with Peirce that a symbol's meaning 'grows' in use and experience. She was also sufficiently aware philosophically to anticipate Whorf's sense of unease about the structure of 'Western' grammar with its flowing time and static space.

Some of these points can be exemplified in the repetition, not of a single word but a whole incident. Stein repeats a circus-clown or Chaplin-like gesture of Martha Hersland throwing an umbrella in the mud several times as she describes her progress from childhood to adulthood. According to Elizabeth Sprigge the incident refers to a moment in Stein's own life.[72] In the text, however, the incident serves many purposes. At its first repetition gesture becomes message but also acquires an aura of symbol. The third time it occurs it suggests a frozen alienation from the poor children outside the rich ten acres. The vaguely erotic sense of frustration is confirmed when in a later incident Martha sees a man hitting a woman with an umbrella – again in a poor area – which then decides her on her college career. The umbrella stands in for a sense of frustration with family, then with class, then with adult relations between the sexes. Martha's refusal of these issues gives her a motion, Stein says, towards the university. The unreflected habit, and the habitual association signalled by the repetitions, will take Martha right into the world of power drives she has reacted against. The narrative irony is that this emotional symbol grows in the author's gaze but not in Martha's.

Saussure said that the life of society, inert by nature, blends with language. Stein's effort was to unscramble that blending and hope for knowledge in the process. How could the artist survive among Sapir's drifting folk, or these Americans in the making? Could the detail, the minute linguistic difference make for a symbolization of the psychologically real, as Whorf was to suggest later? Stein inherited a world whose present Whitney spoke of as the consequence of a 'gradual accumulation of results in one unbroken line of action', and where for Saussure *langue* overcame the event of *parole*. Whitney took the implication to its logical conclusion: 'All form making is accompanied by a gradual and unreflective process.' Stein attempted to represent that 'gradual and unreflective process' as a strategy in her technique of representation. She played with the fact – in Ricoeur's words – that the sentence neither represents a 'state of affairs' nor the word an 'object', to the limit. Many critics have noted her use of the continuous present as creating an effective vehicle for this, but none have noted the problems. Heidegger said that the 'verbal substantive' was the emptiest of all forms. By its very form the verbal substantive coincides with Stein's use of the continuous present to suggest a world in motion, without defining the subjective and objective moments within praxis: 'In a way he has needing knowing every day that he was being living every day' (*Making of Americans*, p. 862). While the implication of such a sentence is clear – the intense almost Puritan need to grasp a reality which the very need frustrates – the emptiness Heidegger complains of is certainly there in the absence of actual content and actual subjective response. As a vehicle for that 'nervous' world it works well. As an attempt to index a truth of the representational process there are problems of endlessly suspended judgement.

Ironically, for a novel deliberately purged of references to all the personal experiences from which it sprang, *The Making of Americans* directs us boldly and intimately to the tale's teller. The presence of the teller is in fact a major content of the story. There is a certain disguise as well, of course, and paradoxically it operates in the very frankness of the self-declarations. The famous 'I am unhappy in all this writing' (p. 340), is not merely a declaration of personal mood but a strategy to bind the reader more closely, through confession, to the very fabric of the tale. It offers the weight of creative difficulty no less than the language itself directs attention to the attempted synthesis of the creative process and the finished creation in all their complexity.

Sterne's *Tristram Shandy* was as we have seen an important model for Stein. Sterne refers to that 'strange state of affairs between the reader and myself'.[73] His aim was, of course, to make it as strange as possible. He informs us that he will start a chapter over again, have a chapter on writing chapters, says how he longs for a new one, tells us that he's in a melancholy frame of mind, admonishes us to start over and read the chapter again, and has a range of tones from the ironic, affectionate and classical 'gentle reader' to the almost bullying and querulous. It is an old trick for the public performer to declare nervousness or uncertainty. It simultaneously defends and engages. The audience is held in any case. Both author and reader are on strange ground, called on to discover or rediscover the endless resourcefulness of language's own image, to paraphrase Foucault, and even more to surrender to a magic time of narrative.

To a degree the past, present and future of any story are not those known in experience, though they claim kinship. Thus the story claims a kind of power in its disposal of life and death. The story-teller herself is not only, in John Berger's words, 'death's secretary',[74] but also life's secretary, building birth and memory into a pattern which momentarily releases us from the process of time and offers knowledge: 'Once an angry man dragged his father along the ground. . .' (*Making of Americans*, p. 3). That 'time' is recognizable but not known. Gradually clues are given, the teller begins the game: 'The old people in a new world, the new people made out of the old, that is the story that I mean to tell, for that is what really is and what I really know' (p. 3). As much as this refers to the content of the 'making' of Americans, it refers as well to the powers of the teller, as if the brave new world of Miranda's gaze were already undercut by the ironic shadowy presence of the world-weary Prospero. In fact the whole novel explores the disjunctions and conjunctions of 'that I mean to tell', 'what really is', and 'what I really know'. In intention, representation, and intelligibility lies the whole difficulty of the art. Stein assumes Adorno's 'darkest secret of first philosophy', the implicit 'I know and you don't' in the claim to represent being, but with varying degrees of confidence. Just as the content of the work will suggest that the 'new world' cannot escape the common fate, so Stein revises technique only to confront in new ways the old difficulties of the teller.

As Stein strove to be truthful in that period of 'paradigmatic uncertainty' in science, art, philosophy and psychology, she could imagine no audience for her efforts:

> Bear it in your mind my reader, but truly I never feel it that there ever can be for me any such creature, no it is this scribbled and dirty and lined paper that is really to be to me always my receiver – but anyhow reader, bear it in your mind – will there be for me ever any such creature, – what I have said always before to you, that this that I write down a little each day here on my scraps of paper for you is not just an ordinary kind of novel with a plot and conversations to amuse you, but a record of decent family progress respectably lived by us and our fathers and mothers. . .
>
> (*Making of Americans*, p. 34)

Stein is saying in effect I can't imagine you because what we assume to be possible (a record of decent family progress respectably lived by us) is neither really known nor has ordinary common-sense conventions for its vehicle.

The passage also shows the effort of imagining a public which does not yet exist. The scribbled, lined and dirty paper gives us a kind of transition to the act. Derrida in a discussion of duration, Rousset, and Corneillean movement provides some helpful ways of focusing this more closely:

> Rousset understands the theatrical or novelistic movement as Aristotle understood movement in general: transition to the act, which itself is the repose of the desired form. Everything transpires as if everything within the dynamics of Corneillean

meaning, and within each of Corneille's plays, came to life with the aim of final peace, the peace of the structural *energeia*: Polyeucte. Outside this peace, before and after it, movement in its pure duration, in the labour of its organization can itself be only sketch or debris.[75]

In representing the transition to the act Stein attempts to make present her own movement; and to own up to the sketch and debris. Since the paper with its lines and dirt promises both order and disorder the scribble with parallel qualities attempts to find some point of identification with it as frame and resistance to its own gesture. The receiver (the absence of audience) anticipates the record because she/he is 'contained within movement in general'. At least that is Stein's hope, which is, however, never really sustained in the book, as if (*pace* Derrida) 'structural *energeia*' could really rule out contradiction.

The record of 'a decent family progress respectably lived' will never achieve 'the peace of the completed act', for many reasons. First, because of the Darwinian paradox: that 'being' will be complete only when the record is fully revealed. As nineteenth-century scientists were quick to point out, this particular form of being escapes empirical truth. In delivering becoming as being (the further paradox of the record of being), Stein by moving beginning and ending into a permanent present runs the risk of dogmatism. First, because psychologically completion is not permitted. Second, because the intuition of being as a sense of the world which escapes expression and therefore permits difference, is made more difficult. Third, because the record is fundamentally different from being, in the sense that it is a concrete and particular gesture of representation within language and makes an appeal to others as other. There is a sense in which Stein wants to control response by making the superior epistemological truth of her technique sufficient by itself to deliver truth of content.

The two temporal modes of continuity and spontaneity within Darwinian theory lead Stein partially to equate nature and culture within a general economics of time. In Stein and in much work inspired by her – large-scale repetitive works in film, in music (one thinks of Steve Brakhage, Warhol, minimalist art in general and Terry Riley), this leads to an attempt to mesmerize the audience.[76] Yet she is equally consumed by the objects of her own gaze:

As I was saying I had heard descriptions of this one, they were ordinary descriptions, they were not very interesting, they had not very much meaning. Then I saw this one, then I looked intensely at this one, then this one was a whole one to me. Then the

whole being of this one was inside me, it was then as possession of
me. I could not get it out from inside me, it gave new meaning to
many things, it made a meaning to me of damnation. I had then to
tell it to this one, that was the only way to loosen myself from this
one who was a whole one in me. I had then to tell this one of the
meaning in damnation that this one being a whole one inside me
had made clear to me. Always then later this one was a whole one
to me, it was then a gentler possession of me inside me than when
this one first was a whole one inside me, a damned one to me. It
was still true to me later inside me the whole of this one but it did
not then possess me.

(*Making of Americans*, p. 314)

There are things here which disrupt that mesmeric automatism of
a general economics of cognitive process, and others which confirm
it. In the absence of content, only the emotional psychology of the
process of understanding and creating remains. It is not unlike
James's descriptions of religious experience; first the sense of disgust
with the meaning of the ordinary world, then the intense vision and
then the altered perception. But there the comparison ends. For Stein
continues by saying that the new vision itself becomes damned and
then finally it fades away. The pattern is familiar from the original
fable (the struggle fades away) and from her description of angry
feeling, analysed above. The key question again is the role of consciousness in what appears to be a natural economics of a psychology
of recognition. I think it occurs at four points. First, in the 'looking
intensely' – Stein gives a superior role to the empiricist category of
'attention'. Second, it is the conscious recognition of the event as
damnation – a value judgement. Third, it is in the need to tell others
– like the Ancient Mariner – of the damnation. Fourth, it is in the
characterization, or rather in the admission, that in losing oneself
(being possessed) one permits the possibility of new meaning. Stein
here takes on the role of the aggressive Gothic teller delivering herself of the compulsions of her experience. Like the Ancient Mariner
she is forever exiled from that 'decent family progress respectably
lived by us'.

The Mariner had the bad habit of stopping one in three, however,
and part of the satire in *The Making of Americans* is directed precisely
against repetitive habits. As in Freud there is both pleasurable and
compulsive repetition. Repetition can help the creative representation of character for Stein, which she attends with all her senses,
taking it away from merely moral or mental habit: 'Soon then it
commences to sound through my ears and eyes and feelings the
repeating that it always coming out from each one, that is them, that
makes then slowly each one of them a whole one' (p. 291). The

emphasis on polymorphous attention and slowness defends the concept of character from Christian soul-essentialisms, the dualisms of the psychologists, psychological types and mechanistic functionaries equally.

Yet the problem of where meaning is to be situated, and at what point, will not go away:

> Always, one having loving repeating to getting completed understanding must have in them an open feeling, a sense for all the slightest variations in repeating, must never lose themselves so in the solid steadiness of all repeating that they do not hear the slightest variation. If they get deadened by the steady pounding of repeating they will not learn from each one even though each one always is repeating the whole of them they will not learn the completed history of them, they will not know the being really in them.
>
> (*Making of Americans*, p. 294)

The hint of didacticism here in these rules for attention does not mask the fact that the problem of predication has not really been confronted, nor indeed the question of how attention alone prevents that deadening of repeating. Attention cannot be heuristic. The best that can be said of Stein here is what Derrida said of Lévi-Strauss, that Stein preserves as an instrument what she doubts as a truth.[77] Her theory is buried in her technique and one wonders whether openness and alertness to variation alone can successfully oppose the steady deadening of repeating.

In addition it is arguable whether Stein's desire to represent the inclusiveness of the world can escape the solipsistic fate of late Romantic individualism attempting to incorporate the rhythms of a world described in terms of a naturalist philosophy. As Stein's representations refine themselves in *The Making of Americans*, the content becomes narrowed to one man's relation to death. In attempting to regularize the dynamic of repetition and variation as an epistemology (indeed as she uses that dynamic to recapitulate the historical development of the novel within the work, from Aristotelian ethical fable to bourgeois romance to scientific naturalism), Stein seems trapped in a downward spiral which 'variation' is powerless to challenge. One of the pleasures of reading those long sentences, in which the variations (negative, positive, with differing degrees of certainty, clarity, with shifting singularities and pluralities of subject and objects, and as modes of feeling, knowledge and decision) are rung on the fixity of statement itself, is the surprising range of moods and the densely intricate meanings which can emerge. On the other hand there is equally a sense in which this language becomes increasingly mirrored on itself. At its most simple Stein hoped that her technique would arbitrate thinking and feeling. For all the steadiness of the sentences' rhythm, the relation of loving to realizing, of knowing to feeling, will not dissolve into a single universal currency of meaning. For these reasons the authorial voice is constantly declaring unhappiness.

Indeed the 'nervousness' of *The Making of Americans* is a reflection of what Marx called 'the hurried nature of society's metabolic process'[78] and its autonomous economy which seemed to so many Americans at this time to fail their civilization's earlier liberal principles. It is a phenomenon which is 'a personal way', 'a family affair', 'a way of living in a national way', 'a way of living in the local way'. As Stein said in *Geography and Plays*: 'In the midst of money we are whistling.'[79]

Finally, as at the end of Part Three on James, one of Stein's more readily accessible and common-sense works will be considered. *Wars I Have Seen* was one directed to a popular audience. Here, among many other things, society's 'nervousness' becomes dramatized in a new way. Stein's personal autobiographical account of social life in Pétain's France had to include the stark historical and political fact of World War II. Here Tocqueville's 'restlessness' and Dr Beard's American 'nervousness' become the 'anxiety' of totalitarian society. Yet the work also comes at the end of a lifetime of writing. No less than her previous works it takes up her multiple concerns, and makes a last statement about history, narrative and time.

Chapter 15
A World Made of Stories

> . . . unfortunate about melodrama: namely that one cannot
> make music, absolute music.
> > EDVARD GRIEG TO FREDERICK DELIUS[1]

'She laughs, she smokes. She tells stories with an American shrewdness in getting the tang and the kick into the telling.' That is how
Sherwood Anderson, as from one story-teller to another, described
Stein. And Eric Sevareid, the American journalist, reported being
'deeply impressed by the finest flow of talk I had ever listened to with
the possible exception of that from Schnabel, the pianist'.[2] It was
by all accounts the way she was, and certainly the way she would
have been pleased to have been seen: a fact that might be noted by
American feminists who have dwelt on the unhappiness of her
sexuality and make historyless, classless, and economically innocent
claims like 'Women are now far more exuberantly expressive'.[3]
While happiness does have a revolutionary quality, such claims
suggest a kind of dogmatism associated with the regulation behaviour of therapeutic culture. There have been few women in the
twentieth century more exuberantly expressive than Stein in certain
moods, but like the great artist she was, she was a woman capable of
'expressing' many different moods in different ways; including that
most un-American of recognitions, as Adams noted: sexual tragedy.

As far as stories are concerned, however, it might also be noted
that in *Geography and Plays* (1922) she said, 'I do not like stories'.[4] For
Stein, narrative engaged the entire spectrum of the contradictions of
her vision. Like Hawthorne, Henry James and Fitzgerald, Stein
placed the enchantment of story – its displacement of time in its own
time – against the pull of a contemporary reality which, to be sure,
could only be described as another story, but one whose time was
unrecoverable and much less enchanting. It was with a sense of
fascinated horror that she was to attempt to find ways of describing a
world which in the '30s and '40s marked one of the blackest periods
of European and American history.

The question of narrative is a multiple question. It involves a generic tradition, an epistemology, a psychology and a politics. So far only some of Stein's more impenetrable works have been considered. However, she was known, and largely still is known, for works which actually became popular in her own lifetime, and which were written in a readily accessible language: *Three Lives* (1909), *The Autobiography of Alice B. Toklas* (1932), *Everybody's Autobiography* (1936). Each of these was published in at least three editions in her lifetime. Stein's own theorizing about narrative and the popular novel is interesting in its own right, for she had a very lively sense of a world changed by mass media, and the ways in which writers might engage with it.

During the nineteenth century history was considered to be the province of narrative. That had already changed or was well on the way to changing, as Henry Adams had realized, by the mid-1880s. Stein too was anxious to take narrative away from history, but she clearly felt the need to define precisely what she meant by both terms:

> Narrative concerns itself with what is happening all the time, history concerns itself with what happens from time to time. And that is perhaps what is the matter with history and that is what is perhaps the matter with narrative. Let us think of newspapers, of novels, of detective stories of biographies of autobiographies of histories and of conversations. It does happen it is bound to happen that the way of telling anything can come not to mean anything to the one telling that thing.[5]

Stein deliberately distinguishes and blurs the two concepts. The result is contradictory. On the one hand the time of story is continuous in its magical ability to offer a world. The world of narrative has many times: the time of flashback, the time of associative ramblings, of characters, of authorial voice. The time of history ('from time to time'); is also diversely based. On the one hand 'from time to time' may involve a change of epoch: classical–medieval or pre-capitalist–capitalist. It may be that 'from time to time' selects significant moments which though non-lineally present will make up an ideological continuity, and so on. There are multiple possibilities. For Stein herself the duality could perhaps be more relevantly exemplified by contrasting the private and public worlds.

Autobiography obviously deals more with the private than with the public. Stein was living in an era where the social increasingly blurred the old sense of private and public, producing something that bore the elements of both but could not be judged in terms of either. Stein's last book, *Wars I Have Seen*, will provide a singular example of this. War was no longer a public event, something men 'went to', but was all around and involved those traditionally exempt: women, children and the old. Stein was searching for a form which could give a sense of this world. Clearly it could neither be simply psychological nor simply historical. The 'way of telling' therefore had to be reinvented, for the old forms were inadequate. Stein said in her work *Four in America* (1932-3, published 1947), 'This is narrative as an index',[6] referring to the last section in that book, 'Or a history of the United States'. Narrative as an index – and she was perhaps recalling Peirce in the choice of the word – was her attempt to combine psychological time with long-term slow structural social change: a pointing of attention significantly. There were no terms with which to include actual politics, but her work is increasingly valuable politically because it registered accurately and without sentiment that sense of life which actual political and technological changes were bringing about. Stein had no theory of the relation of event to history or ideology, but she knew that the common-sense assumptions of narrative and history were no longer in touch with the world she lived in after the 1890s.

So she looked at the assumptions behind the 'telling' of her own world: in newspapers, in novels, in detective stories, in biographies and in autobiographies, in histories and in conversations. Stein's aim was to bring the unconscious assumptions of these generic types of communication into consciousness by attempting in different ways to expose the theories of knowledge on which they relied, including randomizing their hierarchically established claims to truth. Common to all narrative was the question of time:

> That is what narrative is that twenty five years roll around so quickly but that one hundred years do not roll around at all but that they end, the century ends in being an entirely different thing and so any century comes to being and comes to end. That is one of the great difficulties of narratives to begin and to end and I think it has to do with the fact that a century begins and ends but that no part of it begins and ends.[7]

A key problem of ideology is the question of time. Whatever Stein's failures she refused a theology of time – classical cycle, Christian apocalypse, Marxist prophecy, and any Utopia – scientific or un-scientific.

It has already been shown how Stein broke the expected patterns of Aristotelian narrative, substituting those very small-scale moments which were coloured by traditional narrative expectations but which 'added up' to something quite different. In an important interview with Robert Haas, Stein explained her position: 'There should not be a sense of time, but an existence suspended in time', she said; 'You have to denude yourself of time'. But how could the stillness of the artist relate to the world of events within the structure of narrative? Stein could neither quite accept the 'art for art's sake' solution nor commit herself to any contemporary ideology. As well as rejecting destiny, Stein rejected older concepts of characters whose heroic or anti-heroic stances were intimately bound up with the idea of destiny. In this respect Henry James was an important model: 'In the characters of Henry James there is really very little time, the characters do not live very much ensemble lives, but nobody gets excited about the characters'.[8] 'Ensemble' was one word for it. Stein sensed that crushing of the old liberal individual in the new machinations of power. One has only to remember *The Golden Bowl*, where two interlocked couples, four isolated people, unable to live 'ensemble' and flanked by power brokers, dance to the dictates of one man's gold.

Stein also sought for a model where plot was more than a classical system, however rich its generic possibilities. Of the detective story – orginally developed in America by Edgar Allan Poe, but by Stein's time a genre which had swept the popular market – she said: 'The most creative writings [in the twentieth century] were western stories and detective stories, but these were not enough.'[9] Both the detective and the forensic scientist had the grace of their variable classic dealings in the world, but she sensed life was not to be found in a narrative of ritual messages sent from a corpse.

Again with great shrewdness Stein linked changes in fiction with social and technological change. She was perhaps among the first important writers to recognize a change in narrative and character within the relatively new phenomenon of 'publicity', as indeed Henry James had done before her in *The Bostonians* (1886):

> The Duchess of Windsor was a more real person to the public and while the divorce was going on was a more actual person than anybody could create. In the Nineteenth Century no one was played up like that, like the Lindbergh kidnapping really roused people's feelings. Then Eleanor Roosevelt is an actuality more than any character in the Twentieth Century novel ever achieved.[10]

Publicity is of course an experience in which message is presented via mass media to the domestic home. It therefore inherited the mantle of the Gothic novel, directing itself to 'nervousness' about sex, technological disaster, invaders, criminals, and so on. The diversions of Lindbergh and the Duchess of Windsor were politically manipulated stories necessary to an America struggling out of the Depression.

In fact Stein's thoughts about narrative were shaped in relation to the new world of publicity and the genres of popular literature. She found in them that classic, steady experience of the folk. But where was its meaning? In the surface of events, or the slow-moving psychology of group and institutional life? Stein read newspapers differently from others, and she would have sympathized with Mabel Dodge Luhan's ironic comments on her contemporary Hutchings Hawgood ('who dated back to William James and Royce at Harvard, and Wordsworth was his favorite poet'): 'His remarks about news were amusing. He said that real news was connected, not with the weight of the interests of the day, but with such appearances and events as were hopefully insisting on a reawakening of our eternally conservative (though slumbering) ideals.'[11]

The 'time' of the newspaper Stein thought was a false time which writers like Sinclair Lewis employed. It was a time with a past and present but without a future.[12] Newspapers foisted their own spurious present on the past. By claiming to give the truth of the present in formal innocence they failed to represent existence in Stein's own terms: 'in a newspaper there is no beginning and no ending and in a way too there is no going on'. Stein suggests that newspapers are crippled by an enforced mimesis: 'they have to tell a thing that is told as a reality, all this has an awful lot to do with the writing of history'.[13] It is another slant on Stein's steadily held conviction that without awareness of form there can be no significant reality. She had one bleakly amusing comment on it all, however, which is as true now as then: 'Everybody gets so much information all day long that they lose their common sense. They listen so much that they forget to be natural. This is a nice story.'[14]

Getting a lot of information and solving nothing was what the typical policeman in a detective story was supremely good at. Consciously to expose that made a novel more interesting than a newspaper. In any case Stein preferred a good open sense of structure, and a genre where there was a lively sense of play between author and reader. Certainly the unnaturalness of the crime plot, where the factual end begins the work and everything remains to be revealed, would have attracted her. She knew, too, that the detective novel was a product of the impact of newspapers on society and of the chaotic multiplicity of 'information'.

Like Barthes and the rest of us she always relished the sheer pleasure of the text. Indeed Barthes's well-known essay on 'delay' sounds like a summarizing paraphrase of Stein's own meditations on the relations of sentences, narrative, subject – predicate connections, question – statement transpositions, and a historical sense of syntactical change. Here is Barthes, thirty years after *How to Write*:

In short, based on the articulation of question and answer, the hermeneutic narrative is constructed according to our image of the sentence: an organism probably infinite in its expansions, but reducible to a diadic unity of subject and predicate. To narrate (in the classic fashion) is to raise the question as if it were a subject which one delays predicating; and when the predicate (truth) arrives, the sentence, the narrative, are over, the world is adjectivized (after we had feared it would not be). Yet, just as any grammar, however new, once it is based on the diad of subject and predicate, noun and verb, can only be a historical grammar, linked to classical metaphysics, so the hermeneutic narrative, in which truth predicates an incomplete subject, based on expectation and desire for its imminent closure, is dated, linked to the kerygmatic civilization of meaning and truth, appeal and fulfilment.[15]

This essay, reprinted relevantly in a collection of essays on detective fiction, summarizes the structural connections of 'delay' with the very being of the detective story. Stein might have commented that that is what is wrong and that is what is right with detective stories. On the whole Barthes ignores what is wrong with them, and to that extent is less subtle than Stein. Barthes's gesture towards historical dating is pretty arbitrary, given that, for example, the historical grammar of the diad subject and predicate covers virtually the whole of Western history. The apparent abstract precision of 'kerygmatic civilization' hardly distinguishes among civilizations, for there must be few without some structural sense of meaning and truth, appeal and fulfilment.

Hartman similarly fails of precision when he says the 'detective story. . . allows place to turn the tables on time'.[16] The same is true of any narrative with a strong *mise-en-scène*. Stein was much more uneasy than contemporary deconstructionists about conceiving space hermeneutically, especially to the extent of believing that spatial fictions absolutely defeat time. For Stein, Mephistopheles has a way of appearing unexpectedly. For in crime fiction 'space' is hermetically sealed within the closed world of melodrama, as the numerous psychoanalytic studies of the detective story attest. Forensics do not positively guarantee life, they reassure its compulsive and unconscious defeats in a world where spatial demonstrations of all kinds only spuriously conquer time, and history.

The natural life of the increasingly urban folk continued to fascinate Stein, however. She wrote to Van Vechten in 1922: 'I spent the afternoon of the fete of the assumption of the Virgin reading the Bow Boy and it went very well. . . . I like melodrama and background, melodrama is background and so is the rest'.[17] Fifteen years later, in 1937, she wrote of her fascination with drugstores: the only dirty places, she said, in the United States: 'after that I was going in to buy a detective novel just to watch the people sitting on the stools. It was like a piece of provincial life in a real city. . . . I never had enough of going in them'.[18] At worst there is a sense of aesthetic carnival in Stein and Van Vechten, but for Stein at least, melodrama was simply 'background' – that reality to which ritual and psycho-analysis in their different ways responded. Between religion and crime, the Virgin and the Bow Boy, the world delivered itself to the detective story and the newspaper. Was there any way out of a reality so bounded?

At least the detective story set out some interesting problems: the nature of that nervousness which needed to be reassured, the problems of the exceptional person in society, the fascination with, and fear of, death, and the place of eccentricity and deviance. All these could be handled within the terms of the detective story: 'I got a lot of Wilkie Collins out of the Church library at Aix [-les-Bains], of course the Moon Stone when I was young, a little frightening, I remember a larger fat man who moved easily.' Stein may be for-given her lapse of memory, for she is in fact remembering Count Fosco from *The Woman in White*, who has 'the means of petrifying the body after death, so as to preserve it, as hard as marble, to the end of time'. The sense of time here is positively Egyptian, and forensic wish-fulfilment could go no further. Fosco, one of the great villains of nineteenth-century fiction, also enjoys having white mice crawl all over him, loves animals, is immensely fat, 'as noiseless in a room as any of us women', and as Stein remembered, his movements are astonishingly light and easy.[19]

In the third lecture of *Narration: Four Lectures* (1935) Stein talks in detail about newspapers and detective stories. It is the singularity and reductiveness of newspapers, she asserts, that makes them less significant. They have been and 'are very interesting as being one way one variation of one way in it if you like but one way of telling anything of telling everything of telling something'.[20] It is the undifferentiation of content as a result of formal uninventiveness that Stein sees as important here. Everything, anything and something are reduced to that 'one way'. The unfortunate journalists, and to some extent writers of history, are unable to challenge the structure of their own writing: 'after you have done all that hard work you have to write it up as it would be if you had known it all beforehand and that is what really makes it too easy' (*Narration*, p. 38). She continues with more than a hint of humour: 'It takes a tremendously strong personality to break through the events in a newspaper and when they do well it is soon over it is soon smoothed over and even history wishes to change it into something that any one could recover from' (p. 39). In this sense detective stories were already in advance of the newspaper, though they both dealt with a 'natural' consensus about public events. The newspapers responded to 'delay' as fast as possible, detective stories as slowly as possible – indeed they depended on it: 'And so in the newspapers you like to know the answer in crime stories in reading crime and in written crime stories knowing the answer spoils it' (p. 40). Author and reader can sharpen their wits while nature is suspended. It is, she says, 'impossible to hold the attention by telling about the crime you can only hold the attention by telling about detecting' (p. 40). Excitement in life and art are different.

There is difference, too, in terms of their closure. In the first and in newspapers the event is simply complete in some particular dramatic moment, in the second closure has the psychological quality of relief: 'It is not really possible to remember the climax of a real scene because you cannot remember completion but you can remember relief' (p. 41). The emotion is more memorable than the event. The parataxis of event in newspapers represents changelessness within apparent change. Stein is interested in the reverse: change within apparent changelessness, what she called the 'simplicity of something always happening' (p. 43). So Stein relies ultimately on Wittgenstein's 'outward criteria'.

As a writer, however, she had more levels on which to work than the philosopher.

> Think of Defoe, he tried to write *Robinson Crusoe* as if it were exactly what did happen and yet after all he is Robinson Crusoe and Robinson Crusoe is Defoe and therefore after all it is not what is happening it is what is happening to him to Robinson Crusoe that makes what is exciting everyone.
>
> (*Narration*, p. 45)

Stein breaks the illusion of mimesis and ironizes author – character identification. Wilkie Collins made the point precisely in *The Moonstone*. The faithful retainer Gabriel Betteredge solves life's problems by smoking his common-sense English pipe while reading *Robinson Crusoe*. *Robinson Crusoe* is also his way of sobering up after having had 'a drop too much'. Strategically we are asked to believe that the pragmatic, individualist, bourgeois, racially superior, patriarchally psychotic, romantic, adventurous, pet-loving Crusoe (English enough to know how to make himself an umbrella in an emergency) has a neutral perspective on events. Wilkie Collins's affectionate irony, however, suggests that *Robinson Crusoe* befuddles his character's wits as much as his pipe and his beer: that it is an intoxicated perspective. And Stein would have agreed. In its own way, of course, *Robinson Crusoe* is an English version of the American Dream.

It was the 'outside', however, that was crucial in Stein's perception of herself as an author. One aspect of the 'outside' was the different nature of the behaviour of Americans from that of others. Americans were already in a social world far removed from the also fast disappearing private–public world of the Europeans. She recalls how she attempted to explain to doughboys at the end of the First World War about the European sense of privacy: 'because Europeans do not like any body outside to come inside unless they are invited because they like to feel that once inside they are inside and once outside they are outside and they cannot comfortably mix inside and outside'. This mingling of public and private Stein thought was crucial to the whole generic sense of reality of the crime novel, and also to what she called the 'crime hero' of the American newspaper: 'it gets into anybody who can have his picture where it is to be seen by anybody.' She continues:

> Dillinger got to be one so completely that his father naturally could say he was a good boy he always had been a good son. And he was right, that makes of any American a crime hero that his father can say he is a good boy that he has always been a good boy. If they could not say that of him he would not have been on the front page of the news.[21]

It is with rather savage irony that Stein points to society's schizophrenia. Is the good American home life supposed to palliate the public crime? Does an ideology of psychological order sanction actual law-breaking? Stein was right to see the detective novel playing in a social space between public contradiction and private value. When inside is outside and outside inside political value disappears.

Two years later Stein returned to the detective novel in an article for *Harper's*. She praised the abundance of Edgar Wallace, and his fidelity to the money basis of the action he represented in his work:

> You see said Edgar children cannot steal from their father that is French law, a father cannot accuse his children of stealing from him not according to French law so if the father does not give the money to his children then the children can take it from their father and it is not money until they pay it to someone else.

Stein's paraphrase of Edgar Wallace here shows she is still meditating on the relation of public and private, the universal applicability of money, and law. Here public and private are distinguished by law, so that money exchange can have a different legal meaning in the two different domains. For the American it is strange that money and law can have such a variable relation: 'That is what Edgar said to Edgar and after that Edgar said they need hours to think about that. . . .' Wallace is further praised for revivifying the 'old melodrama'. Stein says she does not like his sadism, as she always disliked Dickens's, but she excuses both on the grounds of their 'abundance'.[22]

It was private behaviour that elicited the most significant comment in her meeting with Dashiell Hammett, who told her that men had lost confidence in themselves: 'The men all write about themselves as strong or weak or mysterious or passionate or drunk or controlled by always themselves as the women used to do in the nineteenth century'.[23] Both writers seemed to enjoy the exchange.

As a strategy Stein too stuck to her 'story of existence'.[24] There are hints everywhere that she wanted something more: 'You see it is difficult very difficult that history can even come to be literature. But it would be so very interesting if it could be so very interesting'.[25] Stein was still too much part of the nineteenth century not to be troubled by the nature of historical truth. At least, however, she felt that American writers had managed to separate the 'inside' from the 'outside' and begun to represent a new America in a new language:

> In American writing the words began to have inside themselves these same words that in the English were completely quiet. . . they began to detach themselves from the solidity of anything, they began to excitedly feel themselves the consciousness of completely moving, they began to detach themselves from the solidity of anything, they began to excitedly feel themselves as if they were anywhere or anything, think about American writing from Emerson, Hawthorne, Walt Whitman, Mark Twain, Henry James, myself, Anderson, Wilder and Hammitt [sic] and you will see what I mean, as well as in advertising and in road signs, you will see what I mean, words left alone more and feel that they are moving and all of it is detached and is detaching anything from anything and in this detaching and in this moving it is being in its way creating its existing.[26]

Stein then places herself within an American tradition of writing which dramatizes the relations between sign and society. She senses the unreality of reference when a set of language habits encounter an 'outside' which has changed. It is this unreality of reference which is perhaps captured with black irony in Hawthorne, gnostic transcendentalism in Emerson, uncertain terms of address in Whitman,

wit and cynicism in Twain, and in the very subversion of the
strategy of definition in Henry James. By suspending tradition and
by heuristically equalizing its hierarchies a new range could be
brought in from Shakespeare to Hammett, Cézanne to road signs.
Stein put the world in suspension, that act which reflects the deep
psychology of ontological questioning, by challenging traditional
modes of narration: 'You see I try to convey the idea of each part of a
story being as important as the whole. It was the first time in any
language that anyone had used that idea in literature.'[27] She was
almost right, although a similar case could be made for Ford Madox
Ford's 'impressionism', and the later Henry James as well. Before
any of them, Adams had provided a model in the *Education*, in such
celebrated moments as that on Wenlock Edge. Stein puts it very
much in the spirit of Adams: 'We really now do not really know that
anything is progressively happening and as knowledge is what you
know and as now we do not know that anything is progressively
happening where are we then in narrative writing'.[28]

Stein's explanation here is at least historical. And it insists on
personal discovery of pattern and structure, contrary to some critics
who make Stein's imaginative discoveries into natural fact and then
show her recognizing them: 'The absence of causal and temporal
connection in the American concept of narration made, in Stein's
view, American writing the contemporary writing of the human
mind'.[29] Yet it is easy to see why such statements are so current. On
this basis it is relatively easy to build analogies with Cubism and so
on. 'Spatializing' criticism quickly discovers its own image. Yet no
less than Adams could Stein ignore time. If an ideology of the public
was impossible because the public itself was changing, by that very
fact time came into it. In the new social world time moved more
slowly than in 'history', but it still mattered as the slowly shifting
parameters of family behaviour in *The Making of Americans* showed.
Stein knew that liberal America had disappeared with increasing
speed during the twenty years before and after the First World War.
   Stein's search for a genre which could include melodrama but not
be dominated by it, and which could give a sense of history without
progressivist ideologies, which could be inclusive of public and
private life without the reductive banality of the social time of the
newspapers, and which could challenge an audience out of its
slumber, was perhaps finally found, as for Adams, in autobiography.
In 1941, describing war preparations, she spoke of the French salting
away vegetables in their hot-water bottles. Here in an insignificant
detail was the adaptation of old form to new content, and she commented further: 'in fact life is almost as exciting as the *Swiss Family*

Robinson.[30] Judging the precise humour of that remark is more difficult than might be supposed. It includes hope and despair.

In her penultimate long work, *Wars I Have Seen* (1945), the problem of how to prevent the value of human life from being presented only by melodrama became acute. Indeed the question of the future suddenly became acute: 'Wars', she said, 'do make you interested in prediction and that throws a whole lot of light upon the question of description'.[31] Could wars be dismissed as an uninteresting natural event which took place outside the human mind? Stein had begun her career by describing nervousness in the private domain in order to live a sense of the public reality of America. Now in the public context of war she again turned her attention to daily life. Written in a readily accessible style, *Wars I Have Seen* attempts a narrative of 'events' and 'existence' within a compelling set of historical circumstances.

Wars I Have Seen is Stein's last attempt to render 'society' in terms of her familiar themes and range of materials: portraits, detective-story structures, popular fiction, the tales of the people, the sense of an American writing, melodrama, problems of author and audience, representations of time, and how to promote a way of seeing the world within narrative. The story she tells in this world shows a world organized through terror. She understood that more fully than she was to understand the significance of the atomic bomb. This work is nonetheless important because since 1945 the world has lived with a form of terror disguised as peace for which Stein's and Toklas's existence in the three years of American participation in the war in Europe provides all too apt a model.

Stein's experience of the war as an alien, a Jew, and a woman within a few years of her own death was clearly as an observer. She did not 'see' action, but what she did see was the effect of it in daily life. The activity of the book is therefore minimal; getting food occupies much energy, though like many country people outside the main theatres they had enough of it. They gave their car at a late stage to a Red Cross worker who had had his destroyed in a local raid on Chambéry, and, at least as it appears in the book, that was the limit of their engagement. Francis Rose, the English painter supported by Stein in the '30s, was apparently told by Goering that if France fell 'Gertrude Stein and Alice Toklas woud be safe and never be in financial need', while the reporter Eric Sevareid stated that Stein's works were on Goebbel's blacklist.[32] The two women did survive and so did their paintings, but they had no absolute assurance of either until the end of the war. Of course they had few contacts with resistance fighters, and their courage about them grows as the Maquis become more successful. They do, however, experience the terror of impotence after the Maquis raids, which are then avenged by local Occupation forces.

What is being seen is the effect inside society of a world going to pieces outside, in the terror created by the criminality of Nazi occupation. Stein aimed to write what it felt like. The object described is war without war; in the fullest sense, the 'rumour' of war. All her life Stein had been battling to see it 'as it is' in precisely the sense Arendt meant:

> The tremendous intellectual change which took place in the middle of the last century consisted of the refusal to view or accept anything 'as it is' and in the consistent interpretation of everything as being only a stage of some further development. Whether the driving force of this development was called nature or history is relatively secondary. In these ideologies, the term 'law' itself changed its meaning; from expressing the framework of stability within which human actions and motions can take place, it became the expression of the motion itself.[33]

Wars I Have Seen is in fact the placing of an 'as it is' against law as motion – here easily defined as the internal effects of the 'destiny' of the thousand-year Reich. To see, however, requires a depth of intellectuality resistant to propaganda. Stein's method was to observe behaviour, and, like Adams, she saw a society in which 'reason' (by which was meant consistency) meant 'more police, more regulations, more avoidance of the law, more prisoners'. She continues with this anecdote:

> Nobody does know whether she does know the answer to the questions they asked her. And all the time all around her, there was opening and closing of revolvers and police dogs coming and going and lying down and getting up and suddenly she laughed, quite pleasantly and the man asking her questions said do not laugh at me and she said I am laughing pleasantly that is to say I am laughing at the absurdity of my being here not able to answer the questions you are asking and so she was in prison for two months and then once more they called her to ask questions and as she did not know the answers any more than she had before the man asking said now you can go, and she said where and he said wherever you like and she said you mean I am free and he said yes you are free, and she said but I have no money left, it all went in prison and I have none left for car-fare, and my friends live quite a way off could you give me twenty sous for car-fare, and he said yes he could and she said do, and he gave it to her and she went away and was free. The thing that is most interesting about

government servants is that they believe what they are supposed to believe, they really do believe what they are supposed to believe, which has a great deal to do with wars and wars being what they are.[34]

There is more here than a populist response to 'big government'. Stein is also examining the nature of professionalism and aggressive bureaucracy under general terror. Spontaneously to laugh before bought men becomes a crime in a State interested only in maintaining its own consistency. The official is not a direct enemy – hence he can give his ex-prisoner car fare – he represents the enemy. Stein asks herself further why public sevants 'in the army in every branch of government' (*sic*) often fail to make common-sense judgements. Again Stein's anecdote falls within the culture of professionalism. Her answer is, 'Oh he answered the reason is simple, they are specialists and to a specialist his speciality is the whole of everything and if his speciality is in order and it generally is then everything must be succeeding' (*Wars I Have Seen*, p. 53). Again Stein observes the phenomenon without deepening the explanation, but the writer's observation is accurate. When she attempts more the results are often unsatisfactory. Of the Germans, for example, she says: 'I cannot understand why men have little common sense why they cannot understand when there is no possibility of their winning that they will win, why they cannot remember that two and two makes four and no more' (p. 35).

It was, of course, precisely because two and two makes four that the Germans went on fighting. Arendt gives the reason:

The only capacity of the human mind which needs neither the self nor the other nor the world in order to function safely and which is as independent of experience as it is of thinking is the ability of logical reasoning whose premiss is the self-evident. The elementary rules of cogent evidence, the truism that two and two equals four cannot be perverted even under the conditions of absolute loneliness. It is the only reliable 'truth' human beings can fall back upon once they have lost the mutual guarantee, the common sense, men need in order to experience and live and know their way in a common world. But this 'truth' is empty or rather no truth at all, because it does not reveal anything.[35]

Stein's confusion about common sense and two and two makes four lies at the heart of her work. The precise confusion cannot be resolved purely within her philosophical-linguistic habits of thought. Her commitment to intelligence within the creative act led her both to isolation within the general culture and to designate 'the human mind' in ambiguous terms. On the one hand she characterized the operations of the human mind as a deeply meditative creative activity which struck through customary perception and through the atomization of events to that truth of the secret psychological existence of society. On the other hand she could not give that human mind ontological status because of her prejudice against 'consciousness'. So she was caught between simultaneously needing it and rejecting it.

There are other reasons of course which stand behind this one. Fascinated by history and time, Stein was in fact terrified of it. She could not imagine a contemporary public, only regret a lost one. In the United States (and apparently now in Great Britain) for vast numbers of people anything prefixed by the term 'public' is to be distrusted. There are many obvious historical reasons for that. In an individualist culture, the public realm becomes a space of terror. It appears in an extreme form in *Wars I Have Seen* when Stein registers the shock of encountering the revenge inflicted on French girls who had been with German soldiers: 'naturally it is terrible because the shaving is done publicly. It is as I have often said, life in the middle ages, it certainly is most interesting and logical it certainly is' (p. 243). It is hard to place the ironic tone here. The 'done publicly' is a form of terror which particularly seems to have fascinated Americans from Hawthorne's *Scarlet Letter* to Norman Mailer's account of the execution of Gary Gilmore in *The Executioner's Song*. But it is scarcely a strange paradox, this fear of exposure in a society devoted to publicity. Stein does not mention the fact that resistance fighters moved to stop these revenges, something which would not have happened in the Middle Ages.

The deep structure of *Wars I Have Seen* describes a world caught in a perspective between solitude and loneliness. As such it continues Stein's project begun with *The Making of Americans*. This is not to say that there are not valuable political insights in Stein's book. There are. For example Stein understood very clearly which class Hitler mobilized. No less than Wilhelm Reich she understood that the dictators had capitalised on the frustrations of the lower-middle classes:[36]

> when I was young it was the middle class that is the middle class that had money, and now it is the lower middle class that is in power, and men can have and men will have money, if it is had it would not go on being the lower middle class, because that class has no legend and it has no love interest and it is not timely and it does not like to live and move about and it does not care what it is

all about, it knows what it is and stays there, and that is what the
lower middle class is, and it is they that make the last there is of life
in the nineteenth century because they have no hope and no
adventure. Think of the dictators they are just like that. What did I
say. I said it was just like that.

(Wars I Have Seen, p. 27)

She also knew accurately that Jewish finance was, in world terms,
'only a drop in the bucket' (p. 55), a fact, she adds somewhat
caustically, that Jews don't like to acknowledge because it would
make 'themselves feel less important' which is hard for 'chosen
people' (p. 55). Stein's rigorous critique of the psychology of destiny
extended to her own race. Also she has a sharp eye for nostalgias –
the flip side of destiny seekers – and for the paranoias of those who
cannot perceive any reality other than 'disunity'. Stein describes a
wife's correction of her shopkeeper husband who is complaining of
the disunity of France in this war compared with the First World
War. After the wife speaks of the solidarity of the 'mountain boys',
Stein comments:

> Well after all of course, there is disunion, there are the scared
> middle classes afraid of communism, there are military people
> angry that the army has been taken away from them there are the
> religious old maids and widows who are afraid that in the future
> there will be no religion but as Madame Gallais says the young
> generation are just as united as the poilus in '14–'18 and she is right
> they are.

(Wars I Have Seen, p. 151)

In other words fear creates nostalgia for order in spite of the fact that
new order grows in any case.

This is not to say that Stein is not capable of banality. Her
insistence on nationalist essence is one instance of it. Such characterizations are fine when they register difference as a foreground of
expectation, as in her reporting of an American service man who said
the British got on fine with them once they realized that Americans
were in fact foreign. But statements like 'Germans... are always
choosing someone to lead them in a direction they do not want to go'
(p. 64), quoted without contradiction, are simply silly. Others are
more disturbing. Stein's approval of the Allied tactics of destroying
the civilian base of production before actually fighting (all those fire
raids were not militarily necessary) highlights a contrast which she
sees as the difference between a European and American attitude.
Europeans, Stein says, 'cannot get into the point of America, that
fighting consists in putting the other man out of business' (p. 93).
The stance of the realistic conceals a frightening absolutism.

It is at such moments that Stein's homely explanations fail. Her real strength, however, lies in the delimiting of anxiety and confusion which is the essence of a world controlled by propaganda: 'The French not fighting had plenty of time to worry and to talk and to listen to propaganda and they have gotten so that they do not know what they believe in but they do pretty well know what they do not believe in' (p. 213). Propaganda destroys theorizing along with ideology and puts populations on the defensive. Anxiety is, however, also maintained by actual political acts of terror, from the psychological to the physical. As hope rises for a victory Stein observes: 'every neighbour is denouncing every neighbour for black traffic, for theft' (p. 37). Before that a student with a promising mathematics career is forced to go to Germany to work (p. 38). Eighteen-year-olds have to take a decision whether or not to join the resistance. Small wooden coffins are sent to collaborators: 'They had to find a reliable carpenter to make the coffin but they did find him' (p. 42). Stein and Toklas themselves are told to get ready to leave for Switzerland within twenty-four hours: 'What was so curious in the whole affair was its unreality, like things are unreal when you are a child' (p. 51). In wartime, Stein remarks acutely, everyone has to come into contact with officials and has to learn 'What one did by bribing' (p. 51).

In this context Stein extends the state of war to the state of peace by discussing the two absolutely relevant legal cases which stood on the threshold of twentieth-century history: the Oscar Wilde trial and the Dreyfus case. Significantly they are both again moments of the 1890s, and therefore of Stein's own student days. In the case of Wilde, publicity became an act of terrorization based on sexual fears. In the Dreyfus case there was a 'modern' use of publicity which Arendt has analysed in her book on totalitarianism. It included special-interest press propaganda, 'government' by police, nationalism, a scapegoat class, political ends gained by exploiting the desire of the oppressed to be accepted within existing social paradigms of behaviour, and a ludicrous set of actual events. What Stein captures is the 'feeling' of being in prison: 'And so Oscar Wilde and the Ballad of Reading Gaol was the first thing that made me realize that it could happen, being in prison' (p. 55).

It is the detailing of this feeling that makes *Wars I Have Seen* still worth reading. An eclipse of the moon takes place. Nobody takes much notice: 'Eclipses are an amusement for peace time' (p. 60). Nothing is consistent. A priest denounces Americans and is friendly to Stein (p. 70). There is general fear: the 'word discipline and forbidden and investigated and imprisoned brings horror and fear into all hearts, they do not want to be afraid not more than is necessary in the ordinary business of living where one has to earn one's living and has to fear want and disease and death. There are enough things to be afraid of. . .' (p. 75). When the business of normal life goes on it is something worthy of remark: a local boy forced to work in Germany quits his boss there, finds other employment, and then goes back to his former job after the boss has apologized. Details unconnected with war assume new importance.

So do details connected with it. Stein wryly notes that people can get leather shoes again as soon as the news improves, because shop-keepers do not want to be left with stocks on their hands when the war finishes (p. 123). She notes also huge flocks of wild duck on the Rhône – a result of the absence of the sporting season. As the war closes the occupying forces get simultaneously politer and more random in their shooting habits. Stein is nervous, too, about the presence of American tanks near Chartres, even though 'there are miles more of works of art than even people who are really interested in them can see in their life time. . .' (p. 226). While Stein recognizes that life in the 'unoccupied zone' is very different from that in the occupied north (p. 87), the confidence needed to keep this as steady knowledge is often undermined. She goes to the heart of the matter, however, when she states that the need for enemies is predicated on the fear of death: 'the idea of enemies is awful it makes one stop remembering eternity and the fear of death. That is what enemies are. Possessions are the same as enemies only less so. . .' (p. 36).

Not for the first time, Stein also attempts an explanation within her composition. Throughout the work there is a constant sense that in her terms, the 'nineteenth century' has given way to the 'twentieth century'. What Stein means by these terms becomes clearer in the numerous instances in which the comparison is made:

> There was nothing more interesting in the nineteenth century than little by little realizing the detail of natural selection in insects flowers and birds and butterflies and comparing things and animals and noticing protective coloring nothing more interes-ting, and this made the nineteenth century what it is, the white man's burden, the gradual domination of the globe as piece by piece it became known and became all of a piece, and the hope of Esperanto or a universal language. Now they can do the radio in so many languages that nobody any longer dreams of a single language, and there should not any longer be dreams of conquest because the globe is all one. . . .
>
> (*Wars I Have Seen*, p. 17)

So Stein attempts to give a pattern of changes which includes a scientific theory (evolution), a methodology (comparing things), a politics (the white man's burden), a psychology (dreams of conquest), and a goal (universalization of multiple languages). The degree to which ideas create a politics is questionable, of course. The reverse is at least as true, but what is important here is the stress on the fact that all these changes are interconnected, and that both the content and the style of the interaction had changed significantly in Stein's own time. Stein's insistence on the group nature of the interconnections can be used further as an encouragement to think about the relation of science to methodology and both to politics and imagined goal. Like Adams, Stein saw that new technology plays a role in these changes, altering, in her own example, a drive towards unity of goal.

From Darwin, however, Stein seizes on the role of 'chance' to give a sense of a new reality brought on by her experience of the Second World War: 'This coincidental war this meaningless war, this war that put an end an entire end to the nineteenth century there were so many coincidences and they were the only reality in this time of unreality' (p. 20). Stein is not talking politically here, but in terms of her personal feeling, about the reality she experiences as a result of the political chaos. Chance becomes an order in the givenness of a world not permitted by authority. As she says a little later: 'there is no realism now, life is not real it is not earnest, it is strange which is an entirely different matter' (p. 44). No less than Adams, Stein reflects on a changing psychology marked out by paradigm shifts at every level of human experience and understanding.

Both Adams and Stein were almost unique in their own time and rare in our own for questioning the entire drama of the scientific project. An issue of the United States Information Service magazine, for example, gives a somewhat melodramatic account of a scientist ('his career was almost lost') seeking universal numbers – in this case relating to how a system moves towards chaos.[37] There are double ironies here (the attempt to incorporate chaos as 'order' without distinguishing a heuristic project from one which implies truth), but Stein's response would have been: 'five is there everywhere there are toes. And this has a great deal to so with that, that the nineteenth century believed in science but the twentieth century does not' (*Wars I Have Seen*, p. 56). And Stein was surely right. To the extent that the psychology of endlessly postponed result, the authority of difficult 'languages', the puritanism of specialized singularity and the goal of 'unity' characterize science, Stein predicts an end to reverence.

References to literature also helped Stein to articulate the feeling of war. Literature provides synchronic comparisons and analogies for the feelings that Stein experiences. Shakespeare's *Macbeth* and *Julius Caesar* are singled out to emphasize 'the general confusion, the general fear, the general helplessness, the general nervousness...' (p. 13). Emphasizing the general nature of the confusion is important because terror thrives on undifferentiation. Swift's *Gulliver's Travels* is recalled for speculation on the fear of death and Stein remembers his description of the people 'who never die' (p. 23). James Fenimore Cooper is mentioned a number of times. Cooper's Manichaean vision probably appealed to her and also his sense of decaying conservative values of loyalty such as one finds in *Wyandotte* and *The Hutted Knoll*, which she mentions. *The Spy* is used to illustrate 'everybody denouncing friends and enemies, everybody being hidden in the mountains, patriots, false patriots, bandits making believe being real or false patriots...' (p. 164). Shakespeare, Swift and Cooper were all perhaps at least connected in their political conservatism and their ability to articulate the darkest visions of human life. For Stein these authors and their works helped to lift the burden of being unique in history and to diminish the despair of evil.

At the same time books were a distraction: a real means of suspending the contemporary reality within the secondariness of another. Stein liked to read mystery and spy stories. She declared: 'I want to read them more than ever, to change one reality for another, one unreality for another and so the Spanish–American War made us Americans conscious of being a world power, conscious of the school of realism conscious of England being nineteenth century...' (p. 47). The Spanish–American War here becomes a fiction signalling the decline of European imperialism, and the rise of the imperial United States, though with a different sense of what it meant. She recalls Cummings's *The Enormous Room* when she meets a prisoner who says: 'the worst of being a prisoner was that you were all day and all night always together with seventy other men, men always alone together' (p. 57). Again Stein's feeling is accurate. Enforced sociality is a kind of hell for the 'inner-directed' person, unlike his successor in 'the lonely crowd'.[38]

On actual politics Stein is less good:

> The French dearly love a new form of government, they do love a change... I think I have counted them already in this book, three different varieties of monarchy, two empires three republics, one commune one oligarchy and dictatorship, and now here we are at a fourth republic and everybody is pleased.
>
> (*Wars I Have Seen*, p. 228)

Beneath the humour, however, is a stoic, even cynical belief that the form of government does not matter. Paradoxically Stein's old faith

in the people contributes to this decadent vision. There is a certain
aristocratic belief in the natural ability of the doubtless natural
peasants to resist natural disaster naturally, although fidelity to the
actual exchange of conversation here infringes that serene assumption a little:

> We are not rich like Americans no I said but you can go on
> working the kind of working you do until you are ninety or a
> hundred and you complain but any day is a pleasant enough day
> which it is not in any other country and they said perhaps they
> would like to be rich like Americans. . . .
>
> (*Wars I Have Seen*, p. 138)

Stein is not without her own natural superstitions, and the kindest
thing that can be said of her wheeling on her references to St. Odile
like so many commercial breaks in the narrative, is her faithfulness
perhaps to the fact that superstition is easily aroused under terror.
Perhaps she includes herself then in a kind of Jamesian account
of the role of superstition. In despairing of a future Stein turned
prophetic.

Unlike James, however, the role of belief plays a relatively small
part in Stein's scheme of things. More interesting is the question of
narrative and also, therefore, the role time plays in that narrative.
The role of time cannot but engage the question of history, and as
Stein looks back she has to face the question of public history as well
as the private record: 'I do not know whether to put in the things I do
not remember as well as the things I do remember' (p. 3). As a good
psychologist Stein also knew that age had to do with consciousness
of time. It is well-known subjectively that older people experience a
'more rapid' passing of time than younger people do. There is also
the question of consciousness and its relation to events. Stein
captures terror in her sentence: 'When a baby eats and vomits it is not
war. But when fourteen eats and vomits then it is war' (p. 25).
Subjectively also consciousness can suspend time, and this is precisely the kind of experience of time in which Stein was most
interested:

> And so we were in Vienna and I have never seen it again but it has
> always remained for me something very real. It was there that I
> first came to be and so of course it was real and then there were
> really things, there was a public garden, as formal garden and in a
> kind of way a formal garden pleases a child's fancy more than a
> natural garden. It is more like a garden that you would make
> yourself.
>
> (*Wars I Have Seen*, p. 5)

This apparently simple recollection contains all Stein's favourite themes: memory, time, being, nature, form, the relation of public to private and the innocence necessary to all forms of creativity.

The time of the opening sequences of the book contains in fact many times. There is the gradual awareness of time itself which signals the movement from childhood to adolescence: 'Between the ages of fifteen and twenty three nobody ever can get back in time' (p. 31). Then the future seems more manageable than the actual present. In the narrator's sense of time the past seems more manageable, and her recollections become moving and poigant as they lead back to the present and all its anxiety:

> I had read about fruit trees growing on the sunny side of a wall and I always said when I was fifteen that when I was older and could have it I would have a wall and have fruit trees growing on the sunny side of a wall. I remember the first time I ever saw fruit trees arranged to grow on a wall. It was just after the Spanish–American War and we were in Paris for the exposition and McKinley had just been shot and I saw fruit trees trained to grow on the sunny side of walls and it reminded me of when I was fifteen and I wanted to grow fruit trees on sunny sides of the wall and brother said that he would keep a goat on the wall to eat the fruit trees. And now it is 1943 and there is no milk and we keep a goat.
>
> (*Wars I Have Seen*, p. 34)

The object here inhabits many times, the magic time of the written text, the childhood time of before fifteen, the Spanish–American War, and the present. Ironically the numbered time (fifteen) is never experienced. It is dreamt and remembered only. The deftness of the way psychological time is handled within the narrative here is a reminder of how much Hemingway must have learnt from Stein. As the revery ends present time reappears together with a sense of the weariness of the endless waiting of war.

What is compelling is the pleasure of stories under a general threat of death. It draws us into Stein's narrative time which is in fact almost a thousand and one nights; from April 1942 to the end of the war in 1945. The future is always in doubt and the past, too, gives little comfort: 'the nineteenth century is dead but there is no particular peace for its ashes' (p. 104). In that sense the war she has lived through is qualitatively different from the war of 1914–18: 'Certainly nobody no not anybody thinks that this war is a war to end war. No not anybody, no well no certainly nobody does think about it, they only think about this war ending, they cannot take on the future, no really not, certainly not as warless certainly not as a future' (p. 187).

This sense of an absence of a future is both Stein's strength and her weakness. It is her strength because she has abandoned all mechanisms of determinism: religious, social or scientific. It is her weakness because Stein is open to the same criticism as Faulkner, of whom Sartre said in his famous essay on the eve of the War: 'A closed future is still a future.' 'Even if human reality has nothing more "before" it, even if "its account is closed", its being is still determined by this "self-anticipation". The loss of all hope, for example, does not deprive human reality of its possibilities; it is simply a way of being towards these same possibilities.'[39] There is more ambiguity between Stein's despair and her metaphysics than with Faulkner, however. One senses that she might have understood these words which Sartre quotes from Heidegger's *Sein und Zeit*, and which remind us that the world escapes our despair.

One figure that implausibly connects Stein and Sartre is Richard Wright. The occasion of their correspondence and eventual meeting was in fact *Wars I Have Seen*. On 11 March 1945, Wright's review of Stein's book appeared in *PM Magazine*. He praised the work unequivocally, without evading awkward questions. He praised it for killing the nineteenth century and sending its 'hope, idealism, aspiration, the sense of the future, high-flown metaphysics and all the big, vague, emotional words of our time. . . down the drain of World War II'.[40] Wright accurately pin-pointed Stein's ability to give 'an awful sense of the power of war to kill the soul, of the fear, the rumour, the panic and the uncertainty of war'.

Wright's quotations from the work are a criticism in themselves. As a black American no one knew better than he the nature of war within peace, and life lived under conditions of arbitrary death and fear. Wright picks out Stein's moments as a tribute of one writer to another: 'the air at night, when the moon is bright is full of them going over to Italy to do their bombing and the mountain makes a reverberation as a woman said to me like being inside a copper cooking utensil well when you keep on thinking how quickly anybody can get killed, just as quickly as just very quickly, more quickly even than in a book.' Wright suggests you punctuate with your eyes and interpose with your reading bits from the Old Testament and Hemingway.

He approves of Stein's explanation of the statesmen blundering into war: 'so naturally they believing in what they are supposed to believe make it possible for the country to think they can win a war.' Ruefully, perhaps remembering his own ideological battles of the '30s,

Wright approves of Stein's description of the man who 'was anti-Russian he was anti-Anglo–American he was anti-German he was anti-De Gaulle he was anti-Vichy, he was anti-Pétain he was anti-Maquis. . .'. Wright liked Stein's humour: 'her description of how she welcomed the American troops sounds like steal from Father Divine', and he concludes:

> Wouldn't it be strange if, in 1988, our colleges made the reading of *Wars I Have Seen* mandatory so that our grandchildren might learn how men felt about war in our time? Wouldn't it be strange if Miss Stein's grammarless prose was destined for such a strange destiny? Would it not be strange if anything like that did happen?

Wright's imitation of Stein's prose is not altogether on target here, but it is clear he understands the seriousness of her work.

And then the more difficult questions. Wright says he had read Stein years earlier, having stumbled on *Three Lives* in the Chicago Public Library. Remembering harsh left-wing criticisms of her, that 'her tortured verbalisms were disturbing the Revolution', Wright asks himself, 'Had I duped myself into worshipping decadence?'[41] He answers the question by recalling how he had read Stein's *Melanctha* to blacks in a Black Belt basement in Chicago with immediate enthusiastic response. For Wright at any rate the language took care of criticisms of decadence. In our own time, none the less, it is not difficult to find criticisms of racial stereotyping directed at works like *Melanctha*, and in some ways rightly so.

Stein must first have heard of Wright from Max White, who had attended the New York Writers' Congress and wrote to her in January 1938. He said Wright had 'the clearest and hardest of the minds present', adding that 'I think he's doubtless a left-wing writer. I know he's class-conscious to a degree. . . .'[42] It was not until 2 May 1945 that Stein wrote to Van Vechten about Wright: 'I got one of the soldiers to find me some of his books, the only one they found in the library was Black Boy and I am very enthusiastic, and could you send me through Bianco that and all his other books, I do want to read them.'[43] Stein's enthusiasm accompanied a judgement about Wright's work which has stood the test of time. Her literary judgement, unlike her judgement about painting and painters, never faltered, and she added Wright to the list of American writers she encouraged and recognized. Certainly Wright was a challenge to her entire range of absorbed meditations on what it was to be an American in the twentieth century.

In July 1945 Stein was reading Gunner Myrdal's still magnificent work of 1944, *An American Dilemma*. How she responded to that work will never be known, but it is not difficult to speculate that she would have read Myrdal's words on the psychological characteristics of race with attention, for here were challenges to terms of references (including epistemological and representational problems) over which Stein herself had struggled in the early years of the century: 'Whether underlying capacities and the most general personality traits – speed of reaction for example – differ in average between the two races is not known, but it should not be forgotten that they are never subject to direct observation in the same sense that physical traits are.'[44] Myrdal refers many times in this work to Richard Wright, predicting, for example, that 'the literary product of a Richard Wright will achieve nationwide publicity and acclaim and will affect people as far down as the lower middle classes'. It has been demonstrated that Stein was keenly interested both in publicity and in the lower middle classes, and may have found some reassurance in the following, under the heading, 'glamour personalities':

> When Paul Robeson and Richard Wright sometimes discuss general aspects of the Negro problem, they do so only after study and consideration. These two have deliberately taken up politics as a major interest. They act then in the same spirit and the same capacity as, for instance, Pearl Buck when she steps out of her role as a writer of novels and writes a social and philosophical essay on the woman's problem.[45]

Fresh from reading *Wars I Have Seen*, Wright poured out to Stein his thoughts on politics, writing, and the larger issues of American culture. His letters to her provide a more overtly political context and interpretation for Stein's meditations on the age of anxiety. For Stein, in *Wars I Have Seen* the particular moment of the large general movement from imperialism to totalitarianism was occupied France; for Wright it was the life of black people in the United States. Like Stein, Wright probes beneath solutions provided by orthodox ideologies – none of which, indeed, have proved satisfactory. He describes how blacks are imprisoned in a kind of dream of fear, and how everyone seems helpless, from Communists to the clergy, and from Republicans to Democrats.[46]

Wright locates part of that helplessness in a peculiarly American psychology, and further, like Stein, directs attention to daily life and its essential puritanism. For Americans, Wright argues, nothing can ever be settled or taken for granted. Each day is lived with anxious repetition as if they were still pilgrims arriving in a new country. The result is a country of men and women who appear strong but who in fact are really grown-up babies with guns in their hands.

Like Reich, Wright notes that fascist elements in America see the 'rot' better than liberals and communists, and are more skilled at exploiting it. Like C. Wright Mills, Wright sees the origins of the rot in the mass minds, and in the shocking conformity of American young people who appear without intellectual interests or passion, without initiative in their own beliefs and with no feeling of adventurousness or even rebellion. Like Stein, Wright noted the inertia left by the demise of bourgeois liberalism and its once-believed mandates of romance and adventure. Politically, however, Wright was far from Stein; one can imagine Stein being taken aback by one of Wright's comments to her, to the effect that Roosevelt's death had shaken people's optimism.[47]

Sensing Stein's receptiveness to a sociology of language, Wright makes an analysis of 'jive' speech which he describes interestingly as being outside normal historical development as if synchronically trapped in its own folkiness. It is a mass speech occuring spontaneously in talk and specialized enough to enable blacks to speak it safely within earshot of whites. It arbitrarily selects and varies its vocabulary. He stresses that it has very little to do with African roots, since it is essentially a product of the urban black milieu. Its characteristics are its use of the present tense, and its vivid and descriptive qualities. Ideologically its capacity for racial protest, comedy, bitterness, and celebration of the contemporary moment is somewhat undercut by its infantilism. Formally it often uses simple rhymed couplets which when successful endow its maker with a certain prestige. These rhymes might even eventually find their way into the movies.[48]

These comments can be read in many ways, sociologically, linguistically and politically. They can also be read as an account of the way a performer relates to an audience and on what terms. All the issues looked at in relation to Stein and writing are touched on here: the notion of language and being, language and transformatory process, language and society, and language and speech. Stein's particular interests are therefore touched upon precisely. That continuous present which she hoped would render the moment of meditation is emphasized. Here, too, is speech which reveals ecstatic behaviour distinct from 'common sense' life: 'hepped to the jive'. Here, too, is the emotional curve of language in play as it falls from metaphor to cliché.

It is above all a language for dealing with anxiety. Some fifteen years before Mailer spoke of the White Negro and attempted in the figure of the psychopath to find a model of survival to cope with the emotional effects of living in an increasingly totalitarian world, Wright told Stein about the language of a radically nervous people who hardly know where they belong or where they are going, and have means to articulate either.[49] Above all, in our time, in every urban ghetto, black people live in that war-in-peace which

Stein thought might become, if it was not already, a universal condition. Within the dimensions of this language there was both hope
and desperation, for this was the language of otherwise sane people
who were forced to live in an absolute present because they had been
robbed of their pasts and futures.[50] Here is the dark side of that
'continuous present' which Stein perhaps only renders in the
pervasive melancholy of her tone. Wright gives it inescapably a
political meaning.

Perhaps no one had ever talked to Stein (apart from W. G. Rogers,
who was in any case less acute) so forthrightly across her own
political convictions and so straight and sympathetically to the heart
of what she had in fact herself noted and thought about. Wright went
on to tell Stein about the Father Divine movement, which he argued
was a primitive kind of socialism, though, sensing the prejudices of
his correspondent, he added tactfully that he thought Stein would be
most interested in the kind of language it employed.[51] A letter of
October 1945 shows how well Wright knew Stein's interests. He
tells her how in Quebec, unlike New York, people have found a way
of living a daily life in the city. He speaks, too, of contemporary
political events in America; how the war in Europe had been
psychologically packaged and filed away in a drawer – just as the
Vietnam war was to be during the 1970s and '80s. Wright notes that
how Hitler came to power is forgotten, or is simply attributed to the
'sadism' of the German people, and he continues to argue that
'fascism' is a possibility inside any nation at any time. He continues
that 'isms' represent rather crude attempts to find new codes for
living and for reorganizing ways in which people relate to each
other.[52] It is of course the period just after the ending of the war of
which Wright is speaking: one of the worst chapters in American
history. Externally the policy of Cold War created internally a
terrorized conformity. Wright adds that, in America, if he argued as
he is now arguing to Stein he would be accused of being un-
American, blasphemous, and a threat to the family.

Stein's own life spanned a period even more accelerated in its changes
than Henry Adams's had been. She was born in 1874, within living
memory of the Civil War and at the height of European imperial
power. She died in 1946 not long after the Allied victory in the
Second World War, and the exploding of the atomic bomb at
Hiroshima. Her work, however, took on a range of subjects which
went far beyond the events of her own particular historical life. As
the great American writers have always done, she saw her own
society with an acute sense of its legacies. To the extent that her roots
were in the nineteenth century, she saw that heritage classically in

terms of European civilization's contribution to philosophy, science and the arts. James and Whitehead gave her some terms with which to mediate that tradition in psychology and philosophy. Weininger's characterology helped frame and theorize her readings in eighteenth-century English literature. The artistic milieu of France gave her a place, relatively unencumbered by the restlessness of American daily life, in which to develop her own singularities and from which to view, not the collapsing circus of European civilization as Adams saw it, but the astonishing artistic and scientific achievements of that 'last ten years of bourgeois optimism', in Europe before the First World War.

In this context she used her training in philosophy, psychology and medicine to revise the techniques of prose discourse. The result was a probing – often satiric – of bourgeois consciousness as such; its assumptions about normal common-sense life (and particularly its development in America), its suppression of the irrational, the professionalization of its work habits with the consequent effects on family life and personal experience. Stein hoped that to revise the ways of relating language to traditional philosophical questions of ontology, epistemology and ethics would enable her to produce a new literature adequate to the changes which were taking place in both Europe and America. Her meditations on language closely parallel those of her contemporaries in linguistics – in all the variant forms of that subject.

Only at its most abstract moments did Stein's discourse part with a world. She confronted, no less than Adams, the changes attendant on the shift from nineteenth-century civilization to twentieth-century society: the decline of the family, the rise of the professional, the 'triumph' of the therapeutic, the banalities and possibilities of mass society, the alienation of the serious writer, the problems of conceptualizing the historical process, the rise of popular culture, the space – time of scientific exegesis, the transformation of concepts of the heroic individual, changes in sex roles, social manners, constitutional and legal affairs, religious consciousness and behaviour, and the government of the social world by new media. Her writing at its best gives a sense of what it feels like to survive with wit and intelligence through these changes.

The devotion to the writer's task and a fearless revision of its methods enabled her to register the effects of military occupation in the last years of her life with a sense of prophetic relevance to peace-time conditions. It also made her encounter with Richard Wright a fruitful one and helped make a bridge between two people of very different ideological convictions, but with a clear common cause of describing the new world of twentieth-century society.

Conclusion

Picking Up the Pieces: An Open Conclusion

This study of three major American writers of the modernist period in the multiple contexts of history, science and literature has not been written with the kind of 'objectivity' that assumes an innocent and timeless perspective. The world of the 1980s and 1990s presses on any writer or critic demanding committed, if necessarily open-ended, judgements in even the most analytic of appraisals directed towards the work of the past. What is offered here, by way of conclusion, is a meditation, in contemporary terms, on certain problems which have emerged historically in the course of the study. For there are continuities among problems which not only stretch from the times of Adams, James and Stein to the present, but which move back behind them into the eighteenth century and further.

In recovering historical antecedents, the aim is not to produce the academic's 'truth of origins', but the promise of history itself: that its study might lead to a certain modesty about the claims of the present, including its methods of criticism, that lessons from the past might enable a contemporary generation to avoid the repetition of certain mistakes; that a longer view might enable certain judgements about what is valuable and what is evil about the human condition to be made with more precison and imagination; and finally that an informed discrimination among the options across the whole range of human experience which history offers might be the basis of confronting change and the new with imagination and courage.

In openly insisting on the contemporary relevance of the study, the aim is to demonstrate a continuity of problems and criticisms between the subject studied and the perspectives offered, from the early years of this century to the present. The ambition is not to settle once and for all the traditional quarrels between the humanities and the social sciences, nor even to demonstrate their interdependence in any formal academic way. For the divisions are not even necessarily those which occur between the disciplines, but rather, among 'professional' attitudes held by members of any group within a discipline. Those who refuse to theorize or at least to re-examine the very roots of their own practices, who seek to legitimate every move by reference to a house method, who refuse even to look over the edge of their traditional subject areas, who 'theologize' their logic and who force issues that may need many different theories and empirical untidinesses into monologic abstraction – these are the new policemen of the corporate university. Brandishing prospectuses of their own cost-effectiveness, indeed their own 'cheapness' in more senses than one (interdisciplinary work, purely scientific and humanistic work cannot be readily quantified in the short term), they offer a false security to their masters who, using moralistic slogans of making universities 'relevant to modern needs' – that is, providing professional human tools to manage the status quo of capitalist society – stifle increasingly that *basic human right* to contemplate in independent solitude, or to work in chosen groups without outside pressure, and to think radically, at least for some period in a single working life, in both humanistic and scientific terms about the meaning of nature and the human condition.

The impetus for this study as outlined in the Introduction was derived from Arendt's distinction between the *polis* and *societas*. The following argument addresses itself to those issues of agency and sovereignty in the shift Adams noted in historical description between political narrative and sociological structuralism. Here also, some modern developments in the corporate world, and that world's complete domination of science and technology, will be considered in the spirit of Adams's early observations on just those subjects. Then, taking up the implications of the writings of James and Stein, the notion of 'society' itself will be theorized and discussed more closely. Finally the question of the nature and style of descriptive discourses about the human subject will be raised – and left, in conclusion, open-ended.

I

It was Adams above all, among the three authors studied here, who was concerned with power 'under whatever name it was known'. Here it is pertinent to recall the critics of the 1930s who were less squeamish than most modern academic commentators about including the subject of power in their analyses. In 1939 Robert Lynd was observing that 'We lack a philosophy of the place of Power in modern institutional life', and further drew the conclusion that somehow it got neatly expunged in the not-quite-overlapping fields of economic analyses.[1] C. Wright Mills also was exercised about the disappearance of that public domain in which power was traditionally exercised: 'The transformation of publics into a mass society is one of the keys to the meaning of modern life.'[2] As early as the beginning of the nineteenth century, the ideological ground was being prepared for the change, in the rise of the social sciences in which 'man was not so much invented as discarded, with the new study of the underlying forces that shape our will substituted for the idea of human agency that lay at the heart of the now discarded political sciences'.[3] The new institutional analyses diminished the importance of the individual event, which had been at the heart of the old historical narrative and was further deprived of significance by hours of daily 'news' in the mass media. A Dreyfus affair or a Sacco and Vanzetti trial had engaged whole countries in political debate; now, in the words of one commentator, 'the most stirring events are immediately superseded by other stirring events'.[4]

By the end of the period of this study, however, there were commentators who had begun to see some of the political and social consequences of the changes Adams had so astutely observed. James Burnham's now forgotten book, *The Managerial Revolution* is a more politically-oriented version of Whyte's *The Organization Man* (1945), and exactly contemporary with the Stein–Wright correspondence. Infuriating Right and Left in the process, Burnham argued that while democratic institutions seemed to be *politically* intact, a social and economic revolution had taken place which effectively nullified their original aims and intentions. The new world was a world of managers and the problem was how to describe present localization of sovereignty in relation to traditional sovereign power. That there was a change was incontestable: 'The shift from parliament to bureau occurs on a world-wide scale. Viewed on a world-wide scale, the battle is already over.' Parliament had been the sovereign body of the limited state of capitalism, the new bureaus are 'the sovereign bodies of the unlimited state of managerial society'. In the managerial society politics and economics are 'directly interfused. . . the economic arena is also the arena of the State'. Power seemed to be becoming more and more invisible as the 'captains of industry' became inaccessible to traditional political scrutiny. Writing in the shadow of the fall of the European empires, Burnham noted that the new managers were quite capable of dishing out therapeutic doses of limited democracy while making the free world economically dependent on the 'American central area'.[5]

Many other commentators have since taken up particular aspects of Burnham's analyses. The lateral *community* of interests between government and business is largely secret, though government functions as such are highly publicized, for instance in the areas of 'public expenditure'.[6] The corporations which control investment decisions are the real sources of power. Whether that power is used well or badly is not the issue here; what is important is the significance of the change in relation to public perception of it. Yet the older issues of minorities, the poor, and the quality of life of all workers in contemporary society persist. Historians remind us how close America was to a reopening of the class war in the years 1956–8, yet how, in the wake of the new industrial revolution located in the Sun Belt and classically in Silicone Valley in California, many early twentieth-century gains for working people have been eroded, even removing 'a seventy-year-old restriction on child labor and home work'. In the deluge of 'events' the defeat of American workers is continually overlooked: 'American labor may never have had to face the carnage of a Paris Commune or defeated revolution, but it has been bled in countless "Peterloos" at the hands of Pinkertons or the militia.'[7]

Real power increasingly seems remote from the majority of people. This is reflected in the fact that mass political absenteeism at elections is most marked in the most advanced of capitalist countries such as the United States. For there is no obvious control of the actual shifts of power itself. Even money, as a Marx or Adams would have noted, becomes entirely metaphysical, recirculating without reference to productive investment. In 1980 corporations spent $10 billion suing each other and $83 billion – $11 billion more than the total of new productive investment – in mergers and take-over bids.[8] These figures look puny in the context of the subsequent decade. There are implications here for the professional classes also; there are new hierarchies of pay and conditions of work which cut across traditional assumptions about the nature of their work.

Every new development of the circumstances of power demands legitimation, and the ceremonies of late twentieth-century power with its highly publicized 'big science', technological wizardry, its aura and belief systems induced by mass propaganda methods, would certainly have interested an Adams who sat meditating on the Virgin and the Dynamo, unimpressed by Langley's claims for modern technology. In the history of science, Easlea has noted that Popper's vision of a scientific community of open-minded reasonable men (whatever it was historically) has been replaced by Kuhn's vision of social consensus in scientific practice, involving psychological conversion, the dying-off of dissidents, and retraining of the young by the winning faction.[9] But he does not relate the changes to huge increases in investment in science and the institutionalization of its processes.

In technology proper the staging of space flights at appropriate political moments legitimates that $1 trillion in military expenditure between 1985 and 1987 (comparable in economic impact to the height of the Vietnam war). The Elizabethan procession is replaced by technological dramas which can be used in success or failure. The recent *Challenger* space 'disaster' encompassed all the ritual public acts of ceremonial dismemberment which have been a coercive feature of priestly and autocratic states since time immemorial. For those in power murder is less risky than war,[10] even though in a social technocracy the responsibility for an 'accident' is as difficult to locate as the local effects on populations of far-away economic and management decisions. Carter has noted that the ceremonies take a standard form. Children at the Concord High School, watching the *Challenger* on television with staff members and friends, cheered when they saw the rocket explode, raising their thumbs in a signal of victory in the belief that the explosion was part of the staging.[11]

Adams was particularly sensitive to new theologies. In his own time the social creed was 'Darwinism', neatly and deftly dissected by Adams in his chapter of that title in the *Education*. After Adams and as early as 1937, Thurman Arnold in his book, *The Folklore of Capitalism*, argued that a 'social organization' depended on a 'creed', a set of attitudes based on 'self-interest', an uncritical attitude taken towards institutional habits, and a metaphysic of external power. In an Adamsian vein Arnold continues, and with appropriate irony:

> In our rational and sophisticated age the Devil and Hell become very complicated. The true faith is Capitalism. Its priests are lawyers and economists. The Devil consists of an abstract man called a demagogue. He is the kind of person who refuses to be moved by sound economists and lawyers and who is constantly misleading the people by making the worse appear the better reason.

Better no doubt to stick to Stein's patriarchal family with its 'thrifty head' balancing the budget and saving money for the future.[12]

The legitimating metaphysics vary. Still popular is the war of all against all, in which the natural world is portrayed in anthropomorphic terms. In the 1950s and '60s Ardrey, Morris, Tiger and Fox and Lorenz naturalized a Hobbesian view of nature which was followed by countless nature films repeating the same dreary message.[13] A recent film, *Lions in the African Night*, a joint South African/American venture, is a typical case. The view of nature is projectively malign, and is presumably linked to the need to encourage investment in anti-'violence' technology. The nature-legitimations of social Darwinism were similarly linked to the race terror in Dixie in the late nineteenth century.[14]

It is the relation between the creeds, the ethics and metaphysics of the social and traditional concepts of political power, then, that becomes problematic in the twentieth as well as the late nineteenth century. As Robert Lynd long ago noted, it is not enough to talk about the 'political', the 'economic', the 'social', as if consensus existed as to their precise interactions and roles in the general sovereignty of contemporary polity.[15] The following discussion attempts merely to open up some ways of investigating the social by including the questions of power. If the Arendtian distinction between the *societas* and the *polis* has broken down, will conditions ever again exist for good government? Is it possible to talk effectively about 'social control', and is 'hegemony' a more useful word than 'power' or Marxian 'productive forces'?

Beginning at the traditional starting-point, it is as well to remember that Saint-Simon's social systematizing occurred in the context of the political chaos which followed the French Revolution.[16] It was an American, Edward A. Ross, who first popularized the notion of 'social control' in 1901 in his book, *Social Control: A Survey of the Foundations of Order*. As for William James and Durkheim, 'society' is there to control the animal urges in 'Man':

> The operation of Ross's concept was rather similar to that of Durkheim's *conscience collective*, which was also capable of constraining men's 'animal spirits' with a power directly proportional to the intensity of interaction around its specific form. Family, marriage and religion were accorded this power at a primary level, while at the secondary level professional associations would act in a similar way to counteract the anomie endemic in economic life.[17]

Following Ross, Robert Park in Chicago, like Adams, saw a shift from primary groups of social control (the family, neighbourhood and community) to 'secondary means' of social control – the police, political machine and the courts. Yet as Marxist historians point out, the terms of 'breakdown' are those of biology or psychological pathology. The James–Münsterberg traditions of social discourse ensured just that. Yet the Marxist privileging of the labour–wage relation with gestures towards 'hegemony' shows that the problem of assessing the location and nature of power remains as elusive as ever. The article relied on here attempts on the one hand to show the social as dependent on the political: that 'Leisure time is clearly constricted by type and hours of work', and on the other declares that the social is detached from the political: 'The primary point of a holiday is not political. It is to enjoy yourself, for tomorrow you must work.'[18] Such statements show appalling ignorance of the actual facts of organized leisure, from Coney Island to Disneyland,

and assume that mass tourism from Majorca to Florida to the Indian subcontinent is without political implication.

Because 'beliefs' are independent of actions which may or not follow them, it does not follow that 'belief' does not have a political content, or is pure 'superstructure'. At the root of Marx's own argument is a belief-systems analysis of the nature of the commodity as fetish, and the first volume of *Capital* is, among many other important things, a magnificent barrage against capitalist superstition. Equally the empiricist historian is quick to counter the 'fashionable current of thought nourishing itself in the Freudian analysis of Oedipal conflict and the feminist critique of patriarchal domination', which has '"over-politicized" family social relations, neglecting the collaborative and sacrificial elements of family attachment and overemphasizing the power aspects of family interaction'.[19] Yet neither theoretical nor empirical evidence is advanced for the counter-assertion. That empirical evidence should in all honesty be produced, to counter Freudian theory with revised theory, and give evidence of historical family living in class, economic and social terms. It should also differentiate 'family living' in different cultures under both capitalism and state socialism.

The key problem here is one of linguistic description and representation. Foucault may cavalierly disregard the minutiae of history and economics while offering important ethical and hegemonic critiques. Similarly the empiricist historian may write footnotes like the following: 'For important insights into individual choice and consciousness, see F. M. Dostoevsky, *Notes from the Underground....*'[20] (!) While appreciating the gesture towards literature from a historian, it must be said that it fails of a certain precision.

That there is a significant shift in the way power operates is not in dispute. The countless studies of hidden persuaders, sexist advertising and other media copy, the insidious assumptions of the therapeutic state, and of mass education as well as political studies of 'friendly fascism' may not be ignored. What is at issue is the precise way in which these operate at any given moment and the authority of separate disciplinary codes and practices to lay claim to their description. There is a sense in which the screening of *Dallas* in an African village has replaced the gunboat and district officer, but the terms in which an understanding of that may be begun will require everything from an analysis of the economics of corporate power to a careful consideration of technological and anthropological circumstances in which that power operates.

Yet 'hegemony' is still a difficult term. Too often its *manner* is described rather than the precise way in which it operates. It persuades rather than coerces, it lays out loaded alternatives to control what appears to be freely given consent.[21] What is missing is the notion of 'terror' in the Sartrean sense. Consent may be given without being believed in, as a result of a coercion of which the subject is well aware. A drink in a bar with any American graduate student or pre-tenure professor will show that resentment about economically enforced 'role-playing' is still alive and well even in the United States. Poorly paid workers *and* professionals under capitalism or state socialism from Poland to California are more than aware of the roles they *must* take up to survive the threats of a power system whose parameters are concretely experienced even where they are not always concretely analysed.

Much as some sociology has radicalized its own critique since the 1930s, there are myths which need to be punctured under sober economic analyses. Kolko has demonstrated that, against Riesman's assumptions of a general levelling of income distribution into middle-class generality and Talcott Parsons's assumptions about the massification of status symbols, income distribution in the United States has not significantly altered since 1910 (it is currently getting worse), and that types of cars, for example, are directly related to income.[22] Nonetheless Riesman usefully points out that a certain proletarianization of professionals has taken place both in terms of hours worked and income – though the latter varies very considerably. 'Doctors, civil servants, teachers, school and college administrators, and some groups of managers and intellectuals work almost as long hours as steel workers did in the nineteenth century.'[23] For workers, on the other hand, straightforward political problems of a nineteenth-century kind remain in the struggle for union rights. The shifting of industrial units to the South of the United States has largely been characterized in terms of weather and energy-cost savings. In fact the savings have been guaranteed from largely non-unionized labour. In Anglo-America particularly the attack on the right of workers to protect themselves through unionization is unremitting.

In the current spate of analyses of social engineering, from Szasz to Foucault and beyond, the question of the actual demands of 'efficient' capitalism have sometimes been forgotten. Both asylum and hospital 'relieved the household of obligations that interfered with employment in the market economy'.[24] The author found scrawled in pencil on page 43 of a battered copy of Szasz's *Psychiatric Justice* (1965) in the Yale undergraduate library: 'Cheaper for state if defendant goes to Dept. of Correction, not civil hospital. Worse facilities though.' It is a response which reduces to economic pragmatism the entire human-rights argument of the book. The question of the responsibilities of the household are, however, no easier to determine than that of the State. Usually the household is sentimentalized by government while its members are forced to work longer hours – with predictable effects on 'family life'. Should a daughter in fact give up a rewarding career to look after a senile mother? Governments are notoriously hypocritical about the role of women, and the answers given normally depend on the state of the labour market. Indeed in the current downgrading of work in advanced technological societies, women are often the most victimized of all, and make up a considerable part of that third of the United States labour force (out of a labour force 100 million strong) of wage-earners trapped in a 'low-wage ghetto suspended precariously above the official poverty line'.[25]

It is these questions that purely 'social' and 'economic' analyses fail to answer. In the one 'adjustment' and in the other 'trickle-down' are the gestures paid to the obliterated questions of power in the State. At worst, in both the Soviet Union and the United States, sociology itself and the professional practices it has spawned are used 'as an instrument of State policy, both with respect to domestic problems and as an instrument for international leverage, influence and prestige'.[26]

The beginnings of 'social' analyses and 'social' thinking noted in Münsterberg, and the predication of social and individual change on Darwin-based psychology noted in James and critiqued to a certain extent in Stein, have developed considerably since their time. In the Anglo-American world Szasz's trenchant criticisms of the 1960s and early 1970s are still pertinent. Virchow's famous statement that doctors are the 'natural attorneys of the poor',[27] has developed into the medicalization (to use the current neologism) of the entire social process.

When the psychiatrist takes on the role of social engineer he 'acts as priest and policeman, arbitrator and judge, parent and warden: he coerces, manipulates, punishes and rewards, and otherwise influences and compels people, often by relying on the police power of the state, to play, or to cease to play, certain games'. The denial of moral, personal, political and social problems by 'pretending' (in the words of Szasz) they are 'psychiatric problems',[28] will be noted here and returned to later. Stein laid out the issues more brilliantly than any social scientist in her piece on 'Forensics'. The power of the professional is in fact both underestimated and overestimated. There always exists an uneasy balance between the owner of capital and the expert employed on his or her behalf in any particular instance. Behind the 'medicalization' of society, however, are the economic facts which underlie its influence. In the United States 10 per cent of

GNP is spent on health, and medicine surpasses the construction sector in employment. Its income distribution is hierarchical in the extreme, and in terms of quality of care it generally falls below the more fully nationalized medicine of northern Europe.[29]

It was, however, the emphasis on the 'social' aspects of labour – already exemplified in Münsterberg and noted by Whyte and others – that speeded productivity with fewer chances of labour unrest. In compensation the provision of a 'social' safety net was offered. From the point of view of those in power the emphasis was less on the quality of life and happiness of the people, than on a cost-effective minimum provision to ensure healthy labourers. In such a scheme the old are not as worthy of medical attention, even though they are more fully paid-up either through State or private insurance, than those still young with some years of work to go. The production of anxiety is a covert political function which operates at the level of the social. Viguerie, the publicist for the New Right in the United States, recalled how the discussion of *political* issues had little impact on the mass of the population: 'We talked about the sanctity of free enterprise, about the Communist onslaught until we were blue in the face.' The break-through came with the concentration on 'social issues'. 'It was the social issues that got us this far, and that's what will take us into the future. We never really won until we began stressing issues like bussing, abortion, school prayer and gun control.'[30] Wilhelm Reich, in 1935 in *The Mass Psychology of Fascism*, had observed just this phenomenon, of how racial anxiety, sexual anxiety, moralism and fear of disorder was used by the leaders of the rise of fascism at a classic moment of capitalist collapse in which the revolution 'never happened', and it is still a lesson some Marxists have to learn.

These, then, are some of the ways in which the 'social' may engage with actual operations of political power. Before analysing the nature of the 'social' in more hegemonic ways, two more locii of sovereignty in the contemporary world (ones which had also exercised Adams profoundly) must be looked at. The first is the world-wide development of the 'limited company' (now better known as the corporation). The second concerns what most historians and sociologists, unlike Adams, leave out of their analyses: the effect of science and technology on politics and society.

Is it then possible to locate responsibility for actions in the corporate world? It is axiomatic that when any attempt is made to place responsibility for actions that have gone badly wrong, the accuser is saddled with entertaining a 'conspiracy theory'. 'Conspiracy' is a wonderful word: it smacks of piracy, of smoke-filled rooms, of a priori illegality, like Milton's Devils in *Paradise Lost*, in 'bold conspiracy against Heav'n's King'. Today's managers are reasonable men and their opponents are, as has been shown, demagogues. To be accused of conspiracy is to lose. It transfers blame from the facts of the case to the *behaviour* of the bringer of the case, thus burying ethics and reasonable debate in quasi-clinical accusation. As such it is a familiar right-wing and left-wing device.

Yet in the case of today's corporate world it is hard to pin-point the perpetrators of deeds and decisions when those decisions may bring down a Third World government, starve to death half a million people, throw out of work a community half-way round the world, and kill a President. After all the 'limited company' was designed to limit the responsibility of those who formed its body. It is no less an artificial person than Hobbes's *Leviathan*. One of the raciest descriptions of it was given by Thurman Arnold in 1937: 'A corporate organization is a combination of a municipal election, a historic pageant, an anti-vice crusade, a graduate school seminar, a judicial proceeding, and a series of horse trades, all rolled into one – thoroughly buttered with learning and frosted with distin-guished names.' It is difficult indeed to accuse that lot of premeditated conspiracy. Yet the question of power persists. Indeed at the level of persuasion, as Arnold says, the 'ideal that a great corporation is endowed with the rights and prerogatives of free individuals is as essential to the acceptance of corporate rule in temporal affairs as was the ideal of the divine right of kings in an earlier day.'[31] The ideal is marketed heavily, not least in soap operas where the corporations are dramatized as family businesses, and power is shown as mediated by private psychodramas rather than as a conflict of public interest.[32] Even Shakespeare in one of his more sentimental moments had King Lear go down on his kness and think about the poor for a few lines. Psychodrama, of course, always accompanies the manifestations of power. It prevents, as Michel Serres would say, the master and the slave coming face to face.[33]

The interlocking powers (financial, military, industrial) of the great corporation are fundamentally political. Foreign policy is essentially about safeguarding loans.[34] C. Wright Mills has argued that it is a community of interests, class affiliations, and agreed values rather than direct 'conspiracy' that keeps the system going.[35] From 1945 onwards, as Van der Pilj has shown, American corporate and financial establishments turned European economic develop-ment away from colonialism and cartelism to 'auto-centred growth based on consumer-durable consumption within a European domes-tic market'. Even today Wall Street, money-centre banks and the United States Treasury 'remain sufficiently hegemonic to enforce interest-tribute from the Third World and an unwanted "Marshal Plan in reverse" from Europe and Japan'.[36] Accompanying these Adamsian power plays is a bought press which will always expose particular scandals at particular moments but generally portrays such incidents as arguing for the excellence of public scrutiny and internal policing, or as regrettable deviations within a generally soundly managed system.[37]

In international terms the 'debt-trap', begun in the nineteenth century, has mushroomed almost out of control. The politics of the IMF have come recently under increasing scrutiny. Here again direct 'conspiracy' is not the issue, merely agreed and unwritten rules: the Managing Director of the IMF is always a Western European, and the President of the World Bank is an American.[38] That actual coercion is involved is, however, not in doubt. Crude gunboat diplomacy is a very last option. Susan George has shown why it is not necessary, in her chilling and magnificent book, *A Fate Worse than Debt* (1988). She reports a conversation of Paul Fabre, chief economic correspondent of *Le Monde*, with an American banker (an 'intelligent and sensitive man'), who told him that in the case of a Latin American country's repudiation of debt:

> we have the legal machinery all ready to go. It would be lightning-fast: we would seize all the country's assets on land, on sea and in the air. We would black all the bank accounts of its citizens; not a single one of its ships could dock or a single plane land anywhere outside that country's borders without being immediately sequestered.[39]

Adams spoke of slaughtering a thousand Malays to give them the benefits of flannel petticoats. As the Third World gets poorer the scale of operations of the IMF (backed equally by Western Europe, the United States and Japan) in terms of qualitative malignity surpasses anything accomplished by the old European empires.

Closely linked with, and dependent upon, the growth of economic institutions is what used to be called the 'military–industrial complex'. Adams was above all concerned with the magnitude of force – somewhat clumsily and inconsistently figured as energy output, GNP, blind acceleration of industrial production, and displays of fetishistic magic. Adams was right to see, however, that force was as pan-national as the limited company in its distribution and effects; the Rhine was more modern than the Hudson, and electric lights blazed at Hammerfest. And so it is today. At the level of military technology, too, national and ideological differences are ignored. At the height of the McCarthy era in the United States, one George Tichenor was arguing for the 'militarization of the engineer on the Russian model', at West Point and Annapolis. The depoliticization of the engineer is scarcely a new phenomenon.[40]

Technique (the attitude of mind developed from engagement with technics), as Ellul once said, supersedes liberalism. Veblen, in characteristic vein, described the middle men as follows: 'By settled habit the technicians, the engineers and industrial experts are a harmless and docile sort, well fed on the whole, and somewhat placidly content with a "full dinner pail" which the lieutenants of the Vested Interests allow them.'[41] But the attitudes so bred are not merely passive, as Veblen has suggested. The engineer passed a whole set of attitudes on to sociologists. The engineer, more than the pure scientist, was hooked on the liberal notion that there are salvationary behaviours based on objective and neutral methods. His high priest was B. F. Skinner, in whom the tradition of Münsterberg and others reached its apogee:

> The struggle for freedom has been formulated as a defense of autonomous man rather than as a version of the contingencies of reinforcement under which people live. A technology of behaviour is available which would more successfully reduce the aversive consequences of behaviour, proximate or defend and maximize the achievement of which the human organism is capable, but the defenders of freedom oppose it.[42]

Skinner's famous attacks on literature fulfil Whyte's prophecy of 1935 that 'the climate is now propitious for coming right out and naming the humanities as the enemy'.[43]

At a more profound level the Jamesian identification of meaning with ends is deeply inscribed in the concept of social engineering. This slick, aesthetic reversal of the a priori produces its own monsters. Against this notion it is necessary to place Arendt's much more complex definition of the nature of meaning and its relation to deeds. She argues that it is just this pragmatics of meaning that produces the sense of meaninglessness of the contemporary world:

> Meaning, which can never be the aim of action and yet, inevitably, will arise out of human deeds after the action itself has come to an end, was now pursued with the same machinery of intentions and organized means as were the particular direct aims of concrete action – with the result that it was as though meaning itself had departed from the world of men and men were left with nothing but an unending chain of purposes in whose progress the meaningfulness of all past achievements was constantly cancelled out by future goals and intentions.[44]

It is precisely that 'machinery of intentions' and 'organized means' which is the deep structure of the scientific management movement, that 'systematic philosophy of worker and work', as Braverman has described it, which may well be 'the most powerful as well as the most lasting contribution America has made to Western Thought since the *Federalist Papers*'.[45]

It is the late Lewis Mumford, the heir of Henry Adams, who has been the most trenchant critic of the mega-machine which contemporary life has become and which now threatens actual global existence with its highly productive waste and nauseous materials. To be sure, the drift of Mumford's arguments over the last sixty or more years has been Utopianist and organicist; those arguments have not for the most part included economic and political factors, but have been unerring in directing attention solidly to areas others have ignored. No one has described better the unethical and fetishistic compulsions of technology with more impartiality, nor tried harder to understand what a technology in the service of human wishes might become. He has managed to embody the best features of James's attack on progress and the denial of the person in science. Last of the great American radical critics of the 1930s, this magnificent humanist of technological history has described with increasing relevance the reduction of person to consumer: 'The willing member of megatechnic society can have everything the system produces – provided he and his group have no private wishes of their own, and will make no attempt personally to alter its quality or reduce its quantity or question the competence of its "decision makers". In such a society the two unforgivable sins, or rather punishable vices, would be continence and selectivity.'[46]

Adams's figure of the sleeping child next to the noiseless machine is an image of threatened choice and possible distance under vast compulsion in the relation between human beings and the machine. The logic of the machine, as Marx pointed out, is to feed its own continuity, aggrandizement and consistency. Like the capital which sustains it, it has a life of its own. Alongside the politically direct effects of technology, such as the specialized, highly computerized direct-mail firms serving the interests of corporate-funded political action groups (PACs), or the 'Californization' of politics with the manipulative TV interview; and alongside the directly social affects of technology – car, telephone and ambulance in the medical profession, cars and telephones in policing and crime, [47] there emerges the problem of the relation of the subject to what Guattari has called the totality of structures, to which he gives the name of 'machine'.[48]

As Marx long ago described it, 'Technology reveals the active relation of man to nature, the direct process of the production of his life, and thereby it also lays bare the process of the production of the social relations of his life, and of the mental conceptions that flow from those relations.'[49] The machine itself lost value for every moment it was not being used, and consequently imposed its own demonic time on its operators and a fear of loss of investment on its owner. In our own time the naturalization of the machine in such misleading phrases as 'user-friendly' and 'software' has disguised that aspect of its totality of structures which stand apart from us. Guattari has glossed Adams's image of baby and dynamo acutely: 'The unconscious subject as such will be on the same side as the machine, or better perhaps, *alongside* the machine. There is no break in the machine itself: the break is on either side of it.'[50]

The interlocking aspects of politics, economics, military and industrial planning, technological development and social mythology have been captured in a number of works of literature in our time, and perhaps it is only those which can give a sense of what it feels like to live in the world of the late twentieth century. Dale Carter has deftly interlinked the world of Pynchon's *Gravity's Rainbow* (1973) with the actual history of American politics and technology in the post-war years, and his closing pages describe the sacrifice of Christa McAuliffe, who in her own biography (the all-American childhood, piano and dancing lessons, Girl Scouts, the all-star softball team, the teacher in the public school system) provided 'a morally instructive parable of state'. Much of the training she received 'consisted of stern admonitions' never to touch 'those switches', and Carter comments, 'for the ordinary American citizen wired up to the space shuttle's circuits the controls stayed a long way off.'[51] Mumford has correctly pointed out that the megamachine is common both to the Soviet Union and the United States. In the United States the technologically militarized élites have 'extended their tentacles throughout the industrial and the academic world, through fat subsidies for "research and development", that is, for weapons expansion, which made these once-independent institutions willing accomplices in the whole totalitarian process'.[52]

Has in fact 'society become police', as Adams asserted? It is now time to look at that world of society itself in more detail. To what extent has it become 'totalitarian'? How much has the Jamesian therapeutic vision succeeded and, paradoxically, his horror of the professional been justified? How has the nature of the mass society, and its entertainments, commented on by Stein from detective stories to motor cars – not to mention the general anxiety particularized in Richard Wright's response to her letters – been continued and developed? What has happened to Arendt's notion of the 'private' – the world of independent thinking, love and creativity? And, above all, to what extent is 'society' a monster created by the fusion of he public and private realms?

II

As Simone Weil once remarked: 'It is quite impossible to avoid the social problem. The first duty that it places on one is not to tell lies.'[53] The 'social' in the following account relates specifically to so-called developed societies. Bookchin gives a fair warning that 'the word social should not sweep us into a deluge of intellectual abstractions that ignore the distinctions between one social form and another'. For example the social attitudes of Hopi children observed in schools administered by whites are not comparable with those of their administrators: 'So all-pervasive were their group attitudes. . . that [they]. . . could be persuaded only with the greatest difficulty to keep score in competitive games.'[54]

The arbiters of the social in Western society are the professionals. Without actual political power in the traditional sense, they manage 'society' in endlessly proliferating cadres. From the traditional professional bodies of the law, the army, the church and medicine, professions have multiplied to include most white-collar jobs that require long training (sociologists, economists, psychologists, psychotherapists, and a host of specialized 'consultants' whose business is far from medicine), as well as many of the more highly skilled industrial jobs in engineering and hi-tech software.

There have been numerous descriptions of what a 'profession' is. Most commentators begin with a classification of characteristics, missing the first and most fundamental point that a profession claims, in the first instance, to be politically neutral. Pope's eighteenth-century couplet in the *Essay on Man* sets the conservative tone for both the nineteenth and twentieth centuries:

> For Forms of Government let fools contest;
> Whate'er is best administered is best.

The reaction against the political science of the seventeenth and eighteenth centuries came, understandably, in the wake of the French Revolution and the Terror. The revolutionary philosophy was to be superseded by a 'philosophy of organization'.[55] Hayek called the social philosophy of Saint-Simon and the string of social theorists who followed him, organizing the 'counter-revolution of science'.[56] Social science was pitted against the political memories and political theories of earlier generations, much as Stuart Hughes has shown that Marx was a 'proving ground' for the generation of Durkheim a century later.[57] The legitimation was methodological and, from an astonishingly early moment, 'medical'. In Saint-Simon's words: 'Si les physiologistes et les philosophes veulent aujourd'hui réunir franchement leurs efforts, ils parviendront à ramener toutes les questions politiques à des considérations d'hygiène.'[58] The advice was heeded. As Hughes comments in his classic work, *Consciousness and Society*: 'Sorel, Pareto, Durkheim, Freud, all thought of themselves as engineers or technicians, men of science or medicine.'[59]

As such the aim was to make the profession a hermetically sealed yet indispensable group. The training had to be long and expensive – thus making it difficult for anyone from a working-class background to enter. It was a job for life, it had a common and often esoteric language (mathematics, scientific terms, sociological jargon), which often took long early training to learn. It was on the whole internally policed. Anyone who appealed for any kind of judgement outside its ranks was either speedily disposed of, or censured heavily. It presided over the training of its own members. It was highly specialized and authoritatively certificated by stiff tests. Above all it knew its own boundaries, discouraged 'the interdisciplinary', and refused to comment on anything which it did not feel came within its own preserve. It addressed itself to the carefully demarcated area of the 'social' and was hostile to 'political' issues and questions. Above all it was scientific and objective, and never subjective, emotional, nor involved with problems of power. It could pride itself on knowing more than its masters, whom it knew were dependent on it for expertise to run a complex society, from weapons systems to economics. And it could distinguish itself from the mass of working people on the double basis of the moral superiority of its regularized life-style while offering those same working people 'help'. Its watchword was service, not profit.[60]

Within the professions, of course, there are many hundreds of thousands of people who are kind, decent, law-abiding, and genuinely proud of their hard-won abilities placed at the disposal of society. Teachers and social workers are always badly paid and therefore continuously under attack by the journalistic flunkeys of the rich. Doctors and lawyers are not so badly paid, yet many of them work impossible hours for their monetarily better-rewarded labour. In our own time the democratization of the 'professions' has withdrawn from them much of their original status, and there is increasing proletarization of the middle classes in 1990s Anglo-America, owing to cut-backs in the public sector. In addition, Bledstein notes how certification is now almost universal, a trend begun as early as the nineteenth century when undertakers began calling themselves 'Doctors of Grief'.[61] Workers may also in some advanced industries be paid 'salaries', thereby eroding another traditional status distinction. The whole of the scientific management movement noted earlier in the sections on psychology and on James, was in effect a 'socialization': a word as much abused as the historical euphemisms of 'modernization' and 'industrialization'. The *social* planning of the post-Taylor management systems has also been noted, and Braverman points to its value base: 'The *internal* planning of. . . corporations becomes in effect *social* planning, even though, as Alfred P. Sloan explained, it is based upon the "net return" on "invested capital", which he calls the true measure of efficiency.'[62]

Critiques of the managers of the social realm have not, however, been lacking. Chomsky quotes Peter Berger to the effect that 'As the physicists are busy engineering the world's annihilation, the social scientists can be entrusted with one smaller mission of engineering the world's consent'. Paul Goodman wrote that 'we are artificing a social machine running for its own aggrandizement, in which all citizens are personnel'. Long ago Simone Weil talked about that moral doubleness the profession encourages: 'The fact that men can do their jobs and still be human beings in their private lives shows that the profession puts blinkers over their eyes, that it canalizes individual virtues and that individual virtues do not elevate the profession.'[63] B. F. Skinner's confident vision of 'society' agreeing to 'make behaviour consistent by the use of social engineering', is countered by increasing criticism of scientistic methodology and its appropriateness for the human realm in which 'the concept of the detached non-interfering scientist is a fiction'.[64] Historians quarrel over the legacy of Durkheim, but his attempted mediation of the conservative and collectivist political positions in carving out a 'professional' niche within a university system and in offering support for what was called in the 1930s the 'practical curriculum', is increasingly under critical scrutiny.[65] Others have noted that 'the helping professions are the most effective contemporary agents of social conformity and isolation'. They thus support the existing political structure and are largely immune from political regulation.[66]

While these criticisms remain largely ineffective in actual terms, critics have persisted in undermining the stances of objectivity and conservative characterizations of the domain of nature which have always underwritten professional legitimations. It was Werner Sombart who gave psychological clues to objectivity in the human sciences: '"Objectivity" is the compensation men offer themselves when their capacity to love has been crippled. Thus those who wish to speak in praise of objectivity often know no better way of doing so than to denounce sentimentality.' Gouldner, citing Sombart, points to the political implications, and it is worth quoting him in full:

> Objectivity is the way one comes to terms with and makes peace with a world one does not like but will not oppose; it arises when one is detached from the status quo but reluctant to be identified with its critics, detached from the dominant map of social reality as well as from meaningful alternate maps. 'Objectivity' transforms the nature of exile into a positive and valued *social location*; it transforms the weakness of the internal 'refuge' into the superiority of principled aloofness. Objectivity is the ideology of those who are alienated and politically homeless.[67]

The last two sentences (my emphasis) are particularly important for showing the deep structure of professional ideology. Objectivity of course goes with a 'scientific' view of nature. Traditionally, even where the practice is not philosophically fully acknowledged, scientists have relied on the distinction between nature and mind to permit the one to be scrutinized by the other. Epistemological questions are expunged in order to render the purity of objectivity inviolable.

It was Gertrude Stein who examined the assumptions of the scientific gaze within the formal project of literature's representation of the social process. Like Whitehead she would have dearly loved a correspondence theory between mind and nature, but she was too much aware of the artist's capacity to recreate the world fully to accede to it. In traditional radical European philosophy consciousness is still a valued concept, but nature is characterized as a domain of pure necessity. Sartre began to invalidate this notion, since he claimed correctly that Nature without observers is a transcendental concept, but that such an insight insists on *everything* (including purposive action) being referred back to it. Speaking within the Marxist tradition of dialectics, he claimed that the 'dialectic of nature refers to the totality of material facts – past, present, future – or, to put it another way, it involves the totalization of temporality'.[68]

Strangely, the American ecological critic Bookchin, who in general sets himself in an anti-Marxist tradition and prefers the anarchist tradition of Fourier, Kropotkin and Mumford, also insists, in Sartre's phrase, on a totalizing and historical concept of nature: 'We phase into society as individuals in the same way that society, phasing out of nature, comes into itself', and 'The need to bring a sense of history into nature is as compelling as the need to bring a sense of history into society'. While 'phasing into' is evasive (obviously the nature of production and accompanying social relations must be specified), the same wish to avoid reductive dualisms is in evidence. Nature is not, for either, to be anthropomorphized into a mimetic alibi for society. Bookchin: 'A snarling animal is neither "vicious" nor "savage" nor does it "misbehave" or "earn" punishment because it reacts appropriately to certain stimuli.'[69] Sartre on the other hand, attempting to describe a phenomenon like deforestation as a historical phenomenon, sees such moments as inverted praxis – that is the necessarily negative results of labour returning as a hostile constraint on future action.

Breaking out of this circle of double action is theoretically difficult. Nature is seen simply as a transcendent totality and a practical limit. Bookchin on the other hand takes Sartre's notion – that 'Destruction by Nature is imprecise: it leaves little islands, even whole archipelagos. Human destruction is systematic. . .' – in a much more positive way. Nature may offer a model of freedom as well as of necessity, and its transcendence here consists precisely in the hope it offers of imperfect destructiveness as part of a cycle of renewal. Bookchin also takes the Frankfurt School to task for being unprepared to 'make the claims of nature against the failures of society'.[70] There are weaknesses in Bookchin's argument which leave the questions of power largely untouched; nonetheless he points to major faults in the characterization of nature within the Marxist tradition: faults which it shares with capitalist tradition also; specifically the production process's inevitable seizure of hostile Nature in a hostile manner.

These comments sufficiently introduce that ambiguous naturalization of the social process whose most imporant theorist in the twentieth century has been Talcott Parsons. Rather like William James, Parsons countered that 'gloomy' social theorizing of the Europeans with proposed therapeutic structures in which values were successfully acted out. Theories of power and notions of contradiction are ignored. It was Parsons who laid less stress on the legitimation of science and greater stress on 'professionalism'. Orderly yet 'spiritual', it was neither bureaucratic nor capitalist. In the later period 'socialization' replaces an earlier view of Jamesian voluntaristic action, though recent sociologists have reclaimed the earlier notion.[71]

Parsons's view of the social world straddled a metaphysical contradiction between genetic differentiation and organic single systems – a metaphysics not remote from either Darwin's theory of natural selection or Whitehead's organicism. As Gouldner points out the Parsonian emphasis was on the self-regulation and maintainence of systems.[72] In other words once again the emphasis is on homeostatic models, rather than on ones which include creativity and change. Value is transmitted rather than created. As with Durkheim the implicit opposition, though rarely stated, was Marxism. For from the point of view of the Marxist, Parsons simply moralized the superstructure. The often repressive culture within which Parsons sought to harmonize social roles was unproblematized. Aronowitz makes the point that 'The empirical proof of Parsons's argument resides in the longevity of the social system'.[73] That 'social' time runs more slowly than political time is an argument familiar in the present book, from Lyell to Braudel. Whether it empirically legitimates a hidden conservative politics is nonetheless very much open to doubt.

The mediation of professionalism, however, has been nowhere more marked than in medicine, which in its own way threatens to take over the entire responsibility for maintaining homeostasis within the culture. The links with the actual political structure in terms of economics have already been described. It remains to describe links with society. The effects of the 'medicalization' of culture are almost fashionably under scrutiny at this time, yet certain points can be raised here to show the continuity of debate between James's attempts to introduce the language of therapeutics into the erstwhile religious, philosophical and ethical domains and Stein's attempts to wrench the world of the creative away from the social structures of 'normal life'.

Seen from below, the teacher, the social worker, the lawyer, the doctor, the psychiatrist, the policeman and the priest have enormous power, simply because they have knowledge on which others are dependent – including of course any one of themselves in relation to any other profession.[74] All depend on a notion of society as a kind of organism for whose equilibrium or 'homeostasis' they are responsible. The notion of homeostasis, however – a word invented by Walter B. Canon in a book called *The Wisdom of the Body*, published perhaps classically in 1933 – has a history of its own, for its origins lie in Claude Bernard's concept of the internal environment (*le milieu intérieur*) responding organically to an exterior one; the notion moves, as Russett has shown, as a social concept through the work of, among others, Pareto and L. J. Henderson (who linked equilibrium with system) to Parsons himself.[75]

A history of social medicine has yet to be written, but Roy Porter has shown that the term originated with Jules Guérin (1801–86), and Porter lists some terms which arose more or less synonymously with it: 'social hygiene', 'preventative medicine', 'state medicine', 'sanitary engineering', 'public health'. For many the 'methodology' of social medicine was derived from clinical practice. 'Statistics' provided the 'social post-mortem' and defined the meaning of 'normal' in the measurement of 'health'. From the 1930s to the 1950s historians produced analyses and contemporary accounts of social medicine, 'carrying the implicit polemical argument that it could be a panacea for the ills both of society and of medicine'.[76] The impetus came from Virchow, whose famous statement that doctors are the natural attorneys of the poor has already been cited. It had various fates in various countries, in the eugenics movement in England, social hygiene in France, biotechnical engineering in Germany. The excesses of 'social patholgy' in political terms in the twentieth century are too well known to be insisted upon here. In Jonas's words: 'Especially in the human sphere, experimentation loses entirely the advantage of the clear division between vicarious model and true object.'[77]

Yet for all the importance of more radical analyses, in the 'real world' of psychopathological commentators the nonsense continues unabated. In a recent work by the doctor and priest William Meissner, *The Paranoid Process* (1978), which is the 'fullest clinical statement' of the condition of paranoia, one may find the following:

> As long as the individual sense of self remains congruent and adaptive in the functioning social matrix, we do not tend to regard the sense of self as pathological. . . . Our basic hypothesis with respect to the organization of society is that social processes organize themselves in such a way as to provide appropriate contexts within which the paranoid process comes into play, so as to preserve certain specific adaptive functions within the society and to provide the appropriate context within which individuals may find a sense of appropriate belonging and useful participation. . . . Thus society provides structures and contexts within which the basic mechanisms of the paranoid process can be turned to adaptive and useful purposes.[78]

Such banality dressed up in scientistic language litters the pages of the textbooks of the social sciences, but it is exemplary in its essentialization of the self, its hypostasization of the social, its acceptance of the normal as given, its social-Darwinistic terminology of adaption and context, and its unstated teleology of unspecified utilitarianism and instrumentalism. The evasions can been seen in the title of the section heading from which the passage comes: 'Sociopolitical Adaption'. Here indeed is 'the physician as agent of society'.[79] That the pressure towards homeostasis may equally cause stress and illness, or that normality might not be a condition where nothing ever goes wrong, does not occur to these unruffled spirits.[80]

That role of the social agent has nowhere, even now, been better examined than by Szasz. In spite of certain limitations (the assumption of the mind–body dualism, the Popperian reading of Marx and Freud, and a certain intangible disposition to ignore the role of power, perhaps best seen in his preference for Camus over Sartre), no one has more trenchantly battled against the implicit totalitarianism, in East and West, of the managed society. Long before the structuralist critics of the 1970s, Szasz was describing the therapeutic state and psychiatry as an institution of social control.[81] Furthermore he was insisting that psychiatrists had usurped the realm of strictly moral problems by converting them into medical problems. The Jamesian seamless parallels between mind and body, the abuse of the notion of 'health', all received merciless analytic criticism. Above all, that secretly political cooperation between law and medicine was exposed for what it was: 'the defendant is not a "patient", the prosecutor and his psychiatrists are not his "doctors". The relationship between the defendant and the state (and its representatives) is antagonistic, not cooperative'. There was no 'rational generally accepted method for translating a legal standard into a social act'. In both the United States and the Soviet Union, ethics and due process of law were subject to abuse by medical professional managers. 'Health' was a screen behind which ethical responsibility on both sides could be evaded:

> How do we determine who is fit to stand trial and who is not? Does this subject deserve the attention of the general public, or is it a special problem that concerns only the district attorney, judges, and forensic psychiatrists who must interpret the law? The answer we give reflects the image of social order we envisage.[82]

Szasz challenged also that compelling parallel, as he called it, between bodily and mental illness and the new notion that 'hysteria, neurasthenia, depression, paranoia, and so forth were regarded as diseases that *happened* to people'.[83] The fatalism of the happening gave permission to act out certain roles which lifted ethical responsibility on the grounds of a determined factuality: an excellent way of manipulating other people without being held to account. The professions supplied the ceremony, from the couch to the law court. Increasingly, Szasz argued, medicine itself, and above all psychiatry, 'may come to resemble the profession of law'.[84] Thirty or more years on, the shift is from the 'professional socialization' of young doctors to their 'corporate socialization', the health centre of one era is becoming the 'profit centre' of the next.[85] In this obvious turn for the worse, however, the precise centre of sovereignty might be more clearly exposed.

The key institution of the professionalizing process is of course the university. Nineteenth-century American academic institutions were bought out by the corporations in the 1880s and 1890s, and Cardinal

Newman's ideal of the university disappeared for ever. The process took longer elsewhere. In Great Britain, for example, the final conversion to the 'practical curriculum' will probably be accomplished in the next four or five years. As in most totalitarian states the onslaught on the humanities, powerless though they are, remains a kind of litmus paper with which to gauge the extent of the servitude of the world of learning to its philistine masters. The Skinnerian view that literature, with its commitment to freedom and dignity, is the enemy of the logic of planned behaviour has become generally accepted. William James complained of the 'Ph.D. Octopus' and Stein broke with the behavioural sciences to both criticize and use their basic assumptions in the creation of a literature only now coming to full attention. Neither could possibly have foreseen the extent to which 'men at centres of learning become experts inside administrative machines'. C. Wright Mills added the real reason for the shift: 'The American university system seldom if ever provides political education; it seldom teaches how to gauge what is going on in the general struggle for power in modern society.'[86]

Veblen's classic essay (1918) on the subject gives the details of a process now more or less complete. The clergy have been replaced by businessmen and politicians. A once-subservient administration (in the best sense) has become the most important part of what is a large corporation disposing of huge expenditures and with an attitude to academics commensurate with their inferior salaries, and untidy intellectual habits. The ideal university 'man' still bears the trappings of the country-gentleman class, quiet, self-effacing, 'sound', whose efficiency is measured in the committee room rather than in the classroom. The university PR machine likes non-controversial outside lectures preferably before, in Veblen's words, 'an audience of devout and well-to-do women'. Religious subjects and leftist politics are taboo. (One would add here to Veblen's analysis that under 'friendly fascism' they are permitted at the very expensive universities.) The duties of publicity are large and arduous, continued Veblen, and they are attached to competition between departments: the 'businesslike rivalry between the several schools is perhaps the gravest drawback to the American university situation'. Such rivalry is of course imposed from without, reflecting the divide-and-rule strategy of the paymasters. Veblen gloomily concluded that 'any promise of rehabilitation for the higher learning in the universities can not be attempted in the present state of public sentiment'.[87]

A detailed account of the change from the Merrill Act of 1862 is given in the first part of C. Wright Mills's *Sociology and Pragmatism: The Higher Learning in America* (1964). Mills ends by citing Eliot's inaugural address at Harvard: 'Philosophical subjects should never be taught with authority. They are not established sciences. . . [they are] full of bottomless speculation.'[88] Paul Goodman concluded in the 1960s, 'There is no mass base for university reform in the universities.' The reasons are not hard to find. By 1954 Whyte had observed that 'business administration majors made up the largest single field of undergraduate institutions outside the field of education itself'.[89]

The hierarchy of colleges and schools reflects a class and economic division within society itself.[90] What Galbraith once applied to economists now applies to a whole range of 'personnel' within the university system. Allowing for numerous exceptions, 'they will prove to identify economic goals with all of life. They are not, accordingly, the best proponents of the public, aesthetic, and intellectual qualities on which the quality and safety of life increasingly depend. They are, in the main, the natural allies of the industrial system.' Making up most of the educational and scientific estates, they have a strong tendency to 'surrender to the goals of the industrial system before the battle is joined'.[91] Mostly middle-class and in consequence powerless, academics like to identify with power. This is not crude identification with the wealthy, nor with brutality, nor with politicians necessarily, but with 'the efficient system itself', which, as Goodman saw accurately, is the main factor 'which renders them powerless'.[92]

Yet academics and what freedom they have left must be defended. Recently much publicity has been given to Russell Jacoby's book, *The Last Intellectuals*. It is worth pausing over, as it purports to offer reasons for the decay of the independent intellectual operating outside the university. Its title should sound warning bells. For like *The Last of the Mohicans*, it celebrates as nostalgic, knowing, moralistic sentiment what it fails to analyse politically. Battening on real discontent and frustration, and in many ways giving timely renewed notice to just those extra-academic thinkers on whom the present work also relies, Jacoby's book fails to analyse the politics of university economics, publishing and distribution, just as it fails to analyse the urban-renewal programmes that yuppify the cosy little bohemian centres he is so nostalgic for. Lewis Mumford told the author in 1973 that when he started out he could make enough money from a book that sold under 2,000 copies to live for a year. If men like Mumford lived 'their lives by way of books, reviews and journals', and 'rarely taught in universities',[93] it was because historically it was economically possible to do so. It is no longer possible. Nor were such men as polarized in their attitudes to the academic system as Jacoby's simplistic theses argue. They would have preferred to have the attention of universities and the large audiences which passed through their doors. Jacoby personalizes, and psychologizes, the *trahison des clercs* at every step. And at no point in his argument is the university tenure system examined in terms of its often overt political suppression of the young and the potentially threatening.

The Last Intellectuals is a classic instance of the 'time-delay' strategy of criticism, as well as an attempt to cash in on an increasingly radical intellectual scene. Nowhere in his book does Jacoby take up the cause of neglected artists, writers and radical critics, in or out of universities, who, unpublicized, are working *now*. The precise politics and particular analysis of the acceptable ideologies for contemporary recognition escape the flailing clumsiness of his muscular liberal fundamentalism.

Most of all Jacoby neglects the politics of recognition in a *mass society*: that precise problem which Stein sought to solve in an unsatisfactory way in 1935, after years of neglect. The nature of what mass society actually is has been the subject of much debate, as with its corollary, mass culture. Stein humorously lamented that she would like to have been as popular as Jenny Lind, but she asked in vain for the man who would publish her in series. With familiar sharpness the precise irony of her statement signals most of the problems under discussion here.

In creative terms there has always been a relation between high and low culture. Milton used the great tradition of English folklore as did Shakespeare. Beethoven's last quartets take up the folk tunes of his native land and Bach used popular love songs to harmonize into his finest chorales. Melville drew on a whole range of popular literature for *Moby Dick*, and, post-Dada and Surrealism, serious artists of all kinds have had no problems about the range of materials they can engage with. There is also no question that great art can come from the relatively untutored. A Bunyan can move as much as a Milton, a John Clare as much as a Shelley. In terms of radical criticism also, as the prison literature of the United States shows, insights into politics do not depend on a college education.

Two examples show the distance between contemporary thinkers. Arendt always argued for a tough intellectually demanding approach to intellectual life because she came from a European tradition which actually values thinking. Mass society 'wants not culture, but entertainment, and the wares offered by the entertainment industry are indeed consumed by society just like any other consumer goods'.[94] It was C. Wright Mills who distinguished, in the same spirit, the difference between the public and the mass. The 'public' ensures equality of response between expressing and receiving opinion. Public communications ensure this and action readily follows even against the 'prevailing system of authority'. Influential institutions do not sway or penetrate the public, which remains to a degree autonomous. A 'mass', in contrast, receives the opinions of the few, it is impossible to answer back effectively, action is controlled independently of such reciprocity as is allowed, and institutional opinion is identified with public opinion.[95] Mills was writing in the shadow of the defeat of Nazism and Fascism and in the context of the vast growth of the communications industries.

In contrast, Shils, a Parsonsian apologist for mass society, has argued that élites and mass move 'towards each other' through pop music, that charisma is democratically dispersed inside mass culture, that it is spontaneous and has lifted the lid on impulse, that technological progress ensures the well-being of bureaucracy, and that the lower classes are drenched in civility unlike the 'lower classes of pre-modern society'. No empirical evidence is offered for these moralizing opinions. Here in the great 'mass society' there is more of a sense of attachment to society as a whole, more of 'a sense of affinity with one's fellows', more openness to understanding.[96] Clearly the Europeans are, once more, hopeless pessimists. The argument from pessimism and/or optimism, however, reduces to behaviour and feeling, an issue which needs to be examined carefully with certain distinctions thought out. That 95 per cent of mass entertainment is slush – nasty, brutish, and malign, will not be denied except by slumming liberals. That distinctions can be made within it, and that some of it is marvellous (the author remembers with great happiness the Sergeant Bilko TV series of the 1950s) is equally not to be denied. That important clues to the direction of the culture in social terms can be elicited by looking at westerns or the *Ladies' Home Journal* is also true. But deciding a priori (and it is the a priori that must be emphasized) that gay black women's literature is more important to study than *Don Quixote* is an intellectual fraud, and is degrading for gay black women who also write literature.

The choice is between cultural and critical difficulty (which always resists the demagogue) and sustaining the class, sexual, and economic anxiety under which millions live by cheap ideological characterizations which flatter intelligence, sustain impoverished images of the self, and substitute moralism for analysis. Aronowitz has not only made important distinctions between popular and mass culture, but also has suggested that any teacher who neglects the complete involvement of students in popular entertainment culture will not get very far.[97] Defenders of popular culture endlessly confuse entertainment and popular culture. My own piano teacher holds annual concerts of her pupils in which some black high school students play along with their squeeze-boxes and some play Beethoven sonatas, depending on their skill and experience, which is in process of being encouraged and developed more complexly. The class identification, supported by a snobbish culture, of high culture with high classes and low culture with the lower classes – the whole underlined by economic maldistribution of educational resources – needs to be resisted to the limit.

Mere juxtaposition of the two is not evaluative. One recent apologist speaks of how the 1984 Olympics 'were [not only] accompanied with predictably vulgar hucksterism but also with a first-rate internal festival of classical music, ballet, theatre, folklore, and painting'.[98] The evasion is in the 'were accompanied' and in the 'but also'. Valuation is avoided and neither legitimates the Olympics – one of the great shows of mass society, in which the therapeutic state receives ultimate authentication – hence the fuss over drugs which render its body politic unhealthy in more ways than one. Irrespective of competition, the human body must be displayed in the purity of its perfection as a social icon. The collusion in this mass social event (1988) by social-democratic Norway as by the state socialist USSR enables the autocratic police state of South Korea (backed by the USA) to attain a degree of respectability, and shows the extent to which the 'political' has been swamped by the need for the shows of mass social propaganda in our time. 'Strength through joy', as James's praise of the skiing sisters of Norway anticipated, acts against the 'unhealthy minded', when optimism is official. Leni Riefenstal's *Olympia*, whose epic visual mysticism celebrates a spectacle of exhausted marathon runners falling into the arms of white-uniformed officials with Nazi armbands (accompanied by Herbert Windt's trumpet music), presents the worst consequences of this vision.

It is clear what happens to the 'political' within 'socialization', but what of the 'private'? What happens to the nature of the subject when the 'social' takes over? The civil liberty of the individual is immediately at risk when social professionals take over due processes of law. Stein gave some sense of that institutionalized terror against the private in *The Making of Americans* when she described the life of an ordinary American college. Aronowitz has shown how the lives of 'middle managers' of all kinds – of district sales, service facilities, production superintendents, together with department heads of universities, and directors of research programmes – increasingly lack 'the private dimension'.[99] Stein, it will be recalled, was amazed at the familiarity with which people greeted her after extensive radio and newspaper coverage. Modern commentators have called this

phenomenon a 'para-social' relation between spectator and performer: a compensatory relation which provides the socially and
psychologically isolated 'a chance to enjoy the elixir of sociability'.[100]
Its characteristics are proximity without intimacy.[101]

Such phenomena point to a take-over by the addictive means
of mass communication of personal choice, local loyalty, and the
possibility of different and individual lives. Politically, voter and
party workers scarcely meet face to face. The doorstep conversation
has been replaced by the telephone call, and propaganda by 'mail-
out' joins the other junk mail that litters the post-box. Socially, as
C. Wright Mills wrote, 'to remain local is to fail'.[102]

Whyte warned long ago that the 'peace of mind offered by organization remains a surrender, and no less so than for being offered
in benevolence'. Once within the institution the trap is set. Whyte
quotes from a *Bureau of Naval Personnel Handbook* on 'How to deal
with an obstreperous person'. The narrative goes something as follows: You fail to hear the objections, or misunderstand them, then
recognize the now 'legitimate' objection to 'get him to feel he belongs', Then incite the group against him, endlessly ask him to clarify
the position, turn him into the conference comedian and then sooth
his bruised ego and 'restore him to human society [*sic*] by asking him
questions that he can answer out of special [*sic*] experience'.[103] As
can be seen from this routine of black comedy, specialization is part
of the control system. From the personal point of view, success
depends on specialization, and one commentator adds, 'to crown his
success he must de-specialize – but it is usually too late. This is one
reason why his success is so often a bitter fruit.'[104]

What happens to the 'ethical subject' in these conditions is obvious. Foucault in one of his last interviews said, 'it seems to me
that the question of an ethical subject does not have much of a place
in contemporary political thought.'[105] Bookchin has given the
reasons:

> The Superego is no longer formed by the father or even by
> domineering social institutions; it is formed by the faceless people
> who preside over the records of birth and death, of religious
> affiliation and educational pedigree, of 'mental health' and
> psychological proclivities, of vocational training and job accept-
> ance, of marriage and divorce certificates, of credit ratings, and
> bank accounts; in short of the endless array of licenses, texts,
> contracts, guides, and personality traits that define the status of
> the individual in society.[106]

If those abundant gratifications which 'an industrial society is able to
distribute',[107] are added to this internalized self-repressiveness, it

would appear that the rejoicing in 1984 that Orwell's *1984* had not historically occurred stands as a precise fulfilment of Orwell's predictions. No one had noticed.

Yet, against the managed society and at the personal level, unpredictability with its promise of renewal remains at the heart of all creativity, love, and the ability to recognize and go through with the experience of tragedy. Very little in the contemporary world supports such a view, yet Arendt's classic definition of unpredictability is more important now than at the time it was first formulated:

> Unpredictability is not lack of foresight, and no engineering management of human affairs will ever be able to eliminate it, just as no training in prudence can ever lead to the wisdom of knowing what one does. Only total conditioning, that is, the total abolition of action, can hope to cope with unpredictability.[108]

Such a view may help the recovery of responsibility of a different sort from that traditionally recognized. A contributor to a recent anthology of writings on human emotions talks of Sartre's 'relentless' arguing 'that we are responsible for everything we do and everything we are. And this includes our emotions'. And, he continues, 'Thus Sartre could not disagree more with William James's theory, according to which emotions are largely instinctual, physiological reactions over which we have no control.'[109] The account paraphrases Sartre wrongly and refuses to note that the point of Sartre's account is the 'dramatization' (private or public), post-impact, of the emotional response. The theatre of everyday life needs complex ways in which to assess responsibility, but responsibility remains more important than 'adjustment'.

III

Finally what of the nature of representation and, to use the fashionable term, 'discourse'? In what direction will the nature of social and political theory develop? What of the nature, too, of theories of language and the fate of literature? It was Szasz who, citing Reichenbach, commented that 'there can be no such thing as "body language" though there are body signs'. Such a remark sums up earlier chapters on language in this book and Stein's place among them. Szasz went on to attack the jargon of the human sciences and to cite the work of Charcot, Janet and Freud, making the point that more than changes of words were involved: 'Henceforth persons who imitated illness – for example, who had "spells" – were regarded as genuinely ill, and were called hysterics; and those who imitated physicians – for example who "hypnotised" – were regarded as genuine healers and were called psychotherapists.' Charcot, friend of the Grand Duke Nicholas of Russia, put on splendid shows in which his working-class patients were coached by assistants in the niceties of dramatic representations of hysteria. Enter the physician.[110] No less than Orwell, Szasz noted that 'the language peculiar to totalitarian doctrines is always a scholastic or administrative language'.[111] In Orwell's words, 'Orthodoxy, of whatever colour, seems to demand a lifeless, imitative style. . . . When one watches some tired hack on the platform mechanically repeating the familiar phrases – bestial atrocities, iron heel, bloodstained tyranny, free peoples of the world, stand shoulder to shoulder – one often has a curious feeling that one is not watching a live human being but some kind of dummy. . . .'[112]

The same is true of the specialized languages of literary criticism and the human sciences. Here is a sample: modernization, socialization, legitimation, repressive desublimation, feminization, patriarchy, demagoguery, social base, urbanization, phallocratic, conspiracy theory, literary production, erasure, closure, industrialization, discourse, paranoia, Oedipal, individual and society, the construction of the feminine, and so forth. Not that some of these words do not genuinely refer; a number have been used reluctantly in the present work. In addition a cliché can be used sincerely and new theories need neologisms. Nonetheless the sheer dullness of the incorporated vocabulary betrays anxiety about acceptance, and the fear of re-creation which counters every genuine attempt at analysis. Orwell's tired hacks these days are too young, and to be found in graduate schools terrorized by their tolerant supervisors. The attempts of linguistics to find a truth of language above or below speaking has also powerfully aided the psychological demand that an exact regulated language can be found to reveal the political and social condition in referential purity.

The only comprehensive work to look historically at the rival claims of literature, science, and the social sciences to describe the world, is Wolf Lepenies's *Between Literature and Science: The Rise of Sociology* (1985; trans. 1988). It is not clear whether the rivalry is felt so keenly in literature as in sociology, since 'describing society' is not necessarily the first aim of a writer of literature – though in the world of the origins of sociology, the novel (Dickens and Balzac) could have been said to have done just that. Lepenies traces the fascinating path of their mutual reactions nonetheless. Flaubert's programme for literature Lepenies surmises would have delighted a Durkheim, given the vocabulary of mutual aims.[113] It is a pity, however, not to have on record the resurrected Flaubert's reaction as he read through the last page of *La Suicide*. In spite of all the refer-

ences to Faust, Musset, Lamartine, Chateaubriand, my own response
to this work is not dissimilar to the one given above in relation to
Darwin's work on the emotions, which is similarly studded with
literary names. Sometimes Lepenies's contending duallists are a little
simplistic, and his heart-and-style (literature) versus head-and-truth
(sociology) dualities can leave out the crucial question of strategies
of discourse in which both may make an appeal to heart and head,
within the rhetoric and politics of any specialist discourse claiming
authenticity.

Lepenies is perhaps best on Germany, pointing out Riehl's note
that 'the Weimar classics had shown that poets could also be
scholarly, to the advantage of both science and literature'.[114]
Dilthey's praise of poetry in the same spirit is duly recorded, and also
the decline of the relation between poetry and science, whose
greatest advocate had, of course, been Goethe. Lepenies describes the
competitiveness between history and sociology, Simmel's literary
sociology, the influence of Nietzsche, Weber's 'heroic' Protestant-
ism, Becker's anti-Posivitism, Spengler's 'literary' history, and
Stefan George and his circle's hostility towards sociology, and their
affection for Weber.

In our own time the debates continue: criticism, literature, and
sociology continue fruitfully to poach on each other's fields, and
quarrel with each other. Diggins's article on Adams argues, for
example, that Adams 'believed that the "new science of society"
would prove "hostile" to the older institutions of church, state, and
property', and continues that a Weberian perspective suggests why
the opposite occurred:

> While science may have purged authority from the human and
> spiritual realm, it enabled corporate capitalism, modern politics,
> technology and bureaucracy to be legitimated precisely because
> they became part of the empirical, routine operations of society
> and then took on the status of rational authority.[115]

Adams's *Esther* shows, however, that he was not unaware of the
problem. The rational authority of the Murrays was based on a
Darwinian programme of survival. And from a Weberian perspective Adams did refer to scientists as Cardinals. What is good about
Diggins's comment is the willingness to use Weber synchronically
and historically at the same time. Social scientists themselves are
increasingly calling for the insights of other disciplines to move their
own work away from excessive statistics and scientism.

The theoretical issues a work like this has raised, moving as they do
between methods, philosophies, and metaphoric creativity, are too

large to summarize here. The attitude to traditional philosophy, however, of all the many issues involved, is perhaps the most important. In America the Jamesian tradition continues unabated and its most recent proponent is Rorty. While agreeing about the aridness of much Anglo-American philosophy, sympathizing with the effort to ensure that philosophy plays a role in the general culture, and absolutely agreeing with the need to let intellectual discussion spin out all over the place, it is possible to criticize the tone and style of Rorty's own philosophic discourse. Citing Dewey-style pragmatism as a return to openness and relevance, his own actual mode of argument resembles uncannily James's proto-therapeutics and a somewhat cavalier approach to metaphor. In a way his presentation of the issues, for example in 'Philosophy in America Today', which closes his book *Consequences of Pragmatism* (1982), can be fruitfully read in the light of Lepenies's book. For it is yet another chapter in the debate between science, literature and philosophy, and should be seen historically (a perspective Rorty somewhat underplays) as such.

For all his pleas for tolerance, Rorty has the Jamesian tendency to think in twos and to call for rugged head-bashing compromise. For James's 'empiricist–idealist' divide he substitutes 'Analytic–Continental', with about as much accuracy now as James displayed in the nineteenth century. And 'twos' link his argument together, enabling him to move somewhat breathlessly, for example, in one paragraph from Snow's Two Cultures to Kripke, Kuhn and Rawls versus Heidegger, Foucault and Derrida, and then to talk about a '*political* split because both sides think of themselves as looking out for the interests of the global *polis*, as the leaders who must make articulate to their fellow-citizens the dangers of the time'. Even supposing these irresponsible simplifications were true, the worst inference is that genuine contradiction is somehow simply a matter of psychology (Jamesian 'sentiment of rationality' again coming to the surface). The rhetoric that builds up to this passage depicts 'heavy-breathing' academics 'which academic power cannot fully explain'.[116] It is possible to take the opposite view that in today's corporate university, if and when, intellectually speaking, academics stop getting angry with each other, debate, and therefore freedom, will be over. The quarrels over funding of departments, if linked into these arguments, is an ethical not a philosophical issue. Rorty tends to confuse the two.

One suspects also a rather naïve nationalism in Rorty's arguments. Is it really the case that Dewey, important philosopher as he is, knocks Kant on the head once for all and not only anticipates Foucault, but arrives where Foucault was heading but never quite succeeded? The manneristic synchronism of the argument precludes that patient thoughtfulness and study which Arendt saw as the *sine qua non* of the contemplative life. There seems to be real American–European divide here. In the Western nation which has most seriously failed in relation to communal and public responsibility (and Great Britain is fast catching up with it), there seems to be a sentiment according to which philosophy legitimates itself by a populist manner of address, not by whether it has sometimes difficult and complex things to say about nature, experience and culture. In contrast to capitalist populism, in which everything is made easy for the 'man in the street', the socialist project entails respect for long, slow, difficult learning and for the life of the mind, simply because it can imagine a world in which basic needs are fulfilled. In an anti-capitalist framework, thinking is not legitimated by material ends, simply because the greatest truth about the human condition lies elsewhere. And if the only alternative to that conceived of by capitalist philosophers is characterized as a 'European', superstitious airy-fairyness, in which the 'real world' is ignored, then the paucity of those philosophers' imaginations aids and abets a betrayal not only of intellectual life, in which liberal behaviour is substituted for radical thought, but of a whole range of values which distinguish freedom from necessity.

In Rorty's earlier book, *Philosophy and the Mirror of Nature* (1979), there is further evidence of these matters. But just one point relevant to the argument here will be noted, and that is, that the alternative to intellectualist seems to be 'therapeutic'; it not only informs the substance of the argument but penetrates its mode also, in its examples and analogies. The book is self-confessedly, 'like the writings of the philosophers I most admire, therapeutic rather than constructive'. Against Arendt (whose vigorous defense is not even mentioned), Part Two of the book hopes, like James, to replace a philosophy of representations with 'a pragmatist conception of knowledge which eliminates the Greek contrast between contemplation and action, between representing the world and coping with it'.[117] As with James a mystical and ultimately religious continuity transfers the much-beloved real world to a realm where neither acting nor thinking takes place: the key mode of being in a corporate university.

For those interested in nuances of vocabulary shifts, James's sick- and healthy-minded become Rorty's tender- and tough-minded. But whereas James's 'patients' as least struggled with God as they fought for alternatives, Rorty's 'tender'-minded merely point to 'significance', and the 'tough' ones to 'truth'. The path from one to the other is as smooth as the passage from a lamb to a sheep. Like the irascible James, rolling up his sleeves against the entire 'European' tradition, and fighting off 'neurotics', Rorty knows, in the slogan of the decade, that 'when the going gets tough the tough get going'. The British imperial equivalent in the last century, from the calm superiority of absolute power, was not whether you won or lost, but 'how you played the game'. The two slogans as indicating the passage from confident imperialism to nervous totalitarianism are worthy of that 'contemplation' Rorty so despises.

In Rorty's discussion of the representation of pain, the symptom replaces the sign, as one might expect.[118] The therapeutic vision sees the body as a self-validating construct, never mind concepts of nature, experience and culture. And on it goes. The targets (Hegel, Locke, Kant) are predictable – and add footnotes to well-established Jamesian paradigms of bias, argument and rhetoric. In contrast, a relatively unknown work like Gillian Rose's *Hegel Contra Sociology* (1981) shows just how useful the history and practice of philosophy can be in helping to understand the world and methods of the social. No attempt is made here at a summary, but of relevance to the current argument concerning the more theoretical aspects of the 'social' is the author's careful account of the way the Marburg and Heidelberg Schools each in their own way turned Kant's transcendental logic into *Geltungslogik* (a logic of validity). This is a logic in which 'validity', 'objectification' and 'method' do not have a transcendental or formal status but constitute a 'metaphysics of a new kind'.[119]

Gillian Rose maintains that the development of a scientific sociology was inseparable from this transformation of the neo-Kantians. Arguing that it might have been expected that sociology would have addressed itself to the history and genesis of experience, rather than to that of justification or validity, she notes that in fact:

> the sociology of Durkheim and of Weber endorsed the neo-Kantian critique of psychologism, the derivation of validity from processes of consciousness. Like the neo-Kantians, Durkheim and Weber treated the question of validity as pertaining to a distinct realm of moral facts (Durkheim) or values (Weber) which is contrasted with the realm of individual sensations or perceptions (Durkheim) or from the psychology of the individual (Weber).

It was, continues Gillian Rose, 'the ambition of sociology to substitute itself for traditional theoretical and practical philosophy, as well as to secure a sociological object-domain *sui generis*'.[120]

The first of these ambitions was, of course, precisely what James sought to do for *psychology*, the second he attempted and, to his credit, honestly failed to do. Historically and in theoretical terms the links are intellectually precise. Like James, Durkheim was strongly influenced by the neo-Kantians: 'Durkheim was closely associated with the leading French representatives of German neo-Kantianism: Charles Renouvier, Emile Boutroux.... He was taught by Boutroux at the École Normale Supérieure 1879–1882, and was greatly influenced when a student by the writings of Renouvier.'[121]

The implications for sociology were numerous. Among them was the notion that 'society as a reality *sui generis* is the origin of the validity of judgements.' The essentially moral–metaphysical nature of this notion is clear. Durkheim drew a parallel between the 'postulate' of society and Kant's postulate of God, but as Gillian Rose points out, there is a logical fuzziness in making a postulate constitutive, since Durkheim wanted to make 'society' demonstrative of how experience is possible. In Gillian Rose's words, 'neither a postulate nor constitutive principle can be "easily verified by experience", because they make experience possible or intelligible in the first place.'[122]

In addition to Gillian Rose's argument here, it is pertinent to add that Durkheim's reasoning is in a classic nineteenth-century mode. For 'society' is in fact legitimated as a metaphysic by making it an 'origin'. The argument is in precisely the same order of legitimation as that of the 'social contract' which Durkheim was so anxious to avoid. At least the social contract had been set in the style of a pseudo-historical legal drama, whereas the notion of 'society' is pure metaphysical structure.

For Durkheim the difference between a 'judgement of reality' and a 'judgement of value' was 'not the difference between theoretical and moral judgements as in Kant, but the neo-Kantian difference between a subjectively valid judgement and an objectively valid one'. It was Weber who took up the cause of the 'subjectively valid judgement' with its hoped-for coincidence between belief and will. After a long and complex argument in which Hegel is re-read speculatively, the principle of unity in Durkheim's collective conscience or Parsons's 'pattern maintenance' is shown to be a postulate which reproduces the real dominance of individuals, 'but cannot explain it because the postulate is formal and empty'.[123]

As for action theory, while is seems to be directed to subjectively meaningful ends, or to the sum of legitimations, it reproduces only the illusion of 'free unconstrained action which is the correlate of a formal law...'. Gillian Rose concludes:

Structural sociology is 'empty', action theory is 'blind'. The former imposes abstract postulates on social reality and confirms by simplifying the contradictions of dominant law. The latter confirms social reality as a mass of random meanings in its immediate mode of representation. The lack in both cases of any references to transformative activity, property relations, law and the corresponding media of representation results in the absolutizing of the unconditioned actor on the one hand and of the totally conditioned agent on the other. If actuality is not thought, then thinking has no social import. The suppression of actuality results in sociologies which confirm dominant law and representation and which have no means of knowing or recognizing the real relations which determine that law and the media of re-presentation.[124]

Accompanying the evasions which Gillian Rose describes is a shift in the operations of power between 'society' and knowledge. Lyotard has described some of the changes in ways which help to link (not unify) the disparate aspects of this concluding discussion and also the foregoing commentaries on Adams, James and Stein. The word 'post-modern' has been avoided throughout this book for Orwellian reasons, but there is a very general historical sense in which, to paraphrase James, the way things 'hang together' post-1945 can be described as a 'post-modern condition'. Adams, James and Stein do not 'anticipate' it but they respond to certain aspects of the moments of its inception.

Lyotard notes the shift from the optimism behind the Parsonsian system corresponding to 'the stabilization of the growth economies and societies of abundance under the aegis of a moderate welfare state', to German *Systemtheorie* which is fully technocratic, 'even cynical, not to mention despairing'.[125] That that melancholy is not confined to Germany can be seen from a work like Thomas Pynchon's *Gravity's Rainbow* (1973), where a despair of post-1945 politics and the grand narrative of speculative moral discourse provides the horizon against which social controls are dramatized by means of localized narratives of black humour, the mystification of means inside entropic goals, a fragmentation of narrative in the service of the endlessly repetitive pleasures of commodity fetishisms, and the breakdown of performative criteria inside technological confidence.

The questions of 'language game' and narrative are not confined to literature alone, though literature and its study within related humanities remains the key area of rehearsing resistance (and that certainly includes the simple pleasure of the text) to the 'post-modern' condition. The current shift in emphasis to notions of discourses may lead to an attempt to homogenize and over-abstract different areas of human knowledge, but at best it calls into question the 'unconscious' hierarchy of knowledges which the corporate state promotes. It calls into conflict the metaphysic of liberalized system and problematizes the 'social' as the religion of democracy. It was James who, in writing to Jane Addams, after reading her *Democracy and Social Ethics*, observed: 'The religion of democracy needs nothing so much as sympathetic interpretation to one another of the different classes of which society consists.'[126] This accurate statement, with all the contradictions of class conflict and power relations fully repressed, reaches its apogee in John McDermott's letter to James's old journal *The Nation* in 1966. The inspiration for American intervention in Vietnam 'may have been less to be the world's "policeman" than to be its social worker'.[127]

Lyotard insists that power and knowledge are simply two sides of the same question. He further uses the concept of narrative to contrast the projects of literature and science. As such he makes analytic much of what Stein was doing in her own language games in the early years of this century. For she pitted language games, the problematization of narrator and narration, speculation about the pragmatics of transmission and the claims of story, against the suspended time of scientific language in its claim to speak for the whole of the human world. Further, she ambiguously set 'society' against 'institution', challenged the externalization of the referent in its pseudo-neutrality to parties and the systematics of exchange, and wrested memory from institutional authorization and the continuously unfulfilled dynamics of business and science. Her focus on 'knowledge' in an age of epistemological black-out demanded the return of the speculative against a nostalgia (in a positive sense) for the grand narrative. Ironically, though her actual politics belonged to Jeffersonian America, surviving only as collaborative propaganda in the era of the New Deal, her work has become more important now simply because of the dependence of the 'social' on the technocratically controlled university where 'scientists, technicians, and instruments are purchased not to find truth but to augment power'. Here the argument returns to Adams and a new definition of that difficult word 'force': '"Force" appears to belong exclusively to the fast game, the game of technology.'[128]

Stein showed, against James's intention, though his practice denied it, that 'Social pragmatics does not have the "simplicity" of scientific pragmatics. It is a monster formed by the interweaving of various networks of heteromorphous classes of utterances.'[129] Stein's fidelity to creative language made her a magnificent critic of the social realm. In so far as the legitimation of that realm increasingly turns to the control of discourse and knowledge (indirectly through market criteria), her work is politically valuable.

*   *   *

All three authors studied in this book indicate ways of framing problems of relevance to the late twentieth century. By what intellectual, personal and collective means is that understanding of how the subject comes into history permitted? How is it possible to survive in a world of fragmentary and disconnected explanations? Where does power lie, and how is it to be controlled? The serious questions beneath Adams's melancholy ironies are whether it is possible to talk to each other across the boundaries of training, sex, nationalities and cultures when there are so few shared ideologies and narratives, and none easily valued because of oppressive institutional validations. The field of that particular problem is enormous, ranging from the intellectually atomized members of a contemporary university to personal and private relations.

Adams also insists that it is not possible to talk about politics without talking about technological growth, irrational drives and the new kinds of lives emerging as a result of corporations which have effectively replaced nation-states as sovereign powers. However unsatisfactorily Adams sometimes framed his own answers to these questions, he challenged the 'aura' of science and suggested that 'education' involved a multi-disciplinary effort which would take a lifetime to accomplish, both inside and outside the academy. Adams also defended theorizing and speculation – those activities always designated as 'useless' within the State's desire to produce semi-lobotomized technicians for its control of the productive process. Adams's very 'method' of intellectual enquiry is of increasing democratic relevance in a world of minimal democratic practice. His 'patrician' demand for a high order of generalizing mind and a plurality of methods and fields becomes more not less important in our own time. In Eric Mottram's words, 'Choice not submission is the aim.'[130] The maintenance of that choice becomes increasingly difficult and increasingly urgent in our own culture. Adams's restless intelligence showed that there were just as important lessons to be learned in a Provençal poet as there were in a Kelvin or a Mach. Science was not a priori significant nor poetry a priori insignificant for assessing or even maintaining the value of human life. While Adams squared up to the actual disintegration of liberalism and its dream of bourgeois civilization, and prophesied that the arbitrary nature of law and justice which Stein experienced in France would be extended to civil life (more police, more people in prison), there is, of course, a less satisfactory side to him. He reflected some of the more unattractive features of his historical class: a certain cynicism, anti-Semitism, crass nationalism and occasional sentimentalities which escaped the limits of irony. His melancholy sometimes has the classic features of Sartre's bad faith.

If in Adams the public and private worlds of liberal civilization were shown decadently clinging to their sustaining myths, in James what takes place is the disintegration of an erstwhile Protestant and Romantic (the legacy of transcendentalism) discourse under pressure from Darwin's rewriting of the world picture in metaphysical as well as scientific terms. Whereas James tried to save a moral perspective within what he rightly recognized as a scientific take-over of the very terms for the description of human behaviour, he failed to invent a satisfactory alternative. What it is so important to recognize in the details of the moralistic values James placed against the disintegration of a moral tradition, is that they have become the stock-in-trade of twentieth-century State and commercial discourse. The insistence on the 'brute in man', certain bad features of academic advocacies of 'popular culture', the anti-intellectual impulses of 'real-lifeism', the belief in the therapeutic as a salvationary mode, the advocacy of the ambiguous values of 'professionalism' (with its apolitical stance), the demotion of the contemplative life in the interests of the 'active' life – these are all, it is important to recognize, a kind of collective trope, claiming authority in a world of simple media explanations for human behaviour, of sport and entertainment as primary agents of human value, and of the pressure to devalue education as a difficult enterprise. Of course James would have been horrified by such a world, but the diverse aspects of his individualism, traditionally creditable as they were, offered little protection against its emergence. There is an actual politics, and an English one at that, behind James's work, as the examination of his relation to Locke and Bagehot has shown. The impressive magnitude of James's intellectual effort should not obscure the judgements he actually made. This study has been relatively harsh in its assessment of James because the details of the vast network of issues which his work throws up must be rethought if that crucial moment, when an important Western moral tradition (Christian and Greek) is taken over by the professionalizing discourses of the sciences of society, is to be understood.

In Stein's work the nature of discourse was confronted head-on. The act of withdrawal from the academy and professional life did not mean that she ignored problems of history and psychology problematized by Adams and James. It is not possible to separate discussions of language from philosophy, psychology, biological theories and ideologies. Stein turned to language and literature because she believed they engaged the world more than the psychomedical specialisms in which she had trained, but she did not forget her training either. The classical questions of the relation of language to being, knowledge and society re-emerged consciously in her writing. Stein's project was paralleled in the work of contemporary linguists both European and American. This study has shown that Stein was not some miraculous forerunner of 'modernism', or 'post-modernism', but simply someone engaged in current debates at a particularly exciting time, culturally and intellectually, in a field which happened to be literature. Her deliberations on the relations between language, literature and 'social psychology' drew on her extensive knowledge of Western philosophy, pschology, medicine and biology, as well as on literary traditions. Against current critical trends it has been insisted here that her revised techniques engage new ways of dealing referentially with the historical contents of these disciplines, as a response to her own time. And Stein's work, at its best, exhibits a dazzling combination of high seriousness and sheer *joie de vivre*.

Finally, what of this notion of 'society'? It has been glimpsed in overlapping definitions of it, like planes of Cubist space, in historians, philosophers, social commentators, ethnologists, linguists, creative writers, political theorists and even sociologists. The aim has not been, like Lovejoy with 'romanticisms' and 'pragmatisms', ironically to categorize it out of usefulness. Definitions are continually redefined, as Adams contemplates Morgan, or Locke casts about for an underpinning to his theory of language. Adams challenged the synchronizing impulses of the new modes of ethnology, yet scrutinized them also as possibilities for enlightenment. To what extent did 'society' pose problems for traditional political theories – did it enlarge or diminish their possibilities? Or was 'society' merely an alibi – at worst a vacuum – resulting from the high Victorian consensus about free trade and the liberal entrepreneur at the point of collapse?

Adams was no less aware than Arendt of the potentially totalitarian twentieth century, with its 'social' controlling of the public through the private. Adams's response was to create an ensemble of overlapping explanations, in which multiplicity was accepted as the basis of order on many levels rather than that unitary order dear to the heart of the authoritarian. At a less abstract level he asked whether it was possible for 'social types' to engage in story. In his image of the 'struggling caravan' of American society twisting about 'in search of its tail', Adams denied that 'society' could emancipate itself from time and history.

In James the ambiguous social values of the triumph of the therapeutic and of social sentiment are bounded at one end by Durkheim's institutional statistics and Renouvier's neo-Kantianism and at the other end by the symbolic writhings of that decapitated frog James wrote about on his honeymoon. James's involvement with Lockean philosophy is a reminder that the concept of 'society' as language, field, metaphysic, and political alibi are not entirely twentieth-century problems, and that the drive to characterize political life as drifts, organisms and technological automatisms flatters historical pessimism while mistaking for truths what are at best tough-minded hypotheses. Stein's revision of generic and linguistic possibilities for literature gave her tools that were largely satiric for describing society in many of its darker aspects and in a wide range of human situations, from the family to the occupied nation-state. What is finally clear from this study is that Arendt's political generalizations about our inability even to contemplate the notion of 'freedom' in our own time might be partially challenged by a fearless insistence on the importance, the imaginative ambition – so clearly exemplified in these three writers – of the life of the mind itself.

Notes

The following abbreviations and/or short forms are used throughout for primary sources cited frequently in the Notes or referred to in the text:

	Cited as
Henry Adams: *The Education of Henry Adams* [1907], ed. Ernest Samuels (Boston, 1973)	*Education*
Esther [1884], ed. Robert Spiller (New York, 1938)	*Esther*
Historical Essays (New York, 1891)	*Historical Essays*
History of the United States of America [1884–91] 9 vols. (New York, 1931)	*History*, I–IX
The Letters of Henry Adams, ed. J. C. Levenson, Ernest Samuels, Charles Vandersee, Viola Hopkins Winner, 3 vols.: I (1858–68); II (1869–85); III (1885–92) (Cambridge, Mass., and London, 1983)	*Letters*, I, II, III
Letters of Henry Adams, ed. Worthington Chauncy Ford, vol. II (1892–1918) (Boston and New York, 1938)	*Letters* (ed. Ford), II
Mont-Saint-Michel and Chartres [1904] (New York, 1974)	*Chartres*
Henry Adams and His Friends: A Collection of his Unpublished Letters, ed. Harold Dean Cater (Boston, 1947)	*Unpublished Letters*
William James: *The Letters of William James*, ed. Henry James, 2 vols. (Boston, 1920)	*Letters*, I and II
The Moral Equivalent of War and Other Essays, ed. and introd. John K. Roth (New York, 1971)	*Moral Equivalent of War*

A Pluralistic Universe [1909] (Cambridge,   *Pluralistic*
   Mass., and London, 1977)   *Universe*
Pragmatism [1907] (Cambridge, Mass., and   *Pragmatism*
   London, 1975)
The Principles of Psychology, 2 vols. [1891]   *Principles*, I and
   (Cambridge, Mass., and London, 1981)   II
The Varieties of Religious Experience [1902]   *Varieties*
   (Cambridge, Mass., 1985)
The Will to Believe and Other Essays in   *Will to Believe*
   Popular Philosophy [1896] (Cambridge,
   Mass., and London, 1979)

Gertrude Stein: *How to Write*, pref. and introd.   *How to Write*
   Patricia Meyerowitz (1931; repr. New
   York, 1975)
Letters of Gertrude Stein and Carl Van   *Letters Stein/*
   Vechten, ed. Edward Burns, 2 vols. (New   *Van Vechten*,
   York, 1986)   I and II
The Making of Americans: being the history of   *Making of*
   a family's progress (1925; repr. London,   *Americans*
   1968)
Narration. Four Lectures, introd. Thornton   *Narration*
   Wilder (Chicago, 1935)
Stein [Gertrude] Papers, Yale Collection of   Stein Papers,
   American Literature, Beinecke Library,   Beinecke
   Yale University
Wars I Have Seen (New York, 1945)   *Wars I Have*
                                                        Seen

Sources cited in the Notes in condensed form are listed with full
bibliographical particulars in the Bibliography.

Introduction
[1] Hans Jonas, *Philosophical Essays: From Ancient Creed to Technological Man* (Chicago and London. 1974), p. 14.
[2] Michel Serres, *The Parasite*, trans. Lawrence R. Schehr (Baltimore and London, 1982), p. 29.
[3] Thurman W. Arnold, *The Folklore of Capitalism* (1939: rpr. New Haven, Conn., and London, 1968), p. 121.
[4] James Burnham, *The Managerial Revolution, or What is Happening in the World Now* (Harmondsworth, 1945), p. 67.
[5] Raymond Williams, *Politics and Letters, Interviews with the New Left Review* (London, 1981), p. 325; Paul Ricoeur, *The Rule of Metaphor: Multi-Disciplinary Studies of the Creation of Meaning in Language*, trans. Robert Czerny with Kathleen McLaughlin and John Costello, SJ (London and Henley, 1978), p. 9.
[6] Dorothy M. Emmet, *Whitehead's Philosophy of Organism* (London, 1932), p. 244.
[7] Wilkie Collins, *The Moonstone* (1868; rpr. London and Toronto, 1944), pp. 37–8.
[8] Ricoeur, *Rule of Metaphor*, p. 239.
[9] Carl O. Sauer to Charles Olson, 26 July

1954, published in *New World Journal*, 1. 4 (Spring 1979), p. 161.

[10] *Critical Angles: European Views of Contemporary American Literature*, ed. and introd. Marc Chénetier (Carbondale and Edwardsville, I. 11., 1986), p. xxi.

[11] Brooks Adams, *The Theory of Social Revolutions* (New York, 1913), p. 217.

[12] Alfred North Whitehead, *Adventures of Ideas* (1933; rpr. Harmondsworth, 1948), p. 141.

[13] Paul Radin, *The Method and Theory of Ethnology: An Essay in Criticism* (New York and London, 1933), p. ix.

[14] Vern Wagner, *The Suspension of Henry Adams: A Study of Manner and Matter* (Detroit, 1969), p. 9.

[15] George Orwell, 'Inside the Whale' (1940), in George Orwell, *The Collected Essays, Journalism and Letters of George Orwell*, ed. Sonia Orwell and Ian Angus, vol. I: *An Age like This* (1968; rpr. Harmondsworth, 1970), p. 576.

[16] R.G. Collingwood, *An Autobiography* (Oxford, 1939), p. 107.

[17] Michel Foucault, *Language, Counter-Memory, Practice; Selected Essays and Interviews*, ed Donald F. Bouchard, trans. Donald F. Bouchard and Sherry Simon (Ithaca, NY, 1977), p. 85.

[18] Jacques Ellul, *The Technological Society*, trans. John Wilkinson (New York, 1964), pp. 201, 206.

[19] Marshall Sahlins, *Culture and Practical Reason* (Chicago and London, 1976), p. 108.

[20] H. Stuart Hughes, *Consciousness and Society: The Reorientation of European Social Thought 1890–1930* (New York, 1977), pp. 42, 25.

[21] See Burton J. Bledstein, *The Culture of Professionalism: The Middle Class and the Development of Higher Education in America* (New York, 1976).

[22] Robert L. Church, 'Economists as Experts: the Rise of the Academic Profession in the United States, 1870–1920', in *The University in Society*, ed. Lawrence Stone, vol. II: *Europe, Scotland and the United States* (Princeton, NJ, 1975), pp. 573, 575, 595.

[23] See, for example, Paul A. Samuelson, 'The World Economy at the Century's End' [conference paper], Comite Organizador Local-Colegio Nacional de Economistas (A. C. Mexico, 1980), esp. p. 34. For this reference I am indebted to Professor Gunnar Bramness, Department of Economics, University of Oslo.

[24] Hannah Arendt, *The Human Condition: A Study of the Central Dilemmas Facing Modern Man* (Chicago, 1958), p. 28.

[25] Ibid.

[26] William H. Whyte, *The Oganization Man* (1956; rpr. Harmondsworth, 1960), p. 24.

[27] The phrase was suggested to me by Professor Eric Mottram of King's College, London University.

[28] Jacques Barzun, *A Stroll with William James* (New York, 1983), Gerald E. Myers, *William James, His Life and Thought* (New Haven Conn., and London, 1986); Frank Lentricchia, 'The Return of William James', *Cultural Critique*, 4 (Fall 1986), 5–31.

[29] Jacques Barzun: *Berlioz and the Romantic Century* (1950; rpr. London, 1951); *Darwin, Marx and Wagner: Critique of a Heritage* (Boston, 1941), p. 93. The excesses of Barzun's involvement with James (though understandable for one of his generation when James could be seen as the sweet voice of reason in a disgraceful period of European history) are revealed not so much in the recent book as in the scandalous article he wrote in 1963 defending capital punishment on the basis of a kind of 'sentiment of rationality': Barzun, 'In Favor of Capital Punishment', *American Scholar*, 31 (Spring 1962), 181–91.

[30] Lentricchia's equation, in 'The Return of William James', of theory as such with totalitarian and élitist positions, and the simplistic binary oppositions he maps out to elaborate his case, are something of an intellectual disgrace. The silliness of many of his statements is manifest (for example, that 'theory-desire' is responsible for destroying Vietnamese villages) and is scarcely worth commenting upon. But here is one summarizing statement: 'So the world according to James is a geography of practices adjacently placed: a heterogeneous space of dispersed histories, related perhaps by counterpoint, or perhaps utterly disrelated – a cacophony of stories – but in any case never related in medley' (p. 10). The evasions are typical of one kind of American thinking; the obliteration of actual history and the possibility of actual intelligibility in spatializing paradoxes. Geography buries history in a very American manner. Lentricchia offers only the sentiment of argument in his choice of counterpoint or cacophony, while warning rhetorically against medley. To know the difference between counterpoint and cacophony would involve too much theory and risk making élitists of those who tried! A medley is of course a series of popular and well-known tunes played in sequence and is presumably enjoyed by just those people on whose behalf

Lentricchia vicariously speaks.

[31] Marjorie Perloff, *The Poetics of Indeterminacy: Rimbaud to Cage* (1981; rpr. Chicago, 1983), p. 72.

[32] Linda Mizejewski, 'Gertrude Stein: The Pattern Moves, the Woman behind Shakes It', *Woman's Studies: An Interdisciplinary Journal*, 13 (172): special issue, *The Female Imagination and the Modernist Aesthetic*, ed. Sandra M. Gilbert and Susan Gubar (1986), p. 40.

[33] Catherine R. Stimpson, 'The Somagrams of Gertrude Stein', *Poetics Today*, 6. 1–2 (1985), 79.

[34] Harriet Scott Chessman, *The Public is Invited to Dance: Representation, the Body, and Dialogue in Gertrude Stein* (Stanford, Calif., 1989). I am most grateful to Dr Chessman for letting me read her book at proof stage.

[35] Cyrena N. Padroni, 'Gertrude Stein: From Outlaw to Classic', *Contemporary Literature*, 27. 1 (Spring 1986), 113.

[36] Jean-Paul Sartre, *Critique of Dialectical Reason*, trans. Alan Sheridan-Smith (1960; rpr. London, 1976), p. 55.

[37] Raymond Williams, 'The Uses of Cultural Theory', in *The Politics of Modernism Against the New Conformists* (London, 1989), p. 175.

Chapter 1
Opening the Field

[1] Earl Klee, 'Henry Adams and the Patrician Response to the Liberal Polity', *Humanities in Society*, 3.3 (Summer 1980), 250.

[2] Brooks Adams, 'The Heritage of Henry Adams', in *The Degradation of the Democratic Dogma*, ed. Books Adams (New York, 1919), p. 31.

[3] Ibid., pp. 34, 85.

[4] Ibid., p. 37.

[5] John Quincy Adams, *Report upon Weights and Measures* (Washington, DC, 1821), p. 6. Cited hereafter in the text, as *Report*.

[6] Max I. Baym, *The French Education of Henry Adams* (New York, 1951), p. 16. Baym also notes (p. 9): 'The transition from John to Quincy Adams is the shift from the influence of Voltaire to that of Rousseau, from reason to sensibility.'

[7] Blaise Pascal, *Pensées*, trans. A. J. Krailsheimer (Harmondsworth, 1966), p. 58.

[8] *The Times*, 16 Jan 1981, Parliamentary Report.

[9] Henry Adams to Charles Francis Adams, 27 Jan 1869, in *Letters*, II. 14.

[10] William H. Jordy, *Henry Adams: Scientific Historian* (New Haven, Conn., and London,

1952), p. 181: 'Faithful to his old teacher, then, Adams nevertheless fully justified his assertion to his editors that he "leaned, but not strongly" toward Lyell and Darwin.' There is some controversy between Jordy and Samuels on this point. On the whole I agree with Samuels. Jordy does not make enough of the differences between Lyell and Darwin.

[11] Ernest Samuels, *The Young Henry Adams* (Cambridge, Mass., 1948), p. 167. Cited hereafter as Samuels, I.

[12] Timothy Paul Donovan, *Henry Adams and Brooks Adams: The Education of Two American Historians* (Norman, Okla., 1961), p. 53: '...his orientation was never truly Darwinian.'

[13] Henry Adams, *Historical Essays*, p. 461. Cited hereafter in the text.

[14] Frederic Jameson, *Marxism and Form: Twentieth-Century Dialectical Theories of Literature* (Princeton, NJ, 1971), title-page.

[15] I think these quotations support Samuels rather than Jordy. See n. 10 above.

[16] David Contosta, *Henry Adams and the American Experiment* (Boston and Toronto, 1980), p. 78.

[17] Michael Ruse, *The Darwinian Revolution* (Chicago and London, 1979), p. 97.

[18] Howard E. Gruber, *Darwin on Man: A Psychological Study of Scientific Creativity* (London, 1974), p. 152: 'Throughout the transmutation notebooks the question [of the origin of life] arises in various ways. First of all, how *many* beginnings has life had? Must a coherent theory of evolution postulate only one?'

[19] Adams to Elizabeth Cameron, 2 July 1891, in *Letters*, III. 500.

[20] Adams to Margaret Chanler, 9 Sept 1909, in *Letters* (ed. Ford), II. 524.

[21] Peter J. Bowler, *The Eclipse of Darwinism: Anti-Darwinian Evolution Theories in the Decades around 1900* (Baltimore and London, 1983), p. 107 f.

[22] Adams, *Historical Essays*, pp. 1–79.

[23] G. P. Gooch, *History and Historians in the Nineteenth Century* (London, 1913), p. 17.

[24] *Njals Saga*, trans. Carl. F. Bayerschmidt and Lee M. Hollander (London, 1955), p. 256.

[25] Adams, *Historical Essays*, p. 79.

[26] Ibid.: 'The Bank of England Restriction', pp. 177–278; 'The Legal Tender Act', pp. 279–316; 'The New York Gold conspiracy', pp. 317–66.

[27] Karl Marx, *Capital: A Critique of Political Economy*, vol. I, trans. Ben Fowkes (Har-

mondsworth, 1976), p. 242 and n.

[28] Brooks Adams, *The Gold Standard: An Historical Study*, rev. edn. (Washington, DC, 1895), pp. 18, 29.

[29] Marx, *Capital*, I. 176.

[30] Ibid., I. 242.

[31] See E. P. Thompson, *The Poverty of Theory and Other Essays* (London, 1978), p. 363: '. . . Marx, in his wrath and compassion, was a moralist in every stroke of his pen.' If we read either Marx or Adams only for their more abstract theory, we should miss a great deal of what was valuable in their writing.

[32] C. Wright Mills, *Sociology and Pragmatism: The Higher Learning in America* (New York, 1966), p. 40 f.

[33] R. Buckminster Fuller, *Education Automation: Freeing the Scholar to Return to his Studies* (Carbondale and Edwardsville, Ill., 1962), p. 59.

[34] Stephen Toulmin and June Goodfield, *The Architecture of Matter* (London, 1962), p. 239 f.

[35] See pages 209–241.

[36] Adams to Charles Milnes Gaskell, 17 Sept 1894, in *Letters* (ed. Ford), II. 55.

[37] Auguste Comte, *The Positive Philosophy*, Introd. Abraham S. Blumberg (New York, 1974), p. 406.

[38] Adams to Elizabeth Cameron, 22 Jan 1899, in *Letters*, (ed. Ford), II. 208.

[39] Adams to Cecil Spring-Rice 12 Feb 1897, in ibid., II. 123.

[40] Ibid.

[41] Ernest Samuels, *Henry Adams: The Major Phase* (Cambridge, Mass., 1964), p. 41. Cited hereafter as Samuels, III.

[42] Matthew 6:21.

[43] Adams to Elizabeth Cameron, 10 Apr 1898, in *Letters* (ed. Ford), II. 163.

[44] Gooch, *History and Historians*, p. 30.

[45] Adams to Brooks Adams, 6 May 1899, in *Unpublished Letters*, p. 462.

[46] Marx, *Capital*, I. 240 f.

[47] Brooks Adams, *The Law of Civilization and Decay* (New York, 1895), p. vii.

[48] An excellent discussion of 'organicism' in the nineteenth century may be found in Greta Jones, *Social Darwinism and English Thought: The Interaction between Biological and Social Theory* (Brighton, 1980), p. 160 f.

[49] Adams's annotation is on p. 70 of vol. I of his copy of Karl Marx, *A Critical Analysis of Capitalist Production* (London, 1887). This and other books in Adams's library from which I quote his annotations are in the Massachusetts Historical Society.

[50] Adams's copy of Marx's *Capital*, I. 66.

[51] Adams to Worthington Chauncy Ford, 19

Dec 1898, in *Letters* (ed. Ford), II. 197.

[52] Adams to Brooks Adams, 5 Nov 1899, in ibid., II. 248.

[53] Adams to Brooks Adams, 21 Oct 1899, in *Unpublished Letters*, p. 484: 'Some day I may find it convenient to know about socialist theories; they seem to be now on the verge of ousting all others except the pure capitalistic, which comes to the same result by any road.'

[54] Adams to Henry Cabot Lodge, 2 Jan 1873, in *Letters*, II. 156.

[55] Frederick Engels, *Dialectics of Nature* 2nd rev. edn., trans. Clemens Dutt (Moscow, 1954), p. 40.

[56] Fernand Braudel, *On History*, trans. Sarah Matthews (Chicago, 1980), p. 20.

[57] Samuels, I. 27. Francois Guizot, *Historical Essays and Lectures*, ed. Stanley Mellon (Chicago and London, 1972), p. 144.

[58] See Roland Barthes, *Michelet* (Paris, 1954).

[59] Jules Michelet, *The People*, trans. John P. McKay (Urbana, Ill., Chicago, London, 1973), p. 5.

[60] These debates were sophisticated. Here for example is François Simiand in the *Revue de Synthèse historique*, 6–7 (1903), in an article entitled 'Méthode historique et science sociale...' (pp. 128 ff.) which reviewed works by Lacombe and Seignobos: 'L'oeuvre historique la plus brute, le dépouillement de textes le plus amorphe, le recueil de documents le plus passif, est déjà choix, implique quelque élimination, suppose quelque vue préalable de l'esprit' (p. 131).

[61] Pascal, *Pensées*, p. 232.

[62] Adams to Henry Cabot Lodge, 1 Feb 1878, in *Letters*, II. 333.

[63] Alfred North Whitehead, from *Science and the Modern World* (1925) in *Alfred North Whitehead, An Anthology*, ed. F. S. C. Northrop and Mason W. Gross (New York, 1953), p. 371.

[64] Adams to Sir Robert Cunliffe, 8 Jan 1895, in *Letters* (ed. Ford), II. 63.

[65] Charles Olson, *The Special View of History* (Berkeley, Calif., 1970), p. 27.

[66] Adams to Elizabeth Cameron, 11 July 1895, in *Letters* (ed. Ford), II. 75.

[67] Adams to Henry Osborn Taylor, 17 Jan 1905, in *Unpublished Letters*, p. 559.

[68] John LaFarge, *An Artist's Letters from Japan* (London, 1897), p. 25.

[69] Samuels, I. 133.

[70] Henry Thomas Buckle, *History of Civilization in England*, 2 vols. (1857; rpr. New York, 1858), I. 14. Cited hereafter in the text, as Buckle, I or II.

[71] Adams's own copy of Buckle's *History of*

Civilization in England is the 4th edn. (London, 1864). The underlining is on p. 204 of volume I.

[72] Adams to Elizabeth Cameron, 15 July 1896, in *Letters* (ed. Ford), II. 108.

[73] Adams to Samuel J. Tilden, 24 Jan 1883, in *Letters*, II. 491.

[74] Ernest Samuels, *Henry Adams: The Middle Years* (Cambridge, Mass., 1958), p. 58. Cited hereafter as Samuels, II.

[75] Wagner, *Suspension of Henry Adams*, p. 41.

[76] There is an important article on this subject by Henry S. Kariel, 'The Limits of Social Science: Henry Adams's Quest for Order', *American Political Science Review*, 50 (1956), 1074–92. Kariel argues that Adams was searching for a genuine knowledge of society based on natural law but stopped short of the quietism this implied. Keeping the various contradictions in suspense Adams noted the implicit authoritarianism of the claims of the new social sciences. Levenson has also argued that Adams was 'caught in a stage between the dramatic historian and the social scientist...', See J. C. Levenson, *The Mind and Art of Henry Adams* (Boston, 1957), p. 127. In a letter of 1910 Adams noted, 'All our sociology and psychology is still in dense confusion," in 'Seventeen Letters of Henry Adams', ed., Frederick Bliss Luquiens, *Yale Review*, 10 (Oct 1920), 137.

[77] Henry Adams, review of *The History of the Norman Conquest* by Edward Freeman, *North American Review*, 110 (1870), 351.

[78] George Feaver, *From Status to Contract: A Biography of Sir Henry Maine, 1822–1888* (London, 1969), p. xvi.

[79] Samuels, II. 309.

[80] Lewis Henry Morgan, *Ancient Society* (New York, 1877), p. 302.

[81] Comte, *Positive Philosophy*, p. 507.

[82] Quoted in Robert Mane, *Henry Adams on the Road to Chartres* (Cambridge, Mass., 1971), p. 49.

[83] Guizot, *Historical Essays*, pp. 293, 41.

[84] Stephen Toulmin, *Human Understanding: The Collective Use and Evolution of Concepts* (Princeton, NJ, 1972), p. 385.

[85] Marvin Harris, *The Rise of Anthropological Theory* (New York, 1968), p. 1.

[86] Radin, *Method and Theory of Ethnology*, p. 71.

[87] Ibid., p. 131.

[88] Ibid., p. 253.

[89] Thomas R. Trautmann, *Lewis Henry Morgan and the Invention of Kinship* (Berkeley, Calif., Los Angeles and London, 1987), p. 169. I am most grateful to Marzia Balzani

for drawing my attention to this work.

[90] Mark Poster, *Existential Marxism in Postwar France: From Sartre to Althusser* (Princeton, NJ, 1975), p. 332.

[91] Samuels, I. 252. Samuels argues that Adams never really challenged the theory of an 'Anglo-Saxon' origin for Germanic law.

[92] Adams to Lewis Henry Morgan, 29 Apr 1876, in *Letters*, II. 264.

[93] Adams to Lewis Henry Morgan, 21 May 1876, in *Letters*, II. 268–9.

[94] Henry Adams, *Essays in Anglo-Saxon Law* (Boston, 1876), p. 121.

[95] Ibid, pp. 147, 149, 151.

[96] Lewis Henry Morgan, *League of the Ho-de-no-sau-nee or Iroquois* (Rochester, NY, and New York, 1851), p. 60.

[97] Edward B. Tylor, *Primitive Culture: Researches into the Development of Mythology, Philosophy, Religion, Language, Art and Custom*, 2 vols., 7th edn. (New York, 1924), I. 115. Cited hereafter in the text, as Tylor, I or II.

[98] Jacques Monod, *Chance and Necessity: An Essay on the Natural Philosophy of Modern Biology, trans. Austryn Wainhouse* (New York, 1971), p. 30.

[99] Adams to Elizabeth Cameron, 8 Sept 1891, in *Letters*, III. 544.

[100] Quoted by Baym, *French Education of Henry Adams*, p. 196.

[101] Karl Marx and Frederick Engels, *Selected Works* (London, 1970), p. 499.

[102] For a modern feminist discussion of evolution, matriarchy, and its history see Evelyn Reed, *Woman's Evolution* (New York and Toronto, 1974).

[103] Marx and Engels, *Selected Works*, p. 482.

[104] Ibid., p. 498.

[105] The discussion of Adams's relations with women ranges from the sane and sensitive to the psychologically pedantic. A good instance of the latter is in Joseph F. Byrnes, *The Virgin of Chartres: An Intellectual and Psychological History of the Work of Henry Adams* (London, 1981), p. 86: 'The intensity of Adams's expressed yearning for Elizabeth [Cameron], and the poetry that he quoted on occasion in relation to his feelings for her, lead one to posit the sexual overevaluation called idealization.' Also (p. 124): "The Virgin" took the place of love lost between Henry and Elizabeth.' For a corrective to this nonsense see Ernest Samuels, 'Henry Adams and the Gossip Mills', in *Essays in American and English Literature Presented to Bruce Robert McElderry, Jr.*, ed. Max F. Schulz *et al.* (Athens, Ohio, 1967), pp. 59–75. R. P. Black-

mur's comment: 'Women, for Adams, had instinct and emotion and could move from one to the other without becoming lost in the mid-way bog of logic and fact,' is an elegant deployment of sexist terms for the more sexist characterizations in Adams's work: see R. P. Blackmur, *Henry Adams/R. P. Blackumr*, ed. Veronica Markowsky (New York, 1980), p. 13. For a more negative view of the image projected by Adams see Edward N. Saveth, 'The Heroines of Henry Adams', *American Quarterly*, 8 (Fall 1956), 231–42. There is much valuable information in Thurman Wilkins, *Clarence King: A Biography* (New York, 1958). Inviting Adams to Maxim's in 1897, King offered 'brown girls' as additional entertainment with the comment, 'I will be a second La Farge and never tell' (p. 349). While this arouses speculation as to what Adams and La Farge were up to on their Pacific trip, it is to be noted that Adams turned down the invitation. The two best books on the subject are Eugenia Kaledin, *The Education of Mrs. Henry Adams* (Philadelphia, 1981), and William Dusinberre, *Henry Adams, The Myth of Failure* (Charlottesville, Va., 1980). The pleasures and pains of Adams's love for Elizabeth Cameron are told sympathetically by Arline Boucher Tehan, *Henry Adams in Love: The Pursuit of Elizabeth Sherman Cameron* (New York, 1983).

[106] Sir Cecil Spring-Rice, *The Letters and Friendship of Sir Cecil Spring-Rice, A Record*, ed. Stephen Gwynn (London, 1929), p. 77.

[107] Adams to Elizabeth Cameron, 1 Sept 1901, in *Letters* (ed. Ford) II. 348.

[108] *North Ameican Review*, 114 (1872), 303, 326.

[109] Samuels, III. 287, 289.

[110] Stephen A. Kippur, *Jules Michelet: A Study of Mind and Sensibility* (Albany, NY, 1981), p. 206.

[111] E. Drumont, *La Fin d'un monde* (Paris, 1889), p. 111. The best case for Adams is made by Contosta, *Henry Adams and the American Experiment*, p. 98.

[112] Adams to Rebecca Gilman Rae, 8 Nov 1890, in *Unpublished Letters*, p. 221. While sympathizing with the difficulty of choosing letters for the new standard edition, it does seem a pity that this very lively letter from Samoa has been left out.

[113] Clarence King, *Mountaineering in the Sierra Nevada* (Boston, 1872), p. 103.

[114] Adams to Lewis Henry Morgan, 14 July 1877, in *Letters*, II. 311.

[115] Morgan, *Ancient Society*, p. 61. Cited hereafter in the text, as Morgan.

[116] Marx and Engels, *Selected Works*, p. 530.

[117] [N.D.] Fustel de Coulanges, *The Ancient City: A Study of the Religion, Laws, and Institutions of Greece and Rome*, trans. William Small (Boston, 1874) p. 65. Cited hereafter in the text, as Fustel.

[118] Michel Foucault, *The History of Sexuality*, vol. I, trans. Robert Hurley (New York, 1980), p. 105.

[119] Stanley Moore, 'Marxian Theories of Law in Primitive Societies', in *Culture in History: Essays in Honour of Paul Radin*, ed. Stanley Diamond (New York, 1960), p. 648.

[120] Carl Resek, *Lewis Henry Morgan: American Scholar* (Chicago, 1960), p. 117.

[121] Ibid., p. 153.

[122] Trautmann, *Lewis Henry Morgan*, pp. 172–5, for Trautmann's discussion of Darwin's influence on Morgan.

[123] Adams wrote a book on aristocratic families of the South Seas: *Memoires of Marau Taaroa Last Queen of Tahiti* (Washington, DC, 1893).

[124] Adams to Elizabeth Cameron, 13 Sept 1890, in *Letters*, III. 275.

[125] 'Three times out of four, when I reached any interesting point, I am blocked by the reply that what I ask is a secret': Adams to Elizabeth Cameron, 8 Nov 1890, in *Letters*, III. 330.

[126] *Unpublished Letters*, p. 718, n. 2; Samuels, III. 32.

[127] Jordy's 1952 book, *Henry Adams: Scientific Historian*, is still the only full-length work to take Adams's involvement with science seriously. A new study is needed, however, which will take into account issues in the *philosophy* and *psychology* of the scientific enterprise, for these issues were closer to Adams's concerns than actual science as normally seen by practising scientists.

[128] Adams to Margaret Chanler, 29 Jan 1908, in *Letters* (ed. Ford), II. 489.

[129] Adams to Margaret Chanler, 11 Apr 1909, in ibid., II. 517.

[130] Adams to Simon Newcomb, 15 Aug 1875, in *Letters*, II. 232.

[131] Toulmin, *Human Understanding*, p. 323 f.

[132] Paul J. Hamill, 'Science as Ideology: The Lore of the Amateur, Henry Adams', *Canadian Review of American Studies*, 12. 1 (Spring 1981), 25.

[133] Ibid., p. 24.

[134] Adams to Charles Milnes Gaskell, 14 June 1903, in *Letters* (ed. Ford), II. 407.

[135] Adams to Henry Osborn Taylor, 17 Jan 1905, in *Unpublished Letters*, pp. 558–9.

[136] Engels, *Dialectics of Nature*, p. 133. Compare G. F. W. Hegel, *The Phenomenology of Mind*, trans. J. B. Bailie (London, 1931), p. 195 f.

[137] Lewis Mumford, *Technics and Civilization* (London, 1946), p. 156 f.

[138] Simiand, 'Méthode historique et science sociale. . .', 16.

[139] Adams to Margaret Chanler, 9 Sept 1909, in *Letters* (ed. Ford), II. 524.

[140] E. Gryzanovski, 'Schopenhauer and his Pessimistic Philosophy', *North American Review*, 116 (1873), 43.

[141] Ibid., p. 63.

[142] *Darwin and his Critics: The Reception of Darwin's Theory of Evolution by the Scientific Community*, ed. David Hull (Cambridge, Mass., 1973), p. 302 f. Fleeming Jenkin quotes Thompson (Lord Kelvin) on p. 321.

[143] Samuels, II. 38.

[144] Jordy, *Henry Adams*, p. 231.

[145] Sartre, *Critique of Dialectical Reason*, p. 20.

[146] Jordy, *Henry Adams*, p. 137.

[147] E. Gryzanovski. 'Comtism', *North American Review*, 120 (1875), 258.

[148] Contosta, *Henry Adams and the American Experiment*, p. 34.

[149] Sartre, *Critique of Dialectical Reason*, p. 20.

[150] Toulmin, *Human Understanding*, p. 185.

[151] Louis Zukofsky, 'Henry Adams: A Criticism in Autobiography', *Hound and Horn*, 3. 4 (1930), 63.

[152] Ernest Fenollosa, *The Chinese Written Character as a Medium for Poetry*, ed. Ezra Pound, (1936; rpr. San Francisco, 1968), p. 28.

[153] Jameson, *Marxism and Form*, p. 74.

[154] Walter Benjamin, 'The Work of Art in the Age of Mechanical Reproduction', in Benjamin, *Illuminations*, ed. Hannah Arendt (1970; rpr. London, 1973), p. 219 f. See also Jameson, *Marxism and Form*, p. 74.

[155] Ellul, *Technological Society*, p. 201.

Chapter 2
From Hero to Social Type

[1] Richard C. Vitzthum's book, *The American Compromise; Theme and Method in the Histories of Bancroft, Parkman, and Adams* (Norman, Okla., 1974), praises Adams's 'empirical, pragmatic reasonableness', (p. 167) as the basis of an ethical perspective of patriotism, reasonableness and pragmatism conducted *professionally*. He also claims Adams is a Rankean. The reader is referred to this book as representing the antithesis of what the present study is arguing. Timothy Paul Donovan (see ch. 1, n. 12) makes the point (p. 42) that Adams thought Ranke 'needed tempering with sensibility'. My own view is that Adams uses Rankean sequence as the basis for a narrative strategy. No literary critic (which Vitzthum claims to be) would deny that sequential narrative is biased fundamentally towards value and point of view. Further, the attempt to cover the vacuum created by this sort of criticism is not resolved in pure aestheticism. 'Ethics' as 'tone', which colours 'facts', is a familiar strategy (since William James if not before) of American criticism which combines aestheticism with moralism, in lieu of judgements which radically alter form and engage a more socially-oriented critique.

[2] Quoted in Gooch, *History and Historians in the Nineteenth Century*, pp. 8–9. The following account relies on this still valuable book.

[3] Braudel, *On History*, p. 11.

[4] Gooch, *History and Historians*, p. 581.

[5] Marx and Engels, *Selected Works*, p. 505.

[6] Adams to Sir Henry Maine, 22 Feb 1875, in *Letters*, II. 218–19.

[7] Adams to Justin Winsor, 27 Sept and 29 Sept 1881, in *Letters*, II. 438, 439.

[8] There are bibliographical problems with editions of Adams's *History* (1884–91). The edition used here is the 9-vol. New York edition of 1931: *History of the United States of America*, cited hereafter in the text, with volume number and page.

[9] Clive Bush, 'Gilded Backgrounds; Reflections on the Perception of Space and Landscape in the Early American Republic', in *Views of American Landscape*, ed. M. Gidley and R. Lawson Peebles (Cambridge, 1989), pp. 13–30.

[10] Henry Maine, *Ancient Law* (London, 1861), p. 19.

[11] Henry Adams, *Esther*, cited hereafter in the text.

[12] Matthew Arnold, 'The Scholar Gipsy', in *The Poems of Matthew Arnold*, 2nd edn., ed. Miriam Allott (London and New York, 1979), p. 355.

[13] Richard M. Dorson, *The British Folklorists: A History* (Chicago, 1968), p. 98.

[14] Matthew Arnold, 'Dover Beach', in *Poems*, p. 253.

[15] The most comprehensive work on the subject of the *femme fatale* is still Mario Praz, *The Romantic Agony*, trans. Angus Davidson (London, 1933).

Chapter 3
A Poetics of Social Hegemony

[1] William J. Courtney, 'The Virgin and the Dynamo: The Growth of Medieval Studies

in North America, 1870–1930', in *Medieval Studies in North America: Past, Present and Future*, ed. Francis G. Gentry and Christopher Kleinhenz (Kalamazoo, Mich., 1982), p. 10.

[2] Adams to Charles Milnes Gaskell, 27 Mar 1871, in *Letters*, II. 103.

[3] Whitehead, *Alfred North Whitehead*, p. 416.

[4] As the *Catholic World* once said of *Mont-Saint-Michel and Chartres*: '. . . its whole theme leaves us gasping at its blasphemy': Hugh F. Blunt, 'Mal-Education of Henry Adams', *Catholic World*, 145 (Apr 1936), 46–52. Those in charge of the maintenance of Chartres, however, thought differently and have permitted a stained-glass memorial window to Adams to be inserted in the cathedral. Adams's 'theology' combined heart and head in ways calculated to upset layman and theologian alike. Others have pointed to theologically 'inaccurate' interpretations of the Virgin: John P. McIntyre, 'Henry Adams and the Unity of Chartres', *Twentieth Century Literature*, 7 (1962), 159–71. J. C. Levenson (see ch. 1, n. 76) says Adams never became a convert (p. 271). In the debate between reason and faith Adams clung to Puritan reason. See G. H. Roelofs, 'Henry Adams: Pessimism and the Intelligent Use of Doom', *Journal of Literary History*, 17 (1950), 235. For an argument that Adams was more anti-intellectual than William James, on the other hand, see M. Colacurcio, '*Democracy* and *Esther*: Henry Adams's Flirtation with Pragmatism', *American Quarterly*, 19 (1967), 53–70. Adams himself said (tongue in cheek), 'I am much more shy of my theology than of my architecture or linguistics . . . and should be much mortified if detected in error about Thomas Aquinas, or the doctrine of universals', Adams to Frederick Bliss Luquiens, 27 Feb 1911, in 'Seventeen Letters of Henry Adams', 116.

[5] See Robert Mane, *Henry Adams on the Road to Chartres*. This is a most usefully detailed work, the chief merit of which is to recognize that Adams's *Chartres* is a 'prose poem'. The critical stance is perhaps a little pugnacious and Mane tends to reduce Adams to a follower of Pascal flailing against 'logic'.

[6] Adams to Charles Milnes Gaskell, 1 Sept 1895, in *Letters* (ed. Ford), II. 79.

[7] Henry Adams, *Mont-Saint-Michel and Chartres* [1904], p. 48. Cited hereafter in the text, as *Chartres*.

[8] Jacques Ellul, *Propaganda: The Formation of Men's Attitudes*, trans. Konrad Kellen and Jean Lerner (New York, 1973), pp. 62, 64.

[9] Norman O. Brown, *Love's Body* (New York, 1968), p. 70.

[10] Ibid.

[11] Adams to Charles Milnes Gaskell, 22 Nov 1899 in *Letters* (ed. Ford), II. 249.

[12] See Peter Coveney, *The Image of Childhood: The Individual and Society: A Study of the Theme in Engish Literature*, rev. edn., introd. F. R. Leavis (Harmondsworth, 1967).

[13] R. G. Collingwood, *The Idea of History* (London, Oxford, New York, 1956), p. 189.

[14] Jean-Paul Sartre, *Between Existentialism and Marxism*, trans. John Matthews (New York, 1979), p. 53.

[15] Adams to Rebecca Gilman Rae, 26 Aug 1896, in *Unpublished Letters*, p. 381.

[16] Adams to Charles Milnes Gaskell, 22 July 1904; to John Hay, 29 Aug 1904; to Charles Milnes Gaskell, 19 Aug 1905, in *Letters* (ed. Ford), II. 438, 441 and 458 respectively.

[17] These ideas occurred to the present author while enjoying the privilege of attending Vincent Scully's lectures on American architecture at Yale, 1980–1. My thanks, too, to Joel Pfister for his enthusiasm for American architecture and for our many discussions. See also Ernst Scheyer, *The Circle of Henry Adams: Art and Artists* (Detroit, 1970). Scheyer argues that Adams's Richardson house was, however, one of the least succesful of the latter's designs (p. 148), and also points out that Adams's interest in the 'Romanesque' was initiated by Richardson (p. 107).

[18] Hugo Münsterberg, *The Americans*, trans, Edwin B. Holt (New York, 1905), p. 487.

[19] Agnes Arber, *The Mind and the Eye: A Study of the Biologist's Standpoint* (London. 1954), p. 106. Cited hereafter in the text, as Arber.

[20] Eric Mottram, 'Henry Adams: Index of the Twentieth Century', in *American Literary Naturalism*, ed. Y. Hakutani and L. Fried, (Heidelberg, 1975), p. 105.

[21] Ricoeur, *Rule of Metaphor*, pp. 272–95. Cited hereafter in the text, as Ricoeur.

[22] Collingwood, *Idea of History*, p. 47.

[23] Adams's note in his copy of *Oeuvres de Descartes*, ed. Jules Simon (Paris, 1865), p. 170.

[24] Ibid., p. 205.

[25] Adams's note in his copy of Charles Jourdain, *La Philosophie de Saint Thomas d'Aquin*, 2 vols. (Paris, 1858), I. 213.

[26] Ibid., II. 451.

[27] Adams's underlining in his copy of l'Abbé P. Carbonel, *Histoire de la philosophie*, 2nd edn. (Paris, 1882), p. 320.

[28] Adams's note in his copy of E. V. Maumus, *S. Thomas d'Aquin et la philosophie*

cartésienne, 2 vols. (Paris, 1890), II. 132.
[29] Ibid., II. 156.
[30] Ibid., II. 366–7.
[31] One of the best recent articles on Adams makes excellent use of certain parallels between his thought and that of Hegel. See Joseph G. Kronick, 'The Limits of Contradiction: Irony and History in Hegel and Henry Adams', *Clio*, 11 (4) (Summer 1986), 391–410.
[32] See Olaf Hansen, 'Henry Adams: *Mont Saint Michel and Chartres*,' *Amerikastudien*, 28.3 (1983), 324. Hansen argues that 'The architectural metaphor (ergon) was transformed by Henry Adams into an image in the modern sense, a necessary, unifying concept: fiction becomes a must where historiography reaches its limits.' However, it is not 'unity' as such that a poetic image discloses but a complex way of knowing the world.
[33] William Carlos Williams, *Interviews with William Carlos Williams*, ed. Linda Welshimer Wagner (New York, 1976), p. 29.

Chapter 4
The Arts of Transition: *The Education of Henry Adams*

[1] Henry Adams, The Education of Henry Adams [1907], p. 399. Cited hereafter in the text.
[2] Giambattista Vico, *The Autobiography of Giambattista Vico*, trans. M. H. Fisch and T. G. Bergin (Ithaca, NY, and London, 1944), has a discussion of the philosopher's reputation and reception in the United States by the translators, p. 99 f. Vico was read by John Fisk and Rank Sanborn, the latter a founder of the American Social Science Association. Adams must have known *of* Vico's work, for Frederick H. Hedge, in an article called 'The Method of History', published in the *North American Review* during Adams's editorship, wrote, 'Vico was the first to point out distinctly the analogies and parallelisms in the history of nations, and to show that the progress of society follows a given order; that nations have their necessary pre-appointed course of evolution and revolution; that human history, in short, no less than the material universe, is governed by fixed laws, consequently that history is a science, or that a science of history is possible': *North American Review*, 111 (1870), 313.
[3] Quoted from the *Corpus Hermeticum* in Frances A. Yates, *Giordano Bruno and the Hermetic Tradition* (New York, 1969), p. 243.
[4] Herman Melville, *Moby Dick, or The White Whale*, ed. Luther S. Mansfield and Howard P. Vincent (New York, 1962), p. 421.
[5] Sigmund Freud, *Civilization and its Discontents*, trans. Joan Rivière, rev. James Strachey (1929; rpr. London, 1963), pp. 7, 8.
[6] One might also recall George Inness's famous Lackawanna Valley painting and his statement, 'From that unity of thought mind controls the eye to its own intent within the units of that idea; consequently we learn to see in accord with ideas developed by the power of life, which also leads us through our own affections': quoted in Barbara Novak, *American Painting of the Nineteenth Century* (London, 1969), p. 245.
[7] As well as Murchison and Huxley whom he mentions in the text, Adams knew of Richard Owen. In his library there was a copy of Owen's *Paleontology: or a Systematic Summary of Ancient Animals and their Geological Relation*, 2nd edn. (Edinburgh, 1861). Adams had underlined on p. 159: 'The buckler of *Pteraspis truncatus* has been found in Silurian stratum below the Ludlow bone bed; it is the earliest known indication of a vertebrate animal.' And a few pages later (p. 175), still evincing loyalty to the ideas of Agassiz, he underlines Owen's comment: 'A retrospect of the genetic history of fishes imparts an idea rather of mutation than of progression.'
[8] William Wordsworth, 'Ode: Intimations of Immortality from Recollections of Early Childhood', in *William Wordsworth: The Poems*, ed. John O. Hayden (New Haven, Conn., 1981), pp. 523–9.
[9] Wordsworth, 'Lines Composed a few miles above Tintern Abbey', in ibid., pp. 357–62.
[10] Matthew Arnold's famous lines, 'Wandering between two worlds, one dead/The other powerless to be born...', occur in 'Stanzas from the Grande Chartreuse' (1852, pub. 1855) in *The Poems of Matthew Arnold*, p. 305.
[11] This annotation appears not to be on Samuels's microfilm of the annotations, so it represents a minor find. It occurs on p. 196 of Adams's copy of *Culture and Anarchy* (New York, 1883).
[12] Adams to Elizabeth Cameron, 18 Sept 1899, in *Letters* (ed. Ford), II. 240.
[13] Adams's note in his copy of *Oeuvres de Descartes*, p. xxxi.
[14] See Ernst Scheyer, *The Circle of Henry Adams*, p. 39: Adams was '*a* Hegelian who never *knew what it was*'.
[15] Adams's underlining in his copy of Dr Albert Schwegler, *Handbook of the History of Philosophy*, trans. James Hutchinson Stirling (Edinburgh, 1867), p. 320.

[16] Adams's note in his copy of *Oeuvres de Descartes*, p. 74.

[17] Adams's notes in his copy of Lucien Poincaré, *La Physique moderne* (Paris, 1906), pp. 17, 32.

[18] Jordy, *Henry Adams: Scientific Historian*, p. 233.

[19] Adams's notes in his copy of Karl Pearson, *The Grammar of Science*, 2nd edn. (London, 1900), pp. 12, 179.

[20] Adams's notes in his copy of J.-B. Stallo, *La Matière et la physique moderne*, 3rd edn. (Paris, 1899), pp. 128, III.

[21] Easily the best short article on Adams and science is Joseph Mindel, 'The Uses of Metaphor: Henry Adams and the Symbols of Science', *Journal of the History of Ideas*, 26 (1965), 89–102. Mindel explores the misplaced search for accuracy of Levenson and Jordy by stating that metaphor does not have to be true in order to be useful. Mindel uses contemporary philosophers of science like Nagel, Bridgman and Kuhn to come to the conclusion that many of Adams's insights – including his commentary on thermodynamics – will bear comparison with what Schroedinger and Smith were doing more scientifically. Mindel misses some of the irony, however, in insisting that Adams's application of certain scientific metaphors was too literal. This is certainly true in some but certainly not all cases.

[22] R. G. Collingwood, *The Idea of Nature* (1945; rpr. London, Oxford, New York, 1978), p. 93.

[23] Thomas Carlyle, *On Heroes and Hero Worship and the Heroic in History*, ed. A. MacMechan (Boston, 1901), p. 228.

[24] Adams's notes in his copy of John Trowbridge, *What is Electricity?* (New York, 1896), pp. 4–5. Note also p. 106: 'the spectacle of the transformation of energy by the dynamo in our great cities is impressive.'

[25] *The Gramophone* (Feb, 1983), 973. See also Donovan, *Henry Adams and Brooks Adams*, p. 23: in the new world of the 1890s 'The scientist replaced the priest between humanity and the universe; and while his explanations were usually couched in the terminology of mathematics, they were as esoteric to the layman as the Latin incantations of church liturgy.'

[26] Benjamin, 'The Work of Art in the Age of Mechanical Reproduction', p. 219 f. See also Jameson, *Marxism and Form*, p. 74.

[27] 'Empathy' is a cult word of the 1890s. It comes out of art criticism. Vernon Lee had been expounding it in the Anglo-American villas of Florence in the 1890s; see Ernest Samuels, *Bernard Berenson: The Making of a Connoisseur* (Cambridge, Mass., and London, 1979), p. 152.

[28] Jack Shepherd, *The Adams Chronicles: Four Generations of Greatness* (Boston, 1975), p. 404. See also Lynn Bryce, 'Silent Confluence: Eastern and Western Themes in Adams's Monument at Rock Creek Cemetery', *North Dakota Quarterly*, 51.2 (Spring 1983), 84–93. Bryce gives a detailed breakdown of the actual cost of the monument and argues that Saint Gaudens built the figure of Adams's wife as a kind of synthesis of the Buddhist deity Kannon and the Virgin Mary.

[29] See Marshall McLuhan, *The Gutenberg Galaxy* (London, 1962); Wilhelm Reich, *The Mass Psychology of Fascism*, trans. Vincent R. Cargagno (New York, 1970); David Riesman, with Nathan Glazer and Reuel Denny, *The Lonely Crowd*, abridged edn. with a 1969 Preface (New Haven, Conn, and London, 1980); Max Weber, *The Protestant Ethic and the Spirit of Capitalism*, trans Talcott Parsons (London, 1930). The best article on Adams as 'Index' of the twentieth century is that by Eric Mottram, cited above, ch. 3, n. 20.

Chapter 5
Adams and James

[1] Adams to Elizabeth Cameron, 5 Sept 1917, in *Letters* (ed. Ford), II. 646.

[2] Cited in Adams, *Letters*, II. 363n.

[3] Adams to Charles Milnes Gaskell: 21 Aug 1878, in *Letters*, II. 344, 29 Jan 1882, in ibid., 448.

[4] Adams to William James, 9 Dec 1907, in *Letters* (ed. Ford), II. 485; to Margaret Chanler, 9 Sept 1909, in ibid., 524.

[5] Adams to William James, 9 Dec 1907, in ibid., 486.

[6] F. O. Matthiessen, *Henry James: The Major Phase* (London, New York, Toronto, 1946), p. 119.

[7] Daniel W. Bjork, *The Compromised Scientist: William James and the Development of American Psychology* (New York, 1983). For raging Oedipal struggles see p. 24 f.

[8] Adams to Charles Milnes Gaskell, 19 Dec 1870, in *Letters*, II. 94.

[9] William James, 'The Ph.D. Octopus', in *Moral Equivalent of War*, p. 28. And see Bjork, *Compromised Scientist*, p. 83: 'Tichener produced 56 Ph.Ds, a feat only approached by Cattel at Columbia.'

[10] Edwin Bjorkman, interview with William James, *New York Times*, 3 Nov 1907, p. 8.

[11] Witnessing one of James's attacks of angina pectoris, Freud said, 'I have always wished that I might be as fearless as he was in the face of approaching death': cited in Paul F. Boller, Jr., *American Thought in Transition: the Impact of Evolutionary Naturalism, 1865–1900* (Chicago, 1969), p. 147.

[12] Josiah Royce, *William James and Other Essays on the Philosophy of Life* (New York, 1911), p. 39.

[13] Robert F. Sayre, *The Examined Self: Benjamin Franklin, Henry Adams, Henry James* (Princeton, NJ, 1964), p. 189.

[14] A. A. Roback, *William James, Marginalia, Personality and Contribution* (Cambridge, Mass., 1942), p. 85.

[15] F. T. Hoffman, 'William James and the Modern Literary Consciousness', *Criticism*, 4 (Winter 1962), 1–13.

[16] G. W. F. Hegel, *The Philosophy of History*, trans. J. Sibree (New York, 1956), p. 86.

[17] Bjork, *Compromised Scientist*, p. 164.

[18] These comments are a response to the following two articles, among others: James E. Bayley, 'A Jamesian Theory of Self', *Transactions of the Charles S. Peirce Society*, 12 (Winter 1976), 148–65; and Daniel B. Schirmer, 'William James and the New Age', *Science and Society*, 33 (Fall-Winter 1968), 434–45.

[19] John Patrick Diggins, '"Who bore the failure of the Light": Henry Adams and the Crisis of Authority', *New England Quarterly*, 58.2 (June 1985), 188.

[20] E. L. Rodrigues, 'Out of Season for Nirvana: Henry Adams and Buddhism', in *Indian Essays in American Literature: Papers in Honour of Robert E. Spiller*, ed. Sujit Mukherjee and D. V. K. Raghavachary (Bombay, 1969), pp. 179–94.

[21] Jacques Maritain, *Creative Intuition in Art and Poetry* (New York, 1953), p. 358

[22] Merle Curti, *Human Nature in American Historical Thought* (Columbia, Mo., 1968), p. 83.

[23] Bjork, *Compromised Scientist*, p. 44: 'At the very moment of scientific triumph James wanted release from science.'

[24] John Dewey, *The Influence of Darwin on Philosophy* (New York, 1910), p. 288.

[25] J. C. Levenson, 'Henry Adams and the Culture of Science', in *Studies in American Culture*, ed. Joseph Kwiat and Mary Turpie, (Minneapolis, 1960), p. 136.

[26] See for example, Lynn White, Jr., 'Dynamo and Virgin Reconsidered', *American Scholar*, 27 (1958), 186. White attacks Adams's views on technology vigorously, but his common-sense approach blinds him to the real subtlety of Adams's argument.

[27] John Locke, *An Essay Concerning Human Understanding*, ed. Peter H. Nidditch (Oxford, 1984), pp. 108–9.

[28] John J. McDermott, introd., *The Writings of William James. A Comprehensive Edition* (New York, 1967), p. xxxxiii.

[29] Ralph Barton Perry, *The Thought and Character of William James*, 2 vols. (Boston, 1935), II. 607. Cited hereafter as Perry, I or II.

[30] William James, 'Ten Unpublished Letters from William James, 1842–1910, to Francis Herbert Bradley, 1846–1924', introd. J. C. Kema, *Mind*, 35 (July 1966), 312.

[31] William James, 'On Some Hegelianisms', *Mind*, 7 (Apr 1882), 192.

[32] Jean-Paul Sartre, *Search for a Method*, trans. Hazel E. Barnes (New York, 1968), pp. 10–11, 12–13.

[33] Hughes, *Consciousness and Society*, p. 112.

[34] Adams's copy of James's *Principles of Psychology*, now in the Massachusetts Historical Society, is the 2 vol. Henry Holt & Co. edition of 1902, currently available in a Dover reprint. This edition is cited hereafter in the text as *Principles* (1902). Adams's marginalia were first brought to public attention by Max I. Baym, 'William James and Henry Adams', *New England Quarterly*, 10 (1937), 717–42.

[35] Barzun, *A Stroll with William James*, p. 50.

Chapter 6
William James: *The Self and Politics*

[1] Barzun suspects the disintegration of our culture. He tells us of muggings, teenage pregnancies and worse, 'High progressivism' in higher education. He suspects psychology and softness with criminals. Like most of us (or in his opinion few of us), he suspects and distrusts ideologies. Yet he will have to forgive this writer for finding him as much a 'bundle of contradictions' as his hero. This (in his words) 'thought-cliché' is employed deliberately here because bundles come in different shapes and sizes and have the capacity therefore to be cliché-resistant. Barzun is a clever commentator but he does not always play fair. He diverts us with misapprehensions about the meaning of 'concepts' in popular speech and gracefully sidesteps the entire non-Aristotelian tradition in philosophy to assure us that those concepts mean 'the perception of sameness'. He dismisses all notion of 'principles' with a quotation from Dorothy Sayers which says 'they kill', and reliably informs us that all 'philos-

ophy of history' is a priori systematic distortion. Like James in fact Barzun has very little sense that 'no man is an island': he has little notion that the overworked professor and the embattled teacher of an inner-city school might share a vocation. Barzun, *Stroll*, pp. 60, 157, 253.

[2] William James, *Letters*, I. 158.

[3] Alan Trachtenberg, *The Incorporation of America. Culture and Society in the Gilded Age* (New York, 1982), p. 143.

[4] Adams, *Education*, p. 166.

[5] Dewey, *Influence of Darwin*, p. 242.

[6] Mills, *Sociology and Pragmatism*, p. 267–8.

[7] Perry, I.15.

[8] See Barzun, *Darwin, Marx, Wagner*, p. 358, and Eric Bentley, *A Century of Hero Worship*, 2nd edn. (Boston, 1957), p. 257.

[9] Perry, II. 575.

[10] H. W. Schneider, *Making the Fascist State* (New York and London, 1982), p. 237.

[11] Antonio Gramsci, 'The Study of Philosophy', in *The Modern Prince and Other Writings*, trans. Louis Marks (New York, 1957), p. 74.

[12] Jean-Paul Sartre, *Nausea*, trans. Robert Baldick (Harmondsworth, 1965), p. 162.

[13] Barzun, *Stroll*, p. 108.

[14] Mills, *Sociology and Pragmatism*, p. 260. An important chapter in Mills's book, on James's 'Psychological Liberalism', seems to have been deliberately ignored by all the commentators of the 1980s.

[15] Ibid., p. 262.

[16] James, *Letters*, I. 252.

[17] Samuel H. Levinson, *The Religious Investigations of William James* (Chapel Hill, NC, 1981), p. 24.

[18] Levinson, *Religious Investigations*, pp. 9 and 10, 64.

[19] Perry, I. 253.

[20] Here James, of course, shared Adams's views. See Kaledin, *Education of Mrs. Henry Adams*, p. 137.

[21] Alice James, *The Diary of Alice James*, ed. Leon Edel (New York, 1934), p. 8.

[22] William James, 'The Gospel of Relaxation', in *Moral Equivalent of War*, p. 53.

[23] Wells Twombly, *200 Years of Sport in America: A Pageant of a Nation at Play* (New York, 1976), p. 124.

[24] Perry, I. 695.

[25] Alice James, *Diary*, p. 114.

[26] *New York Evening Post*, 4 Mar 1899, p. 4.

[27] William James, 'The Philippines Again', letter to *New York Evening Post*, 10 Mar 1899, p.4.

[28] William James's address to the Anti-Imperialist League, published as 'Speech of Professor William James', *Evening Post* (New York), 3 Dec 1903, p. 8. Cited hereafter in the text, as 'Speech'.

[29] *Evening Post* (New York), 4 Dec 1903, p. 6.

[30] A. O. Lovejoy, *The Thirteen Pragmatisms and Other Essays* (Baltimore, 1963), p. 41. See also Stephen J. Whitfield, '"Sacred in History and in Art": The Shaw Memorial', *New England Quarterly*, LX. 1 (Mar 1987), 18, for James's 'unexpected blind spots on the issues of racism, women's rights, British oppression of the Irish, and British Imperialism in general' and George A. Garrison and Edward H. Madden, 'William James – Warts and All', *American Quarterly*, 29 (Summer 1977), 207–21.

[31] Harriet Beecher Stowe, *The Minister's Wooing* (London, 1859), p. 15.

[32] Mills, *Sociology and Pragmatism*, p. 64.

[33] Ibid., p. 87.

[34] James, *Letters*, I. 247; Mills, *Sociology and Pragmatism*, p. 87.

[35] Edward C. Moore, *American Pragmatism: Peirce, James and Dewey* (New York, 1961), p. 78.

Chapter 7
America and Europe

[1] See Perry, I. 3–78.

[2] Ibid., I. 88.

[3] The following account is based on Perry's still invaluable critical anthology.

[4] H. W. Schneider, *A History of American Philosophy*, 2nd edn. (New York and London, 1963), p. 105 f.

[5] William James, 'The Social Value of the College Bred', in *Moral Equivalent of War*, p. 17.

[6] George Santayana, *Character and Opinion in the United States* (London, 1920), p. 43.

[7] George Miller Beard, *American Nervousness Its Causes and Consequences...* (New York, 1881).

[8] James William Anderson quotes a letter of James to Hodgson of 1869, 'I have consequently made up my mind to lose at least a year now in vegetating and doing nothing but survive', in '"The Worst Kind of Melancholy": William James in 1869', *Harvard Library Bulletin*, 30.4 (Oct 1982), 369. The most illuminating study of the profession of illness in relation to James is Howard M. Feinstein, *Becoming William James* (Ithaca, NY, and London, 1984). Feinstein covers in detail subjects like the strenuous life, the gospel of relaxation, the notion of invalidism (with foreign travel to spas) conferring status in a

work-oriented culture. The choice seems to have been between rebellion and masochism, or, as Feinstein puts it, between 'crime and punishment' (p. 202).
[9] Henry James to William James, 26 Dec 1882, in Henry James, *Letters*, ed. Leon Edel vol. I (London, 1975), pp. 393–6.
[10] Perry, II. 227.
[11] Daniel Goleman has discussed the correctives now being applied to E. G. Boring's behaviourally-biased *History of Experimental Psychology* (1950) and Eugene Taylor's discovery and publication of unpublished notes of James which indicate that James 'saw the subconscious as the key to mental healing', in *New York Times* (*Science Times*), 1 Oct 1958. See Eugene Taylor, 'William James on Psychopathology: The 1896 Lowell Lectures on "Exceptional Mental States"', *Harvard Library Bulletin*, 30.4 (Oct 1982), 455–79. The lectures are now published: *William James on Exceptional Mental States*, ed. Eugene I. Taylor (New York, 1984).
[12] Perry, I. 415.
[13] Richard A. Hocks, *Henry James and Pragmatistic Thought. . .*(Durham, NC, 1974).
[14] Perry, I. 301.
[15] James, *Letters*, II. 152.
[16] From ibid., I. 161, 232, 288, and II. 152, 305.
[17] This paragraph is, with some additions, based on Cranston's standard biography: Maurice Cranston, *John Locke. A Biography* (Oxford and New York, 1985).
[18] Cranston, *John Locke*, pp. 120, 35, 279.
[19] See Kenneth Dewhurst, *John Locke, Physician and Philosopher. A Medical Biography* (London, 1963).
[20] J. R. Kantor, *The Scientific Evolution of Psychology*, 2 vols, (Chicago, 1969), II. 71. This work, an example of a very positivistic history of psychology, does make the point, however, that the development of 'psychological man' with Locke was owing to political theories and needs.
[21] Cranston, *John Locke*, p. 92.
[22] James, *Letters*, I. 164.
[23] John Stuart Mill, *The Autobiography of John Stuart Mill* (New York, 1924), pp. 94, 99.
[24] James, *Letters*, II. 259, 316.
[25] Ibid., II. 242.
[26] Ibid., II. 241, 260.
[27] Ibid., I. 307; II. 21, 22.
[28] Ibid., II. 206.
[29] Perry, I. 355, 320 f.
[30] The following account relies principally on E. G. Boring's classic *History of Experimental Psychology*, 2nd edn. (New York, 1950), and

A Source Book in the History of Psychology, ed. R. T. Herrnstein and E. G. Boring (Cambridge, Mass., 1965). These two indispensable works are, however, very much biased towards a positivist view of the subject and towards behaviourist psychology in general (see above, n. 11). The selection in the following account of issues relevant to James is entirely my own.
[31] James, *Letters*, I. 196.
[32] R. I. Watson, *The Great Psychologists*, 3rd edn. (Philadelphia, New York, Toronto, 1971), p. 255.
[33] Cf. B. F. Skinner, *Beyond Freedom and Dignity* (New York, 1971).
[34] James, *Letters*, I. 263–4.
[35] Boring, *History*, p. 317.
[36] Daniel N. Robinson, *Towards a Science of Human Nature: Essays on the Psychologies of Mill, Hegel, Wundt and James* (New York, 1982), p. 132.
[37] *A History of Psychology in Autobiography*, ed. Carl Murchison, 2 vols. (New York, 1961), I. 398.
[38] Watson, *Great Psychologists*, p. 292.
[39] James, *Letters*, I. 91.
[40] *The Nation*, 5 (1867), 432.
[41] James, *Letters*, II. 233.
[42] Perry, I. 159.
[43] James, *Principles*, I. 134.
[44] Ibid., I. 210–11.
[45] *Source Book*, ed. Herrnstein and Boring, p. 205.
[46] Gaston Bachelard, *The Psychoanalysis of Fire*, trans. Alan C. M. Ross (Boston, 1964), p. 11.
[47] Hans Aarsleff, *From Locke to Saussure: Essays on the Study of Language and Intellectual History* (London, 1982), p. 153.
[48] *Source Book*, ed. Herrnstein and Boring, p. 275.
[49] R. D. Laing, *The Voice of Experience* (Harmondsworth, 1983), p. 163.
[50] James, *Letters*, II. 115.
[51] Perry, I. 260; James *Letters*, II. 63.
[52] James, *Letters*, I. 287.
[53] Mark Schwen, 'Making the World: William James and the Life of the Mind', *Harvard Library Bulletin*, 30. 4 (Oct 1982), 439.
[54] Perry, I. 323.
[55] James, *Pluralistic Universe*, pp. 98, 118.
[56] Jean-Paul Sartre, *The Psychology of Imagination* (London, 1972), p. 2.
[57] Perry, II. 607 f., 636.
[58] Theodore Adorno, *Against Epistemology: A Metacritique; Studies in Husserl and the Phenomenological Antinomies*, trans. Willis Domingo (Oxford, 1982), pp. 45, 46.

[59] Samuel Langhorne Clemens [Mark Twain] *The Adventures of Huckleberry Finn*, ed. Sculley Bradley, Richmond Croom Beatty, E. Hudson Long, Thomas Cooley (New York, 1977), p. 132.

[60] Harriet Beecher Stowe, *Life and Letters of Harriet Beecher Stowe*, ed. Annie Fields (London, 1898), p. 289.

[61] Quoted from Oliver Wendell Holmes, *Medical Essays 1842–1882* (1883), in Ivan Illich, *Limits to Medicine* (London, 1976), p. 146.

[62] Henry James, *Washington Square* (London, 1967), pp. 197, 199.

[63] Illich, *Limits to Medicine*, p. 45.

[64] Ibid., pp. 7, 96, 6, 99, 41, 8.

[65] Foucault, *The Birth of the Clinic: An Archaeology of Medical Perception*, trans. A. M. Sheridon Smith (1973); rpr. New York, 1975), pp. 197, xiv.

[66] Lorraine J. Daston, 'The Theory of Will versus the Science of Mind', in *The Problematic Science: Psychology in the Nineteenth Century*, ed. William R. Woodward and Mitchell G. Ash (New York, 1982), p. 91.

[67] Douglas Guthrie, *A History of Medicine*, rev. edn. (London, 1958), p. 241.

[68] Illich, *Limits to Medicine*, p. 39; Foucault, *Birth of the Clinic*, pp. 97, 98.

[69] Illich, *Limits to Medicine*, pp. 30, 121.

[70] Dewhurst, *John Locke*, p. 38.

[71] Guthrie, *History of Medicine*, p. 246.

[72] Foucault, *Birth of the Clinic*, p. 96.

[73] Locke, *Essay Concerning Human Understanding* (see above, ch. 5, n. 27), pp. 410–11. Cited hereafter in the text of this chapter as *Essay*.

[74] Cranston, *John Locke*, p. 107.

Chapter 8
Philosophizing a Social Pathology

[1] Jones, *Social Darwinism and English Thought*, pp. xii, 14.

[2] Peter Brent, *Charles Darwin: 'A Man of Enlarged Curiosity'* (London, 1981), p. 43.

[3] Collingwood, *Idea of Nature* (London, Oxford, New York, 1960), p. 133; Jones, *Social Darwinism*, p. 17.

[4] Bowler, *Eclipse of Darwinism*, p. 119.

[5] Jones, *Social Darwinism*, pp. 28, 53.

[6] Bowler, *Eclipse of Darwinism*, p. 18.

[7] Philip P. Wiener, *Evolution and the Founders of Pragmatism* (Cambridge, Mass, 1949), p. 70.

[8] Moore, *American Pragmatism*, p. 89.

[9] Wiener, *Evolution and Pragmatism*, p. 99.

[10] Bowler, *Eclipse of Darwinism*, p. 23 f.

[11] Agassiz's copy of Charles Darwin, *On the Origin of Species by Means of Natural Selection* (London, 1859), is in the Natural History Library, Harvard. I am most grateful to the librarian, Jennifer Fewell, for help with Agassiz's handwriting. Page references in the text and notes are to this copy and edition, cited hereafter as *Origin*.

[12] Darwin, *Origin*, p. 129 (Agassiz's note): 'Does the excellence of the classification make it less likely to be the result of intelligent creation? More likely to be the result of physical causes?'

[13] Ibid., p. 133: 'Why not say that animals meant to live in cold climates are created with warm fur?' Agassiz writes, against Darwin's, 'Thus it is well known to furriers that animals of the same species have thicker and better fur the more severe the climate is under which they have lived . . .'.

[14] For a lively account of Marian Hooper and the Agassizs' school see Otto Friedrich, *Clover* (New York, 1979), pp. 48–53.

[15] Adams to Alexander Agassiz, 12 Apr 1903, in *Unpublished Letter*, p. 539.

[16] Adams to Charles Milnes Gaskell, 14 June 1903, in *Letters* (ed. Ford), II. 407.

[17] Bowler, *Eclipse of Darwinism*, p. 107.

[18] *Darwin and his Critics*, ed. Hull, p. 153.

[19] David S. Barber, 'Henry Adams's *Esther*: the Nature of Individuality and Immortality', *New England Quarterly*, 45 (1972), 231.

[20] Bowler, *Eclipse of Darwinism*, p. 48.

[21] Charles Lyell, *Principles of Geology, or Modern Changes of the Earth and its Inhabitants*, 7th edn. (London, 1847), p. 1.

[22] Mindel, 'Uses of Metaphor in Henry Adams', 101.

[23] Adams, pp. 225, 231.

[24] Perry, I. 5.

[25] James, *Letters*, I. 54: 'All theory is grey, dear friend/But the golden tree of life is green.'

[26] Gruber, *Darwin on Man*, 2nd edn. (Chicago, 1981), p. 86.

[27] James, *Letters*, I. 62.

[28] Perry, I. 225.

[29] James, *Letters*, II. 2; Perry, I. 209.

[30] James, *Letters*, II. 344.

[31] Walter Bagehot, *Physics and Politics: or Thoughts on the Application of the Principles of 'Natural Selection' and 'Inheritance' to Political Society* (London, 1872), pp. 208–9.

[32] Henry Adams, *A Letter to American Teachers of History* (Washington, DC, 1910), p. 12; cited hereafter in the text. It should be clear that I disagree with the following: 'James is the scientist; Adams only gave the appearance

of being scientific', in Ralph Maud, 'Henry Adams: Irony and Impasse', *Essay in Criticism*, 8 (1958), 383. The first clause depends on the definition of scientist, the second addresses a wrong question.

[33] E. O. Wilson, *Sociobiology: the New Synthesis* (Cambridge, Mass., 1975). The marketing of this book in post-Vietnam-war American needs careful study. For a critique see Stephen Jay Gould, *Ever Since Darwin: Reflections on Natural History*, (1978; rpr. Harmondsworth, 1980), pp. 251 f.

[34] Jones, *Social Darwinism*, p. 41.

[35] Harris, *Rise of Anthropological Theory*, pp. 122–3.

[36] Jones, *Social Darwinism*, p. 4.

[37] U. J. Jensen, 'Introduction: Preconditions for Evolutionary Thinking', in *The Philosophy of Evolution*, ed. U. J. Jensen and R. Harré (Brighton, 1981), p. 19.

[38] Charles Darwin, *The Life and Letters of Charles Darwin*, 3 vols. (London, 1887), III. 189.

[39] Engels, *Dialectics of Nature*, p. 186.

[40] Jones, *Social Darwinisn*, p. 72.

[41] Ibid., p. 71.

[42] See for example Gregory Bateson, *Steps to an Ecology of Mind* (St. Albans and London, 1973).

[43] Michael Ghiselin, *The Triumph of the Darwinian Method* (Berkeley, Calif., and Los Angeles, 1969), p. 60.

[44] Ludwig Wittgenstein, *Tractatus Logico-Philosophicus*, trans. D. F. Pears and B. F. McGuinness (London, 1961), p. 25.

[45] Norbert Wiener, *The Human Use of Human Beings* (1954; rpr. London, 1968), pp. 35, 36.

[46] *Philosophy of Evolution*, ed. Jensen and Harré, p. 164.

[47] S. Toulmin, 'Human Adaptation', in ibid., p. 186.

[48] Dewey, *Influence of Darwin on Philosophy*, p. 8. Cited herefater in the text, as *Influence*.

[49] This is Darwin's phrase: *Origin*, p. 90.

[50] Stanley Edgar Hyman, *The Tangled Bank: Darwin, Marx, Frazer and Freud as Imaginative Writers* (New York, 1962), pp. 22, 33.

[51] Ghiselin, *Triumph of the Darwinian Method*, p. 29.

[52] Perry, II. 89.

[53] Jones, *Social Darwinism*, p. 134.

[54] Ibid., p. 14.

[55] H. Standish Thayer, introd., *Pragmatism: The Classic Writings*, ed. Thayer (New York and Toronto, 1970), p. 20.

[56] William James, 'Great Men and Their Environment' (1880), in James, *The Will to Believe*, p. 163. Unfortunately James scholars

cannot simply work from the Harvard standard edition; it is important to read chronologically. I have reinstated in square brackets a phrase from the original article which, it will be readily seen, is of the utmost importance to the field of ideas with which James was dealing, and of clear importance to the argument here. Note that the original title of the article was 'Great Men, Great Thoughts and the Environment' (*The Atlantic Monthly*, 46 (Oct 1880), 441–59). The article has received some recent attention. See Robert J. Richards, 'The Personal Equation in Science: William James's Psychological and Moral Uses of Darwinian Theory', *Harvard Library Bulletin*, 30. 4 (Oct 1982) [James Special Issue], 387–419, which gives a useful outline of the connections between James and Darwin but attempts no critique of the respective positions.

[57] James, *Letters*, I. 203.

[58] James, *Will to Believe*, p. 165.

[59] Ibid., p. 170.

[60] Ibid., p. 171.

[61] Jones, *Social Darwinism*, p. 42.

[62] *Dictionary of National Biography*, ed. Leslie Stephen (1885), under Bagehot.

[63] Bagehot, *Physics and Politics*, p. 13. See Shlomo Avineri, *The Social and Political Thought of Karl Marx* (Cambridge, 1968), p. 42. Avineri argues that Marx comes near Bagehot's distinction between the real and apparent British Constitution in his separation of socio-economic and political spheres. It should be added that Bagehot is perhaps a forerunner of theorists of hegemonic controls.

[64] Geoffrey Best, *Mid-Victorian Britain, 1851–1875* (London, 1971), p. 236.

[65] Ibid., pp. 238, 257.

[66] W. L. Burn, *The Age of Equipoise: A Study of a Mid-Victorian Generation* (London, 1964), p. 18.

[67] *New Encyclopaedia Britannica*, 15th edn. (1982), under Bagehot. See also ibid., 13th edn., under Bagehot: 'To a certain extent, the *Physics and Politics*... "caught on" in a new direction, and Darwin himself was greatly interested.'

[68] Bagehot, *Physics and Politics*, p. 10. Cited hereafter in the text, as *Physics*.

[69] James, *Principles*, I. 126. Cited hereafter in the text.

[70] James, *Will to Believe*, p. 184.

[71] Adams to William James, 27 July 1882, in Adams, *Letters*, II. 466.

[72] Jones, *Social Darwinism*, p. 138.

[73] William James, 'The Sentiment of Rational-

ity', in James, *The Will to Believe* (1979 Harvard edition, cited hereafter in the text), p. 57. This later version of the essay begins with extracts from the original article published in *Mind*, 4 (July 1879), and continues with an article called 'Rationality, Activity and Faith', which appeared in the *Princeton Review* (July 1882).

[74] Aristotle, *On the Art of Poetry*, trans. Ingram Bywater (Oxford, 1920), p. 78.

[75] Walt Whitman, 'Preface, 1855', to *Leaves of Grass* (1st edn., in Whitman, *Leaves of Grass*, ed. Harold W. Blodgett and Scully Bradley (New York, 1965), p. 727.

[76] James, *Will to Believe*, pp. 64–5. Discussing James's 'Address at the Emerson Centenary in Concord', Dana Brand has pointed out that '. . . for James Whitman is not a complex and contradictory poet': Brand, 'William James's Reformulation of Emerson and Whitman', *ESQ; A Journal of the American Renaissance*, 31. 1 (1st Quarter 1985), 45.

[77] Daston, 'Theory of Will versus the Science of Mind', p. 94.

[78] Ralph Waldo Emerson, 'Nature' (1836) in *Collected Works of Ralph Waldo Emerson*, vol. I: *Nature, Addresses, and Lectures* (Cambridge, Mass., 1971), p. 7.

[79] Frederick Pollock, 'Evolution and Ethics', *Mind*, I. 3 (1876), 344.

[80] Ibid. Pollock's article is cited also in Jones, *Social Darwinism*, p. 38.

[81] Dewey, *Influence of Darwin on Philosophy*, p. 2.

[82] Perry, II. 24; Gay Wilson Allen, *William James, A Biography* (London, 1976), p. 518.

[83] Bentley, *Century of Hero Worship*, p. 257.

Chapter 9
The Principles of Psychology

[1] Adorno, *Against Epistemology*, p. 14.

[2] See Karl Pribham and Merton Gill, *Freud's Project Reassessed* (London, 1976).

[3] Perry, II. 173.

[4] John E. Smith, *Purpose and Thought: The Meaning of Pragmatism* (London, 1979), pp. 85.

[5] Ibid, pp. 94, 95.

[6] Lovejoy, *Thirteen Pragmatisms*, p. 48.

[7] Richard W. F. Kroll in an article on Locke and Gassendi speaks of '. . . the current trends in the history of ideas, of denying any simple division between developments in continental and British philosophies in the late nineteenth and early eighteenth centuries': Kroll, 'The Question of Locke's Relation to Gessendi', *Journal of the History of Ideas*, 45 (July–Sept 1984), p. 339.

[8] Watson, *Great Psychologists*, p. 207.

[9] Morton White, *Science and Sentiment in America: Philosophical Thought from Jonathan Edwards to John Dewey* (New York, 1972), p. 177. And see also Frank Lentricchia, 'The Romanticism of William James', *Salmagundi*, 25 (1974), 92, 96, 97.

[10] For example, Craig R. Eisendrath, *The Unifying Moment: The Psychological Philosophy of William James and Alfred North Whitehead* (Cambridge, Mass., 1971), p. 28.

[11] James, *Will to Believe*, p. 198 n.

[12] William James, *The Meaning of Truth* (Cambridge, Mass., and London, 1975), pp. 30–1.

[13] James, *Pluralistic Universe*, pp. 49, 44.

[14] Jean Wahl, *The Pluralist Philosophies of England and America*, trans, Fred Rothwell (London, 1925), p. 3.

[15] D. B. Klein, *A History of Scientific Psychology* (London, 1970), p. 383.

[16] Hans Linschoten, *On the Way toward a Phenomenological Psychology*, ed. A. Giorgi (Pittsburgh, Pa., 1968), p. 81.

[17] Richard I. Aaron, *John Locke* (Oxford, 1955), p. 34; Klein, *History of Scientific Psychology*, p. 366.

[18] Daniel N. Robinson, *An Intellectual History of Psychology* (New York and London, 1981), p. 215.

[19] Kroll, 'Locke's Relation to Gassendi', p. 343.

[20] White, *Science and Sentiment in America*, p. 172

[21] Gerald E. Myers, 'William James's Theory of Emotions', *Transactions of the Charles Peirce Society*, 2 (Winter 1969), p. 68.

[22] James, *Will to Believe*, p. 76 f.

[23] Robert S. Harper, 'The Laboratory of William James', *Harvard Alumni Bulletin*, 52 (5 Nov 1949), 170.

[24] Eisendrath, *Unifying Moment*, p. 27. The following pages seek to extend further Eisendrath's accurate observations.

[25] Cranston, *John Locke*, p. 279.

[26] Locke, *Essay*, p. 43, Cited hereafter in the text, as *Essay*.

[27] George Herbert, 'The Pulley', in *The Works of George Herbert*, ed. F. E. Hutchinson (Oxford, 1945), p. 159.

[28] Lorraine J. Daston's discussion followed here: Daston, 'Theory of Will . . .', pp. 92 f.

[29] Ibid., p. 103.

[30] Cranston, *John Locke*, p. 274.

[31] Santayana, *Character and Opinion in the United States*, p. 75.

[32] Thayer, in *Pragmatism: The Classic Writings* ed. Thayer, p. 36.

[33] James, *Will to Believe*, pp. 26–7.

[34] James, *Pragmatism*, p. 31.

[35] Adorno, *Against Epistemology*, p. 43.

[36] Sidney Kaplan, 'Taussig, James and Peabody: A "Harvard School" in 1900?', *American Quarterly*, 7 (Winter 1955), 319, 326.

[37] Dewey, *Influence of Darwin*, pp. 267, 269.

[38] Smith, *Purpose and Thought*, p. 48: 'Where philosophical world formulas are invoked, Dewey questioned whether the pragmatic method is supposed to discover or indicate in terms of consequences for life the value of some formula whose logical content is already fixed, or whether it is supposed to criticize, revise or ultimately constitute the meaning of the formula. Dewey rightly perceived that James was often using the method in the first way whereas Dewey himself wanted to confine it to the second.' My own feeling is that Dewey simplifies James on this issue.

[39] Lovejoy, *Thirteen Pragmatisms*, p. 40.

[40] Henry S. Levinson, *Science, Metaphysics, and the Chance of Salvation: An Interpretation of the Thought of William James* (Missoula, Mont., 1978), p. 6.

[41] J. B. Watson, *Psychology from the Standpoint of a Behaviorist* (Philadelphia and New York, 1919), pp. xi, xii, 364.

[42] *Pragmatism: The Classic Writings*, ed. Thayer, p. 343.

[43] Max C. Otto *et al.*, *William James, the Man and Thinker: Addresses delivered at the University of Winsconsin in Celebration of the Centenary of his Birth* (Madison, Wisc., 1942), p. 69. James M. Edie's recent book, *William James and Phenomenology* (Bloomington, Ind., and Indianapolis, 1987), argues (p. 78) that: 'Consciousness *as a function* is prior to the dichotomy of subject and object; it is "subjective and objective both at once"; it is "entirely impersonal...pure experience". One feels that what James primarily lacked for a more adequate solution to this problem was precisely the Husserlian and Sartrean distinction between the pre-reflexive (pre-personal, not-yet-reflected) consciousness and the fully reflexive, judging consciousness.' However, it is a large assumption that James would have welcomed these more modern 'solutions', given his disposition to replace consciousness with the divided kingdom of physiological attention and mystical experience.

[44] Eisendrath, *Unifying Moment*, pp. 44, 105. McDermott, introd., *Writings of William James*, p. xxxvii.

[45] Eisendrath, *Unifying Moment*, p. 97.

[46] Ibid., p. 54.

[47] James, *Pluralistic Universe*, p. 83.

[48] Lentricchia, 'Romanticism of William James', p. 86.

[49] Levinson, *Science, Metaphysics...*, p. 10.

[50] James, *Pragmatism*, pp. 97–8: 'leading that is worth while'.

[51] Santayana, *Character and Opinion*, p. 151.

[52] Sartre, *Psychology of Imagination*, p. 98.

[53] Linschoten, *Phenomenological Psychology*, pp. 55, 94, 122, 198, 249.

[54] Bruce Wilshire, *William James and Phenomenology: A Study of 'The Principles of Psychology'* (Bloomington, Ind., and London, 1968), p. 8.

[55] James M. Edie, 'William James and Phenomenology,' *Review of Metaphysics*, 23 (1970), p. 517.

[56] Jean-Paul Sartre, *The Transcendence of the Ego: An Existentialist Theory of Consciousness*, ed., trans. and introd. Forrest Williams and Robert Kirkpatrick (New York, 1957), pp. 105–6.

[57] Whitehead, *Alfred North Whitehead. An Anthology*, p. 540.

[58] Locke, *Essay*, pp. 116, 411.

[59] Christopher Hill, *The World Turned Upside Down: Radical Ideas during the English Revolution* (1972; rpr. Harmondsworth, 1975), pp. 221, 367.

[60] Hill, *World Turned Upside Down*, pp. 392–3. See also James Tully's review of Neal Wood, *The Politics of Locke's Philosophy: a Social Study of 'An Essay Concerning Human Understanding'* (Berkeley, Calif., 1983) in *Political Theory*, 12. 1 (May 1984), pp. 286–90.

[61] Sartre, *Nausea*, p. 126.

[62] James, *Pluralistic Universe*, p. 112.

[63] Martin Heidegger, *On the Way to Language*, trans. Peter D. Hertz (San Francisco, 1971), pp. 35–6.

[64] Bertrand Russell, review of *Essays in Radical Empiricism*, *Mind*, 21 (Oct 1912), pp. 571–5.

[65] James, *Meaning of Truth*, p. 32.

[66] Charlenne Haddock Seigfried, *Chaos and Context: A Study in William James* (Athens, O., 1978), p. 93.

[67] James, *Pragmatism*, p. 4.

[68] John C. McDermott, *The Culture of Experience* (New York, 1976), p. ix.

[69] Ibid., pp. 186, 113.

[70] John Dewey, *The Quest for Certainty* (London, 1930), p. 20, cited in Smith, *Purpose and Thought*, p. 96.

[71] C. Wright Mills, *The Sociological Imagination* (New York, 1959), p. 99.

[72] Ralph Waldo Emerson, 'Self Reliance'

(1840), in *The Collected Works of Ralph Waldo Emerson*, vol. II, (Cambridge, Mass., and London, 1979), p. 29; Walt Whitman, 'Song of Myself', in Whitman, *Leaves of Grass*, p. 29.

[73] Herman Melville, *The Confidence Man: His Masquerade* (Evanston, Ill., and Chicago, 1984), p. 112.

[74] Adams, *Education*, p. 249.

[75] Charles Darwin, *The Descent of Man*, 2nd edn. (London, 1888), p. 91.

[76] V. P. Bynack, 'Noah Webster's Linguistic Thought and the Idea of an American Culture', *Journal of the History of Ideas*, p. 14 (Jan–Mar 1985), pp. 111–13.

[77] James, *Pragmatism*, p. 88, *Pluralistic Universe*, p. 87.

[78] Linschoten, *Phenomenological Psychology*, p. 122.

Chapter 10
War and Peace in the Global Psyche

[1] Barzun, *Darwin, Marx, Wagner*, p. 93.

[2] Jones, *Social Darwinism*, pp. 124–5, 126.

[3] Julien Benda, *The Great Betrayal [La Trahison des clercs]*, trans. Richard Aldington (London, 1928), pp. 105–6.

[4] James, *Will to Believe*, pp. 171, 55, 160–1.

[5] Stephen Crane, *Great Battles of the World* (London, New York, Toronto, 1914), p. 84.

[6] Ralph Barton Perry, *The Present Conflict of Ideals: A Study of the Philosophical Background of the World War* (New York, 1918), p. 145.

[7] James, *Moral Equivalent of War*, p. 7.

[8] Ibid., p. 9.

[9] Ibid., p. 10.

[10] Myers, *William James, His Life and Thought*, p. 444.

[11] Ibid., p. 602

[12] James, *Moral Equivalent of War*, p. 14. James's advocacy of a sort of socialist equilibrium probably owes something to H. G. Wells, but he never really got as far as even Well's gradualism. Wells: 'It is very easy for writers like myself to deal in the broad generalities of Socialism and urge their adoption as general principles; it is altogether another affair with a man who sets himself to work out the riddle of the complications of actuality in order to modify them in the direction of Socialism': H. G. Wells, *First and Last Things; A Confession of Faith and Rule of Life* (1908; repr. London, 1929), p. 86.

[13] James, *Pragmatism*, p. 39.

[14] James, *Pluralistic Universe*, p. 18.

[15] James, *Pragmatism*, pp. 55, 56.

[16] James, *Varieties of Religious Experience*, p. 46.

[17] Ibid., p. 135.

[18] Levinson, *Religious Investigations of William James*, gives a good critique of the *Varieties* in religious terms, and also summarizes other religious commentary.

[19] James, *Varieties*, p. 134.

[20] Ibid., p. 67.

[21] Sartre, *Psychology of Imagination*, p. 6. Cited hereafter in the text, as *Imagination*.

[22] Sigmund Freud, *The Interpretation of Dreams*, trans. James Strachey (Harmondsworth, 1980), p. 76.

[23] Ibid., p. 628 f.

[24] Ibid., p. 628.

[25] Maurice Merleau-Ponty, *Phenomenology of Perception*, trans. Colin Smith (London and Henley, 1978), p. 337.

[26] Ibid., pp. 337, 344–5.

[27] James, *Varieties*, p. 134.

[28] Ibid., p. 135.

[29] Merleau-Ponty, *Phenomenology*, pp. 342–3. The phrase is Saussure's. See Ferdinand de Saussure, *Course in General Linguistics*, Charles Bally *et al.*, trans. Wade Baskin (London, 1974), p. 4.

Chapter 11
Gertrude Stein and the Legitimation of Society

[1] Stein to Robert Bartlett Haas, 23 (?) Jan 1938 (Stein Papers, Beinecke).

[2] Samuel's, II. 648. Berenson actually read some of Gertrude Stein's work – probably the early 'portraits' – as a letter of 23 Nov 1912 to her attests: 'As for your own prose I find it vastly more obscure still. It beats me hollow, & makes me dizzy to boot. So do some of Picasso's by the way': (*The Flowers of Friendship: Letters Written to Gertrude Stein*, ed D. Gallup (New York, 1953), p. 66. Note also a letter from Leo Stein to Mabel Weekes, 19 Sept 1902: 'I have also met Mrs Berenson's sister (Dora Russell) and brother-in-law (Bertrand Russell), a young mathematician of genius. Mrs Russell is a reformer and is now nursing her nerves. . . . Gertrude has put Berenson on eggs and milk, under which he is flourishing like a Green Bay Tree': Leo Stein, *Journey into the Stein: Being the Letters, Papers and Journals of Leo Stein*, ed. Edmund Fuller (New York, 1950), p. 10. In the 1970s there was something of a critical contretemps between two American commentators on Adams and Stein. James M. Cox argued that 'Stein is the woman whom Adams had tried to imagine emerging from the American

scene': Cox, 'Autobiography and America', *Virginia Quarterly Review*, 47 (Spring 1971), 227. William Wasserstrom argued that 'only a woman with a male sensibility was qualified to deny Adams's libel on America', and further that 'it is barely conceivable to think of the Steins, both Leo and Gertrude – whose acquaintance with Bernard Berenson had drawn them to Cézanne and inspired their historic first great act of acquisition – as ignorant of Adams's ideas': Wasserstrom, 'The Sursymamericubealism of Gertrude Stein', *Twentieth-Century Literature*, 21 (Feb 1975), p. 97.

[3] For a brief discussion see Clive Bush, 'Towards the Outside: The Quest for Discontinuity in Gertrude Stein's *The Making of Americans: Being a history of a family's progress*', *Twentieth-Century Literature*, 24. 1 (Spring 1978–9), pp. 25–57.

[4] Chessman, *Public Is Invited to Dance*, p. 157.

[5] For Richard Wright's links with Stein see the end of Chapter 15. See also Hugh MacDiarmid (Christopher Murray Grieve), 'Gertrude Stein', in *At the Sign of the Thistle* (London, 1934), pp. 33–56: '. . . a determination to reject all such auto-deception of the mind and concentrate, or, rather re-concentrate, on the essence of our psychical plight, and what T. E. Hulme said of the necessary preliminary preparation for an understanding of the religious attitude can be applied to Miss Stein's work, regarded as spadework, pioneering, towards a dynamic literature – a literature that will do what literature has never done in the past, act directly on present consciousness, circumvent all those elements which have hitherto protected the inertia, the refusal to think, to experience. . . .'

[6] Stein to Carl Van Vechten, [postmark 22 Dec 1935], *Letters Stein/Van Vechten*, I. 468.

[7] Dolores Klaich, *Woman + Woman: Attitudes Towards Lesbianism* (New York, 1974), p. 202, and p. 214: 'since their deaths we have learned that Toklas not only typed Stein's manuscripts but did a lot of heavy editing, suggesting, arguing, even actual writing. . . . Any resemblance between Toklas's relation with Stein and a butch–femme relationship is pure myth. . . . Toklas was one strong dyke.' For the other view see Eliot Paul (not sympathetic to Stein and probably not to be trusted), 'Gertrude, Alas, Alas', *Esquire*, 26 (July 1946), 62: 'Gertrude dominates Alice, makes all the decisions, takes all the praise or blame.'

[8] Ernest Hemingway, *Selected Letters 1917–1961*, ed. Carlos Baker (New York, 1981), p. 650.

[9] Gertrude Stein's seriousness about her lectures is not in doubt. Ulla Dydo writes of her Cambridge lecture of 1926, 'She must have sensed as soon as she received the invitation that the temptation to please an audience would interfere with composition and that a live audience would make her personality rather than her words the focus of attention': Dydo, 'Landscape is Not Grammar: Gertrude Stein in 1928', *Raritan*, 7. 1 (Summer 1987), 99.

[10] F. Piraro suggests that Stein's experience with a black midwife in Baltimore was a profound '*expérience médicale*' which affected her early work: for example the opening pages of *A Long Gay Book*. Certainly *A Long Gay Book* can be read as a defense of the erotic and creative life as against the pure 'nature' of motherhood and babies 'with no conscious feeling in them'. See Piraro, 'The Last Years of Gertrude Stein', *Europe – Revue littéraire mensuelle*, 63. 676 (1985), p. 96.

[11] Oscar Wilde, *An Ideal Husband, A Play* (London, 1909), Act I, p. 31.

[12] Stein to W. G. Rogers, (?) Nov 1938 (Stein Papers, Beinecke). Stein's politics is receiving some attention. But careful distinctions need to be made in judging the relations between art and life. Catherine R. Stimpson is a case in point when she says: 'Sociologically, Stein's handling of her energies shows the limits of her imagination. . . at heart she was apparently unable to picture a world in which men, and an exceptional woman, did not plumb language and culture': Stimpson, 'Stein, Toklas, and the Paradox of the Happy Marriage', in *Mothering the Mind: Twelve Studies of Writers and Their Silent Partners*, ed. Ruth Perry and Martine Watson Brownley (New York and London, 1984), p. 131. I think Stimpson is wrong about Stein's attitudes to non-writers, and moralistic, by implication, about the necessary withdrawal from the world of the serious artist: notwithstanding exceptions like a William Carlos Williams or a Muriel Rukeyser.

[13] Stein to W. G. Rogers, (?) 1936: 'they [Latins] do not believe in majorities because in a latin country there is no such thing' (Stein Papers, Beinecke).

[14] Gertrude Stein, 'Money', *Saturday Evening Post*, 13 June 1936, p. 88.

[15] W. G. Rogers, *When This You See Remember Me* (New York and Toronto, 1948), p. 25.

[16] Gertrude Stein, *How Writing is Written: The Previously Unpublished Writings of Gertrude Stein*, 2 vols (Los Angeles, 1974), II. 55. Stein was responding to a questionnaire circulated among writers by *Partisan Review*.

The questions were tedius and tendentious, i.e. 'How would you describe the political tendency of American writing as a whole since 1930? How do you feel about yourself? Are you sympathetic to the current tendency towards what may be called "literary nationalism"....?' Stein replied, 'Writers only think they are interested in politics, they are not really, it gives them a chance to talk and writers like to talk but really no writer is really interested in politics.'

[17] Stein to Robert Bartlett Haas, 23 Jan 1938 (Stein Papers, Beinecke).

[18] Kenneth Rexroth, introd. to *A Return to Pagany: The History, Correspondence, and Selections from a Little Magazine 1929–1952*, Ed. Stephen Halpert with Richard Jones (Boston, 1969), p. xiv.

[19] Henry David Thoreau, *Walden*, ed. J. Lyndon Shanley (Princeton, N.J., 1962), p. 8; Gertrude Stein, 'English and American Language in Literature', *Life and Letters Today*, 13 (Sept 1935), p. 22.

[20] Gertrude Stein, 'I Came and Here I Am', *Hearst's International Cosmopolitan*, Feb 1935, p. 168.

[21] Stein to Robert Bartlett Haas, 13 Sept 1937 (Stein Papers, Beinecke).

[22] Wordsworth, *The Poems*, ed. Hayden, p. 871.

[23] Alfred North Whitehead, from *Science and the Modern World*, in *Whitehead: An Anthology*, ed. Northrop and Gross, p. 444.

[24] Charles Darwin, *The Expression of the Emotions in Man and Animals* (1872; repr. Chicago and London, 1965), pp. 279, 327.

[25] Ibid., p. 280.

[26] For a discussion of Emerson's phrase see Hans Aarslef, *The Study of Language in England, 1780–1860* (Princeton, N.J., 1967), p. 243.

[27] I am thinking of the effect of Horne Tooke on English philology in the first thirty years of the nineteenth-century. See Aarslef, *Study of Language*, p. 73.

[28] Charles Darwin, *Metaphysics, Materialism and the Evolution of Mind: Early Writings of Charles Darwin*, ed. Paul H. Barrett with a commentary by Howard E. Gruber (Chicago, 1980), p. 74.

[29] Merleau-Ponty, *Phenomenology of Perception*, p. 53.

[30] Jacques Derrida, *Of Grammatology*, trans. Gayatri Chakravorty Spivak (Baltimore and London, 1976), p. 49.

[31] James, *Principles*, II. 1064.

[32] Ibid., II. 1072.

[33] Ibid., II. 1082.

[33] Jean-Paul Sartre, *Sketch for a Theory of the Emotions*, trans. Philip Mairet (London, 1971), pp. 27, 28. See also a very acute article by Jerome Neu, 'A Tear is an Intellectual Thing', *Representations*, 19 (Summer 1987), pp. 35–6: 'Why do we cry? My short answer is: because we think' (p. 35). Neu also comments: 'Sartre gives us a sense of being more responsible for our lives than we might like to believe', suggesting that Sartre exaggerates our capacity to take responsibility. My own sympathies, as should be clear, are with Sartre.

[35] Sartre, *Sketch*, p. 91.

[36] A. A. Roback states that 'immediately preceding World War I, Münsterberg rated as the foremost psychologist of his time': Roback, *History of American Psychology*, rev. edn. (New York, 1964), p. 200. The most complete account of James's relation with Münsterberg is in Bjork, *Compromised Scientist*, pp. 43 f.

[37] Münsterberg, *The Americans*, p. viii. Cited hereafter in the text.

[38] Hugo Münsterberg, *Business Psychology* (Chicago; 1915), p. 184. Cited hereafter in the text.

[39] Mumford, *Technics and Civilization*, p. 385.

[40] Ellul, *Technological Society*, p. 133. Ellul attacks Taylor's notion that an industrial plant is a 'closed organism'.

[41] Wiener, *Human Use of Human Beings*, pp. 131 f.

[42] See the whole of ch. 4 of Harry Braverman's *Labor and Monopoly Capital: The Degradation of Work in the Twentieth Century* (New York, 1974), pp. 85 f.

[43] Whyte, *Organization Man*, p. 39.

[44] The most famous of these factory 'accidents', the 'Triangle' fire of 1911, occurred four years before Münsterberg published his book on business psychology. See Leo Stein, *The Triangle Fire* (Philadelphia and New York, 1962).

[45] The famous phrase is the title of ch. 8 of *The Varieties of Religious Experience*.

[46] The Solomons/Stein articles first appeared in the *Psychological Review*, Sept 1896 and (Stein only) May 1898. The text used here is Gertrude Stein [With Leon Solomons], *Motor Automism* (New York), 1969, so cited hereafter in the text.

[47] B. F. Skinner, 'Has Gertrude Stein a secret?', *Atlantic Monthly*, 153 (Jan 1934), 50–7.

[48] *Flowers of Friendship*, ed. Gallup, p. 99 n. In the Stein Papers (Beinecke) is correspondence between A. N. and Evelyn Whitehead and Stein and Toklas stemming from this occasion. Evelyn Whitehead's letters form the

bulk of it and, taken together, make an extraordinarily moving record of one woman's
war. Whitehead himself appears rather aloof
and engrossed in philosophy, but it is clear
that Evelyn Whitehead could write about
her personal problems, financial worries and
anxieties for her sons (one was lost in an
aeroplane accident) to Stein and Toklas. A
sympathetic feminist might make much of
this triangle between male philosopher, gay
writer and mate, and harassed and anxiety-
stricken wife. Stein and Toklas did not visist
the Whiteheads again, but sent aid during the
scarce war years.
[49] Victor Lowe, *Understanding Whitehead*
(Baltimore, 1962), p. 267.
[50] Collingwood, *Idea of Nature*, p. 171.
[51] Ivor Leclerc, 'Form and Actuality', in *The
Relevance of Whitehead*, ed. Ivor Leclerc (London and New York, 1961), p. 172.
[52] Gottfried Martin, 'Metaphysics as *Scientia
Universalis* and as *Ontologia Generalis*', in
ibid., p. 309.
[53] Quoted from James's 'Notes for the Psychological Seminary', in *Some Problems in
Philosophy*, by Eugene Fontinell, who gives
an extended discussion of the notion of 'field':
Fontinell, *Self, God and Immortality: A
Jamesian Investigation* (Philadelphia, 1986),
p. 27.
[54] Victor Lowe, 'The Influence of Bergson,
James and Alexander on Whitehead', *Journal
of the History of Ideas*, 10 (Apr 1949), 267–96.
Lowe partially changed his mind in his 1962
book, *Understanding Whitehead* (see n. 49), and
argued, p. 193, that Bergson's influence may
have been more profound.
[55] Whitehead, *Adventures of Ideas*, p. 268.
[56] Alfred North Whitehead, *The Concept of
Nature* (1920; repr. Cambridge, 1982), 3, 144,
150.
[57] Alfred North Whitehead, *The Aims of
Education and Other Essays*, in *Whitehead: An
Anthology*, ed. Northrop and Gross, p. 142.
[58] Lowe, *Understanding Whitehead*, p. 37.
[59] Whitehead, *Adventures of Ideas*, p. 217.
[60] Lowe, *Understanding Whitehead*, p. 341.
[61] Charles Hartshorn 'Whitehead and Contemporary Philosophy', in *Relevance of Whitehead*, ed. Leclerc, pp. 21–43.
[62] Lowe, *Understanding Whitehead*, p. 50.
[63] Ibid., pp. 29, 40.
[64] Whitehead, *Adventures of Ideas*, p. 211.
Dorothy Emmet speaks of there being 'no
dualism between the realm of Being and
Becoming', and characterizes Whitehead's
theory of knowledge 'as a particular kind of
correspondence theory': Emmet, *Whitehead's*

Philosophy of Organism, pp. 134, 171.
[65] Whitehead, *Adventures of Ideas*, p. 288, cited
by Leclerc, in 'Form and Actuality', in
Relevance of Whitehead, ed. Leclerc, p. 184.
[66] Martin Jordan, *New Shapes of Reality:
Aspects of Whitehead's Philosophy* (London,
1968), p. 173.
[67] Whitehead, *Science and the Modern World*, in
Whitehead: An Anthology, ed. Northrop and
Gross, pp. 371, 372.
[68] Lowe, *Understanding Whitehead*, p. 223.
[69] Cited from *Science and the Modern World* in
Emmet, *Whitehead's Philosophy of Organism*,
p. 92.
[70] Jordan, *New Shapes of Reality*, p. 153.
[71] Lancelot Law Whyte, *The Unconscious
Before Freud* (London, 1962): brief qoutations
in this passage cited from pp. 136, 151, 155,
171, 175, 176.
[72] Jordan, *New Shapes of Reality*, p. 43.
[73] Whitehead, *Adventures of Ideas*, p. 312.
[74] Locke, cited in Emmet, *Whitehead's Philosophy of Organism*, p. 100.
[75] Lowe, *Understanding Whitehead*, p. 245.
[76] Whitehead, *Adventures of Ideas*, p. 15. Cited
hereafter in the text, as *Adventures*.
[77] Clive Bush, 'Cultural Reflections on
American Linguistics from Whitney to
Sapir', *Journal of American Studies*, 22. 2 (Aug
1988), pp. 185–212.
[78] A. H. Johnson, 'Whitehead on the Uses of
Language', in *Relevance of Whitehead*, ed.
Leclerc, pp. 125 f. Owing to its brevity, the
article (pp. 125–41) is discussed hereafter
without recourse to page references.
[79] Alfred North Whitehead, *Symbolism, Its
Meaning and Effect* (London, 1927), p. 38,
cited by Johnson (see n. 78).
[80] Lowe, *Understanding Whitehead*, p. 242.
[81] Max Bense, 'Kosmologie und Literatur:
über Alfred N. Whitehead und Gertrude
Stein', *Texte und Zeichen*, 3 (1957), pp.
512–25.

Chapter 12
Indices of an Approach to Stein
[1] Walter Benjamin, 'On Language as Such
and on the Language of Man' (1916), in
Benjamin, *One Way Street and Other Writings*
(London, 1978), p. 166.
[2] Saussure, *Course in General Linguistics*,
p. 107.
[3] 'It was Heraclitus who first appealed to
words as embodying the nature of things,
and his influence on Plato is manifest in the
Cratylus': C. K. Ogden and I. A. Richards,
The Meaning of Meaning: A Study of the

Influence of Language upon Thought and of the Science of Symbolism (1923; repr. London, 1972), p. 32.

[4] Martin Heidegger, *An Introduction to Metaphysics*, trans. Ralph Manheim (New Haven, Conn., and London, 1959), p. 13.

[5] Heidegger, *On the Way to Language*, p. 81.

[6] Martin Heidegger, *Poetry, Language, Thought*, trans Albert Hofstadter (New York, 1975), p. 108.

[7] Ernst Cassirer, *Language and Myth*, trans. Susanne K. Langer (New York, 1946), p. 75.

[8] Foucault, *Language, Counter-Memory, Practice*, ed. Bouchard, p. 55.

[9] Ibid., p. 51. Foucault's remarks occur in a discussion of Bataille's *Histoire de l'oeil*: 'On the day that sexuality began to speak and be spoken, language no longer served as a veil for the infinite; and in the thickness it acquired on that day we now experience finitude and being. In its dark domain, we now encounter the absence of God, our death, limits and their transgression.'

[10] Aarsleff, *From Locke to Saussure*, p. 52.

[11] Heidegger, *Introduction to Metaphysics*, p. 53.

[12] Heidegger, *On the Way to Language*, pp. 23–4; Ricoeur, *Rule Of Metaphor*, p. 297.

[13] Maurice Merleau-Ponty, *Signs*, trans. and introd. Richard C. McCleary (Evanston, Ill., 1964), p. 43.

[14] Heidegger, *On the Way to Language*, p. 123.

[15] V. N. Volosinov, *Marxism and the Philosophy of Language*, trans. Ladislav Matejka and I. R. Titunik (New York and London, 1973), p. 19.

[16] Foucault, *Language, Counter-Memory, Practice*, p. 30.

[17] William Dwight Whitney, *The Life and Growth of Language* (London, 1889), p. 145.

[18] Benjamin, *One Way Street*, p. 111.

[19] Merleau-Ponty, *Signs*, p. 98.

[20] Ricoeur, *Rule of Metaphor*, p. 37.

[21] Saussure, *Course in General Linguistics*, p. 40; Benjamin Lee Whorf (An American Indian Model of the Universe', in *Selected Writings*, ed. and introd. John B. Carroll (Cambridge, Mass., 1956), p. 59.

[22] Ricoeur, *Rule of Metaphor*, p. 304.

[23] Ogden and Richards, *Meaning of Meaning*, p. 302. (The spa town of Cheltenham, once largely populated by retired colonials, now has a thriving Asian community.)

[24] Ibid., p. 96.

[25] Ibid., p. 135.

[26] Ricoeur, *Rule of Metaphor*, p. 305.

[27] Maurice Merleau-Ponty, *Consciousness and the Acquisition of Language*, trans. Hugh J. Silverman (Evanston, Ill., 1973), p. 6.

[28] Whitney, *Life and Growth of Language*, p. v.

[29] Paul Feyerabend, *Against Method* (London, 1978), p. 15.

[30] Aarslef, *From Locke to Saussure*, p. 251.

[31] Lewis Mumford, *The Pentagon of Power* (London, 1971), p. 115.

[32] Aarslef, *From Locke to Saussure*, p. 318.

[33] J. P. Mayer, 'More on the History of the Comparative Method: The Tradition of Darwinism in August Schleicher's work', *Anthropological Linguistics*, 8 (1966), 1–12.

[34] Merleau-Ponty, *Consciousness*, p. xxxvii; Aarslef, *From Locke to Saussure*, p. 164.

[35] R. H. Robbins, *A Short History of Linguistics* (London, 1969), p. 150.

[36] Aarslef, *From Locke to Saussure*, p. 164.

[37] Charles S. Peirce, *Philosophical Writings*, ed. Justus Buckler (New York, 1955), pp. xiv, 114.

[38] Ibid., p. 115.

[39] Wittgenstein, *Tractatus*, p. 19, Jean Piaget, *The Language and Thought of the Child*, trans. Marjorie and Ruth Gabain, 3rd edn. (London, 1971), p. 4.

[40] Whorf, *Language, Thought and Reality*, pp. 158, 55.

[41] William Dwight Whitney, *Whitney on Language: Selected Writings*, ed. Michael Silverstein (Cambridge, Mass., and London, 1971), pp. 22, 73.

[42] Whitney, *Life and Growth of Language*, p. 90.

[43] Ibid., p. 50.

[44] Ibid.

[45] Clive Bush, *The Dream of Reason* (London and New York, 1977), p. 87; Whitney, *Life and Growth of Language*, p. 225.

[46] Whitney, *Life and Growth of Language*, p. 283.

[47] Ogden and Richards, *Meaning of Meaning*, p. 76.

[48] Alfred Korzybski, *Science and Sanity: An Introduction to Non-Aristotelian Systems and General Semantics*, 4th edn. (Lakeville, Conn., 1958), pp. 130, 20.

[49] Aarslef, *From Locke to Saussure*, p. 155.

[50] Saussure, *Course in General Linguistucs*, pp. 84, 8.

[51] Ibid., pp. 161, 163.

[52] Ricoeur, *Rule of Metaphor*, p. 119.

[53] Whorf, *Language, Thought and Reality*, p. 36.

[54] Aarslef, *From Locke to Saussure* (citing Locke, as in the following discussion), pp. 27–8.

[55] Merleau-Ponty, *Signs*, p. 48.

[56] Heidegger, *On the Way to Language*, p. 74.

[57] Adorno, *Against Epistemology*, p. 23.

[58] Volosinov, *Marxism and the Philosophy of Language*, p. 12.
[59] Aarslef, *From Locke to Saussure*, p. 26.
[60] Locke and Leibniz, cited by Aarslef, ibid., pp. 57, 85.
[61] Ogden and Richards, *Meaning of Meaning*, p. 321.
[62] Whitney, *Life and Growth of Language*, p. 311.
[63] Leonard Bloomfield, *Language* (1933; repr. London, 1979), pp. 408, 28.
[64] Ibid., p. 48.
[65] Robbins, *Short History*, p. 188.
[66] Bush, 'Cultural Reflections on American Linguistics'.
[67] Saussure, *Course in General Linguistics*, p. 198.
[68] Edward Sapir, *Culture, Language and Personality*, ed. David G. Mandelbaum (Berkeley, Calif., Los Angeles, and London, 1956), p. 9.
[69] Ibid., pp. 14, 76, 71.
[70] Edward Sapir, *Language: An Introduction to the Study of Speech* (1921; repr. New York and London, 1949), p. 155.
[71] Ibid., pp. 154, 150.
[72] Cited in *Sexual Stratagems: The World of Women in Film*, ed. Patricia Erens (New York, 1979), p. 24.
[73] Sapir, *Culture, Language and Personality*, p. 172.
[74] Ibid., pp. 73, 69, 70.
[75] Ibid., p. 17.
[76] Robbins, *Short History*, p. 25.
[77] Ibid., pp. 81, 87.
[78] G. A. Padley, *Grammatical Theory in Western Europe 1500–1700: The Latin Tradition* (Cambridge, 1976), p. 60.
[79] Robbins, *Short History*, p. 138.
[80] Ibid., p. 26.
[81] Padley, *Grammatical Theory*, p. 32.
[82] Ogden and Richards, *Meaning of Meaning*, p. 334.
[83] Darwin, *Metaphysics, Materialism and the Evolution of Mind*, p. 122.
[84] Whitney, *Life and Growth of Language*, p. 301.
[85] Ibid., p. 210.
[86] Saussure, *Course in General Linguistics*, p. 125.
[87] Ricoeur, *Rule of Metaphor*, p. 218.
[88] A. Korzybski, *Manhood of Humanity: The Science and Art of Human Engineering* (New York, 1921).
[89] Korzybski, *Science and Sanity*, p. 57.
[90] Ricoeur, *Rule of Metaphor*, p. 248.
[91] Cassirer, *Language and Myth*, p. 12.
[92] Heidegger, *Introduction to Metaphysics*, p. 55.
[93] Whorf, *Language, Thought and Reality*, p. 158.
[94] Ibid., p. 153.
[95] Ibid., p. 248.
[96] Ibid., P. 260.
[97] Volosinov, *Marxism and the Philosophy of Language*, p. 110.
[98] Ricoeur, *Rule of Metaphor*, p. 129.
[99] Volosinov, *Marxism and the Philosophy of Language*, p. 61.
[100] Merleau-Ponty, *Signs*, p. 97.
[101] Ibid., p. 63.
[102] Ibid., p. 102.
[103] Saussure, *Course in General Linguistics*, p. 74.
[104] Frederic Jameson, *The Prison House of Language: A Critical Account of Structuralism and Russian Formalism* (Princeton, N.J., 1972), p. 27.
[105] *Emil Durkheim on Institutional Analysis*, ed., trans. and introd., Mark Traugott (Chicago and London, 1978). Cited hereafter in the text, as *Durkheim*.
[106] Jean-Paul Sartre, *Literary and Philosophical Essays*, trans. Annette Michelson (London, 1968), p. 136.
[107] Volosinov, *Marxism and the Philosophy of Language*, p. 89.
[108] Merleau-Ponty, *Consciousness*, p. 10.
[109] Whorf, *Language, Thought and Reality*, p. 40.

Chapter 13
How to Write

[1] Cited in Wendy Lois Steiner, 'Gertrude Stein's Portrait Form' (Ph.D. diss., Yale University, 1974), p. 180.
[2] Gertrude Stein, Notebook 'N' (Stein Papers, Beinecke).
[3] Gertrude Stein, 'Poetry and Grammar,' in Stein, *Look at me now and here I am: Writings and Lectures* (London, 1967), p. 140.
[4] See entry for 'Grammar' in Noah Webster, *An American Dictionary of the English Language* (1821; repr. New York and London, 1970).
[5] Stein to Virgil Thompson, 7 Oct 1928 (Stein Papers, Beinecke).
[6] Gertrude Stein, *Useful Knowledge* (New York, 1928), p. 104.
[7] James R. Mellow, 'Gertrude Stein Rediscovers America', *Columbia Forum*, NS 3 (Winter 1974), 22.
[8] Steiner, 'Gertrude Stein's Portrait Form', pp. 221, 87. Steiner discusses the critics' use of the 'movie metaphor'.
[9] Gertrude Stein, 'Christian Berard', in *Portraits and Prayers* (New York, 1934), p. 77.

[10] 'Sentence', in Webster, *American Dictionary*.

[11] Stein, 'Poetry and Grammar', p. 126.

[12] Gertrude Stein to Sherwood Anderson, Feb 1929, in *Anderson/Stein*, ed. Roy L. White (Chapel Hill, N.C., 1972), p. 68.

[13] Allen Fisher, *unpolished mirrors A–H* (London, 1979–81); Chessman, *The Public Is Invited to Dance*, p. 93.

[14] Ezra Pound, in Fenollosa, *Chinese Written Character*, ed. Pound, p. 10.

[15] Stein, *How to Write*, p. 20. Cited hereafter in the text.

[16] See Harriet Chessman's discussion of Ida and Stein's use of language as a mode of being using psychoanalytic theory. It is one of the best discussions along these lines, though the question of representation is not finally confronted: Chessman, *Public Is Invited to Dance*, p. 169.

[17] Picasso, however, was not too pleased about the colours Toklas used: Linda Simon, *The Biography of Alice B. Toklas* (Garden City, N.Y., 1977), p. 144.

[18] Gertrude Stein, 'Henry James', in Stein, *Four in America* (New Haven, Conn., 1947), p. 119.

[19] William Carlos Williams, *Paterson, Books I–V* (London, 1964), p. 28.

[20] Cited in Eric Mottram, *Towards Design in Poetry* (London, 1977), p. 19.

[21] Merleau-Ponty, *Consciousness*, p. 6.

[22] Ulla Dydo, 'Must Horses Drink, or "Any Language Is Funny If You Don't Understand It"', *Tulsa Studies in Women's Literature*, 4. 2 (Fall 1985), 275.

[23] S. C. Neuman, *Gertrude Stein, Autobiography and the Problem of Narration* (Victoria, B.C., 1985), p. 53.

[24] J. M. D. Olmsted and E. Harris Olmsted, *Claude Bernard and the Experimental Method in Medicine* (London, New York, Toronto, 1962), p. 171.

[25] Adorno, *Against Epistemology*, p. 26.

[26] BBC News, 23 July 1985: obituary for Professor Keith Simpson.

[27] 'Report of a Joint Committee of the General Council of the Bar of England and Wales, The Law Society and the British Medical Association', *Medical Evidence in Courts of Law* (London, 1965), p. 10.

[28] Foucault, *Birth of the Clinic*, pp. 145, 126.

[29] Marie-Claire Pasquier, 'Gertrude Stein: Ecouter, parler, voir', *Les Temps modernes*, 419 (June 1981), p. 2168.

[30] Foucault, *Birth of the Clinic*, pp. 160, 129.

[31] Stein, *Narration*, p. 31.

[32] Gertrude Stein, *Everybody's Autobiography* (1937; repr. New York, 1964), p. 26; *Forensic Fables by O.* (1926; repr. London, 1961).

[33] Chessman, *Public Is Invited to Dance*, p. 155, Commenting on Stein's essay 'American Crimes and How They Matter' (1935), Harriet Chessman shrewdly observes, 'To close a "case" may represent only another version of warmongering, not because it actually solves or reveals anything, but because it destroys the mystery of dialogic relation.' I would see that less of a 'mystery', however, than a life-oriented, open-ended possibility of human exchange which resists those who have power to close cases arbitrarily.

[34] Paul Bowles, *Without Stopping: An Autobiography* (1972; repr. New York, 1985), p. 120. This is one of the most amusing episodes in a remarkable autobiography. See also Chessman, *Public Is Invited to Dance*, p. 162, for tracing of 'I am because my little dog knows me' to the English folk rhyme 'Lawkamercyme'.

[35] See Toulmin, *Human Understanding*, pp. 88–9.

Chapter 14
Decline in the West: *The Making of Americans*

[1] Hannah Arendt, *The Origins of Totalitarianism* (1951; repr. Cleveland and New York, 1967), p. 351.

[2] Stein, *Everybody's Autobiography*, p. 207.

[3] Kenneth Rexroth, introd., *Return to Pagany*, ed. Halpert and Jones, p. xv. And see further, p. xv: 'For this self-evident truism he was broken by the East German government and became a not person, like the folk singer, Wolf Bierman, who sings precisely of the soul of man under Socialism, the human self-alienation that still endures behind the interpersonal iron curtains of slogans and shibboleths.'

[4] Stein to Carl Van Vechten, postmark 17 Mar 1924, in *Letters, Stein/Van Vechten*, I. 94. The story of the publication of *The Making of Americans* is told in Gillian Hanscombe and Virginia L. Sayers, *Writing for Their Lives, The Modernist Women, 1910–1940* (London, 1987), pp. 223 f.

[5] Malcolm Bradbury, *The Modern American Novel* (Oxford, 1984), p. 40: 'better to have read than to read'.

[6] Charlotte Kretzoi, 'Gertrude Stein's Attempt at "The Great American Novel"', *Studies in English and American* (Budapest), 4 (1978), 27.

[7] See above, p. 284.

[8] See above, p. 285.

[9] From the Radcliffe mss, reproduced in Rosalind S. Miller, *Gertrude Stein: Form and*

Intelligibility (New York, 1949), p. 121.

[10] See above, p. 277.

[11] Stein, Notebook marked 'C', n.d. (Stein Papers, Beinecke).

[12] Leon Katz, 'The First Making of *The Making of Americans*: a Study Based on Gertrude Stein's Notebook and Early Memoirs of her Novels, 1902–1908' (Ph.D. diss., Columbia University, 1963), p. 196.

[13] Stein to W. G. Rogers, (?) Dec 1938 (Stein Papers, Beinecke).

[14] Neil Schnitz, 'Portraits, Patriarchs, Mythos: The Revenge of Gertrude Stein', *Salmagundi*, 40 (1978), 75.

[15] For a sympathetic account of this process of evaluation and the early years see Ulla E. Dydo, 'To Have the Winning Language: Texts and Context of Gertrude Stein', in *Coming to Light: American Women Poets in the Twentieth Century*, ed. Diane Wood Middlebrook and Marilyn Yalom (Woman and Culture Series) (Ann Arbor, Mich. 1985), pp. 4–20.

[16] Stein, *Useful Knowledge*, pp. 64–8.

[17] Stein, Notebook (small grey), 2, n.d. (Stein Papers, Beinecke).

[18] Gertrude Stein, 'Your United States', *Atlantic Monthly* (Oct 1937), 463.

[19] Arendt, *Origins of Totalitarianism*, p. 52.

[20] Pasquier, 'Gertrude Stein: Écouter, parler, voir', 2164.

[21] Stein, Miscellaneous notes for *A Long Gay Book*, 34 [Papers numbered by Leon Katz] (Stein Papers, Beinecke).

[22] Stein, Notebook 'C' n.d.: inside back cover (Stein Papers, Beinecke).

[23] Stein, Notebook 'B' (red), n.d. (Stein Papers, Beinecke).

[24] Stein, 'Your United States', 464.

[25] William Carlos Williams, 'The Work of Gertrude Stein', *Pagany*, 1 (Jan–Mar 1930), 44.

[26] Stein, Notebook (small grey), 14, n.d. (Stein Papers, Beinecke).

[27] Williams, 'Work of Gertrude Stein', 45.

[28] Stein, Notebook (small black), (?) 1904 (Stein Papers, Beinecke).

[29] Katz, 'First Making of *The Making of Americans*', p. 277.

[30] Stein, *Narration*, p. 60.

[31] Stein to Carl Van Vechten, 18 Apr 1916, in *Letters Stein/Van Vechten*, I. 53.

[32] Katz, 'First Making of *The Making of Americans*', p. 12.

[33] Stein, *Narration*, p. 26.

[34] Otto Weininger, *Sex and Character* (London and New York, 1906), p. 95.

[35] Ibid., p. 97.

[36] Stein, *Making of Americans*, p. 345; this work cited hereafter in the text. See also bp Nichol's criticism of Bridgeman's dismissal of Stein's emotional 'substances' as a 'theory of rumours', in 'Excerpts from some beginning writings on Gertrude Stein's Theories of Personality', *White Pelican*, 3 (Autumn 1973), 17.

[37] Weininger, *Sex and Character*, p. 128.

[38] Ibid., pp. 152, 182.

[39] Marianne Moore, cited in John Malcolm Brinnin, *The Third Rose, Gertrude Stein and Her World* (1959; repr. London, 1960), p. 96.

[40] Katz, 'First Making of *The Making of Americans*', p. 291.

[41] Arnold Hauser, *The Sociology of Art*, trans. Kenneth J. Northcott (London, Henley and Melbourne, 1982), p. 3.

[42] Stein, *Narration*, pp. 5, 25.

[43] Aristotle *on the Art of Poetry*, trans. Ingram Bywater (1920; repr. Oxford, 1959), pp. 40 f.

[44] Stein, 'English and American Language in Literature', 21.

[45] Stein, *Narration*, p. 30.

[46] Stein, 'English and American Language in Literature', 19.

[47] Oswald Spengler, *The Decline of the West*, trans. Charles Francis Atkinson, 2 vols. (1918 and 1922; repr. London, 1932), I. 8, 19.

[48] Ibid., I. 370, 424.

[49] Marjorie Perloff, 'Poetry as Word System: The Art of Gertrude Stein', *American Poetry Review*, 8 (1979), 34.

[50] William Burroughs and Brion Gysin, *The Third Mind* (New York, 1978), p. 61.

[51] Spengler, *Decline of the West*, II. 24.

[52] G. W. F. Hegel, *Hegel's Logic*, trans. William Wallace (1873; repr. Oxford, 1975), p. 174.

[53] Bush, 'Towards the Outside: The Quest for Discontinuity in *The Making of Americans*', 28.

[54] Katz, 'The First Making of *The Making of Americans*', p. 248.

[55] Gyula Illyes, *People of the Pusta*, trans. G. F. Cushing (Budapest, 1967), p. 144.

[56] Aristotle, *The Nicomachean Ethics*, trans. H. Rackham (Cambridge, Mass., London 1934), p. 407.

[57] Ibid., pp. 285, 391. The predication of the states of the body on the passions in fact goes back to Aristotle and reappears, causally reversed, in the Elizabethan theories of humours. The James–Lange theory of the emotions follows the Aristotelian sequence. The 'Fluid' and 'Solid' characters of *The Making of Americans* also ultimately have their source in Aristotle and the Elizabethan

humour tradition, a fact not noted by L. Ruddick, 'Fluid Symbols in American Modernism – William James, Gertrude Stein, George Santayana and Wallace Stevens', in *Allegory, Myth and Symbol*, ed. M. W. Bloomfield (Cambridge English Studies, vol. 9) (Cambridge, Mass., 1981).

[58] Aristotle, *Nicomachean Ethics*, p. 407.

[59] W. F. R. Hardie, *Aristotle's Ethical Theory* (Oxford, 1968), pp. 12, 224.

[60] Norman O. Brown, *Life Against Death: The Psychoanalytical Meaning of History* (New York, 1959), p. 96.

[61] Ibid., p. 96.

[62] Brown, *Life Against Death*, pp. 108, 107.

[63] Louis Zukofsky, '*A*' *1–12* (1959; repr. London, 1966), pp. 174–5.

[64] Zukofsky, '*A*', pp. 176, 242.

[65] Arendt, *Human Condition*, p. 41.

[66] Bledstein, *Culture of Professionalism*, pp. 19, 31.

[67] Ibid., pp. 93, 40.

[68] Ibid., p. 113.

[69] Ibid., p. 306.

[70] Fuller, *Education Automaton*, p. 58.

[71] Whitehead, *Adventures of Ideas*, p. 280. See above, ch. 11, p. 290.

[72] Elizabeth Sprigge, *Gertrude Stein, Her Life and Work* (London, 1957), p. 14.

[73] Laurence Sterne, *Tristram Shandy*, ed. Howard Anderson (1760; repr. New York and London, 1980), p. 206.

[74] John Berger in *About Time*, dir, Michael Dibb and Christopher Rawlance, Channel 4 TV (UK), 23 May 1985.

[75] Jacques Derrida, *Writing and Difference*, trans. Alan Bass (1967; repr. Chicago, 1978), p. 21.

[76] Suggested by Professor Eric Mottram after a paper given by the author to the Graduate Seminar at King's College, London University, 9 May 1985.

[77] Jacques Lacan, *Ecrits: A Selection*, trans. Alan Sheridan (London, 1977), p. 284.

[78] Marx, *Capital*, I. 217.

[79] Gertrude Stein, *Geography and Plays* (1922; repr. New York, 1968), p. 407.

Chapter 15
A World Made of Stories

[1] *Delius. A life in letters*, ed. Lionel Carley, vol. I: 1862–1908 (London, 1983), p. 28.

[2] Stein, *Anderson/Stein*, ed. White, p. 9; Eric Sevareid, *Not So Wild A Dream* (1946; repr. New York, 1976), p. 89.

[3] Catherine R. Stimpson, 'The Mind, Body, and Gertrude Stein', in *Gertrude Stein: Modern Critical Views*, ed. Harold Bloom (New York, 1986), p. 143.

[4] Stein, *Geography and Plays*, p. 132.

[5] Stein, *Narration*, p. 30.

[6] Stein, *Four in America*, p. 201.

[7] Ibid., p. 2.

[8] Robert Bartlett Haas, 'Gertrude Stein Talking. A Trans-Atlantic Interview', *Uclan Review*, 9 (Spring 1963), 40, 41.

[9] Ibid., 41.

[10] Ibid., 42.

[11] Mabel Dodge Luhan, *Movers and Shakers*, vol. III of *Intimate Memories* (New York, 1963), p. 53.

[12] Robert Bartlett Haas, 'Gertrude Stein Talking [Part 2]', *Uclan Review*, 9 (Winter 1964), p. 46.

[13] Stein, *Narration*, pp. 37, 35.

[14] Gertrude Stein, 'Reflections on the Atomic Bomb', *Yale Poetry Reveiw*, 7 (1947), 4.

[15] From Roland Barthes, *S/Z*, trans. Richard Miller (1974), in *The Poetics of Murder: Detective Fiction and Literary Theory*, ed. Glenn W. Most and William W. Stowe (San Diego, Calif., 1983), p. 119.

[16] Geoffrey Hartman, 'Literature High and Low: The Case of the Mystery Story', in *Poetics of Murder*, ed. Most and Stowe, p. 216.

[17] Stein to Carl Van Vechten, late Aug 1923, in *Letters Stein/Van Vechten*, I. 86.

[18] Stein, 'Your United States', 462.

[19] Stein to Carl Van Vechten, 20 Jan 1938, in *Letters Stein/Van Vechten*, II. 588. Wilkie Collins, *The Woman in White* (1859; repr. London, 1910), pp. 193,194.

[20] Stein, *Narration*, p. 33. Cited hereafter in the text.

[21] Gertrude Stein, 'American Crimes and How They Matter', *New York Herald Tribune*, 16 Mar 1935, p. 29.

[22] Gertrude Stein, 'Why I Like Detective Stories', *Harper's Magazine* (Nov 1937), 70, 104.

[23] Stein, *Everybody's Autobiography*, p. 5.

[24] Gertrude Stein, review of Sherwood Anderson's *A Story-Teller's Story*, *Ex Libris*, 2 (Mar 1925), 177.

[25] Stein, *Narration*, p. 54.

[26] Stein, 'English and American Language in Literature', 24.

[27] Cited in Katz, 'The First Making of *The Making of Americans*', p. 90.

[28] Stein, *Narration*, p. 17.

[29] Shirley Swartz, 'Between Autbiographies: Gertrude Stein and the Problem of Audience', *White Pelican*, 3 (Autumn 1973), 46.

[30] Stein to Robert Bartlett Haas, 29 Sept 1941 (Stein Papers, Beinecke).

[31] Stein to Robert Bartlett Haas, 11 July 1940 (Stein Papers, Beinecke).

[32] Cited from Francis Rose, *Saying Life: The Memoires of Sir Francis* (London, 1961), and Eric Severeid, *Not So Wild A Dream* (New York, 1946), in Maureen R. Liston, *Gertrude Stein. An Annotated Critical Bibliography* (Kent, O., 1979), I-B-ii-75/I-B-ii-80.

[33] Arendt, *Origins of Totalitarianism*, p. 477.

[34] Stein, *Wars I Have Seen*, p. 52. Cited hereafter in the text.

[35] Arer.dt, *Origins of Totalitarianism*, p. 477.

[36] Reich, *Mass Psychology of Fascism*, p. 13.

[37] James Gleik, 'The Riddle of Chaos', *Dialogue*, 68 (1985), 57–63.

[38] Riesman, *Lonely Crowd*, p. 158.

[39] Sartre, *Literary and Philosophical Essays*, p. 87.

[40] Richard Wright, 'Gertrude Stein's Story is Drenched in Hitler's Horrors' [note Wright's original title which was, 'Gertrude Stein Kills the 19th Century'], *PM Magazine*, 11 Mar 1945, 15. Further quotations in the text are all from p. 15.

[41] Ibid., See, for example, Michael Gold, *Change the World!* (New York, 1936). Contemporary criticism is not much more subtle. But whereas Gold at least had some of the best insights of orthodox Marxism – and his anger is legitimate against Stein's overt political position – a recent article, hostile to the Stein–Wright connection, confines itself to distinctly 'bourgeois influence' and 'psychological' connections. My point is that Stein and Wright shared certain political insights as a result of an imaginative confrontation of twentieth-century social changes, even though these insights are not recognized as 'political' by conventional Marxists, nor apparently by some critics who write about Afro-American literature. See E. E. Miller, 'Richard Wright and Gertrude Stein', *Black American Literature Forum*, 16. 3 (1982), 107–12.

[42] *Flowers of Friendship*, ed. Gallup, p. 326.

[43] Stein to Carl Van Vechten, 2 May 1945, in *Letters Stein/Van Vechten*, II. 771.

[44] Gunnar Myrdal with Richard Sterner and Arnold Rose, *An American Dilemma: The Negro Problem and Modern Democracy*, 2 vols. (New York and London, 1944), I. 152.

[45] Myrdal, *American Dilemma*, II. 656, 735.

[46] Richard Wright to Gertrude Stein, 27 May 1945, (Richard Wright Papers, Beinecke).

[47] Ibid.

[48] Richard Wright to Gertrude Stein, 23 June 1945 (Richard Wright Papers, Beinecke).

[49] Ibid. Norman Mailer, 'The White Negro: Superficial Reflections on the Hipster', *Dissent*, Summer 1957, 276–93, repr. in Mailer, *Advertisements for Myself* (New York, 1957).

[50] Richard Wright to Gertrude Stein, 23 June 1945 (Richard Wright Papers, Beinecke).

[51] Ibid.

[52] Richard Wright to Gertrude Stein, 29 Oct 1945 (Richard Wright Papers, Beinecke).

Conclusion

[1] Robert S. Lynd, *Knowledge for What? The Place of Social Science in American Culture* (1939; repr. New York, 1964), p. 141.

[2] Mills, cited in Stanley Aronowitz, *The Shaping of American Working-Class Consciousness* (New York, 1973), p. 323.

[3] Robert Wokler, 'Saint-Simon and the Passage from Political to Social Science', in *The Language of Political Theory in Early-Modern Europe*, ed. Anthony Pagden (Cambridge, 1987), p. 327.

[4] D. Aberle and Kaspar D. Naegele, 'Middle-Class Fathers' Occupational Role and Attitudes towards Children', in *America as a Mass Society*, ed. Philip Olson (London, 1963), p. 416.

[5] Burnham, *Managerial Revolution*, pp. 127–8, 135, 220.

[6] Braverman, *Labor and Monopoly Capital*, p. 268; Aronowitz, *Shaping of American Working-Class Consciousness*, p. 269.

[7] Mike Davis, *Prisoners of the American Dream: Politics and Economy in the History of the U.S. Working Class* (London, 1986), pp. 139, 16.

[8] Ibid., pp. 3, 215.

[9] Brian Easlea, *Liberation and the Aims of Science: An Essay on Obstacles to the Building of a Beautiful World* (London, 1973), p. 17.

[10] Serres, *The Parasite*, p. 222.

[11] Dale Carter, *The Final Frontier* (London, 1988), p. 260.

[12] Arnold, *Folklore of Capitalism*, pp. 25, 5, xiv.

[13] Aronowitz, *Shaping of American Working-Class Consciousness*, p. 115.

[14] Davis, *Prisoners of the American Dream*, p. 40.

[15] Lynd, *Knowledge for What?*, p. 151.

[16] Cynthia E. Russett, *The Concept of Equilibrium in American Social Thought* (New Haven, Conn., 1966), p. 34.

[17] Gareth Stedman Jones (citing Ross), 'Class Expression versus Social Control? A Critique of Recent Trends in the Social History of "Leisure"', in *Social Control and the State*, ed. Stanley Cohen and Andrew Scull (1983; repr. Oxford, 1985), p. 44.

[18] Ibid., pp. 45, 48 and 49.
[19] Michael Ignatieff, 'State, Civil Society and Total Institutions: A Critique of Recent Social Histories of Punishment', in *Social Control and the State*, ed. Cohen and Scull, p. 98.
[20] John A. Mayer, 'Notes towards a Working Definition of Social Control in Historical Analysis', in *Social Control and the State*, ed. Cohen and Scull, p. 38, n. 47.
[21] *American Media and Mass Culture: Left Perspectives*, ed. Donald Lazere (Berkeley. Calif., Los Angeles, London, 1987), p. 241.
[22] Gabriel Kolko, 'The American "Income Revolution"', in *America as a Mass Society*, ed. Olson, pp. 103–4 and 113.
[23] David Riesman, 'The Suburban Dislocation', in *American as a Mass Society*, ed. Olson, p. 297.
[24] Paul Starr, *The Social Transformation of American Medicine* (New York, 1982), p. 75.
[25] Ibid., p. 208.
[26] Alvin W. Gouldner, *The Coming Crisis of Western Sociology* (New York, London, 1970), p. 158.
[27] Cited in Dorothy Porter and Roy Porter, 'What was Social Medicine? An Historiographical Essay', *Journal of Historical Sociology*, I. 1 (Mar 1988), 95.
[28] Thomas S. Szasz, *The Myth of Mental Illness: Foundation of a Theory of Personal Conduct*, rev. edn. (New York, 1974), pp. 260, 182.
[29] Davis, *Prisoners of the American Dream*, p. 214.
[30] Ibid., pp. 113, 170.
[31] Arnold, *Folkore of Capitalism*, pp. 230, 185.
[32] Donald Lazere, 'Conservative Media Criticism: Heads I Win Tails You Lose', in *American Media and Mass Culture*, ed. Lazere, p. 91.
[33] Serres, *The Parasite*, p. 58.
[34] Peter Körner et al., *The IMF and the Debt Crisis*, trans. Paul Knight (London and Atlantic Highlands, N.J., 1986), p. 61.
[35] C. Wright Mills, *The Power Elite* (New York, 1959), pp. 20–1.
[36] Kees van der Pijl, *The Making of an Atlantic Ruling Class*, cited in Davis, *Prisoners of the American Dream*, p, 189; Davis, *Prisoners*, p. 233.
[37] Peter Dreier, 'The Corporate Complaint against the Media', in *American Media and Mass Culture*, ed. Lazere, p. 77.
[38] Körner et al., *IMF and the Debt Crisis*, p. 47.
[39] Susan George, *A Fate Worse than Debt* (Harmondsworth, 1988), p. 68.
[40] Whyte, *Organization Man*, p. 88. And see Bush, *Dream of Reason*, p. 55, for my discussion of Melville's carpenter in *Moby Dick*.
[41] Ellul, *Technological Society*, p. 296: 'The Technician rejects both the school of natural law and the historical school...'; Thorstein Veblen, 'The Technicians and Revolution', in *The Portable Veblen*, ed. Max Lerner (New York, 1950), p. 441.
[42] Skinner, *Beyond Freedom and Dignity*, p. 124. This passage and the attendant argument is discussed in Noam Chomsky, *For Reasons of State* (London, 1973), p. 116.
[43] Whyte, *Organization Man*, p. 88.
[44] Hannah Arendt, *Between Past and Future: Eight Exercises in Political Thought*, rev. edn. (Harmondsworth, 1977), p. 78.
[45] Braverman, *Labor and Monopoly Capital*, p. 88.
[46] Mumford, *Pentagon of Power*, p. 332.
[47] Starr, *Social Transformation of American Medicine*, p. 70.
[48] Félix Guattari, *Molecular Revolution*, trans. Rosemary Sheed (Harmondsworth, 1984), p. 117.
[49] Marx, *Capital*, I. 493n.
[50] Guattari, *Molecular Revolution*, p. 112.
[51] Carter, *Final Frontier*, pp. 257–9.
[52] Mumford, *Pentagon of Power*, p. 266.
[53] Simone Weil, *Lectures on Philosophy*, trans. Hugh Price (London, 1978), p. 139.
[54] Murray Bookchin, *The Ecology of Freedom: The Emergence and Dissolution of Hierarchy* (Palo Alto, Calif., 1982), pp. 48, 45.
[55] Alexander Pope, *Essay on Man*, Epistle III, ll. 303–4, cited in Wokler, 'Saint-Simon and the Passage from Political to Social Science', in *Language of Political Theory*, ed. Padgen, p. 337; see also Wokler, 'Saint-Simon...', p. 334.
[56] Cited by Thomas S. Szasz, *Ideology and Insanity: Essays on the Psychiatric Dehumanization of Man* (New York, 1970), p. 219.
[57] Hughes, *Consciousness and Society*, p. 74.
[58] Wokler, 'Saint-Simon....', p. 336.
[59] Hughes, *Consciousness and Society*, p. 36.
[60] Bledstein, *Culture of Professionalism*, pp. 34, 87. See also the definition of a profession by William J. Goode, 'Community Within a Community: The Professions', in *America as a Mass Society*, ed. Olson.
[61] Bledstein, *Culture of Professionalism*, p. 5.
[62] Braverman, *Labor and Monopoly Capitalism*, pp. 268–9.
[63] Noam Chomsky, *Problems of Knowledge and Freedom: The Russell Lectures* (London, 1972), p. 60; Paul Goodman, *People or Personnel/Like A Conquered Province* (New York, 1968), p. 134; Weil, *Lectures on Philosophy*, p. 130.
[64] Skinner, cited in Aronowitz, *Shaping of*

American Working-Class Consciousness, p. 115; Easlea, *Liberation and the Aims of Science*, p. 152.

[65] 'Practical Curriculum' in Whyte, *Organization Man*, p. 83. For recent important work on Durkheim see Wolf Lepenies, *Between Literature and Science: the Rise of Sociology* [*Die Drei Kulturen*, 1985], trans. R. J. Hollingdale (Cambridge, 1988).

[66] Murray Edelman, 'The Political Language of the Helping Professions', in *Language and Politics*, ed. Michael J. Shapiro (Oxford, 1984), p. 60.

[67] Gouldner, *Coming Crisis of Western Sociology*, p. 103, citing Sombart.

[68] Sartre, *Critique of Dialectical Reason*, pp. 28–9.

[69] Bookchin, *Ecology of Freedom*, pp. 33, 34, 27.

[70] Sartre, *Critique*, p. 163; Bookchin, *Ecology of Freedom*, p. 273.

[71] Gouldner, *Coming Crisis....*, pp. 139, 155, 143; Simon Clark, *Marx, Marginalism and Modern Sociology. From Adam Smith to Max Weber* (London and Basingstoke, 1982), p. 6.

[72] Gouldner, *Coming Crisis....*, p. 231.

[73] Aronowitz, *False Promises: The Shaping of American Working-Class Consciousness*, p. 58.

[74] Starr, *Social Transformation of American Medicine*, p. 4.

[75] Russett, *Concept of Equilibrium in American Social Thought*, pp. 19, 112.

[76] Dorothy and Roy Porter, 'What was Social Medicine', pp. 91, 90.

[77] Jonas, *Philosophical Essays*, p. 106.

[78] William Meissner, M.D., S.J., *The Paranoid Process* (New York, 1978), pp. 802, 807. Cited by Steve Want in a paper entitled, 'Paranoia: A History of Discourses', delivered to the English Graduate Seminar, Kings College, London University, 26 May 1988.

[79] Szasz, *Myth of Mental Illness*, p. 61.

[80] Alfred H. Katz, 'The Social Causes of Disease', *New Society*, 23 Jan 1969, p. 125.

[81] Thomas Szasz, *Law, Liberty and Psychiatry* (1965; repr. New York, 1968), p. 212.

[82] Thomas Szasz, *Psychiatric Justice* (New York, 1956), pp. 36, 27, 11.

[83] Szasz, *Myth of Mental Illness*, p. 12.

[84] Szasz, *Psychiatric Justice*, p. 57.

[85] Starr, *Social Transformation of American Medicine*, p. 448.

[86] Mills, *Sociological Imagination*, p. 99.

[87] Veblen, 'The Higher Learning', in *Portable Veblen*, ed. Lerner, pp. 526, 538.

[88] Mills, *Sociology and Pragmatism*, p. 64.

[89] Goodman, *People or Personnel/Like a Conquered Province*, p. 289; Whyte, *Organization Man*, p. 13.

[90] Edward Greer, 'The Public Interest University', in *Up Against the American Myth*, ed. Tom Christoffel *et al.* (New York, 1970), p. 341.

[91] John K. Galbraith, *The New Industrial State* (1967; rpr. Harmondsworth, 1969), pp. 385, 383.

[92] Goodman, *People or Personnel/Like A Conquered Province*, p. 343.

[93] Russell Jacoby, *The Last Intellectuals* (New York, 1987), p. 17.

[94] Arendt, *Between Past and Future*, p. 205.

[95] Mills, *Power Elite*, pp. 303–4.

[96] Edward Shils, 'The Theory of Mass Society', in *America as a Mass Society*, ed. Olson, pp. 37–8.

[97] Aronowitz, *False Promises: The Shaping of American Working-Class Consciousness*, p. 100.

[98] Lazere, in *American Media and Mass Culture*, p. 2.

[99] Aronowitz, *Shaping of American Working-Class Consciousness*, p. 275.

[100] Donald Huton and R. Richard Wohl, 'Mass Communication, Para-Communication Interaction', in *America as a Mass Society*, ed. Olson, p. 55.

[101] Joseph Bensman and Bernard Rosenberg, 'Mass Media and Mass Culture', in *America as a Mass Society*, ed. Olson, p. 171.

[102] Mills, *Power Elite*, p. 39.

[103] Whyte, *Organization Man*, pp. 372, 55.

[104] John R. Seeley, R. Alexander Sim and E. W. Loosley, 'Career Orientations', in *America as a Mass Society*, ed. Olson, p. 427.

[105] Michel Foucault, *The Final Foucault*, ed. James Bernauer and David Rasmussen (London, Cambridge, Mass., 1988), p. 18.

[106] Bookchin, *Ecology of Freedom*, p. 139.

[107] Gouldner, *Coming Crisis of Western Sociology*, p. 276.

[108] Arendt, *Between Past and Future*, p. 60.

[109] *What is an Emotion: Classic Readings in Philosophical Psychology*, ed. Cheshire Calhoun and Robert C. Solomon (New York and Oxford, 1984), p. 244.

[110] Szasz, *Myth of Mental Illness*, pp. 108, x, 17 f.

[111] Szasz, *Psychiatric Justice*, p. 37.

[112] George Orwell, 'Politics and the English Language', in *Inside the Whale and Other Essays* (1962; repr. Harmondsworth, 1981), p. 152.

[113] Lepenies, *Between Literature and Science*, p. 7.

[114] Ibid., p. 201.

[115] Diggins, '"Who Bore the Failure of the Light": Henry Adams and the Crisis of Authority', 190.

[116] Richard Rorty, *Consequences of Pragmatism (Essays: 1972–1980)* (Minneapolis, 1982), pp. 228, 229.

[117] Richard Rorty, *Philosophy and the Mirror of Nature* (Princeton, N.J., 1979). pp. 7, 11.

[118] Ibid., p. 80.

[119] Gillian Rose, *Hegel Contra Sociology* (London, 1981), p. 13.

[120] Ibid., pp. 13, 14.

[121] Ibid., p. 14.

[122] Ibid., pp. 15, 16.

[123] Ibid., pp. 17, 213.

[124] Ibid., pp. 213, 214.

[125] Jean-François Lyotard, *The Post-Modern Condition: A Report on Knowledge*, trans. Geoff Bennington and Brian Massumi (Manchester, 1984), p. 11.

[126] William James to Jane Addams, 17 Sept 1902, in *William James: Selected Unpublished Correspondence*, ed. Rederick J. Down Scott (Columbus, 1986), p. 293.

[127] Stuart Creighton Miller, *'Benevolent Assimilation': The American Concept of the Philippines, 1889–1903* (New Haven, Conn., 1982), p. 269. For McDermott's letter see *The Nation*, 25 July 1966.

[128] Lyotard, *Post-Modern Condition*, pp. 89, 46.

[129] Ibid., p. 65.

[130] Mottram, 'Henry Adams: Index of the Twentieth Century', 97.

Bibliography

Articles in edited collections are listed under the author's names, except in the case of multi-contributor volumes from which more than one article is cited; these last are listed under the name of the volume editor only.

Aaron, Richard I., *John Locke* (Oxford: Clarendon Press, 1955)

Aarsleff, Hans, *From Locke to Saussure: Essays on the Study of Language and Intellectual History* (London: Athlone Press, 1982)

Aarslef, Hans, *The Study of Language in England, 1780–1860* (Princeton, NJ: Princeton University Press, 1967)

Adams, Brooks, *The Gold Standard: An Historical Study*, rev. edn. (Washington, DC: D.C.R. Beall, 1895)

Adams, Brooks 'The Heritage of Henry Adams', in *The Degradation of the Democratic Dogma*, ed. Brooks Adams (New York: Macmillan, 1919)

Adams, Brooks, *The Law of Civilization and Decay* (New York: S. Sonnenshein, 1895)

Adams, Brooks, *The Theory of Social Revolutions* (New York: Macmillan, 1913)

Adams, Henry, *The Education of Henry Adams*, ed. Ernest Samuels (Boston: Houghton Mifflin, 1973)

Adams, Henry [ed.], *Essays in Anglo-Saxon Law* (Boston: Little Brown, 1876)

Adams, Henry, *Esther*, ed. Robert Spiller (New York: Scholars' Facsimiles and Reprints, 1938)

Adams, Henry, *Henry Adams and his Friends: A Collection of his Unpublished Letters*, ed. Harold Dean Cater (Boston: Houghton Mifflin, 1947)

Adams, Henry *Historical Essays* (New York: Charles Scribner, 1891)

Adams, Henry, *History of the United States of America*, 9 vols. (New York: Charles Scribner's Sons, 1931)

Adams, Henry, *A Letter to American Teachers of History* (Washington, DC: J.H. Furst, 1910)

Adams, Henry, *Letters of Henry Adams*, ed. Worthington Chauncy Ford, vol. II: *1892–1918* (Boston and New York: Houghton Mifflin, 1938)

Adams, Henry *The Letters of Henry Adams*; ed. J. C. Levenson, Ernest Samuels, Charles Vandersee, Viola Hopkins Winner, 3 vols.: I (1858–68); II (1869–85); III (1886–92) (Cambridge, Mass. and London: The Belknap Press of Harvard University Press, 1982–3)

Adams, Henry [ed.], *Memoirs of Marau Taaroa Last Queen of Tahiti*, by Queen Marau (Washington, DC: Privately Printed, 1893)

Adams, Henry, *Mont-Saint-Michel and Chartres* (New York: Gordon Press, 1974)

Adams, Henry, review of *The History of the Norman Conquest* by Edward Freeman, *North American Review*, 110 (1870), 351

Adams, Henry, 'Seventeen Letters of Henry Adams', ed. Frederick Bliss Luquiens, *Yale Review*, 10 (Oct 1920), 111–30

Adams, John Quincy, *Report upon Weights and Measures* (Washington: Gales and Seaton, 1821)

Adorno, Theodor, *Against Epistemology: A Metacritique; Studies in Husserl and the Phenomenological Antinomies*, trans. Willis Domingo (Oxford: Basil Blackwell, 1982)

Allen, Gay Wilson, *William James, A Biography* (London: Hart-Davis, 1967)

Anderson, James William, '"The Worst Kind of Melancholy": William James in 1869',

Harvard Library Bulletin, 30.4 (Oct 1982), 369–86

Arber, Agnes, *The Mind and the Eye: A Study of the Biologist's Standpoint* (London: Cambridge University Press, 1954)

Arendt, Hannah, *Between Past and Future: Eight Exercises in Political Thought*, rev. edn. (Harmondsworth: Penguin Books, 1977)

Arendt, Hannah, *The Human Condition: A Study of the Central Dilemmas Facing Modern Man* (Chicago: University of Chicago Press, 1958)

Arendt, Hannah, *The Origins of Totalitarianism* (1951; repr. Cleveland and New York: Meridian Books, 1967)

Aristotle, *Aristotle on the Art of Poetry*, trans. Ingram Bywater, pref. Gilbert Murray (1920; repr. Oxford: Clarendon Press, 1959)

Aristotle, *The Nicomachean Ethics*, trans. H. Rackham (Cambridge, Mass.: Harvard University Press; London: Heinemann, 1934)

Arnold, Matthew, *Culture and Anarchy* (New York: Macmillan, 1883)

Arnold, Matthew, *The Poems of Matthew Arnold*, 2nd edn., ed. Miriam Allott (London and New York: Longman, 1979)

Arnold, Thurman W., *The Folklore of Capitalism* (1939; repr. New Haven and London: Yale University Press, 1968)

Aronowitz, Stanley, *False Promises: The Shaping of American Working-Class Consciousness* (New York: McGraw-Hill, 1973)

Avineri, Shlomo, *The Social and Political Thought of Karl Marx* (Cambridge: Cambridge University Press, 1968)

Bachelard, Gaston, *The Psychoanalysis of Fire*, trans. Alan C. M. Ross, pref. by Northrop Frye (Boston: Beacon Press, 1964)

Bagehot, Walter, *Physics and Politics: or Thoughts on the Application of the Principles of 'Natural Selection' and 'Inheritance' to Political Society* (London: Henry S. King, 1872)

Barber, David S., 'Henry Adams's *Esther*: the Nature of Individuality and Immortality', *New England Quarterly*, 45 (1972), 227–40

Barthes, Roland, *Michelet* (Paris: Seuil, 1954)

Barthes, Roland, *S/Z*, trans. Richard Miller (New York: Farrar, Streus and Giroux, 1974)

Barzun, Jacques, *Berlioz and the Romantic Century* (1950; repr. London: Gollancz, 1951)

Barzun, Jacques, *Darwin. Marx, Wagner: Critique of a Heritage* (1941; repr. New York: Doubleday, 1958)

Barzun, Jacques, 'In Favor of Capital Punishment', *American Scholar*, 31 (Spring 1962), 181–91

Barzun, Jacques, *A Stroll with William James* (New York: Harper and Row, 1983)

Bateson, Gregory, *Steps to an Ecology of Mind* (St. Albans and London: Paladin, 1973)

Bayley, James E., 'A Jamesian Theory of Self', *Transactions of the Charles S. Peirce Society*, 12 (Winter 1976), 148–65

Baym, Max I., *The French Education of Henry Adams* (New York: Columbia University Press, 1951)

Baym, Max I., 'William James and Henry Adams', *New England Quarterly*, 10 (1937), 717–42

Beard, George Miller, *American Nervousness, Its Causes and Consequences . . .* (New York: G.P. Putnam, 1881)

Benda, Julien, *The Great Betrayal [La Trahison des Clercs]*, trans. Richard Aldington (London: George Routledge, 1928)

Benjamin, Walter, 'On Language as Such and on the Language of Man' (1916), in Benjamin, *One Way Street and Other Writings*, introd. Susan Sontag, trans. E. Jephcott and K. Shorter (London: New Left Books, 1978)

Benjamin, Walter, 'The Work of Art in the Age of Mechanical Reproduction', in Benjamin, *Illuminations*, ed. and introd. Hannah Arendt (1970; repr. London: Fontana, 1973)

Bense, Max, 'Kosmologie und Literatur: über Alfred N. Whitehead und Gertrude Stein', *Texte und Zeichen*, 3 (1957), 512–25

Bentley, Eric, *A Century of Hero Worship*, 2nd edn. (Boston: Beacon Press, 1957)

Best, Geoffrey, *Mid-Victorian Britain, 1851–1875* (London: Weidenfeld and Nicholson, 1971)

Bjork, Daniel W., *The Compromised Scientist: William James and the Development of American Psychology* (New York: Columbia University Press, 1983)

Bjorkman, Edwin, interview with William James, *New York Times*, 3 Nov 1907

Blackmur, R. P., *Henry Adams/R. P. Blackmur*, ed. Veronica Makowsky (New York: Harcourt Brace Jovanovich, 1980)

Bledstein, Burton J., *The Culture of Professionalism: The Middle Class and the Development of Higher Education in America* (New York: W.W. Norton, 1976)

Bloomfield, Leonard, *Language* (1933; repr. London: George Allen and Unwin, 1979)

Blunt, Hugh F., 'Mal-Education of Henry Adams', *Catholic World*, 145 (Apr 1936), 46–52

Boller, Paul F. Jr., *American Thought in Transi-*

tion: the Impact of Evolutionary Naturalism, 1865–1900 (Chicago: Rand McNally, 1969)

Boring, E. G., A History of Experimental Psychology, 2nd edn. (New York: Appleton-Century Crofts, Meredith, 1950)

Bookchin, Murray, The Ecology of Freedom: The Emergence and Dissolution of Hierarchy (Palo Alto, Calif.: Cheshire Books, 1982)

Bowler, Peter J., The Eclipse of Darwinism: Anti-Darwinian Evolution Theories in the Decades around 1900 (Baltimore and London: John Hopkins University Press, 1983)

Bowles, Paul, Without Stopping: An Autobiography (1972; repr. New York: Ecco Press, 1985)

Bradbury, Malcolm, The Modern American Novel (Oxford: Oxford University Press, 1984)

Brand, Dana, 'William James's Reformulation of Emerson and Whitman', ESQ; A Journal of the American Renaissance, 31.1 (1st quarter 1985), 38–48

Braudel, Fernand, On History, trans. Sarah Matthews (Chicago: University of Chicago Press, 1980)

Braverman, Harry, Labor and Monopoly Capital: The Degradation of Work in the Twentieth Century (New York: Monthly Review Press, 1974)

Brent, Peter, Charles Darwin: 'A Man of Enlarged Curiosity' (London: Heinemann, 1981)

Brinnin, John Malcolm, The Third Rose, Gertrude Stein and her World (1959; repr. London: Weidenfeld and Nicholson, 1960)

Brown, Norman O., Life Against Death: The Psychoanalytical Meaning of History (New York: Vintage Books, 1959)

Brown, Norman O., Love's Body (New York: Vintage Books, 1968)

Bryce, L., 'Silent Confluence: Eastern and Western Themes in Adams's Monument at Rock Creek Cemetery', North Dakota Quarterly, 51.2 (Spring 1983), 84–93

Buckle, Henry Thomas, History of Civilization in England, 2 vols. (1857; repr. New York: D. Appleton, 1858)

Burn, W. L., The Age of Equipoise: A Study of a Mid-Victorian Generation (London: George Allen and Unwin, 1964)

Burnham, James, The Managerial Revolution, or What is Happening in the World Now (Harmondsworth: Penguin Books, 1945)

Burroughs, William, and Gysin, Brion, The Third Mind (New York: Viking Press, 1978)

Bush, Clive, 'Cultural Reflections on American Linguistics from Whitney to Sapir', Journal of American Studies, 22.2 (Aug 1988), 185–212

Bush, Clive, The Dream of Reason: American Consciousness and Cultural Achievement from Independence to the Civil War (London: Edward Arnold; New York: St. Martins Press, 1977)

Bush, Clive, 'Gilded Backgrounds; Reflections on the Perception of Space and Landscape in the Early American Republic', in Views of American Landscape, ed. M. Gidley and R. Lawson Peebles (Cambridge: Cambridge University Press, 1989), 13–30

Bush, Clive, 'Towards the Outside: The Quest for Discontinuity in Gertrude Stein's The Making of Americans: being a history of a family's progress', Twentieth-Century Literature, 24.1 (Spring 1978–9), 25–57

Bynack, V. P., 'Noah Webster's Linguistic Thought and the Idea of an American Culture', Journal of the History of Ideas, 14 (Jan–Mar 1985), 99–114

Byrnes, Joseph F., The Virgin of Chartres: An Intellectual and Psychological History of the Work of Henry Adams (London: Fairleigh Dickinson University Press; Associated University Presses, 1981)

Calhoun, Cheshire, and Solomon, Robert C., eds., What is an Emotion: Classic Readings in Philosophical Psychology (New York and Oxford: Oxford University Press, 1984)

Campbell, Lewis and Garnett, William, The Life of James Clerk Maxwell, with a selection from his correspondence and occasional writings, and a sketch of his contribution to science. (London: Macmillan, 1882)

Carbonel, l'Abbé P., Histoire de la philosophie, 2nd edn. (Paris: Sequin Frères, 1882)

Carlyle, Thomas, On Heroes and Hero Worship and the Heroic in History, ed. A. MacMechan (Boston: Ginn, 1901)

Carr, E. H., What is History? (Harmondsworth: Penguin Books, 1983)

Carter, Dale, The Final Frontier (London: Verso, 1988)

Cassirer, Ernst, Language and Myth, trans. Susanne K. Langer (New York: Harper, 1946)

Chenetier, Marc, ed., Critical Angles: European Views of Contemporary American Literature (Carbondale and Edwardsville: Southern Illinois University Press, 1986)

Chessman, Harriet, The Public is Invited to Dance: Representation, the Body, and Dialogue in Gertrude Stein (Stanford, Calif.: Stanford University Press, 1989)

Chomsky, Noam, For Reasons of State (London: Fontana, Collins, 1973)

Chomsky, Noam, *Problems of Knowledge and Freedom: The Russell Lectures* (London: Fontana/Collins, 1972)

Church, Robert L., 'Economists as Experts: the Rise of an Academic Profession in the United States, 1870–1920', in Lawrence Stone (ed.), *The University in Society*, vol. II: *Europe, Scotland and the United States from the 16th to the 20th Century* (Princeton, NJ: Princeton University Press, 1975), 571–609

Clark, Simon, *Marx, Marginalism and Modern Sociology. From Adam Smith to Max Weber* (London and Basingstoke: Macmillan Press, 1982)

Cohen, Stanley and Scull, Andrew, eds., *Social Control and the State, Historical and Comparative Essays* (1983; repr. Oxford: Basil Blackwell, 1986)

Colacurcio, M., '*Democracy* and *Esther*: Henry Adams's Flirtation with Pragmatism', *American Quarterly*, 19 (1967), 53–70

Collingwood, R. G., *An Autobiography* (Oxford: Oxford University Press, 1939)

Collingwood, R. G., *The Idea of History* (London, Oxford, New York: Oxford University Press, 1956)

Collingwood, R. G., *The Idea of Nature* (1945; repr. London, Oxford, New York: Oxford University Press, 1960, 1978)

Collins, Wilkie, *The Moonstone* (1868; repr. London and Toronto: Dent, Everyman's Library, 1944)

Collins, Wilkie, *The Woman in White* (1859; repr. London: Everyman's Library, 1910)

Comte, Auguste, *The Positive Philosophy by Auguste Comte, with a New Introduction* by Abraham S. Blumberg (New York: AMS Press, 1974)

Contosta, David, *Henry Adams and the American Experiment* (Boston and Toronto: Little, Brown, 1980)

Courtney, William J., 'The Virgin and the Dynamo: The Growth of Medieval Studies in North America, 1870–1930', in *Medieval Studies in North America: Past, Present and Future*, ed. Francis G. Gentry and Christopher Kleinhenz (Kalamazoo, Mich.: Medieval Institute Publications, 1982), 5–22

Coveney, Peter, *The Image of Childhood: The Individual and Society: a Study of the Theme in English Literature*, rev. edn., introd. F. R. Leavis (Harmondsworth: Penguin Books, 1967)

Cox, James M., 'Autobiography and America', *Virginia Quarterly Review*, 47 (Spring 1971), 252–77

Crane, Stephen, *Great Battles of the World* (London, New York, Toronto: Hodder and Stoughton, 1914)

Cranston, Maurice, *John Locke. A Biography* (Oxford and New York: Oxford University Press, 1985)

Curti, Merle, *Human Nature in American Historical Thought* (Columbia: University of Missouri Press, 1968)

Darwin, Charles, *The Descent of Man*, 2nd edn. (London: John Murray, 1888)

Darwin, Charles, *The Expression of the Emotions in Man and Animals* (1872; repr. Chicago and London: University of Chicago Press, 1965)

Darwin, Charles, *The Life and Letters of Charles Darwin including an autobiographical chapter, edited by his son, Francis Darwin*, 3 vols. (London: John Murray, 1887)

Darwin, Charles, *Metaphysics, Materialism and the Evolution of Mind, Early Writings of Charles Darwin*, transcribed and annotated Paul H. Barrett, commentary Howard E. Gruber (Chicago: University of Chicago Press, 1980)

Darwin, Charles, *On the Origin of Species by Means of Natural Selection* (London: John Murray, 1859)

Daston, Lorraine J., 'The Theory of Will versus the Science of Mind', in *The Problematic Science: Psychology in the Nineteenth Century*, ed. William R. Woodward and Mitchell G. Ash (New York: Praeger, 1982), 88–112

Davis, Mike, *Prisoners of the American Dream: Politics and Economy in the History of the U.S. Working Class* (London: Verso, 1986)

Delius, Frederick, *Delius. A Life in Letters*, ed. Lionel Carley, vol. I: *1862–1908* (London: Scolar Press, 1983)

Derrida, Jacques, *Of Grammatology*, trans. Gayatri Chakravorty Spivak (Baltimore and London: Johns Hopkins University Press, 1976)

Derrida, Jacques, *Writing and Difference*, trans. Alan Bass (1967; repr. Chicago: University of Chicago Press, 1978)

Descartes, René, *Oeuvres de Descartes*, ed. Jules Simon (Paris: Bibliothèque-Charpentier, 1865)

Dewey, John, *The Influence of Darwin on Philosophy* (New York: Henry Holt, 1910)

Dewey, John, *The Quest for Certainty* (London: G. Allen and Unwin, 1930)

Dewhurst, Kenneth, *John Locke, Physician and Philosopher. A Medical Biography* (London: Wellcome Historical Medical Library, 1963)

Diggins, John Patrick, '"Who bore the failure of the Light": Henry Adams and the Crisis of Authority', *New England Quarterly*, 58.2 (June 1985), 165–92

Donovan, Timothy Paul, *Henry Adams and*

Brooks Adams: The Education of Two American Historians (Norman: University of Oklahoma Press, 1961)

Dorson, Richard, M., *The British Folklorists: A History* (Chicago: University of Chicago Press, 1968)

Drumont, E., *La Fin d'un monde* (Paris: A. Savin, 1889)

Durkheim, Emile, *Emile Durkheim on Institutional Analysis*, ed., trans., and introd., Mark Traugott (Chicago and London: University of Chicago Press, 1978)

Dusinberre, William, *Henry Adams, The Myth of Failure* (Charlottesville: University Press of Virginia, 1980)

Dydo, Ulla, 'Landscape is Not Grammar: Gertrude Stein in 1928', *Raritan: A Quarterly Review*, 7.1 (Summer 1987), 97–113

Dydo, Ulla, 'Must Horses Drink, or "Any Language Is Funny If You Don't Understand It"', *Tulsa Studies in Women's Literature*, 4.2 (Fall 1985), 272–80

Dydo, Ulla E., 'To Have the Winning Language: Texts and Context of Gertrude Stein', in *Coming to Light: American Women Poets in the Twentieth Century*, ed. Diane Wood Middlebrook and Marilyn Yalom (Woman and Culture Series) (Ann Arbor: University of Michigan Press, 1985), 4–20

Easlea, Brian, *Liberation and the Aims of Science: An Essay on Obstacles to the Building of a Beautiful World* (London: Chatto and Windus for Sussex University Press, 1973)

Edie, James M, 'William James and Phenomenology', *Review of Metaphysics*, 23 (1970), 481–526

Edie, James M., *William James and Phenomenology* (Bloomington and Indianapolis: Indiana University Press, 1987)

Eisendrath, Craig R., *The Unifying Moment: The Psychological Philosophy of William James and Alfred North Whitehead* (Cambridge, Mass.: Harvard University Press, 1971)

Ellul, Jacques, *Propaganda: the Formation of Men's Attitudes*, trans. Konrad Kellen and Jean Lerner (New York: Vintage Books, 1973)

Ellul, Jacques, *The Technological Society*, trans. John Wilkinson, introd. Robert K. Merton (New York: Vintage Books, 1964)

Emerson, Ralph Waldo, 'Nature', (1836) in *The Collected Works of Ralph Waldo Emerson*, vol. I; 'Self Reliance' (1840), in ibid., vol. II, introd. Joseph Slater (Cambridge, Mass., and London: Harvard University Press, 1971, 1979)

Emmet, Dorothy M., *Whitehead's Philosophy of Organism* (London: Macmillan, 1932)

Engels, Frederick, *Dialectics of Nature*, 2nd rev. edn., trans. Clemens Dutt (Moscow: Progress Publishers, 1934)

Erens, Patricia, ed., *Sexual Stratagems: The World of Women in Film* (New York: Horizon Press, 1979)

Feaver, George, *From Status to Contract: A Biography of Sir Henry Maine, 1822–1888* (London: Longmans, 1969)

Feinstein, Howard M., *Becoming William James* (Ithaca, NY, and London: Cornell University Press, 1984)

Fenollosa, Ernest, *The Chinese Written Character as a Medium for Poetry*, ed. Ezra Pound (1936; repr. San Francisco: City Lights, 1968)

Feyerabend, Paul, *Against Method* (London: Verso, 1978)

Fisher, Allen, *unpolished mirrors A-H* (London: Spanner, 1979–81)

Fontinell, Eugene, *Self, God and Immortality: A Jamesian Investigation* (Philadelphia: Temple University Press, 1986)

Foucault, Michel, *The Birth of the Clinic: An Archaeology of Medical Perception*, trans. A. M. Sheridan Smith (1973; repr. New York: Vintage Books, 1975)

Foucault, Michel, *The Final Foucault*, ed. James Bernauer and David Rasmussen (Cambridge, Mass. and London: MIT Press, 1988)

Foucault, Michel, *The History of Sexuality*, Vol. I, trans. Robert Hurley (New York: Vintage Books, 1980)

Foucault, Michel, *Language, Counter-Memory, Practice: Selected Essays and Interviews by Michel Foucault*, ed. Donald F. Bouchard, trans. Donald F. Bouchard and Sherry Simon (Ithaca, NY: Cornell University Press, 1977)

Freud, Sigmund, *Civilization and its Discontents*, trans. Joan Rivière, rev. James Strachey (1929; repr. London: Hogarth Press, 1963)

Freud, Sigmund, *The Interpretation of Dreams*, trans. James Strachey (Harmondsworth: Penguin Books, 1980)

Friedrich, Otto, *Clover* (New York: Simon and Schuster, 1979)

Fuller, R. Buckminster, *Education Automation: Freeing the Scholar to Return to his Studies* (Carbondale and Edwardsville: Southern Illinois University Press, 1962)

Fustel de Coulanges, N. D., *The Ancient City: A Study of the Religion, Laws, and Institutions of Greece and Rome*, trans. William Small (Boston: Lee and Shepherd, 1874)

Galbraith, John K., *The New Industrial State* (1967; repr Harmondsworth: Pelican Books, 1969)

Gallup, Donald, ed., *The Flowers of Friendship: Letters to Gertrude Stein* (New York: Alfred A. Knopf, 1953)

Garrison, George A., and Madden, Edward H., 'William James – Warts and All', *American Quarterly*, 29 (Summer 1977), 207–21

George, Susan, *A Fate Worse than Debt* (Harmondsworth: Penguin Books, 1988)

Ghiselin, Michael, *The Triumph of the Darwinian Method* (Berkeley and Los Angeles: University of California Press, 1969)

Gleik, James, 'The Riddle of Chaos', *Dialogue*, 68 (1985), 57–63

Gold, Michael, *Change the World!* (New York: International Publishers, 1936)

Gooch, G. P., *History and Historians in the Nineteenth Century* (London: Longmans, Green, 1913)

Goodman, Paul, *People or Personnel/Like A Conquered Province* (New York: Vintage Books, 1968)

Gould, Stephen Jay, *Ever Since Darwin: Reflections on Natural History*, (1978; repr. Harmondsworth: Pelican Books, 1980)

Gouldner, Alvin W., *The Coming Crisis of Western Sociology* (New York, London: Basic Books, 1970)

Gramsci, Antonio, 'The Study of Philosophy', in Gramsci, *The Modern Prince and Other Writings*, trans. Louis Marks (New York: International Publishers, 1957)

Greer, Edward, 'The Public Interest University', in *Up Against the American Myth*, ed. Tom Christoffel, with David Finkelhor, Don Gilbarg (New York: Holt Rinehart Winston, 1970), 338–43

Gruber, Howard E., *Darwin on Man: A Psychological Study of Scientific Creativity. Together with Darwin's Early and Unpublished Notebooks*, transcribed and annotated by Paul H. Barrett. Foreword by Jean Piaget (London: Wildwood House, 1974); 2nd edn. (Chicago: University of Chicago Press, 1981)

Gryzanovski, E., 'Comtism', *North American Review*, 120 (1875), 237–81

Gryzanovski, E., 'Schopenhauer and his Pessimistic Philosophy', *North American Review*, 117 (1873), 37–79

Guattari, Félix, *Molecular Revolution*, trans. Rosemary Sheed (Harmondsworth: Penguin Books, 1984)

Guizot, François, *Historical Essays and Lectures*, ed. Stanley Mellon (Chicago and London: University of Chicago Press, 1972)

Guthrie, Douglas, *A History of Medicine*, rev. edn. (London: Nelson, 1958)

Haas, Robert Bartlett, 'Gertrude Stein Talking. A Trans-Atlantic Interview', *Uclan Review*, 9 (Spring 1963), 40–8; [Part 2], 9 (Winter 1964), 40–8

Hamill, Paul J. 'Science as Ideology: The Lore of the Amateur, Henry Adams', *Canadian Review of American Studies*, 12.1 (Spring 1981), 22–35

Hanscombe, Gillian, and Sayers, Virginia I., *Writing for Their Lives: The Modernist Women, 1910–1940* (London: Women's Press, 1987)

Hansen, Olaf, 'Henry Adams: *Mont Saint Michel and Chartres*', *Amerikastudien*, 28.3 (1983), 323–34

Hardie, W. F. R., *Aristotle's Ethical Theory* (Oxford: Clarendon press, 1968)

Harper, Robert S., 'The Laboratory of William James', *Harvard Alumni Bulletin*, 52 (5 Nov 1949), 169–73

Harris, Marvin, *The Rise of Anthropological Theory* (New York: Columbia University Press, 1968)

Hauser, Arnold, *The Sociology of Art*, trans. Kenneth J. Northcott (London, Henley and Melbourne: Routledge and Kegan Paul, 1982)

Hedge, Frederick H., 'The Method of History', *North American Review*, 111 (1870), 311–29

Hegel, G. W. F., *Hegel's Logic*, trans. William Wallace (1873; repr. Oxford: Clarendon Press, 1975)

Hegel, G. F. W. *The Phenomenology of Mind*, trans. J. B. Bailie (London: Allen and Unwin, 1931)

Hegel, G. W. F., *The Philosophy of History*, trans. J. Sibree, introd. C. J. Friedrich (New York: Dover, 1956)

Heidegger, Martin, *An Introduction to Metaphysics*, trans. Ralph Manheim (New Haven and London: Yale University Press, 1959)

Heidegger, Martin, *On the Way to Language*, trans. Peter D. Hertz (San Francisco: Harper and Row, 1971, 1982)

Heidegger, Martin, *Poetry, Language, Thought*, trans. Albert Hofstadter (New York: Harper Colophon Books, 1975)

Hemingway, Ernest, *Ernest Hemingway; Selected Letters 1917–1961*, ed. Carlos Baker (New York: Scribners, 1981)

Herbert, George, *The Works of George Herbert*, ed. F. E. Hutchinson (Oxford: Clarendon Press, 1945)

Herrnstein, R. T. and Boring, E. G., eds., *A Source Book in the History of Psychology* (Cambridge, Mass.: Harvard University Press, 1965)

Hill, Christopher, *The World Turned Upside Down: Radical Ideas during the English Revolution* (1972; repr. Harmondsworth: Penguin Books, 1975)

Hocks, Richard A., *Henry James and Pragmatistic Thought. . .* (Durham, N.C.: University of North Carolina Press, 1974)

Hoffman, F. T., 'William James and the Modern Literary Consciousness', *Criticism*, 4 (Winter 1962), 1–13

Holmes, Oliver Wendell, *Medical Essays 1842–1882*, vol. IX in *The Writings of O. W. Holmes* (London: Sampson Low, 1891)

Hughes, H. Stuart, *Consciousness and Society: The Reorientation of European Social Thought 1890–1930* (New York: Vintage Books, 1977)

Hull, David, ed., *Darwin and his Critics: The Reception of Darwin's Theory of Evolution by the Scientific Community* (Cambridge, Mass.: Harvard University Press, 1973)

Hyman, Stanley Edgar, *The Tangled Bank: Darwin, Marx, Frazer and Freud as Imaginative Writers* (New York: Atheneum, 1962)

Illich, Ivan, *Limits to Medicine* (London: Marion Boyars, 1976)

Illyes, Gyula, *People of the Pusta*, trans. G. F. Cushing (Budapest: Corvina Press, 1967)

Jacoby, Russell, *The Last Intellectuals* (New York: Basic Books, 1987)

James, Alice, *The Diary of Alice James*, ed. Leon Edel (New York: Dodd, Mead, 1934)

James, Henry, *Letters*, ed. Leon Edel, vol. I (London: Macmillan, 1975)

James, Henry, *Washington Square*, introd. Leon Edel (London: Bodley Head, 1967)

James, William, 'Great Men, Great Thoughts and the Environment', *Atlantic Monthly*, 46 (Oct 1880), 441–59

James, William, *The Letters of William James*, ed. Henry James, 2 vols. (Boston: Atlantic Monthly Press, 1920)

James, William, *The Meaning of Truth* (Cambridge, Mass. and London: Harvard University Press, 1975)

James, William, *The Moral Equivalent of War and Other Essays*, ed. and introd. John K. Roth (New York: Harper and Row, Harper Torchbooks, 1971)

James, William, 'On Some Hegelianisms', *Mind*, 7 (Apr 1882), 186–208

James, William, 'The Philippines Again', Letter to *The New York Evening Post*, 10 Mar 1899, p. 4

James, William, *A Pluralistic Universe* (Cambridge, Mass., and London: Harvard University Press, 1977)

James, William, *Pragmatism* (Cambridge, Mass., and London: Harvard University Press, 1975)

James, William, *The Principles of Psychology*, 2 vols. (1891; repr. Cambridge, Mass. and

London: Harvard University Press, 1981)

James, William, review of Hermann Grimm, *Unüberwindliche Machte*, *The Nation*, 5 (1867), 432

James, William, 'Speech of Professor William James – Counsel to forget Yesterday and its Sins and Work for the Future, the Watchword to be, "Independence for the Philippine Islands"', *The Evening Post (New York)*, 3 Dec 1903, p. 8

James, William, 'Ten Unpublished Letters from William James, 1842–1910, to Francis Herbert Bradley, 1846–1924', introd. J. C. Kema, *Mind*, 35 (July 1966), 309–31

James, William, *The Varieties of Religious Experience* (Cambridge, Mass.: Harvard University Press, 1985)

James, William, *The Will to Believe and Other Essays in Popular Philosophy* (Cambridge, Mass., and London: Harvard University Press, 1979)

James, William, *William James on Exceptional Mental States*, ed. Eugene Taylor (New York: Charles Scribner's Sons, 1984)

James, William, *William James: Selected Unpublished Correspondence*, ed. Rederick J., Down Scott (Columbus: Ohio State University Press, 1986)

Jameson, Frederic, *Marxism and Form: Twentieth-Century Dialectical Theories of Literature* (Princeton, NJ: Princeton University Press, 1971)

Jameson, Frederic, *The Prison House of Language: A Critical Account of Structuralism and Russian Formalism* (Princeton, NJ: Princeton University Press, 1972)

Jensen, U. J., and Harré, R., eds., *The Philosophy of Evolution* (Brighton, Sussex: Harvester Press, 1981)

Jonas, Hans, *Philosophical Essays: From Ancient Creed to Technological Man.* (Chicago and London: University of Chicago Press, 1974)

Jones, Greta, *Social Darwinism and English Thought: The Interaction between Biological and Social Theory* (Brighton, Sussex: Harvester Press, 1980)

Jordan, Martin, *New Shapes of Reality: Aspects of Whitehead's Philosophy* (London: George Allen and Unwin, 1968)

Jordy, William H., *Henry Adams: Scientific Historian* (New Haven and London: Yale University Press, 1952)

Jourdain, Charles, *La Philosophie de Saint Thomas D'Aquin*, vol. I (Paris: Hachette, 1858)

Kaledin, Eugenia, *The Education of Mrs. Henry Adams* (Philadelphia: Temple University Press, 1981)

Kantor, J. R., *The Scientific Evolution of Psychology*, 2 vols. (Chicago: Principia Press, 1969)

Kaplan, Sidney, 'Taussig, James and Peabody: A "Harvard School" in 1900?', *American Quarterly*, 7 (Winter 1955), 315–31

Kariel, Henry S., 'The Limits of Social Science: Henry Adams's Quest for Order', *American Political Science Review*, 50 (1956), 1074–92

Katz, Alfred H., 'The Social Causes of Disease', *New Society*, 23 Jan 1969, p. 125

Katz, Leon, 'The First Making of *The Making of Americans*: A Study Based on Gertrude Stein's Notebooks and Early Memoirs of her Novels, 1902–1908' (Ph.D. diss., Columbia University, 1963)

King, Clarence, *Mountaineering in the Sierra Nevada* (Boston: J. R. Osgood, 1872)

Kippur, Stephen A., *Jules Michelet: A Study of Mind and Sensibility* (Albany: State University of New York Press, 1981)

Klaich, Dolores, *Woman + Woman: Attitudes Towards Lesbianism* (New York: Simon and Schuster, 1974)

Klee, Earl, 'Henry Adams and the Patrician Response to the Liberal Polity', *Humanities in Society*, 3.3 (Summer 1980), 243–63

Klein, D. B., *A History of Scientific Psychology* (London: Routledge and Kegan Paul, 1970)

Körner, Peter, with Gero Maass, Thomas Siebold, Rainer Tetzloff, *The IMF and the Debt Crisis*, trans. Paul Knight (London and Atlantic Highlands, NJ: Zed Books, 1986)

Korzybski, Alfred, *Manhood of Humanity: The Science and Art of Human Engineering* (New York: E. P. Dutton, 1921)

Korzybski, Alfred, *Science and Sanity: An Introduction to Non-Aristotelian Systems and General Semantics*, 4th edn. (Lakeville, Conn.: International Non-Aristotelian Library, 1958)

Kretzoi, Charlotte, 'Gertrude Stein's Attempt at "The Great American Novel"', *Studies in English and American* (Budapest), 4 (1978), 7–34

Kroll, Richard W. F., 'The Question of Locke's Relation to Gassendi', *Journal of the History of Ideas*, 45 (July–Sept 1984), 339–59

Kronick, Joseph G., 'The Limits of Contradiction: Irony and History in Hegel and Henry Adams', *Clio: A Journal of Literature, History and the Philosophy of History*, 11.4 (Summer 1986), 391–410

Lacan, Jacques, *Ecrits: A Selection*, trans. Alan Sheridan (London: Tavistock, 1977)

LaFarge, John, *An Artist's Letters from Japan* (London: T. Fisher Unwin, 1897)

Laing, R. D., *The Voice of Experience* (Harmondsworth: Pelican Books, 1983)

Lazere, Donald, ed., *American Media and Mass Culture: Left Perspectives* (Berkeley, Los Angeles, London: University of California Press, 1987)

Leclerc, Ivor, ed., *The Relevance of Whitehead: Philosophical Essays in Commemoration of the Centenary of the Birth of Alfred North Whitehead* (London: George Allen and Unwin; New York: Macmillan, 1961)

Lentricchia, Frank, 'The Return of William James', *Cultural Critique*, 4 (Fall 1986), 5–31

Lentricchia, Frank, 'The Romanticism of William James', *Salmagundi*, 25 (1974), 81–108

Lepenies, Wolf, *Between Literature and Science: the Rise of Sociology [Die Drei Kulturen, 1985]*, trans. R. J. Hollingdale (Cambridge: Cambridge University Press, 1988)

Levenson, J. C., 'Henry Adams and the Culture of Science', in *Studies in American Culture*, ed. Joseph Kwiat and Mary Turpie (Minneapolis: University of Minnesota Press, 1960)

Levenson, J. C. *The Mind and Art of Henry Adams* (Boston: Houghton Mifflin, 1957)

Levinson, Henry S., *Science, Metaphysics, and the Chance of Salvation: An Interpretation of the Thought of William James* (Missoula, Mont.: Scholars Press for the American Academy of Religion, 1978)

Levinson, Samuel H., *The Religious Investigations of William James* (Chapel Hill: University of North Carolina Press, 1981)

Linschoten, Hans, *On the Way toward a Phenomenological Psychology*, ed. A. Giorgi (Pittsburgh, Pa.: Duquesne University Press, 1968)

Liston, Maureen R., *Gertrude Stein. An Annotated Critical Bibliography* (Kent, O.: Kent State University Press, 1979)

Locke, John, *An Essay Concerning Human Understanding*, ed. Peter H. Nidditch (Oxford: Clarendon Press, 1984)

Lovejoy, A. O., *The Thirteen Pragmatisms and Other Essays* (Baltimore: John Hopkins Press, 1963)

Lowe, Victor, 'The Influence of Bergson, James and Alexander on Whitehead', *Journal of the History of Ideas*, 10 (Apr 1949), 267–96

Lowe, Victor, *Understanding Whitehead* (Baltimore: Johns Hopkins University Press, 1962)

Luhan, Mabel Dodge, *Intimate Memories*, vol. III: *Movers and Shakers* (New York: Harcourt Brace, 1936)

Lyell, Charles, *Principles of Geology, or Modern Changes of the Earth and its Inhabitants*, 7th edn. (London: John Murray, 1847)

Lynd, Robert S., *Knowledge for What? The Place of Social Science in American Culture* (1939; repr. New York: Grove Press, 1964)

Lyotard, Jean-François, *The Post-Modern Condition: A Report on Knowledge*, trans. Geoff Bennington and Brian Massumi, foreword Frederick Jameson (Manchester: Manchester University Press, 1984)

McDermott, John J., *The Culture of Experience* (New York: New York University Press, 1976)

McDermott, John J., introd., *The Writings of William James. A Comprehensive Edition* (New York: Random House, 1967)

MacDiarmid, Hugh [Christopher Murray Grieve], 'Gertrude Stein', in MacDiarmid, *At the Sign of the Thistle* (London: Stanley Nott, 1934)

McIntyre, John P., 'Henry Adams and the Unity of Chartres', *Twentieth Century Literature*, 7 (1962), 159–71

McLuhan, Marshall, *The Gutenberg Galaxy* (London: Routledge and Kegan Paul, 1962)

Mailer, Norman, 'The White Negro: Superficial Reflections on the Hipster', *Dissent*, (Summer 1957), 276–93, repr. in *Advertisements for Myself* (New York: Putnam, 1957)

Maine, Sir Henry, *Ancient Law* (London: John Murray, 1861)

Maine, Sir Henry, *The Early History of the Property of Married Women as collected from Roman and Hindoo Law. A Lecture* (Manchester: A. Ireland, 1873)

Mane, Robert, *Henry Adams on the Road to Chartres* (Cambridge, Mass.: Harvard University Press, 1971)

Maritain, Jacques, *Creative Intuition in Art and Poetry* (New York: Pantheon, 1953)

Marx, Karl, *Capital: A Critique of Political Economy*, vol. I, introd. Ernest Mandel, trans. Ben Fowkes (Harmondsworth: Penguin Books, 1976)

Marx, Karl and Engels, Frederick, *Selected Works* (London: Lawrence and Wishart, 1970)

Matthiessen, F. O., *Henry James: The Major Phase* (London, New York, Toronto: Oxford University Press, 1946)

Maud, Ralph, 'Henry Adams: Irony and Impasse', *Essays in Criticism*, 8 (1958), 381–92

Maumus, E. V., *S. Thomas d'Aquin et la philosophie cartésienne*, vol. II (Paris: V. Lecoffre, 1890)

Mayer, J. P., 'More on the History of the Comparative Method: The Tradition of Darwinism in August Schleicher's work', *Anthropological Linguistics*, 8 (1966), 1–12

Meissner, William, *The Paranoid Process* (New York: Jason Aaronson, 1978)

Mellow, James R., 'Gertrude Stein Rediscovers America', *Columbia Forum*, NS 3 (Winter 1974), 22–9

Melville, Herman, *The Confidence Man: His Masquerade* (Evanston, Ill., and Chicago: Northwestern University Press and The Newberry Library, 1984)

Melville, Herman, *Moby Dick, or The White Whale*, ed. Luther S. Mansfield and Howard P. Vincent (New York: Hendricks House, 1962)

Merleau-Ponty, Maurice, *Consciousness and the Acquisition of Language*, trans, Hugh J. Silverman (Chicago: Northwestern University Press, 1973)

Merleau-Ponty, Maurice, *Phenomenology of Perception*, trans. Colin Smith (London and Henley: Routledge and Kegan Paul, 1962, 1978)

Merleau-Ponty, Maurice, *Signs*, trans. and introd. Richard C. McCleary (Evanston. Ill.: Northwestern University Press, 1964)

Michelet, Jules, *The People*, trans. John P. McKay (Urbana, Chicago, London: University of Illinois Press, 1973)

Mill, John Stuart, *The Autobiography of John Stuart Mill* (New York: Columbia University Press, 1924)

Miller, E. E., 'Richard Wright and Gertrude Stein', *Black American Literature Forum*, 16.3 (1982), 107–12

Miller, Rosalind S, *Gertrude Stein: Form and Intelligibility* (New York: Exposition Press, 1949)

Miller, Stuart Creighton, *'Benevolent Assimilation': The American Concept of the Philippines, 1889–1903* (New Haven: Yale University Press, 1982)

Mills, C. Wright, *The Power Elite* (New York: Oxford University Press, 1959)

Mills, C. Wright, *The Sociological Imagination* (New York: Oxford University Press, 1959)

Mills, C. Wright *Sociology and Pragmatism: The Higher Learning in America* (1964; repr. New York: Oxford University Press, 1966)

Mindel, Joseph, 'The Uses of Metaphor: Henry Adams and the Symbols of Science', *Journal of the History of Ideas*, 26 (1965), 89–102

Mizejewski, Linda, 'Gertrude Stein: the pattern moves, the woman behind shakes it', in *The Female Imagination and the Modernist Aesthetic*, ed. Sandra M. Gilbert and Susan Gubar, special issue, *Woman's Studies: An Interdisciplinary Journal*, 13. 172 (1986), 34–44

Monod, Jacques, *Chance and Necessity: An Essay on the Natural Philosophy of Modern Biology*, trans. Austryn Wainhouse (New York: Alfred A. Knopf, 1971)

Moore, Edward C., *American Pragmatism: Peirce, James and Dewey* (New York: Columbia University Press, 1961)

Moore, Stanley, 'Marxian Theories of Law in Primitive Societies', in *Culture in History: Essays in Honour of Paul Radin*, ed. Stanley Diamond (New York: Columbia University Press, 1960), 642–59

Morgan, Lewis Henry *Ancient Society* (New York: Henry Holt, 1877)

Morgan, Lewis Henry, *League of the Ho-de-no-sau-nee or Iroquois* (Rochester: Sage and Brother; New York: M. H. Newman, 1851)

Most, Glenn W. and Stowe, William W., eds., *The Poetics of Murder: Detective Fiction and Literary Theory* (San Diego, Calif.: Harcourt Brace Jovanovich, 1983)

Mottram, Eric, 'Henry Adams: Index of the Twentieth Century', in *American Literary Naturalism: A Reassessment*, ed. Y. Hakutani and L. Fried (Heidelberg: Carl Winter Universitätsverlag, 1975), 90–105

Mottram, Eric, *Towards Design in Poetry* (London: Writers Forum, 1977)

Mumford, Lewis, *The Pentagon of Power* (London: Secker and Warburg, 1971)

Mumford, Lewis, *Technics and Civilization* (1934; repr. London: George Routledge and Sons, 1946)

Münsterberg, Hugo, *The Americans*, trans. Edwin B. Holt (New York: Williams and Norgate, 1905)

Münsterberg, Hugo, *Business Psychology* (Chicago: La Salle Extension University, 1915)

Murchison, Carl, ed., *A History of Psychology in Autobiography*, 2 vols. (New York: Russel and Russel, 1961)

Myers, Gerald E., 'William James's Theory of Emotions', *Transactions of the Charles Peirce Society*, 2 (Winter 1969), 67–89

Myers, Gerald E., *William James, His Life and Thought* (New Haven and London: Yale University Press, 1986)

Myrdal, Gunnar, with Richard Sterner and Arnold Rose, *An American Dilemma: The Negro Problem and Modern Democracy*, 2 vols. (New York and London: Harper, 1944)

Neu, Jerome, 'A Tear is an Intellectual Thing', *Representations*, 19 (Summer 1987), 35–61

Neuman, S. C., *Gertrude Stein, Autobiography and the Problem of Narration* (Victoria, BC: University of Victoria Press, 1985)

Nichol, b p, 'Excerpts from some beginning writings on Gertrude Stein's Theories of Personality', *White Pelican*, 3 (Autumn 1973), 15–23

Njals Saga, trans. from the Old Icelandic with introduction and notes by Carl. F. Bayerschmidt and Lee M. Hollander (London: Allen and Unwin, 1955)

Novak, Barbara, *American Painting of the Nineteenth Century* (London: Pall Mall Press, 1969)

O. [pseud.], *Forensic Fables by O.* (1926; repr. London: Butterworths, 1961)

Ogden, C. K. and Richards, I. A., *The Meaning of Meaning: A Study of the Influence of Language upon Thought and of the Science of Symbolism* (1923; repr. London: Routledge and Kegan Paul Ltd., 1972)

Olmsted, J. M. D. and Olmsted, E. Harris, *Claude Bernard and the Experimental Method in Medicine* (London, New York, Toronto: Apelard-Schuman, [1962]

Olson, Charles, *The Special View of History* (Berkeley, Calif: Oyez, 1970)

Olson, Philip, ed., *America as a Mass Society* (London: Free Press of Glencoe, Collier-MacMillan, 1963)

Orwell, George, 'Inside the Whale' (1940), in *The Collected Essays, Journalism and Letters of George Orwell*, ed. Sonia Orwell and Ian Angus, vol. I: *An Age like This* (1968; repr. Harmondsworth: Penguin Books, 1970)

Orwell, George, 'Politics and the English Language', in Orwell, *Inside the Whale and Other Essays* (1962; repr. Harmondsworth: Penguin Books, 1981)

Otto, Max C., *et al.*, *William James, the Man and Thinker: Addresses delivered at the University of Wisconsin in Celebration of the Centenary of his Birth*, introd. George C. Sellery and Clarence A. Dykstra (Madison: University of Wisconsin Press, 1942)

Owen, Richard, *Paleontology: or a Systematic Summary of Ancient Animals and Their Geological Relation*, 2nd edn. (Edinburgh: Adam and Charles Black, 1861)

Padley, G. A., *Grammatical Theory in Western Europe 1500–1700: The Latin Tradition* (Cambridge: Cambridge University Press, 1976)

Padroni, Cyrena N., 'Gertrude Stein: From Outlaw to Classic', *Contemporary Literature*, 27.1 (Spring 1986), 98–114

Pascal, Blaise, *Pensées*, trans. A. J. Krailsheimer (Harmondsworth: Penguin Books, 1966)

Pasquier, Marie-Claire, 'Gertrude Stein: Écouter, parler, voir', *Les Temps Modernes*, 419 (June 1981), 2159–73

Paul, Elliot, 'Gertrude, Alas, Alas', *Esquire*, 26 (July 1946), 62

Pearson, Karl, *The Grammar of Science*, 2nd edn. (London: Adam and Charles Black, 1900)

Peirce, Charles S., *Philosophical Writings of Peirce*, ed. Justus Buckler (New York: Dover, 1955)

Perloff, Marjorie, *The Poetics of Indeterminacy: Rimbaud to Cage* (1981; repr. Chicago: Northwestern University Press, 1983)

Perloff, Marjorie, 'Poetry as Word System: The Art of Gertrude Stein', *American Poetry Review*, 8 (1979), 33–5

Perry, Ralph Barton, *The Present Conflict of Ideals: A Study of the Philosophical Background of the World War* (New York: Longmans, Green, 1918)

Perry, Ralph Barton, *The Thought and Character of William James*, 2 vols. (Boston: Little, Brown, 1935)

Piaget, Jean, *The Language and Thought of the Child*, Marjorie and Ruth Gabain trans. 3rd edn. (London: Routledge and Kegan Paul, 1971)

Piraro, F., 'The Last Years of Gertrude Stein', in *Europe–Révue littéraire mensuelle*, 63.676 (1985), 89–101

Poincaré, Henri, *La Science et l'hypothèse* (Paris: Flammarion, 1902)

Poincaré, Lucien, *La Physique moderne* (Paris: Flammarion, 1906)

Pollock, Frederick, 'Evolution and Ethics', *Mind*, I.3 (1876), 334–45

Porter, Dorothy and Roy, 'What was Social Medicine? An Historiographical Essay', *Journal of Historical Sociology*, I.1 (Mar 1988), 95

Poster, Mark, *Existential Marxism in Postwar France: From Sartre to Althusser* (Princeton, NJ: Princeton University Press, 1975)

Praz, Mario, *The Romantic Agony*, trans. Angus Davidson (London: Oxford University Press, 1933)

Pribham, Karl and Gill, Merton, *Freud's Project Reassessed* (London: Hutchinson, 1976)

Radin, Paul, *The Method and Theory of Ethnology: An Essay in Criticism* (New York and London: McGraw-Hill, 1933)

Reed, Evelyn, *Woman's Evolution* (New York and Toronto: Pathfinder Press 1974)

Reich, Wilhelm, *The Mass Psychology of Fascism*, trans. Vincent R. Carfagno (1935; repr. New York: Farrar, Straus and Giroux, 1970)

'Report of a Joint Committee of the General Council of the Bar of England and Wales, The Law Society and the British Medical Association', *Medical Evidence in Courts of Law* (London: British Medical Association, 1965)

Rexroth, Kenneth, introd. to *A Return to Pagany: The History, Correspondence, and Selections from a Little Magazine 1929–1952*, ed. Stephen Halpert, with Richard Jones (Boston: Beacon Press, 1969)

Richards, Robert J., 'The Personal Equation in Science: William James's Psychological and Moral Uses of Darwinian Theory', *Harvard Library Bulletin* [James Special Issue], 30.4 (Oct 1982), 387–419

Ricoeur, Paul, *The Rule of Metaphor: Multi-Disciplinary Studies of the Creation of Meaning in Language*, trans. Robert Czerny with Kathleen McLaughlin and John Costello, SJ (London and Henley: Routledge and Kegan Paul, 1978)

Riesman, David, with Nathan Glazer and Reuel Denny, *The Lonely Crowd*, abridged edn. with a 1969 Preface (New Haven and London: Yale University Press, 1980)

Roback, A. A., *History of American Psychology*, rev. edn. (New York: Collier Books, 1964)

Roback, A. A., *William James, Marginalia, Personality and Contribution* (Cambridge, Mass.: Sci-Art Publishers, Harvard Square, 1942)

Robbins, R. H., *A Short History of Linguistics*, rev. ed. (London: Longmans, Green, 1969)

Robinson, Daniel N., *An Intellectual History of Psychology* (New York: Macmillan; London: Collier-Macmillan, 1981)

Robinson, Daniel N., *Towards a Science of Human Nature: Essays on the Psychologies of Mill, Hegel, Wundt and James* (New York: Columbia University Press, 1982)

Rodrigues, E. L., 'Out of Season for Nirvana: Henry Adams and Buddhism', in *Indian Essays in American Literature: Papers in Honour of Robert E. Spiller*, ed. Sujit Mukherjee and D. V. K. Raghavachary (Bombay: Popular Prakashan, 1969), 179–94

Roelofs, G. H., 'Henry Adams: Pessimism and the Intelligent Use of Doom', *Journal of Literary History*, 17 (1950), 214–39

Rogers, W. G., *When This You See Remember Me* (New York and Toronto: Rinehart and Co., 1948)

Rorty, Richard, *Consequences of Pragmatism (Essays: 1972–1980)* (Minneapolis: University of Minnesota Press, 1982)

Rorty, Richard, *Philosophy and the Mirror of Nature* (Princeton, NJ: Princeton University Press, 1979)

Rose, Francis, *Saying Life: The memoirs of Sir Francis Rose* (London: Cassell, 1961)

Rose, Gillian, *Hegel Contra Sociology* (London: Athlone/Humanities Press, 1981)

Royce, Josiah, *William James and Other Essays on the Philosophy of Life* (New York: Macmillan, 1911)

Ruddick, L. 'Fluid Symbols in American Modernism – William James, Gertrude Stein, George Santayana and Wallace Stevens', in *Allegory, Myth and Symbol*, ed. M.W. Bloomfield (Cambridge English Studies, vol. 9), (Cambridge, Mass., 1981)

Ruse, Michael, *The Darwinian Revolution* (Chicago and London: Chicago University Press, 1979)

Russell, Bertrand, review of William James, *Essays in Radical Empiricism*, in *Mind*, 21 (Oct 1912), 571–5

Russett, Cynthia E., *The Concept of Equilibrium in American Social Thought* (New Haven, Conn.: Yale University Press, 1966)

Sahlins, Marshall, *Culture and Practical Reason* (Chicago and London: University of Chicago Press, 1976)

Samuels, Ernest, *Bernard Berenson: The Making of a Connoisseur* (Cambridge, Mass., and London: The Belknap Press of Harvard University Press, 1979)

Samuels, Ernest, *Henry Adams*, vol. I: *The Young Henry Adams;* vol. II: *The Middle Years;* vol. III: *The Major Phase* (Cambridge, Mass.: Harvard University Press, 1948–1964)

Samuels, Ernest, 'Henry Adams and the Gossip Mills', in *Essays in American and English Literature Presented to Bruce Robert McElderry, Jr.*, ed. Max F. Schulz *et al.*, (Athens, O.: Ohio University Press, 1967)

Samuelson, Paul A., 'The World Economy at the Century's End' [conference paper]. Responsable de la Publicacion: Comite Organizador Local-Colegio Nacional de Economistas (A.C. Mexico, Agosto de 1980)

Santayana, George, *Character and Opinion in the United States* (London: Constable, 1920)

Sapir, Edward, *Culture, Language and Personality*, ed. David G. Mandelbaum (Berkeley, Los Angeles, London: University of California Press, 1956)

Sapir, Edward, *Language: An Introduction to the Study of Speech* (1921; repr. New York and London: Harcourt Brace Jovanovich, 1949)

Sartre, Jean-Paul, *Between Existentialism and Marxism*, trans. John Matthews (New York: Morrow Quill Paperbacks, 1979)

Sartre, Jean-Paul, *Critique of Dialectical Reason*, trans. Alan Sheridan-Smith (1960; repr. London: New Left Books, 1976)

Sartre, Jean-Paul, *Literary and Philosophical Essays*, trans. Annette Michelson (London: Hutchinson, 1968)

Sartre, Jean-Paul, *Nausea*, trans. Robert Baldick (Harmondsworth: Penguin Books, 1965)

Sartre, Jean-Paul, *The Psychology of Imagination* (London: Methuen, 1972)

Sartre, Jean-Paul, *Search for a Method*, trans. Hazel E. Barnes (New York: Vintage Books, 1968)

Sartre, Jean-Paul, *Sketch for a Theory of the Emotions*, trans. Philip Mairet, pref. Mary Warnock (London: Methuen, 1971)

Sartre, Jean-Paul, *The Transcendence of the Ego: An Existentialist Theory of Consciousness*, ed., trans. and introd. Forrest Williams and Robert Kirkpatrick (New York: Farrar, Straus and Giroux, 1957)

Saussure, Ferdinand de, *Course in General Linguistics*, ed. Charles Bally, Albert Sechehaye, Albert Reidlinger, trans. Wade Baskin; introd. Jonathan Culler (London: Fontana Collins, 1974)

Saveth, Edward N., 'The Heroines of Henry Adams', *American Quarterly*, 8 (Fall 1956), 231–42

Sayre, Robert F. *The Examined Self: Benjamin Franklin, Henry Adams, Henry James* (Princeton, NJ: Princeton University Press, 1964)

Scheyer, Ernst, *The Circle of Henry Adams: Art and Artists* (Detroit: Wayne State University Press, 1970)

Schirmer, Daniel B., 'William James and the New Age', *Science and Society*, 33 (Fall-Winter 1968), 434–45

Schneider, H. W., *A History of American Philosophy*, 2nd edn. (New York and London: Columbia University Press, 1963)

Schneider, H. W., *Making the Fascist State* (New York and London: Oxford University Press, 1928)

Schnitz, Neil, 'Portraits, Patriarchs, Mythos: The Revenge of Gertrude Stein', *Salmagundi*, 40 (1978), 69–91

Schwegler, Albert, *Handbook of the History of Philosophy*, trans, James Hutchinson Stirling (Edinburgh: Edmonston and Douglas, 1867)

Schwen, Mark, 'Making the World: William James and the Life of the Mind', *Harvard Library Bulletin*, 30.4 (Oct 1982), 427–54

Seigfried, Charlenne Haddock, *Chaos and Context: A Study in William James* (Athens, O.: Ohio University Press, 1978)

Serres, Michel, *The Parasite*, trans. with notes, Lawrence R. Scher (Baltimore and London: Johns Hopkins University Press, 1982)

Sevareid, Eric, *Not So Wild A Dream* (1946; repr. New York: Atheneum, 1976)

Shapiro, Michael J., ed., *Language and Politics* (Oxford: Basil Blackwell, 1984)

Shepherd, Jack, *The Adams Chronicles: Four Generations of Greatness* (Boston: Little, Brown, 1975)

Simiand, François, 'Méthode historique et science sociale, étude critique d'après les ouvrages récents de M. Lacombe et de M. Seignobos', *Revue de Synthese historique*, 6–7 (1903), 1–22

Simon, Linda, *The Biography of Alice B. Toklas* (Garden City, NY: Doubleday, 1977)

Skinner, B. F., *Beyond Freedom and Dignity* (1971; repr. Harmondsworth: Pelican Books, 1973)

Skinner, B. F., 'Has Gertrude Stein a Secret?' *Atlantic Monthly*, 153 (Jan 1934), 50–7

Smith, John E., *Purpose and Thought: The Meaning of Pragmatism* (London: Hutchinson, 1979

Spengler, Oswald, *The Decline of the West*, trans. Charles Francis Atkinson, 2 vols. (1918 and 1922; repr. London: George Allen and Unwin, 1932)

Sprigge, Elizabeth, *Gertrude Stein, her Life and Work* (London: Hamish Hamilton, 1957)

Spring-Rice, Sir Cecil, *The Letters and Friendship of Sir Cecil Spring-Rice, A Record*, ed. Stephen Gwynn (London: Constable, 1929)

Stallo, J.–B., *La Matière et la physique moderne*, 3rd edn. (Paris: Germer Baillière, 1899)

Starr, Paul, *The Social Transformation of American Medicine* (New York: Basic Books, 1982)

Stein, Gertrude, 'American Crimes and How They Matter', *New York Herald Tribune*, 16 Mar 1935, p. 29

Stein, Gertrude, *Anderson/Stein* [Letters], ed. Roy L. White (Chapel Hill: University of North Carolina Press, 1972)

Stein, Gertrude, 'Christian Berard', in Stein, *Portraits and Prayers* (New York: Random House, 1934)

Stein, Gertrude, 'English and American Language in Literature', *Life and Letters Today*, 13 (Sept 1935), 22

Stein, Gertrude, *Everybody's Autobiography* (1937; repr. New York: Vintage Books, 1964)

Stein, Gertrude, *Four in America*, introd. Thornton Wilder (New Haven, Conn.: Yale University Press, 1947)

Stein, Gertrude, *Geography and Plays* (1922; repr. New York: The Something Else Press, 1968)

Stein, Gertrude, *How to Write*, pref. and introd. Patricia Meyerowitz (1931; repr New York: Dover Publications, 1975)

Stein, Gertrude, *How Writing is Written: The Previously Unpublished Writings of Gertrude Stein*, 2 vols. (Los Angeles: Black Sparrow Press, 1974)

Stein, Gertrude, 'I Came and Here I Am', *Hearst's International Cosmopolitan*, Feb 1935, 168

Stein, Gertrude, *The Letters of Gertrude Stein and Carl Van Vechten*, vol. I: *1913–1935*; vol. II: *1935–1946*, ed. Edward Michael Burns (Irvington, NY: Columbia University Press, 1986)

Stein, Gertrude, *Look at me now and here I am: Writings and Lectures by Gertrude Stein*, ed. Patricia Meyerowitz (London: Peter Owen, 1967)

Stein, Gertrude, *The Making of Americans: being the history of a family's progress* (1925; repr. London: Peter Owen, 1968)

Stein, Gertrude, 'Money', *Saturday Evening Post*, 13 June 1936, 88

Stein, Gertrude [with Leon Solomons], *Motor Automism* (New York: Phoenix Book Shop, 1969)

Stein, Gertrude, *Narration*. Four lectures by Gertrude Stein with an introduction by Thornton Wilder (Chicago: University of Chicago Press, 1935)

Stein, Gertrude, 'Reflections on the Atomic Bomb', *Yale Poetry Review*, 7 (1947), 3–5

Stein, Gertrude, review of Sherwood Anderson's *A Story-Teller's Story*, *Ex Libris*, 2 (Mar 1925), 177

Stein, Gertrude, *Useful Knowledge* (New York: Two Rivers Books, Payson and Clarke, 1928)

Stein, Gertrude, *Wars I Have Seen* (New York: Random House, 1945)

Stein, Gertrude, 'Why I Like Detective Stories', *Harpers* (Nov 1937), 70

Stein, Gertrude, 'Your United States', *Atlantic Monthly* (Oct 1937), 463

Stein, Leo, *Journey into the Self: Being the Letters, Papers and Journals of Leo Stein*, ed. Edmund Fuller, introd. Van Wyck Brooks (New York: Crown, 1950)

Stein, Leo, *The Triangle Fire* (Philadelphia and New York: J.B. Lippincott, 1962)

Steiner, Wendy Lois, 'Gertrude Stein's Portrait Form' (Ph.D. diss., Yale University, 1974)

Sterne, Laurence, *Tristram Shandy*, ed. Howard Anderson (1760; repr. New York and London: W.W. Norton, 1980)

Stimpson, Catherine R., 'The Mind, Body, and Gertrude Stein', in *Gertrude Stein: Modern Critical Views*, ed. and introd. Harold Bloom (New York: Chelsea House, 1986)

Stimpson, Catherine R., 'The Somagrams of

Gertrude Stein', *Poetics Today*, 6. 1–2 (1985), 67–80

Stimpson, Catherine R., 'Stein, Toklas, and the Paradox of the Happy Marriage', in *Mothering the Mind: Twelve Studies of Writers and Their Silent Partners*, ed. Ruth Perry and Martine Watson Brownley (New York, London; Holmes and Meier, 1984)

Stowe, Harriet Beecher, *Life and Letters of Harriet Beecher Stowe*, ed. Annie Fields (London: Sampson Low, Marston, 1898)

Stowe, Harriet Beecher, *The Minister's Wooing* (London: Sampson and Low, 1859)

Swartz, Shirley, 'Between Autobiographies: Gertrude Stein and the problem of audience', *White Pelican*, 3 (Autumn 1973), 41–9

Szasz, Thomas S., *Ideology and Insanity: Essays on the Psychiatric Dehumanization of Man* (New York: Anchor Books, 1970)

Szasz, Thomas S., *Law, Liberty and Psychiatry* (1965; repr. New York: Collier Books, 1968)

Szasz, Thomas S., *The Myth of Mental Illness: Foundation of a Theory of Personal Conduct*, rev. edn. (New York: Harper and Row, 1974)

Szasz, Thomas S., *Psychiatric Justice* (New York: Macmillan, 1956)

Taylor, Eugene, 'William James on Psycho-pathology: The 1896 Lowell Lectures on "Exceptional Mental States"', *Harvard Library Bulletin*, 30.4 (Oct 1982), 455–79

Tehan, Arline Boucher, *Henry Adams in Love: The Pursuit of Elizabeth Sherman Cameron* (New York: Universe Books, 1983)

Thayer, H. Standish, ed., *Pragmatism: The Classic Writings* (New York and Toronto: Mentor Books, New American Library, 1970)

Thompson, E. P., *The Poverty of Theory and Other Essays* (London: Merlin Press, 1978)

Thoreau, Henry David, *Walden*, ed. J. Lyndon Shanley (Princeton, NJ: Princeton University Press, 1962)

Toulmin, Stephen, *Human Understanding: The Collective Use and Evolution of Concepts* (Princeton, NJ: Princeton University Press, 1972)

Toulmin, Stephen and June Goodfield, *The Architecture of Matter* (London: Hutchinson, 1962)

Trachtenberg, Alan, *The Incorporation of America. Culture and Society in the Gilded Age* (New York: Hill and Wang, 1982)

Trautmann, Thomas R., *Lewis Henry Morgan and the Invention of Kinship* (Berkeley, Los Angeles and London: University of California Press, 1987)

Trowbridge, John, *What is Electricity?* (New York: D. Appleton, 1896)

Tully, James, review of Neal Wood, *The Politics of Locke's Philosophy: a Social Study of 'An Essay Concerning Human Understanding'* (1983), in *Political Theory*, 12.1 (May 1984), 286–90

Twain, Mark [Samuel Langhorne Clemens], *The Adventures of Huckleberry Finn*, ed. Sculley Bradley, Richmond, C., Beatty, E., Hudson Long, Thomas Cooley (New York: W.W. Norton, 1977)

Twombly, Wells, *200 Years of Sport in America: A Pageant of a Nation at Play* (New York: McGraw Hill, 1976)

Tylor, Edward B. *Primitive Culture: Researches into the Development of Mythology, Philosophy, Religion, Language, Art and Custom*, 2 vols., 7th edn. (New York: Brentano's, 1924)

Veblen, Thorstein, 'The Technicians and Revolution' in *The Portable Veblen*, ed. Max Lerner (New York: Viking Press, 1950)

Vico, Giambattista, *The Autobiography of Giambattista Vico*, trans. M. H. Fisch and T. G. Bergin (Ithaca, NY, and London: Cornell University Press, 1944)

Vico, Giambattista, *The New Science of Giambattista Vico*, abridged trans. of the 3rd edn. (1744), Thomas Goddard Bergin and Max Harold Fisch (Ithaca, NY, and London: Cornell University Press, 1970)

Vitzthum, Richard C., *The American Compromise; Theme and Method in the Histories of Bancroft, Parkman, and Adams* (Norman: University of Oklahoma Press, 1974)

Volosinov, V. N., *Marxism and the Philosophy of Language*, trans. Ladislav Matejka and I. R. Titunik (New York and London: Seminar Press, 1973)

Wagner, Vern, *The Suspension of Henry Adams: A Study of Manner and Matter* (Detroit: Wayne State University Press, 1969)

Wahl, Jean, *The Pluralist Philosophies of England and America*, trans. Fred Rothwell (London: Open Court, 1925)

Wasserstrom, William, 'The Sursymameri-cubealism of Gertrude Stein', *Twentieth-Century Literature*, 21 (Feb 1975), 90–106

Watson, J. B., *Psychology from the Standpoint of a Behaviorist* (New York: J.B. Lippincott, 1919)

Watson, R. I., *The Great Psychologists*, 3rd edn. (Philadelphia, New York, Toronto: J. B. Lippincott, 1971)

Weber, Max, *The Protestant Ethic and the Spirit of Capitalism*, trans. Talcott Parsons (London: George Allen and Unwin, 1930)

Webster, Noah, *An American Dictionary of the English Language by Noah Webster*, introd. Mario Pei (1821; repr. New York and London: Johnson Reprint, 1970)

Weil, Simone, *Lectures on Philosophy*, trans. Hugh Price, introd. Peter Winch (London: Cambridge University Press, 1978)

Weininger, Otto, *Sex and Character*, Authorized Translation (London: Heinemann; New York: G.P. Putnam's Sons, 1906)

Wells, H. G., *First and Last Things: A Confession of Faith and Rule of Life* (London: Watts, 1929)

White, Lynn, Jr., 'Dynamo and Virgin Reconsidered', *American Scholar*, 27 (1958), 183–94

White, Morton, *Science and Sentiment in America: Philosophical Thought from Jonathan Edwards to John Dewey* (New York: Oxford University Press, 1972)

Whitehead, Alfred North, *Adventures of Ideas* (1933; repr. Harmondsworth: Penguin Books, 1942, 1948)

Whitehead, Alfred North, *Alfred North Whitehead, An Anthology*, ed. F. S. C. Northrop and Mason W. Gross (New York: Macmillan, 1953)

Whitehead, Alfred North, *The Concept of Nature* (1920; repr; Cambridge: Cambridge University Press, 1982)

Whitehead, Alfred North, *Symbolism, Its Meaning and Effect* (London: Macmillan, 1927)

Whitfield, Stephen J., '"Sacred in History and in Art": The Shaw Memorial', *New England Quarterly*, 60.1 (March 1987), 3–27

Whitney, William Dwight, *The Life and Growth of Language* (London: Kegan Paul, Trench, 1889)

Whitney, William Dwight, *Whitney on Language: Selected Writings of William Dwight Whitney*, ed. Michael Silverstein, introd. Roman Jacobson (Cambridge, Mass. and London: MIT Press, 1971)

Whitman, Walt, *Leaves of Grass*, ed. Harold W. Blodgett and Scully Bradley (New York: New York University Press, 1965)

Whorf, Benjamin Lee, 'An American Indian Model of the Universe', in *Language, Thought and Reality: Selected Writings of Benjamin Lee Whorf*, ed. and introd. John B. Carroll (Cambridge, Mass.: MIT Press, 1956)

Whyte, Lancelot Law, *The Unconscious Before Freud*, Foreword Edith Sitwell (London: Tavistock, 1962)

Whyte, William H., *The Organization Man* (1956; repr. Harmondsworth: Pelican Books, 1960)

Wiener, Norbert, *The Human Use of Human Beings: Cybernetics and Society* (1954; repr.

London: Sphere Books, 1968)

Wilde, Oscar, *An Ideal Husband, A Play* (London: Methuen, 1909)

Wilkins, Thurman, *Clarence King: A Biography* (New York: Macmillan, 1958)

Williams, Raymond, *Politics and Letters: Interviews with the New Left Review* (London: Verso, 1981)

Williams, Raymond, 'The Uses of Cultural Theory', in *The Politics of Modernism: Against the New Conformists* (London: Verso, 1989)

Williams, William Carlos, *Interviews with William Carlos Williams*, ed. Linda Welshimer Wagner (New York: New Directions, 1976)

Williams, William Carlos, *Paterson. Books I–V* (London: Mac-Gibbon and Kee, 1964)

Williams, William Carlos, 'The Work of Gertrude Stein', *Pagany*, 1 (Jan–Mar 1930), 44

Wilshire, Bruce, *William James and Phenomenology: A Study of 'The Principles of Psychology'* (Bloomington and London: Indiana University Press, 1968)

Wilson, E. O., *Sociobiology: the New Synthesis* (Cambridge, Mass.: Harvard University Press, 1975)

Wittgenstein, Ludwig, *Tractatus Logico-Philosophicus*, trans. D. F. Pears and B. F. McGuinness, introd. Bertrand Russell (London: Routledge and Kegan Paul, 1961)

Wokler, Robert, 'Saint-Simon and the Passage from Political to Social Science', in *The Language of Political Theory in Early-Modern Europe*, ed. Anthony Pagden (Cambridge: Cambridge University Press, 1987)

Wordsworth, William, *William Wordsworth: The Poems*, ed. John D. Hayden (New Haven, Conn.: Yale University Press, 1981)

Wright, Richard, 'Gertrude Stein's Story is Drenched in Hitler's Horrors', *PM Magazine*, 11 Mar 1945, p. 15

Yates, Frances A. *Giordano Bruno and the Hermetic Tradition* (New York: Vintage Books, 1969)

Zukofsky, Louis, *'A' 1–12* (1959; repr. London: Jonathan Cape, 1966)

Zukofsky, Louis, 'Henry Adams: A Criticism in Autobiography', *Hound and Horn*, 3.4 (1930), 63

Index